More Praise for *The FBI War on T*
and the author (continued from back

"Incredible! <u>Wow</u>. [*The FBI War on*
revolutionary investigative journalism. It's what the Movements have been needing to raise consciousness regarding various operations by the reactionaries and their agents."

-Sanyika Shakur (aka 'Monster' Kody Scott). Best-selling author of *Monster: The Autobiography of an LA Gangmember*. Shakur turned into a radical leftist while in prison and developed political plans with Tupac for reducing drug dealing and drug violence in American cities.

"I'm already on page 70 - and that is a miracle with all the reading I generally have to do, but this book is WOW."

-Rebecca S. Myles, News Reporter/ :Producer/ Anchor/ Engineer, WBAI Pacifica Rdio 99.5 FM New York City

"Everytime I re-read it, I find something new. John Potash has researched extensively on the acts of political state repression on culture. This book must be read by everyone into HipHop culture, but especially by people who are serious about creating a new and better world."

-Orlando Green, National Treasurer of the National HipHop Political Convention and co-founder of HipHop Sustains.

"I love this book. Its painful truths are part of a national healing process that is long overdue. What these murder victims had in common was Blackness and leadership, a combination so terrifying to Uncle Sam that he sends out his goons when he thinks he sees it. To read this book is to learn why some of the greatest music, art, and oratory of the 20th Century was never composed at all. The lawless "intelligence community" - what Theodor Adorno called "the werewolves who emerge in the night whenever someone has to be done away with" - destroyed these men and robbed America. A Black President is a great a step forward but our path, like that of South Africa, had better include a phase of truth-telling about the role of American authorities --persons and programs inside CIA, FBI, and certain police departments--in our nation's racist horrors past and present, or we will never reach the social maturity of real peace. This book by John Potash is part of the same national healing process as the great "Unspeakable" trilogy by James W. Douglas on the murders of President Kennedy, Dr. King, and Malcolm X. Read it and pass it on."

-James Hecht, PhD. Senior Staff Writer, <u>www.fromthewilderness.com</u>, author of *Limousine, Midnight Blue*.

"For John Potash, with more thanks than I can say. We move on!"

-Julia Wright, journalist, daughter of the first best-selling African-American novelist, Richard Wright, after this author presented a paper at the 100-year celebration of her father's birth. This was part of a panel: "Richard Wright: An Inconvenient Hero." It consisted mostly of sons and daughters of activist figures targeted by U.S. intelligence such as Wright and Stretch Johnson along with Ethel and Julius Rosenberg.

"Enlightening, stimulating, incredibly detailed and painstakingly researched...a masterly presentation."

-Ahati N. N. Toure, PhD. Assistant Professor of Africana History and Black Studies, Department of History, Political Science, and Philosophy, Delaware State University. Author of *John Henrik Clarke and the Power of Africana History*. Praise given of a presentation by the author of *The FBI War on Tupac Shakur and Black Leaders* regarding the book, to his class.

"John Potash is arguably the definitive voice on Tupac Shakur's death."

-Dedon Kamati, host of *Freedom Now* on KPFK Los Angeles and former Black Panther.

"My friends and I from the U.S. Intelligence community all read this book and picked it apart to try and find errors in it, but none of us could find any."

-Mill Butler, who spent years doing U.S. Intelligence contract work in the Washington D.C. area.

'#3 in Top Ten books for Summer/Fall Reading 2012.' –**Chris Stevenson**, *BlackCommentator.com"*

The FBI War on Tupac Shakur and Black Leaders

U.S. Intelligence's Murderous Targeting of Tupac, MLK, Malcolm, Panthers, Hendrix, Marley, Rappers & Linked Ethnic Leftists

by
John Potash

Foreword by Pam Africa
with Mumia Abu-Jamal
Afterword by Fred Hampton, Jr.

Progressive Left Press Baltimore, MD

Library of Congress Cataloging-in-Publication Data

Potash, John
The FBI War on Tupac Shakur and Black Leaders: ***U.S. Intelligence's Murderous Targeting of MLK, Malcolm, Panthers, Hendrix, Marley, Rappers & Linked Ethnic Leftists*** **/ by John Potash; Foreword by Pam Africa with Mumia Abu-Jamal; Afterword by Fred Hampton, Jr.**
p.cm.
Includes footnotes.
ISBN 09791469-0-9

1st limited Progressive Left Press printing September 2007
1st bulk printing, January 2008
2nd (final) printing October 2008
3rd printing October 2009
4th printing April 2010
5th printing December 2010
6th printing September 2011
7th printing August 2012
8th printing June 2013
9th printing March 2014
10th printing May 2015

For information regarding special discounts for bulk purchases, please contact Progressive Left Press at (410)960-7744, or jpota4@aol.com **& put "tupac book" in subject. Also see** www.fbiwarontupac.com **which is likely in need of updating.**

Contents

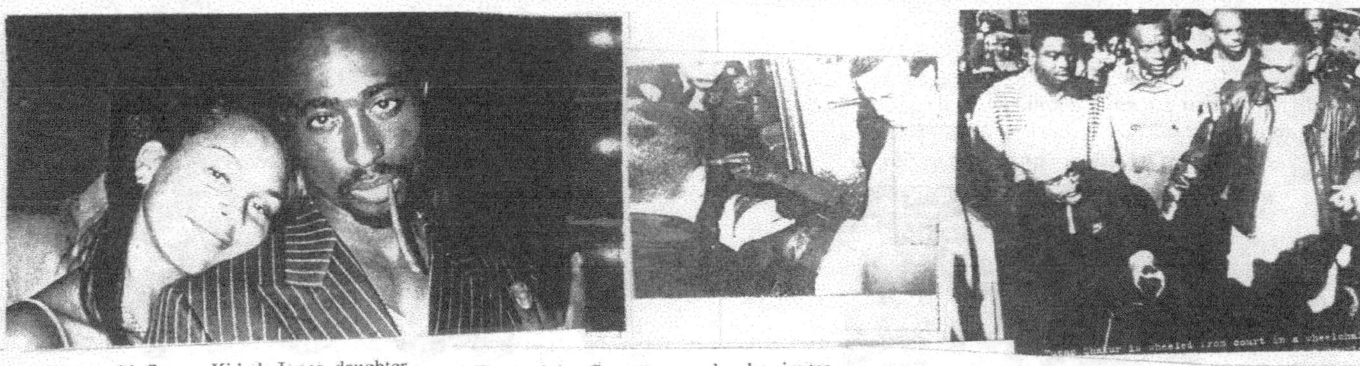

1.Tupac with fiancee Kidada Jones, daughter of music mogul & Vibe owner, Quincy Jones.

2.Tupac giving finger to press horde minutes after he took four bullets in New York.

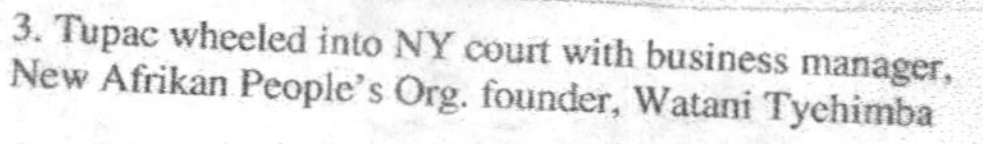

3. Tupac wheeled into NY court with business manager, New Afrikan People's Org. founder, Watani Tyehimba

Tupac speaking at Los Angeles voter registration rally with Snoop Doggy Dogg.

4.Tupac speaking for Brotherhood Crusade, LA group fighting anti-affirmative action bill.

Tupac with his mother, Afeni Shakur.
©Landov Photos, from Jamal Joseph's *Tupac Shakur Legacy*

5. NY Black Panther leaders, Afeni Shakur arrested with husband, Lumumba by NYPD.

6. Tupac with friend, actor Mickey Rourke, at a benefit for El Salvador.

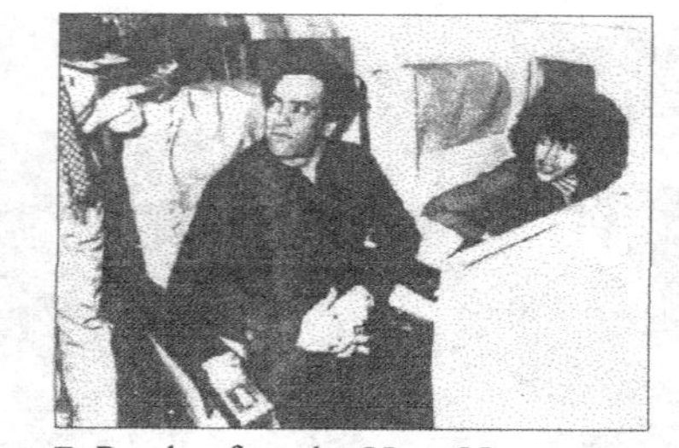

7. Panther founder Huey Newton & Elaine Brown, his one-time lover. Brown said that she kept her ex-lover, a CIA spy, as her advisor.

8. FBI San Francisco chief Held lead attack on Tupac's godfather, LA Panther head G. Pratt, oversaw Bay area for Newton's murder, & Oakland attacks on Tupac, before retiring due to J. Bari's lawsuit.

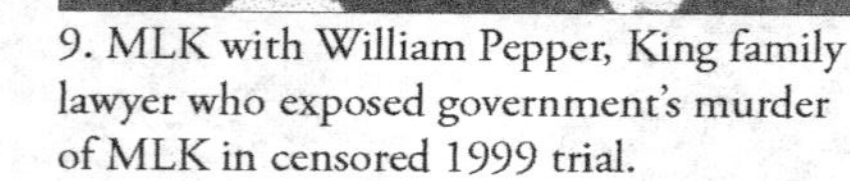

9. MLK with William Pepper, King family lawyer who exposed government's murder of MLK in censored 1999 trial.

10. Jimi Hendrix with fiancee, M. Danneman, who died just after her expose on government foul play & Hendrix's radical politics was released.

11

~~EYES ONLY~~

APPROVED FOR RELEASE 1993
CIA HISTORICAL REVIEW PROGRAM

9 June 1965

MEMORANDUM FOR : Chief, Security Research Staff

SUBJECT : [redacted]
(Conversation with 8 June 1965,
Washington, D.C.)

1. On 8 June 1965, the writer met with Mr. [redacted] at the Hilton Hotel, Washington, and had a long discussion with him beginning at approximately 1:15 and ending at 5 p.m. [redacted] comments covered a wide range of matters, but basically they can be broken down into 3 main topics:

(a) His attitude towards the FBI;

(b) His thoughts concerning the writing of a series of books with the protagonist a CIA agent; and

(c) Comments on the Negro Civil Rights Movement, the various personalities connected with it, and some of Mr. Kennedy's opinions and theories regarding future events connected with the Civil Rights Movement.

Each of the above will be discussed separately.

Mr. [redacted] attitude towards the FBI

2. Sometime back, Chief, SRS, decided that it would be advantageous to have Mr. [redacted] give information, particularly regarding the Civil Rights Movement, to agents of the FBI in New York City, particularly if this information concerned domestic or local events and activities. Chief, SRS, felt that it would be a faster means of communication than heretofore used wherein Mr. [redacted] communicated with SRS officers who, in turn, passed the information to either the FBI or areas where it was useful.

3. Mr. [redacted] made it very clear that he did not wish to communicate with FBI agents, that the Civil Rights Movement should be regarded as an international situation because of the Communist directed infiltration into the movement, and that he felt in some respects that he was being "downgraded" by being used as a source by the FBI and not in a higher echelon

~~EYES ONLY~~

SECRET

12

CIA HISTORICAL REVIEW PROGRAM

SUBJECT: Notes Made During Conversations with [redacted] in New York City 2 February 1965

APPROVED FOR RELEASE 1993
CIA HISTORICAL REVIEW PROGRAM

1. Harry Belafonte had two children by his first wife, Marguerite, who is a negress. The boy Adrian, now about 12, has been placed by Belafonte into a boarding school somewhere. The daughter "Sharie" now goes to New Lincoln High School in New York City. She is about 14 years old and Belafonte is having a great deal of trouble with this girl being apparently a delinquent and other problems.

2. Belafonte's current wife, Julie Robinson, who is white is the daughter of a Communist Party member and she herself is a Communist. Julie will not have anything to do with Belafonte's daughter Sharie. Julie Robinson is Jewish, a notorious lesbian, a professional dancer, and has had a great many affairs.

3. Marguerite, the negro first wife of Belafonte, was probably Communist approved for Belafonte. She is a teacher by profession and now runs a model agency apparently in New York City. Rumor has it that she is trying to get married to a doctor or dentist who resides in Washington, D.C.

4. [redacted] has found out a great deal of information which would indicate that Belafonte is about to lose a large personal fortune in investments that he made in Guinea, and also is "losing his shirt" in some "Tanganyika Project". Details of these situations are not fully known but it would appear that the loss of money in these projects for Belafonte is a "hold" which the Communists (probably the Chinese Communists) have over Belafonte.

5. [redacted] reported that Belafonte is going on a 17-week tour and doing odd jobs such as a performance at the Latin Casino at Cherry Hill, New Jersey. These are spots that Belafonte normally would not touch but he needs money and hence takes these engagements. In fact, he had to break through a picket line at the Cherry Hill Casino to perform there.

6. Harry Belafonte, according to [redacted] has bankrolled "SNICK" as well as Martin Luther King possibly and probably with Sidney Portier the negro actor who is a Communist and also with Sammy Davis Jr. Portier is reportedly "shacking" with Dinne Carol, who is a well-known negro popular singer.

7. A source described Belafonte as a founder of "SNICK". Incidentally Belafonte is now on his 7th psychiatrist.

8. Source states Martin Luther King is a homosexual and a "Switch Hitter".

11. CIA document from FOIA request for novelist Jay Richard Kennedy's file. J.R. Kennedy (see name accidentally not blacked out at arrow) became Harry Belafonte's manager (before Belafonte caught on) to spy on the civil rights movement as Belafonte consistently helped MLK. Panther Elaine Brown said Kennedy was her life-long mentor, supporting top Panthers such as K. Cleaver and G. Pratt's claim she was a spy.

12. J.R. Kennedy helped create many of the rumors about black actors (see above). Other documents in this file discussed "if MLK was assassinated" and dated 1965.

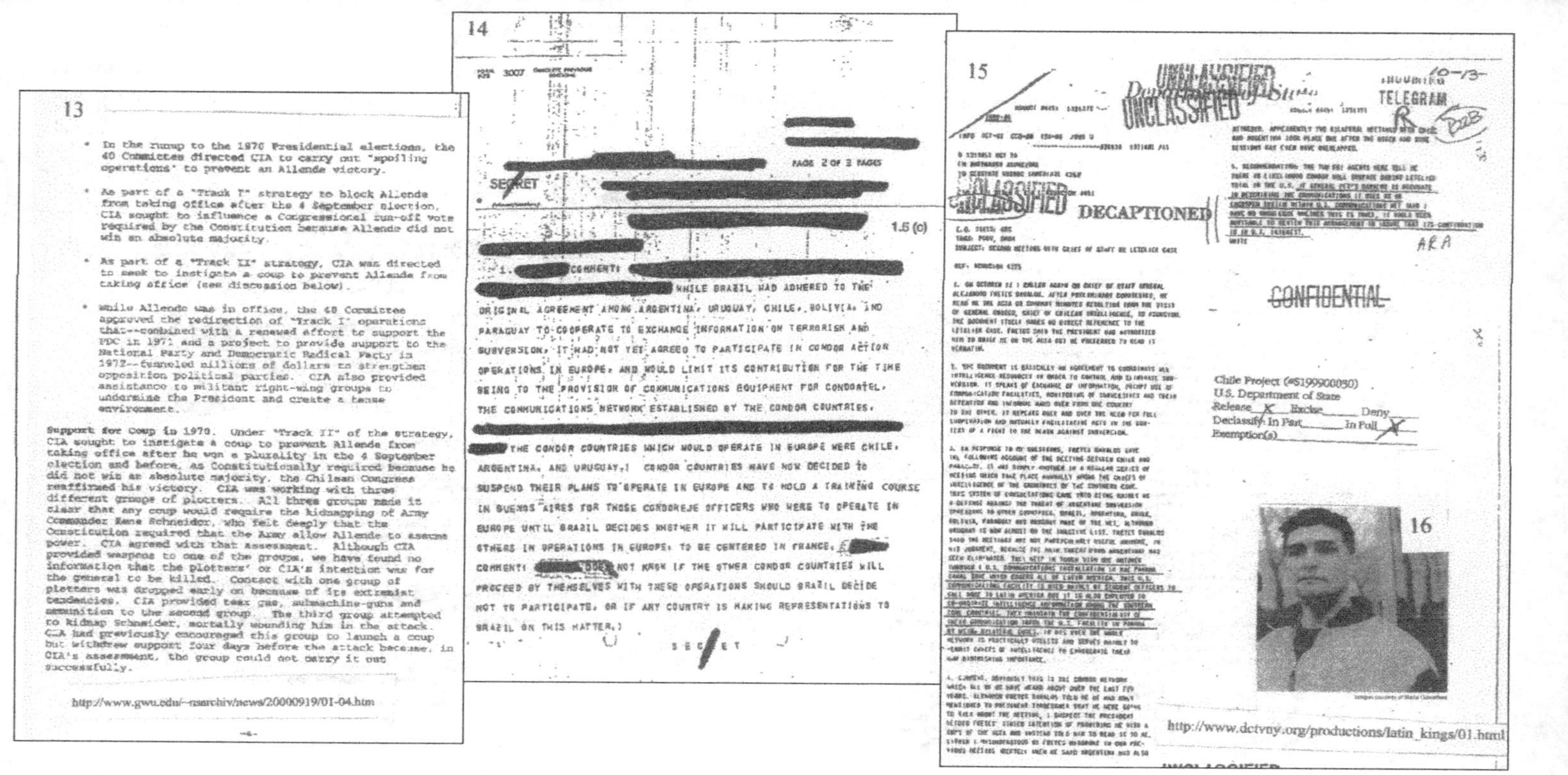
13

- In the runup to the 1970 Presidential elections, the 40 Committee directed CIA to carry out "spoiling operations" to prevent an Allende victory.
- As part of a "Track I" strategy to block Allende from taking office after the 4 September election, CIA sought to influence a Congressional run-off vote required by the Constitution because Allende did not win an absolute majority.
- As part of a "Track II" strategy, CIA was directed to seek to instigate a coup to prevent Allende from taking office (see discussion below).
- While Allende was in office, the 40 Committee approved the redirection of "Track I" operations that--combined with a renewed effort to support the PDC in 1971 and a project to provide support to the National Party and Democratic Radical Party in 1972--funneled millions of dollars to strengthen opposition political parties. CIA also provided assistance to militant right-wing groups to undermine the President and create a tense environment.

Support for Coup in 1970. Under "Track II" of the strategy, CIA sought to instigate a coup to prevent Allende from taking office after he won a plurality in the 4 September election and before, as Constitutionally required because he did not win an absolute majority, the Chilean Congress reaffirmed his victory. CIA was working with three different groups of plotters. All three groups made it clear that any coup would require the kidnapping of Army Commander Rene Schneider, who felt deeply that the Constitution required that the Army allow Allende to assume power. CIA agreed with that assessment. Although CIA provided weapons to one of the groups, we have found no information that the plotters' or CIA's intention was for the general to be killed. Contact with one group of plotters was dropped early on because of its extremist tendencies. CIA provided tear gas, submachine-guns and ammunition to the second group. The third group attempted to kidnap Schneider, mortally wounding him in the attack. CIA had previously encouraged this group to launch a coup but withdrew support four days before the attack because, in CIA's assessment, the group could not carry it out successfully.

http://www.gwu.edu/~nsarchiv/news/20000919/01-04.htm

-4-

14

3007

PAGE 2 OF 3 PAGES

SECRET

1.5 (c)

1. COMMENT: WHILE BRAZIL HAD ADHERED TO THE ORIGINAL AGREEMENT AMONG ARGENTINA, URUGUAY, CHILE, BOLIVIA AND PARAGUAY TO COOPERATE TO EXCHANGE INFORMATION ON TERRORISM AND SUBVERSION, IT HAD NOT YET AGREED TO PARTICIPATE IN CONDOR ACTION OPERATIONS IN EUROPE, AND WOULD LIMIT ITS CONTRIBUTION FOR THE TIME BEING TO THE PROVISION OF COMMUNICATIONS EQUIPMENT FOR CONDORTEL, THE COMMUNICATIONS NETWORK ESTABLISHED BY THE CONDOR COUNTRIES.

THE CONDOR COUNTRIES WHICH WOULD OPERATE IN EUROPE WERE CHILE, ARGENTINA, AND URUGUAY.) CONDOR COUNTRIES HAVE NOW DECIDED TO SUSPEND THEIR PLANS TO OPERATE IN EUROPE AND TO HOLD A TRAINING COURSE IN BUENOS AIRES FOR THOSE CONDOREJE OFFICERS WHO WERE TO OPERATE IN EUROPE UNTIL BRAZIL DECIDES WHETHER IT WILL PARTICIPATE WITH THE OTHERS IN OPERATIONS IN EUROPE, TO BE CENTERED IN FRANCE. COMMENT: DOES NOT KNOW IF THE OTHER CONDOR COUNTRIES WILL PROCEED BY THEMSELVES WITH THESE OPERATIONS SHOULD BRAZIL DECIDE NOT TO PARTICIPATE, OR IF ANY COUNTRY IS MAKING REPRESENTATIONS TO BRAZIL ON THIS MATTER.)

SECRET

15

UNCLASSIFIED

Department of State

TELEGRAM

UNCLASSIFIED

DECAPTIONED

CONFIDENTIAL

ARA

Chile Project (#S199900030)
U.S. Department of State
Release X Excise ___ Deny ___
Declassify: In Part ___ In Full X
Exemption(s) ___

16

http://www.dctvny.org/productions/latin_kings/01.html

13-15. These three U.S. Intelligence documents support how U.S. Intelligence helped orchestrate the coup of Chile's democratically elected leftist president, Dr. Salvadore Allende (13). Then they aided the multinational assassination operation directed at Latin American leftists worldwide, Operation Condor, based in Chile under coup leader and dictator Augusto Pinochet (14, 15).

16. The picture is of Antonio King "King Tone" Fernandez. The Young Lords advised him to lead the 3,000 member Almighty Latin King and Queen Nation (ALKQN) to convert from a gang to an activist group. Former Panthers advised the Bloods and Crips that Tupac also encouraged to convert to activism.

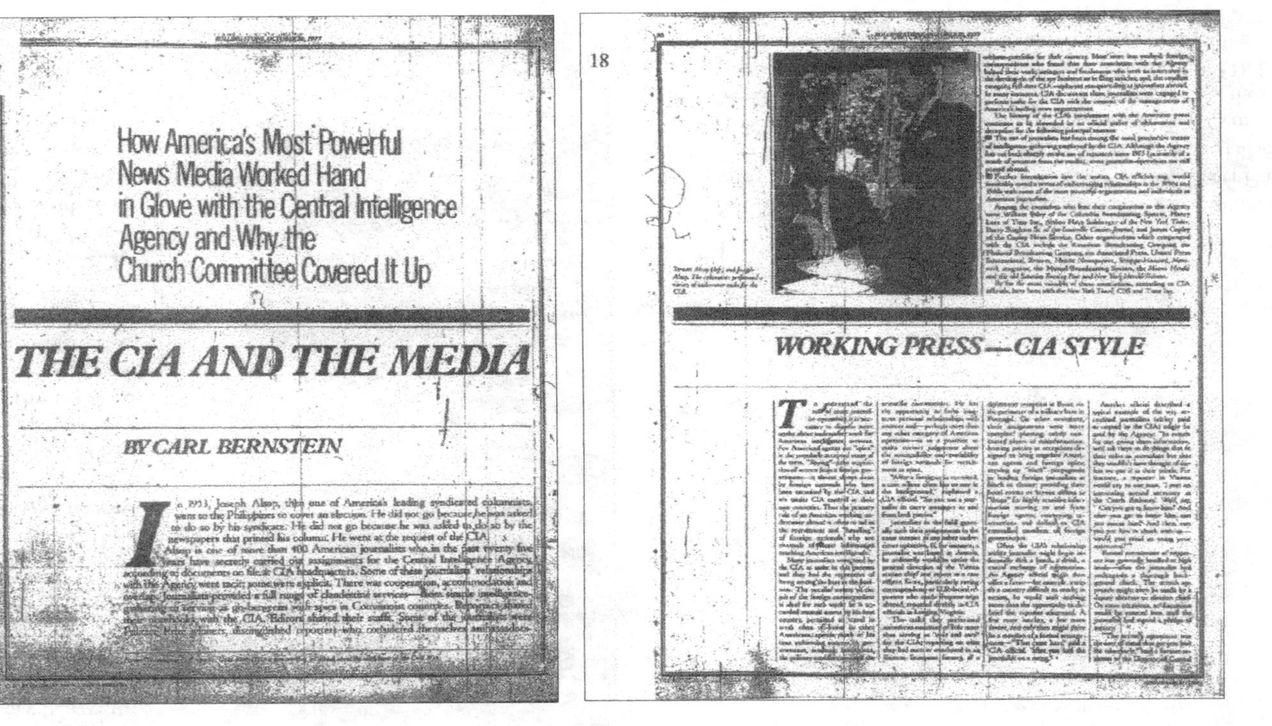

17

How America's Most Powerful News Media Worked Hand in Glove with the Central Intelligence Agency and Why the Church Committee Covered It Up

THE CIA AND THE MEDIA

BY CARL BERNSTEIN

In 1953, Joseph Alsop, then one of America's leading syndicated columnists, went to the Philippines to cover an election. He did not go because he was asked to do so by his syndicate. He did not go because he was asked to do so by the newspapers that printed his column. He went at the request of the CIA.

Alsop is one of more than 400 American journalists who in the past twenty-five years have secretly carried out assignments for the Central Intelligence Agency, according to documents on file at CIA headquarters. Some of these journalists' relationships with the Agency were tacit; some were explicit. There was cooperation, accommodation and overlap. Journalists provided a full range of clandestine services—from simple intelligence-gathering to serving as go-betweens with spies in Communist countries. Reporters shared their notebooks with the CIA. Editors shared their staffs. Some of the journalists were Pulitzer Prize winners, distinguished reporters who considered themselves ambassadors-

18

WORKING PRESS—CIA STYLE

17,18. Carl Bernstein could only publish his seminal article on the CIA's control of the media in Rolling Stone, despite his recent Watergate fame in 1977. It came out of a Congressional Committee's (mostly hidden) findings after activists burglarized an FBI office in 1971. It detailed how "well over 400" members of the media lived double lives in their work for the CIA. Note this author's asterisk next to the part saying the closest work was with the New York Times, CBS, and Time, Inc. At Time, Inc., the Vice-President went back and forth as head of U.S. Intelligence's Psychological Warfare, supporting that he used his many media outlets for that purpose. Time Warner bought control of Tupac's record labels, censored him and fought release of songs, as Warner had with Jimi Hendrix.

19. Most of this comes from a book by Jonn Christian, a former ABC Newsman, and an FBI agent-turned journalist, William Turner. They cite the many witnesses who said convicted assassin Sirhan Sirhan was two or more feet away from RFK, while the fatal shot came an inch away from RFK's head. RFK then grabbed the tie of the "guard" in that position—the real suspected assassin, Thane Cesar. Reports said this was a Robert Maheu operation (see document on Maheu to right). Picture by of Ted Charach, shows coroner Thomas Noguchi at press conference showing where the gun must have been to shoot RFK. An official court report at bottom says bullet fired from one inch away, behind RFK's right ear. Charach photo by Thomas Smith comes from Thom White, "RFK Assassination Far from Resolved," Citizine. 6/5/05

19

Page 7 of 11

Ted Charach holding a picture of Coroner Thomas Noguchi indicating a bullet that struck Robert Kennedy at point blank range in the back of the head.
Photo by Thomas Smith.

EXTRA
RFK IS DEAD

5. Thane Eugene Cesar (right) with fellow Ace Security guards moments after the shooting. Note his missing clip-on tie.

6. Robert Kennedy lies dying on the floor of the kitchen pantry of the Ambassador Hotel. Note clip-on tie near his right hand.

Charach photo by Thomas Smith comes from Thom White, "RFK Assassination Far from Resolved," *Citizine*. 6/5/05

20

MORI DocID: 1451843

SECRET
EYES ONLY

SUBJECT: Johnny Roselli

1. In August 1960, Mr. Richard M. Bissell approached Colonel Sheffield Edwards to determine if the Office of Security had assets that may assist in a sensitive mission requiring gangster-type action. The mission target was Fidel Castro.

2. Because of its extreme sensitivity, only a small group was made privy to the project. The DCI was briefed and gave his approval. Colonel J. C. King, Chief, WH Division, was briefed, but all details were deliberately concealed from any of the JMWAVE officials. Certain TSD and Communications personnel participated in the initial planning stages, but were not witting of the purpose of the mission.

3. Robert A. Maheu, a cleared source of the Office of Security, was contacted, briefed generally on the project, and requested to ascertain if he could develop an entree into the gangster elements as the first step toward accomplishing the desired goal.

4. Mr. Maheu advised that he had met one Johnny Roselli on several occasions while visiting Las Vegas. He only knew him casually through clients, but was given to understand that he was a high-ranking member of the "syndicate" and controlled all of the ice-making machines on the Strip. Maheu reasoned that, if Roselli was in fact a member of the clan, he undoubtedly had connections leading into the Cuban gambling interests.

5. Maheu was asked to approach Roselli, who knew Maheu as a personal relations executive handling domestic and foreign accounts, and tell him that he had recently been retained by a client who represented several international business firms which were suffering heavy financial losses in Cuba as a result of Castro's action. They were convinced that Castro's removal was the answer to their

00012

SECRET
EYES ONLY

20. This CIA document shows how the CIA has worked with the Mafia on operations, such as attempting to assassinate Cuba's leader Fidel Castro. Note its Las Vegas Mafia. That R. Maheu, suspected of aiding RFK's assassination, is named. Some top suspects in Tupac's murder in Vegas include a U.S. Intelligence/Mafia collaboration. Also, the top police suspects came from Los Angeles's Rampart Division, one of 18 LAPD divisions, which covered up RFK's murder. From gwu.edu/~nsarchive/NSAEBB?NSAEBB222/index.htm

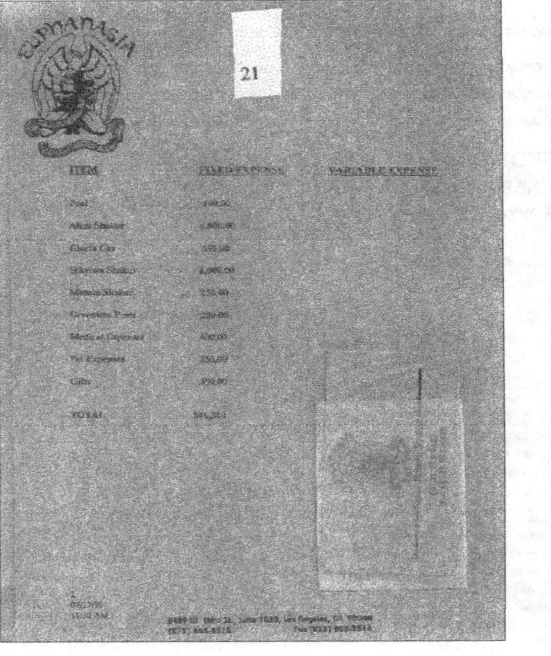

EUPHANASIA

21

ITEM	FIXED EXPENSE	VARIABLE EXPENSE
[illegible]	[illegible]	
Afeni Shakur	[illegible]	
Gloria Cox	[illegible]	
Sekyiwa Shakur	[illegible]	
Mutulu Shakur	[illegible]	
Geronimo Pratt	[illegible]	
Medical Expenses	[illegible]	
Pet Expenses	[illegible]	
Gifts	[illegible]	
TOTAL	[illegible]	

21. This page is from Tupac's business started in the last months of his life. It shows that he had sent regular payments to some of his imprisoned revolutionary family members. These included his imprisoned revolutionary stepfather, Mutulu Shakur, who was a cofounder of the Republic of New Afrika. Tupac also sent regular payments to his godfather, LA Panther leader Geronimo Pratt (Ji Jaja).

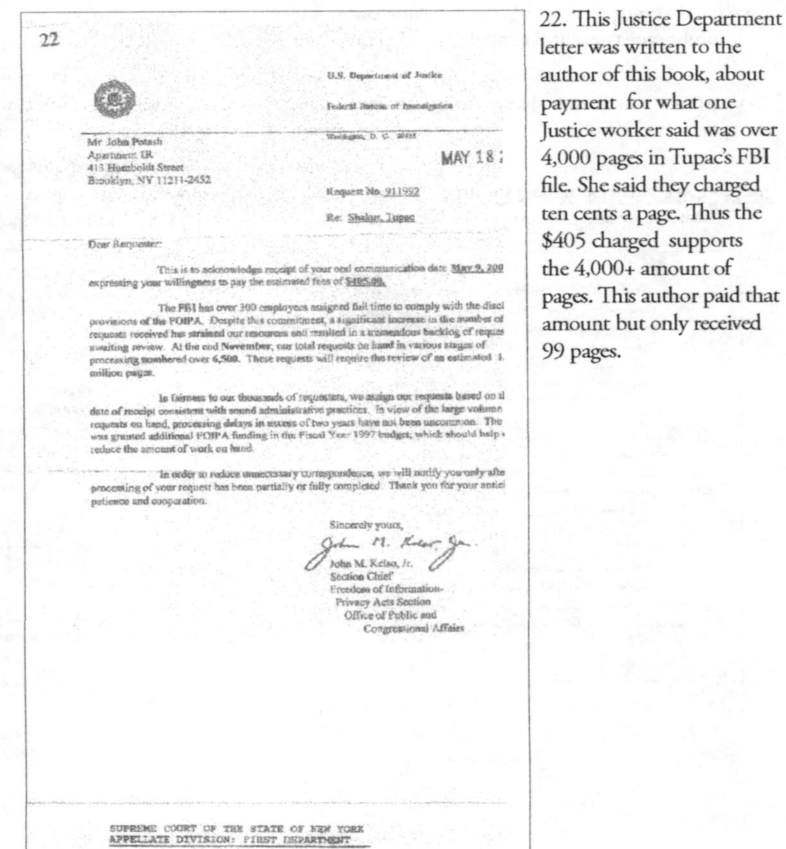

22

U.S. Department of Justice

Federal Bureau of Investigation

Washington, D. C. 20535

Mr. John Potash
Apartment 1R
413 Humboldt Street
Brooklyn, NY 11211-2452

MAY 18 :

Request No. 911992

Re: Shakur, Tupac

Dear Requester:

This is to acknowledge receipt of your oral communication date May 9, 200 expressing your willingness to pay the estimated fees of $405.00.

The FBI has over 300 employees assigned full time to comply with the discl provisions of the FOIPA. Despite this commitment, a significant increase in the number of requests received has strained our resources and resulted in a tremendous backlog of reques awaiting review. At the end November, our total requests on hand in various stages of processing numbered over 6,500. These requests will require the review of an estimated 1. million pages.

In fairness to our thousands of requesters, we assign our requests based on tl date of receipt consistent with sound administrative practices. In view of the large volume requests on hand, processing delays in excess of two years have not been uncommon. The was granted additional FOIPA funding in the Fiscal Year 1997 budget, which should help reduce the amount of work on hand.

In order to reduce unnecessary correspondence, we will notify you only afte processing of your request has been partially or fully completed. Thank you for your antici patience and cooperation.

Sincerely yours,

John M. Kelso, Jr.
Section Chief
Freedom of Information-
Privacy Acts Section
Office of Public and
Congressional Affairs

SUPREME COURT OF THE STATE OF NEW YORK
APPELLATE DIVISION: FIRST DEPARTMENT

22. This Justice Department letter was written to the author of this book, about payment for what one Justice worker said was over 4,000 pages in Tupac's FBI file. She said they charged ten cents a page. Thus the $405 charged supports the 4,000+ amount of pages. This author paid that amount but only received 99 pages.

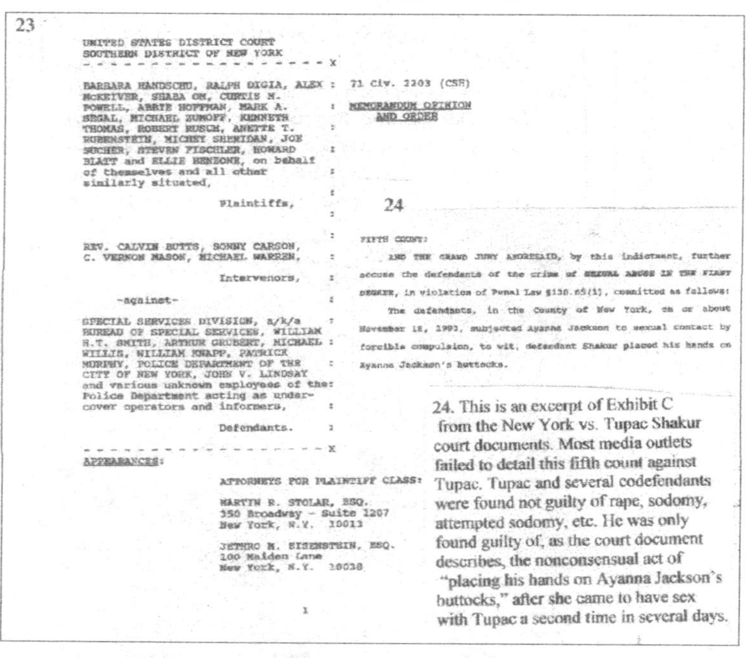

23

UNITED STATES DISTRICT COURT
SOUTHERN DISTRICT OF NEW YORK
- x

BARBARA HANDSCHU, RALPH DIGIA, ALEX : 71 Civ. 2203 (CSH)
McKEIVER, SHABA OM, CURTIS M.
POWELL, ABBIE HOFFMAN, MARK A. : MEMORANDUM OPINION AND ORDER
SEGAL, MICHAEL ZUMOFF, KENNETH
THOMAS, ROBERT RUSCH, ANETTE T.
RUBENSTEIN, MICHEY SHERIDAN, JOE
SUCHER, STEVEN FISCHLER, HOWARD
BLATT and ELLIE BENZONE, on behalf
of themselves and all other
similarly situated,

Plaintiffs,

REV. CALVIN BUTTS, SONNY CARSON,
C. VERNON MASON, MICHAEL WARREN,

Intervenors,

-against-

SPECIAL SERVICES DIVISION, a/k/a
BUREAU OF SPECIAL SERVICES, WILLIAM
H.T. SMITH, ARTHUR GRUBERT, MICHAEL
WILLIS, WILLIAM KNAPP, PATRICK
MURPHY, POLICE DEPARTMENT OF THE
CITY OF NEW YORK, JOHN V. LINDSAY
and various unknown employees of the
Police Department acting as under-
cover operators and informers,

Defendants.
- x

APPEARANCES:

ATTORNEYS FOR PLAINTIFF CLASS:

MARTIN R. STOLAR, ESQ.
350 Broadway - Suite 1207
New York, N.Y. 10013

JETHRO M. EISENSTEIN, ESQ.
100 Maiden Lane
New York, N.Y. 10038

1

24

FIFTH COUNT:

AND THE GRAND JURY AFORESAID, by this indictment, further accuse the defendants of the crime of SEXUAL ABUSE IN THE FIRST DEGREE, in violation of Penal Law §130.65(1), committed as follows:

The defendants, in the County of New York, on or about November 18, 1993, subjected Ayanna Jackson to sexual contact by forcible compulsion, to wit, defendant Shakur placed his hands on Ayanna Jackson's buttocks.

24. This is an excerpt of Exhibit C from the New York vs. Tupac Shakur court documents. Most media outlets failed to detail this fifth count against Tupac. Tupac and several codefendants were found not guilty of rape, sodomy, attempted sodomy, etc. He was only found guilty of, as the court document describes, the nonconsensual act of "placing his hands on Ayanna Jackson's buttocks," after she came to have sex with Tupac a second time in several days.

25

THE PEOPLE OF THE STATE OF NEW YORK,

-against-

TUPAC SHAKUR,

Defendant-Petitioner.

AFFIDAVIT

New York County
Indictment No. 11578/93

Appellate Division
Case No. ________

STATE OF NEW YORK)
) ss.:
COUNTY OF NEW YORK)

BARBARA J. JUSTICE, M.D., being duly sworn deposes and says:

1. I am a physician licensed to practice medicine in the State of New York and specialize in general surgery. I am currently affiliated as a surgical fellow at Harlem Hospital. I have extensive experience in trauma surgery involving gunshot wounds.

2. On December 9, 1994, Tupac Shakur (hereinafter the "patient") came under my medical care as a result of multiple bullet wounds to his head, scrotum and right thigh sustained on November 30, 1994. The patient was first treated at the Bellevue Hospital Center where he had a surgical repair of the scalp and scrotal injuries as well as repair of a major blood vessel in his right thigh.

3. Specifically the patient suffered two entrance gunshot wounds to the back of his head, and two exit wounds which went through the top of his scalp. A third bullet penetrated the exterior surface of his right hand. A fourth bullet struck the patient in the base of his penis, and proceeded through his scrotum. Either that bullet or a fifth bullet entered his right thigh, severing the profundus femoral artery.

23. This court document originally involved a class action suit against New York for it's murderous "political police" Intelligence division—Bureau of Special Services (BOSS). Like most police intelligence divisions, BOSS had officers who also worked for the FBI. Abbie Hoffman was a plaintiff and Tupac's New York lawyer, Michael Tarif Warren was an Intervenor, regarding this lawsuit against the NYPD for Cointelpro-type "Black Desk" activities in the '80s.

24. This is an excerpt of Exhibit C from the New York vs. Tupac Shakur court documents. Most media outlets failed to detail this fifth count against Tupac. Tupac and several codefendants were found not guilty of rape, sodomy, attempted sodomy, etc. He was only found guilty of, as the court document describes, the nonconsensual act of "placing his hands on Ayanna Jackson's buttocks," after she came to have sex with Tupac a second time in several days.

25. Above is an excerpt of the continuation of the second page cut and pasted with the first page showing the doctor's court deposition regarding Tupac's Times Square recording studio lobby shooting in New York. The document details that the "muggers" had a clear motive of killing Tupac, using a known U.S. Special Forces style of one shot to get him on the ground and then two shots in the head. Tupac miraculously survived.

Author's Preface

I got into this book project after researching the New York Panther Shakur family for an activist novel. When New York gunmen shot Tupac Shakur in November of '94, *The Washington Post* commented on "another strange twist" regarding police behavior and Tupac. Wondering if the police targeted Tupac as they did his family, I called Tupac's activist New York trial lawyer, Michael Tarif Warren. He adamantly agreed with this idea. Warren consistently provided me with information and encouragement since then.

That spring of '95, I published an article suggesting a latter-day FBI Cointelpro targeting of Tupac, in a Washington D.C. political prisoner-supporting magazine, *Claustrophobia*. By 1996 I had started a national social work school newspaper, *Social Justice Action Quarterly*, which I ran for four years while getting a masters at Columbia University. I also published an unrelated article in the internationally distributed *Z Magazine* that year, just before Tupac's murder. *Z*, *Covert Action* and other left-wing political magazines had rejected my '95 and '96 article submissions on Tupac. But *Z* may have shared it with Christian Parenti as he asked Assata Shakur about this "rumored" theory in a 1997 *Z* interview. Assata said she agreed that the FBI could have targeted Tupac.

In 1999, *Covert Action Quarterly* (CAQ) published my article on the FBI targeting Tupac and other black leaders. Co-founded by Phillip Agee, a 12-year CIA official who blew the whistle on his agency's illegal operations, CAQ required similar meticulous documentation as this book contains. Shortly before then and since, Tupac's lifetime family friend and business manager, Watani Tyehimba, has been a major source of information and encouragement for me on this book. Tyehimba's fellow New Afrikan People's Organization founding leader, Tupac's national attorney Chokwe Lumumba, gave me helpful information, as did Tupac's Atlanta trial lawyer, Ken Ellis.

On Black Panther information, former New Haven Panther George Edwards and Panther National Communications Secretary Kathleen Cleaver were very helpful. Cleaver, an attorney on the faculty of Emory University Law School, offered consistent encouragement, insight, and a referral to her book editor. Fellow die-hard activist Edwards kindly donated copies of his own research documents, as well as giving insight, critiques and help. Also thanks to International Concerned Family and Friends of Mumia Abu-Jamal director, Pam Africa, for her promotional aid and Foreword (also to Razzakahn for his help in that endeavor). Thanks to Mumia Abu-Jamal for his flattering remarks and contribution to the Foreword. And thanks to Fred Hampton, Jr. for his Afterword to this book.

Further thanks for others' unpaid help in varied ways: my wife, Janine, for her tireless editing; professors Dennis Brutus and the late Richard Cloward; *CovertAction Quarterly*'s, Bill Schaap, Ellen Ray and, particularly, Lou Wolfe; *Claustrophobia*'s Brad, Bobby and David; Mike Turner, formerly with the law firm Stillman and Friedman; and FAIR's Steve Rendall.

A final thanks to Afeni Shakur, along with her (and Tupac's) personal assistant, Molly Monjauze, and former Panther-turned Tupac Foundation director, Thomas McCreary, for their warmth in our brief talks. All of Tupac's mentors and friends passed on their inspiring passion for a better world that allowed them to persevere despite U.S. Intelligence's opposition.

In 2005, I started distributing a plastic binder-bound version of this book manuscript. I revised that version over a half dozen times before printing 50 copies of a "perfect bound" paperback version in October of 2007. This is the second (and likely last) edition of the perfect bound paperback version of the book. I'm now moving on to an activist novel with equal amounts of research and some themes mentioned in this book.

On one last note, *The FBI War on Tupac Shakur and Black Leaders* originally ran up to 700 pages. I condensed the book into this smaller package to make it more affordable. Virtually every paragraph has an endnote but, with limited time and resources, I was unable to reproduce new words that began and ended every paragraph of newly condensed information. So please disregard the occasional incorrect wording that starts some of these endnote references and please excuse this imperfection.

John Potash, January 2008

This second printing includes corrections of multiple typos in the previous edition. It also includes new information on Richard Wright (Ch.38), Paul Robeson (Ch.40), Jam Master Jay Mizell (Ch.33), and on the FBI deputizing over 20,000 business leaders (Ch.40). Thanks to Afrikan World Books www.afrikanworldbooks.com and www.akpress.com for distribution. Also thanks to Pacifica's WPFW's Jared Ball, along with WOLB's Nati and Daren Muhammad, for their radio interviews. Further thanks to Everyone's Place and Robin's Books for their book talks. And final thanks to Julia Wright for inviting me to speak at the 100 year Celebration of her father Richard Wright, and Kaleem Ashref for his audio web interview on http://americaetc.googlepages.com John Potash, 10/2008

3rd printing thanks to Pacifica New York WBAI Evening News' Rebecca Myles, Interim Manager Tony Bates and Education at the Crossroads' Basir Mchawi. Thanks to Washington WPFW's Voices with Vision and Naji Mujahid. ***DVD now available.*** John P. 10/2009

4th printing thanks to Gopal Matlock and assistant producer, and Dedon Kamathi, host of "Freedom Now" on Los Angele's KPFK radio station, part of the Pacifica network at 90.7. I also wanted to thank the people that interviewed me for internet podcasts or internet radio in the last year. These include Mike McCann, Gus of C.O.W.S. radio, and Simone of www.blackwomenin communication.com, Jeff Long for his Redacted News blog posting, Thomas Good Next Left Notes for his support and jpplaya for turning my presentation into youtube videos. Thanks to Matt and Elaine Sullivan and Lou Wolfe of Rock Creek Free Press for printing two of my articles based on this book. A special thanks to Sanyika Shakur as well as Professor Grif of Public Enemy for discussing my book throughout his speaking tour. John P. 4/2010

The 5th printing includes new information on the Baltimore Black Panthers in Chapter 3. It also contains new information on Jimi Hendrix and Bob Marley, as well as Public Enemy (Ch.32). While this printing was underway, a filmmaker sent me copies of government documents that show Jimmy 'Henchman" Rosemond was working as a police informant/agent. This filmmaker also said he had documents showing that Haitian Jacques Agnant (Tupac: "Knew he was working for the Feds" Ch.18) was put on trial and sentenced with those three gunmen in a seperate incident. Other people have sent me news, such as Ras Ceylon and his Throwback Records being raided by the DEA and his record studio office in shambles due to it. And, New York's The Brecht Forum was broken into and their computers stolen. And there's the case of Michael Jackson. Please excuse this writer from not having the time to keep adding any more to this book. People are also giving me conflicting reports on the source of a quote from Tupac's Makavelli CD about "We must fight for Mumia..." They say it's either Khalid Muhammad or Louis Farrakhan. I can't find a solid reference as to which answer is right. The next book is under way with some overlapping material but important new information on a new subject.

Thanks to Brett McCabe of *The City Paper*, Baltimore, for his interview and article on this author and book in June 2010. Andy Rubin of Cyclops Books and Records for two showings of the 85 minute film/DVD based on this book. Cornell Dews and AllHipHop.com for their interview and article in June of 2010. Sister Fay and her Sisterspace and Books in Washington DC for hosting a film showing of the DVD based on this book. Cincinnati Radio host Nathan Ivey, for several interviews on 101.1 WIZF fm radio as well as his 1230AM

WDBZ. Umar Abdullah-Johnson of "The Umar Johnson Show"Wednesdays @ 6pm 1540AM/WNWR Philadelphia. Sanyika Shakur (aka Monster Kody Scott) for his gracious letter from jail praising this book (which this writer temporarily misplaced, but will find). Rasheed Barnwell of Real Talk Radio in Gary, Indiana (reaching Southside Chicago) for his radio interview. Ural Garrett of OnWaxMagazine.com for his interview. Thanks to Darren Muhammad of Black Anti-Defamation Urban League(BADUL) and WOLB, as well as BADUL Director Leticia Fitts, for their numerous forums for me presenting my work.

More thanks to Pam Africa, for all her tireless work that included setting up and promoting a film showing at Dowling's Palace in Philadelphia. Bluestockings Bookstore Café in New York and Boston's Lucy Parsons Center for their book talks and film showings. Former Panther George Edwards for organizing a showing of the film in New Haven, CT (as well as contributing to the Boston film showing) and Tom Flickin and his Flickin Media Group, for helping promote the New Haven showing. Paul Scott for discussing the book in his OpEd, Winter in America. Michael Richardson for reviewing the film in the Boston Progressive Examiner. GL Henderson for his internet radio interview. Zo Williams and Felicia Morris of Voice of Reason program on "The Foxxhole with Jamie Foxx" station on Sirius106/XM149 satellite radio. French TV/film producer Alex Jordanov for his interview for a TV film on Tupac with 3e Oeil Productions. Thanks to Tyson Gravity of Black and Nobel Books for coming down to Baltimore to try and film an interview (we'll make it happen). Further thanks to writer/filmmaker Alexander McLean for his interview due on film/youtube at underyourskin.net. And, last but definitely not least, a special thanks to Professor Griff of Public Enemy for his consistent promotion of the book on his speaking tour and radio interviews. For anyone else, if I forgot you, contact me and I'll thank you in the next printing.

John Potash December 2010

For this 6th printing, thanks again to Alex Jordanov for giving me and the theme of my book national exposure in France with his nationally televised documentary, *Tupac: L'Assassination D'une Icon* (The Assassination of an Icon)on Troisieme Rue. And thanks again to Daren Muhammad of *State of the City* WFBR 1590am noon Tuesdays to Saturdays, for interviews, as well as Latecia Fitts also of BADUL for the Baltimore forums. Thanks to Sama'an Ashrawi and Chris Sakaguchi of the radio station at The University of Texas at Austin's 91.7 KVRX Tuesday 11pm show for an interview. Thanks also to Dominique DiPrima Host/Producer *The Front Page* 102.3 KJLH radio Thursday early morning show in Los Angeles. Esowan Books in Los Angeles and

Marcus Books in San Francisco (and Oakland) for giving me the forum for showing parts of my film. Thanks also to the Los Angeles Sentinel for the advance coverage of my LA event at Esowan. Also thanks to Muz Wear Urbn Grmnts for the T-shirt collaboration of the cover of this book. Please buy this shirt and help get the word out. Thanks to Tyson Gravity and Hakim Green of Black and Nobel Books for the interview, filmed and posted on your website. Asher Underwood for the interview and great work with Shawn Sparxx on truthabouttupac.com Also to Deodon Kamati, host/producer of *Freedom Now* on Saturdays 5pm KPFK in Los Angeles. Since last printing, Dexter Isaacs has written a letter to Allhiphop.com saying James "Henchman" Rosemond offered him $2500 to fatally shoot Tupac in the New York recording studio. Rosemond admitted he was who Tupac described as Haitian Jacques Agnant's associate that lured Tupac with huge money to that recording studio. I've been given copies of government documents by a top TV documentary producer in France, Alex Jordanov. They show Rosemond collaborating with the government in 1997 and '98.

John Potash, September 2011

For this 7th printing: thanks to John Judge and everyone else at the Committee for Political Assassinations (COPA) for inviting me to speak at your fall of 2011 conference. Thanks to Joe Green for the work with COPA and interview in the San Diego Examiner, reprinted on COPA's website. Vinny Eastwood for his New Zealand radio interview as well as Infinity Radio for getting the interview out further and American Freedom Radio for getting the interview out around the U.S. Everyone at Black and Nobel Books for another presentation at your Philadelphia bookstore. Thanks to Dedon Kamati of Freedom Now on KPFK Los Angeles for another radio interview. Thanks to Dequi Kioni-Sadiki of Where We Live on WBAI New York for the radio interview with myself, Maurice "Mopreme" Shakur, and Dharuba Bin Wahad. Thanks to Chris Stevenson for picking this book as #3 on his Top 10 Summer/Fall books to read on Blackcommentator.com and for his two interviews on BlogTalkRadio. Thanks to Sanyika Shakur (aka "Monster" Kody Scott) for the recommendation of this book in his interview with the San Francisco Bay View newspaper. A final word of apology and regret to Watani Tyehimba about losing touch and not getting more information on how his son, Yakhisizwe, followed Tupac to Death Row and then died around the time of Tupac's death. Mainstream media continues to hide such information and I wish I could fill in even more of the picture to get as much of the story out there as possible to help stop these horrors from continuing. This will be in the Tupac section of the next book. As I approach the final drafts of my next book, this will likely be the last printing of this one.

John Potash June 2012.

For this 8th printing: thanks to John Judge and the Committee on Political Assassinations for inviting me to talk with Congresswoman Cynthia McKinney et al at Howard University for Malcolm X's birthday event. Thanks to David of Under the Pavement Radio 96.9 FM, Manchester, England for the interview. Thanks Paul Allen Billings of The Beat, 103.7 FM, Western Michigan Radio for his Drive at Five interview. Thanks Ron Mba Herd II of W.E. A.L.L. B.E. blogtalkradio. And thanks again to Darin Muhammad for his State of the City interview on 1590 AM in Baltimore.

John Potash June 2013.

For this 9th printing: I'm happy to announce that Trine Day will be publishing my next book, tentatively titled: **Drugs as Weapons Against Us**: *The CIA's Murderous Targeting of SDS, Panthers, Hendrix, Lennon, Cobain, Tupac & other Leftists*. It will be released in the fall of 2014. Thanks to *Z* magazine for their 2013 printing of my article "The FBI War on the Shakurs," regarding the war on Assata and Tupac. Thanks again to John Judge and the Committee of Political Assassinations (COPA) for having me speak on the FBI's Counterintelligence Program at the 50th Anniversary of John F. Kennedy's assassination conference in Dallas in 2013. And thanks for having me speak on the Malcolm X panel at the University of the District of ColumbiaLawSchool in 2014. It's very sad that John Judge had a stroke shortly after that event. For more information and to contribute to helping him, see COPA website politicalassassinations.com. Thanks to Netfa Freeman and *Voices With Vision* radio program, WPFW, 89.3 FM in WashingtonD.C. for having me on your show again, in 2014. Thanks to SGTReport.com for an interview in 2013. This printing has a few changes. I'll be attempting to add the information on Watani Tyehimba's son being found dead soon after Tupac's death, in Chapter 26. This author will relate more recent developments since the last printing. This author feels it's too overwhelming to change the book with each new development, except as when revisions on pertinent past history deserve changing. Great news came with Baltimore Black Panther Marshall Eddie Conway's release from prison in 2014. Very sad news came with the passing of Tupac's national lawyer, Chokwe Lumumba, after he had been elected mayor of Jackson, Mississippi. One of Tupac's bodyguards, Frank Alexander, also sadly died in 2013.

John Potash March 2014

For 10th printing: R.I.P. Committee On Political Assasinations director John Judge. Info on Yakhisizwe Tyehimba as the Director of Security for the New Afrikan Panthers when Tupac was Chair of the group has been added to Chapter 11. Thanks to Ed Opperman and John B. Wells (Caravan To Midnight), Race for the Times and Down the Rabbit Hole, for the interviews. New book **Drugs as Weapons Against Us** hopefully will be available by the end of May 2015.

Foreword

By Pam Africa with contribution and essay by Mumia Abu-Jamal

I've spent the last few decades organizing, first nationally, and then worldwide, to gain Mumia Abu-Jamal's release, along with the release of eight brothers and sisters of MOVE and other political prisoners (see Ch.17). In the summer of 1999, an award-winning magazine, *Covert Action Quarterly*, came out with a very important cover story on "Mumia and the Media." I read many of the very informative articles in that magazine, which required that its authors provide footnotes for all its facts. These articles ranged from an alert about political prisoner Leonard Peltier of the American Indian Movement, to an article on WBAI director, the late Samori Marksman and his close associate, Elombe Brath, as well as the militarization of the police and an attack on MOVE.

Then I decided to read the article "Tupac's Panther Shadow: The Political Targeting of Tupac Shakur." I didn't know much about this controversial young rapper but after reading this article I realized I had to know more. So I called one of the publishers, Louis Wolfe. I thanked him for the many educational articles in that #67, 1999 issue. I liked the magazine so much that I made the cover page into a T-shirt for fundraising at our 1999 Millions for Mumia demonstration. Wolfe gave me two boxes of *Covert Action* for fundraising as well. We received an overwhelming response to John Potash's article on Tupac. Wolfe told John how important I thought his article was.

Six years later, I was fortunate to meet John Potash in Harlem, New York, where I was co-hosting the Coalition to Free Mumia Abu-Jamal informational fundraising forum. Upon introducing himself, I immediately greeted him with a warm hug. John then gave me a copy of his book manuscript for The FBI War on Tupac Shakur and Black Leaders. I led John to my comrade Fred Hampton, Jr. and introduced them for the first time. Fred had already received a copy of John's book from Smitty, an elder Black Panther from New Jersey. Like myself, Fred was pleased to meet John Potash.

I took my copy of his book with me when I flew to a Mumia event in San Francisco. On the plane, I started reading parts that interested me. I quickly realized that everything in the book interested me, so I started from the beginning. Once arriving in California, I kept reading every chance I got. I needed to read more. I felt driven to complete this manuscript and couldn't put it down.

Simply put, The FBI War on Tupac Shakur and Black Leaders is one of the most important books I ever read. I quickly placed this manuscript amongst the books that Mumia must read and urged other supporters to do so. I called John and asked for more copies of the book manuscript, which he sent me.

During a visit with Mumia, we talked about John's book. I asked for comments on the book. Without hesitation, Mumia said, "Remarkable! Pam, It's truly remarkable work." Mumia wrote a book called *Death Blossoms: Reflections from a Prisoner of Conscience* in 1996, from which we selected one of his chapters, titled, "Objectivity and the Media," to be part of this foreword (see below).

I proceeded to take copies of *The FBI War on Tupac Shakur and Black Leaders* manuscript with me around the world. In France, I gave it to my sister in struggle, Julia Wright, a freelance journalist and frontline activist who heads our International Concerned Friends of Mumia Abu-Jamal in that country. She's also the daughter of the famous mid-century novelist and Pan-Africanist Richard Wright (Ch.38). I gave it to Amiri Baraka and his wife. I gave it to Michael Franti, Herman Ferguson, and Black Panthers now living in other countries. I also talked to Kathleen Cleaver who said this book manuscript had to be published. Through this book, Dharuba Bin Wahad, former Black political prisoner who did over 28 years in prison, learned of the over 4,000 page FBI file on Tupac. He also wanted people to know how political prisoners put protection on Tupac while he was incarcerated (this is explained in the book). Everyone who read it had been asking, "When is this writer going to publish it? When can I get the final edition?"

One person I gave it to, Omi Raheem, immediately contacted John to say she wanted to buy 10 copies of the manuscript before it was published. Omi is a former Queens, New York Black Panther who was a friend of Afeni Shakur's. Like many Panthers, she had rushed to Afeni's side as soon as she heard Tupac was shot. Omi gave her copies of John's book to loved ones as educational gifts. Another friend, Razzakahn read my copy and said it was excellent. He purchased several copies for friends, and more copies for his teenage grandchildren and incarcerated inmates. Omi also brought over four DVDs on Tupac because I wanted to know more about him after reading the early edition of this book. I witnessed the birth of this book from a seed, with *Covert Action Quarterly*, and now the baby is ready for the world. This book bridges the generation gap, from U.S. Intelligence's assassinations of Malcolm X, Martin Luther King and Jimi Hendrix, to Bob Marley, today's political rappers, and today's black political leaders.

It's so thorough that it leaves no room for doubt as to how treacherous this government is. For example, I can't disagree with the evidence on Mumia Abu-Jamal. As detailed in here, the evidence supports that U.S. Intelligence used psychological profiling on Mumia.

The evidence further supports that they used similar psychological profiling in 1993 to set up the police shooting at Tupac Shakur in Atlanta. The chapter on Mumia touches on our MOVE organization, which I'll discuss further, starting with our web page introduction:

"The MOVE organization is a family of strong, serious, deeply committed revolutionaries, founded by a wise, perceptive, strategically-minded black man named JOHN AFRICA. MOVE work is revolution. JOHN AFRICA's revolution, to stop man's system from imposing on life. To stop industry from poisoning the air, water, and soil, and to put an end to the enslavement of all life. Our work is to show people how rotten and enslaving the system is. And that the system is the cause of homelessness, unemployment, drug addiction, alcoholism, racism, domestic abuse, AIDS, crime, war and all the problems of the world. We are working to demonstrate that people not only can fight the system, they must fight the system, if they ever want to free themselves from endless suffering and oppression."

Our MOVE organization had experienced a brutal attack by Philadelphia police in 1977 and '78. City officials spent ten months illegally trying to evict us from our home and eventually turned off our water. They then surrounded our house with a four block-wide blockade and wouldn't allow anyone to bring in food, while also checking every Philadelphia resident that tried to come in (For further details, www.onamove.com, onamovellja@aol.com, and tel#215-387-4107). They surrounded the house with snipers and, amidst unloading a fusillade of bullets on our house, police shot their own cop. They blamed everyone in the house, but it later came out that he was shot with a police bullet (however the convicted MOVE members remain in prison today despite this exonerating evidence).

After the murder of Black Panther Fred Hampton at his home in 1969, Chicago police didn't tear the house down and it came back to haunt them with an outside investigation and lawsuit. In our 1978 situation, Philadelphia police ended up bulldozing the house while we were in it, both to get us out and destroy the crime scene evidence. When we finally emerged from the house, young Delbert Africa came out shirtless with his hands raised. Police viciously beat, stomped and near-fatally shot him. Then they dragged his body through the street. The cops later found out that television cameras had recorded it. Other men were also beaten viciously and nine MOVE members and three supporters were arrested.

On May 13, 1985, in a desperate attempt to murder JOHN AFRICA, police used a bogus warrant (which was later found to be invalid) and other trumped up reasons to surround our house and try to force us out with water cannons, ammunition and explosives. The police fired over 10,000 rounds of ammunition at the house and then dropped a bomb from a helicopter on the roof. They then ordered the firemen not to put hoses on the ensuing fire, leading to the deaths of 11 black men, women and children. The fire ended up consuming two square blocks of Philadelphia, destroying 61 homes and leaving 250 people homeless. The only adult MOVE member to survive, Ramona Africa, was the only one ever charged for the events of that day. She maxed out her seven-year sentence on charges of inciting a riot when it was the police that illegally invaded and bombed our home, viciously murdering 11 of my brothers and sisters.

Tupac died just before he planned to talk with Mumia in jail. One of our top organizers from the International Concerned Family and Friends of Mumia Norwalk Chapter, the late Susan Burnett, knew Tupac Shakur all his life and knew of his importance. Susan had just finished arranging for Tupac to get on Mumia's visitor list as the two wanted to talk. Susan had married Black Panther Ali Bey Hassan (aka Iverson Burnett) who organized with Tupac's mother Afeni Shakur. The government put Afeni and Ali Bey both on trial in 1971, as part of the New York Panther 21 who a jury acquitted. Tupac often stayed at the Burnetts' house when he was younger and stayed in touch with them. The government targeted and eliminated their Norwalk Chapter, which represented both Mumia and other political prisoners (Mumia referred to Susan and Ali Bey as the dynamic duo).

In another example of how the sons and daughters of important leaders get attacked, John F. Kennedy, Jr.'s death deserves attention because I think that was a U.S. Intelligence assassination. Mumia's former lawyer, Leonard Weinglass, had just finished an interview that appeared in John F. Kennedy Jr.'s magazine George. JFK, Jr., a young leftist with the ability to get his message to a wide audience, was doing research for an article on our MOVE organization just before he was assassinated. While John Potash covered the assassination of Robert F. Kennedy, similar tactics were used in JFK, Jr's death. Just like they did with Tupac and many black leaders, they tried to demonize JFK, Jr. after his death. [for more on JFK, Jr.'s assassination, see "You CAN Handle the Truth, Who Killed JFK Jr?" youtube.com].

The so-called "powers that be" only let influential leaders go so far with their leftist work. Once they cross a certain line, conservative forces have their political police, the vast U.S. Intelligence network, to take these people down. *The FBI War on Tupac Shakur* connects the dots, drawing them into one large, consistent, still-running plan by the reactionary forces that dominate the government's executive branch. This plan includes assassinating leftist leaders, particularly those of color. These assassinations include political leaders, musicians, and others. Most of those they don't kill get incarcerated for the rest of their lives.

This book further shows how these conservative forces so easily work hand-in-hand with the corporate media to demonize leaders and destroy the way people remember them. For example, everyone should know that the *2008 Guinness Book of Records* has included the MOVE organization under the section on cults. It lists May 13, 1985, the day 11 MOVE members died, as one of the largest "mass suicides." We are not a cult, we are an organization, and we certainly did not commit suicide. Philadelphia police dropped a bomb on our house. This is just another example of how the government works with the media. They also mislabel a murderous attack on the Symbionese Liberation Army, in the 1970s, as a cult mass suicide. The media further tries to erase or rewrite the real history of the government trying to kill one of the greatest black leaders, JOHN AFRICA.

How this system gets away with the horrors upon our people is through a lack of knowledge and a lack of media attention to the horrors this system has committed. One goal of corporate media and all of corporate American agencies—governmental and military, locally, nationally and internationally—is to stop people by demonizing anyone, any age, anywhere through lies, fear, and intimidation. This book is one you must read. It's another informed way of finding out how this government really works and its devastating effects on people. There isn't one person I know who has picked up this book and read one page anywhere in this book and wasn't compelled to read on. Their first question was "Where can I get it?"

As one of many unaware people, this book made me aware. I only wish that so many other misinformed people could learn what this book teaches. The late C. Delores Tucker headed Philadelphia's chapter of Martin Luther King Jr. Center for Social Change. Governmental corporate America misused C. Delores Tucker who, willingly or unwillingly, led the attack against Tupac. I wish she could have read this investigative, fact-filled book and understood that Tupac was a victim. He made some mistakes in his life, but like Martin Luther King Jr., he was a victim who raised the consciousness of people to resist and expose the wrongs of this government. Like Martin, Tupac was assassinated as he reached a new level of consciousness combined with influence, which was very threatening to those in power. Both had a way of attracting people and speaking directly to them and both were murdered in the prime of their lives.

Tupac lives through those who know him and those that are learning about him like myself. This book helps people see that Tupac was much more than a rapper, and that Martin Luther King Jr. said much, much more than "I have a dream." It is a tool to connect people to the past and help us understand who these people really were and why they were targeted.

This book will be on my table with other books to make people aware of Corporate American gangsters and their murderous political police henchmen. We in MOVE will never allow people to forget who JOHN AFRICA is and what this government did on May

13th, 1985.On the MOVE and LONG LIVE JOHN AFRICA, The Power of Truth is Final.

Pam Africa January 2008

(Book author's note: MOVE members capitalize their group's name and their founder's name to counter the media censorship of them.)

A Call To Action:

"The choice, as every choice, is yours: to fight for freedom or be fettered, to struggle for liberty or be satisfied with slavery, to side with life or death. Spread the word of life far and wide. Talk to your friends, read, and open your eyes even to doorways of perception you feared to look into yesterday. Hold your heart open to the truth."
--Mumia Abu-Jamal

As stated above, political prisoner, cause-celebré, Mumia Abu-Jamal asked that the following essay, "Objectivity and the Media," originally published as a chapter in his book, *Death Blossoms* (2005), to be included as an addition to Pam Africa's Foreword. A page titled "Dialogue," in that book, preceded it and will introduce it.

Dialogue

In our country alone there are over a million men and women—not even counting juveniles—in prisons. There are an estimated three million homeless people. Poverty is widespread, and fear is the national currency. People seek the security of love, yet at the same time they are isolated, alienated—even from themselves. Isolation and alienation are barriers, forces of division. What shatters these barriers is dialogue.

Even in a free democracy, the State always attempts to control dialogue—to decide for its own interests the limits of allowable discourse. In order to be heard, one must have wealth, power, influence, rank. It's the same with the media. The media always quotes the same roundtable of "experts." Where are the voices of the poor, the excluded, the powerless? Absent those voices, absent a recognition of their worth, there can be no true dialogue, and thus no true democracy.

Objectivity and the Media

Objectivity in journalism is an illusion, a hollow word, yet it becomes so real to its perpetrators, who have been poisoned with the lie from the first day of journalism school, that they end up not only believing in it, but letting it form the whole foundation of their profession. It's always been a great ideal, but in reality it's a misguided belief. And they end up using it to justify everything they do.

When you look at news today—I'm talking now about national network newscasts—it is astounding that what used to make the local news, if that, is now considered as having national importance. Local crime stories, especially the most lurid ones, become national news stories not because of anything extraordinary about them, but because that is the stuff that sells. It's the old jingle: "If it bleeds, it leads." They don't feed the public pieces that stimulate intelligent thought, pieces that might make people talk or even ask questions about the fundamental relationships of power, rank, and status in this country. They're more interested in sensation.

It's almost as if the average newscast has been reduced and molded to fit Hard Copy or some other such show like that. The end product is trash, but it is trash that has been carefully designed to attract you emotionally, to touch you sensationally, to get you looking (but not thinking). It doesn't provoke you or encourage you to question the fundamentals. The real issues behind a story are often ignored. They're not considered important enough to be raised. That's why many people –not only MOVE, but other groups who are misunderstood and misrepresented—share MOVE's "f.t.p." attitude toward the media: Fuck the press!

By the seventies people began to admit that the media was in the hip-pocket of big business. Well, today the media is big business. The major media organizations are not just controlled by it—they are part of it. Many of them are owned by huge multinational corporations. And if you think they don't control what comes over the air, you're in for a surprise. If I control your paycheck, I tell you what to say and what not to say.

When Rizzo was mayor, he was always taking the Philadelphia media to task and – especially during the time of the 1978 MOVE confrontation – accusing them of stirring things up with their advocacy journalism. They lacked objectivity, he complained. Well, Rizzo was right on one count, because, as I said earlier, journalistic "objectivity" is non-existent. Who's objective? But as far as the slant of their advocacy goes, I don't know who Rizzo thinks they were advocating. It sure wasn't MOVE.

Neither the brutal police assault on the MOVE compound in August 1978 nor the bombing of their new compound in May 1985 – in which eleven of their members were killed, and a whole neighborhood was destroyed – could ever have happened without the media. It was in their interest to create the fires of carnage and hatred, and feed those fires. The media built the scaffolding around the MOVE standoff, and the information they disseminated became the catalyst for the final conflagration. The next step after that was for them to whitewash the whole thing to save face for the "investigative" commission.

The frightening thing is that the press's involvement in the MOVE debacle was in no way unique; it is instructive for the present, the future, and for any number of contexts and loci, not just racist Philadelphia. Don't forget – two things always define the media's perspective: money and power. And the resulting "blindness" is therefore often willful.

I remember being down in Philadelphia at my petition hearing in the fall of 1995 – I was being shuttled back to the prison, and the sheriff had turned the radio on. The newscaster was announcing that ABC had just been acquired by the Disney Corporation. I laughed. I was in the back of the van laughing and laughing and thinking to myself that it won't be long before they have Mickey Mouse and Donald Duck on the evening news.

On a deeper level, of course, it's no laughing matter. When the power of the press is exercised in concert with the political machinery that is in place today – I'm talking about the right wing shift in American politics – what you have is a dangerous, malevolent concoction. It might sound paranoid, but that's what you have.

Just recently there's been considerable controversy about the planes that were shot down over Cuba. The alternative press is asking some interesting questions, but what about the mainstream media? There's a whole history to this incident that is being withheld by the government and the press. I can't help wondering about the fact that when Cuba was the whorehouse of the Caribbean – when it was a Mafia safe-haven – you didn't hear anybody talking about invading Cuba or changing the government. It was only when a government of the Cubans' own choice rose to power and said that they were no longer willing to be our whorehouse – "We are an independent sovereign country, and we will have the government we want, not the government that you want" – that our government began plotting to kill President Castro and to destroy Cuba through an economic blockade that, according to international law, amounted to an act of war. Has our government, our press, acted on the right side of history? Have they stood on the right side of fundamental justice?

Cuba's only one of many examples. Fundamentally, the United States Government has allied itself for decades with some of the darkest forces in history for the sake of economic gain, for political self-interest, for the protection of the status quo. And it continues to do so, domestically as well. That's why we have the likes of David Duke running for governor and the likes of Pat Buchanan running for President (in spite of having Klansmen on his staff). It's why everybody is talking about welfare queens and slamming the poor. It is also why the safest political platform of the decade is based on promises of "getting tough on crime." Their line is that it's okay to despise the poor, because they have it "too good" anyway. Besides, they claim, it's the poor, the minorities who are causing a rise in violent crime: "What we need is more executions. What we need to do is start chopping people's heads off..." The level of political discourse in our country is anti-life. And the press is not innocent.

Mumia Abu-Jamal, 2005

The FBI War on Tupac Shakur and Black Leaders

U.S. Intelligence's Murderous Targeting of Tupac, MLK, Malcolm, Panthers, Hendrix, Marley, Rappers & Linked Ethnic Leftists

Introductory Summary

Years of accumulated evidence supports that the FBI orchestrated the murder of rap icon Tupac Shakur, and that they used similar tactics to murder other leftist black leaders. Thousands of pages of U.S. Intelligence documents, court testimony and agents' disclosures reveal how the FBI and other intelligence agencies have waged war on black leaders.[1] A review of Black Panther progeny Tupac Shakur's life and times highlights how the FBI maintained the use of similar targeting tactics throughout the last four decades of this war. It also shows how U.S. Intelligence focused on musicians and on aiding conservative corporate control of the media. The evidence supports that U.S. Intelligence murderously targeted political and cultural leftist leaders, including Malcolm X, Martin Luther King, Black Panthers, Jimi Hendrix, Bob Marley and activist rappers.

The U.S. Intelligence targeting of Tupac and his Shakur family provides a window into intelligence targeting of leftist black leaders from 1965-2005. U.S. Intelligence (Defense, CIA, FBI and police intelligence) historically opposed leftists—those working to make changes in society to gain a more equitable sharing of wealth and resources.[2] The CIA's leadership, the director of all intelligence agencies until 2001, was comprised of the wealthiest American families. Their founders also saved thousands of Nazis and supervised these Nazis as they worked on intelligence projects.[3]

To stop leftists from achieving their goals of opposing America's wealthiest, U.S. Intelligence used tools ranging from propaganda to violence.[4] With historical prejudices not too disimilar from the Nazis they protected, U.S. Intelligence brandished particularly brutal violence against many black leftists. Evidence also supports their violent targeting of ethnic leftist leaders linked to Tupac's activism and targeting. These include Latino gang leaders-turned activists, as well as Robert F. Kennedy and environmental leader Judi Bari.

The Shakurs worked in many legitimate radical political organizations in the '60s, from Malcolm X's OAAU to the socialist Black Panther Party. U.S. Intelligence's murder of Malcolm X and many Panthers led the Shakurs to a more revolutionary perspective by the time Tupac was born in the '70s. Tupac Shakur's Black Panther mother, Afeni Shakur, raised Tupac as her "revolutionary black prince." Afeni's radical activist partner, Mutulu Shakur, and her Black Panther friends also served as Tupac's mentors throughout his childhood. This helped Tupac gain his own revolutionary leadership position before his rap career.

Tupac left this position for the entertainment world, but U.S. Intelligence focused more on him as he used his fame to further his political agenda. When Tupac's career took off immediately, U.S. Intelligence increased their tactics in proportion to his increasing wealth and influence. Tupac used his success to aid a national revolutionary group of former Panthers, led by his business manager, Watani Tyehimba, and national lawyer, Chokwe Lumumba. He hid his revolutionary agenda behind a "gangsta rap" façade as part of a political plan to aid the growing movement of gangs' leftist politicization.[5]

Media-censored eyewitness accounts support Tupac Shakur confidantes' reports of how U.S. Intelligence targeted Tupac. Evidence suggests that this targeting included up to six police intelligence murder attempts before he was jailed on an apparent frame-up. Prison "penal coercion" and police agents that filled the ranks of Death Row Records then helped manipulate Tupac in order to distort his political goals and create conflicts among rappers. Upon Tupac's signaled departure from Death Row, evidence supports that intelligence agents killed Tupac to stop him from aiding his extended family's goals, to curtail gangs' activist conversions, and to aid the police rap units' targeting of many top rappers with political links.[6]

A review of the last four decades details U.S. Intelligence's use of overlapping tactics and agents against the Shakurs and other black leaders. While this review attempts comprehensiveness, it remains merely a sampling of targeted leaders and attacks on the black community. The sampling stopped many months before this book's publication date and includes a diverse range of left-leaning to socialist, local to national, cultural and political leaders. A subtext of this book also examines how wealthy, prejudicial conservative forces have controlled virtually all of mainstream media in order to veil or hide most of this information.

1-US Intelligence vs. Newton/Seale's Black Panthers' Aid to Blacks; Shakurs Lead Harlem

> "Racism plus capitalism breeds fascism when the avaricious businessmen refuse to give control to the unemployed workers and their unions...Fascism breeds when the lazy, tricking, demagogic politicians lie and mislead people about the sufffering that Black people are subjected to, that Brown peoples are subjected to, that any color or minority group peoples, or any poor White peoples are subjected to...[by brutal] pig cops...'Pig' [refers to] people who systematically violate peoples' constitutional rights." Bobby Seale, 1969,70. Speech and interview excerpts, *The Black Panthers Speak.*[7]

Tupac Shakur's family had involvement in radical black activist organizations that experienced much government oppression. Afeni Shakur gave birth to Tupac in 1971, three years after she married a fellow Harlem Black Panther, Lumumba Shakur, the Harlem chapter's founding leader. Lumumba's brother, Zayd Shakur, also organized with them in the New York Panthers. Their Black Panther group had started across the country almost five years before Tupac's birth.

Huey Newton and Bobby Seale started the Black Panther Party for Self Defense in 1966 to counter a century of violence against blacks that the U.S. ignored or aided.[8] For example, the National Association for the Advancement of Colored People (NAACP) recorded nearly 5,000 mob lynchings of blacks from 1900-1950. Black socialist W.E.B. Du Bois founded the NAACP. U.S. agents spied on Du Bois and revoked his passport.[9]

In the 1950s, U.S. Intelligence agencies (CIA, FBI, police intelligence, etc.) began collaborative operations against leftists that were particularly violent against blacks.[10] Socialists and other leftists wanted more power for poorer workers. After World War II, the wealthiest families of the American corporate elite had started the supervising Intelligence agency—the Central Intelligence Agency (CIA)—to counter any leftist activism at home or abroad as it threatened their wealth and political dominance (Ch.19).

The FBI's Counter Intelligence Program (Cointelpro) typefied these collaborative operations. In response to the '50s civil rights movement, southern racists began a long series of bombings of black churches and civil rights headquarters. Later investigations found that Cointelpro agents took part in many of these actions (Ch.19).

Lumumba Shakur had formerly been a member of Malcolm X's organization in New York. In 1965, Malcolm X's assassination played an important part in reshaping black organizations. Many believed the accumulating evidence that U.S. Intelligence played a role in Malcolm's assassination (Ch.8). Several black activist groups soon emerged with a more radical stance. Stokely Charmichael (name later changed to Kwame Toure) and H. Rap Brown helped lead the Student Nonviolent Coordinating Committee (SNCC) around that time. Black college students had started SNCC in 1960 as an integrated group helping blacks register to vote in the south.[11] SNCC had worked closely with Martin Luther King's Southern Christian Leadership Coalition (Malcolm X also had spent many hours aiding SNCC leaders he crossed paths with in Africa before his death). Several years after Malcolm's death and murders of its members, SNCC decided to change the "Nonviolent" part of its name to "National," and then decided to exclude whites from their membership.[12]

SNCC leaders first used the symbol of the black panther. They started an Alabama political party that used a black panther logo on a flag in 1965. Herman Ferguson and Maxwell Stanford, Jr. (Muhammad Ahmad) also organized the Revolutionary Action Movement (RAM) that year. RAM was a semiclandesitine, black nationalist and Marxist group that elected Robert Williams its International Chairman and Malcolm X its International Spokesman. Williams had led a local NAACP chapter in the South, wrote the book, *Negroes with Guns*, and organized armed units to protect civil rights workers before his exile in Cuba. Also inspired by Stokely Charmichael's use of the black panther, Stanford helped start RAM's Black Panther Party in Philadelphia and New York, while other chapters included California by mid-1966.[13]

Later in 1966, Bobby Seale, a 29 year-old graduate student in engineering, had attended RAM meetings while studying at Merritt College in Oakland, California. Huey Newton, a 24 year-old law student, was also studying at Merritt when he met Seale at an Afro-American Association meeting. They both disagreed with some of RAM's and the Afro-American's discreet tactics. Newton and Seale reportedly believed that these two groups relied on an underground status that didn't include enough of a militant self-defense in response to the rampant police brutality the two activists had personally experienced. So, in October of 1966 Seale and Newton started their own group in Oakland that they called The Black Panther Party for Self Defense.[14]

They decided that Seale should have the title Chairman and Newton Minister of Defense. As it was legal to openly carry guns in public at this time, Seale and Newton believed that Black Panther Party members should keep themselves armed and defend themselves against unwarranted police attacks. Newton instructed Panthers on their legal rights early in their membership. He also led them in countering incidents of police brutality in their Oakland neighborhood. Newton had his Panthers surround the police with guns pointed while he recited the victim's legal rights.[15]

Huey Newton and Bobby Seale officially registered their group as a political organization. Their main activities involved starting programs to provide political education to their community and free services to poor blacks. They provided political education classes that taught black history and the plight of the black man in the Western world. They also talked to their membership about changing society to change their situation. They based their teachings on books by writers such as black liberation theorist Franz Fanon, Chinese revolutionary communist leader Mao Tse Tung and Cuba's socialist revolutionary Che Guevera, along with speeches by Malcolm X. Newton, Seale and later Panther leaders required much reading when Panthers first joined the group.[16]

Seale and Newton created their free services as part of a Ten-Point Program. This program listed the Black Panther Party's aims and desires for their community. The first five points included self-determination, full employment, a form of reparations for the "robbery" by the capitalists in their community, decent housing and education that included black history. The second five points included military service exemption, an end to police brutality and murder, freedom for blacks incarcerated by the racist judicial system, trial by juries of black peers and for basic needs to be met. To address the last point they started "survival" programs, such as free children's breakfast programs and free health clinics. They also addressed community issues, such as the need for a traffic light on a corner where kids were regularly getting hit by cars. They further created a newspaper that helped other Black Panther Party chapters duplicate these programs. It had a circulation of 125,000 copies a week by 1970.[17]

U.S. Intelligence targeted both the RAM-based and Seale/Newton-based Black Panther organizations from their inceptions. Some Americans only came to know anything about this targeting when anti-war activists eventually burglarized an FBI office in 1971. The activist burglars confiscated thousands of documents, and then copied them for politicians, reporters and scholars. These documents from the Counter Intelligence Program files provided the first proof of such operations and the first notion that such a program had an official name. Still, media and politicians continued to cover up many details of Cointelpro.[18]

On the second anniversary of Malcolm X's assassination in February of 1967, the RAM-based Panthers invited Malcolm's widow, Betty Shabazz, to speak at a memorial event. Newton and Seale's Panthers joined as Shabazz's security, armed with shotguns and pistols while wearing their standard black attire of berets and leather jackets. Best-selling author Eldridge Cleaver covered the event as an editor at San Francisco-based *Ramparts* magazine. Cleaver saw Huey Newton stand down police and counter their racial epithets by using words such as "pigs" rather than curse words that, because of obscenity laws, could have brought on his arrest at that time. This led the *Ramparts* editor to join the Panthers as their Minister of Information.[19]

The Black Panther Party for Self Defense's national leadership gained publicity that helped them build new chapters in the eastern states. Later in '67, Bobby Seale and Huey Newton made Student National Coordinating Committee (SNCC) leaders Stokely Charmichael and H. Rap Brown honorary Panther leaders on the East Coast. Other SNCC members also began starting Panther chapters in Chicago and eastern cities.[20]

In the spring, Oakland police broke into the home of Newton's neighbor and destroyed his property near the Black Panther Party for Self-Defense's office. Newton went to the house, asked the police if they had a search warrant, and they placed Newton under arrest.[21] This was the first of several specious arrests. When Seale went to bail Newton out on one such charge, police arrested Seale on an antiquated law barring guns near a jail.[22]

Police failed to keep Newton and Seale imprisoned for long, but attacks continued upon their release. On October 27, 1967, the last night of Huey Newton's probation for a 1964 conflict, one of a long line of bizarre shootings involving Panthers occurred. An Oakland police officer pulled over the car Newton drove, accompanied by two passengers. At a later trial it was revealed that the officer had a list of Black Panther license plates on him and another police car followed him. While accounts differ on the details of what happened, a shoot-out ensued that left one officer dead. Another officer and Newton were wounded. Newton left the scene for a hospital where police soon found, beat and jailed him. Details of the incident support Newton's claim of not having a gun when police shot him.[23]

After over four years of legal battles, the state dismissed all the charges against Huey Newton. In that time, a "Free Huey" movement gained international stature while Panther chapters rose in many cities nationwide. Newton later attained his CIA file that said he was on a U.S. Intelligence "hit list." This supported that the October of '67 shooting was a police intelligence murder attempt.[24]

2-The 1968 U.S. Intelligence Assassination of Martin Luther King, Jr.

> "Human progress never rolls in on the wheels of inevitability. It comes through the tireless efforts and the persistent work of dedicated individuals. [Many] say the Negro must lift himself by his own bootstraps. They never stop to realize that no other ethnic group has been a slave on American soil. [They don't] realize that the nation made the black man's color a stigma...Two thirds of the people of the world go to bed hungry [while America spends] millions of dollars a day to store surplus food...And maybe we spend far too much of our national budget establishing military bases around the world rather than bases of genuine concern and understanding...I am convinced that [the Vietnam War] is one of the most unjust wars that has ever been fought in the history of the world...It has strengthned the military-industrial complex...Every time we kill one we spend about five hundred thousand dollars while we spend only fifty-three dollars a year for every [poor] person...And we force young black men and young white men to fight and kill in brutal solidarity...We are coming to Washington in a Poor People's Campaign." Martin Luther King, Jr. 1968. Excerpt "Remaining Awake Through a Great Revolution."

While formerly on the other end of the spectrum regarding civil rights struggle tactics, Martin Luther King had moved closer to the Black Panther's perspective by 1968. Martin Luther King, Jr. won a Nobel Peace Prize in 1964 after close to a decade of non-violent civil rights organizing. Martin Luther King (hereafter, "King" or "MLK") helped spearhead many marches and rallies to end segregation and gain voting rights that were denied to so many poor blacks in the American South.[25] That civil rights work involved marches that led to many arrests and beatings by local police. CIA documents and FBI agents revealed how U.S. Intelligence stated that their goal was to destroy the increasingly radical Martin Luther King. They had made MLK their number one black activist target.[26]

Historians have debated what most helped get national civil rights legislation passed during King's life. Top sociologists Piven and Cloward effectively argued that riots contributed the most to the passage of national civil rights laws. Mainstream history texts rarely cover the vast violence by racist whites that spurred riotous reactions by black communities. For example, in 1963 a gunman killed Medgar Evers, secretary of the Mississipi NAACP. Also in Mississippi that year, police and Ku Klux Klan killed one black and two Jewish SNCC activists. The accumulation of these murders helped spark riots in black areas.

Militantly racist whites also used other means of violence against blacks. Between June and October of 1964, twenty-four Black churches were bombed in Mississippi alone. Partly in response to these events, Americans held 1,412 separate demonstrations in 1963 according to the U.S. Justice Department. Researchers documented a nationwide series of riots after police brutalized black leaders at some of the peaceful demonstrations. The largest of the riots were in New York, Chicago, Maryland, Philadelphia and New Jersey in the first half of 1964. Whether responding to riots or sincere about civil rights, President John F. Kennedy initiated the Civil Rights Act just before his assassination in November of 1963. Congress passed the Act and President Johnson signed it in July of 1964.[27]

Despite police continually arresting and badly beating him, MLK called for nonviolent civil disobedience. But King also defended rioters' actions in saying, "A riot is the language of the unheard."[28] Blacks rioted in a particularly large number of cities in the summer of 1967. U.S. Intelligence interviewed 500 jailed blacks in the largest of those riots—a violent outburst in Detroit. When U.S. Intelligence asked the rioters who most inspired them, Intelligence analysts stated their surprise that most responded with MLK rather than younger SNCC firebrands such as Stokely Charmichael and H. Rap Brown.[29]

Several decades after King's April of 1968 assassination, his widow Coretta Scott King and most of the Kings' adult children hired attorney William Pepper to represent them. Pepper aided them in filing a civil lawsuit against Memphis rooming house owner Lloyd Jowers and his government co-conspirators in MLK's assassination. They filed this lawsuit mostly due to a 20-year investigation that Pepper, a former friend of MLK, had undertaken into the real perpetrators of King's assassination.

William Pepper worked as a journalist in Vietnam, an experience that led to anti-war activism beside Martin Luther King, Jr . Pepper then went to law school and, after MLK's death, had accepted the official version of the assassination. In 1977, MLK's closest civil rights associate, Rev. Ralph Abernathy, asked Pepper to represent long-believed sole assassin James Earl Ray who was serving a life sentence for allegedly shooting King from the third floor bathroom of Lloyd Jower's rooming house. Ray hoped that his case could be reassessed and Abernathy believed that Pepper would help them find out who really orchestrated the assassination.

Pepper took the case and first published a book on his MLK assassination investigation in 1995, titling it *Orders to Kill*. Warner Books then bought the rights to *Orders to Kill* and published it in 1998 (as Ch.20 suggests, Warner likely had ulterior motives as it appeared to decrease the book's circulation). *Orders to Kill* detailed the U.S.

Intelligence documents, government whistleblowers, and other evidence supporting that U.S. Intelligence assassinated Martin Luther King.[30]

In his introduction to *Orders to Kill*'s 1998 edition, MLK's son, Dexter Scott King, said that U.S. Intelligence orchestrated the assassination of his father in 1968 for several reasons. Their top motive was to stop MLK's civil rights work and anti-Vietnam war organizing. They also wanted to halt MLK's mobilization of an interracial poor people's coalition that planned to camp in front of the White House to redirect money from the war to the poor, and to decrease King's influence over the 1968 presidential election.[31] Pepper and others found government-documented evidence that a dozen government intelligence agencies coordinated their plotting against King before his death. Many witnesses and much evidence supported how they worked with police and contracted the Mafia to aid the fatal shooting of MLK in Memphis.[32]

On April 4, 1968, a gunman fatally shot Martin Luther King. He had just come out of his Memphis hotel room and onto the third floor balcony that faced the back bushy area of Lloyd Jowers' rooming house whose ground was at about MLK's room level. Pepper published photos of an identified CIA agent lowering himself to the street from the wall extending down from that rooming house backyard within minutes of the assassination. The government claimed James Earl Ray shot from the rooming house's bathroom window. A photo's confirmation helped lead undercover black Military Intelligence agent Marrell McCollough to admit that he raced to Martin Luther King seconds after his shooting. McCollough was the first to kneel over King, checking him for life signs and reporting his death.[33]

A former Naval Intelligence agent-turned reporter aided Pepper by interviewing two Special Forces Group (SFG a.k.a. Green Berets) snipers, hiding out in separate Latin America countries by that 1980s time period. The two independently corroborated each other's information that they were stationed atop Memphis' Illinois Central Railroad Building. Other snipers were reportedly located in two different positions, including J.D. Hill who said he was perched on a water tower with his rifle site on King. They all said they were to keep MLK and his associate, Andrew Young, in their rifle sites as they waited for a signal to shoot. One of the three SFG snipers provided a copy of his Army Intelligence orders paper that day which Pepper included in his book. It proved Naval Intelligence aid and top Pentagon command knowledge of the operation. Pepper verified its shorthand through others that worked in the Pentagon.[34]

Pepper said that these Special Forcers Group (SFG) officers had been active in the 5th SFG conducting cross-border covert operations in Vietnam, from 1965-66. Throughout 1967, the US Strike Command (CINCSTRIKE), with Army Intelligence, the CIA and FBI members, responded to the urban riots. CINCSTRIKE deployed these SFG snipers in their 902nd division to do covert operations as part of small "Alpha team" units in cities where riots erupted. Their bosses gave them photographs of black militants and community leaders that were to be killed if an opportunity arose in the course of the riot.[35]

Coretta Scott King and her children, who had also grown into accomplished black leaders, had William Pepper represent them partly to help publicize Pepper's findings. The King family's lawsuit against Lloyd Jowers and his government intelligence co-conspirators in MLK's assassination came to trial in 1999. That trial brought over 70 of Pepper's witnesses under oath. While Pepper couldn't get all his interviewees to the courtroom, at the trial he presented videotaped messages along with 4000 pages of documents that included declassified government intelligence papers to support the King family's case.[36]

William Peppper's findings first became public in Britain. The BBC aired a September 1989 documentary on MLK. In that show, Mafia boss Sam Giancana's occasional driver, Myron Billet, claimed to witness the CIA and FBI offering a million-dollar murder contract on King to New York and Chicago Mafia bosses. He said they rejected it.[37]

The BBC documentary also showed James "Ricco" Kimbel, who offered evidence that he worked with the Mafia as a CIA and FBI asset. He said New Orleans Mafia boss Carlos Marcello accepted the CIA/FBI contract on King. Kimbel also said that he worked with Memphis Mafia bosses Frank and Sal Liberto who helped carry out the assassination on behalf of Marcello. Kimbel further said that he flew two army snipers to Memphis as part of the operation. Kimbel and Myron Billet signed affidavits on their claims.[38] As Pepper explained in his book, "the Marcello/Liberto/Memphis assassination operation provided the Government with a plausibly deniable alternative to the use of its own trained professionals who were waiting in the wings and ultimately not required.... Organized crime [the Mafia] frequently fulfills this need and insulates federal, state, and/or local public officials and agencies from responsibility."[39]

Pepper tried to get his information to the public in many ways. In 1993 he agreed to defend long-believed assassin James Earl Ray in a television trial (Ray never actually had a trial as he was strong-armed into a plea bargain to avoid execution). Home Box Office (HBO) and Thames Production of London agreed to co-produce it. The jury at the trial found Ray not guilty. While the trial lasted for 50 hours over ten days, it was aired in a three-hour show on April 4, 1993, the 25th anniversary of the assassination. Virtually no media covered the event except NBC's *Today Show*.[40]

Out of fear of harsher charges due to Pepper's accumulated evidence, Lloyd Jowers then admitted to part of his role in MLK's assassination. On ABC's *Prime Time Live* in 1993, Jowers told Sam Donaldson that Mafia boss Frank Liberto paid him $100,000 for his part in MLK's murder. Jowers also cleared James Earl Ray. Jowers' employee at the time of the assassination, Willie Akin, supported Jowers' account on *Prime Time Live*.[41]

Jowers gave further details independently to Pepper, Dexter King and Ambassador Andrew Young. The three tape-recorded their discussion with Jowers and later authenticated it when they replayed it at the 1999 trial. Jowers said that five people involved in MLK's assassination planned it at his rooming house. These included an Intelligence/Mafia liaison named Raul Pereira, Military Intelligence agent Marrell McCollough and a Memphis police sharpshooter, Lt. Earl Clark. Besides Jowers, Young and King, another 1999 trial witness said he heard Liberto tell someone by phone to "shoot [him] on the balcony" the day of King's death. Several more witnesses also testified that Liberto admitted his role in King's assassination. And witness James Milner said that Lloyd Jowers told him how a law enforcement officer fired the fatal shot at MLK.[42]

Two women closely connected to some of these named figures in MLK's assassination backed Jowers' account, while also further implicating him. Jowers' girlfriend at the time, a waitress at his rooming house's grill named Betty Spates, said she saw Jowers bring a rifle in from his backyard seconds after the assassination.[43] Glenda Grabow, a long-time associate of Raul Pereira (better known by his first name), signed affidavits to that fact that Raul stated that he killed King. Grabow had also aided Raul's many illegal activities, including gun-running. She said that two of Raul's cousins participated in their illegal activities and told her that Raul played a part in King's assassination.[44]

Other witnesses at the trial testified that Memphis police chiefs cooperated with U.S. Intelligence and Mafia-contracted individuals in the assassination operation. For example, two detectives, one a captain, testified as to how Memphis Police superiors ordered him to withhold the usual black security team for King.[45] Amongst much more evidence, former Memphis Intelligence officers Jim Smith and Eli Arkin, along with former Fire Department captain Carthel Weeden, testified to their parts in aiding army and military officials with the audio and visual surveillance of MLK prior to and during his assassination. Arkin said these officials were from the 111th Military Intelligence Group (MIG) who had partly based themselves in his office.[46] Undercover agent Marrell McCollough worked for the 111th MIG before getting a promotion to the CIA following MLK's death.[47]

Furthermore, videotape of known police intelligence informant Rev. Billy Kyles showed him accidentally admitting to his role in the assassination. In cross-examining Kyles at the trial, one of

William Pepper's assistant defense attorneys played a videotape of the reverend making a public speech in 1981 about his being with MLK on that assassination day. Kyles said he was standing outside King's hotel room door and knocked to bring King out of his room and onto the hall balcony. Kyles then seemed to get carried away in that public speech and said in the tape, "...only as I moved away so he could have a clear shot, the shot rang out," leaving the judge and jury looking stunned. When the attorney asked him who he meant could have a clear shot, Kyles had a hard time answering but finally said that he supposed it would have been James Earl Ray.[48]

Other testimony came from diverse sources. Due to a scheduling conflict, *New York Times* reporter Earl Caldwell could not attend the trial, but he gave videotaped testimony that included the prosecutor cross-examining him on his statement in a pre-trial hearing. Caldwell said that his *Times* editor shocked him by saying he was sending Caldwell to Memphis to "nail" (write an attack article on) King. Caldwell further stated that he saw a shooter in the bushes behind Jowers' rooming house. Another witness signed an affidavit as to having seen smoke come from that backyard bushes location just after the fatal shot was fired at MLK. For years, officials claimed that James Earl Ray fired from that rooming house's third floor bathroom.[49]

Testimony continued from Cab driver Louie Ward who testified that a fellow cabdriver saw MLK get shot, and then saw a man immediately jump down from the rooming house's backyard wall and run to a waiting police car. Ward said he saw the cab driver repeat the story to police officers twice. The fellow cabdriver at the scene died later on that assassination night, apparently either falling or being pushed out of a speeding car. Also, a police officer claimed to have guarded fresh footprints in the backyard of the rooming house and police made a cast of the prints but never investigated them thereafter.[50]

Two judges took the stand to add testimony about the alleged murder weapon used in MLK's assassination. Criminal Court Judge Joe Brown, who had presided over several mid-'90s hearings reexamining the assassination evidence, testified that ballistics experts showed how authorities accepted the wrong rifle as the murder weapon. Judge Arthur Hanes, Jr. testified that as a lawyer on James Earl Ray's case he interviewed a man who had the alleged murder weapon in his store during the assassination, exempting it from the crime. Another witness, James McCraw, had given a deposition saying that Lloyd Jowers showed him the real murder weapon and McCraw's housemate testified that McCraw admitted disposing of the weapon for Jowers. An ignored FBI report also said the alleged murder rifle failed an accuracy test and didn't match the fatal bullets in MLK.[51]

Amongst several dozen more witnesses, key testimony came regarding the U.S. Intelligence operatives who disclosed their roles in the assassination operation. Former CIA operative Jack Terell, an expert witness for the ABC television network as a whistle-blower in the Iran-Contra scandal, testified by videotape because he was bed-ridden with liver cancer. Terell said that in 1975, his close friend, J.D. Hill, seemed to want to unburden himself and admitted his role: having MLK in his gun scope as a backup Army Special Forces Group (SFG) sniper in the MLK assassination. Hill's murder after his admissions sent the other snipers in his unit, described above and below, into hiding.[52]

Stanford History Professor Clayborne Carson, the 15-year director of the MLK Papers Project, read interviews of the other assigned Army SFG snipers, having already noted their historical significance. As part of his trial testimony, Carson read an interview of a sniper who said that fellow government agents "would not be wearing ties," and Marrell McCollough was the only person close to MLK's body not wearing a tie. Carson further read the sniper's statements that they would be radioed on whether to fire backup shots or disengage (leave). Apparently, McCollough's job was to rush to the body, confirm the death, and signal that confirmation to the Military Intelligence Group agents conducting the surveillance. They then communicated to the backup snipers to disengage since the first shots killed King.[53] McCollough's role gained importance in scrutiny of Malcolm X's assassination (Ch.8).

Prof. Carson last read the interview statements of an intelligence agent photographer positioned on a fire station roof who first got pictures of King falling and then took pictures of the actual shooter. He said that agent gave them to a military Colonel and kept the still unreleased negatives which showed James Earl Ray wasn't the shooter. Black leader Andrew Young was also a target in their sights, staying in King's hotel.[54]

The jury in that 1999 trial delivered a guilty verdict against Lloyd Jowers and concluded U.S. "governmental agencies were parties to this conspiracy." When William Pepper published his last book about the trial and his investigation, *An Act of State: The Execution of Martin Luther King*, Coretta Scott King and the U.S. Attorney General at the time of MLK's assassination, Ramsey Clark, wrote supportive statements for the book's cover. Pepper and Clark have both said how wealthy corporations have too much control over the media in most democracies so that the research and ideas in books such as Pepper's would receive little attention or support (Ch.19).[55] Virtually all American media sources heavily censored this trial. For example, *The New York Times* had an article on the trial's verdict on its front page, but spent much of the article belittling the King family's claims and minimizing the trial's importance.[56] MLK's family has the entire trial transcript on The King Center's website.[57]

3-U.S. Intelligence Starts Murderous Targeting & Harassment Arrests of Panthers

> "Rulers perceive the greatest threat to be the national liberation movements around the world, particularly in Asia, Africa, and Latin America. In order for them to wage wars of suppression against these national liberation movements abroad, they must have peace and stability and unanimity of purpose at home. But…[American Blacks] too, demand liberation." Eldridge Cleaver, *The Black Panther* newspaper, 1969.

> "The systematic attempt to liquidate the leadership of the Black Panther Party starting with the bullet fired into Huey P. Newton in October is but the most advanced stage of a national conspiracy in the mother country against black people in the colony…The assassination of Dr. King was a move on a national scale similar to the attempted assassination of Eldridge Cleaver on a local scale; both attacks were against the politics of coalition. [Both King and Cleaver joined diverse groups] into a single movement against poverty and racism." Kathleen Cleaver, *The Black Panther*, 1968.[58]

Black Panther leaders strongly suspected that U.S. Intelligence orchestrated Martin Luther King's assassination. They also strongly suspected that police particularly targeted them for arrest and murder. Later revealed FBI documents detailed the U.S. Intelligence's "harassment arrest" strategy. Other documents, mentioned previously, showed that they had a hit list of black leaders and they had Huey Newton on that list.[59]

Several pages of FBI documents described how they instructed local police intelligence units to employ a "harassment arrest" strategy against RAM and other black activist groups in 1967. The pages detailed their strategy of draining black activists of their time, money, and freedom. These FBI documents detailed how the FBI worked with Oakland police in using this strategy against the Panthers there, and how police worked with the FBI against other black activist groups nationwide thereafter.[60]

U.S. Intelligence increased the violent nature of their attacks in direct proportion to the perceived threat of the Black Panthers' expansion and success with their programs. After police wounded and jailed Panther cofounder Huey Newton, U.S. Intelligence next focused on the remaining Panther leaders. By the end of '67, Bobby Seale and Eldridge Cleaver made alliances with white radicals to form the Peace and Freedom Party presidential ticket. The group made Cleaver their U.S. presidential candidate and Students for a Democratic Society cofounder Tom Hayden their vice-presidential candidate. In the first two months of 1968, police raided and ransacked Eldridge Cleaver and his wife Kathleen's Oakland, California home. Kathleen Cleaver was the Communications Secretary for the Panthers, making statements on national television. A month later, police arrested 25 Panthers in the area, including Seale and Panther Office Chief David Hilliard.[61]

When Martin Luther King's assassination occurred on April 4, 1968, Eldridge Cleaver worried that, with Seale and Newton in jail, police would use any excuse to kill him and any remaining Panther leaders. Just after the assassination, blacks responded by rioting in over 100 cities, setting various sections of most major urban areas in flames. Despite having the largest per capita black population, Oakland remained calm. The Black Panthers had spread the word that police would use the excuse of a riot to kill their membership.[62]

Police took matters into their own hands. On April 6 they shot at Cleaver and several other original Panthers. Police reported a gunman in the neighborhood as the reason to fire over 1,000 rounds of ammunition for 90 minutes at a house in whose basement cowered Cleaver and 18 year-old fellow Panther Bobby Hutton. Another 20 minutes of tear gas shells caused a fire, and one hit Cleaver in the chest. While also suffering a gunshot wound in the foot, Cleaver told Hutton they needed to come out naked with their hands up to save themselves. He said that if they didn't, police could use the excuse that they were carrying guns, in order to shoot them. Naked, Cleaver survived and was arrested, but the more modest Hutton came out behind him only shirtless with his arms raised and was fatally shot.[63]

With Hutton's murder, the FBI and California police intelligence had begun their murderous decimation of the Northern California Black Panthers. Several undercover agents ended up revealing how they set up Panther Field Marshall, George Jackson, in the San Francisco Bay area's San Quentin Prison. Jackson's prison books, *Soledad Brothers* and *Blood in My Eye*, inspired many. Professor Angela Davis taught at UCLA when she headed Jackson's defense committee, before the university's dismissal of her for such radical work. Attacks on Jackson culminated with his eventual murder in prison in 1971.[64]

FBI and police began focusing on other chapter leaders to follow through on FBI Director J. Edgar Hoover's orders to "destroy" and "eradicate" Panther chapters' programs in 27 cities.[65] Various sources estimated that the New York Black Panther membership ranged from 400 to well over 800 members months after its April of 1968 inception. New York Panther leaders claimed a much higher membership, saying they signed up 800 new members in a single month. This caused immediate work against the New York Panthers by the FBI as it quickly became the largest Panther chapter.

The New York Police Department had a special intelligence unit working against leftist political groups called the Bureau Of Special Services (BOSS). Government officials assigned Lieutenant Angelo Galante to supervise a new BOSS unit focusing on the New York Panthers. Galante's background underscores U.S. Intelligence's concerns about the New York Black Panther chapters. Galante previously worked for the Office of Strategic Services (OSS) and the agency the OSS evolved into—the CIA. He specialized in fighting against revolutionary guerilla forces behind enemy lines.[66]

BOSS first mass-arrested members of a SNCC-based midtown Manhattan Panther chapter. When those Panthers went to trial, a mob of "off-duty" police beat them with clubs and blackjacks *inside* the courthouse hallway. Undercover agents also helped entrap the Brooklyn Panthers. The Brooklyn Panther chapter included Afeni Shakur's lifetime friend, Thomas McCreary (Tupac mentioned him in his song "Wordz of Wisdom").[67]

BOSS assigned at least six undercover agents to the Harlem and Bronx New York Black Panther chapters. Several of these agents even helped Lumumba Shakur and Sekou Odinga found these Panther chapters. At least one of the agents had originally joined Malcolm X's Organization of Afro-American Unity (Ch.8), where Lumumba Shakur and Sekou Odinga were previously involved in activism.[68]

Lumumba's father Saludine "Abbah" Shakur (James Coston) had first taken the name Shakur, Arabic for "the Thankful," in the early '60s. Living in Harlem, Abbah Shakur joined Malcolm X's OAAU from its start, before Lumumba (born Anthony Coston) and Lumumba's teen friend Sekou Odinga (Nathaniel Williams) followed suit. Odinga started a Bronx Panther chapter and Lumumba started the Harlem Panther chapter. Abbah and his adopted son Mutulu Shakur (Jeral Williams) joined the Revolutionary Action Movement (RAM) and Abbah initiated a RAM-based Panther chapter.[69] In the 60s, these activists had shed what they called their "slave names"—the names of their ancestors' slave masters—for those of African independence leaders, such as the Congo's Patrice Lumumba and Guinea's Sékou Touré.[70]

Police duplicated the Newton/Seale scenario of arresting one leader who came to bail out another (Ch.1) when the Harlem and the Bronx chapters showed the most growth in '68.[71] By November of 1968, police arrested Harlem Panther leader Lumumba Shakur when he came to bail out Bronx Panther leader Sekou Odinga. Police had charged Odinga with driving a stolen car and planning a bank robbery in Stamford, Connecticut because he was armed, as most Panthers were, reportedly for self-defense. Police dropped the bank robbery charge but kept the car theft charge. Lumumba went to bail Odinga out, traveling with two women, three kids and a gun. Police placed

Lumumba in jail and charged him, too, with planning a bank robbery. Apparently, none of these charges led to convictions.[72]

Tupac Shakur's mother, Afeni Shakur (born Alice Williams), said in her autobiography that she couldn't believe these arrests. Afeni had first been emboldened by the American Indians fighting off the Ku Klux Klan in her hometown of Lumberton, North Carolina. She moved to New York as a 13 year-old in 1960 and she joined the Panthers in '68. With a precocious intellect, Afeni wrote an article that won her a citywide journalism award that year. Afeni soon married Lumumba and changed her name. Afeni saw Sekou Odinga as her mentor and said that he was such a beautiful, pure person that she couldn't believe it when police arrested him and Lumumba on incomprehensible charges.[73]

Meanwhile, three hours south of New York in Baltimore, Maryland, a Panther reported that the National Security Agency (NSA) joined the FBI in their Counter Intelligence Program (Cointelpro) targeting of him. In his book, *The Greatest Threat,* Baltimore Black Panther Marshall Eddie Conway reported that the NSA, located in nearby Fort Meade, Maryland, had undercover agent Warren Hart start a Black Panther Party chapter in Baltimore. Hart started it with other fellow agents before real activists joined. Conway said he acted as "Lieutenant of Security in Maryland and that led me to exposing the agent provocateur." Conway further said that Hart and his fellow agents also set up a fake White Panther Party in Baltimore.

The NSA apparently started the fake Baltimore Panther chapter to lure radical activists into the group and then frame them for arrest. Conway cited how in "1969, six Panthers were arrested for allegedly assaulting police who were arresting a seventh Panther. This Panther was later revealed by *The Baltimore Sun* to be working for the Police Department."

After Panther Eddie Conway exposed the NSA's role in the Baltimore Black Panthers, Cointelpro targeted him. They arrested Conway at his job and charged him with the murder of one police officer and the attempted murder of two others. While Conway awaited trial, a judge ordered Conway's release, saying there wasn't any evidence to hold him. The prison decided to change his jail cell mate. People told Conway this new cell mate worked for the government.

In court, the government claimed this jail cell mate, Charles Reynolds, was a Morgan State University college student and one-time offender. Reynolds said Conway confessed to the crime. Conway saw the set up and said he refused to participate in the "circus" trial. Investigators later found out that Reynolds was a career criminal and paid professional informant, immediately released after the trial to later live in Detroit. With no physical evidence linking him to the crime, the court convicted Eddie Conway, giving him a sentence of life plus 30 years.[74]

4-FBI Agents in LA Cultural Group Attack Panthers: LA Murders & NY 21 Set-up

> "[Racist policemen] must withdraw immediately from the black community, cease the wanton murder and brutality of black people, or suffer the wrath of the armed people. [Huey Newton] was free enough to realize this and free enough to express this." Alprentice "Bunchy" Carter, *The Black Panther*, 1969.[75]

The Los Angeles Black Panther chapter had formed soon after the Oakland chapter. The LA Panthers had to deal with a new FBI strategy. M. Wes Swearingen, who worked in the FBI's LA Counter Intelligence Program (Cointelpro) unit, described his unit's murderous machinations. He said the FBI paid informant members of the United Slaves Organization, a Black cultural nationalist group, to murder LA Panther leaders Alprentice Bunchy Carter and Jon Huggins. These United Slaves murderers, first reported as George and Larry Stiner, shot them on the UCLA campus in January of 1969 (note that the FBI commonly calls these undercover agents "informants"—a cover-up name that hides both their employment by the FBI and the insidious nature of their murderous actions).[76]

Other whistleblowers elaborated on this. LA police intelligence agent Louis Tackwood also revealed the regular money, guns, drugs and orders he gave to United Slaves leader Ron Karenga to attack the Panthers.[77] Tackwood testified to this in court and before a Senate Intelligence committee. He further passed a polygraph test. Various aspects of Karenga's life contradict his supposed cultural revolutionary persona. A *Wall Street Journal* article detailed Karenga's ownership of gas stations. The *Journal* further noted Karenga's ties to the LA mayor and the Rockefellers, along with his secret meetings with Governor Ron Reagan and the police chief following MLK's assassination.[78]

While *The Wall Stree Journal* article may have been a false smear of Karenga, later events suggest otherwise. After the Carter and Huggins murders, the FBI's United Slaves informants murdered four more Black Panthers.[79] Furthermore, Swearingen verified D'Arthard Perry's claims that the FBI then engineered the prison break of several United Slaves murderers.[80] And finally, New Haven Panther George Edwards said that he attained a U.S. Intelligence document reporting Karenga's meetings with Governor Reagan, funding by the Rockefellers, and the Stiners work with U.S. Intelligence.[81]

It's important to note some debate as to whether the United Slaves (US) was a legitimate Black Nationalist cultural group or an FBI front. When Huggins and Carter were killed, they had left a tape saying that if anything happened to them, they wanted Panther Elmer

"Geronimo" Pratt to take over, and Pratt took over as the LA Panther leader.[82] Years later, Geronimo Pratt said that US as a group shouldn't be held accountable for the FBI agent infiltrators who carried out these murders of Panthers. Geronimo, who later changed his last name to Ji Jaga, said that an undercover agent in the Panthers started the conflict that led to Carter and Huggins' murders when that agent slapped a United Slaves member.[83]

Geronimo gave a more detailed description of this undercover agent in an email that Kathleen Cleaver helped distribute. Geronimo said that in 1968, as he helped Bunchy Carter with security when Eldridge Cleaver was giving a speech at UCLA, a young woman named Elaine Brown ran up to the security gate crying and begging to meet Cleaver. After discussion with Cleaver, Carter allowed it. Pratt said that Brown had sex with Cleaver and then had sex with LA leader John Huggins while his wife Erika was pregnant. Pratt said he was more suspicious of Brown with each of these incidents.

Pratt further said that the murderous January of '69 UCLA between the United Slaves (US) and Panthers was carefully prearranged. He said Elaine Brown slapped a US member with whom she had also been having sex. She then immediately ran from the US member to Huggins, saying that the US member was attacking her. Pratt said Huggins took out his gun and shot at the purported attacker. The US member proceeded to shoot and kill Huggins and Carter. Pratt claimed that Elaine Brown then testified in court and falsely accused George and Larry Stiner. Pratt accused Brown of working as an undercover federal agent and wrecking further havoc amongst the Panthers thereafter, as he tried to get her expelled from all Panther chapters (Ch.s 6,10).[84]

Other credible witnesses hold Geronimo in high regard while still giving a different view. For example, FBI whistleblower M. Wes Swearingen worked in the Los Angeles Cointelpro unit at the time. He said the Stiners were "informers" (getting paid by the FBI) and an FBI agent named Eric Galt arranged the Stiners' murder of Carter and Huggins. Swearingen further said that "Darthard Perry, a self-admitted and publicly acclaimed informer for the FBI, filed an affidavit in a Black Panther Party lawsuit against the government charging that he knew the United Slaves members who were responsible for the murders of the Panthers were FBI informers."[85]

The Stiners went to jail in 1969. Perry claimed the FBI engineered their prison break from San Quentin in 1974, never seeing jail again. New Haven Panther George Edwards, who also has great respect for Pratt, says he trusts Pratt's statements about the Carter and Huggins shooting. Edwards said that he only disagrees with Pratt's account about the Stiners. Edwards said that, along with the fact that he saw an Intelligence document which implicated their work with the

Stiners, these brothers were identical twins and wouldn't have escaped for good so easily without government help.[86]

Thus, most sources agree that U.S. Intelligence orchestrated the murders of LA Panther leaders Carter and Huggins. The disagreement only lies in which particular individuals or groups remain responsible. Many people support that the FBI at least ran their murderous operations inside the United Slaves through undercover infiltrators without a number of United Slaves members realizing it. This appears similar to U.S. Intelligence targeting the Nation of Islam's Elijah Muhammad, while also infiltrating both the Nation of Islam and Malcolm X's group to predominantly target Malcolm X (Ch.8).[87] During Pratt's LA Panther leadership, the FBI agents, purportedly in the United Slaves, continued murdering Panthers with little-to-no retaliation (Pratt apparently didn't want to buy into the FBI's "divide and conquer" strategy, having blacks kill each other).[88]

Whether the FBI set up the Los Angeles-based United Slaves as a front for intelligence operations, or had agents infiltrate an already established group, evidence supports that U.S. Intelligence later ran a similar operation in Los Angeles during the '90s. A police whistleblower found much evidence that undercover police agents in Los Angeles-based Death Row Records were involved in similar activities against Tupac Shakur and the rap community nationwide. Other evidence supports that U.S. Intelligence supervised these agents involved in some of Death Row's illicit operations (Ch.s 22-5).[89]

Several disclosures and findings support that the FBI used undercover agents in the United Slaves (US) to target the New York Panthers at the same time as they targeted the LA Panther chapter. FBI informant D'Arthard Perry said that the FBI used US infiltrator Claude Hubert to kill several LA Panthers and then transferred him to New York City.[90]

Furthermore, on January 17, 1969, the day United Slave FBI infiltrators murdered LA leaders Carter and Huggins, police shot at Bronx Panther leader Sekou Odinga and two other Panthers while they were parked near the Harlem river. Odinga and Panther Kuwasi Balagoon escaped. Police arrested 19 year-old female Panther Joan Bird whom they found cowering in the shot up car. They then beat her up in the precinct.[91] (Also, undercover police agent Ralph White shot a gun in the Black Panther office when Harlem leader Lumumba Shakur was in there around this same date.[92])

These mid-January attacks appeared to be the culmination of a bi-coastal operation using various FBI undercover agents in the United Slaves and the Panthers to frame and kill the Black Panther leadership in Los Angeles and New York. The police officers' shooting at Odinga, Balagoon and Bird was part of an elaborate FBI and BOSS undercover agent plot against the New York Panthers. Police made a specious claim that they thwarted the three Panthers' attempt to shoot police coming out of a precinct, despite that the precinct was 560 yards away (5 ½ football fields) and the Panthers' rifle didn't have a telescopic sight.[93]

It appears more than a coincidence that United Slave leader Ron Karenga was scheduled to speak as an honorary chair of a Harlem cultural festival the day that cops shot at Odinga—January 17. U.S. Intelligence used his speaking engagement as part of their excuse for attacking the New York Panthers. Police claimed that Sekou Odinga, Harlem Panther leader Lumumba Shakur and 19 other leading Panthers had planned to bomb and shoot at police precincts to upstage Ron Karenga's visit.[94] New Haven Black Panther George Edwards attended that event and reported Karenga's security harassing him and his fellow Panthers there. He also heard Karenga's verbal attacks of the Panthers at that event.[95]

The FBI had planned this mid-January incident long in advance. First, undercover BOSS agent Ralph White attained work in Lumumba Shakur's office at the Elsmere Tenants Council, a Bronx antipoverty agency. Then, several days before police shot at Odinga, FBI agent Roland Hayes finalized his work with Ralph White and his fellow BOSS undercover agent, Eugene Roberts, to plant dynamite at Lumuba's Elsmere Tenants Council office as a frame-up. Attorneys pressured Agent Ralph White to admit in court that he fired a gun in the back room of Shakur's office near this time. Was White trying to set up an "accidental" shooting of Lumumba on the day of shootings at Odinga, Carter and Huggins?[96] The FBI appeared to try and assassinate the leaders of the two largest chapters in the country on the same day.

Failing to murder the New York leaders that day, FBI and police then used these January incidents to launch a mass arrest of the New York Black Panther leadership, over two months later. On April 2, 1969, police led a 5 a.m. mass arrest of Sekou Odinga, Lumumba and Afeni Shakur, along with others identified as the top 21 NYC Panther leaders, dubbed the New York Panther 21. They were charged with hundreds of counts relating to the alleged police precinct-shooting plans and for planning to bomb public places around New York City.

Only Sekou Odinga evaded the April 2 police sweep by climbing out of his third story window and escaping to Algeria. Once there he joined Eldridge and Kathleen Cleaver, who had formed a Panthers-in-exile group. Police had charged Eldridge with firing back at the cops after they had fired a fusillade of bullets at him, just before they murdered Panther Bobby Hutton (Ch.3). Eldridge had jumped bail and Kathleen went with him to the African country that granted them asylum.[97]

5-FBI/Cops Murder Hampton as He Politicized Gangs and Shoot at War Vet Pratt

> "You can jail a revolutionary, but you can't jail the revolution. You can run a freedom fighter around the country but you can't run freedom fighting around the country. You can murder a liberator, but you can't murder liberation."
>
> Fred Hampton, 1970, speech excerpt from *The Black Panthers Speak.*

The FBI's Counterintelligence Program (Cointelpro) continued coordinating their attacks in several of the largest cities' chapters. On April 2, 1969, as police intelligence mass-arrested the New York Panther 21, the FBI had a key agent initiate an assault on the Chicago Panthers. On that day, an undercover FBI agent in the Chicago Panthers, William O'Neal, personally started an armed clash between the Chicago Panthers and Chicago's largest gang, the Blackstone Rangers (later changed to El Rukn). The FBI gave O'Neal a pay raise for his purposeful "provocation" that successfully ended the Chicago Panthers' progress at politicizing the Blackstone Rangers and merging with them.[98]

Chicago's charismatic Black Panther leader, Fred Hampton, developed this merge. Hampton proved dangerous in the FBI's perspective for several reasons. Hampton rallied people with persuasive speeches and built alliances with many other radical groups.[99]

But the FBI appeared most concerned with Hampton's ability to make connections with and politicize the leaders of Chicago's huge, well-armed gangs. Hampton convinced Chicago's 3,000 member Blackstone Rangers gang to make the conversion to a radical political force as a new Black Panther chapter.[100] This would have effectively doubled the national size of the Black Panther Party, which had an estimated 2,000-5,000 members in 40 chapters by the end of 1968.[101] The merge got far enough that the gang changed its name to The Black P. Stone Nation.[102]

After Panther infiltrator William O'Neal reported the pending merge in December of '68, the FBI quickly orchestrated actions to thwart it. They sent off fake letters to many people involved in the merge in order to sabotage it. O'Neal also verbally exacerbated tensions between the groups' leaders before he initiated the armed conflict. O'Neal further destroyed merger negotiations with two other Chicago gangs, the Vice Lords and the Mau Maus.[103]

O'Neal next damaged Panther work with other radical political groups. He sent racially prejudiced messages to the white radicals in the national Students for a Democratic Society (SDS) office in Chicago to damage that collaboration. SDS had grown into the largest anti-war goup by late 1968 (estimated to have 350 chapters).[104]

The FBI also helped O'Neal end discussions of a collaborative rainbow coalition between the Panthers, SDS, the Young Lords (a Latino group modeled after the Panthers who supported Puerto Rican independence), and another white group.[105]

The FBI had the same motives and used similar tactics for targeting the Chicago Panthers as they would Tupac Shakur years later. Tupac also instituted a plan to radicalize gangs (Ch.14). The FBI worked with police gang intelligence units against the Chicago Panthers and recruited undercover Panther infiltrator William O'Neal by letting him off of several criminal charges. Evidence supports that U.S. Intelligence similarly let record producer Suge Knight off of criminal charges and had him work with police gang intelligence units against Tupac (Ch.s 22,23).[106]

Researchers rarely mention how much the Panthers' potential to politicize gangs likely concerned the FBI in many cities. Reportedly, Bunchy Carter had previously headed the several thousand strong Clausson gang. This may have motivated his early murder by the FBI—one of the first Panther murders.[107] Motives to heavily focus on New York Panther leaders Lumumba Shakur and Sekou Odinga likely included their former New York leadership in gangs estimated as 10,000 strong. Also, Afeni Shakur had led a female gang affiliated with one of the male gangs.[108]

It's further interesting to note Lumumba's belief regarding U.S. Intelligence's perspective on gangs. He said that when he was active in gangs, U.S. Intelligence encouraged non-political gang violence for a "bad-nigger-kill-bad-nigger" population control of young blacks. Lumumba said the Navy aided this by offering unlimited weapons for easy pilfering from the Brooklyn Navy Yard when he was a gang leader.[109]

By December of '69, the 21 year-old Chicago leader Fred Hampton had risen to the top of the national ranks of the Black Panther Party. Newton, Seale and the New York Panther leadership were in jail. Eldridge and Kathleen Cleaver were in Algeria. Oakland's David Hilliard led the Panthers National Office and was assigning Hampton to the Central Committee and as a national spokesman, with LA Panther leader Geronimo Pratt next in line. Groups such as the UCLA Law Students Association invited Hampton and other Panthers to give talks nationwide.[110]

On December 3, 1969, FBI and police conducted the most brutal of all their armed attacks on Panther locales. Ex-FBI agent Wes Swearingen said that his former partner, Chicago FBI supervisor Gregg York, told him how his unit convinced Chicago police to make a twilight raid on the Panthers, assassinate Fred Hampton in particular, and attempt to murder many other Panthers.[111] Trial transcripts and evidence supported this admission. After the FBI made up a claim that the Panthers killed a cop, police raided Hampton's home with artillery that included a machine gun. They wounded many Panther members sleeping there. They also killed Hampton who remained asleep in his bed after an undercover agent in the Panthers drugged the punch he had with dinner. In that raid, police further murdered a visiting southern Illinois Panther captain, Mark Clark.[112]

A future FBI assistant director came in for the cover-up while his son led attacks in Los Angeles. High level FBI supervisor Richard G. Held came in as the new Chicago chief while his son, Richard W. Held, supervised the LA FBI Cointelpro unit. Only after many years did a federal judge rule that the operation was an FBI conspiracy and award the survivors close to $2 million.[113]

Richard W. Held orchestrated the attempted murder of LA Panther leader Geronimo Pratt with a raid of the LA Panther office only several days after the Chicago raid. The FBI likely had added concern about Pratt because he was a highly decorated Vietnam War veteran. Police marksmen shot up Pratt's bed through his window. Pratt luckily slept on the floor that night due to back injuries from the war and remained unharmed, though police arrested him for possibly harboring a fugitive (Ch.6).[114] Held's targeting later included environmentalist Judi Bari, Huey Newton and possibly Tupac (Ch.s 11-13).

6-FBI Sets Up Fugitive Raids & Manufactures East/West Panther Feud in NYC

U.S. Intelligence appeared to take advantage of their April mass-arrest of the New York Panther 21 leaders to set up a "fugitive operation." Researchers have found evidence that U.S. Intelligence planned to have a Panther commit murder and then visit the Chicago, LA and other Panther chapters, so that police could then raid those chapters in pursuit of him. Just weeks after the April of '69 NY Panther 21 arrest, George Sams came to the New York Panthers alleging that the National Black Panther office in Oakland had sent him. Sams, who had a long criminal record and some history of mental illness, had been officially expelled from the Panthers before this.[115] But police attacks, arrests of Panthers around the country, as well undercover agent infiltrators at many offices, hurt the Panthers' ability to verify Sams' statements. Sams' actions, evidence, and later government admissions support the claims of many that Sams worked undercover for the FBI.

In mid-May of '69, Oakland Central headquarters Panther Field Marshall Landon Williams drove George Sams, Oakland Panther Rory Hyathe, and New York Panther Alex Rackley from New York City two hours north to New Haven, CT Panther office. Landon Williams and Hyathe only stopped in New Haven briefly and left Sams and the much younger Rackley at the New Haven office. Erika Huggins, the wife of slain LA Panther leader John Huggins, had started a Black Panther chapter there.

Panther national cofounder Bobby Seale had visited the New Haven office just days previously as he was giving a speech at nearby Yale University. When Sams and Rackley got to that office, Sams put a gun to Rackley's head, and similarly held a gun to New Haven Panther George Edwards. He ordered other New Haven Panthers to tie them up, claiming they were undercover FBI agent infiltrators. Edwards, an Air Force veteran and highly committed Panther, told his fellow New Haven Panthers that Sams better shoot him now or let him go. Edwards saved himself. Rackley ended up fatally shot. [116]

Huey Newton said at a press conference that George Sams was an FBI agent that the FBI apparently then cut from employment.[117] Several aspects of events following this murder support his statement. First, George Sams proceeded to travel to many Panther offices, allegedly on the run from the FBI and police. Police and FBI then used the excuse of trying to apprehend Sams to go on murderous raids of over eight Panther offices around the country, such as those in Chicago and Los Angeles that left Hampton dead and Pratt's bed shot up.[118] All of these raids came just *after* visits by Sams. Professor and playwright Donald Freed's published account said that an armed Sams actually walked right through the police and FBI line in Chicago. Police used the charge of harboring the "fugitive" Sams as a reason for jailing

Panthers in all the cities' Panther offices they raided. Legal expenses bankrupted most of these chapters.[119]

Also, when police finally took Sams in custody, they charged Bobby Seale and eleven of the top New Haven Panthers with the murder of Alex Rackley. Similar to how New York kept the Panther 21 in jail awaiting trial for up to two years, New Haven kept Seale and New Haven chapter founder Erika Huggins in jail for 18 months awaiting trial. One report said that Sams was the only first-hand witness called into the courtroom. That the prosecution reported basing their charges on material provided by "a trusted ten-year informant" provides strong evidence that this was Sams.[120] The judge dismissed the charges against Seale and Huggins. New Haven Panther Captain Lonnie McLucas was acquitted of murder and other charges but convicted of conspiracy to murder and got 12 years in jail. Ultimately, Sams ended up in prison for ordering the shooting. Newton said it was because the FBI abandoned him.[121] Sams received a life sentence but was granted parole after four years.[122]

The FBI had also used various tactics to pit many Black Panther leaders against each other. Jailing various leaders helped the FBI gain success with these strategies. It similarly helped them with divisive strategies they used on Tupac in the '90s. While Huey Newton was in jail, the FBI first created conflicts between him and his honorary East Coast Panther leaders who also led SNCC, Stokely Carmichael and H. Rap Brown. The FBI divided Newton from the SNCC leaders with the use of undercover agents and fake letters they wrote. They sent letters in the names of these leaders to each other, or signed them as anonymous sources.[123]

But a key "divide and conquer" strategy they used against the Panthers evolved into the East Coast versus West Coast feud, pitting the New York Panther 21 against the Oakland National office. The FBI first set up this feud by using fake letters and other tactics to pit Huey Newton against Minister of Information Eldridge Cleaver in Algeria. Mainstream media aided them in this effort.[124] The FBI also created fake letters and used undercover agents to divide Newton's Oakland office from Afeni's imprisoned New York 21. The FBI's media collaborators then helped this become the East versus West war—a strategy later used against Tupac Shakur and other rap figures (Ch.s 21, 34).[125]

Murders of important Panthers on both coasts began. For example, someone killed Black Panther newspaper editor Sam Napier, and the other Panther faction was blamed. Undercover agents reportedly influenced Newton to believe that Geronimo Pratt and his wife, Sandra, sided with Cleaver and the New York 21 (Ch.10). Professor Ward Churchill and researcher Jim Vander Wall said a statement of expulsion of Pratt and most of the New York 21 in *The Black Panther* newspaper "was apparently proposed and prepared by

Elaine Brown, widely suspected among former party members of having been a police agent." [126]

Years later, Pratt said that Newton told him how Elaine Brown manipulated him, particularly before a key televised debate with Eldridge Cleaver. Newton only realized it after the expulsions, at which time he tried to expel Brown, but her backers convinced him otherwise.[127] While Pratt hid from California police just after his expulsion, his pregnant wife Sandra was murdered. Panther Communications leader Kathleen Cleaver said that when she came back to the U.S. from Algeria she barely avoided murder in the East versus West war. Evidence suggests that undercover agents perpetrated most of this East/West war's murders.[128]

Lumumba Shakur's brother, New York Panther Zayd Shakur, led the New York Panthers while Lumumba, Afeni, and Sekou Odinga were in jail. Zayd worked hard to quell the East versus West feud. When he found his fellow New York Panthers murdered for unknown reasons and police were arresting Panthers without substantiation, he went underground.[129] As the New York Panther 21 went to trial by 1971, the FBI had achieved their goal of neutralizing much of the Black Panther leadership across the country through the use of harassment arrests, imprisonment, murder and undercover agent influence.[130]

7-Multi-ethnic Revolts in US as Afeni Shakur Leads Panther 21 Tragicomic Trial

> "Black Panther historians argue themselves over the beginning at the spirit of the Black Panther Party. Some say it had its beginnings around 400 years ago when you first decided we were not human beings. Others attribute it to the 100 million or so that you killed on slave ships. Others to Gabriel Prosser, Denmark Vesey, Nat Turner and of course [military general and Haitian slave rebellion leader] Toussaint L'Ouverture. Some even say it began at the time of the fugitive slave act and the Dred Scott decision. But…all agree on the modern adaptation of it—that Franz Fanon put it on paper, that Malcolm X put it into words, and that Huey P. Newton put it into action."
>
> Afeni Shakur, *Rat*, 1970. *The Black Panthers Speak.* [131]

Individuals from racially diverse revolutionary groups soon crowded the underground due to the FBI's Cointelpro repression. The Weather Underground (a.k.a. Weathermen) led a "cadre" organization of mostly white revolutionary anti-war and anti-racism groups nationwide. Other Panther-aligned groups modeled their programs after the Panther programs and experienced similar, though less brutal, repression. These included the aforementioned Puerto Rican Young Lords, The White Panthers in Detroit, and the American Indian Movement (AIM), as well as socialist, communist and anarchist groups.[132]

While space precludes extensive details, the U.S. Intelligence attacks on AIM were particularly brutal. Besides the typical assassinations, U.S. Intelligence used other tactics against AIM in a reign of terror starting in the early '70s. For example, when the last national AIM leader, John Trudell, protested on the U.S. Capitol steps and burned an American flag, his house was burned down within hours. His pregnant wife, mother-in-law and three young children died inside (see notes).[133]

Another infamous U.S. Intelligence attack on AIM gained internationl attention partly through actor/producer Robert Redford's documentary, *Incident at Oglala.* In that 1975 South Dakota incident, an FBI force attacked an AIM house on the Pine Ridge Reservation. Two FBI agents and an AIM member were killed. AIM member Leonard Peltier languishes in jail despite a federal prosecutor admitting that the government "doesn't know who shot the agents." Numerous international groups, leaders and celebrities have attempted to gain Peltiers' release with documents to help prove his innocence, to no avail.[134]

The fear of being drafted into possible slaughter during the Vietnam War, radicalized white Americans. After its 1960 inception, the predominantly white Students for a Democratic Society (SDS) had gone from being a group that organized around civil rights and economic issues, to the largest antiwar organization in the country with an estimated membership between 80-100,000 at its peak by the end of 1968. In its final year, 1969, the SDS leadership split due to a disagreement in tactics, though undercover FBI infiltrators helped magnify these divisions. At least half of the SDS leaders formed a new group they called The Weathermen (later Weather Underground for feminist reasons), which started to embrace militant tactics.[135]

Other civil rights activists and anti-war activists also became disillusioned by the seemingly small effect of their peaceful protests, while violent attacks on leftist groups went unprosecuted. Racists and reactionaries, either working for U.S. Intelligence or unprosecuted by U.S. courts, conducted hundreds of bombings and murders. These included bombings of black churches and buildings as well as murders of blacks and their white activist supporters.[136] Blacks reacted partly by rioting, which some leading sociologists claimed was the key to getting civil rights legislation passed.[137] At least several groups of activists began retaliating by planting their own time bombs in buildings of companies connected to Vietnam War atrocities. These activists called to get the bomb sites evacuated and spare people physical harm.[138]

The Weather Underground used this bomb planting tactic. They also used a myriad of other tactics that included newspaper and book publishing in response to the U.S. military and police assaults on black and third world people. In response to Fred Hampton and Mark Clark's murders, for example, they blew up Chicago police cars and a Haymarket Square police statue. They also claimed to always evacuate people from the area of bombings and proceeded to carry out at least 20 more bombings in the early '70s. These were a small percentage of an estimated several thousand student-linked political bombing incidents, in a two year period alone, to protest the Vietnam war and racist government actions.[139]

The Weather Underground, the Panthers and other revolutionary groups survived for a number of years because of above ground support. Various celebrities, politicians and activists helped them. These included actors such as Donald Southerland, Jane Fonda Marlon Brando and Jean Seberg (who was particularly targeted amongst actors), politicians Tom Hayden and Shirley Chisolm, and musicians such as John Lennon, Jimi Hendrix (Ch.38), and composer Leonard Bernstein. Bernstein held fundraisers for the New York Panthers and helped accumulate money towards their huge bail.[140]

The New York Panther 21 gained huge international publicity. Several books exclusively covered them in various ways. As time went on from the arrest to the end of the trial, the 21 Panther defendants dwindled down to about 13. Some were held on charges elsewhere while others, such as Dharuba (born Richard Moore) and Cetewayo (born Michael Tabor) gained release on bail and escaped to join Odinga and the Cleaver faction in Algeria. The indictment counts also dwindled down from 30 counts charged to each defendant, to 12 for each.[141]

Afeni Shakur rose to stardom as a leader and her own trial lawyer during this time. The New York 21 had chosen Afeni for first release on the raised bail. They made her their spokesperson and Harlem leader as they awaited trial for close to two years. During this release, Afeni became pregnant with Tupac. Most media reports claim New Jersey Panther Billy Garland was Tupac's father. Lumumba, still jailed, divorced Afeni upon hearing the news of her pregnancy.

After several months the judge then revoked all bail and Afeni was back in prison. Afeni fought to keep her pregnancy while studying to defend herself in court as her own attorney. She petitioned for a daily glass of milk and an egg to keep her fetus healthy as she studied law books in prison. She had time, as a major publisher said the Panther 21 trial was the longest trial in the history of the state and, possibly, the longest trial in the history of the U.S. [142]

Afeni was up against a lot. The Assistant District Attorney (ADA) prosecuting the case, Joseph Phillips, introduced six undercover agents as witnesses. The judge showed his continual bias throughout the trial, from setting each Panther's bail at an exorbitant $100,000 to prompting ADA Phillips about what to say. A former Justice Department lawyer also complained that the judge and prosecutor met nightly to improperly confer on how to gain a guilty verdict. (Regarding the bail, when Phillips showed a film in the court, *The Battle of Algiers,* as evidence the Panthers used this movie to learn bombing tactics, several Panthers with obstructed views responded, "We paid $100,000 for a ticket and can't see the movie."). [143]

But Afeni's legal study paid off, as did her brilliant court queries. When the judge denied most every legal motion by Afeni, she showed the jury how he had completely stopped listening to what she was even saying. The judge had denied several objections by Afeni to the district attorney's lies and illegal tactics. So, Afeni finally queried, "May we ask the district attorney to cooperate in having a just trial?"

"Request denied," said the judge, causing Panther-supporting courtroom spectators to erupt with laughter. Jurors later said they took particular note of this response by the judge. They also would note being "thrilled" when 23 year-old Afeni, only 5'4" and 5-8 months pregnant with Tupac during the trial, told the rotund, white ADA Phillips to sit down during the trial.[144] Books documented these and other moments where various Panthers entertained their courtroom supporters by mocking the prosecutors (see endnote).[145]

Many revolutionary anti-war Panther supporters watched the New York 21 trial closely in the courtroom and the news. But one group took action against the judge's particular show of bias. Early in the trial someone set off a bomb at the judge's home. Two reports cited the Weather Underground as planting this bomb.[146]

In the end, half of the drained and embattled Panther defendants finally found freedom after 2 years of incarceration. The jury went out to decide their verdict for about two hours. When they came back, the court clerk repeated each of the 12 counts individually for all 13 defendants, saying, "How do you find, sir?"

To each count of every defendant, 156 total, the foreman of the jury responded, "Not guilty." Afeni Shakur sobbed quietly, as did Panther defense attorney Gerald Lefcourt and several jurors. Spectators called out, "Right on!" and "Power to the people!" Many jurors and writers credited Afeni's trial work for getting all of the Panther 21 off. Lumumba Shakur and five others remained in jail, as the state had lodged warrants against them for other crimes.[147]

8-Malcolm X's Assassination: Panther Infiltrator's Role Similar to Agent in MLK's

> "You are out of touch with reality. For a few in several smoke filled rooms, you're calling that remaining free while the masses of the people—white and black, red, yellow and brown and vulnerable—are suffering in this nation.... The seal and the constitution reflect the thinking of the founding fathers that this was to be a nation by white people and for white people. Native Americans, blacks and other non-white people were to be the burden bearers for the real citizens of the nation."
>
> Malcolm X speech excerpted and played in Tupac Shakur's, "White Man's World," under alias Makavelli, *Don Killuminati: The 7 Day Theory*, 1996.

> "No Malcolm X in my history text, why is that?
> 'Cause he tried to educate and liberate all blacks."
>
> Tupac Shakur, "Words of Wisdom," *2Pacalypse Now*, 1991.

Not long before the jury went into deliberations on their verdict at Afeni Shakur's New York Panther 21 trial in early 1971, one of the Panther 21 defense attorneys cross-examined undercover agent Eugene Roberts and reopened an important chapter of history. Afeni and Lumumba Shakur, as well as Huey Newton and so many other Black Panther leaders, had looked to Malcolm X as their inspiration. In her New York trial, Afeni implied that the Nation of Islam wasn't the real force behind Malcolm's assassination.

Among the undercover police agents infiltrating the New York Black Panthers, Eugene (Gene) Roberts and two others were there from its inception. Bureau Of Special Services (BOSS) agent Roberts had formerly infiltrated Malcolm X's Muslim Mosque Number One. In 1964, Malcolm X attempted to rebuild this Mosque after Elijah Muhammad excommunicated him. Malcolm also started the activist group, Organization of Afro-American Unity (OAAU) that year. Roberts had become one of Malcolm X's bodyguards, moving up to the top among Malcolm's OAAU security.[148]

After Panther 21 defense attorney Carol Lefcourt cross-examined Gene Roberts on his testimony regarding the Panthers, her husband and fellow attorney Gerald Lefcourt asked Roberts about a different subject.

"Isn't it a fact that you helped murder Malcolm X?"

"YES!" Afeni cried out from her chair.[149]

Much research backed defense attorney Lefcourt's accusation. Closer scrutiny of Malcolm X's life leading up to his murder supports that U.S. Intelligence orchestrated his assassination. With the compendium of evidence that the U.S. military intelligence apparatus effected Martin Luther King's assassination (Ch. 2), it's important to note an FBI memorandum of 3/4/68. It discussed the "long range goals" including: "Prevent the rise of a 'messiah' who could unify, and electrify, the militant black nationalist movement. Malcolm X might have been such a 'messiah'; ... Martin Luther King, Stokely Charmichael and Elijah Muhammad all aspire to this...[particularly] King... should he abandon his supposed 'obedience' to 'white liberal doctrines' (nonviolence)...."[150] This and other documents showed how Malcolm X had clearly emerged as U.S. Intelligence's top threat.[151]

Malcolm X's life path to become this top threat also overlapped the Shakurs' lives several times before Gene Roberts joined the Panthers. Afeni's father-in-law, Abbah Shakur, had joined Marcus Garvey's Universal Negro Improvement Association (UNIA) in its founding location of Harlem. Malcolm X's father, Earl Little worked as a preacher and led a chapter of Marcus Garvey's UNIA in Lansing, Michigan during the 1920s.[152]

The UNIA gained widespread appeal in the 1920s and '30s, reaching a million members amongst northern U.S. blacks.[153] Garvey orignally started his UNIA with its black pride activism in his birth country of Kingston, Jamaica before re-starting it in Harlem. Garvey's life appeared to reflect the effect of government oppression of many black leaders and groups to come after him. He first supported socialists and anti-colonialists worldwide. He had a successful international shipping company that helped distribute his *Negro World* newspaper to the Caribbean and Africa, where other UNIA chapters started. When both British and U.S. Intelligence officials (including emerging FBI leader J. Edgar Hoover) corroborated against him, he took on a more conservative, capitalist but nationalist stance to allow himself back into the U.S. Nonetheless, Garvey was shot, imprisoned, deported and exiled for his activist work.[154]

Born in 1925, Malcolm X described race relations in Lansing growing up. The town's segregationist and racist rules included banning blacks from East Lansing after dark. When leaders such as Earl Little organized for any changes, racist whites threatened them. For example, the white Black Legion, Lansing's Ku Klux Klan, threatened Little and then burned his house down in 1929. In 1931, when Malcolm was 6, his father was found dead with a crushed skull and his body almost cut in half, reportedly due to being laid on street car tracks. Malcolm's mother, Louise Little, paid for the funeral through a small insurance policy. A larger company wouldn't pay on Little's life insurance because they called it a suicide.[155]

By the start of the '60s, FBI documents later made public revealed that U.S. Intelligence wrote up to several reports a week on Malcolm X (a.k.a. El-Hajj Malik El-Shabazz) due to his radical influence over blacks.[156] Malcolm's influence over large numbers of American blacks first came through his Nation Of Islam (NOI) leadership as its national spokesman. The FBI began their surveillance file on him early in the 1950s.[157] From the late '50s on, Malcolm X's leadership of the New York NOI mosque also helped him meet with third world revolutionaries and African leaders in the New York-based United Nations.

The CIA grew concerned about Malcolm's influence amongst these leaders. African leaders soon hosted Malcolm X and had him take part in their political decisions. From the mid-1800s to the mid-1900s, European nations had invaded and forcibly taken Africa's riches of oil, diamonds and other minerals until independence movements drove the European colonizers out. After WWII devastated most European countries, it expedited the chances for African independence movements to gain control of their countries and U.S. corporations saw a chance to gain control of African wealth through more subtle means. Malcolm's input about racism in the U.S. threatened to sabotage multinational corporations' hundred million-dollar deals.[158]

Malcolm X criticized America's capitalist system as exploiting people in general but he believed that its historical racism kept people of color particularly disadvantaged. And, with a huge media presence, he expressed his ideas to large forums. But NOI leader Elijah Muhammad disagreed with Malcolm's leftist political activism. Muhammad restricted Malcolm's political activities, leading him to split with the NOI in 1964.[159]

African leaders helped fund Malcolm's travels and he started a new activist group in '64, which he named the Organization of Afro-American Unity (OAAU) in connection with the Organization of African Unity (OAU).[160] African presidents had invited Malcolm as the only American allowed in their OAU meetings because they recognized him as the leader of black American interests.[161] Malcolm also maintained his position of militant self-defense while he began directly collaborating with Martin Luther King's group and other civil rights movement leaders.[162] RAM leader Maxwell Stamford reported Malcolm X saying that the non-equality of African women in African organizations hindered the liberation movement and he wanted to practice equality and give them more leadership in his OAAU.[163]

The Shakurs, an activist family, joined Malcolm's Harlem-based OAAU several years before co-founding Black Panther chapters. After his years in Marcus Garvey's UNIA, Abbah Shakur joined Malcolm X's New York City OAAU. Lumumba Shakur joined the OAAU after his father, and Lumumba's teen friend Sekou Odinga also joined the OAAU.[164] Undercover police agent infiltrator Gene Roberts joined the OAAU at its inception and rose to the leadership ranks of its Harlem-based security force. He then followed Lumumba into the Harlem Black Panthers (Abbah Shakur helped found a RAM-based New York Panther chapter). By working for the New York Police department's Bureau of Special Services (BOSS), Roberts also worked for the FBI's Counter Intelligence Program (Cointelpro) against Malcolm X and the Black Panthers, while the CIA superiors supervised the entire U.S. Intelligence apparatus.[165]

U.S. Intelligence had made several attempts on Malcolm's life early in his development. As early as 1958, New York detectives shot up Malcolm X's office, for which the city settled with Malcolm in a $24 million lawsuit.[166] FBI undercover agent, John X Ali, who infiltrated the Nation Of Islam (NOI), could provide the floor plan since he was living with Malcolm at the time.[167]

Agent John X Ali also reportedly played a part in orchestrating the firebombing of Malcolm's house in 1965. Ali had risen to a national secretary assignment, one of the highest leadership positions in the NOI.[168] NOI leader Elijah Muhammad's son, Wallace Muhammad, said several FBI undercover agents in the NOI national staff helped Ali make that rise, as also attested to by FBI documents.[169]

Malcolm X believed that U.S. Intelligence further set up his near-fatal poisoning in Cairo, Egypt late July of 1964. He said CIA agents made their presence obvious to try and intimidate him as he traveled through Africa. They didn't want him to present a planned United Nations appeal to African leaders that the U.S. was violating American blacks' human rights. At a Cairo restaurant, Malcolm said that just as he felt the poison in his food, he realized that he recognized the waiter as someone he saw in New York. Rushed to the hospital, he was barely saved by a stomach pumping. The attending doctor said there was a toxic substance in his food. Malcolm had been concerned about NOI death threats, but he knew that they didn't have a global spy capacity.[170]

Several other disclosures support Malcolm's belief that this was a CIA attempt on his life. A high level African diplomat later said that the French Counter-Espionage Department reported that the CIA planned Malcolm's murder, and France barred Malcolm for the first time in fear of getting scapegoated for the assassination.[171] The FBI Director wrote a confidential memo on Malcolm's travel plans through Britain and France. He sent it to the CIA Director, the Army Intelligence (Intel) chief, the Naval Intel Director, and the Air Force Counterintel chief, as well as Intel chiefs in London and Paris.[172] One such memorandum on Malcolm and African leaders went directly to the CIA director of covert action, Richard Helms, who had a key role in assassination plots.[173]

Furthermore, FBI and police behavior around Malcolm X's assassination on February 21, 1965, supports their role in it. An FBI document said [undercover agent] John Ali met with Talmadge Hayer (a.k.a. Thomas Hagan), one of the gunmen that shot Malcolm X, the night before the assassination. Hotel information on Ali's stay in New York those days supports this.[174] At the Audubon Ballroom hall where Malcolm X gave his last speech, uniformed police left the area despite usually filling inside and outside the halls where Malcolm gave speeches.[175]

When cross-examined at the New York Panther 21 trial in 1971, undercover police agent Gene Roberts said he was the first to arrive at Malcolm's body and he "proceeded to give Malcolm X mouth-to-mouth resuscitation."[176] But Roberts revealed more, in interviews decades later, which supports that his real role appeared to be checking Malcolm X's vital signs to confirm the assassination's success. Roberts described the actions of Joan Roberts who was with him at the event. When Malcolm X was shot, Malcolm's wife Betty Shabazz first tried to cover her daughters and screamed, "They're killing my husband!" [177] When the shooting stopped, Shabazz, a nurse, went to run to her husband, but Joan Roberts grabbed her. Shabazz struggled to get free, threw Roberts into a wall and ran to Malcolm.[178] Gene Roberts said he was there checking Malcolm's pulse. He turned to Shabazz and said Malcolm was dead.[179]

Roberts admission bore even more importance due to its historical parallels. As previously noted, attorney William Pepper extensively documented revelations on the role of undercover infiltrator, Military Intelligence agent Marrell McCullough in Martin Luther King's assassination (Ch.2). McCullough disclosed how he raced to and knelt over Martin Luther King as he lay bleeding from the fatal shooting. Pepper noted that McCollough was "apparently checking him for life signs," making sure the assassination was successful and signaling to Military Intelligence that "the army snipers there as backup shooters [weren't needed as]...the contract shooter [hadn't]...failed to kill King." They then communicated to the Special Force Group snipers who were waiting for their shooting orders that they could disengage.[180]

Police officials' admissions and later events supported the malevolent roles of the Roberts. Without Gene Roberts' disclosure at the Shakurs' Panther trial six years later, no one would have known he worked undercover for the BOSS police intelligence unit. New York's *Herald Tribune* also said a "high police official" confirmed that several undercover BOSS agents were in the Ballroom audience at the assassination.[181]

And finally, despite some admissions, police and media's cover-up actions were extensive. For example, New York's *Herald Tribune* and *The New York Times* reported that just after the shooting of Malcolm, police detained two people that the crowd grabbed. A later *Herald Tribune* edition said the crowd only grabbed one, without acknowledging their earlier account. The *New York Times* later edition dropped the second suspect from its subheading, but still quoted Patrolman Thomas Hoy who said that, while one subject was grabbed by Malcolm's supporters, he grabbed a second suspect being chased by some people. Hoy further said, "the crowd began beating me and the suspect" in the Ballroom. In the following days, no mention was made of the second suspect in the mass of media's accounts.[182]

The media also largely ignored the circumstances around the death of Malcolm's close ally, Leon 4X Ameer. Mainstream media alleged that he died of an overdose of sleeping pills less than twenty days after Malcolm's assassination. This happened just after Leon 4X announced plans to produce tapes and documents of Malcolm's proving the government was responsible for his assassination.[183] Soon after Malcolm's murder, a partially deleted FBI memo noted the CIA's desire to get rid of Malcolm. It said a *Life* magazine reporter agreed with a source that the reporter should "check out Washington and the CIA because they wanted Malcolm out of the way because he 'snafued' African relations for the U.S."[184] risking deals worth vast amounts of money for top American corporations.

9-Cointelpro Continued: Mutulu Called Terrorist; Assata & Black Liberation Army

> "Chemical warfare began to change the shape and attitude of the brothers and sisters who participated in, what we called then, the revolution. Whether it be the civil rights aspect of integrating into or assimilating into America, or the revolutionary nationalist fight for self-determination and/or liberation by nationhood. ...[Our] ability to fight chemical warfare was a significant contribution. ...So the Lincoln Detox became not only recognized by the community as a political formation but its work in developing and saving men and women...we began to move around the country and educated other communities around acupuncture drug withdrawal." Mutulu Shakur[185]

Arguably one of the single most important historical factors aiding the New York Panther 21 and other embattled Black Panthers was the continuing change in the political climate towards black revolutionaries. The activist burglary of an FBI office had a huge effect. In March of 1971, two months before the Panther 21 trial ended, activists broke into a Media, Pennsylvania FBI office. They removed a thousand documents and exposed the FBI Counter Intelligence Program, a vast program against law-abiding citizens protesting against the Vietnam War and for civil rights and economic justice. The documents also showed the FBI's sophisticated tactics and collaborative work with local police and many mainstream media outlets nationwide. The activists' distribution of these documents forced Congress and mainstream media outlets to at least acknowledge some of these brutal FBI illegalities with Cointelpro.[186]

For public relations' sake, the FBI officially ended Cointelpro in 1971. Agents and events support that the program continued. For example, former Cointelpro agent M. Wesley Swearingen said that the FBI actually continued the program under different names.[187] Various judges later agreed that an FBI/police Cointelpro continued against black activists.[188]

More and more U.S. Intelligence agents ended their careers and risked their lives to reveal how their groups initiated the terrorism against leftists. In 1973, Louis Tackwood, the agent working in Los Angeles' version of BOSS, the Criminal Conspiracy Section (CCS), described how the FBI had a liaison agent in CCS and vice versa. Tackwood gave hours of description that became the book, *The Glass House Tapes.* CIA agents such as Phil Agee and Victor Marchetti also published exposés on the Central Intelligence Agency. Marchetti's book came out only after court-enforced CIA deletions. Agee circumvented CIA censorship by first publishing his book in England.[189]

Afeni Shakur kept up her activism after giving birth to Tupac Amaru Shakur on June 16, 1971, a month after her release from prison following her trial acquittal. She immediately set him on a revolutionary course. Calling him her "black prince of the revolution," she named him after the last Incan leader to die trying to fight off the Spanish invaders. She also named her close friend, LA Panther leader Geronimo Pratt, Tupac's godfather (some sources say Afeni further named her close friend Assata Shakur as Tupac's godmother).[190]

By that time, police began new attacks on Geronimo Pratt. Wes Swearingen and other agents testified that LA FBI informants set Pratt up on a murder frame-up. In his memoir, former FBI agent Swearingen said he looked into the FBI's file on Pratt and saw that they had on audiotape that Pratt was hundreds of miles away in Oakland just before and after the murder.[191] An FBI-paid lawyer had infiltrated Pratt's defense counsel, according to the California Attorney-General's office in a declaration filed in court, and the FBI paid another person on Pratt's defense team. This led to Pratt's conviction and imprisonment for over 25 years.[192]

Afeni regularly traveled to the West Coast to help with Pratt's legal defense team of activist lawyers who helped Pratt for years. While they initially failed to acquit Pratt, the lawyers did uncover the various forces teamed up against him and eventually exonerated him. A judge finally ruled in his favor (Geronimo dropped his birth name and changed his last name to ji Jaga by that time). The U.S. ended up awarding Pratt several million dollars for false imprisonment. Pratt's lawyers found that the CIA had joined forces with the FBI in their attacks on Pratt. *New York Times* journalist Seymour Hersh found that the CIA went against its charter (to not work against Americans inside U.S. borders) by spying on many American leftists inside the U.S.[193]

Afeni continued her activism and accepted invitations to speak at Harvard, Yale, and many other colleges nationwide. With the assistance of Lumumba's adopted brother, Mutulu Shakur, she then worked on an historic lawsuit against the New York police. This suit gained the broadest restriction on any city's police intelligence activities.[194]

By 1973 Afeni moved in with Mutulu, a cofounding leader of the Republic of New Afrika (RNA).[195] The RNA was politically aligned with the Panthers, had similar goals and experienced similar police repression. The RNA formed in 1968 when 500 grassroots activists had met in Detroit to declare independence for the black nation inside the U.S. The following year, police attacked the RNA convention at Rev. C.L. Franklin's ("Queen of Soul" Aretha's father) New Bethel Church in Detroit. Police fired 800 rounds in the church and then held 150 people incommunicado before a judge set up court in the police station and got most of them released.[196]

Lumumba and Mutulu's brother, NYC Panther Zayd Shakur, started a new militant self-defense group. Zayd, who had gone underground after having his life threatened trying to mend the East/West Panther rift, worked with Panther Sekou Odinga to form the Black Liberation Army (BLA). The BLA reportedly protected activist leaders from armed police assault by regularly positioning snipers in various rooftop locations.[197]

Afeni and Zayd's close NYC Panther friend Assata Shakur (born Joanne Chesimard) had quit the Panthers because of the East/West feud. The respect Assata attained amongst other Panthers due to her vast political knowledge and speaking abilities led to continued targeting despite her exit from the group. She continued finding white detectives following her around her Harlem neighborhood. One day in 1970, she saw her picture on the front page of the *Daily News* saying police wanted her for questioning regarding a cop's murder. In fear, she joined her close friend Zayd in his underground hiding. Tupac knew Assata as his aunt.[198]

The FBI started a propaganda campaign against Assata Shakur, calling her "the revolutionary mother hen" of the Black Liberation Army. They accused the BLA of murdering a number of New York City police officers (most of these accusations came with little evidence and few valid convictions). The FBI conducted a nationwide manhunt for Assata in 1972.[199] Posters with her face appeared in police precincts and banks that cited her involvement in serious criminal activities, putting her on the FBI's most wanted list; and to all levels of police she became a shoot-to-kill target.[200]

In May of 1973, New Jersey police pulled over Zayd and Assata Shakur's car. Police fatally shot Zayd, while wounding Assata and former Panther 21 member Sundiata Acoli. Shots from one of the three killed a police officer. Assata said that police proceeded to beat her at the scene and torture her in a hospital. She said that in the hospital, she was only saved from more torture when a white nurse intervened. But, she said, prison officials used torturous tactics on her thereafter.[201]

New Jersey police charged Assata with killing the police officer. The case didn't reach trial for four years because prosecutors brought Assata to trial six times for alleged involvement in a half dozen other major criminal actions spanning from 1971 to 1973. They failed to gain a conviction at any of those hearings.[202]

By 1976, Assata's lead trial lawyer, Stanley Cohen, reported several breakthroughs in her case, and was found dead from a physical attack soon after with all his papers stolen.[203] At the trial, Assata's other lawyers presented tests and medical experts to prove her innocence in court. For example, Assata's fingers tested negative for gun residue when police coducted it. That test and doctors' findings supported that police shot Assata while she was in a seated position with her hands raised and that the bullet immediately severed a median nerve that wouldn't have allowed her to pull a gun trigger. Nonetheless, prosecutors won a conviction against her for killing the police officer during that '73 stop.[204]

Mutulu Shakur's life-long activism put him under constant FBI surveillance. His work with the Revolutionary Action Movement and leadership of the Republic of New Afrika likely brought on this surveillance. Mutulu's FBI file revealed that agents' reports on him were delivered to the FBI Director every 3 months since he was 19 years old. Mutulu Shakur also cofounded and directed the National Task Force for Cointelpro Litigation and Research.[205]

Afeni Shakur worked with Mutulu on his Cointelpro Litigation and Research activities, the success of which was supposed to stop the Counter Intelligence Program (Cointelpro). While traveling to Los Angeles to aid in Geronimo Pratt's defense, Afeni also advocated for the Panther perspective as she worked on an historic New York lawsuit brought on by a wide-array of anti-war activists, such as Abbie Hoffman.[206] Similar to a lawsuit taking place in Chicago after Fred Hampton's murder, the New York lawsuit accused the New York police department of violating the legal rights of New York activists with everything from illegal spying to perpetrating violence against activists. After close to a decade, a judge agreed with most of the lawsuit's charges and the suit's lead lawyer, Barbara Handschu, helped the group gain the most restrictions on police intelligence of any city nationwide. This forced the NYPD to "officially" end it's police Cointelpro activities.[207] In the 80s, the judge for that case found that the NYPD had continued its Cointelpro activities with a police unit targeting blacks called The Black Desk.[208]

Mutulu Shakur made his living by using a Canadian degree in acupuncture to successfully combat the heroin epidemic. The CIA and military caused this epidemic by trafficking heroin out of the Vietnam area during the war and beyond.[209] Mutulu helped direct the Bronx's Lincoln Detox, where he and other activists also politically educated clients. These activists were linked to black nationalism, the Latino community's Young Lords, and the white SDS/Weather Underground. They said that they were fighting the "chemical warfare" being waged on their communities. Despite its reported success, New York City de-funded Lincoln Detox. Mutulu continued his work anyway, founding a national acupuncture group. He was invited to China to further his work with acupuncture. The Zimbabwe Afrikan National Union also invited Mutulu to visit their country in 1980, because of his continued political leadership.[210]

The FBI said Mutulu founded the Revolutionary Armed Task Force (RATF)—a rainbow coalition of activists from the BLA and

Weather Underground, as well as an Italian revolutionary and the Young Lords (on others, see notes).[211] Reports said some RATF worked at Lincoln Detox and took extreme measures when the city tried to close it. The government charged the group with robbing banks to support Lincoln Detox when the city barred its funding. The FBI also accused RATF (one activist said this was the BLA's Multinational Task Force) of breaking Assata Shakur from jail and helping her gain exile status in Cuba. A judge then convicted members of RATF on a failed bank truck robbery that killed a police officer and a guard. Police went after Mutulu, not for any involvement in the actual crime, but for being a "co-conspirator."[212]

It's likely not a coincidence that by 1980, U.S. Intelligence started using the label "terrorist" for their assault on radical leftists. New York closed its Bureau Of Special Services Cointelpro unit, but they created several new ones that carried out similar duties as BOSS. One New York unit that had started in 1971, the year BOSS disbanded, was the similarly undercover Street Crime Unit. Another unit created in 1980 was the Joint Terrorist Task Force which New York and U.S. Intelligence started in response to the RATF and BLA. California had started a similar ad hoc unit out of Los Angeles. The FBI utilized these Task Forces as more openly-formed amalgams of national, state and city police agent units that were formerly run covertly. Echoing the more universal erosion of constitutional rights to come after 9/11/01, California and New York labeled Mutulu Shakur and other activists "terrorists" to justify the joint work against them that violated their constitutional rights.[213]

10-FBI Queried Tupac as CIA-Linked Dealer Hooked Afeni, Agent Hooked Newton

> "Even though you were a crack fiend, I always knew you were a black queen,"
>
> Tupac Shakur, "Dear Mamma," *Me Against the World*, 1995.

> "Couldn't survive in this capitalistic government
> 'Cause it was meant to hold us back with ignorance
> Drugs and sneak attacks in my community,
> They killed our unity
> But when I charged them they cried immunity."
>
> Tupac Shakur, "Panther Power"(1989) *Tupac Shakur: The Lost Tapes*, 1998

In 1981, the FBI charges against Mutulu Shakur sent him into hiding and onto its Most Wanted list. The FBI visited Tupac at school to question him about his stepfather Mutulu's whereabouts. Mutulu later said that Tupac became politically precocious by this time through attending political meetings with him. Tupac also experienced the deaths of his parents' revolutionary friends and imprisonment of his aunt Assata. Also in '81, Rev. Herbert Daughtry said he asked 10 year-old Tupac what he wanted to be when he grew up. Tupac responded, "a revolutionary." Daughtry said this reflected his mother's revolutionary view of the world in "wanting to make a complete change for the better."[214]

The FBI continued targeting Afeni Shakur. They reportedly visited her job sites for many years and intimidated employers into firing her or not hiring her. The beleaguered Shakurs moved dozens of times, but Afeni managed to stay politically active, writing a chapter of a book, *Human Rights for Everybody*, co-written by other activists including her ex-husband Lumumba Shakur, Howard Zinn, Noam Chomsky, Grace Paley, and Juan Jose Pena.[215]

By 1982, a drug dealer named Kenneth "Legs" Saunders (a.k.a. Legs McNeil) entered Afeni's life. After moving through dozens of homes and homeless shelters, Afeni moved into Legs' home.[216] Legs eased Afeni's poverty while she tried to raise Tupac and his younger sister Sekyiwa. Sekyiwa was Afeni's daughter by Mutulu. Afeni said Legs got her into using crack, "That was our way of socializing. He would come home late at night and stick a pipe in my mouth." [217]

Much research supports that U.S. Intelligence inserted Legs into beleaguered Afeni's life. Radio reporter Richard Boyle, who covered the trial of Vietnam Veterans Against the War leaders in the '70s, said that an undercover female government agent moved in with the anti-war group's leader. He said this wasn't uncommon since U.S.

Intelligence "often uses women, or men, to get in personal relationships with their targets."[218]

Legs' connections support that this was his role in '82. He was an associate of New York drug lord Nicky Barnes.[219] Barnes assisted the first national "Black drug kingpin," Frank Matthews, who worked untouched for years. The Justice Department indicted Matthews' entire network in '73, but dropped charges on nine of them due to their CIA ties. Matthews left the U.S. with millions of dollars. Barnes took Matthews' place from '73 into the late 80s. Barnes' ability to remain jail-free suggested he was either one of the nine with CIA ties or that he had similar U.S. Intelligence support. Professor Clarence Lusane said that Barnes won so many "acquittals on gun, narcotics, bribery and murder charges," the *New York Times* called him "Mr. Untouchable."[220]

Afeni Shakur's relationship with Barnes' associate, Legs, only ended when she made her move to Baltimore. She reported that after several years with Legs, when she moved to Baltimore, he apparently went to jail for credit card fraud. When she called to talk to him in jail, the prison officials claimed he died of a crack-induced heart attack.[221]

About the same time as Nicky Barnes and Legs' were dealing cocaine, the CIA was running a California-based cocaine trafficking operation with a similar network that also later affected Afeni and Tupac. As supported by a CIA Inspector General's findings, during that mid-80s time period, U.S. Intelligence supplied the nation's West Coast-based top drug trafficker, "Freeway" Ricky Ross.[222] A longtime probation officer for Ross said that drug lord Michael Harris was one of two top dealers buying from Ross and learning from him. Harris later provided seed money for the Death Row Records music label that produced Tupac's last two CDs (Ch.22).[223]

Other examples of U.S. Intelligence's use of undercover agents support that an intelligence group inserted Legs into Afeni's life. *The New York Times* described how an FBI "informant" (paid FBI employee) became the boyfriend of Malcolm X's daughter, Qubilah Shabazz, and then ensnared her in a plot to assassinate Nation Of Islam leader Louis Farrakan. The boyfriend convinced Shabazz that Farrakan plotted against her mother, Betty Shabazz. The article claimed that the elder Shabazz blamed Farrakan for some aspect of Malcolm X's death. It's possible that the boyfriend also contributed to Shabazz's apparent drug problem as the government agreed to drop the charges if Shabazz agreed to see a psychiatrist and get drug treatment.[224]

U.S. Intelligence also used similar tactics against Huey Newton. Black Panther cofounders Newton and Bobby Seale had originally barred any Panthers' use of drugs. That attitude changed with the huge use of marijuana among youth, but no reports were found of Panthers receiving drug-dealing charges. Reports cited various undercover agents trying to get close to Newton after he was released from prison. One in particular, Earl Anthony, said he worked for the FBI and CIA as he dealt bulk weed to Newton.[225] Seale said Newton started selling cocaine at this time. Newton claimed he wasn't involved in heavy drugs and cited the FBI's failed attempts to arrest him for drugs.[226] Several sources claim that Black Panther Elaine Brown helped get Newton using cocaine. Geronimo ji Jaga (formerly Pratt) said Newton told him in 1988 that Brown "kept cocaine and sexy women on him everyday/night." [227]

As previously discussed, evidence supports many Panthers' belief that Elaine Brown, Huey Newton's lover around 1970, was an undercover agent (Ch.s 4, 6). Panthers such as Communications Secretary Kathleen Cleaver and New Haven Panther George Edwards added to researchers' claims that Elaine Brown was "widely suspected among former [Black Panther] party members of having been a police agent." Brown became Newton's lover just after his prison release.[228] Other evidence that Elaine Brown helped Earl Anthony influence Huey Newton's drug involvement includes her arrest for cocaine possession in 1976. Unlike other Panthers who often received heavy sentences for small charges, a judge only sentenced Brown to complete "a series of yoga lessons." [229]

Cleaver and Edwards believe Brown's spy work led to murders of Panthers. Many Panthers more particularly believed that Brown influenced Newton to expel Geronimo and his wife, Nsondi (Sandra "Red" Pratt) from the Black Panther Party, after which pregnant Nsondi was found bullet-riddled and stuffed in a sleeping bag on a roadside. Reportedly there was no serious police investigation of her murder.[230]

Geronimo reported Huey Newton telling him that it took many months for him to come out of his drug and sex euphoria and realize he was surrounded by agents. Newton said he first began to suspect when it came out during Geronimo's trial that Brown's name was on a receipt from a paint shop that changed the color of Geronimo's car. Newton said she also testified against the United Slaves members who weren't the ones who pulled the trigger on Bunchy Carter and John Huggins. Newton said he became convinced she was an FBI agent and put Brown in a "Panther jail," but his "advisors" eventually got her back involved in the Panthers against his wishes (Pratt also noted Brown receiving psychiatric treatment at UCLA which he called a "prerequsite for patsies of Elaine's type.") [231]

While Earl Anthony's book, *Spitting in the Wind*, appears part disclosure and part cover-up, it supports former Panthers' claims about Elaine Brown. Anthony represented Brown as a committed Panther who linked him with another "committed activist," Jay Richard Kennedy. He failed to mention, and his fact-checking editors failed to disclose, that a popular book, David Garrow's *Bearing the Cross: Martin Luther King, Jr. and the Southern Christian Leadership Conference,* named J.R. Kennedy as a top CIA informant four years prior to Anthony's publication. FOIA-released CIA documents back this claim, as does the

King family lawyer, William Pepper, in his book *Orders to Kill*. Brown said that before Newton, Jay Kennedy had been her lover for two years. Anthony appeared to be trying to protect the covers of both Brown and Kennedy with this "committed activist" description.[232]

The CIA documents, Brown's incidental disclosures, and whistleblower reports further support Brown's likely U.S. Intelligence work. The CIA documents on Jay Kennedy verified that he was a CIA-supported writer who had infiltrated the civil rights movement by the start of the '60s. Kennedy got himself in a position as a manager for a longtime Martin Luther King supporter, entertainer Harry Belafonte, before Belafonte fired him (Ch.40).[233] Brown incidentally revealed evidence of her undercover work when she cited Jay Kennedy as a lifelong mentor whom she went to for guidance as late as the '90s, despite that the published reports on Jay Kennedy's CIA work started appearing in the mid-80s.[234] The surrounding of Newton with government agents fits with CIA whistleblower John Stockwell's statement that U.S. Intelligence used such agents in psychological warfare against Huey Newton until his death.[235]

Earl Anthony published several books that appeared to mix information with "disinformation," such as the notions described above. Elaine Brown continued lecturing and similarly writing both information and disinformation in books and for newspapers. Brown's negative reflections on Huey Newton in her *A Taste of Power: A Black Woman's Story* contradicts accounts by top women in the Panthers such as Afeni Shakur and Kathleen Cleaver (whose account holds particular validity given the Cointelpro-induced animosity provoked in Newton towards Eldridge Cleaver). Many other books on the Panthers also contradict Brown's accounts.[236]

Elaine Brown's later statements and activist work provide more contradictions on her real motives. In a 2003 lecture of Brown's, she rejected the idea of many undercover agents in the Panthers, despite that a number of agents openly testified against the Panthers in trials and that evidence supported the fact that many more agents were never revealed. Brown's defenders might say her work of heading the Oakland Panthers when Newton fled the country in the '70s, her work on behalf of prisoners, and her writing on behalf of black activists support good intentions. While certainty is hard to come by in these assessments, evidence of Brown's past misdeeds undermine any purportedly good intentions with her later activist work.[237]

11-Tupac's Panther Leadership & Newton's Panther Renewal, "Anniversary" Murder

> "The United States was transformed at the hands of the ruling circle from a nation to an empire...The United States as an empire necessarily controls the whole world either directly or indirectly...The ruling reactionary circle, through the consequences of being imperialists, transformed the world...They laid seige upon all communities of the world, dominating the institutions to such an extent that the people were not served by the institutions in their own land. The Black Panther Party [wanted to] reverse that trend and lead people to...seize the means of production and distribute the wealth and the technology in an egalitarian way to the communities of the world."
>
> Huey Newton, *To Die for the People: Writings and Speeches*, ed. Toni Morrison

> "...they loved the sight
> of your dimming and flickering starlight...
> they wanted 2 c your lifeless corpse
> This way u could not alter the course
> Of ignorance that they have set
> 2 make my people forget...
> I had loved u forever because of who u R
> And now I mourn our fallen star"
>
> Tupac Shakur, excerpt of "Fallen Star (4 Huey P. Newton)," *The Rose That Grew From Concrete*, Tupac's Collected Poems.

In the mid-80s, Tupac Shakur had his acting debut as a 13 year-old in Harlem. In 1984, Tupac starred in a production of *A Raisin in the Sun* held at the Apollo Theater as a political benefit for Jesse Jackson's presidential run. Within another year, Afeni Shakur moved Tupac and his sister Sekyiwa to Baltimore. Afeni then successfully fought to get Tupac into the magnet public high school, The Baltimore School for the Arts, where Tupac studied acting, dance, Shakespeare and writing for three years. Tupac also started activist groups there that worked on anti-violence campaigns and AIDS prevention education. [238]

While living in Baltimore, Tupac Shakur attended meetings of the New Afrikan Panthers, a group that helped inspire his development of activist work in school. The New Afrikan Panthers included young blacks ranging from their mid-teens to late-twenties that comprised the young adult section of the revolutionary group, the New Afrikan People's Organization (NAPO). Afeni's close friend, ex-Black Panther Watani Tyehimba, helped found NAPO and served as its security director. Tupac lived with Tyehimba for long stretches in 1985 and '86. Another important activist who was part of the Republic of New Afrika, attorney Chokwe Lumumba, also helped found NAPO and served as its chairman. The New Afrikan Panthers and NAPO had chapters in ten cities nationwide.[239]

In New York at this time, law officials spread a wide net over the activist community and jailed many who had any association with the Revolutionary Armed Task Force that they linked to the Brinks Bank truck robbery, Assata's escape and Mutulu Shakur's Lincoln Detox.[240] In early 1986 a judge jailed Watani Tyehimba for not giving a grand jury information on the whereabouts of Mutulu Shakur. Tyehimba said that with no previous criminal record, "I was held in Civil Contempt of Court, which is less than a misdemeanor, but was still housed as though I was a convicted criminal for 14 months, including 23 hours a day lockdown for the first 40 days."[241]

Later in '86, five years after the Brinks robbery attempt, government police finally caught Mutulu Shakur. Mutulu evaded the authorities longer than any of the other activists charged as being an RATF member.[242] Three days before Mutulu's capture, his brother, Lumumba Shakur, Afeni's ex-husband and the founding Harlem Panther leader, was found dead in Louisiana. Mutulu suspected that a police informant learned of Mutulu's whereabouts and decided to target both brothers. It also suggests that Lumumba helped his brother in hiding.[243]

A judge's acknowledgement of the FBI's Counterintelligence Program's continuance against Mutulu failed to keep Mutulu out of prison. Despite the FBI claiming to have disbanded Cointelpro, a federal judge said that the FBI violated Mutulu's rights with their Cointelpro actions.[244] Still, Mutulu started serving a sixty-year sentence in August of 1988 for "conspiracy" to commit armed robbery and murder (not for actually committing the crimes). The court also found Mutulu guilty of aiding Assata Shakur's prison escape. Some said this came without concrete evidence linking him to the actual undertaking.[245] A parole board repeatedly denied Mutulu parole, partly because, like Geronimo Pratt, he wouldn't renounce his politics.[246]

In 1987, a Baltimore teen living near Tupac was murdered. Afeni decided to move the family to Marin City, near Oakland, and into the house of Geronimo Pratt's second wife, Linda Pratt. A couple of weeks after Tupac's move, gunmen shot two of Tupac's activist Baltimore friends in the head.[247] But Oakland was also dangerous for the Shakurs. Afeni didn't realize that residents had nicknamed the northern California city Cokeland in those days. While living with Pratt, Tupac excelled in school and read voraciously. He also directed and starred in Shakespeare plays that he rewrote with modern dialogue.

Tupac got into conflicts with his mother due to her drug problem, but never lost sight of his goals. When Afeni's crack problem intensified, Tupac left home and high school in his senior year. He remained virtually homeless until taken in by his eventual first manager, Leila Steinberg. Tupac quickly impressed the similarly political Steinberg with his photographic memory and his precocious ability to plainly communicate a Marxist analysis of America's class system and other political issues. For example, in an interview for a video while he was a little known teen in high school, Tupac explained that "for the upper class," George H.W. Bush, was "a perfect president…that's how society is built. The upper class runs [society] while…the middle class and lower class, we talk about it." Tupac also read hundreds and hundreds of graduate school level books as a teen, from socialist and anarchist classic texts, to philosophical treatises, poetry, Shakespeare, and cutting-edge contemporary books on alternative historical analyses, feminism, and psychology.[248]

Tupac further kept up his later renowned, packed schedule of productivity. He assisted Steinberg in her after-school activist art programs. Tupac wrote much poetry, led several rap musical groups and recorded his first album. He dedicated one of his poems to Huey Newton and titled a new song of his "Panther Power." Tupac coupled his art with attending New Afrikan Panther meetings and he was elected the youngest-ever national chairman, at 17. He stayed in that leadership position for almost two years. Tupac was NAPO's top newspaper distributor in California and helped create their *Panther Power* mini-newspaper insert. Yakhisizwe Tyehimba, son of Tupac's mentor Watani, was Security Director of the New Afrikan Panthers under Tupac[249]

During Tupac's leadership tenure in 1988, police arrested Huey Newton on a minor charge that put him in prison with Geronimo Pratt (ji Jaga). Newton had endured two decades of constant arrests on apparent frame-ups, yet he still earned a doctorate, wrote several books, and started a Panther-inspired school for children in Oakland. Huey Newton displayed his vast intellect in the books he wrote along with the books published of his conversations with renowned psychologist Erik Erikson and his speeches edited by future Nobel Prize for literature winner, Toni Morrison..[250]

In prison, Geronimo Pratt took Newton under his wing (reportedly Newton was in drug withdrawal in prison) and the two compared their intelligence files. They commiserated about how the FBI and CIA set them against each other for the last 18 years. On August 22, 1988, the day officials were to release Newton from prison, he chose to remain incarcerated and announced a press conference for the following day. There, he said that he wouldn't leave prison until officials freed Pratt. Then Pratt asked Newton to leave and help him from the outside.[251]

Once out, Huey Newton worked for Pratt's release while also likely consulting with and possibly gaining inspiration from Tupac. Most black political prisoners started identifying themselves as "New Afrikans" around this time. Newton worked with Geronimo's lawyer and made speeches for Pratt's release. New Afrikan Panther leader Tupac said he consulted with Geronimo as well as the "Panther Minister of Defense," which had been Newton's official Panther position. In the summer of '89, Newton called East Coast Black Panthers who had restarted a Black Panther newspaper and said he wanted to reunite the Black Panthers, which, with Tupac's group, would have spanned two generations.[252]

U.S. Intelligence reportedly still had Newton under surveillance and these moves likely contributed to his early death. On August 22, 1989, exactly one year after Huey Newton refused prison release on Pratt's behalf, a gunman murdered Newton in Oakland. A minor conviction for gun possession led Newton to stay unarmed, while undercover police continued watching his every move. The assailant shot Newton three times, including twice in the head as he lay on the ground.[253]

In addition to its anniversary timing, many other aspects of Newton's murder suggest that it was a U.S. Intelligence assassination. The *San Francisco Examiner* caught Oakland Police Lt. Mike Sims in a number of lies about the murder. When Sims repeatedly said the police had "no suspects, no clues," the *Examiner* reported that police had been videotaped arresting three men near the scene within minutes of the murder. Then Sims said only two were arrested, neither of whom were linked to Newton's murder. Oakland Police corrected Sims the following day, saying the two were suspects, though they only named and charged one. As detailed more later, it's also important to note that Richard Held spoke with Lt. Sims at his press conference regarding Newton (Ch.12)[254]

The FBI and police claimed that the accused shooter, Tyrone Robinson, appeared to have acted in self-defense when Newton pulled a gun after an argument over money he owed Robinson for cocaine. But this claim is contradicted by the earlier police statement that they didn't find a gun belonging to Newton at the scene and the account doesn't explain why the shooter would put two extra bullets in Newton's head as he laid on the street from the first bullet. As a Special Forces commando described for an unrelated article, putting two extra bullets in the head is a signature move in a combat military execution (later attempted on Tupac, Ch.18).[255]

Furthermore, witness Michelle Johnson, who lived just across the street from where Newton was killed, gave a description of the murder that was consistent with a murder setup. Johnson heard a brief argument and recognized one of the two men as Huey Newton. The other man ordered Newton into a car. Newton protested, "Man, I ain't getting in your car." She next heard shots, peeked out her window and saw Newton slumped on the sidewalk. This first-hand account refutes that Newton was killed over drugs, instead showing that Newton's assailants had kidnapping and murder plans.[256]

Johnson's description, along with more aspects of the murder, supports the contentions of Newton's brother and area activists that the FBI murdered Newton.[257] That Newton was murdered exactly a year after refusing his prison release and calling a press conference on behalf of Pratt also deserves more scrutiny. Examples of such a "threat-timed" targeting tactic further support that U.S. Intelligence was involved in murdering Huey Newton. Newton's close friends said that the police had Newton under constant surveillance. A former CIA agent said that the CIA made Newton a life-long focus. These factors, alone, support that U.S. Intelligence set up his assassination.[258]

Several other black leaders' assassinations came with similar anniversary timing as Newton's death. Martin Luther King's family lawyer, William Pepper, emphasized that U.S. Intelligence orchestrated Martin Luther King's assassination exactly one year after he officially announced his opposition to the Vietnam War.[259] A gunman assassinated Congo president Laurent Kabila on January 16, 2001. It was on this exact date forty years before that the U.S. aided the assassination of Kabila's former comrade, and Congo's first independently elected president, Patrice Lumumba, according to CIA documents.[260] This apparent tactic engenders a conscious or subconscious warning with regard to an incident whose timing marks the anniversary date of a previous incident. U.S. Intelligence also appeared to use this tactic against Tupac Shakur (Chs. 13, 26).

12-Evidence FBI Set Up Armed Attacks on Tupac after Newton & Judi Bari

"I see no justice, all I see is niggas dying fast;
The sound of a gun blast, then watch the hearst pass…
Just another day in the life 'G,' gotta step lightly
'cause cops try to snipe me…
Fuck you to the Marin County Sheriff Department.
Fuck you to the FBI. Fuck you to the CIA.
Fuck you to the B-U-S-H.
Fuck you to all you racist, redneck mothafuckers!"
Tupac Shakur, *2Pacalypse Now*, "I Don't Give a Fuck" 1991.

The other key figure quoted in the cover-up of Huey Newton's death, Richard W. Held, had a serial killer's resume. As son of an FBI Assistant Director, Held gained high leadership status at a young age. At 27 he headed the FBI Counter Intelligence Program unit in L.A. and directed the FBI-paid informants in the United Slaves who murdered the Panthers. Held also framed Geronimo Pratt after Held failed in his attempt to murder the LA Panther. He then directed infiltration and murder within the American Indian Movement, and covered up FBI murders of Puerto Rican independence activists.[261]

The FBI sent Richard Held to head the San Francisco office as Special Agent in Charge (SAC/Director) in 1985 where his cover-up activities suggest that he continued his murderous Cointelpro work. When Held came to the San Francisco area he took over his earlier duties of targeting Pratt. Newton's support of Pratt posed a setback to Held's sabotage of Pratt's defense team. This work included FBI infiltration in the '80s.[262] In 1989 Held made statements to the media blaming Newton's murder on a botched drug deal without providing any evidence.[263] Police immediately followed Held's lead and made statements that contradicted the strong evidence that the shooter only had Newton's murder in mind when he tried to remove Newton from the more visible area before putting two extra bullets in his head.[264]

The year after Newton was murdered, a bomb went off under the car seat of successful environmental leader, Judi Bari. Evidence and disclosures eventually indicated that the FBI was likely behind this bombing. Bari headed the Earth First! environmental group's Redwood Summer campaign. The car bomb that exploded in May of '90 paralyzed Bari from the waist down. She and her wounded fellow activist passenger, Darryl Cherney, launched a lawsuit. While working on that suit, a reporter asked Bari about the FBI's search for the bomber. Reflecting her label as "queen of the quip" she said, "I hope the FBI find their man. And when they do, I hope they fire him."[265]

The government eventually agreed to settle the suit for several million dollars. A judge noted how the FBI directed the Oakland police to say Bari was transporting the bomb to use against the logging industry she battled. Researchers have accumulated much evidence to support that Richard Held actually directed the 1990 operation to plant the bomb, which had a motion-detection trigger, under Bari's seat. This was the second attempt on her life. Months before the bombing, a logging truck had nearly killed her and her three young kids when it ran them off a highway. Someone also nailed a picture of Bari to her door with crosshairs over her face and feces smeared on it (see cover photo). The crosshairs are reportedly a known FBI threat tactic.[266]

After the bombing, Judi Bari chronicled dozens of murderous Cointelpro-type tactics the FBI used against her, and her section of Earth First, leading up to the car bomb incident.[267] This research supported Bari's lawsuit, which had gained enough congressional support to take the area FBI supervisor, Richard Held, and his collaborator in the Oakland police, Lt. Mike Sims, to court. Held and Sims had extensively collaborated with the Newton murder cover-up a year earlier. Former colleagues and writers say the Bari suit sent Held into early retirement in 1993, though not before three armed and murderous attacks took place on new entertainment star Tupac Shakur in Held's Bay area.[268]

Many aspects of Tupac Shakur's time in the San Francisco Bay area support that Richard Held kept a close eye on him. Held returned to Geronimo Pratt's locale and continued with FBI cover-up work on Pratt's case. As Held led the FBI fight against Pratt's defense team that Newton aided with public speeches, Tupac performed musical benefits to raise money for his defense and discussed strategy with his godfather, Pratt.[269]

Tupac Shakur only left his national leadership of the New Afrikan Panthers due to a break into the music world, but he didn't give up his activism. Grammy-nominated Digital Underground (DU) took him on their national rap tour in 1990. He then recorded with and joined DU on their world tour in 1991. Tupac also started a new activist project at that time called The Underground Railroad to nurture young black activist leaders.[270]

As soon as Tupac's impending stardom became apparent, police assaults began with telltale timing. By 1991 Tupac landed a solo record deal for his *2Pacalypse Now* and a top movie role in *Juice*. His first radical political single had its world premier on MTV in mid-October. Several days after his video's release, Oakland police stopped Tupac for jaywalking, beat his head against the pavement and choked him until he was unconscious. Both of these police brutality tactics have led to victims' deaths. Tupac sued for $10 million and received a $15,000 settlement several years later.[271]

The timing of a second armed attack just after another major entertainment release also suggests Cointelpro-ace Richard Held's orchestration. In January of 1992, strangers conducted a drive-by shooting of Tupac's limousine. The limousine was taking him from his San Francisco premiere in his debut movie, *Juice,* to its after-party. Luckily no one got hit.[272]

Evidence and witnesses of another drive-by shooting reveals that police have conducted drive-by murders in unmarked cars. In an early 90's incident, an officer shot a police cadet scheduled to testify against the LAPD in a racial police brutality case involving a pro football player. The officer claimed self-defense, while witnesses described a drive-by execution of the cadet with no evidence of him firing. After witnesses implicated several Los Angeles police officers, the LAPD was forced to admit that their officers used an unmarked car in the fatal shooting.[273] This gives further credence to Held having orchestrated the second armed attack on Tupac.

13-LA Riots; FBI Targets Fred Hampton, Jr, NAPO's Tupac in Marin & Musicians

> "We cannot afford the luxury just to look at Hip Hop as some kind of abstract phenomena. We have an obligation similar to the way Harriet Tubman utilized negroe spirituals and the way the late, great Nat Turner utilized the church. We have a responsibility. There's too many of us in Sing Sing for us to be kept hold by Bling Bling. We know what Che Guevara said about the Cuban Revolution—'The role of the propagandist is as important as the role of the guerilla.' So we're going to hold those cats accountable. We knew in the '60s it was The Movement, first, that had James Brown say 'I'm black and I'm proud.' You're going to see that same type of resistance, that same type of community from the streets, reinforcing some forces that at some point want to use Hip Hop as a tool, not just using Hip Hop as some abstract type of thing."
>
> Fred Hampton, Jr. 2006 interview.[274]

Tupac Shakur gave the FBI another reason to target him; he started funding the New Afrikan People's Organization's leadership by the beginning of 1992. When Tupac sued the Oakland police for brutality, he hired NAPO national chair Chokwe Lumumba. He kept him as his consulting lawyer from then on. Tupac then officially hired his regular assistant and mentor, Watani Tyehimba. He made the ex-Panther and NAPO security director Tyehimba his business manager. Tupac also promoted the New Afrikan Panthers in his lyrics and spoke at NAPO gatherings.[275]

While Tupac worked on his second film in Los Angeles at the end of April of 1992, John Singleton's *Poetic Justice,* sections of the city rioted in response to the acquittal of the four white cops caught on video beating motorist Rodney King. It was the largest riot since the '60s and sparked smaller riots in several other cities.[276]

Historically, U.S. Intelligence put huge resources into targeting the forces playing a part in riots. In the '60s, U.S. Intelligence documents revealed research into which prominent activist figures most inspired the rioters. When their results pointed to Martin Luther King, U.S. Intelligence put more resources into targeting him (Ch.2).[277] Mike Davis, author of the best-selling book, *City of Quartz*, wrote how U.S. Intelligence used the 1992 LA riots as an opportunity to wage full scale war on communities of color, particularly chapters of two LA gangs declaring peace and becoming radicalized by former Black Panthers.[278]

After the 1992 riots, which raged for several days, evidence supports that U.S. Intelligence also targeted particular activists whose parents were Panther leaders, including Chicago's Fred Hampton, Jr.

and Tupac Shakur. The slain Chicago Black Panther leader's son, Fred Hampton, Jr., held a rally to protest the Rodney King police acquittal. Hampton, Jr. was Chicago's 22 year-old National People's Democratic Uhuru Movement leader. Hours after the rally, police and FBI agents picked Hampton up as he was walking with his three year-old daughter and arrested him on several charges. Hampton said the police officer that led FBI agents in arresting him, Joseph Grubesette, had also arrested his Panther leader father.[279]

Police accused Hampton of "firebombing" a store and lesser charges. Police reportedly based their claims only on a bottle filled with gasoline found intact at the store. Police didn't present fingerprints, eyewitnesses, or any other physical evidence at the trial. The trial judge asked how police could charge Hampton with arson at a store when they couldn't even show that a fire ever occurred there. Nonetheless, the government's claim that Hampton had a "predisposition" to commit the crime led to a conviction and an 18-year sentence for "aggravated arson."

During his nine years in prison, Fred Hampton, Jr. reported what he believed were government murder attempts behind bars. Hampton also said that a New York attorney who worked to defend him from continued police attacks, was herself murdered and all of her legal papers on his case were stolen. Assata Shakur said the FBI had similarly orchestrated the murder of her lawyer, whose wife found him killed in their home and all of Assata's trial papers missing (Ch.9). This supports Hampton's belief that a latter-day FBI Cointelpro orchestrated all these attacks. He further published pictures of his damaged car and grazed neck when gunmen shot at him and his mother, the first of two murder attempts in 2002. At that time Hampton worked as National Chairman of the Prisoners of Conscience Committee (Hampton also often cited Tupac's importance as an activist). Attacks would continue on his POCC (Ch.40).[280]

With Tupac's widespread fame by 1992, they wouldn't have targeted him as brazenly as they did Hampton. But U.S. Intelligence had a particular longtime concern about political musicians and more sophisticated strategies for attacking them. An exposed intelligence document reviewed by a 1976 congressional committee examining the FBI's Counterintelligence Program detailed many tactics used against political musicians. It instructed agents to:

> "Show them as scurrilous and depraved. Call attention to their habits and living conditions, explore every possible embarrassment. Send in women and sex, break up marriages. Have members arrested on marijuana charges. Investigate personal conflicts or animosities between them. Send articles to the newspapers showing their depravity. Use narcotics and free sex to entrap. Use misinformation to confuse and disrupt. Get records of their bank accounts. Obtain specimens of their

> handwriting. Provoke target groups into rivalries that may result in death." [281]

Evidence supports that U.S. Intelligence used most of these tactics against Tupac. Intelligence-linked conservatives such as Pat Buchanan blamed rappers for the LA riots and U.S. Intelligence particularly targeted those singing about the Rodney King incident.[282] Tupac emerged as a public figure, agitator and critic in 1992. His solo debut, *2Pacalypse Now,* released in November of '91, was becoming a gold record. It included song lyrics with militant responses to police brutality, such as "I remember Rodney King and I blast on his punk ass" [the cop]. [283] Critical acclaim for his *Juice* role and starring in Academy Award-winner Singleton's next film increased his acting offers.

Rolling Stone magazine gave Tupac and several other rappers paragraphs of space to comment on the King verdict and the riots. Tupac said

> "The difference between 1992 and the Watts riots twenty-seven years ago is AK-47s, crack, unemployment. Those people wanted to see tomorrow—now people really don't care. It was like getting slashed with a knife. The Latisha Harlins decision [in which a Korean grocer got five years probation in the fatal shooting of a fifteen-year-old black girl] came, and we took that. When they gave the grocer probation and then sent a black man to jail for shooting a dog, we took that shit. When we went to the Rodney King trial every day and saw them call us gorillas, we took that. But this verdict was like Marie Antoinette saying, 'Let them eat cake.' America's got to feel what it is to live in the ghetto for three days. We get looted, we get beat down, we get grabbed out of trucks every day. It's hypocritical to be sensitive to white victims but not to us. I feel for the Koreans who lost their businesses and for the people who got hurt, but I feel more for my people." [284]

With Tupac's fame, any new attack on him would require less obvious police actions. Evidence suggests that U.S. Intelligence used sophisticated tactics in a bizarre attack on Tupac at the Marin Fest in August of 1992. Researchers indicated that U.S. Intelligence used an anniversary threat-timing tactic in their assassination of Martin Luther King. Evidence also suggested the use of this tactic in Huey Newton's assassination (Ch.11). Thus, the Marin Fest coordinators' scheduling of the event on August 22, the anniversary of Newton's murder, was the first indication that U.S. Intelligence may have planned a third attempt to murder Tupac at this event.

A documentary video, *Thug Immortal*, provided a detailed account of the Marin Fest and showed other aspects of the event that suggest U.S. Intelligence made a third attempt on Tupac's life there. This video, along with *Tupac: Resurrection*, showed Tupac performing at a previous outdoor concert, singing his radical epithet, "Panther Power," which railed against America's "capitalistic" system, rapping it's "time to change the government now, Panther Power!"[285] In '92, Marin invited Tupac to the festival as an honorary guest.

The producers of *Thug Immortal* also presented an eyewitness, Marku Reynolds, who gave a detailed account of the attack on Tupac at that event. Reynolds said Charles "Man-Man" Fuller and Mutulu Shakur's son, Maurice "Mopreme" Harding, were body-guarding Tupac. Reynolds described how, as an old Marin neighborhood friend of Tupac's, he was joking with Tupac while the entertainer signed autographs, when a threatening group of men came over. He said one of them rushed at Tupac without provocation, but Fuller stopped him. Then another went around them and punched Tupac. Reynolds described and reenacted how Harding used a gun to try and ward them off, firing a warning shot straight up toward the sky. Seconds later, other gunshots sent Harding and Tupac running for their jeep. Reynolds said he never saw a gun in Tupac's hands.[286] One of the gunshots fatally hit a five-year-old boy a block away.[287]

Reynolds further detailed that right after the shots ended, a number of men ran after Tupac and Harding's jeep. Reynolds described how one person, who apparently stopped Tupac from closing his jeep door, punched Tupac many times in front of police. Others tried to turn the jeep over as Harding started driving away. A group of assailants with an estimated 200 others following, attacked Tupac with bottles, bricks and stones. Harding tried to drive his jeep through the crowd as the mob followed the jeep until it pulled in front of a police precinct a few blocks away. There, many kept attacking Tupac and not Harding who had the gun.[288]

Marku Reynolds described how he saw police standing around Tupac's jeep holding shotguns. Despite this armed police presence, the assailants continued attacking Tupac and destroying his jeep in the process. Tupac then crawled under a parked police car. After additional police units pulled up, police started dispersing the crowd. Police proceeded to only arrest Tupac and Maurice Harding. They released Tupac after several hours and didn't charge him with a crime. They originally charged Harding with shooting the boy, until witnesses cleared him and he was released without any charges.[289]

Eyewitness accounts support that the person who punched Tupac did so to set up his murder. Reynolds saw Harding's warning shot to the sky fail to scare off that attacker's group, and he heard more shots that sent Harding and Tupac running. This supports that the group had guns and fired at Tupac (A *Thug Immortal* technician or editor distinctly cut out an important part of Reynolds' account—what happened between Harding's shot and Harding running). Other eyewitnesses also supported that this group of attackers shot at Tupac when the witnesses came to the police after the incident. These witnesses said they saw the shooter of the 5 year-old boy. When police showed them a line-up with Harding, they said he wasn't the one who fired the fatal shot (Harding was recognizable since he lived in Marin City).[290]

Furthermore, police actions suggest their link to an FBI-planned murder attempt. That police at the Marin Fest merely watched people punch Tupac and try to overturn his jeep, without intervening, suggests foreknowledge. Police standing around with shotguns when Harding's jeep reached the precinct also failing to stop the attack also suggests a stand down order. It appeared that police only breached this order when Tupac got out of the jeep and crawled under the police car, risking damage to the vehicle by the mob. While they may have only been waiting for additional police units to arrive, that they only arrested the victims and not any of the assailants—top culprits for the boy's murder—provides more support of certain police authorities' foreknowledge. Then police and prosecutors dropped all charges against Harding and made no charges against anyone else at the scene (Was this to avoid details coming out in a trial? Prosecutors similarly dropped a case involving Tupac in Atlanta faster than expected, Ch.16).[291]

FBI Cointelpro veteran Richard Held's tactics and expertise show his fingerprints on this event and may better explain these bizarre circumstances. As previously detailed, much evidence implicated Held in the murderous attacks on Huey Newton and Judi Bari in that San Fracisco Bay area within the last several years (Ch.12). Bari wrote detailed articles of how Held used similar Cointelpro tactics against the Black Panthers, the American Indian Movement and her group. She cited these tactics as including intimidation, propaganda in the media and fake vigilantes (to create a "lynch-mob mentality"), as well as local police and government complicity.[292]

Upon closer scrutiny, Richard Held appeared to use all these tactics around this Marin Fest event. For example, local government complicity could have come in having Tupac invited as an honorary guest at the event and holding it on the third anniversary of Newton's murder. The FBI previously used a black community cultural fest, the Harlem Festival, in orchestrating an attack on Afeni Shakur's New York Panthers (Ch.4). FBI supervisor Richard Held continued his work against Pratt and Newton in that San Francisco Bay area when Newton joined Pratt's defense team. Tupac had also done benefits for his godfather, Geronimo Pratt, there (Ch.12).[293] This further suggests one use of the "intimidation" factor Judi Bari mentioned as its threat-timing gives a conscious or subconscious warning. Within several years, two other key people in Tupac's life were later murdered on important threat-timed dates (Ch. 26).

Regarding Bari's mention of Richard Held's "propaganda in the media" Cointelpro tactic, other researchers and former coworkers of Held's attested to how he "specialized" in media manipulation.[294] Held appeared to manipulate Marin's local media leading up to the Marin Fest. Reynolds and others reported that some people in Marin were saying that Tupac made many negative remarks about Marin residents to the media.

The *Thug Immortal* filmmakers implied that the people promoting these rumors apparently quoted a local paper's distortion of a national magazine's interview of Tupac. In the magazine interview, Tupac discussed his teen homelessness in Marin City and his mother's drug dealers as, "shitty, dumb niggas who had women, rides, houses, and I ain't have shit. They used to dis me because I was at the bottom." Tupac said he got "love" from people in Marin City, "but it was the kind of love you give a dog or a neighborhood crack fiend." (This self-deprecating statement went along with his previously saying that as a teenager, "I hated myself, I used to keep it a secret.").

The local Marin newspaper "spun" this interview by implying that Tupac denigrated Marin City residents as mostly dogs and crack fiends. Some people further hyped this newspaper's allegations of Tupac putting down Marin, and they threatened Tupac when he visited in the weeks leading up to the Marin Fest.[295] These false rumor tactics are also referred to as "whisper" campaigns in political battles. The allegations provided the Marin Fest assailants a cultivated excuse for attacking Tupac, shielding the FBI from suspected orchestration.

The allegations may have further provided a "fallback" plan, in case the attackers failed to fatally shoot Tupac. Judi Bari had detailed Held's FBI Cointelpro tactic of cultivating a lynchmob mentality. This gained more immediacy when the Marin Fest crowd was led to believe Tupac, not the attackers, was to blame for the child's shooting. Marku Reynolds lent particular credibility to his description and the use of this tactic when he cited his own bizarre behavior. Despite saying that he was a friend of Tupac's, he never saw Tupac holding a gun, and he only saw Harding shoot a warning shot straight up, Reynolds joined the crowd in angrily going after Tupac. The assailants were the top suspects for influencing the crowd to develop this lynch-mob mentality.[296] (The media continued to blame Tupac for the boy's murder despite that eyewitnesses said Harding hadn't even fired the fatal shot, leading to the dropped charges. On U.S. Intelligence and the media, Ch.19).[297]

And finally, exactly a month later, Vice-President Dan Quayle condemned Tupac's lyrics in a well-publicized speech.[298] Tupac had only released one album by that time. That the second-highest ranking Replublican critiqued a new rapper's lyrics suggests that U.S.

Intelligence continually increased both the priority they gave to attacking Tupac and the number of different tactics they used against him.

14-Gang Peace, Monster/Sanyika, & Tupac's "Thug Life" Plan to Radicalize Gangs

> "They'll let you go as far as you want, but as soon as you start asking too many quesitons, boom, the block will come down…I don't think Bush is a bad president because for the upper class, he's a perfect president. And that's how society is built. The upper class runs [society] while…the middle class, we're just lost; we're going through the motions. We're the worker bees and they get to live like royalty."[299]
>
> Interview of Tupac when he was 17, before he decided on his gangsta persona.

U.S. Intelligence had another important reason to murder Tupac Shakur in 1992. The entertainer worked with his stepfather Mutulu Shakur in helping to politicize the Bloods and Crips gangs. In 1991, gang leaders finally took action regarding police execution-style shootings of their fellow gang members after witnesses told Crip leader Dewayne Holmes that police shot his unarmed cousin. Former Black Panthers and others helped the largest Bloods and Crips gang chapters call a peace truce by April of '92. At that truce meeting, a few days before the riots, they vowed to fight racism instead of each other.[300] Black entertainers, politicians and religious leaders such as Harry Belafonte, Jesse Jackson and Louis Farrakhan also successfully helped this gang peace truce spread through a majority of the LA gang chapters and then throughout the U.S.[301]

Tupac and Mutulu aided this peace truce in at least two ways. First, imprisoned Mutulu helped broker the Bloods/Crips peace truce in the federal prison system.[302] Then he developed a new hidden political plan with Tupac. They devised their "Thug Life Movement" as a plan with several goals. It included having Tupac take on a "gangsta" persona for the purpose of appealing to gang members and then politicizing them. Thug Life also tried to get gang members to abide by codes of conduct that decreased black victimization. It further tried to persuade gang members to make legal money through making music. A final goal involved politicizing other rappers. And, while some of Tupac's early lyrics sounded as if they advocated violence for it own sake, they actually called for armed rebellion to oppose racist and economic oppression of "the masses, the lower classes" by the upper class.[303]

Several disadvantages of this plan included the creation of a negative image of Tupac that both hurt his appeal to mainstream society and allowed detractors more reason to criticize him. Tupac's critics, some of whom were amongst the overlapping U.S. Intelligence and media groups (Ch.19), easily used this against him. Still, Tupac's later increased use of terms such as "bitch" and "'ho," albeit regrettable, might be better understood as the regular street slang amongst much of his audience. Various negative forces would also come into his life to increase this lyrical tendency, but black feminists such as Bell Hooks spoke out on Tupac's behalf, and Danyel Smith described Tupac's first three CD's lyrics about women as "uplifting, pro-choice and anti-abuse."[304]

One defense lawyer, Iris Crews, stated having a hard time joining Tupac's case, on one of the rapper's many low-level criminal charges, until she could find out who he really was. She said, "Had he been this foul-mouthed, woman-hating kid, I wouldn't have done it." But instead she recalled how one day in a court recess, she saw Tupac with his extended family of children climbing all over him. Tupac said to her, "If I don't work, these kids don't eat." Crews said he'd been deprived of his own childhood and, "at twenty, he had twenty people to support."[305]

Tupac had a growing fan base to politically influence and his stepfather had a solid black activist base. Writers said Mutulu was "revered" among black nationalists. Mutulu also gained respect amongst Bloods and Crips leaders who had converted to activism. Tupac and Mutulu drew up a specific "Code of THUG LIFE" that consisted of 26 points for gang members. These included not endangering innocent people with their drug dealing and shooting, along with prohibiting ever working with the government. It was used to help increase the number of gang sects taking part in the Bloods/Crips peace truce. In 1992, at a "Truce Picnic" in California, Tupac was reportedly instrumental in getting rival Bloods and Crips gang members to sign the Code of THUG LIFE.[306]

Mutulu and Tupac further inspired former Crip gang leader "Monster" Kody Scott to change his name to Sanyika Shakur as he joined the New Afrikan Movement (Tupac later said he planned an activist collaboration with Sanyika). Sanyika's book, *Monster*, detailed his and other gang members' embrace of black nationalism and revolutionary socialism.[307] After the LA riots, Bloods and Crips including Sanyika Shakur (as Monster Kody Scott) first revealed gang community improvement plans in the *Nation* magazine. This included a written proposal from the Bloods and Crips truce leaders.[308]

Government officials didn't appreciate Sanyika Shakur's politicization. After Sanyika Shakur first made his political conversion in the late '80s, prison officials placed him in solitary confinement for years. They then revoked his bail in the mid-90s after his book's publication.[309]

Gang peace summits and conversions to Panther-inspired radicalism spread eastward. For example, Bloods and Crips called a gang peace truce in Atlanta. In New York, the Latin Kings acquired Panther-linked Young Lords consultants in their reported conversion to political activism. Later in New York, a Bloods leader rallied his group around Panther books and espoused unity with Latinos (Ch.36).[310] Bloods and Crips gang leaders even traveled to England and spoke to a socialist Black group called Panther.[311]

U.S. Intelligence and conservative government forces had many reasons to find the movement of gang members converting to leftist political activism a huge concern. The Bloods and Crips not only encompassed a large majority of the estimated 100,000 gang members in Los Angeles,[312] but reports acknowledged how the two gangs had spread to states across the U.S. from Texas to New York. Studies showed 1,100 individual Bloods and Crips gangs active in 115 cities nationally.[313] By 1995, the Bloods and Crips were even reportedly active in all four branches of the armed services and at more than 50 military bases around the U.S.[314]

U.S intelligence reacted to these gang activist conversions in several ways. The LAPD framed gang peace leaders and they mass-arrested gang unity meeting participants. U.S. Intelligence further used the LA riots as an opportunity to wage full-scale war on the gangs declaring peace and becoming "radicalized" by former Panthers. The CIA director worked with the FBI director, who sent many extra agents to work with police. They did this through their anti-gang Operation Hammer as well as a post-riot program launched by President Bush called Weed and Seed.[315]

Also, by a Presidential Executive Order, federal authorities formed Joint Task Force—Los Angeles (JTF-LA). This task forced echoed the Joint Terrorist Task Force used in New York against Tupac's stepfather Mutulu Shakur. The JTF-LA used U.S. Army and Marine forces, as well as aid from the national guard, the FBI and the Bureau of Alcohol, Tobacco and Firearms, in working with Los Angeles police. The California National Guard commander, Major General James Delk, now retired, said that gang members' opposition led his group's role to be "more akin to low intensity conflict (or urban warfare) than riot control."[316]

Prison officials collaborated with U.S. Intelligence objectives in the federal prison system. They put Mutulu Shakur in the country's most restrictive confines, apparently due to gang work with young blacks and his work with Tupac. Out of concern over his "outside contacts and influence over the younger black element," prison officials transferred Mutulu to the most maximum-security underground prison in Colorado.[317] U.S. Intelligence later used such prison placement and anti-gang forces against Tupac.

15-Tupac's FBI File, Republican Attacks, Harassment Arrests & Specious Lawsuits

"I never had a record until I made a record." Tupac Shakur, 1994 quote.

U.S. Intelligence and their Republican (GOP) political supporters increased their focus on Tupac Shakur. The Los Angeles FBI office continued accumulating documents that eventually came to over 4,000 pages in their file on Tupac, according to a Freedom Of Information Act (FOIA) Justice Department worker. They guarded this file closely as a FOIA request only released 99 partially deleted pages.[318]

But any documentation of operations against Tupac Shakur remained unavailable because of legal changes President Ronald Reagan made in the '80s. Reagan and Bush began keeping documentation of U.S. Intelligence operations under wraps and outside of FOIA requests' reach through President Reagan's Executive Order 123333. The order "'privatized' NSC [National Security Council] intelligence operations and permitted agencies other than the CIA to carry out 'special operations' without reporting its activities…[allowing] any private enterprise the NSC set up, to carry out covert operations."[319]

U.S. Intelligence began using new strategies against Tupac and enlisted the White House for help. While Tupac had only one CD, George Bush, Sr.'s Vice-President Dan Quayle focused on him and one other amongst the many so-called "gangsta" rappers. As previously mentioned, on September 22, exactly one month after the Marin Fest attack (see timing tactic discussion in Chs. 12, 13, 26), Quayle made a widely publicized speech, saying that Tupac's CD "has no place in our society." *Billboard* also noted how in that speech Quayle used the same words that he used in a speech against rapper Ice-T three months earlier.[320]

This repeated statement supports that Intelligence planned the speeches to help bring the ensuing censorship of Ice-T and Tupac. Ice-T had joined Tupac in railing against the government in *Rolling Stone*'s post-riot issue, except Ice-T more directly called for taking the riot to the White House. Like Tupac, Ice-T also proposed a violent response to the Rodney King police brutality incident, in his song "Cop Killer."[321]

The case of Ice-T appeared to show Time Warner's true intent in supporting U.S. Intelligence's repressive agenda (Ch.20). Ice-T had sung the song "Cop Killer" with his band, Body Count, at every stop of the sold-out '91 Lollapalooza Tour. No police complaints ensued. He then released the song on his band's CD, which hovered between #32 and #45 on the Billboard charts for weeks. The LA riots ended in early

May of '92, and two Texas police groups held a press conference in June protesting the CD. After many congressmen joined the protest over the next 45 days, Ice-T announced his removal of the song from the album. Despite largely increased sales from the publicity, Time Warner dropped Ice-T within six months.[322]

Tupac likely brought on Quayle's denunciation for several reasons. Some included Tupac's attacks of George Bush in his debut CD's lyrics. Tupac was also about to release his second CD with more attacks on Bush and Quayle just before the presidential election. These critiques mentioned Republican leaders by name while also saying "they've got money for war but can't feed the poor." Between Tupac's debut CD on Interscope Records and the release of his second CD, Time Warner increased its ownership of Interscope's music label from 25% to 50%.[323] Time Warner then delayed Tupac's second CD's release for a year, well after the election.[324]

Other Republican politicians also singled out Tupac in their speeches. Republican presidential candidate Bob Dole and former Bush cabinet member William Bennett said Time Warner needed to ban Tupac's recordings. A former Pennsylvania state office holder who headed a private group she called the National Congress of Black Women, C. Delores Tucker, joined Bennett in a suspicious campaign against Tupac (see below).[325]

Politicians were brought into the tactical strategy more officially in 1993. Sundance Award-winner Nick Broomfield, who produced the documentary *Biggie and Tupac*, said that a bipartisan Senate subcommittee formed out of concern over rap's subversive elements in '93. He also said that the FBI began spying on rappers that year (though they clearly started in 1988 or earlier).[326]

The U.S. Intelligence document outlining the tactics for use against political musicians included orders to "send articles to the newspapers" smearing them, using "narcotics and free sex to entrap" them, arrest them "on marijuana charges" and "provoke target groups into rivalries" (Ch.13).[327] New police intelligence units formed to target rappers. New York had a rap intelligence unit trained in the FBI's Counter Intelligence Program tactics that started at least as early as 1995. That unit subsequently trained police in Los Angeles and Atlanta (Ch.30).[328]

After Quayle's public denouncements of Tupac, police appeared to use the FBI's harassment arrest strategy against him.[329] In line with Tupac's popular quote, "I never had a record until I made a record," the power that increasing fame brought the radical rap star also brought on more police attacks. In Los Angeles, where the FBI accumulated their file on Tupac, police arrested the rap and film star about a half dozen times on crimes such as public drunkenness, gun possession (common among celebrities to arm themselves against stalkers) and marijuana possession. Except for a fight with the Hughes brothers directorial team in '94, most of the charges were dismissed.[330]

These harassment arrests and public denouncements further appeared to have the purpose of leading people to believe Tupac invited strangers' armed attacks, because of his purported "criminal" behavior. Like the armed attacks after his MTV debut and his movie debut premiere, another conflict occurred in 1993 while Tupac was in L.A.. In March, Tupac was filming his first "live" network television musical performance on the set of *In Living Color*. In between takes he took a break with a friend and went to their limousine parked just outside. Tupac reported that the limousine driver started screaming at his friend as if to instigate a fight. He said the driver then attempted to use a gun on them. Police confirmed finding a gun at the scene that didn't belong to Tupac or his friend, supporting Tupac's account and making it the fourth attack by an assailant with a gun.[331] Police detained Tupac and interrupted his television performance.

In Atlanta, police similarly took Tupac away from a national rap convention just before his featured speeches, two years in a row. Police arrested Tupac for marijuana possession, then public drunkenness, and next for allegedly slapping a female fan who wanted his autograph. Two of these arrests occurred one year apart during Atlanta's "Jack the Rapper" national rap convention which scheduled Tupac to speak in '92 and '93. Tupac lost much time and money before judges dismissed the charges.[332]

The FBI appeared to have another strategy. They apparently used the Republican denunciations and harassment arrests for a second reason—to get Tupac's shows canceled. In interviews, Tupac said many venues canceled his concerts due to police citing their risk of turning riotous. The FBI had previously used this tactic on other musicians. The FBI first tried to use this tactic against the top-selling rap group N.W.A. in 1988. After the FBI sent N.W.A. a warning letter about their "Fuck the Police" song, the FBI then sent faxes to the police department in every city that N.W.A. toured. They told police to find an excuse to cancel each show (though few were at that time). After success against Tupac, they tried to use it against the rap tour of top political musical group Rage Against the Machine when they toured with rap group Wu Tang Clan. Rage lead singer Zach De La Rocha said that police called concert venues and said they wouldn't provide security because the show posed too much risk of a riot occurring.[333]

By the mid-to-late '70s, researchers found that U.S. Intelligence started a new version of the harassment arrest strategy in the form of a harassment lawsuit strategy. As early as the '70s, Cointelpro researchers found that the "U.S. Justice Department brought many activists to trial, often on unprosecutable conspiracy charges in order to deplete the funds and energy of the left." [334] A vast number of civil suits began against Tupac and continued against other wealthy, leftist-linked black entertainers (Chs. 30-34). Over a dozen people risked sanction and penalization for "frivolous" lawsuits when they filed seemingly specious civil suits against Tupac starting in 1992. Did U.S. Intelligence advise certain plaintiffs to take the risk of financial penalties? The bizarre nature of several lawsuits, along with links to U.S. Intelligence and top conservative figures, suggests such a new intelligence tactic. For example, C. Delores Tucker, who had joined in television advertisements against rappers with President Bush's drug czar, William Bennett, filed a civil lawsuit claiming Tupac's lyrics hurt her sex life.[335]

Most of the other lawsuits appeared just as specious and had similar high level conservative links. Vice-President Dan Quayle's public denunciation of Tupac came in support of a multi-million dollar lawsuit a Texas police officer's widow filed against Tupac. Quayle claimed that "*2Pacalypse Now* bore some responsibility for the fatal shooting of [this] Texas state trooper." [336] Also, the Atlanta autograph-seeker, as previously mentioned, filed suit alleging that Tupac slapped her. Witnesses said that the woman hounded Tupac as he was rushing to an appointment, a female associate of Tupac's intervened, and the autograph-seeker started a fight with her. They said that Tupac merely got in between the two to stop the fight. A judge dismissed the case.[337]

Furthermore, a woman claimed she was shot and paralyzed at a Tupac concert because Tupac created a "riotous atmosphere" at the show.[338] And finally, the limo driver who Tupac said tried to use a gun on him during his first live network television musical performance joined the others in suing the rapper.[339] The driver did this despite that the police report backed Tupac's claim that he tried to use the gun on Tupac. This scenario of an apparent attempt on Tupac's life leading to a lawsuit would repeat itself in Atlanta that year.

U.S. Intelligence attacks continued in direct proportion with Tupac's ever-increasing wealth and influence. His trials and tribulations kept him on edge. *The Source* magazine reported one particular incident that may have particularly concerned the intelligence community. It occurred when Tupac exploded in anger and alluded to a latter-day Black Liberation Army. The incident also displayed the devotion members of the Nation of Islam security team had for Tupac.

This incident came about when Tupac awaited trial for the sole charge he agreed he was guilty of—a fistfight on a film set with young black directors Albert and Allen Hughes. *Source* magazine reporter Dream Hampton followed Tupac at the time. On the day of the trial in a Los Angeles courthouse, Tupac stood outside the courtroom with Hampton and others. He saw the Hughes brothers surrounded by the Nation of Islam's security-for-hire Fruit of Islam (FOI). Tupac walked up to one of the bow-tied FOI and asked why they were protecting the Hughes Brothers from him. Accusations between the brothers and Tupac ensued, when an FOI guard pushed Tupac and he charged the group. Tupac backed the brothers and their four guards against the wall.

"You gon' need mothafuckin' Farrakhan to calm me down! You got that? Farrakhan! You beanpie-slinging, bowtie-wearing bitches! You wear bowties! Remember that! I'll have niggas from Crenshaw wit AK's and rags up here! Nigga you don't even know who you fucking with—these roots run deep!" Tupac's threats apparently alluded to the modest 'rags' attire of his former New Afrikan Panther group in the Crenshaw neighborhood of Los Angeles who lived as revolutionaries and likely backed it up with AK-47 military rifles if ever needed for self-defense. Later in the courtroom, two of the FOI guards assured Tupac they were fans of his despite that the Hughes brothers hired them. The judge in the case sentenced Tupac to 15 days in jail.[340]

16-Atlanta Police Shoot at Tupac & Target H. Rap Brown; FBI's Grisly Cover-ups

"How long will it last 'til the poor get more cash
Until then, raise up!
Tell my young black males, blaze up!...
Pump ya fists like this
Holla if ya hear me—PUMP PUMP if your pissed!
To the sell-outs living it up
One way or another you'll be giving it up, huh
I guess 'cause I'm black born
I'm supposed to say peace, sing songs, and get capped on
But it's time for a new plan, BAM!
I'll be swingin' like a one man, clan."

Tupac Shakur, "Holler If Ya Hear Me," *Strictly 4 My N.I.G.G. A.Z*, 1993.

One of the most straightforward police attempts to murder Tupac Shakur occurred in 1993. Tupac had recently moved to Atlanta, buying a house for his mother and sister. He partly did this to be near his business manager, Watani Tyehimba, who also helped lead the New Afrikan People's Organization (NAPO) from there.[341] Witnesses support that "off-duty" cops shot at Tupac after the unarmed rapper finished a Halloween night concert at an Atlanta college.

The incident started as Tupac drove back from his performance. Tupac's car, followed by an entourage of 3-6 cars, stopped at a traffic light near a hotel driveway. A black driver with no connection to Tupac said he pulled into that driveway to turn around when two white cops on foot in civilian clothes, with two women, screamed racial slurs at the black driver. One of the cops also punched him.[342]

White and black bystanders at the scene, among others, said that Tupac rolled down his window and asked what was going on. When one of the white men took out a gun, Tupac rolled his window back up. A white couple also stopped at the traffic light in their car, said they saw a group of whites run over to Tupac's car, looking like "a white gang attacking a black man." One of the men broke Tupac's passenger window with the butt of his gun and shot at him.[343]

Tupac rolled out of his car in time to avoid getting shot. The off-duty cop firing his gun brought Tupac's security guards out of their cars. Tupac grabbed one of their guns and fired three shots back. The people exiting the entourage of several cars sent the white group running with the gunman reportedly running partially backwards still aiming behind him at Tupac. Tupac's shots hit the two men in the leg, butt and back. Police arrested Tupac for attempted homicide.[344]

The white officers said one of the women was one of the officer's wives and the black motorist nearly hit her, but the woman would never speak to this. Those officers also made conflicting reports. They first wrote a police report that described Tupac's group responding to the incident as "niggers came by and did a drive-by shooting." They then changed that to Tupac's group getting out of their cars, surrounding and threatening them, then shooting at them.[345]

Many aspects of the incident and post-shooting events contradict the police account and support that police planned this attempt to kill Tupac. During the entire conflict, the officers never identified themselves as police.[346] The officers also discredited themselves by lying in saying they didn't have a gun on them that night. Furthermore, immediately after the incident, Atlanta police went directly to Tupac's hotel room to arrest him, despite that Tupac had registered himself in six rooms under aliases. Such an action supports that he was under close police surveillance.[347]

Most importantly, prosecution dropped their charges against Tupac when the biggest revelations came to light in court. The state prosecutor's own witness said that the gun one of the cops used on Tupac had been taken from the other cop's police evidence locker.[348] In another trial, a police supervisor explained that officers use such "throwaway guns" for the ease of hiding them after killing someone.[349]

These factors and others support that this was a botched police operation to kill Tupac (the fifth gun-wielding assault). These police officers failed to identify themselves, as if to hide the fact. It's common knowledge that shooting a cop can lead to a death sentence and lawyers say that cops would announce "police" to protect themselves on- or off-duty.[350] Also, police had previously used "off-duty" cops in attacks on Black Panthers.[351]

Attacks on former Student Nonviolent Coordinating Committee leader H. Rap Brown in Atlanta in this '90s time period further supports that these Atlanta police were carrying out a U.S. Intelligence operation against Tupac Shakur. The FBI continued using its Counterintelligence Program tactics against H.Rap Brown from the '60s to the '90s. U.S. Intelligence made Brown a huge Cointelpro target while he led SNCC with Stokely Charmichael in the late '60s, and the Black Panthers made Brown an honorary Panther leader.[352]

In 1967, U.S. Congress used an incident to aid the FBI targeting of H. Rap Brown. An hour after Brown spoke at a summer rally in Maryland, two black auxiliary police officers shot at the SNCC leader, grazing his head. Blacks reacted by rioting. When later asked about the truth of rumors that organizers snuck him out of town in a coffin, Brown replied, "I've never said. The government probably would have liked me to leave in a coffin." U.S. Congress then passed the Rap Brown Amendment, making it illegal to go across state lines and give a speech that "provokes" a riot.[353]

When prosecutors brought Brown to trial in 1970, the FBI appeared to target two of his SNCC successors, Ralph Featherstone and Che Payne. A fatal bomb detonated in their car as they headed for the courthouse to support Brown. The FBI was similarly implicated for using this tactic in planting the car bomb that paralyzed Judi Bari in 1990 (Ch.12).[354]

After five years imprisonment in the '70s, Brown moved to Atlanta, Georgia. In Atlanta, H. Rap Brown changed his name to Jamil Al-Amin and became the city's imam (spiritual leader) of the second largest community of traditional Muslims in the United States.[355] Imam Jamil Al-Amin rose to national prominence as an Islamic leader. He chaired Atlanta's Council of Imams, a member of the National Community that has 30-40 affiliate mosques across the country with 20,000-30,000 followers and, unlike the Nation Of Islam, was the sect that most Muslims in the world follow. Muslim leaders credited Al-Amin for helping increase membership at many of their mosques.[356] Al-Amin's work included successfully clearing drugs out of neighborhoods, according to the daily *Atlanta Journal-Constitution*.[357]

In 1993, when Atlanta police attacked Tupac, they were also targeting Imam Jamil Al-Amin in several ways. From '92-'95, Atlanta police intelligence worked with the FBI in infiltrating Al-Amin's mosque, allegedly to investigate a possible homicide. Several years and tens of thousands of documents failed to produce any charges.[358] In 1995, a man was shot in a park near Al-Amin. Police first claimed Al-Amin shot him, but ended up dropping the charge when the man claimed police forced him to say that Al-Amin shot him.[359]

Then, in 1999, U.S. Intelligence appeared to wage their largest attack on Imam Jamil Al-Amin. Police claimed that Al-Amin fatally shot a police officer.[360] Jamil Al-Amin's problems with the law that year started when he was driving a friend's car and a police officer pulled him over. Al-Amin had a police badge a local mayor had given him as an honorary auxiliary officer for helping to get drug dealers out of a neighborhood. The officer that pulled Al-Amin over charged him with theft and impersonating a cop.[361]

Police then said that Jamil Al-Amin missed his court date for that charge. Al-Amin said he never received the notice in the mail. Atlanta police sent two black cops out to arrest Al-Amin with a note that the Iman was armed and dangerous. One of these cops said Al-Amin fatally shot his fellow officer.[362] Much evidence supports that this was not Al-Amin and that these officers were sent after, or must have come upon, a different person. The officer said he shot and wounded Al-Amin. Police investigators also said Al-Amin left a trail of blood from where he was shot. Upon arrest several days later, Al-Amin didn't have a mark on his body, but he still ended up on death row for allegedly killing a police officer. Former Tupac manager Watani

Tyehimba and Tupac's New York lawyer Michael Tarif Warren have worked to help Jamil Al-Amin's defense appeals.[363]

Media organizations claimed that the FBI couldn't have continued their Cointelpro targeting of H. Rap Brown (Al-Amin) in Atlanta because blacks had gained leadership positions in that city. Events both before and after Jamil Al-Amin's Atlanta conviction undermine this claim. For example, a strip club owner tried to pay an FBI informant $20,000 to rough up Atlanta's Black mayor, Bill Campbell, yet the FBI failed to inform the mayor. Mayor Campbell called the FBI "the forces of evil," in 2001, recalling their surveillance of Rev. Martin Luther King Jr.[364] After leaving office in 2002, federal authorities leveled a seven-count indictment against Campbell, alleging bribes, illegal campaign contributions, and filing false income tax returns.[365] After a seven-year FBI and IRS investigation of Campbell, a jury found him not guilty on all charges except three counts of tax evasion. Nonetheless, the trial judge sentenced Campbell to 2 ½ years in prison and to pay $63,000, on $160,000 of unreported income and a fine.[366]

Also, at least one racist police intelligence operation further undermined the argument that blacks in higher office could stop U.S. Intelligence operations. A white police whistleblower in charge of investigating the murders of 29 black children in Atlanta from 1979-1981 presented a large amount of evidence that the Ku Klux Klan carried out those murders. He presented evidence detailing how the FBI and state intelligence agents in the Georgia Bureau of Investigation maintained a cover-up for the KKK. This whistleblower further noted how intelligence agents collaborated with the KKK in dealing arms and drugs, supposedly to set the group up for arrest. Yet police, the GBI nor the FBI filed any charges against the white supremacist group.[367]

The FBI and Atlanta police ended up saying that they arrested the man responsible for these child murders. Prosecutors gained a conviction of Wayne Williams, a black man, for the murder of two adults in the '80s. Atlanta prosecutors claimed during the trial that they had evidence supporting that Williams had also murdered the 29 black children, though Williams was never officially charged with those murders. An FBI agent even contradicted the evidence convicting Williams of the adult murders, saying that his fellow agents fabricated their claim of hearing Williams throw his victims' bodies over a bridge, the major evidence against Williams.[368]

A member of the original police task force that investigated the child murders, Louis Graham, was named Dekalb County police chief at the end of 2004. At a press conference, the police chief became openly tearful in announcing that he was reopening the case in 2005, saying "I don't think Wayne Williams is responsible for anything…I made my mind up 20 years ago and I feel that way today." Chief Graham believed his fellow investigators suppressed evidence that the

KKK committed the murders.[369] These incidents show how despite blacks attaining increasingly higher offices in Atlanta politics and in the police department starting in the '80s, the racist white power structure continued to work with U.S. Intelligence behind their backs.

17-Psychological Profiling of Tupac? Police Profiling Attempt to Murder Mumia

> "It is that all-American corporationism that transforms rap's grittiness into a gutter of materialism: a woman, a living being, reminds a man of a thing—a car. That to me is more perverse than the much-criticized 'bitches and 'hos' comments...Tupac Shakur's 'Dear Mamma' and 'Keep Your Head Up' are shining examples of artistic expressions of loving oneness with one's family and people. Creative, moving, loving, funky, angry and real are that young man's work, as is a fair amount of the genre. Like any art form in America, it is also a business with the influences of the market place impacting upon its production. The more conscious its artists, the more conscious the art. Keep ya' head up."
> Mumia Abu-Jamal, Prison Radio.[370]

> "We must fight for brother Mumia, we must fight for brother Mutulu...we must fight for brother Geronimo Pratt, we must fight for the countless political prisoners."
> On Tupac Shakur, "White Manz World," *Don Killuminati, the 7 day theory*, 1996.

Regarding the Atlanta officers' assault on Tupac, Tupac's lawyer Chokwe Lumumba supports that Atlanta police intelligence may have used psychological profiling on Tupac to attempt his murder. Lumumba said police started using psychological profiling on political activists at the same time they started using it on common criminals in the early '70s. Lumumba believed that police may have attacked the black motorist to lure Tupac into a shooting.[371]

The previously mentioned information that U.S. Intelligence waged psychological warfare on Huey Newton suggests that they first used profiling on the Panther cofounder in the '70s.[372] Newton wrote about the use of this profiling tactic in an incident where police shot up the door of his next-door neighbor in 1973. Newton believed it was an attempt to lure him into defending the neighbor and getting shot himself. He later found out that the FBI rented that neighbor's apartment.[373]

Evidence also supports the use of such psychological profiling to attempt the murder of Philadelphia Black Panther cofounder Mumia Abu-Jamal (born Wesley Cook). Mumia had become a prestigious journalist by 1981. Evidence of the early U.S. Intelligence targeting of Mumia included the FBI labeling him a top threat in 1973, an FBI picture of Mumia with the word "dead" written on the back, and Mayor Frank Rizzo publicly threatening him in 1978. Rizzo worked as police commissioner before and after his stint as mayor. By that time, Mumia highlighted activists on his National Public Radio shows and exposed police brutality against predominantly black organizations such as MOVE. [374] He also won a Peabody Award for outstanding journalism and was elected chair of the Philadelphia Association of Black Journalists.

In 1981, evidence and witnesses support that U.S. Intelligence used psychological profiling to attempt Mumia Abu-Jamal's murder in a bizarre, uncertain sequence of events. At this time Mumia was moonlighting as a cab driver while working as a journalist. After he was robbed twice in his cab, Mumia carried a gun in the car. Virtually everyone with knowledge of a late night December shooting incident agree to the following facts. While working in downtown Philadelphia, Mumia heard gun shots and then saw his brother, William Cook, staggering. Mumia got out of his cab and went towards him. A police officer fired his gun at Mumia, leaving him slumped on the street, and other gunshots had fatally wounded Officer Daniel Faulkner.[375]

Mumia Abu-Jamal's trial came quickly, despite his need for time to both recuperate and work on his defense. The trial judge, Albert Sabo, created many problems for Mumia. For example, he wouldn't allow Mumia to represent himself and the judge unconstitutionally removed Mumia from the courtroom for a length of the trial. Mumia's court-assigned public defender was only given $800 for all the expert witnesses combined, and testified that he hadn't been able to interview any witnesses in advance. When an 85% white jury convicted Mumia, the judge, Albert Sabo, sentenced him to death. Sabo led the nation in death sentences and incidentally revealed his plans for Mumia in the judicial chambers.[376] A court clerk signed an affidavit stating that just before the trial he overheard Judge Sabo discuss how he planned to help prosecution in the case, saying, "I'm going to help them fry the nigger."[377]

After years of appeals amidst what grew into a massive international movement to stop Mumia's execution, physical evidence that wasn't revealed until after the trial cleared Mumia while impugning the police. Police didn't test Mumia's gun after the incident to see if it had been used, nor did they test Mumia's hand for nitrate residue that would have been there if he fired it, according to an expert.[378] Police also tried to hide the medical examiner's report on the fatal bullet having been a .44 caliber that Mumia's .38 caliber gun couldn't have fired.[379] The pages of Mumia's FBI file they allowed to be released also incriminated their involvement in an operation against Mumia. The last page showed that the FBI monitored his prison visitors as late as 1991.[380] The file also exposed two attempts to frame him while he was in the Panthers—once for robbery and another time for murder.[381]

In those following years, many witnesses gave testimony that also both exonerated Mumia and supported that the incident was part of a huge operation. Police claimed they had two witnesses who said they saw Mumia shoot the officer and another two who said they heard him confess in the hospital. Police gained this testimony by threatening to end these witnesses' livelihood. For example, cabdriver Robert Chobert was on probation for a felony arson conviction and had two other convictions for driving while intoxicated which could have cost him his taxi license, making him very susceptible to police pressure.[382]

Another key prosecution witness, prostitute Veronica Jones, testified about police similarly threatening her to previously make false statements. At a '95 hearing, she made statements clearing Mumia and said that police told her they had given another prostitute, Cynthia White, favors for providing false testimony. White had 38 previous arrests and was wanted on three open cases.[383]

Also, police alleged that Mumia confessed to the murders, yet their witnesses—Faulkner's partner Gary Bell and hospital security guard Priscilla Durham—said Mumia made the confession when he first arrived at the hospital. Police only claimed this after Mumia filed a charge of police brutality, two months after the shooting. Bell told ABC's *20/20* (in 1999) that he didn't mention the confession for two months because it shocked him so much that he suppressed it. Durham first lied in saying she never knew Faulkner and then claimed Mumia screamed the confession at a time when many police officers were in Mumia's hospital room, none of whom heard it. The police officer assigned to follow Mumia to the hospital and sit with him in his room, Gary Wakshul, wrote in his report that Mumia made no comments there. Two attending doctors reported not hearing any confession and finding that Mumia was barely conscious at the reported time of the alleged confession.[384]

Years after the shooting, a startling affidavit came from Arnold Beverly, a career hit man serving time in jail. Beverly said that the Mafia paid him to shoot Faulkner and that another paid gunman also shot the cop. He said the Mafia told him that they did so on behalf of other police who were receiving Mafia payoffs and that Faulkner threatened these transactions. Beverly said other cops were at the scene to back him up and provided help with his getaway.[385] Mumia's release campaign chair Pam Africa said Beverly passed two lie detector tests with this affidavit.[386]

More affidavits and witnesses support that Mumia didn't shoot Officer Faulkner, but they also support that Faulkner had a malevolent assignment before his own shooting. An affidavit of Mumia's brother, Billy Cook, described the scene that night, saying his childhood friend Kenneth "Poppi" Freeman was with him and led him towards the area where the shooting would take place. Despite that Cook worked the same late hours as his brother, Cook said he had never crossed paths with Mumia at that time of night. Freeman led him to the area, reportedly to get some beer. Officer Faulkner tailed Cook on that street and pulled him over.

Cook said that he wasn't sure where his license and registration were and Freeman gave him something to show Faulkner. Faulkner then had him get out of the car and words were exchanged. Faulkner suddenly beat him over the head with a stick or flashlight until he was bleeding. Cook said he then went back into his car to find his registration in the back seat, with Freeman still sitting in the passenger seat. Cook said that while searching for his registration he heard shots fired and saw flashes of a gun out of the corner of his eye about where Faulkner had been standing. He looked up and Freeman was gone, with his passenger door open. Cook then got out of his car. He was still bleeding and disoriented.[387]

In his own affidavit, Mumia Abu-Jamal said that he often chose that exact area to station his cab because it was a popular club spot at 13th Street and Locust, with a lot of people on foot. He was filling out his log/trip sheet when he heard some shouting. He glanced into his rear view mirror and saw a flashing dome light of a police cruiser, which he said wasn't unusual. He continued to fill out his log sheet when he heard what sounded like gun shots. He looked again into his rear view mirror and saw people running up and down Locust. He scanned the area and recognized his brother standing in the street staggering and dizzy. He ran out of his cab towards him when he saw a uniformed cop turn toward him gun in hand, saw a flash and went down on his knees.[388]

Billy Cook said that when he first saw his brother, he was running. He was feet away from him. Cook added, "We hadn't made any plans to meet that night." Cook further said that Mumia had nothing in his hands when, "I heard a shot and saw him stumble."

Cook also said Freeman was armed that night with a .38 caliber gun. Apparently after Mumia's conviction, Freeman told Cook "about a plan to kill Faulkner" and that he "participated in the shooting," of Officer Faulkner. Cook said Freeman told him he "was connected and knew all kinds of people" after being in the army.[389] It's possible that police intelligence involved Freeman in a plan to kill Faulkner without telling him that the plan included the shooting of Mumia.

Other witnesses backed Billy Cook's account. Added up, these accounts suggest that police intelligence set the scene up this way as part of a psychological profiling operation to lure Mumia out of his car to be shot. The operation appeared to include the murder of Officer Faulkner, which police could then blame on Mumia. A police captain witness for the prosecution said that a driver's license with the name Arnold Howard was found on Faulkner at the scene and some detectives did pursue reports that Faulkner's shooter fled the scene.

Arnold Howard testified that he had given his license to Ken Freeman.[390]

Further cover-up ensued. Three years later, Philadelphia police tried to serve an illegal warrant on the activist organization that Mumia supported, MOVE, at their city rowhouse. The warrant was later found to be invalid. Police infamously dropped a C-4 military explosive from a helicopter on the roof of the house. The FBI and Bureau of Alcohol, Tobacco and Firearms, agencies that joined forces against rappers and Panthers, gave Philly police this explosive for use against MOVE. The explosion caused raging flames and police wouldn't let firefighters put hoses on the fire for several hours. Eleven men, women, and children of MOVE (and their pets) burned to death. The ensuing fire also burned down two whole city blocks. Only two survived and police jailed one of them.[391] *The Village Voice* said that the following day, Freeman was "discovered dead in Philadelphia under mysterious circumstances."[392]

In a 1995 appeals hearing summary, both prosecution and defense witnesses backed Cook's statement. These witnesses said that Officer Daniel Faulkner beat Billy Cook in front of Mumia, after ordering a paddy wagon to the scene.[393] Credible witness William Singletary also supported Cook's statement and Mumia's innocence. Singletary, a black businessman and decorated Vietnam veteran with friends in the Philadelphia Police Department, said he told police what he saw at the shooting scene but detectives tore up the transcript of his first statement and threatened him into signing a false statement. Singletary gave a description of Ken Freeman getting out of a Volkswagon, shooting at Faulkner and fleeing. Singletary also said that he saw Mumia approach the scene without a gun and that he saw Officer Faulkner shoot Mumia (It's uncertain if this was Faulkner or a different cop).

Singletary further said he saw other police arrive and beat Mumia, who was slumped wounded on the ground. Singletary also added to the discrediting of top prosecution witness Cynthia White. He said that she came up to him after the shooting and asked him what had happened. White witness Deborah Korvansky and black witness Dessie Hightower corroborated Singletary's account of seeing the man who fit Freeman's description fleeing the scene.[394]

Mumia Abu-Jamal's case remains on appeal due to the global public protest that has united entertainers, writers and politicians worldwide in support of Mumia (see endnote).[395] The international coverage also brought more witnesses and evidence to light. By the end of the '90s, Mumia had problems with one of his lead lawyers and changed his counsel, suggesting similar FBI tactics used to sabotage Geronimo Pratt's legal defense in the '70s.[396] Mumia Abu-Jamal still sits on death row amidst appeals. Despite his desensitizing confines, he continues his prolific writing that includes several books and countless articles. He can also be heard giving his regular political commentaries from prison on the Pacifica radio network in New York, Washington DC, LA, San Francisco and Houston.

18-NYPD Agent: Sex Frame-up, Cover-up and Link to Tupac's NYC Shooting

> "Listen while I take you back and lace this rap
> A real live tale about a snitch named Haitian Jack
> Knew he was working for the feds, same crime, different trials…
> Set me up, wet me up, niggas stuck me up
> Heard the guns bust but you tricks never shut me up."
> Tupac Shakur, "Against All Odds," *Don Killuminati, the 7 day theory,* 1996.

Two weeks after the 1993 Halloween night Atlanta attack, a new "friend" of Tupac's, Jacques Agnant (a.k.a. Nigel, name Ricardo Brown used in court, "Haitian Jack"), helped set up Tupac's most serious legal charge in New York. Agnant, a purported music promoter who originally came from Haiti, often traveled with his associate, "Trevor" (real name Rick Alinzey). They escorted Tupac to a Greenwich Village dance club in mid-November. That weeknight in the club started out great for Tupac as several professional athletes approached him to say they were fans. Then Agnant and Trevor introduced Tupac to a 19 year-old black Naval Yard employee named Ayanna Jackson. Jackson said that she was with a man she'd been dating for 2-3 months. Within minutes, she danced with Tupac, put her mouth on his penis on the dance floor, then left her date to have sex with Tupac at his hotel.[397]

In the several days following the dance club and late night tryst, Ayanna Jackson left messages on Tupac's hotel answering service about wanting repeat sex. When she came over again, Agnant, Trevor and Tupac's road manager, Charles "Man-Man" Fuller, entered her and Tupac's room. She made several forced sodomy charges against Tupac, Agnant, and Fuller, though she later said Fuller only watched. Police also charged Tupac with illegal gun possession. Trevor eluded arrest.[398] One of the first of many questions about Jackson's honesty regarding the incident came when a female doctor examined Jackson at a hospital after the charges and said that there was no evidence of forced sexual activity, as Tupac claimed.[399]

Tupac had become accustomed to police arrests and media groups' seemingly biased criminal portrayal of him by this time. He came to use some of this media as sound bites in his songs and video. One of his music videos had the actual footage of police arresting him outside the hotel. The cops weren't in uniform, one of the first clues that they were part of New York's infamous Street Crime Unit. They walked Tupac into a police van as television news cameras filmed the scene. Just before sitting down, Tupac leaned back out of the van, looked into a TV camera, and facetiously proclaimed, "Guilty."[400]

Tupac's New York trial attorney for this case, Michael Tarif Warren, had personal experience as the target of New York police intelligence while also gaining notoriety for his activism and success. Warren, a former SNCC organizer, knew much about police intelligence work, as the New York Police Department's Black Desk unit had illegally spied on his Black Liberation Movement work in the '80s.[401] He also represented Mumia Abu-Jamal as his European spokesman in the '90s. Warren later represented a majority of the Central Park jogger rape defendants and had their convictions overturned in 2002, by gaining evidence that supported the real attacker's confession.[402]

Michael Tarif Warren claimed that Haitian music promoter Jacques Agnant worked for police intelligence to orchestrate Tupac's arrest. Warren's suspicions of Agnant's police intelligence links started when the attorney went to put up Tupac's bail. Warren saw a Policemen's Benevolent Association (PBA—a national police group) representative bail out Agnant.[403] Agnant then had a longtime PBA lawyer represent him.[404] Warren later got Agnant's rap sheet that showed Agnant's long list of arrests up and down the East Coast on major charges, all dismissed. "This was a sure sign Agnant was a police agent," said Warren.[405]

Such accumulating evidence supported that U.S. Intelligence set up the incident with Tupac and Ayanna Jackson. The aforementioned Intelligence memorandum regarding political musicians specifically addresed this tactic. It instructed agents to "Send in women and… [use] free sex to entrap" (Ch.13).[406]

Another sign of U.S. Intelligence involvement came when police and the prosecuting district attorney proceeded to use all means possible, legal or not, to keep Tupac Shakur in jail after he was bailed out while awaiting the trial. First, police wrote in their interview of Jackson that she spat semen on her dress and the bedspread after the alleged forced oral sex (sodomy). Instead of trying to verify her claims, police never sent her dress to the evidence lab to test it for semen.[407]

Then, police pretended to hold the hotel phone messages supporting Tupac's defense, before a police source leaked to reporters that the officers actually erased them.[408] Police also unsuccessfully tried to intimidate women to denigrate Tupac by saying publicly before the trial that Tupac sexually assaulted them.[409] In another failed attempt to jail Tupac, the Assistant District Attorney (ADA) Melissa Mourges tried to have Tupac's bail revoked, claiming he harassed Jackson before the trial.[410]

Among many past examples, U.S. Intelligence similarly destroyed evidence that would have exonerated Tupac's godfather, Geronimo Pratt. At the exact time in 1969 when police alleged Pratt murdered a Los Angeles woman, the FBI had him on live audio surveillance tape when they were spying on a Panther conference that

Pratt was attending many hours north in Oakland. When Pratt's defense team finally got the tape records, it was only missing the minutes of Pratt's talk at the conference. The FBI claimed those parts of the tape were accidentally destroyed (Ch.9).[411]

At Tupac's trial, defense attorneys Michael Tarif Warren and Robert Ellis caught two police officers making a number of false statements under oath. For example, Ellis forced the immediate officer on the scene, Officer Craig McKernan, to admit he made a false claim in his pretrial testimony. At the trial, McKernan admitted that he formerly claimed Jackson said Charles Fuller took part in touching her and now he agreed that Jackson said Fuller only watched. Then, after going over Det. Kimberly Slimak's past work as an undercover prostitute, Warren forced her to admit that she misled a grand jury in implying that she personally recovered the guns at the hotel scene. She ended up agreeing that in actuality, another police officer said he found guns. She didn't even see him pick them up, but they gave her the guns and she then brought them in.[412]

The state's case became even weaker with Ayanna Jackson's testimony. First, attorneys caught Jackson contradicting many aspects of written police notes on her account that night, despite a number of pretrial meetings she had with ADA Mourges. Jackson further described different guns at the scene than the ones police said they found there, backing Warren's claim that the guns were planted. And, she said she spat Tupac and Jacques Agnant's sperm on her clothes and the bedspread. The bedspread came up negative for sperm.[413]

ADA Mourges apparently got desperate and made unsupported claims. For example, just after arresting Tupac at the hotel scene, police took the underwear he had on and, upon testing it, they found it contained no traces of semen. Despite that the tested underwear also matched Jackson's description of it, Mourges said that police tested the wrong underwear of Tupac's without giving a reason for such a claim.[414]

While the jury deliberated a verdict, ADA Mourges offered a mistrial, apparently due to how poorly she saw the case going. Mourges offered this mistrial after admitting her office withheld evidence from the defense, allegedly because they just found misplaced pictures at that time. Even though he would have automatically avoided jail, Tupac refused the mistrial offer, believing he had won the case and wanting to clear his name of the charges. ADA Mourges may have offered this mistrial to avoid Tupac's acquittal on all counts, as it would have decreased any negative publicity against Tupac and hurt Jackson's coming civil suit.[415]

The jury found Tupac not guilty of all the major charges including forced sodomy, attempted sodomy, assisting forced sodomy, and gun possession. This upheld the doctor's finding that there was no evidence of forced sodomy. Since the police said they found guns in

Tupac's hotel room, the jury finding supported attorney Warren's contention that police must have planted these guns. Nonetheless, the jury found Tupac guilty on three counts of sexual abuse, specifically detailed as one count of touching Jackson's butt against her will and two counts of assisting Jacques Agnant's touching her butt against her will.[416]

Michael Tarif Warren also cited the District Attorney's mission to put Tupac in jail and the judicial irregularities that aided this mission. The judicial bias never reached the level of Afeni Shakur's New York Panther 21 trial, but it had a grave effect on Tupac's life. While making an appeal on the sexual abuse conviction, Warren sought bail for Tupac. Warren cited many ways the District Attorney made the denial of Tupac's bail a top priority. The DA claimed that Tupac would try to skip bail and flee. This claim was highly dubious considering that as an entertainer, Tupac would lose his main source of income if he fled. The judge's improprieties included allowing the jury to consider a second count of Tupac assisting Agnant's touching of Jackson' butt, despite the fact that Jackson said Agnant only touched her once and ADA Mourges gave no evidence of Agnant touching her another time.[417]

As seen in Panther frame-ups and trials, the prosecutor showed preferable treatment for suspected police agent Jacques Agnant. First, Warren said that prosecution showed their bias in favor of Agnant in allowing him to sever his case from Tupac's. They then allowed Agnant to plea-bargain down to two misdemeanors. ADA Melissa Mourges' cover-up statements regarding her office's incredible leniency towards Agnant supports their roles in this targeting. *New Yorker* editor Connie Bruck noted how Mourges said her office let Agnant off easy because Jackson didn't want to go through the trauma of another trial. Bruck noted, however, that Jackson had already planned another trial with a civil suit against Tupac.[418]

Furthermore, other aspects of Jackson's actions that came out in the trial suggests Jackson was more perpetrator than victim. While men's abuse of women in our society *does* deserve more attention,[419] Jackson's actions support that she collaborated with a U.S. Intelligence attack on Tupac. First, by her own admission and witness reports, Jackson didn't try to leave the hotel when she was alone in the hallway after the alleged assault.

Then, despite claiming that she was traumatized by the hotel sex incident, 19 year-old Jackson immediately called and employed high profile lawyer, Michael Kaplan. Attorneys say that police and prosecution normally speak on behalf of victims alleging crimes. A victim only retains a lawyer if they decide to file a civil lawsuit, almost exclusively after the criminal case goes to trial, to bar the appearance of a money motivation for the claim. Also, defense attorneys need to take time reviewing a case before accepting it and addressing the media about it. After the late-night incident and arrest, Kaplan spoke to the media on Jackson's behalf early the following day and proceeded to file a civil suit. This suggests pre-incident planning.

When questioned about her retention of Kaplan by defense attorneys at the trial, Jackson lied, saying she doesn't know anyone named Michael Kaplan. And finally, Jackson undermined her purported long-term trauma when admitting that between the time of the incident and the trial, she saw Tupac's new movie on which she knew Tupac was working when he allegedly sodomized her against her will.[420]

Ayanna Jackson's actions long after the trial continued to suggest her purposeful involvement in a frame-up. For one, Jackson didn't file a civil suit against Agnant, despite his reported display of wealth.[421] Then, in 1995 Jackson allegedly authored a letter to *Vibe* magazine. That letter, written from her first person perspective but signed "anonymous," appeared to be co-written by a libel lawyer in the way it strongly implied that Tupac and the others raped her without quite saying it actually happened. For example, in the letter Jackson said she "did not deserve to be gang-raped" (a *Vibe* editor chose to extract and highlight this statement in a box on the page). Jackson further described assisted forced sodomy. This first assertion had astutely careful phrasing since, of course, noone *deserves* to be gang-raped, but this claim and the forced sodomy assertions were contradicted by the jury's verdict. No one was ever even charged with rape nor convicted of forced sodomy or assisting forced sodomy.[422] Journalists later repeated such falsehoods as truth (Ch.19).

During the deliberation of the Jackson sexual assault trial, a sixth armed attack on Tupac occurred. All six physical attacks by armed assailants had aspects suggesting U.S. Intelligence orchestration or police cover-up. Jacques Agnant's link to this event, the gunmen's actions, and police inaction support that U.S. Intelligence attempted to murder Tupac yet again in New York City on November 30, 1994.

By the end of November, Tupac had dumped Agnant as a friend, but Tupac's cousin saw Agnant following Tupac.[423] Several nights later, Agnant's associate Booker called Tupac. Booker offered him $7,000 to come to a Times Square recording studio and provide vocals for another rapper.[424] Upon arriving, alleged muggers shot Tupac four-to-five times in the lobby. Contrary to media accounts, a doctor's report gave details that depicted how these gunmen conducted a military-style execution. After the shooters put one bullet through Tupac's scrotum, sending him to the ground, they put two bullets in his head as he lay face down on the floor.[425]

Many curious aspects of this attack include a gunman waiting in the studio for Tupac, the items left behind, and the police presence. First, someone had let one of the gunman into the locked Quad Studios. With dozens of artists, from Madonna to the Rolling Stones, recording hit records at Quad Studios, it had tight security with a video camera surveillance of the locked doors allowing only the artists recording in the studio to buzz someone into the studio front doors. This supported that someone knowingly admitted the gunman into the lobby.[426]

Secondly, police maintained that the incident was "simply another Times Square mugging."[427] These alleged "muggers" took other jewelry but left a diamond-encrusted Rolex watch on Tupac. With guns in hand they then ran out the door into the extremely well lit Times Square area where a police car reportedly hovering nearby failed to go after them.[428]

Even the usually censorial mainstream media cited how a particular amount of police foul play accumulated up to this point. Before the virtually complete media censorship on police foul play in Tupac's trials and tribulations, a few mainstream journalists reported yet another odd aspect of police involvement in this incident. For example, The *Washington Post* commented how "in another strange twist" to Tupac's trial, the same officers immediately arriving on the scene had first arrived at his alleged sexual assault scene.[429] An NYPD officer implicated these officers as part of the Street Crime Unit, the unit believed to have taken over some Counter Intelligence Program duties.[430] A former police detective later said that he worked for New York's official "Rap Unit" found to have targeted rappers and that plainclothes Street Crime Unit members took part in that unit (Ch.30).

Furthermore, a security officer reported that the lobby's surveillance camera videotape caught the whole shooting incident, but the police investigator told him he didn't want to see the tape.[431] Afeni Shakur and attorney Michael Tarif Warren thought police set up the shooting, and the two removed Tupac from the hospital against doctors' orders because of the large police presence at the hospital.[432] They moved him to another hospital where Tupac received a phone call making a death threat. Afeni and Warren accepted an offer by Tupac's friend, *A Different World* actress Jasmine Guy, and moved him into her apartment. Despite the entrance and exit holes in Tupac's head, the bullets miraculously failed to hit his brain and he survived.[433]

Tupac had first rejected the notion that Jacques Agnant (a.k.a. Nigel) was a police agent. But he eventually said it in lyrics implying that Agnant set the shooting up with his associate Booker on behalf of the FBI. In the last CD he finished producing, due out within two months of his death, Tupac rapped with slang about "Haitian Jacques" working for the FBI to set him up for that shooting (see quote at start of chapter).[434]

19-Wealthiest Start CIA Who Hire Nazis and Help Corporations Control Media

"My message to the censorship committee
Who's the biggest gang of niggaz in the city?
The critics or the cops? The courts or the crooks,
don't look so confused, take another look...
All you punk police will never find peace on the streets 'til the niggaz get a piece, Fuck 'em, they kill you to control you
Pay top dollar for your soul
Real niggaz don't fold, straight souljah!"
Tupac Shakur, "Soujah's Revenge," *Strictly 4 My N.I.G.G.A.Z*, 1993.

In lyrics such as these, Tupac used slang to reflect his belief that the media, police and many court officials often worked as extensions of U.S. Intelligence. (He also urged people to fight for their piece of the economic pie—possibly with the dual slang of "piece" to mean a gun—in self-defense as revolutionaries). Many researchers backed Tupac's insinuation about linked corruption between the media, police, and the government justice system. The mechanisms for these groups' overlapping linked control of public information help explain why "alternative" media joined mainstream media in covering up important aspects of Tupac's Times Square shooting. While Intelligence agents were instructed to "send articles to the newspapers" for the purpose of smearing political musicians, the media work against Tupac was much more extensive.[435]

Media organizations had covered-up many other periods and events in Tupac Shakur's life that U.S. Intelligence wanted censored. For example, ten years of research failed to uncover a single article or book that gave a full explanation of Tupac's New Afrikan Panther leadership in NAPO (Ch.11). Virtually all media had failed to report bystanders' accounts of the Atlanta police shooting incident despite that defense attorneys and prosecutors easily obtained them. Similarly, most New York media failed to question police statements that the Times Square incident was only a random mugging. Only years later did an investigating reporter print in her book that police refused to look at the music studio lobby's security videotape of the assailants.[436]

Michael Tarif Warren said that he and the other defense lawyers believed one of the worst cases of cover-up regarding the shooting came from a young black reporter named Toure. Toure said in a *Village Voice* article that, "It's really irrelevant who shot Tupac. It makes just as much, and as little, sense to argue that Tupac orchestrated the incident."[437] With this statement Toure knowingly referred to the 4-5 bullets, two of which went in and out of Tupac's head.[438] Tupac said that reading those lines just made him start "crying like a baby."[439]

Warren said that he and all of the other defense attorneys believed Toure was a government agent.[440]

Some leftist information that wouldn't get published in daily newspapers still comes out in *The Village Voice*. But wealthy conservative businessmen influenced its content by this mid-'90s time period. Wealthy owners bought out *The Village Voice* in the '80s and they eventually bought most other weeklies such as *The LA Weekly*. They proceeded to replace liberal editors with conservatives.[441] These sources offer few articles that differ much from the daily newspapers whose owners also sit on the boards of large, mostly conservative corporations (see below).[442]

Investigative books and articles also support Warren and the other defense lawyers' assertions that Toure worked for the intelligence community. Warren said they believed this partly due to the *Voice* piece and partly because they saw Toure sitting in the front-row for the entire sexual assault trial, and "completely misrepresent it."[443] Research on U.S. Intelligence and the media, as well as a personal interview with Toure, support their belief that he directly or indirectly worked for U.S. Intelligence.

A review of U.S. Intelligence's leadership control helps show how they gained power over most media outlets. The history of U.S. Intelligence as reflected by insiders and researchers supports that the elite multinational corporate owners set up the Central Intelligence Agency. Through the National Security Act of 1947, the CIA leadership ruled over all other 14+ intelligence agencies (though changes occurred after 2000) These agencies included the FBI, NSA, Army Intelligence, Naval Intelligence, etc.[444]

The highest-ranking CIA whistleblower, former assistant Deputy Director Victor Marchetti, was a 14-year CIA veteran. He wrote that CIA leaders came from the wealthiest families, some of which had led the Office of Strategic Services (OSS) wartime intelligence group. Marchetti reported that virtually the entire CIA leadership and middle ranks were filled with white, male, Protestant family members of corporate moguls and it remained that way with few exceptions. British editor Frances Stonor Saunders also pored through government documents to make this similar claim.[445]

Furthermore, the CIA was highly sympathetic to Nazis. In 1999, the U.S. government released over 240,000 federal documents on the post-WWII time period. President George W. Bush had CIA, FBI and Pentagon officials publish limited summaries of the documents in a book, *U.S. Intelligence and the Nazis*. Media groups briefly covered the book, which left out any mention of the Bush family. Nonetheless, *United Press International* (UPI) and *The Times* of London, referenced the documents cited by the book as saying that the CIA hired over 100 Nazi war spies and other war criminals. These included five key associates of infamous Nazi leader, Adolph Eichman, and top Nazi spy,

Renald Gehlen, as West Germany's new spy leader. *The New York Times* said that the CIA gave at least two of these Nazis citizenship. *The Times* implied that this meant CIA employment in Washington. Many of these war criminals were charged with killing thousands of Jews. The British equivalent of the CIA, MI6, also hired many Nazi agents, including one responsible for killing close to a 100 British agents.[446]

Researchers had revealed more extensive aspects of CIA/Nazi work in the '80s. Award-winning investigative reporter Christopher Simpson published, *Blowback: America's Recruitment of Nazis,* in 1988. *Blowback* listed hundreds of government archival files and thousands of documents, among its copious citations. Simpson said two of the half-dozen U.S. Intelligence operations protecting and employing Nazis were code-named "Sunrise" for spies, and "Paperclip" for scientists. He named Robert Lovett, Allan Dulles (both business associates of the Harriman, Rockefeller and Bush families), and OSS agent Frank Wisner as key U.S. Intelligence leaders pushing to hire Nazis to do CIA work in the U.S., Europe, Latin America (Ch.35) and the Middle East. Simpson summarized that "hundreds, and perhaps thousands, of such recruits were SS [Nazi elite guard] veterans." These included the Nazi security's most murderous, such as top Adolph Eichman aid Alois Brunner. The Simon Wiesenthal Center estimated that Brunner was "personally responsible for the murder of 128,500 people" in the Nazi's genocide.[447]

The relationship of the Nazis working for the CIA was similar to the local collaborations between Southern police and Ku Klux Klansmen. Counter to popular beliefs, the CIA and FBI appeared to carry out racist practices just as much if not more than most local police. The *New York Times* and other media groups have conceded that police actions in southern cities aided the KKK in killing civil rights workers, such as the infamous Schwerner, Goodman, Cheney murders (made famous in the movie *Mississippi Burning*, which showed the FBI as rescuing blacks).[448]

Primary sources such as witnesses documented in Howard Zinn's *A People's History of the United States*, say the FBI actually helped the KKK. *The Baltimore Sun* provided another example. It reviewed a University of Delaware professor's book, *The Informant,* that used FBI files, trial transcripts and interviews amongst its sources. *The Sun* summarized that book's chronicling of an FBI undercover agent in the Ku Klux Klan, Gary Thomas Rowe, "in the vicinity of just about every conflagration of racial violence in the virulently segregated Alabama of the early 1960s. He was around for beatings, bombings, ultimately even murder." The book said he virtually never arrested anyone and kept several top Klansmen from getting arrested after their brutal crimes.[449]

The history of the CIA work for multinational corporate interests also reveals their vast control over information. High-ranking CIA official, Victor Marchetti concurred with Frances Stonor Saunders on the CIA's beginnings. They also concurred with how U.S. Intelligence generally acts as agents of these corporations rather than working on behalf of all Americans' interests. President Harry Truman started the Office of Policy Coordination (OPC) in 1948. Under former OSS agent Frank Wisner, the OPC merged with the CIA in 1951 and the OPC grew rapidly. In 1952, Wisner supervised 2,800 personnel in the U.S. and 3,100 overseas working on psychological warfare operations with an $82 million budget. Saunders detailed how their budget and personnel increased annually.[450] After other media sources disclosures, *The New York Times* said that Wisner also had kept a highly secret "Propaganda Assets Inventory," representing a network of more than 800 news and public information organizations and individuals. These non-personnel assets became part of the CIA's opinion-making propagandists within both American and international mainstream media.[451]

A mere glimpse of this sort of ownership comes from the example of William Casey, who was in and out of U.S. Intelligence for years before he became CIA director under President Reagan. Casey led a group of Intelligence officials that founded the Capital Cities media company in 1954. Capital Cities bought the ABC television network in 1985.[452]

Frances Stonor Saunders reviewed troves of buried archival U.S. Intelligence documents that explained their goals. For example, in a 1950 "NSC Directive," the U.S. Intelligence umbrella group, the National Security Council, described its

> "psychological warfare... [through] propaganda... to influence [people's] thoughts and actions... [so that] the subject moves in the direction [they] desire for reasons which he believes to be his own."[453]

The CIA, OPC, and groups with similar right-wing, hyper-capitalist agendas spent huge sums of money to influence national and international opinion by funding writers, musicians, people in stage production, film industry figures, and visual artists. Starting in the '50s, their ever-increasing expenditures funded a vast network of these artists. Partly through the use of many foundations that continue today, most artists didn't realize they were being funded, influenced, and censored by the CIA.[454]

One of these foundations, the Madison Center for Educational Affairs (MCEA) that was founded in 1953, made student recruitment its top emphasis. The CIA had already sponsored student newspapers since the late '40s.[455] The MCEA added more money to that effort and gained jobs at top media posts for its recruits to do their bidding, with job stability and advancement dependent on their cooperation. The MCEA said that "at a university of 10,000, there are perhaps 30 or 40 right-leaning students willing to take a stand." The MCEA gave these small student groups funds for newspapers that amplified their voices to make them appear larger and influence other students.[456]

By the 1980s, people of color represented barely 5% of all professional journalists and the MCEA seized an opportunity. MCEA started a "Student Forum"—an association of minority students of color "who do not support the radical agenda." The Forum had conservative black Supreme Court Justice Clarence Thomas attend its founding conference.[457] By the '90s, MCEA changed its name to the Intercollegiate Studies Institute (ISI) and supported 50-75 newspapers with a circulation of 300,000 to 400,000 at top colleges nationwide.[458] While MCEA/ISI graduates aren't known, Toure's history further suggests that he might be one of many writers and editors of color who used their media positions to cover up politically sensitive details on Tupac's life. In a telephone interview, Toure revealed he had no college journalism training or newspaper experience other than his own off-campus publication, when he graduated from Atlanta's Emory University in 1987. Within little time, Toure obtained a position at the top-selling music magazine, *Rolling Stone,* and then MTV. While at MTV, owned by corporate conglomerate Viacom, Toure wrote freelance articles such as the *Village Voice* piece on Tupac which stated Tupac may have set up his own shooting for publicity's sake.[459] Toure later boasted of writing a review that he said had "ended the career" of top political rap group Public Enemy (Ch.32).

This coupled with other revelations of CIA spy work on Americans locally, particularly blacks (see below), supports that the media worked against local black activists.[460] Suspected U.S. Intelligence collaborator Toure's work gained much corroboration amongst high circulation media. For example, *Village Voice* editors failed to fact check when another writer, likely persuaded by Toure, later repeated Ayanna Jackson's false claim that Tupac held her down while another guy forced her into sexual acts. Other media added to the stated falsehoods regarding this incident, including *People* magazine, which claimed that Tupac raped Jackson.[461] It bears repeating that court documents state that the jury found Tupac innocent of forcibly sodomizing or raping Jackson. And they found him innocent of assisting any forced actions. The jury only convicted Tupac for placing "his hands on Ayanna Jackson's buttocks" and aiding Jacques Agnant as he "placed his hands" there.[462]

U.S. Intelligence perpetrated this type of cover-up regarding events in Tupac's life and other targets' lives with ease. U.S. Intelligence leaders had such extensive control over the media that they boasted about it. In the '50s, CIA propaganda chief Frank Wisner said that he could "play the media like a mighty Wurlitzer." Former veteran

CIA agent Ralph McGehee obtained a CIA memo in '91 claiming the agency had representatives in every media outlet in the country who help spin and censor the news.[463]

Also, Watergate muckraking reporter Carl Bernstein wrote a seminal 1977 expose on the media. Despite his earlier '70s Watergate fame, only *Rolling Stone* magazine published this revealing article. A Senate Intelligence Committee forced CIA Director George Bush, Sr. to admit that "more than 400 journalists had lived double lives, maintaining covert relationships with the CIA," Bernstein wrote. Others in the CIA told Bernstein that the number was far higher. The Senate Committee found that virtually all of the leading media companies have top executives, editors and journalists who are paid by the CIA to, for example, reprint CIA written articles verbatim under their names. Other disclosures included the fact that some of these media and CIA employees were first hired by the media, while others were first hired by the CIA. He also found that their duties "fell under the category of 'covert operations,' rather than 'foreign intelligence.'" The covert ops category implied work inside the U.S. against Americans, which went against the CIA's mandate.[464]

As previously noted, the CIA supervised the whole of U.S. Intelligence and its leadership came from the families that owned the multinational corporations. Ben Bagdikian, dean of the University of California-Berkeley School of Journalism, explained how multinational corporate owners gained even tighter controls over public information. During a sabbatical to study the media industry, Bagdikian set out to research another topic before he found out about the ever-consolidating media ownership. Bagdikian detailed how the media industry experienced a huge consolidation trend approaching "monopolization" by a smaller and smaller number of controlling multinational corporations.

Bagdikian, a Pulitzer Prize-winning former reporter, further explained that most major media outlets have directors on their company boards that also sit on the boards of these major multinational corporations. For example, the Board of Directors of *Time* magazine and the industry standard-bearer *New York Times* also sit on corporate boards involved in military defense contracting, oil, and pharmaceuticals, as well as banks, finance and insurance companies. Bagdikian explained that under law, "the director of a company is obliged to act in the interests of his or her own company."[465]

Thus, for example, a director of both a defense company and a media group should oppose the promotion of Tupac due to his lyrics. Tupac's "money for war but can't feed the poor" lyrics criticized government policies that enriched defense companies and neglected others. He also advocated for organizations of the less privileged to get more from the rich and preached for armed self-defense.[466]

The rare disclosures by *The New York Times* and other mainstream news sources usually came *despite* their ownership's political agenda. These disclosures do come more often in *The New York Times* than the more blatantly conservative news sources such as *The New York Post*, but editors usually limit the content of the disclosures or print other articles that contradict the disclosures. Yale-trained political science professor Michael Parenti explained mainstream media's occasional disclosures by brashly stating in his introduction, "like any liar the press is filled with contradictions...without a word of explanation."[467]

Bagdikian further noted the historical precedent for corporate media control. He detailed how the reform-minded journalism of the early 1900s helped elect reformist politicians such as President Theodore Roosevelt. But, he added, the Rockefeller and J.P. Morgan interests bought control of the most influential media outlets. These conservative robber barons installed their own managers and stopped them from publishing information that could hurt their profits or promote populist politicians (Film, *America: Freedom to Fascism*, by the director of *Trading Places* also cites this information, first stated in the Capital by U.S. Congressman Oscar Callaway in 1917).[468]

The world's most famous scientist also weighed in on this issue. Albert Einstein published a 1949 article, "Why Socialism?" in a new magazine. He started with a defense of his ability to discuss economic and social issues. He cited the fact that conquering peoples monopolized land ownership and established a "priesthood from their own ranks. The priests, in control of education, made the class division of society" permanent, and people are, "to a large extent unconsciously, guided in their social behavior." He stated the need to advance beyond this "predatory phase of human development," "and we should not assume that experts are the only ones who have a right to express themselves on questions affecting the organization of society." He later noted the development of "an oligarchy of private capital" which "cannot be effectively checked even by a democratically organized political society." "Private capitalists inevitably... control, directly or indirectly, the main sources of information (press, radio, education)" drastically reducing people's ability to make informed "use of political rights."[469]

In the later 1900s, to further tighten the elite's control of public information, U.S. Intelligence also gained direct ownership over the vast majority of information sources. For example, one of their own publications, *Armed Forces Journal International*, revealed that the Pentagon (military intelligence) published 371 magazines in 1971, making it 16 times larger than the nation's biggest publisher that year. This number increased to 1,203 different periodicals by 1982.[470] The quantity suggests that these 1200 magazine and journal titles straddled many areas of life, thus controlling information that could make it to the pages of news, fashion and sports magazines crowding book chain outlets.

In the mid-70s, a Senate intelligence committee issued a report stating that the CIA owned outright, "more than 200 wire services, newspapers, magazines, and book publishing complexes," according to Professor Michael Parenti in his book, *Inventing Reality,* and *Washington Post* reporter Morton Mintz in his book, *Power Inc.* Following these reports and Carl Bernstein's *Rolling Stone* exposé, *The New York Times* published one of its few disclosures, the aforementioned piece by Crewden, on the CIA and the media. The *Times* reported another fifty media outlets run by the CIA and added that the CIA secretly commissioned over 1,200 books by '77, including 200 in 1967 alone. Mintz quoted a Senate Select Committee on Intelligence Activities 1976 report describing how the CIA promoted their own propaganda in that a book written "by one CIA operative was reviewed favorably by another CIA agent in *The New York Times.*"[471]

Another apparent tactic for corporations' conservative media control comes through advertising. Disclosures from media insiders present general agreement on advertisers' huge influence over media content. For example, *New York Times* publisher Arthur Ochs Sulzburger openly admitted that he had his editors put forth the auto industry line in censoring auto safety and pollution issues because otherwise it "would affect the advertising." Another *Times* staff member said that stories on the automobile industry in the early '70s were "more or less put together by the advertisers."[472] A CBS television news veteran supported this notion in saying that advertising agencies and their affiliates are "always taken into account," when it came to programming decisions, in order not to offend them.[473]

One of the most well known media insiders, Dan Rather, described the media's conservative censorship in stark terms. Rather started in journalism working for United Press International in the 1950s. His journalistic achievements had him move up to CBS Southern Bureau chief and then anchorman on the *CBS Evening News* in 1981. He remained in that position until 2005. In 2002, the BBC (British Broadcasting Corporation) interviewed Dan Rather about the media's aid in the suppression of dissent in the United States. Rather said, "What you have here is a miniature version of what you have in totalitarian states."[474]

20-US Intelligence & Mafia Shaped R&B/Rock; CIA & Time Warner's Rap Grip

Amongst all of the arts, U.S. Intelligence and top conservative corporations appeared particularly concerned about popular youth music. Various writers believe that U.S. Intelligence thought that rock music and then rap would supersede U.S. Intel's attempt to influence people's opinions. Books cite how the FBI now openly admits having started files on musicians such as Elvis Presley in the mid-'50s and other musicians thereafter. Despite such admissions, researchers such as London's *Daily Mail* and *Sunday Express* legal correspondent, Fenton Bresler, said he fought for years with numerous Freedom Of Information Act requests to get copies of even a small percentage of The Beatles singer John Lennon's FBI and CIA files. Young conservative Ralph Reed, who headed the Christian Coalition and was a leader in the Republican Party, alluded to music when he said in 1996 "the future is an endless and vicious culture war."[475]

In the early '50s, white Jewish Cleveland disc jockey Allan Freed was credited with introducing rock music to large white audiences. White crooners such as Perry Como dominated pop radio at the start of that decade. Freed was the first large city deejay to introduce danceable black rhythm and blues musicians to white audiences in 1951 at a time when most stations only allowed white musicians who covered their songs. Freed was credited with coining the term "rock and roll" in '51, which he borrowed from slang by blacks for sex. Freed, under the moniker Moondog, drummed pencils and howled to songs. He inspired other small stations nationwide to develop his R&B format, soon forcing large stations to follow suit.[476]

In '52 Freed's soaring influence was apparent. That year, 25,000 people, two-thirds white, came to a 10,000-seat arena for Freed's first concert.[477] Freed's career continued skyrocketing before it ended abruptly due to bribery charges in 1960.

Some researchers believe U.S. Intelligence used Allan Freed for his influence, without Freed realizing it, and then set up an early end to his career. One example of U.S. Intelligence's stake in the music world may be indicative. Former OSS agent John Elroy McCaw attended meetings of the U.S. Intelligence umbrella group, the National Security Council as he served on their Advisory Council. He also owned WINS, one of New York City's top music stations.[478]

Events suggest that John McCaw and U.S. Intelligence obtained help in the music world from a common collaborator—organized crime. As seen above in the MLK assassination (Ch.2) and with drug trafficking (Ch.10), U.S. Intelligence collaborations with the Mafia had a long history. And, at least with drug trafficking, the Genovese Mafia family was central to that history.[479]

Fredric Dannen's widely acclaimed bestseller, *Hit Men*, documents the vast number of organized crime figures in the music world, such as Morris Levy. Dannen said Levy was a Genovese Mafia associate who owned top New York jazz clubs and song publishing rights. Levy signed a deal with Allan Freed and influenced him to accept a deejay offer at WINS. McCaw offered Freed a huge salary to join WINS in 1954 and Freed's program became #1 within months. With the help of Freed's popularity, Levy started the jazz and rock record label, Roulette Records, in 1956. An Assistant U.S. Attorney claimed that Roulette Records was also a way station for heroin trafficking (A well-substantiated drug-trafficking charge was also made against the key rap label that undermined Tupac, Death Row Records, Chs.23,28).[480]

After Freed helped make WINS the country's most popular music station, McCaw implemented changes at the station in 1957 that shaped the rock music world. WINS lead the nationwide promotion of the Top 40 music format. This format helped large money interests gain the most dominant influence and control over top music sales through promotion money and radio play menus.[481] It would further aid censorship of political songs by barring them from the radio play menus.

That Paramount Pictures paid Allan Freed $29,000 a day to make a teen movie in 1957 exemplified Freed's immense success in the music world.[482] Powerful forces started a continuous assault on Freed the following year. In 1958, when violence occurred outside a Boston arena at a Freed show, authorities indicted Freed for inciting a riot (Police Intelligence later used this charge against H. Rap Brown, Jimi Hendrix, Tupac and others, and Mafia further meddled in these musicians' lives).[483]

While charges were eventually dropped for the Boston incident, other attacks were more serious. McCaw fired Freed in '58 for unknown reasons. The day he was fired, a gunman, allegedly an upset concert promoter, looked for Freed in the WINS studio before Freed escaped.[484] Freed went to work for WABC but in 1959 researchers believe Freed was set up and scapegoated when Orrin Hatch's congressional committee focused exclusively on him in the "payola" scandals. The term implied a bribe to play certain songs. Morris Levy, the source of much of the payola (bribe) money to play his records, was never called to testify. *Hit Men* author Fredric Dannen said that these deals weren't illegal then and were only considered misdemeanors thereafter. Nonetheless, the scandal effectively ended Freed's career.[485]

John McCaw's four sons followed in their U.S. Intelligence-advising father's footsteps. They gained influence over the media by way of large ownership in cable television networks and other communications companies. The sons accumulated a net worth of at least $750 million, each.[486] Other U.S. Intelligence leaders set up similar spheres of influence in music and entertainment.[487]

The Mafia continued influencing music ownership and work in music clubs, labels and promotion. It also controlled record distribution and music tours through its power in the Teamsters Union.[488] At least one publisher, Lou Wolfe of Covert Action Quarterly, further said that the Mafia owned East/West, the sole magazine distributor to kiosks and newsstands. Wolfe further believed that East/West collaborated with the CIA in barring his and most other leftist magazines.[489]

When Time Inc. and Warner merged in the 1980s, it became the world's largest media conglomerate, which gave it vast power to censor Tupac and cover up events in his life.[490] Both Time and Warner have a history of supporting conservative Republicans, such as backing Richard Nixon's presidency. Warner also showed its loyalty to U.S. Intelligence regarding a book, *Counter-Revolutionary Violence*, by professors Noam Chomsky and Ed Herman, printed by Warner subsidiary, Warner Modular Books. After its printing, the parent company destroyed 10,000 copies because it criticized U.S. Intelligence policies.[491]

Of 17 media companies he listed as working closely with the CIA in his seminal article, "The CIA and the Media," Carl Bernstein said that CIA officials singled out Time, Inc. as doing the most collaborative work with the CIA. Bernstein said that *Time* (and ex-*Life*) magazine founder, Henry Luce, was close friends with CIA Director Allan Dulles. The vice-president of Luce's Time-Life media company, Charles Douglas (C.D.) Jackson dualed as a leader of U.S. Intelligence. He co-authored "a CIA-sponsored study recommending the reorganization of the American Intelligence services."[492]

British editor Frances Stonor Saunders also confirmed that the Time-Life vice-president, C.D. Jackson, had a huge historical role in shaping U.S. Intelligence, particularly regarding culture manipulation. By poring through a huge library archive of Jackson's papers, Saunders found that during his decades-long career at Time-Life, Jackson took several breaks for U.S. Intelligence leadership work. He was deputy chief of the Psychological Warfare Division. He then had a job as an " 'outside' director of CIA covert operations." He further worked as Special Adviser to the President [Eisenhower] for Psychological Warfare. Jackson proposed and authored the consolidation of the Psychological Warfare and the propaganda units to become a major function of the newly created CIA. He further headed CIA front groups, such as The Congress of Cultural Freedom, which obtained vast amounts of money to influence all facets of the arts.[493]

C.D. Jackson embodied the violently anti-Semitic, racist, anti-Communist belief system typical of certain elite families with whom he helped start the CIA. The rabid anti-communist agenda they carried out, which barred thousands of people from work, exemplified Jackson and his Psychological Warfare Division's opinion and influence. They "blacklisted" a particularly large amount of people in Hollywood and the arts for any link to communism.[494] This showed their concern for anyone infringing on their own attempt to shape people's hearts and minds.

U.S. Intelligence accomplished their goals partly through intimidation. The first half of the 20th century included two famous executions. FBI Director J. Edgar Hoover helped direct the targeting in both instances prior to starting his Counter Intelligence Program. C.D. Jackson helped orchestrate the later execution.

The U.S. government conducted the first execution after the 1919 Palmer raids rounded up thousands of anarchists, socialists, and other labor activists. A majority of those rounded up had migrated from Italy. In 1920, police arrested anarchist labor organizers Nicola Sacco and Bartolomeo Vanzetti. Despite massive evidence of their innocence that included a confession of the actual killer, and an international outcry, the government executed the two in 1927. All accounts suggest much advanced planning and the use of the public event to intimidate others away from leftist activism.[495]

C.D. Jackson's government memoranda showed that he and his Intelligence unit also planned the second execution long in advance. The indictment of Julius and Ethel Rosenberg, the parents of two small children (later anti-death penalty activists, Robert and Michael Meeropol) provided another warning of what the government can do to Communists. In a highly controversial conviction of giving atomic secrets to the Soviet Union, they were the first people ever executed for espionage during peacetime. A later book published by Doubleday revealed taped sessions supporting that U.S. Intelligence fraudulently manufactured its key evidence against the Rosenbergs.[496]

One of C.D. Jackson's other propaganda projects financed black musicians, writers and actors who didn't comment on U.S. racism, eroding the livelihood of activist black writers and performing artists.[497] Time and Warner's actions showed that its top executives, who took over after its long-time Vice-President, C.D. Jackson, had similar goals as they attempted to contain rap activist Tupac Shakur. As mentioned, after Tupac's debut Interscope Records CD, Time Warner bought another 25% of Interscope for a controlling share.[498] Time Warner then excluded songs and censored lyrics on Tupac's second and third CDs. They further withheld the release of these CDs for a year each (several reasons might be knowledge of the U.S. Intelligence murder attempts on Tupac as well as Tupac's anti-Bush lyrics coming out just before the '92 presidential election).[499]

Time Warner appeared to have bigger sights on rap in general. First they partnered with the generally well-meaning jazz star-turned music mogul, Quincy Jones, to found *Vibe*. It soon was the top-selling rap magazine.[500] The positive aspect of *Vibe* and other corporate rap magazines was that their financial resources gave black musicians much higher visibility with the magazines' large distribution. The negative aspect of these magazines was that Time Warner and large corporate advertisers appeared to infuse them with the similar conservative agenda presented in their other mainstream publications (on advertisers control, Ch.19). Quincy Jones said he knew little about the industry, which allowed Time Warner to install most of the editors in *Vibe*. (Jones had such little content control that he had to write a letter to the magazine to voice his opinions in one issue).[501]

Tupac confidants Watani Tyehimba and Michael Tarif Warren support that Time Warner and large corporate advertisers who helped fund higher distribution for other rap magazines politically censored much information on Tupac's life.[502] *Vibe* printed similar information as the white-owned, *The Source,* rap magazine. Like many mainstream magazines, *The Source* censored most radical political information (in 2006 these white owners were pushed out by a new board). Time Warner had similar content control over close to 25 other magazines it owned, including *Time, Life,* and *People*.

Rap started dominating music sales by the early '90s and Time Warner dominated rap by that time.[503] After several '80s rap albums broke into the top of Billboard sales charts, including radical political rap, media giant Time Warner began heavily buying into the industry.[504] In 1992, the *Los Angeles Times* said Time Warner's vast record label ownership included "the great bulk of the rap stars."[505] Within eight more years, Time Warner had ownership of twenty formerly independent rap labels,[506] as well as most of the rock music labels (see endnote).[507] But Time Warner provided huge initial funds to promote its rap label, Death Row Records. Death Row, Tupac's next label, had links to both U.S. Intelligence and the Mafia, aiding intelligence operations (Ch.s 22-8).[508]

21-Penal Coercion and FBI Cointelpro Tactics Set Up East/West Rap Feud

Tupac Shakur suffered through a long painful recovery from his four or five bullet wounds. Despite requests from doctors for Tupac to continue bed rest near a hospital, a judge forced Tupac to recover while behind bars. About a week or two after Tupac was shot, a court judge forced him to await his sentencing in jail.

Near the time of Tupac's sentencing, highly suspected undercover agent Jacques Agnant only received two misdemeanors in a plea bargain regarding the heavier charges for which Tupac was acquitted. Meanwhile, with respect to Tupac's conviction on lesser charges of "sexual abuse"—touching following consensual sex, the judge gave Tupac a 1 ½ to 4 ½ year prison sentence at the start of '95. This discrepancy is particularly noteworthy given Tupac only having two misdemeanors on his record versus Agnant's lengthy rap sheet.[509] Tupac's severe sentencing, prison placement, and oncoming prison manipulation suggest further U.S. Intelligence influence.

The judge gave Tupac an exorbitant bail to pay—a Counterintelligence tactic used against his mother. Legal experts wrote how during Afeni Shakur's Panther 21 trial, the judge did Intelligence's bidding by requiring a vast amount of money for bail and directly collaborated with the prosecution in an attempt to gain a guilty verdict.[510] Tupac's judge set bail at $3 million. He refused Tupac's offer of a $1.3 million bail package, despite that only 10% of bail is usually needed for release with a bail bond. Defense attorney Michael Tarif Warren also argued that, as a high profile entertainer, Tupac would jeopardize any future in his professional livelihood if he jumped bail and fled. The judge refused to acknowledge this.[511]

Tupac's third CD, *Me Against the World*, debuted on top of the pop music charts while he was in jail 45 days after his sentencing hearing. Interscope Records ended up selling 2 million copies of the CD in seven months. Many reporters tried to get interviews with Tupac, giving him more of a mouthpiece for his leftist political views. In one interview, Tupac asked, "What did the USA just do, flying to Bosnia ['95, before full-scale bombing]?" Adding, it has "no business over there." Tupac further said, "America is the biggest gang in the world. Look how they didn't agree with Cuba, so [they] cut them off."[512] Cuba had given a safe haven to his ex-Panther aunt Assata Shakur, as well as other black radicals.[513]

Early in March of '95, prison officials distanced Tupac from the New York media by transferring Tupac from Rikers Island to Clinton Correctional Facility in upstate Dannemora, New York, a maximum-security prison about 9 hours north of New York City. It's uncertain whether plans for Tupac's prison transfer were already in motion, but *Me Against the World* was released February 27 and

Tupac's new prison card issue date was 3/8/95. This suggested that the CD's chart-topping week at least hastened the transfer of Tupac away from New York City's interviewing journalists. This prison placement cut down on Tupac's publicity and visits.[514]

At Clinton, officials used the same political prisoner tactics on Tupac as they had on Black Panthers and ethnically diverse activists associated with the Revolutionary Armed Task Force linked to Mutulu Shakur. More intensive political intelligence work in the prisons started in the '70s, according to a special investigative committee of the California State Legislature. They found that the U.S. Department of Corrections had a "Special Services Division" to carry out operations on prisoners.[515] Researchers working from divergent groups, such as the Bureau of Prisons and Amnesty International, described several particular prison tactics as akin to both "torture" and "brain washing," and referred to them as "penal coercion."[516]

University of Wisconsin Professor Alfred McCoy put the "penal coercion" techniques in proper perspective. In his book, *A Question of Torture*, McCoy presented the decades of research the CIA conducted to perfect their techniques at breaking down prisoners with various forms of torture. McCoy found that the CIA came out with their leading manual on effecting these goals that was titled, *Kubark Counterintelligence Interrogation* handbook. The *Kubark* book explicitly cited the importance of using the "penal coercion" techniques developed by the Bureau of Social Science Research, headed by Albert Biderman.[517]

A 1983 *Amnesty International Report on Torture* presented the original documents on these CIA-cited techniques, "Biderman's Chart on Penal Coercion" (which writers Churchill and Vander Wall reprinted in their, *The COINTELPRO Papers*). Biderman listed eight general penal coercion methods prison officials used to psychologically tear down individuals in order to manipulate them. These *methods* are: isolation, monopolization of perception, induced debility, threats, occasional indulgences, demonstrating 'omnipotence,' degradation, and enforcing trivial demands. The *techniques* used to aid these included solitary confinement, restricted movement, exploitation of wounds, death threats, occasional favors, demonstrating complete control over victim's fate, personal hygiene prevention, taunts, denial of privacy and enforcing minute rules.[518]

Reports demonstrated that prison officials used many of these *techniques* and harsher techniques for accomplishing all eight penal coercion *methods* on Tupac. One of Tupac Shakur's appeal lawyers, Stuart Levy, visited Tupac at Clinton's Dannemora prison site and stated his disbelief. Levy said that prior to one of his visits, "Tupac had a rectal search when he came in [to the visiting area]...we spent six hours there in full view of the guards. Then the guards started saying 'Tupac! Tupac!' in this falsetto voice, putting up their fingers with these plastic gloves, waving them—'It's time! It's time!' Why a second rectal search, when he'd been sitting there in plain view with his lawyer, why, except to humiliate him?"[519] These rectal searches aided many aspects of penal coercion, such as the induced debility.

The *Amnesty International Report* described this induced debility's purpose as weakening "mental and physical ability to resist."[520] Prof. McCoy noted how the CIA's *Kubark* research stated that the most long-lasting penal coercion torture techniques came from the victims playing a part in their own pain. Thus, Tupac may have had to endure these painful anal probes in order to see visitors while he was in solitary confinement for eight months. McCoy reprinted Biderman's penal coercion note that "the threat to inflict pain…can trigger fears more damaging than the immediate sensation of pain."[521]

In a court affidavit, the doctor that attended to Tupac long-term after his Times Square shooting described his still healing groin and head wounds. The doctor also noted that Tupac suffered from Post-Traumatic Stress Disorder (PTSD) after the shooting.[522] Tupac's PTSD symptoms continually had him waking up sweating and screaming.[523] Family friend Yaasmyn Fula, who visited Tupac often, said he had both "guards threatening to kill him, [and] inmates threatening to kill him."[524] Tupac confirmed this. Regarding the guards, he said one showed him a Ku Klux Klan T-shirt, saying, "We are the biggest gang in town. Don't ever forget it." [525] One of Tupac's revolutionary uncles in his prison eventually quelled prisoners' threats.[526]

Prison officials used isolation and monopolization of perception on Tupac by placing Tupac in solitary confinement 23 hours a day for eight months, allegedly for flunking a drug test. They further limited his ability to shower, only granting him an indulgence when news reports said Madonna was coming to visit him.[527] Many reported a vastly negative change in Tupac after prison.[528]

Tupac's confidantes believed that the penal coercion techniques helped U.S. Intelligence manipulate Tupac in other ways. Watani Tyehimba and Michael Tarif Warren say the techniques aided an attempt to have Tupac believe that his friend, rapper Biggie Smalls (a.k.a. Notorious B.I.G., born Christopher Wallace) or Biggie's producer, Sean "Puffy" Combs, orchestrated the Times Square shooting. [529] This eventually became known as the East Coast versus West Coast rap war since Tupac was most affiliated with California while Biggie and Puffy were based in New York.

Evidence supports that U.S. Intelligence had historically created an East Coast versus West Coast Panther war around 1970. The FBI influenced Oakland, California-based Huey Newton, while he was in and out of jail, to come into conflict with Afeni Shakur's New York Panther 21 fellow prison inmates. As previously detailed, this evolved into the East versus West Panther war that later had Geronimo Pratt and the New York Panther 21 aligned with Eldridge Cleaver (Ch.6).[530]

To set up the Panther war, the FBI wrote fake letters from the imprisoned NY Panther 21 and they used undercover agents to pass on false information to both Newton and the NY Panther 21. U.S. Intelligence then used journalists to collaborate in magnifying the conflict into the "East/West Panther war." And finally, the FBI used the created feud to cover up their murders of Panthers.[531]

Evidence suggests that the FBI similarly instigated a conflict between Tupac and Biggie to create a war in the rap world. Recall that U.S. Intelligence agents were instructed to "Obtain specimens of their handwriting [apparently to generate dissension through fake letters]. Provoke target groups into rivalries," regarding political musicians (Ch.14).[532]

The FBI remains the most likely culprit for writing anonymous letters to Tupac and paying prisoners that Tupac said had influenced him to believe that Biggie and Puffy were behind his shooting. Tupac's road manager, Charles "Man Man" Fuller, said that Tupac got anonymous letters in prison saying Biggie set up the Times Square shooting. Strangers in jail also told Tupac that Biggie had him shot.[533] U.S. Intelligence's Special Services Division of the Department of Corrections had a history of placing undercover agents and informants in prison to carry out this kind of work.[534]

Tyehimba tried to convince Tupac that Biggie likely had no part in the shooting. Biggie had visited Tupac in the hospital and also wrote him letters in prison saying he had no connection to the shooting. Tyehimba's words couldn't counteract so many people and letters saying Biggie *was* connected to the shooting. Tupac was largely convinced by the fall of '95. Still, Tupac's biological cousin, Billy Lesane, said that Tupac eventually came to think that Biggie simply should have either warned him or worked harder to help find out who shot him.[535]

The media escalated the East versus West rap war even before Tupac ever blamed Biggie for his shooting. By the summer of '95, media outlets began discussing an East versus West rap war that had nothing to do with Tupac or Biggie. Journalists then appeared to take several quotes of Tupac's out of context to magnify the assertions of suspected agent Jacques Agnant's associate Booker, who said Tupac blamed Biggie for his shooting. Agnant and Booker, who offered Tupac the $7,000 to come to the studio, were the prime suspects for setting up that shooting. With these suspected intelligence agents' help, several journalists hyped this conflict as the peak of an East/West rap war.[536]

22-Death Row Signs Him Up: Record Label as U.S. Intelligence Front Versus Tupac

Tupac's jail conditions also helped Intelligence influence Tupac to finally sign with Death Row Records. Death Row made several overtures to Tupac to sign with them, but he refused from 1993-95. Death Row paid Tupac $200,000 for one song, and both Death Row owners regularly traveled from Los Angeles to visit Tupac in the upstate New York prison where he was being held. Tupac manager Watani Tyehimba couldn't understand why Time Warner-Interscope also pushed for Tupac to switch from Interscope to their Death Row subsidiary as early as '93.[537]

Time Warner's aforementioned history of sharing leaders such as C.D. Jackson with U.S. Intelligence, along with its '90s purchase of rap companies, support that it aided U.S. Intelligence goals to manipulate Tupac and rap (Ch.20). Tupac finally stopped rejecting Time Warner's requests to sign with its subsidiary, Death Row. Tupac had spent 10 months in jail. The Appeals Court refused Tupac's $1.3 million bail offer for those many months that he waited for his appeal trial. But within days of Tupac's September of 1995 signing with Death Row Records, the Court of Appeals accepted virtually that same bail offer and released Tupac.[538] Death Row claimed to solely provide the bail money at this time (though writers said Interscope/Time Warner actually did so).[539] Few besides U.S. Intelligence could influence the Court of Appeals.

Other findings further support the notion that Death Row Records dualed as a front company for various U.S. Intelligence operations. Pulitzer Prize-winning writer Gary Webb first incidentally linked Death Row Records to the CIA from the record company's inception. Webb quoted the probation officer of national crack trafficker Freeway Ricky Ross. That probation officer said that Death Row silent partner Michael "Harry-O" Harris was one of Ross' two understudies.[540] The *New Yorker* magazine and other media described how Vice-President George Bush helped run key components of the CIA/Contra/Crack operations with CIA Director William Casey.[541] Webb detailed the CIA cocaine trafficking network, and a CIA Inspector General backed his findings in 1998.[542] Webb said Ross was their national point man, trafficking "multimillion-dollar cocaine shipments across America."[543] This would have made Michael Harris and Death Row Records important assets.

Ricky Ross worked closely with CIA-collaborating cocaine traffickers such as Daniel Blandon and Ron Lister in the '80s. Also, at that time, Lister met regularly with former CIA Covert Operations director Bill Nelson. Nelson had worked under George H. W. Bush at the CIA.[544]

As Vice-President, Bush appeared to renew that relationship when researchers say he also oversaw the National Security Council, which supervises the CIA.[545] This became the Iran-Contra-Crack scandal of the '80s that involved illegal arms sales to Iran, as well as drug trafficking profits, to illegally provide funds to the Nicaraguan Contras. The Contras tried to overthrow the socialist Sandinistas that had usurped the Nicaraguan governance in 1979 from a U.S.-backed brutal dictator, and then won an '84 election. U.S. Congress held hearings investigating Reagan/Bush officials and CIA-linked associates indicted on drug trafficking, murder and related charges. Some were convicted but Bush pardoned many others as President from '88-'92. Retired U.S. Navy Lt. Commander Al Martin, who worked in the Office of Naval Intelligence, blew the whistle on Iran-Contra. Martin detailed how Bush, Sr. oversaw most of these operations before Bush, Jr. nominated Iran-Contra co-conspirator Bill Gates to Secretary of Defense.[546]

Of further note, Death Row silent partner Michael Harris' work with Ricky Ross in this CIA-supplied network on the West Coast reflected a similar CIA cocaine network on the East Coast which affected Afeni Shakur's life. The primary owner of Death Row Records was attorney Dave Kenner. He represented drug kingpin Harris. Kenner introduced Harris to Death Row's managing partial owner, Suge Knight. Kenner then created a shell company with oversight ownership to gain ultimate control.[547]

As previously detailed, a member of the crack dealing East Coast network also appeared to do undercover work against the Shakur family. Ken "Legs" Saunders, got close to Afeni Shakur and sabotaged her life by repeatedly pushing crack on her in the '80s (Ch.10). This bore a striking similarity to the way Kenner got close to Afeni's son Tupac and subsequently manipulated him to fulfill U.S. Intelligence goals.[548] Also, the insertion of a spy as an activist entertainer's manager had at least one historical precedent with CIA spy Jay Richard Kennedy becoming a manager for activist entertainer Harry Belafonte (Ch.s 10, 40).[549]

A white Los Angeles police whistleblower, Detective Russell Poole, provided the best evidence that Death Row Records both produced rap albums and provided cover for U.S. Intelligence operations run by many working inside the record company. Death Row started its operations in early 1992 during George H.W. Bush's presidency. Poole found that "dozens and dozens" of his fellow police department officers were doing more that just moonlighting as security guards at Death Row Records.[550] Poole investigated Death Row with fellow LA Officer Ken Knox. When the two asked their superiors about all the cops working for Death Row, they were "told that some of these cops who worked for Death Row weren't considered security guards, but were more like confidants or troubleshooters or *covert agents*" [emphasis added].[551]

Suge Knight's apparent police intelligence collaboration likely started around 1990, as seen in his 11 guilty pleas from 1990-1995, mostly on violent charges, without the authorities ever revealing he violated his earlier probation. In 1990, a judge had issued him a 2-year suspended sentence and 3 years' probation for felony assault with a deadly weapon. Knight pled guilty to at least five more criminal charges within the next two years, but he never spent a day in jail during that time.[552]

From 1993-1995, Knight violently assaulted people many times without police charging him with a crime. For example, a security guard said Knight pounded him at black musician Prince's Glam Slam Club, causing spleen injuries that required multiple surgeries in 1993. Witnesses said Knight got into a shoot-out at the same club and beat up a music promoter inside the club seven months later.[553] As previously noted, Intelligence used the tactic of recruiting someone facing jail time to acquire agent infiltrators against the Panthers, such as one recruited in 1968 and used against Fred Hampton's Panthers in Chicago (Ch.5).[554]

Some writers suggested that one California assistant state's attorney, Lawrence Longo, protected Knight after the Death Row manager gave his daughter a recording contract. But interactions with any of the Longos only started in the middle of 1995, where as only one of Knight's eleven guilty pleas came after 1992. In a 1995 trial on a 1992 case, some writers believe Longo got Knight a suspended sentence despite very credible charges. In that case, two Death Row-contracted music employees brought police (curiously accompanied by the FBI) back to Death Row studios to show them the bullets lodged in a wall where they said Knight shot at them after first beating them. Knight received one of many suspended sentences at the trial (One of Knight's consulting attorneys who only represented him for that charge, Johnnie Cochran, said Longo was at first only a "low man on the totem pole" for that case. And then Longo was removed from the case).[555]

Desperate to get out of prison, Tupac signed a record deal with Death Row. This led to a tearful parting with his manager Watani Tyehimba. Tyehimba said he knew enough about Death Row Records that involving himself or his New Afrikan People's Organization with the record company could risk their safety. While Tyehimba's son continued to work for Tupac, Watani Tyehimba had to resign as business manager. Tupac's top legal consultant, NAPO Chair Chokwe Lumumba, also had to stop working with Tupac for this reason.[556]

Death Row owners Suge Knight and Dave Kenner appeared to continue the prison authorities' penal coercion tactics on Tupac. Two documented penal coercion tactics (previous chapter) involved physical threats and demonstrations of omnipotence by those making the threats.[557] Among other actions, Death Row made Tupac watch the physical beatings of Death Row employees who showed signs of leaving the record company.[558] Knight also led Tupac to take several trips with him to Hawaii as if to isolate Tupac further.[559]

Knight further appeared to use weed (marijuana) and alcohol in an attempt to manipulate Tupac. Evidence and disclosures suggests that U.S. Intelligence previously had agents try to use drugs and alcohol to manipulate Huey Newton upon his prison release, as well as Afeni Shakur (see above).[560] Death Row supplied Tupac with constant alcohol and weed.[561] Tupac had a higher risk of inheriting a susceptibility to addiction due to his mother's addiction.[562] Also, before entering prison, Tupac had reported a daily weed habit.[563] U.S. Intelligence appeared to use Tupac's and other musician's influence to help popularize marijuana in a black community where it fell way behind in usage compared to the white community, at the end of the '80s.

Others further described Tupac as having marijuana and alcohol abuse problems. A close friend, Jada Pinkett Smith, described Tupac as brilliant, well-read, and both a brother and father to her. But she also said that Tupac later became an addict and an alcoholic—"he was high all the time."[564] Closer to the time Tupac was breaking from Death Row, that behavior appeared to change. Possibly due to the insistence of his fiancée, Kidada Jones, among others, Tupac began trying to avoid alcohol and marijuana by the end of the summer of 1996. Rap music mogul Russell Simmons said that, at one party, Tupac danced with a woman in a wheel chair for four hours rather than drink and smoke with everyone.[565]

23-Death Row Police Goals: Target Tupac & Rap, Traffic Drugs, End Gang Truce

"When they ask me when will the violence cease?
When your troops stop shootin' niggas down in the streets
Niggas had enough, time to make a difference
Bear witness, own our own business…
Take the evil out the people they'll be actin' right
'Cause both Black and White is smokin' crack tonight
And the only time we deal is when we kill each other
It takes skill to be real, time to heal each other…
And ain't a secret don't conceal the fact
the penitentiary's packed, and it's filled with Blacks…
Cops give a damn about a Negro
Pull a trigga, kill a nigga, he's a hero…
Rather be dead then a poor nigga…
and if I die, I wonder if heaven's got a ghetto…
Just think, if niggas decide to retaliate (soulja in the house)."

"I Wonder if Heaven's Got a Ghetto," Tupac Shakur, *R U Still Down? [Remember me]*. Released in 1997.

Dave Kenner and Suge Knight appeared to have an agenda to negatively manipulate rap from the time they first founded the record label at the end of 1991. Suge Knight first divided top '80s rappers such as N.W.A., whom the FBI had targeted with a warning letter and attempts to cancel their concerts in the late '80s (Ch.15). After influencing rappers D.O.C and Andre "Dr. Dre" Young to leave N.W.A., Knight got Dr. Dre involved in negative promotion and behaviors. After Dre rapped against marijuana use on an NWA track, "Express Yourself," Knight convinced Dre to promote weed use, titling his CD after the slang name for particularly strong weed—*The Chronic*.[566] Knight also started public brawls around Dre, in which only he, not Dre, avoided arrest.[567]

Suge Knight next set his sights on getting East Coast rappers linked to activism to leave their labels and join Death Row. Knight tried to get New York's Def Jam rappers to sign to his label. Def Jam produced top political rappers Public Enemy and former N.W.A. star Ice Cube. Suge Knight and Death Row also attempted to use strong arm tactics to sign New York rappers Wu Tang Clan, who were affiliated with Black Liberation Movement leader Sonny Carson and Panther-inspired Hip Hop activists, Zulu Nation. Def Jam and Wu Tang Clan rebuffed Knight's advances.[568]

Suge Knight and Death Row further tried to disrupt rap events. Knight instigated violence in rap venues nationwide. These included the national rap convention in Atlanta at which Tupac was to speak, and in Miami where rap group 2 Live Crew had a music label.[569] That

Knight provoked violent conflicts at these events, yet police failed to arrest him much of the time, provides further evidence of his U.S. Intelligence-linked work.

As detailed in previous chapters, FBI Cointelpro undercover agents aided U.S. Intelligence in pitting activist leaders and groups against each other, such as creating the East/West Panther war, as an apparent excuse for agents' murders of Panthers (Ch.6). Similarly, Death Row's Suge Knight helped instigate the East/West rap war. Knight initiated these actions before Tupac had even signed with Death Row and before Tupac directly accused Biggie and his producer, Sean Puffy Combs, of orchestrating his shooting in Times Square. Knight criticized Combs at an awards ceremony in the summer of '95 and he blamed Combs for the murder of a Death Row associate. Knight also threatened and beat rap industry figures associated with Combs' Bad Boy Records. Combs had no past trace of such violent behavior.[570]

Knight and his employees, on the other hand, had a violent history. Knight was charged with many attacks and his police guards were highly suspected of murdering rap manager Bruce Richardson, who was popular with both Bloods and Crips gang members. Richardson, a 6'5" black belt, easily defended himself against Knight and his guards in public, after Richardson had confronted Knight about stealing rappers. When Richardson ended up dead in his home, Tupac called the rap manager's father to tell him he had no part in the murder. Tupac wouldn't say the same about Knight.[571]

Knight and others at Death Row appeared to use FBI Cointelpro tactics in trying to create divisions among top rap figures, particularly between Tupac and anyone else. Death Row apparently influenced Tupac to switch from writing songs promoting other rappers, to penning lyrics that attacked other rappers. Knight fueled the notion in Tupac's mind that Biggie and Combs set up his shooting. In doing so, he continued the likely U.S. Intelligence agenda involving the paid inmates and fake letters in jail, to promote this unsubstantiated claim about Biggie and Combs. Knight also continually encouraged violence between Death Row and Bad Boy Records.[572] Knight even convinced Tupac to turn against the rap producer he formerly idolized, Dr. Dre, after Dre split with Knight and Death Row early in 1996.[573]

Furthermore, Los Angeles police detective Russell Poole found evidence that police working inside Death Row Records were trafficking cocaine and guns. In documented interviews, one Tupac bodyguard at Death Row, former police and FBI employee Kevin Hackie, told Det. Poole that some of Suge Knight's closest associates were trafficking drugs and guns. Hackie identified three police officers who were close associates of Knight's and worked with Death Row in these activities: Reggie Gaines, David Mack and Ray Perez. Poole found abundant evidence of these officers' involvement in drug dealing, as well as in laundering money.[574]

Bodyguard Kevin Hackie said that Suge Knight and his Death Row security director, former cop Reggie Wright Jr., also had a history with Knight's drug dealing friends. Hackie said that when Reggie Wright Jr. worked for the Compton, California police, he ripped off drug dealers and helped Knight's dealing friends when they got in trouble. And, finally, a female Death Row employee told police detectives that she could provide information that Death Row owner Dave Kenner "was a major drug dealer." While police superiors said they failed to substantiate her claim, they also told Poole to drop his findings. Police further failed to act on other informants' reports of Death Row's drug and gun trafficking, and money laundering.[575]

While Death Row participated in these criminal operations, they also aided another U.S. Intelligence objective. Writers and activists, such as best-selling author Mike Davis, said police worked with the FBI in framing individuals who helped lead the Bloods and Crips gang peace summit and conversion to activism. Despite that Crips gang leader Dewayne Holmes led the drive for gang members to shift their work into legal community businesses, a judge jailed him on a ten-dollar theft charge at a gang unity dance. Congresswoman Maxine Waters and former governor Jerry Brown spoke on behalf of Holmes but couldn't keep him from getting a multi-year jail sentence for petty theft.[576]

Furthermore, people convicted of murdering unarmed gang peace leaders got off easy.[577] Under Operation Hammer, LA police agents targeted the gangs coordinating the peace summits. That operation included 100 FBI agents assigned to assist them after the LA riots (Ch.s 13, 14).[578]

Regarding these police activities, Det. Russell Poole failed to comment on what appeared to be a larger goal of Death Row Records on behalf of U.S. Intelligence—ending the gang peace truce. At least several moonlighting police officers in Death Row Records worked in these groups to disrupt gang peace summit events. One group included the aforementioned Death Row-linked Raphael "Ray" Perez, who worked for the elite undercover CRASH (Community Resources Against Street Hoodlums) anti-gang unit in the Rampart precinct.[579] A government report said that Operation Hammer was run inside of Perez's CRASH undercover anti-gang unit.[580]

"Former" LA cop Reggie Wright, Jr. supervised Death Row's moonlighting cops. Wright's father, Reggie Wright, Sr. was the Compton Police Gang Chief (Compton is a black city in Los Angeles County where rappers N.W.A. started). He formerly worked with his son in Compton, and likely directed him later.[581] Similarly, in the '60s Richard W. Held had led the LA's FBI Cointelpro unit and directed his agents inside the "black nationalist cultural group," the United Slaves, to murder Panthers (Ch.5), before targeting Newton, Bari and Tupac

(Ch.s 10-12). Held was also directed by his father, one-time FBI associate director, Richard G. Held.[582]

Wright and Perez supervised the dozens of police officers following Suge Knight's orders. These orders included conducting anti-gang peace truce work inside Death Row. Early on, Suge Knight had hired many Bloods and Crips gang members from his teen Compton neighborhood to work at Death Row Records, though he subsequently showed favor to his friends in the Bloods.[583] Compton's gang leaders were some of the first to ratify the 1992 gang peace truce and conversion to activism.[584] Insiders described how Knight provoked huge brawls between Crips and Bloods at his recording studio and further used his armed moonlighting police gaurds to protect him as he assaulted anyone who tried to stop the fights.[585]

At least one of these conflicts ended up with Death Row-employed Bloods murdering a Crip in the presence of, if not with the active participation of, Death Row cops. At a Soul Train Music Awards after-party that Death Row held, a group of Death Row Bloods killed a Crip named Kelly Jamerson. Some of these Bloods could have been undercover cops, as some Death Row cops were known to dress in Bloods colors. Jamerson had flashed a gang sign to Death Row rapper Snoop Dogg, a former Crip, and the Bloods beat Jamerson to death. Witnesses gave reports about this murder to uniformed police, but the police department never followed up.[586] In a separate incident, when a Death Row Crip said he communicated with a gunman by cell phone, in an attempt to retaliate against Knight for hunting him down, a police car immediately intervened as if monitoring his phone.[587]

24-Death Row Lines Him Up: FBI Watch Radical Tupac's Murder in Mobland

By August of 1996, Tupac Shakur appeared to have had more success at divorcing himself from the effects of Death Row's coercive tactics. In interviews, Tupac talked about how he would soon leave Death Row. He settled down, moving in with his fiancée, Kidada Jones, the daughter of *Vibe* magazine-owning, music-producing mogul Quincy Jones. Kidada said that Tupac also had found a new apartment for them to move into so they could get out of their Death Row-leased home. And, she said, he talked about having kids.[588]

While many said Tupac's energy was lower and his mood dimmer due to his concerns about his enchainment to Death Row, he started regaining his more fun-loving side that summer of '96. In one video, Tupac was filmed working in the studio. Grabbing a Death Row employee wearing a tank-top and pointing to the young guy's Chinese letters tattoo, Tupac said the guy had "Chinese letters like he's been somewhere. Shit, you ain't never left the block." Looking right into the video camera, Tupac pointed at the tattoo and added, "You know what this says? 'Two egg rolls with hot sauce, to go.'"[589]

In Tupac Shakur's last month he also marked his return to radical leftist politics. Tupac completed production of his last CD, *don killuminati: the 7 day theory*, and it included one of his most explicitly radical political tracks since his first CD. Besides his track "Against All Odds," which, as mentioned earlier, named "Haitian Jacques" Agnant as working for the FBI to set up his shooting (Ch.18), his "White Manz World" included excerpts of radical activist speeches.

"White Manz World" included excerpts from one of his own speeches, as well as one from a Malcolm X speech. In his own speech he dedicated himself to his Panther political prisoner mentors—Mutulu Shakur, Geronimo Pratt, Sekou Odinga and Mumia Abu-Jamal. The Malcolm X excerpt quoted, "the masses of the people—white and black, red, yellow and brown and vulnerable—are suffering in this nation....Native Americans, blacks and other non-white people were to be the burden bearers for the real citizens of the nation."[590] Tupac further signaled a return to leftist activism in his interviews. He discussed some of his political plans, including finishing a movie script he was writing about his mother's Black Panther experience. He also planned to organize around independent electoral politics and to open community centers.[591]

By this time, Tupac defied continued Intelligence attempts to keep rappers in conflict, saying he wanted to re-unify East and West coast rappers. Tupac said that his "W" hand signs didn't stand for "the West" anymore, but for "War" on behalf of a unified Black America.[592] He also talked about politicizing various ethnic groups, reading Mao Tse Tong and returning to his family's political work, which, once having left Death Row, he could do again with his revolutionary mentors in the New Afrikan People's Organization.[593]

By his 25th birthday in June of '96, Tupac Shakur had reached megastardom. Tupac's first Death Row release, *All Eyez On Me*, debuted in January of '96 as a chart-topping double CD with $10 million in sales—the second highest first week sales ever at that time (only topped by *The Beatles Anthology* in '95).[594] It had sold 7 million units by August.

Tupac's percentage of profit would soon massively increase by producing his own CDs as he had imminent exit plans from Death Row Records. He had started his own record and film production company, headed by imprisoned ex-Bronx Panther leader Sekou Odinga's wife, Yaasmyn Fula.[595] By that summer, Tupac argued with Knight about the advance money his contract promised, almost to the point of getting into a fistfight.[596] At the end of August, Tupac finished the CD he claimed should have completed his 3 CD contract and fired his contracted lawyer, Death Row co-owner Dave Kenner.[597]

Ten days after Tupac fired Dave Kenner, concretely signaling his Death Row departure, he was scheduled to attend a Mike Tyson boxing match with Suge Knight in Vegas. Tupac tried to back out of attending, even though he usually congratulated his fan and friend, Tyson, just after the matches.[598] Tupac was wary of this event's timing and locale. Death Row employees said that Kenner's connection with a New York Mafia family was common knowledge, as was the New York Mafia's gambling-based development of Vegas.[599]

U.S. Intelligence had a history of collaborating with the Mafia in various operations. A researcher got family members of one Albert Carone to provide statements and official documents showing how Carone had straddled the Mafia, the U.S. military (as a colonel), and New York police.[600] Among other instances, Martin Luther King's family trial lawyer, William Pepper, provided two examples of such corroborative work, each backed by press reports from the BBC (Ch.2). Pepper explained how Mafia work against MLK provided the CIA with "an officially deniable local contract and assassination operation ostensibly carried out exclusively by organized crime."[601]

Death Row had many links to Mafia figures who, in turn, had links to U.S, governmental agencies. Several researchers mentioned Death Row's links to the Genovese Mafia family,[602] the Mafia family with the longest history of U.S. Intelligence work.[603] Death Row attorney Oscar Goodman acted as the consigliere for the Mafia, keeping members jail-free for years. Goodman was elected mayor of Las Vegas by the end of the '90s. Goodman's partner, Death Row attorney Dave Chesnoff, was a former assistant U.S. attorney. [604] CIA documents also detailed how the Intelligence Agency contracted Las Vegas businessman, Johnny Roselli, who was "a high-ranking member of the 'syndicate'" to orchestrate Cuban leader Fidel Castro's assassination.[605]

Despite his worries about Vegas as a setup, Tupac decided to attend the Tyson fight with Knight on September 7, 1996. Tupac finally decided to go partly due to a benefit concert that he was scheduled to take part in later that night in Vegas. The benefit show stemmed from a summer trial in Los Angeles for weed possession that an elderly white judge had presided over. After reading a report on Tupac's life, the judge called him "remarkable" and sentenced him to do the benefit concert, shocking an LA District Attorney who tried to get Tupac's bail revoked.[606]

That weekend, Death Row made several changes to leave Tupac virtually unprotected for the first time. A day before Tyson's boxing match, Death Row fired one of Tupac's two main bodyguards, Kevin Hackie. The reasons given for this vary, but Hackie reportedly had been encouraging Tupac to move to Atlanta. Suge Knight and Reggie Wright found out about this and fired Hackie.[607] The following day, Tupac's other bodyguard, Frank Alexander, said that Reggie Wright told him he couldn't carry his gun because Death Row had forgotten to register it. Wright further gave Alexander a cell phone with a dead battery.[608]

Hours before the Saturday night Tyson fight, Suge Knight held a party with much reported alcohol and weed at his Vegas mansion. Moonlighting Las Vegas cops attended this party with the moonlighting LA cops in Death Row.[609] They then went to the MGM Grand Hotel which housed the boxing arena where they watched Tyson knockout his opponent in the first round.

After the match, the Death Row group walked through the MGM's huge lobby. Death Row employee Travon Lane and others influenced Tupac to join them in a conflict with a young guy they saw standing in the lobby named Orlando Anderson. The Death Row employees convinced Tupac that Anderson had previously been with several Crips who attacked them. That Tupac may have drank or smoked at the party, as well as the fact that two Crips had once punched him for no reason, may have helped the Death Row group get Tupac to join in this beating. Tupac also was less than a year removed from his 10 months of imprisonment. The group briefly attacked Anderson in the hotel lobby and then left, unstopped by the many guards and police who immediately came to the scene.[610]

Soon after the incident, the large Death Row entourage began the drive to Tupac's post-match benefit concert. Many disclosures about the drive support that it was a U.S. Intelligence-planned procession to Tupac's murder. Knight convinced Tupac to drive with him rather than taking the Hummer Tupac had originally planned to drive. A Death Row bodyguard also said that the security for the drive was unlike any he had previously done for Death Row. He said that two armed bodyguards would normally ride in the car with Knight and

Tupac, but no one rode with them on this occasion. Unarmed guard Alexander followed in the car behind Knight and Tupac.[611]

Just-fired bodyguard Kevin Hackie, who also worked for the FBI but had grown loyal to Tupac (Ch.25), claimed that he had FBI documents to prove that an FBI agent and an ATF agent were in the entourage of cars following Knight and Tupac.[612] *Las Vegas Sun* police reporter Cathy Scott concurred about the FBI presence. She wrote that it had been widely printed that Tupac "was under surveillance by the FBI at the time of his shooting."[613] Many reports also placed Death Row's Los Angeles police officers, such as Richard McCauley, accompanying other Death Row security in Vegas.[614]

Tupac sat in the passenger seat as Knight, followed by the Death Row entourage, stopped at a light by a crowded sidewalk in front of the Maxim Hotel just off The Strip (Las Vegas Boulevard). With a Death Row car in front of them and behind them, Death Row employee Travon Lane pulled up to the left of Knight and Tupac, but a little ahead of them. A car full of women stopped just behind Lane's car. The women grabbed Tupac's attention by calling out to him. Just then, a white Cadillac stopped to Tupac's right partly ahead of him and one or two gunmen from the car fired over thirteen rounds. Four bullets hit Tupac, including two in the chest. Knight's forehead was reportedly cut, though most say that only a ricocheting bullet fragment or glass shard hit him. Reports also claimed that no guards in the following cars fired at the assailants. The Cadillac fled from the scene and was never apprehended.[615]

25-Knight/Death Row Aid Murder & Police Cover-up, Reignite Bloods/Crips War

"In the event of my demise
When my heart can beat no more
I hope that I die 4 a principle
or a belief that I had lived 4
I will die before my time
because I feel the shadow's depth
so much I wanted 2 accomplish
before I reached my death
I have come to grips with the possibility
and wiped the last tear from my eyes
I loved all who were positive
in the event of my demise."

Tupac Shakur, "In the Event of My Demise," from *The Rose That Grew from Concrete*, his collected poems.

The scenario of Tupac Shakur's shooting both suggested Suge Knight's involvement and suggested that he was a low man on the U.S. Intelligence's operation hierarchy. While 170-pound Tupac was hit four times, 330-pound Knight miraculously avoided getting directly hit by any of the 13+ bullets.[616] The danger of the scenario suggests Knight didn't know how precarious it would be, but the care the gunmen took not to hit Knight supports that they must have done so on purpose.

Tupac reportedly tried to jump into the back seat and Knight said in a police interview that he pulled him down. Knight implied that he tried to cover Tupac's body with his own, thereby risking taking the bullets himself, despite their recent fights and Tupac leaving his label.[617]

Knight's actions immediately following the shooting implicate him more forcefully. After the shooting stopped, Knight did a U-turn and raced in the opposite direction from the closest hospital, which was located on the block of the club holding the benefit show. Knight worked several years to purchase that club and went to college in the small town of Vegas, supporting that he knew of the hospital. Knight also failed to call for an ambulance with a cell phone on his dashboard.[618]

Knight drove wildly through lights and over concrete medians back towards the MGM Hotel. Many in the Death Row entourage followed him, as did two cops on bicycles at the scene. Knight flattened all of his tires on the medians and stopped when he got stuck on one. Police surrounded his car, ordered all at the scene to lie on the street, and then paramedics helped take blood-drenched Tupac to a hospital.[619]

Veteran *Las Vegas Sun* police reporter Cathy Scott described Vegas police actions as aiding the escape of Tupac's murderers. Scott presented a "long list of questionable decisions" by police.[620] First, the bike cops were within yards of the shooting and failed to secure the scene. They also either failed to call in the location or the police chiefs ignored their calls.[621] Then, police lost the opportunity to gather evidence and witnesses due to the fact that they searched for evidence for 20 minutes at the location where Knight ended up getting his car stuck on an embankment several miles from the shooting scene.

Scott said that police officials further decided to go against other standard procedures. They didn't put out an All Points Bulletin, they didn't use a police helicopter to search for the killers, and they didn't take any aerial photos.[622] These actions occurred despite Las Vegas cops saying that Tupac's shooting was the biggest murder case in Vegas history.[623]

Such cover-up appeared to continue for months. Eyewitnesses to the shooting said that Vegas police ignored them, and some officers contradicted official police statements that said they had no forthcoming witnesses. [624] Tupac's back-up rappers and bodyguard in the car following his all said they saw the assailants. Rappers Yafeu Fula and Malcolm Greenridge both said they thought they could identify the shooter, while bodyguard Frank Alexander said he saw the assailants before the gunfire. Police appeared to ignore the three's assertions until the *Los Angeles Times* reprinted their statements. [625]

Police then failed to cooperate with media groups trying to assist with the investigation, including TV's *Unsolved Mysteries'* coverage of the murder and promotion of the police call-in tip line. Police reporter Cathy Scott said that police shows like *Unsolved Mysteries* usually help police, and this particular show inspired many phone calls. These calls included one that appeared to be a good tip. Police later reported that they got "too many calls" and stopped answering phones on this tip line. [626]

Furthermore, Los Angeles police officer Ken Knox found fellow LA police officer Richard McCauley working at the front desk in the Death Row Records recording studio in early 1996. Knox reported this to his superiors whom he successfully influenced to officially reprimand McCaulley. A police chief ostensibly ordered him to quit this side work. Many witnesses and hotel records showed that McCaulley was still working for Death Row in Las Vegas when Tupac was shot there.[627] Despite this open defiance of an order, McCaulley was promoted to sergeant shortly after Tupac's murder.[628] It's also interesting that McCaulley's father, Richard McCaulley, Sr., was a veteran LAPD officer, just as was Death Row Security Chief Reggie Wright Jr.'s father was chief of the Compton gang unit.[629] Like the Held father and son FBI leaders, recruitment of veterans' sons may have ensured more loyalty (Ch.5, 12)

The details about a possible police operation against Tupac came out much later. Las Vegas police investigators of Tupac Shakur's murder told white Los Angeles police detective Russell Poole that they had loads of evidence in Tupac's murder and that they didn't plan to follow up on any of it. The Vegas detectives told Poole that police superiors said they were not supposed to actually investigate Tupac's murder.[630]

U.S. Intelligence appeared to have several motives for helping Knight and Death Row cops orchestrate Tupac Shakur's murder. U.S. Intelligence first feared Tupac's political use of his new mega-stardom financed by his large wealth and power. While he was alive, each of Tupac's solo CDs sold more than double the preceding one. Producing his own CDs would exponentially increase Tupac's already multimillion-dollar profits. He also had movie role offers pouring in, and his planned marriage to Kidada Jones would have had him marrying into her *Vibe*-owning father Quincy's wealth and influence.[631]

Tupac's expanding influence and appeal, which went well beyond black America, also would concern U.S. Intelligence. Tupac's fans included fashion designers who feted Tupac and Kidada, a model, with free clothes, and mainstream magazines that ran features on him. Tupac also starred in two new films, *Gridlock'd* and *Gang Related,* both of which hit theaters within months of his death. His close friends ranged from black entertainers and pro athletes to Madonna, Mickey Rourke and Interscope Entertainment mogul Ted Fields.

Furthermore, about 70% of people who bought his albums were white. Many entertainment stars cited Tupac's incredible charm that even won over the elderly white judge who sentenced him to do the benefit concert scheduled after the Vegas Tyson fight. That judge was so moved by Tupac that he wouldn't cancel a post-death review hearing on the case just so he could be around people who knew the rapper.[632]

As mentioned before, by the last months of his life, Tupac had many activist projects. Tupac promised to set up a new community center after each CD, the first of which had already opened in LA. Tupac also stated his intent of returning to his family's revolutionary politics. In one of his last interviews he said that now he would "mix the street life with respected, known, and proven military philosophy." And finally, he stated his plans to collaborate with LA Crip gang leader-turned author, Sanyika Shakur (a.k.a. Monster Kody Scott), a converted revolutionary socialist. This would have particularly set off U.S. Intelligence alarms.[633]

Regarding Tupac's plans with Sanyika Shakur, U.S. Intelligence had yet another motive for murdering the rap star. They apparently saw an opportunity to both end Tupac's goal of radicalizing gangs while also using his shooting to re-ignite the Bloods versus Crips gang war with the aid of Death Row and Suge Knight. Eyewitness Frank Alexander believed Suge Knight had paid alleged Crip Orlando Anderson to wait for the Death Row group in the hotel lobby after the Tyson fight and take a beating from them as a cover-up reason for

Tupac's murder.[634] Det. Russell Poole said that Alexander and Tupac's other bodyguard, Kevin Hackie, both said that they believed Knight, Reggie Wright, Jr. and Anderson all helped set up Tupac's murder. Documentary director Nick Broomfield got Hackie to say on film that Death Row was behind Tupac's murder.[635]

Years after Tupac's death, Hackie disclosed publicly that he had worked undercover for the FBI the whole time he worked for Death Row, from 1992 to 1996.[636] He had apparently become close to Tupac and defied his employer in telling Tupac to move to Atlanta and avoid Las Vegas. Afeni Shakur concurred with Hackie about Tupac's animosity towards Knight, saying Tupac's work for Knight was living "in bondage." Tupac's Aunt Yaasmyn [Fula] agreed with Hackie on Tupac trying to go to Atlanta instead of Vegas his last weekend. Hackie encouraged Tupac to move near his family and mentors in Atlanta, likely for protection. NAPO Security Director Watani Tyehimba lived there near Afeni, while Tyehimba's son worked for Tupac in LA. Death Row fired Hackie days before the Vegas shooting. After Poole tried to use his reports from Hackie against Death Row cops, Hackie said authorities framed him and he spent months in jail.[637]

Hackie disclosed working undercover for the FBI when he sat as part of a panel discussion for a presentation of the DVD *Tupac: Assassination,* and got into a debate with a police officer in the audience.[638] This DVD presented Death Row bodyguard Michael Moore who was a back-up guard for Tupac. Moore also backed Frank Alexander's assertion that Reggie Wright told all of the Death Row bodyguards they were not to carry guns that night due to a lack of state permits. Moore said this shocked him and he, alone, said that he has a personal gun and permit. Moore said he then debated Wright all day about guarding Tupac, as the regular substitute for the recently fired Hackie. Moore finally gave in and left Tupac's side to go directly to Club 661 with Wright. Moore said that at about the time Tupac was shot, he heard a voice come over Wright's radio saying, "Got him!"[639]

Within several days of Tupac's shooting, Knight visited the Las Vegas police department at least twice and talked to the FBI at least once. Sources described only one of these three communications as related to the shooting. One reason given for talking to the FBI, including reporting as an ex-felon in a new state, remains dubious since Knight owned a house in Vegas and often traveled there.[640]

But most curiously, within those first 72 hours after Tupac was shot and he lay dying in the hospital, Knight was talking to the FBI and the police. Knight was also helping to restart the Bloods versus Crips gang war in that short time period. Suge Knight and Death Row Bloods members' actions motivated these gang killings on September 9 in L.A., two days after Tupac's shooting.[641]

In L.A., a Compton police informant's affidavit stated that Suge Knight and his anti-gang CRASH unit confidantes helped spark the war by having their Bloods spread the rumor that lobby scuffle victim Anderson killed Tupac. Anderson lived with his uncle, known Compton Crip Dwayne Keith "Keffy-D" Davis. Death Row employees such as Travon Lane who encouraged Tupac's scuffle with Anderson, along with Bloods working at Death Row, quickly spread the word that the Compton Crips killed Tupac.[642]

Poole said that another police informant claimed that Knight delivered an entire load of AK-47 assault rifles to Bloods gang members at the Nickerson Gardens housing project in L.A. the night after Tupac was shot. The following night, the Bloods versus Crips violence started. It began with shootings of Compton Crip leaders within a 5-10 minute drive of the Nickerson Gardens Bloods.[643] The Bloods and Crips gang sets living in the Nickerson Gardens project in the Watts area of LA had been the first to agree to the peace truce several years before. Other Watts gangs and Compton's Bloods and Crips gang sets were the next to join the truce.[644] The murders revived the Bloods/Crips gang war after their several-year truce and political activist conversion (Ch.14).[645]

In Las Vegas, hospital spokesmen held press conferences for the mass of national and international reporters asking about Tupac's health status. Political activists, entertainers and athletes joined Tupac's family and extended family at the hospital.

Fiancée Kidada Jones described sitting by Tupac's bedside, asking Tupac if he knew she loved him. She said he gave a slight head nod and movement of his foot. Kidada then played Don McLean's "Vincent," a song Tupac loved because it was about Vincent Van Gough, whose art Afeni Shakur had given him as a kid. McLean sang, "now I understand, what you tried to say to me, how you suffered for your sanity, how you tried to set them free. They would not listen they did not know how, perhaps they'll listen now."

People close to the reignited Bloods/Crips gang violence might have felt this way about Tupac as they soon spread a message to stop the violence. Tupac slipped into a coma, his heart failed several times, and Afeni Shakur decided to pull the life support on September 13, 1996.[646] Twenty Crips and Bloods died in the revived gang war in the seven days after Tupac's shooting. But on September 13, while many mourned Tupac's death, activists spread the word that the Crips may not have been behind Tupac's murder, and the shootings ended.[647]

26-Threat-Timing Tactic in Murder of Top Witness, a Panther's Son; Suspect Killed

"In time I learned a few lessons, never fall for riches
Apologize to my true sisters, far from bitches
Help me raise my Black nation
Reparations are due, it's true...
Especially Black, bear with me, can't you see
We're under attack
I never meant to cause drama
To my sister and Mama
Will we make it to better times
in this white man's world...

This is dedicated to my motherfuckin' teachers: Mutulu Shakur, Geronimo Pratt, Mumia Abu-Jamal, Sekou Odinga."

Tupac Shakur, "White Man'z World," *Makavelli: Don Killuminati, The 7 Day Theory*, released 8 weeks after his death, 11/5/96.

"Tupac Amaru Shakur – Assassinated by COINTELPRO."
Mutulu Shakur, www.daretostruggle.org

The cover-up of Tupac's murder appeared as large of an operation as the accumulated attempts to murder him, and it continued for years. *Las Vegas Sun* reporter Cathy Scott heavily investigated Tupac's murder and found out that Yafeu Fula was a forthcoming witness. After Scott pressed police spokesmen on the issue of Fula, they admitted to her that he said he thought he could identify Tupac's murderer in a photo line-up. But in press conferences police maintained that there were no forthcoming witnesses. Scott detailed how police then proceeded to ignore Fula for two months. [648]

In November of '96, the night of Mike Tyson's next boxing match, a gunman shot Yafeu Fula in the head in his girlfriend's stairwell while he reportedly wore a bullet-proof vest.[649] This suggests that U.S. Intelligence's used their threat-timing tactic (Ch.11). Media repeated police saying Fula's murder was drug related, despite no evidence to support the claim and Fula not having a criminal record.[650]

U.S. Intelligence had several reasons to use a timing tactic on Tupac's backup rapper Fula. Fula was the top witness in Tupac's murder. Fula also represented another radical political potential entertainment star, as he had Hollywood good looks and his father was the imprisoned former Bronx Black Panther leader, Sekou Odinga. Also, Yafeu's mother, Afeni's longtime friend Yaasmyn, managed Tupac's new record company.[651]

Past incidents suggest they had already used this tactic regarding Tupac (Ch.11-2). As mentioned, gunmen had attacked Tupac on the anniversary of Huey Newton's death and other gunmen murdered the top forthcoming witness to Tupac's previous New York shooting, Randy "Stretch" Walker, exactly one year after gunmen shot Tupac in Times Square.[652] As previously detailed about Newton and MLK's deaths, the use of this threat timing would provide a conscious or subconscious warning to others.

Other murders linked to Tupac's support a continuing cover-up around Tupac's death. Increasing evidence supported that hotel lobby-beating victim, Orlando Anderson, played a part in Tupac's murder. As mentioned, Death Row bodyguard and eyewitness Frank Alexander believed that Death Row paid Anderson to take that beating as a set up for Tupac's murder.[653] Anderson contradicted himself as to why he was at the MGM. He was also caught lying about how he got a Tyson fight ticket. Many said that Anderson acted very strangely the night of his assault at the MGM Grand hotel. MGM security said Anderson didn't want to file a complaint or say who attacked him, and they said he "wasn't angry at all—he just wanted out of there." A friend said he saw Anderson a few minutes after the incident, and he "didn't appear to be too upset about what happened, "saying 'everything was cool.'"[654]

Reports on the next two days after the shooting further incriminated Anderson. An affidavit filed in court by Compton, California police said that the Tupac-murdering gunmen's vehicle was taken to an auto shop in Anderson's Compton neighborhood two days after the shooting (Vegas detectives reportedly had a vast amount of such evidence they purposely ignored, Ch.25).[655] Also, within 48 hours of Tupac's shooting, a woman saw Anderson transporting guns into his Crip uncle Keffy-D Davis's house with other known Crips that day. The gang peace truce ended that night in Compton. Police found many arms and ammunition in Keffy-D's house as well as a house from which Crip Jerry "Monk" Bonds reportedly fled. [656]

Several key people believed Anderson played a role in Tupac's murder set up. Det. Russell Poole believed Suge Knight staged the lobby scuffle with Anderson to have "it on [hotel security] videotape to set up a motive for the killing of Tupac Shakur that would point the blame at the Compton Crips." [657] Filmmaker Nick Broomfield referred to Anderson as the Lee Harvey Oswald of Tupac's murder. During off-film interviews with Orlando Anderson's friends, family, and lawyer, Broomfield learned that Anderson received payments from an unknown source, and that he'd acquired a very expensive car shortly after Tupac's murder.[658] Also, Afeni Shakur filed a wrongful death lawsuit, claiming that Anderson shot her son and that Crip Jerry Bonds drove the gunman's car.[659]

Further investigation into Orlando Anderson's life supported the police intelligence funding to which Broomfield alluded. Writers said Anderson lacked the regular gang trappings. Friends said that he didn't drink, smoke, use drugs, or sport tattoos, and he didn't have any criminal convictions. He did appear to attain illicit funds from somewhere. Anderson, known also as "Baby Lane," lived a lower middle-class lifestyle in the Compton area of Los Angeles. He fathered four children by the age of 23 and had never been gainfully employed. He had never filed a federal tax return and had no obvious means of support. Anderson was also starting up his own record company without any known source of financing.[660]

Death Row guard Kevin Hackie believed Death Row killed Orlando Anderson as further cover-up. A gunman murdered Anderson in May of '98 at a Compton car wash. Police reported that it happened in a shootout over money. The shooting ended in two other deaths and one arrest.[661] Russell Poole said he found a mixed amount of reliability among police department reports and found more consistent credibility in informants such as Hackie, who believed the Death Row Security Director and "former" police officer Reggie Wright participated in Anderson's murder. Hackie said Wright owned a champagne-colored Chevy Blazer that matched the description of the suspect's car in the Anderson shooting.[662]

U.S. Intelligence also appeared to target other important people close with Tupac besides just Yafeu Fula. Tupac's political mentor and business manager, Watani Tyehimba, had a son, Yakhisizwe Tyehimba. He was close to Tupac's age and kept working closely with Tupac in Los Angeles. Yakhisizwe ended up dead shortly after Tupac's murder."

27-FBI & ATF Watch Again as Death Row Cops are Nailed in Biggie's Murder

Six months after Tupac Shakur's murder, a gunman murdered chart-topping rapper Biggie Smalls (a.k.a. Notorious B.I.G., born Christopher Wallace). The gunman fatally shot Biggie from his car after midnight on March 9, 1997 in Los Angeles, a few months after the murder of Yafeu Fula and a year before that of Orlando Anderson.

Los Angeles police detective Russell Poole first took an interest in Biggie's murder investigation after he investigated the murder of Death Row cop Kevin Gaines. Working on that case led to him stumbling upon the corrupt activities of Death Row's Los Angeles police officers. In doing so, he gained an assignment as an investigator in Biggie's case—the next Tupac-linked murder.[663]

Poole proved a highly credible source on the activities of the Los Angeles police. Poole's father worked for decades in the LAPD, and Poole himself had 10 years of homicide investigation experience. During those years, he received regular commendations and promotions to reach the high level Bureau of Special Operations. Poole's investigation led filmmaker Nick Broomfield to feature him in a major theatrical release, *Biggie and Tupac*. *Rolling Stone* and *Esquire* magazine writer Randall Sullivan also featured Poole in his book, *LAbyrinth* (2002). Both film and book came after Poole's resignation due to the LAPD stonewalling his investigation.[664]

Poole's investigation, with the help of fellow officer Ken Knox, accumulated direct witnesses and solid evidence that LAPD cops working with Death Row orchestrated Biggie's murder and trafficked drugs (As detailed, Poole had also found evidence that Death Row cops orchestrated Tupac's murder). According to Poole, these cops murdered Biggie to further divert people's attention. They wanted to make it look as if Tupac's murder stemmed from the East/West rap rivalry. When Poole communicated these findings to his LAPD superiors, they ignored his reports, transferred him to another division, and threatened him.[665]

Biggie was murdered when a gunman pulled up next to his car and fatally shot him outside an Automotive Museum party in early March of 1997. Quincy Jones' Quest Records and *Vibe* magazine held the party in conjunction with the Eleventh Annual *Soul Train* Music Awards. Many Los Angeles police officers were present at the high publicity event, including some who were moonlighting as bodyguards for the record label that produced Biggie, Sean "Puffy" Combs' Bad Boy Records. But few attempted to pursue the gunman, and the guards reportedly couldn't even get a partial license plate number or a good enough description for police to trace the gunman's car.[666]

Biggie's friends, rapper James "Lil' Caese" Lloyd and Damien "D-Rock" Butler, were riding in the back seat of Biggie's car when he was murdered. They described the shooter for a police artist to make a composite sketch of the gunman the next day. When *Las Vegas Sun* reporter Cathy Scott asked the Los Angeles police for a copy of the sketch, they said it wasn't kept on file. That sketch took 36 months to get into the media and then only when it was leaked.[667] Butler and Lil' Caese Lloyd's police sketch of the killer reportedly matched Harry Billups (a.k.a. Amir Muhammad)—a close friend of Death Row cop David Mack.[668]

Another witness more clearly identified Billups. Filmmaker Broomfield showed a photo line-up to Eugene Deal, a New York State Parole Officer working as a bodyguard for Sean Puffy Combs. From that line-up Deal picked Harry Billups as Biggie's killer. Deal's description of the killer also matched Lloyd's description of Biggie's murderer.[669]

Det. Poole presented witness Damien Butler another photo line-up and Butler identified police officer David Mack as standing just outside the Automotive Museum party in streetclothes, shortly before Biggie's murder.[670] More evidence indicting Mack was that Biggie's murderer used a German made brand of bullets rarely found in LA, yet Mack had them in his home.[671] And, Mack owned a dark-colored Chevrolet Impala, the type that Biggie's assailant used for the drive-by murder, but LAPD superiors wouldn't allow Det. Poole to do forensic tests on Mack's car.[672]

People also saw Orlando Anderson at Biggie's murder scene. As previously detailed, evidence supports Anderson's work with Suge Knight in the Vegas lobby scuffle to help set up a false "gang retaliation" motive for Tupac's murder. That people saw Anderson with his Crip uncle, Keith Davis, and the Death Row cops, furthers the evidence of connections between the Death Row cops and the murders of Biggie and Tupac.[673]

Other prominent witnesses to Death Row's murder of Biggie included Death Row accountant Mark Hylland. Hylland described how Suge Knight, accompanied by Death Row's police associates Raphael "Ray" Perez and Dave Mack, gave him money to obtain the gun that they said they would use to kill Biggie. Hylland gave details of these incidents on film for Nick Broomfield as well as for Det. Poole when he was officially investigating the murder. Poole found that Hylland's story matched his airline flights and hotel stays from LA to Phoenix, where Hylland said a Phoenix cop gave him the murder weapon, with which he apparently drove back to LA.[674]

Most importantly, similar to reports of an FBI agent amongst the Death Row entourage tailing Tupac's car at his murder scene, an FBI agent was present at Biggie's murder. Det. Russell Poole and Nick Broomfield confirmed the *Los Angeles Times*' report that New York police agents were present when the gunman shot Biggie.[675] Poole and Broomfield further confirmed that one agent was a New York detective who also worked for the FBI and took pictures of Biggie minutes before his shooting.[676] Award-winning reporter Cathy Scott further said it became widely reported that the FBI watched both Biggie and Tupac's murders. She also said that FBI agents told her they are supposed to stop their surveillance and intervene if a crime takes place during their surveillance.[677]

In his book *LAbyrinth*, Randall Sullivan reported on Poole's investigation. Poole gave Sullivan copies of all his police documents and they backed Sullivan's note that the FBI/New York detective taking pictures of Biggie within minutes of his murder was Det. Oldham. Accompanying Oldham was another member of the New York police working with a federal agency, Special Agent Timothy Reilly of Alcohol, Tobacco and Firearms (ATF).[678] Former FBI informant Kevin Hackie, who claimed to have documents proving that an FBI agent followed in the line of cars behind Tupac's when he was murdered, also claimed that agent was accompanied by an ATF agent.[679]

Larry Shears, a former ATF agent, said that the ATF had a history of placing murder contracts on left-wing activists. In the '70s, Shears testified in court that the ATF contracted out the [unconsumated] murders of Black Panther Eldridge Cleaver and labor organizer Caesar Chavez. The ATF also collaborated with the FBI to target Huey Newton at that time.[680] And finally, the FBI and ATF worked in the riot unit Joint Task Force-LA that waged a war on gangs just *after* the riots and Bloods/Crips peace truce.[681]

In their questioning of Biggie's friends, police incidentally revealed agents' surveillance of Biggie within minutes of his murder. Lil' Caese Lloyd, one of the passengers sitting behind Biggie, said that police showed him these FBI photos of the Museum party. "Do you know who this is?" they asked him, not realizing that they were pointing at Lloyd himself. The photos were taken "as late as ten minutes before the killing," according to a *Los Angeles Times* story.[682]

For his documentary, *Biggie and Tupac*, Nick Broomfield filmed his discussions with Biggie's mother, Voletta Wallace, who asked Biggie's old friend Lloyd to come over and talk with Broomfield. Lloyd told Broomfield about the police showing him the pictures. Broomfield then tracked down the FBI/NYPD Detective Oldham who took the pictures. Broomfield filmed at least one scene that was both grave and humorous. He showed himself driving through traffic as he called Det. Oldham with his cell phone, miking both sides of the conversation. Broomfield asked if this was "Detective..." blanking out the name. Oldham said "yes" and confirmed that he was the one who took the pictures in L.A., but he wouldn't say why he was investigating Biggie Smalls. Oldham said he couldn't talk because he was in court at Sean Puffy Combs' gun possession trial and, despite three years passing, Biggie's murder was an open case.

Then Broomfield dodged Oldham's attempt to get information and further exposed him for a comic moment in this serious film:

"Where did you get my number?" asked Oldham.

Broomfield remained quiet.

"Where did you get my number?" Oldham repeated.

"Sorry?" responded Broomfield, feigning poor reception.

"Where did you get my number?"

"Where did I get your number?"

"Yes."

"Your number was one of the numbers I was given as somebody who was actually following Biggie at the time that he was shot and who might be able to give me some information."

"Who gave you my number?"

"You know I just… Sorry?"

"Who gave you my number?"

"I really don't know off hand who that was."

"Okay, well when you figure it out, beep me. I'll call you back and we'll talk."[683]

28-Media Aids LAPD Rampart Cover-up of Death Row Cop Murders, Trafficking

Many insiders blamed the heads of Death Row for Tupac's murder. Tupac's bodyguards Frank Alexander and Kevin Hackie said Security Director Reggie Wright and Executive Director Suge Knight threatened their lives if they said anything about Tupac's murder. The two bodyguards also said they believed that Knight and Wright orchestrated Tupac's murder. Nick Broomfield described the long depression and paranoia Alexander exhibited after going against Death Row and talking to Det. Russel Poole. This likely led to his changing reports, in a book and movie, about what happened. Still, his statement to Poole stands as his first report. Hackie said he also believed Death Row orchestrated Biggie's murder to make people believe Puffy and Biggie killed Tupac. Others, such as Death Row's former rapper Snoop Dogg, stated his belief that Suge Knight had Tupac killed.[684]

These accounts received little attention from most media organizations. As explained earlier, conservative corporate media owners have had a shared political agenda with U.S. Intelligence who, as the CIA was pressured to admit in 1977, dually employ well over 400 media figures (Ch.19). Except for the investigation by *Las Vegas Sun* reporter Cathy Scott, virtually all media groups cooperated extensively with the cover-up of Tupac's murder by Las Vegas police, Death Row cops, and top Los Angeles Police Department officials. Media sources such as the *LA Weekly* repeated false claims exemplified by Sgt. Richard McCaulley's statement that he was the sole officer working for Death Row. LAPD officers Russell Poole, Ken Knox, and even Death Row security chief Reggie Wright, cited many LAPD officers working with Death Row Records.[685]

The largest apparent cover-up story on Tupac's murder was a widely reprinted *Los Angeles Times* article by Chuck Philips. Philips wrote that Biggie Smalls brought a gun to Las Vegas and then paid the Crips a million dollars to kill Tupac with that gun. Philips said it was all set up between the lobby scuffle with Orlando Anderson and the shooting. But Philips had apparently revealed his biased support of Suge Knight in advance. When Philips' article came out, Randall Sullivan's book was already in stores reporting Philips' previous statement vowing to vindicate Suge Knight in the Biggie murder case.[686] (Also note that Russell Poole had given copies of all his police files to the *LA Times* but nothing came of it).

Veteran mainstream magazine journalist Robert Sam Anson wrote a long dismissal of Chuck Philips' piece, for *Vibe*. Anson's article pointed out how Philips claimed to have many sources but named few of them. Anson's article also quoted Randall Sullivan questioning Phillips' lack of witnesses to the 395-pound, easily recognizable Biggie's presence in Vegas the weekend of Tupac's murder.[687]

Vibe further interviewed people in Vegas and found that the timing of Philips's explanation also did not pan out. And finally, lawyers for Biggie Small's mother, Voletta Wallace, sent much proof of Biggie's presence in the New York area the night of Tupac's murder, but the press barely mentioned it. [688] Other writers similarly dismissing Philips' piece included noted former *Vibe* writer Kevin Powell and Hip Hop writer Davey D.[689]

In 2008, Philips again published what the *LA Times* called a long investigative article on Tupac. That article claimed to have FBI documents and informants confirming that Sean P. Diddy Combs orchestrated Tupac's shooting in New York. Within ten days other news sources showed that the article's alleged FBI documents were likely fake and the alleged informant lacked credibility. The LA Times apologized for the article, admitted that Philips couldn't substantiate most of the article's premises, and they retracted the story. They never explained why they didn't fact check the article which glaringly misinterpreted some of Tupac's lyrics by leaving lines out. (They also likely knew that the article's web printing attained over a million hits before they retracted it, so the damage was already done.)[690]

Meanwhile, it seems telling that author Randall Sullivan had three conservative groups trying to stop him or smear him in the time between his publishing an article on Death Row cops' corruption and the release of his book on the subject, *LAbyrinth*. Sullivan first published his findings in an extensive *Rolling Stone* article that announced *LAbyrinth*'s coming release. Sullivan expressed his particular surprise that the *LA Times* joined Death Row Records and the LAPD in trying to persuade him to leave out much information from *LAbyrinth*. Sullivan said that when he refused to edit out parts of his book, these groups then tried to discredit him.[691]

Furthermore, Death Row's whistleblowing accountant Mark Hylland revealed other corrupt activities of the LAPD officers working with Death Row. Hylland said he worked to launder drug money for two Death Row cops, including David Mack, who he and others implicated in Biggie's murder. A police investigator found a long paper trail backing up Hylland's claim of laundering money for Mack and three other Death Row-linked cops, including Mack's longtime partner, Ray Perez, and two others (Kevin Hackie also said Perez was Suge Knight's close confidant). Hylland said the four cops made a fortune dealing drugs and had a real estate scam involving Hispanic gang members they had arrested in the Rampart Division. [692]

When Det. Russell Poole came forward with his findings, the Los Angeles District Attorney's office appeared to force the LAPD superiors to stop stonewalling Poole and investigate their own officers' illegal activities. An LA Assistant District Attorney, for one, cited

Poole's work as opening the lid on Los Angeles Police Department's "worst scandal in decades"—the Rampart Scandal. Los Angeles police superiors first formed a Robbery/Homicide Task Force, allegedly to follow up on Poole's investigative findings. The Task Force's name was changed to the Rampart Task Force when it found that many of the cops involved, such as Death Row-linked Perez, came from the special, anti-gang CRASH unit (Community Resources Against Street Hoodlums) located inside the Rampart precinct.[693]

Poole said that the Rampart Task Force became intent on covering up his findings. These findings, which focused on the illegal activities by Death Row-linked cops, included the murders of Tupac Shakur and Biggie Smalls. Poole said the Task Force completely diverted its attention away from the murders of Tupac and Biggie. The Task Force also worked to hide the scandal of Death Row cops' drug and gun trafficking, and their restarting the gang war. The Rampart Task Force initially made CRASH cop Ray Perez its star witness. This allowed Perez to protect most of his fellow Death Row-linked cops involved in the illegal activities while getting dozens of other cops suspended for such activities.[694]

Poole resigned from the LAPD, got censored in media coverage and ended up filing a lawsuit against the LAPD. He said that he saw this as his last resort to get some information to the public. Poole also stated that everyone around him told him not to share his information with the FBI, but he did anyway, in a case of false hope. Poole later decided to help out Biggie Smalls' bereaved mother, Voletta Wallace, in a wrongful death lawsuit against the LAPD.[695]

Wallace's lawsuit, filed with Biggie's wife Faith Evans, reached trial in June of 2005. By the first week of July, the judge declared a mistrial because the LAPD withheld documents from the Wallace family. These documents revealed that an LAPD informant told police that officers Raphael Perez and former officer David Mack acknowledged working for Death Row and murdering Biggie. This also supported Wallace's claim that they hired Mack's college roommate Amir Muhammad (a.k.a. Harry Billups) to pull the trigger.[696]

Wallace and Evans probably received one of their biggest judicial decisions in January of 2006. Their trial judge ordered the city of Los Angeles to pay the family $1.1 million in legal costs. The judge made the order due to her finding that the LAPD intentionally witheld tapes and over 200 pages of documents that supported the Wallace's charges, after they were "found hidden" in two drawers of an LAPD detective.[697]

A month before, Randall Sullivan published his most far-reaching article on the case in *Rolling Stone* magazine. The article detailed that the hidden documents related to assorted hearings and investigations regarding prison inmate Kenneth Boagni. Boagni said that Raphael Perez confessed to his involvement in crimes that included the murder of Biggie when they were cellmates. A panel member overseeing one of those hearings said he found Boagni "totally credible" but said that an LAPD representative quickly cut Boagni off.[698]

Sullivan packed much into his 23-page article, including testimony from the Wallace/Evans trial against Los Angeles. Several other witnesses' testimony stood out. For example, another witness at the Biggie family trial said his brother worked with Amir Muhammad/Harry Billups as part of a group of contract killers. A cellmate of Suge Knight's named Mario Ha'mmonds also testified that Suge Knight said he had Biggie killed with the help of "Reg," [Reggie Wright Jr] as well as Mack and Muhammad, both of whom Ha'mmonds said he previously met through Knight before their jail stints. Ha'mmonds further said that Bay Area rappers Too Short and E-40 offered him money to kill Knight because he killed Tupac.

The judge rescheduled the Wallace/Evans retrial for late 2006 (and then apparently rescheduled it again). The plaintiffs' attorney said political figures called the Wallace family attorney. They worried that he would win the case and the jury would award the rappers' estimated lost earnings to his family. They said that those lost earnings were estimated at over $360 million and could bankrupt the city.[699]

Wallace, Poole and media spokesmen who presented Poole's story, Randall Sullivan and Nick Broomfield, did great work at uncovering what happened in Tupac and Biggie's murders. Their suppositions only appeared to fall short in not fully presenting LAPD superiors' motives for their cops' work in Death Row. In summary, this work included murdering Tupac, covering it up with Biggie's murder, trafficking drugs and guns, and restarting the Bloods/Crips gang war (As previously noted, U.S. Intelligence has a history of trafficking drugs and guns, particularly into black and Latino neighborhoods). Sullivan suggested that LAPD superiors covered up Poole's findings for racial reasons and out of embarrassment. Broomfield alluded to a U.S. Intelligence operation when he referred to Anderson as the Lee Harvey Oswald of Tupac's murder case in a post-film release interview (True or not, many are aware of researchers' claim that Oswald was a patsy for some U.S. Intelligence leaders who they say orchestrated President Kennedy's assassination).[700]

29-Despite Knight's Imprisonment, Death Row & Feds Targets Afeni, Snoop Dogg and Dre

The murder of Tupac, attacks on rap figures, and provocation of Bloods/Crips gang members appeared to be the key objectives of Death Row director Suge Knight. Only after Knight accomplished these tasks did a judge finally sentence him to jail, suggesting U.S. Intelligence partly gave up on him. Judges had previously allowed Knight to stay out of jail for seven years, despite at least nine guilty pleas or convictions, ranging from shooting at the Stanley brothers to beating a club security guard seriously enough to send him to the hospital in critical condition. Within 45 days of Tupac's death, Knight received a 9-year prison sentence for kicking Orlando Anderson in the MGM hotel lobby the night of Tupac's murder.[701]

Poole and his collaborating LA police officer, Ken Knox, revealed enough in their investigations to help send several Death Row figures to jail, but intelligence operations continued. When Knight and several of his corroborating cops went to prison, Reggie Wright, Jr. took the helm.[702] Det. Russell Poole and the police partner of CRASH anti-gang unit cop Ray Perez said that Perez worked with Wright in Death Row Records' criminal operations. Poole and Perez's partner also said that Perez regularly stole cocaine from dealers and the police evidence locker, and then resold it. They also said Perez had shot at unarmed gang members. Perez ended up doing three years jail time on a five-year sentence for one count of cocaine theft. He then got a two-year sentence for shooting an unarmed gang member.[703]

After his October of '96 incarceration, Knight gained release from prison in August of 2001. In 2003 he violated his parole for punching a nightclub valet and did ten more months in jail.[704] Knight's imprisonment suggests he remained lower on the totem pole regarding U.S. Intelligence operations at Death Row Records. Dave Kenner and Reggie Wright, Jr. likely had the upper hand in directing the U.S. Intelligence work. As previously detailed, Kenner was the attorney for national cocaine trafficking Freeway Ricky Ross' associate, Michael Harris, and had the indirect link to Intelligence. He had also set himself up as the primary owner of Death Row Records and had represented many Mafia figures (Ch.s 22, 24). Reggie Wright, Jr., through his Compton police gang unit chief father, also wielded much power and remained free of any legal charges.

Death Row Records' actions involving Tupac's estate further supports that they had a U.S. Intelligence agenda. Death Row tried to devalue the estate that former Black Panther Afeni Shakur had inherited from her son. While working for her son in his last years of life, Afeni, with her imprisoned former partner Mutulu Shakur, aided the successful campaign to gain Geronimo (Pratt) ji Jaga's prison release in 1997, after his 1970 frame-up (Ch.9). U.S. Intelligence had used vast resources in their 20-year campaign to keep ex-Panther leader Geronimo ji Jaga incarcerated. Tupac recorded three songs a day in the 11 months between his prison release and death. Afeni Shakur won a lawsuit to obtain the master tapes of these songs, which had an estimated worth of over $100 million. But Death Row defied the judge's orders, delivering only a third or fewer of Tupac's hundreds of unreleased songs.

Death Row also allowed over a hundred songs on closely guarded master tapes to reach the underground bootlegging market. One bootlegged CD became Europe's top seller. With little-to-no profit to be made by the original release of these bootlegs, only U.S. Intelligence had a motive to devalue Afeni's estate and confound her future activism.[705]

Besides the apparent targeting of Biggie, Orlando Anderson, and Afeni's estate, Death Row also created problems for Tupac's backup group, The Outlawz. Evidence supported that U.S. Intelligence had murdered the rap group's Yafeu Fula by the end of '96 (Ch.26). The Outlawz then claimed that Death Row stymied their new work and filed a lawsuit against the record label in 2000.[706]

U.S. Intelligence appeared to further focus on Tupac's Death Row friend, chart-topping rapper, Snoop Dogg (Calvin Broadus). Snoop had accompanied Tupac at activist rallies where they spoke in support of various progressive causes.[707] Snoop also defied Suge Knight's attempts to heighten the East vs. West rap war. Snoop agreed to a unity pact and joint tour with New York's Sean Puffy Combs shortly after Tupac's death.[708] Reports claimed that Suge Knight regularly bullied Snoop and badly beat Snoop's cousin, RBX, at gunpoint when RBX tried to stop Knight from beating up Crip gang members working at Death Row.[709]

More serious attacks on Snoop started when he left Death Row Records for another music label in 1998. At a concert on his first tour with the new label, a crowd of Death Row guards attacked Snoop backstage. Snoop ran to police for help. Rather than taking the attackers into custody, police arrested Snoop for weed possession.[710] Then, Suge Knight used the FBI's "bad jacketing" Cointelpro tactic of implying that Snoop Dogg was a police informant. Death Row also physically threatened the rapper on their website. Police later charged Snoop's bodyguards with illegal gun possession charges, causing them to go unarmed. Months later, in 2003, gunmen shot at Snoop's car.[711]

British authorities aided the U.S. in attacking rappers (see similar collaboration against Jimi Hendrix, Ch.37). First they banned Snoop Dogg from entering the United Kingdom (England and Northern Ireland) in 2006. They purportedly did this due to a fight in a British airport. Within 10 days, the U.S. denied a visa for Britain's female rapper MIA to enter the U.S. due to the political contents of her lyrics.[712]

Evidence suggests that U.S. Intelligence may have used a harassmant lawsuit tactic against Snoop Dogg as he faced a number of specious lawsuits from 2000-2006 (possibly stronger cases on the use of this tactic, Ch.15, 32). For example, in 2005 the lawyer for a makeup artist dismissed her $25 million lawsuit with prejudice that contended Snoop Dogg drugged and raped her. Under these "with prejudice" conditions she could never refile her suit nor threaten Snoop again. Snoop was never charged with a crime and he said the woman had been trying to extort $5 million from him since 2003.[713]

With virtually all the notable rappers having abandoned Death Row by the late 90s, one of the only rappers who stayed, Kurupt, deserves scrutiny. Kurupt's real name, itself, may or may not be a bizarre coincidence. Kurupt was apparently born Ricardo Brown, Jr. Jacques Agnant had used the name Ricardo Brown when he appeared in court in connection with the sexual assault charge he appeared to help arrange against Tupac. Brown (Agnant) must have shown a driver's license or other document to prove his name. Attorney Michael Tarif Warren and Tupac were convinced after an investigation that Jacques Agnant was an FBI agent. Only after Warren's investigation was Brown's real name of Jacques Agnant revealed. Warren had also found that police had arrested Agnant numerous times up and down the East Coast for major crimes, though all the charges had been dismissed. Kurupt got his break in LA but originally grew up in Philadelphia, within the vicinity of Agnant.[714]

Kurupt collaborated with Suge Knight in promoting dissension in rap. As an older teen, Kurupt moved to LA, where he befriended Snoop Dogg and joined in his back up group, Tha Dogg Pound. After Snoop's breakout albums, Tha Dogg Pound produced their own album and a 25-year-old Kurupt subsequently cofounded his own music label in Philadelphia in 1998. That same year, Kurupt "called out" married rapper, DMX, for allegedly flirting with Kurupt's ex-fiancee, Foxy Brown, who was on Def Jam Records.

Kurupt said on MTV that his "specialty is battle rap." In 2001, Kurupt joined with Suge Knight's attack on Snoop Dogg, calling his former friend a "snitch" (police informant) in a rap song. Kurupt also defended Knight's release of Tupac's songs attacking Biggie and Bad Boy Records that year. In 2002, Knight and Dave Kenner appointed Kurupt senior vice-president of Death Row Records, which had changed its name to Tha Row.[715]

In 2005, police intelligence work appeared to continue at Tha Row/Death Row. Legendary rap producer, Dr. Dre had left Death Row in 1996, abandoning any stake in the record company he made hugely profitable to avoid any retaliatory acts by Death Row. Dre then founded Aftermath Records, which also became very successful. Dre produced 50 Cent and Eminem. While only Eminem became the more radically political of the two, one-time collaborators 50 cent and Eminem both supported the Hip-Hop Summit Action Network and both produced free Tupac songs on behalf of Afeni Shakur.[716] The Vibe Music Awards granted Dre a Lifetime Achievement Award at their ceremony in 2005. According to police accounts, as Dre went to accept the award, a man seated near the front row named Jimmy Johnson went up to the microphone and punched him. Johnson said that Suge Knight paid him $5,000 to assault Dre. Dre had a restraining order on Knight due to past threats.[717]

30-FBI and New York's National Police Cointelpro Targeting of Rappers

Leaks eventually led to findings that by the mid-90s, U.S. Intelligence had combined their '60s Counter Intelligence Program (Cointelpro) against leftist blacks and their targeting of musicians into an official New York police rap intelligence unit.[718] In the spring of 2001, *New York* magazine and other media revealed that the New York Police Department had directed a rap intelligence unit to compile a database containing more than 40 rappers, including Jay-Z, DMX, Sean "Puffy" Combs and Wu Tang Clan rapper ODB's cousin Frederick Cuffie. A police source said the unit distributed information on rappers nationwide. This included distributing their photos and information on their vehicles and record labels to precincts around the country. NYPD spokesman Sergeant Brian Burke first denied the charges. He then admitted that the Police Commissioner launched it, citing rappers' "reckless behavior." Journalists helped police minimize these disclosures by referring to the activity as merely "rapper profiling."[719]

A 2004 leak by a Miami police officer led to a series of articles that revealed much more. These articles began with a Miami police whistleblower saying that New York's rap unit trained other police departments to help them develop rap intelligence units nationwide.[720] The training included distributed binders on rap industry figures that had detailed personal information dating back to 1995, suggesting that the New York unit's collection of data started at least that early.[721] One journalist reported that in some California communities the police chief determines what rap acts are allowed to perform.[722]

After this leak in Miami, former NYPD detective Derrick Parker disclosed information about his work in the New York rap unit. Parker said that his New York unit started well before Biggie Smalls's spring of '97 murder.[723] Reporter Dasun Allah interviewed Derrick Parker while investigating that rap unit for articles in the *Village Voice* and *The Source*. Allah stated that Derrick Parker was trained in the FBI's Cointelpro tactics.[724] (*The Source* appeared to print one of its few revelatory articles to make up for the criticisms it received from the Hip Hop Summit Action Network, see Ch.33. Also note that Dasun Allah rose, briefly, to Editor-in-chief, but was fired by his top editor/publisher within a year or two. That publisher was then ousted himself. Months later, Allah was sentenced to 6 months jail time for a suspiciously motiveless assault).[725]

Parker's disclosures further support evidence that New York police targeted Tupac Shakur with a frame-up and then a murder attempt. Parker said that several undercover units, including the Street Crime Unit, had officers who also worked in the rap intelligence unit.

Parker said that a particular [former] Street Crime Unit officer arrested many rappers.[726]

The Street Crime Unit was thought to have replaced the FBI-overlapping, Panther-targeting BOSS unit. The NYPD disbanded BOSS in 1971, when the FBI "officially" ended its Counter Intelligence Program (Cointelpro), after the activist raid on an FBI office that year exposed the program. Nonetheless, former Cointelpro agents said that the FBI continued Cointelpro activities after 1971, but just used different names (Ch.9). Researchers believe that the Street Crime Unit, which started in 1971, continued BOSS activities. A police officer named Heinz inadvertently admitted that one or more officers who had Tupac under surveillance were part of the Street Crime Unit. These cops also had erased voice mail tapes that supported Tupac's defense in the sexual assault charge and they refused the evidence on a security camera videotape of the gunmen shooting Tupac in the Times Square recording studio (Ch.18).[727]

Parker contradicted some NYPD officials' denials of "exporting" their rap cops, saying that the NYPD sent him down to Houston and Miami to aid police in this work.[728] Events support that these New York-trained rap unit officers used the same murderous Cointelpro tactics that had been used against the Panthers. *The Miami Herald* failed to note but incidentally revealed the important timing of rap murders *after* the Miami police had been trained by the New York unit to focus on rappers in the summer of 2001. The *Herald* article noted no problems with rappers in Miami until a September 2001 murder of a popular rap DJ, a January 2002 murder of a hip-hop promoter and a September 2003 murder of a rap record company owner.[729]

Furthermore, *The Miami Herald* stated that the NYPD had trained police officers from "other major cities like Los Angeles and Atlanta."[730] New York, Atlanta and Los Angeles were the three cities where, as previously detailed, police officers were either directly involved in, passively watched, or covered up the murder and attempted murders of Tupac Shakur.

A final key support for the existence of this new Cointelpro against rappers came from filmmaker Nick Broomfield, writer Randall Sullivan, and former Det. Russell Poole. They helped reveal that some cops on this New York police intelligence rap unit also worked for the FBI. For example, as mentioned earlier, the NYPD's Det. Oldham took pictures of New York rapper Biggie minutes before his death in LA and monitored Sean Puffy Combs' gun possession trial in New York, three years later (Ch.s 27,32). Det. Oldham's dual role as an FBI agent aided the ease of his work in other jurisdictions such as LA.[731]

31-Targets: Spearhead, Rage Against the Machine, Wu Tang, Dead Prez, The Coup

"Organize the hood under I Ching banners,
Red, Black and Green instead of gang bandannas
FBI spying on us through radio antennas
I'll take a slug for the cause like Huey P.
While all you fake niggas try to copy Master P…
Bring the power back to where the people live
I'm sick of working for crumbs and filling up the prisons
Dying over money and relying on religion
For help. We do for self like ants in a colony
Organize the wealth into a socialist economy
A way of life based on the common need
And all my comrades are ready
We just spreading the seed."

Dead Prez "Police State." *Let's Get Free*, 2000.

As previously mentioned, in a memorandum revealed by a Senate Intelligence committee in 1976, U.S. Intelligence detailed particular tactics to use against political musicians. The excerpt of that memo on '60s anti-war musicians bears repeating. It directed agents to "show them as scurrilous and depraved. Call attention to their habits and living conditions, explore every possible embarrassment. Send in women and sex, break up marriages. Have members arrested on marijuana charges. Investigate personal conflicts or animosities between them. Send articles to the newspapers showing their depravity. Use narcotics and free sex to entrap. Use misinformation to confuse and disrupt. Get records of their bank accounts. Obtain specimens of their handwriting. Provoke target groups into rivalries that may result in death" (Ch.13).[732]

Evidence detailed above supports that U.S. Intelligence used these tactics to target Tupac from 1991-1996. Even a small sampling of news in the music world presents evidence supporting that U.S. Intelligence also used these tactics against other black musicians with links to leftist political activists. Tupac's friend Michael Franti, a politically radical San Francisco musician, headed an auspicious political rap debut in 1991, The Disposable Heroes of Hiphoprisy (Sunday morning news shows interviewed Franti due to his excellent political lyrics). After Franti ended work with his partner in Disposable Heroes and started the band Spearhead, he said that intelligence agents showed a group member's mother years of surveillance pictures they'd taken of Spearhead. These included pictures at Seattle's riotous World Trade Organization protests that Spearhead members supported. Franti further noted how British press reported that MTV had sent emails to their affiliates banning any bands' videos that had anti-war messages.

Their multinational corporate owner Viacom apparently had a pro-war agenda.[733]

While U.S. Intelligence unsuccessfully tried to get N.W.A.'s rap shows canceled in '88, they had a larger program and more success against Tupac in '93 (Ch.15). They also worked to cancel the shows of Oakland-based political rapper Paris, according to at least one news article, likely due to his 1992 lyrical attack on the President, "Bush Killa." (Paris also produced a Public Enemy comeback CD in 2005).[734] As mentioned, police intelligence further tried to cancel the shows of radical activist musicians, Rage Against the Machine, when they toured with rappers Wu Tang Clan in 1998. Stadium managers first canceled their shows when police wouldn't provide security, stating too much risk of a riot, but Rage's threat to file lawsuits got the tour shows re-instated.[735] Rage Against the Machine collaborated with several rappers, such as Public Enemy's Chuck D at a Mumia Abu-Jamal benefit that police also unsuccessfully tried to cancel.[736]

U.S. Intelligence put much focus on Wu Tang Clan for several reasons. Besides touring with Rage, the Grammy nominated Wu Tang Clan worked with a founding member of the Republic of New Afrika, Brooklyn's Sonny Carson (Mwalimu Amiri Abubadiki). Carson had also worked with Tupac's New York lawyer Michael Tarif Warren on black liberation causes. Papa Wu, the brother of one of Wu Tang's lead rappers, Ol' Dirty Bastard (ODB, birth name, Russell Jones), founded a music studio with Carson in the Bedford Stuyvesant neighborhood of Brooklyn. Wu Tang also worked with the Panther-inspired, worldwide hip hop activist organization, Zulu Nation.[737]

U.S. Intelligence had many reasons for concern over Sonny Carson's work with rappers topping the pop charts. As detailed more later, Zulu Nation revered Carson and the group was inspiring new chapters worldwide (Ch.36). Also, Carson's son, Lumumba Carson, had started a highly influential Brooklyn group called Blackwatch. That group was one of the first to explicitly meld Black Nationalist politics with Hip Hop. Blackwatch spawned many activist rappers, including Lumumba Carson's own group, X-Clan, where Carson took on the moniker, Professor X. X-Clan's late '80s start had them reach #11 on Billboard's Rap/R&B charts, before their early '90s break up.[738]

Rap activists report that the music industry aided the more subtle attacks on rappers. For example, Public Enemy's former member, Professor Griff, said that people in the record industry tried to create a conflict between his group and X-Clan.[739] Time Warner did buy up a majority of rap labels and the CIA architect who headed Psychological Warfare, C.D. Jackson, also headed Time Inc. (Ch.20). Thus, the company had a long commitment to placing U.S. Intelligence agents and carrying out such operations against black activist musicians as an extention of its Cointelpro tactics (also see Chs.6, 34).

In the late '90s, events supported Wu Tang Clan rapper ODB's claims that the FBI had targeted him. ODB, Wu Tang's more eccentric rapper, told friends and relatives that the FBI killed Tupac for being a rap activist. He changed his name in the futile hope of avoiding being framed or murdered due to his own activism. From 1998-99, police arrested ODB four times around the country on trivial charges, suggesting their use of the FBI harassment arrest strategy. In the summer of '98, strangers broke into ODB's New York home and shot him, but he survived.[740]

Later, possibly using a version of the U.S. Intelligence threat-timing tactic, police orchestrated their most blatant and deadly attack on ODB and his rapper cousin, Fred Cuffie, on Martin Luther King's birthday. As mentioned, it was later revealed that the NYPD rap intelligence unit had a file on Cuffie (Ch.30). On that mid-January night in '99, two plainclothes New York Street Crime Unit cops wearing bulletproof vests and driving an unmarked car in Brooklyn, sirened ODB to pull over. One of the officers put a gun to the head of ODB's passenger, Cuffie. The other cop told ODB to get out of the car, according to the rappers. Out of fear, ODB stepped on the gas and fled. The cops then fired at the rappers.[741]

A different group of uniformed cops then came upon the rappers, surrounding ODB's car just outside his aunt's boarding home. These Street Crime Unit cops that had shot at the rappers likely didn't want to reveal their identity after their apparently unprovoked murder attempt. While the new group of cops didn't find a gun on ODB or Cuffie, the Street Crime cops claimed ODB was driving with his headlights off and that the rapper fired at them first. A police source said ODB's lights were on and a grand jury ruled in favor of ODB and Cuffie's account. Months after that New York shooting, police arrested ODB and held him on $115,000 bail for wearing a bulletproof vest.[742]

In 2000, *The Village Voice* said the FBI had paid an undercover agent to become a Wu Tang Clan manager. *The Voice* reported that a confessed bank robber and Ecstasy drug-dealing young Mafia kingpin, Michael Caruso, had gone undercover to work for the FBI. The *Voice* said Caruso's work appeared to include becoming a personal manager for Wu Tang Clan. Caruso said he managed two Wu Tang rappers. The FBI said they and the Bureau of Alcohol, Tobacco and Firearms (ATF) were investigating Wu Tang on suspected gunrunning, but the FBI never charged anyone with a crime.[743] *The Source* rap magazine ran an interview of Caruso joking about the charge of his FBI spy work months later, but Caruso failed to say that Wu Tang immediately fired Caruso after reading the *Voice* article, and the interviewer failed to mention it.[744]

From 1999-2004, police subjected ODB to trivial arrests, and prison doctors reportedly forced medications on ODB in jail. Still, most of his solo CDs topped the pop music sales charts. In 2004, ODB died just before his 36th birthday. It mysteriously took over a month for a coroner to announce that ODB died from a heart attack due to mixing cocaine with a prescription painkiller.[745] Sonny Carson's business partner, Papa Wu (a.k.a. Freedom Allah), disagreed with the coroner's report, saying that his brother ODB was drug free at the time of his death. Papa Wu also implied political reasons for his brother's death, saying that he and ODB were attending activist rallies together at that time.[746]

Large police groups such as the Policemen's Benevolent Association (PBA) and the Fraternal Order of Police (FOP) also helped local and federal intelligence agencies target black activist celebrities. *The Village Voice* said the PBA tried to ban entertainers throughout New York City, including Rage Against the Machine and New York rapper Mos Def, because of their support for political causes. Most of the PBA and FOP censorship took place in the New York area, but they had a strong national reach. The PBA even protested a Bruce Springsteen tour when he sang about police brutality against blacks. *The Voice* also said that the FOP "compiled a list of hundreds of artists, celebrities, and venues" working on black activism nationwide, especially rap groups aiding Mumia.[747]

The PBA particularly focused on banning the annual activist conference Black August that often set up concerts in New York City and Havana, Cuba. At the 2000 event in New York, the PBA effectively pressured venue owners to cancel their deals with Black August organizers, reportedly due to the presence of Dead Prez, an activist rap group they had hounded. Dead Prez had collaborated with Fred Hampton, Jr. and supported his National People's Democratic Uhuru Movement and Prisoners of Conscience Committee.[748]

Other rap shootings suggest that U.S. Intelligence continued murderous attacks on rappers in many cities nationwide. For example, One of the top rap activists, Boots Riley, formed The Coup. Riley also served on the central committee for the Progressive Labor Party, headed the International Committee Against Racism, and helped publicize campaigns by organizations such as the Women's Economic Agenda Project, the International Campaign to Free Geronimo Pratt, and anti-police brutality groups. While Riley's rap group, The Coup, had never got close to top ten pop chart sales, their star was rising with the help of their newest member and hype man, Tarus Jackson. Riley started appearing on various national news shows as he and Jackson did a 36-city, three-week tour by mid-November 2005. Just at the end of it, two gunmen forced their way into Jackson's home and murdered him.[749]

32- NYPD vs Hip-Hop Summit Rap Moguls Russell Simmons and Sean Puffy Combs; Targeting Public Enemy

> "1. We want freedom and the social, political and economic development and empowerment of our families and communities; and for all women, men and children throughout the world. 2. We want equal justice for all without discrimination based on race, color, ethnicity, nationality, gender, sexual orientation, age, creed or class 3. We want the total elimination of poverty. 4. We want the highest quality public education for all… 6. We want universal access and delivery of the highest quality health care for all…10. We want the progressive transformation of American society into a Nu America as a result of organizing and mobilizing the energy, activism and resources of the hip-hop community at the grassroots level throughout the United States…"
>
> Excerpt of Hip Hop Summit Action Network's "What We Want."

In 1999, after Tupac and Biggie's murders, rap mogul Russell Simmons and many activists convened "Hip-Hop Summits" to end any perceived conflicts between East and West Coast rappers, and to create unity amongst rappers. Simmons had a vast influence amongst rappers that stemmed from his co-founding of one of the most successful rap labels, Def Jam Records. Def Jam launched top rap groups, including the group Run-DMC headed by Simmons' brother, Joseph "Reverend Run" Simmons. Def Jam also produced Public Enemy, LL Cool J, the Beastie Boys, DMX and Jay-Z.

By 2001, Russell Simmons turned the Hip-Hop Summit conferences into an organization called the Hip-Hop Summit Action Network (HSAN). HSAN's Board of Directors consisted of a multiracial group of top rap record label owners. These included a Def Jam director, Kevin Liles, and Damon Dash of rapper Jay-Z's Roc-a-Fella Records, as Simmons' co-chairs. The board also included Bad Boy Entertainment founder Sean "Puffy" Combs (later changed to P. Diddy) and white Warner executive, Lyor Cohen. Political leaders such as former Congressional Black Caucus leader and NAACP Director Kweisi Mfume and NAACP director-turned Nation Of Islam leader, Benjamin Muhammad (formerly Chavis) also sat on the board. The board further included Columbia University professor Manning Marable.

HSAN developed an ambitious 15-point goal statement similar to the Black Panthers Ten Point Program, called "What We Want." While not containing all of the overt socialist politics nor the militant self-defense tactics of the Panthers' Program, their 15-point goal statement included Panther-like radical leftist ideas such as "the total elimination of poverty...racism and...bigotry." It also called for universal health care, equal justice without discrimination, African American reparations, voter enfranchisement and the end of companies' environmental polluting of poor neighborhoods.[750] By requiring voter registration of a concert attendee or an attendee's friend, HSAN further tried to effect electoral politics by registering close to 100,000 new voters a month, "incidentally" mostly Democrats, from 2003-2004.[751]

While HSAN lacked many of the Panthers' activist community survival programs, its directors' and rapper volunteers' vast wealth, influence, leadership and experience made HSAN an imposing force. Queens, New York native Russell Simmons had enormous success by the turn of the century. In 2001, his various companies' annual sales had reached close to $500 million.[752] Russell Simmons also gained huge wealth by starting the Phat Farm clothing line and Rush Communications, which made $192 million in '01. The *New York Times* called Rush Communications "one of the biggest Black-owned companies in the world."[753] Simmons used his mogul status to get mainstream media coverage of his activist speeches nationwide.[754]

Most of the chart-topping rappers in the country worked with the Hip Hop Summit Action Network in various ways. And many of them appeared to be subjected to corrupt attempts by police, the FBI and government prosecutors to put them in jail. While Simmons sold his portion of Def Jam for $100 million in 1999, he stayed linked with many Def Jam artists who spoke at HSAN conferences. The NYPD had many of these rappers on the NYPD rap intelligence database and the rappers came under attack amidst government foul play.

The government put large resources into attacks on HSAN board director Sean Puffy Combs. As the rap mogul owner of Bad Boy Records, Biggie Smalls's label, Combs had an estimated worth of $400 million dollars by 2001,[755] a portion of which he had donated to activist groups in the late '90s.[756] U.S. Intelligence appeared to target Combs with much fewer assaults but similar tactics as used on Tupac. These included an early FBI investigation and arrest[757] as well as a one-sided attempt to drag him into the manufactured Tupac vs. Biggie East/West conflict. By the fall of 1999, Combs was helping Simmons with some aspects of organizing HSAN. Combs' huge finances and high esteem for producing rap talent made him a formidable HSAN member. In October of '99, gunmen inexplicably shot at Combs' recording studio.[758]

But the most infamous incident involving Sean Puffy Combs came in December of 1999. Closer scrutiny of this attack suggests that U.S. Intelligence first attempted to murder Combs in the guise of a robbery, and then they used many government resources in an attempt to imprison Combs. As mentioned, the NYPD rap unit already had a profile on Combs. Combs had helped launch the career of film and music star, Jennifer "J-Lo" Lopez, and had a relationship with her in '99. One of Combs' new rappers, 19 year-old Jamal "Shyne" Barrow, accompanied them and their bodyguards when they went to a Manhattan dance club one night. Original accounts of what transpired indicated that an argument with several people in the club led a stranger to throw a stack of money at Combs. A fight ensued, and gunshots wounded several bystanders.[759]

Prosecution ended up keeping their top witness, Mathew "Scar" Allen, from testifying in person. Witnesses said that Allen, a convicted felon wanted on three unrelated warrants, started the altercation with Puffy. But the judge allowed prosecutors to present Allen's absent testimony against Combs in court through videotape. He also allowed Jennifer Lopez's absent testimony supporting Combs by this means. Witness Tavon Terrence Jones described seeing a man with no resemblance to Puffy Combs shoot in the crowded bar. Other witnesses said that this shooter was Allen. Jones said he heard the man [Allen] talk in the bathroom of robbing Combs.[760]

That prosecution only had the top shooting suspect as their main witness, combined with more evidence gathered by Combs' lawyers, further supports that U.S. Intelligence was the top suspect in setting up the incident. The longtime New York District Attorney, Robert Morgenthau, notorious for aiding U.S. Intelligence in trials against Assata Shakur in the '70s and Tupac Shakur in the '90s, initially filed many charges against Combs. Morgenthau eventually dropped all but a gun possession charge.

Combs' high-powered legal defense team then revealed various links between U.S. Intelligence and the witnesses that prosecutors used for that lone charge. Morgenthau's prosecutors claimed that a "street person" saw a black man in Puffy Combs' car throw a gun out the window when driving away from the club incident. Combs' lawyers, Benjamin Brafman and Johnnie Cochran, said this street person gave the gun to a friend. "That friend is apparently a career informant who was working with a task force of federal and city agents…this professional informant, in turn, gave the weapon to Detective Andrew Vargas, who lists his law enforcement address [as] 26 Federal Plaza—the building in which the New York office of the Federal Bureau of Investigation is located," said Brafman and Cochran.[761]

Several other aspects of the trial support that U.S. Intelligence set up the incident. First, the FBI agent who was at least found to have passively watched Biggie's murder, Det. Oldham, said he was watching the Combs trial (Ch.27).[762] Also, a television news report said that in no other gun possession case in the country had prosecutors called so many witnesses to testify.[763] A veteran cop with the NYPD's anti-gang unit said "Morgenthau wants Puff Daddy [Combs]." The cop provided his own half-revealing reason, saying that since the sensational Tupac "rape" trial the "attention-grabbing Morgenthau seems eager to send an A-list celebrity like Combs to prison." As with Tupac, Morgenthau rejected any deal that didn't involve jail time.[764]

Furthermore, police tested Combs and rapper Shyne Barrow's hands for gunpowder residue after their arrests, but they failed to process the test kits. Prosecutors said that they did this because the tests are unreliable. Defense lawyers said it underscored their clients' innocence.[765] On March 16, 2001, the court acquitted Sean Puffy Combs of all charges. The court acquitted Shyne Barrow of the most serious charges: attempted murder and intentional assault in the first degree. But his conviction on three lesser assault charges, including reckless endangerment and possession of a weapon, led to the judge giving him a 10-year jail sentence.[766]

Despite the trial outcome, and similar to what happened to Tupac, "gold-digging" lawsuits piled up against Combs and other rappers. Prosecutors or government-linked defense attorneys may have influenced these seemingly specious suits as part of a "harassment lawsuit strategy" (Ch.15). Shooting victim Natania Reuben had testified against Combs, yet she also undermined her credibility by filing a $150 million lawsuit against Combs before any trial verdict. Reuben's lawsuit and other claimants' suits amounted to $850 million of lawsuits against Puffy by that time.[767]

Russell Simmons experienced police attention after his HSAN conferences drew tens of thousands, many of whom registered as new voters in 2004.[768] That year, police pulled over his wife's car near their house and arrested her when they allegedly found a bag of weed in a passenger's purse. The police revealed that this wasn't an incidental arrest when they asked her whether Russell was home.[769] Kimora Lee Simmons later received six months of probation as a first time offender when she pled guilty to careless driving for not pulling over fast enough in that incident.[770] Such police focus works as a not-so-subtle warning that if the targeted person continues their leftist activism, police will continue their harassment.

New York targeting apparently started early on with seminal political rap group, Public Enemy (PE). In 1989, Eddie "Professor Griff" Griffin, said that a journalist took statements he made about Jews out of context. A media focus on his remarks eventually led PE's MC Chuck D to expel Professor Griff from the group. In the following years, Griff ended up visiting Holocaust Museums, starting a Bridging the Gap program between blacks and Jews, working for the Free Mumia movement and other activist causes. In the 1990s, Griff reported a gunman shooting at him and getting poisoned. Griff rejoined the group in the next decade.

In a 2007 interview, veteran rap journalist Davey-D detailed getting an email from *Rolling Stone* writer, Toure, in 2002. Suspected agent Toure had covered up both Tupac's New York shooting and trial

(Ch.19). Davey D quoted Toure as boasting that "My review ended the career of Public Enemy." Also, in 2008, Professor Griff's home exploded due to excessive gas pressure. After an inquiry, the utility company never gave the name of their worker involved. And finally, Congresswoman Cynthia Mickinney found documents showing PE was under police surveillance.[771]

33-FBI/Cops Frame & Murder? HSAN's Jay-Z, DMX, Eminem, Jam Master Jay & Mos Def

Many Hip-Hop Summit Action Network supporting rappers came under attack in various ways. Some of these rappers' legal teams uncovered a large amount of foul play amongst police and government prosecutors in relation to these attacks, which suggests more U.S. Intelligence targeting. A mere sampling of news articles and research on other rappers reveals a glimpse of how widespread this targeting had become. The targeting of less political rappers included chart-topping rappers Jay-Z and DMX. While rappers such as these may have written some lyrics that were overly materialistic or that used derogatory street lingo for women, the Hip-Hop Summit's possible conversion of them to a leftist agenda would have concerned U.S. Intelligence. Attempted frame-ups by U.S. Intelligence could help curtail these rappers from having extra time and money to continue supporting such activist groups.

One example of police intelligence foul play concerned another rap mogul in the NYPD rap unit database, Jay-Z (Shawn Carter). Jay-Z co-directed Def Jam subsidiary Roc-A-Fella Records with HSAN board member Damon Dash. New York police claimed to have witnesses that saw Jay-Z stab a record producer in a dance club in late 1999. As evidence against him, prosecutors showed a judge part of a film of Jay-Z at the club. Jay-Z's attorney, Murray Richman, said he secured the rest of the tape that prosecutors had withheld. The tape showed Jay-Z in the opposite corner of the room from where the stabbing occurred.[772]

Jay-Z is not as political as some previously mentioned rappers. Rappers including Talib Kweli, Common, KRS-1, and Immortal Technique, among others, have been much more politically active. Most of these rappers' activism included their support for politically exiled former Panther Assata Shakur. Many of these musicians experienced problems with police, though they may have not been as heavily targeted without as much wealth and power. More research is needed on them.

But rappers such as Jay-Z sold many multiplatinum records and showed some of his emerging leftist politics with his HSAN support. Jay-Z also had videos that displayed Cuban revolutionary Che Guevera on his shirt, and a mural in spanish paying homage to Tupac. This combined with his several-hundred million-dollar worth, and Dash's HSAN Board director position, helped make Jay-Z a target. In 2001, the NYPD said that the Street Crime Unit watched as Jay-Z's bodyguard got out of his car and put a gun in his waistband. Jay-Z, his bodyguard and two companions were all arrested even though the weapon was found on the guard and not in the car. This arrest occurred three days before Jay-Z's stabbing charge trial, in which he was acquitted.[773]

Evidence also supports the notion that the NYPD targeted Def Jam's activist-linked rap and film star DMX (Earl Simmons) with harassment arrests.[774] Like Jay-Z, DMX had many chart-topping CDs. Police focus on DMX may have stemmed from his HSAN aid and collaborations with Rage Against the Machine.[775] In 1999 alone, the NYPD rap unit, which already had a profile on DMX, arrested him three times on a series of bizarre charges. Police arrested him for swearing at one of his concerts in Trinidad, and for health violations over a kennel of dogs he kept. Police again arrested DMX when a gunman shot the rapper's uncle who worked as his manager. The rapper was later cleared of most charges. [776]

In 2000, police charges continued. They charged DMX for weed and guns found in someone else's car. They also charged DMX with rape. His lawyer said evidence and witnesses supported that he wasn't even in the same state where the rape occurred. A DNA test of semen samples exonerated DMX.[777]

Conservative forces further attacked HSAN-supporting white rapper Eminem (born Marshal Mathers). As mentioned, Eminem produced several free songs of Tupac's for Afeni Shakur (Ch.29) and supported her major motion picture release, *Tupac: Resurrection* (The film was one of the only documentaries to ever open in the box office top ten, despite a limited theatrical release in 2003).[778] At about the same time, Eminem wrote a song saying that he didn't care about "dead presidents [dollars]" he only wanted to see the president [Bush] dead. The Secret Service launched an investigation on him. [779]

Eminem also had mutiplatinum sales on his 2004 release, *Encore*. Eminem had tried to sway the presidential election in the fall of 2004 by releasing another song and video highly critical of President Bush. The CD's song "Mosh," and its accompanying video, encouraged young people to storm the White House and overthrow the Bush government for lying about the reasons for the Iraq war. Eminem produced this album just before he volunteered his time for free to produce *Loyal to the Game*, an album of Tupac Shakur's music for Afeni that also topped the music sales charts.[780] Eminem further worked on a collaborative song with Mos Def and Jadakiss, in a rap written by Immortal Technique where the Bush administration is blamed for bringing down the World Trade Center on 9/11/01 (for more on 9/11, see Ch.36).[781]

The Source magazine then tried to discredit Eminem, resulting in a disagreement with the Hip-Hop Summit Action Network (HSAN). HSAN president Benjamin Muhammad said that *The Source* magazine attempted to divide HSAN's racially integrated political movement by attacking Eminem, who avidly supported HSAN. *The Source*'s white owner and editor produced and distributed a free CD with its magazine in which a young Eminem said, "Black girls are stupid."[782] Scholars on racism say that the prejudicial American media and other factors make racism among whites almost universal to varying degrees.[783] But Eminem's life history growing up in black communities and his continued work with black artists suggests that he was far less racist than most whites. Eminem said he regretfully taped the derogatory lyrics after a breakup with a black girlfriend in his youth.[784]

Starting at the end of 2005, strangers shot members of Eminem's rap group, D12, whose CDs had sold over 4 million copies each since 2001. In December of '05, someone shot and wounded D12 rapper Obie Trice as he was driving on a Detroit-area highway. On April 12, 2006, someone fatally shot D12 rapper Proof (DeShaun Holton). Proof was Eminem's best man at his wedding, and his right-hand man onstage. Proof had a musical legacy as his father played in Marvin Gaye's band. Less than a week before Proof's murder, *Rolling Stone* published an article about him and his new solo CD where Proof made reference to his song "Kurt Kobain," with the suspicious assertion, "The circumstances of Kurt's death are freaky to me. I don't think he killed himself." Others have published suspicions of police foul play in Cobain's death (Ch.40).[785]

Details on rapper Proof's shooting show some similar signs of Intelligence targeting as other cases. First, one of the people involved in the shooting was a former U.S. Army seargent, as had been the case in another circumstance of political targeting. In that case, a former member of the army murdered an influential black New York City councilman—the first such shooting ever in City Council chambers (Ch.37). Secondly, the gunman shot Proof three times in the head and chest, suggesting another case of a military style execution that had killed Panther founder Huey Newton and almost killed Tupac (Chs.11, 18).[786]

As mentioned above, besides the project with Eminem and Immortal Technique, Mos Def took up many political causes and the national police group, PBA, banned a number of his shows. Mos Def continued with his activism despite the risks of derailing his ever-increasing stardom which included a number of movie roles to go along with his rap album sales. Mos Def worked with the Hip-Hop Summit Action Network and Fred Hampton, Jr.'s Prisoners of Conscience Committee (POCC). He also worked on Assata Shakur's case and the former Black Panthers being retried for a 35-year-old crime, dubbed the San Francisco 8. He had planned to sing his song, "Katrina Clap," protesting the Bush administration handling of Hurricane Katrina and its victims, at MTV's Video Music Awards. When VMA organizers canceled his performance at the last minute, Mos Def set up a truck to play his song outside the awards show and was arrested for doing so.[787]

Attacks on other less traditional black leaders continued. More U.S. Intelligence tactics used against political musicians appeared to be used against other black leaders with links to entertainment and activism. Women made questionable sexual assault accusations against several black entertainers. For example, one woman waited a year before she claimed that HSAN's Board member Damon Dash had raped her. Another woman waited a year before alleging that Bill Cosby sexually fondled her when she had worked with him at Temple University. Cosby had previously been smeared by *Time* magazine, which showed major insensitivity just after Cosby's son Ennis was murdered in Los Angeles. On their magazine's cover, they included a tabloid-like accusation of a woman who claimed Cosby had fathered her child. Cosby had previously provided several million dollars for Spike Lee's film *Malcolm X* to finish production.[788]

In 2003, more attacks on rappers culminated in the unsolved death of the deejay Jam Master Jay (Jay Mizell). He had worked as the original deejay for Run-DMC, the rap group cofounded by HSAN chairman Russell Simmons' brother Joey "Run" Simmons. By the time of his death, newspapers such as *The Baltimore Sun* credited Jam Master Jay for creating "rap with a social conscience."[789]

While evidence remains uncertain, details of Jam Master Jay's murder suggest another possible U.S. Intelligence orchestrated professional hit. Witnesses said gunmen somehow got through the locked doors of Jam Master Jay's Queens, New York studio. They killed him in a professed military-style—two bullets in the head. As previously noted, gunmen had fired two shots in the head of two past political targets—Tupac and Huey Newton. The assailants then left without money or jewelry, similar to how gunmen left the diamond Rolex watch in Tupac's near-fatal New York shooting.[790]

In December of 2007 an MTV News reporter interviewed Jam Master Jay's brother, Marvin Thompson, and JMJ's close friend, business partner Randy Allen. In that television interview, reprinted on MTV's website, Allen described how he was in the next room of the recording studio when the gunman shot JMJ. Both Thompson and Allen confirmed that a security camera caught the assailants on videotape.[791] Similar to Tupac's New York recording studio near-fatal shooting, neither the media nor police made any mention of the murderer on videotape. And, police surely saw the JMJ recording studio security camera, but they either suppressed its evidence or purposely failed to press anybody for its contents.

34-FBI-Fostered Rap Feuds? Shots at Biggie Witnesses, 50 Cent, Nas & Lil' Kim

"I'm American too, but I aint with the president's crew
What you peddlin' and who you peddlin' to?
You aint got the ghetto with you
Try'na lead my sheep to the slaughterhouse
We ain't got no choices who to choose
Ten years ago they were trying to stop our voices
And end Hip-Hop, they some hypocrites
Condoleeza Rice...if she ever really care about poor schools
She gotta prove that she aint just another Uncle Tom fool...
Need a truce with the gangs and some food for the hungry...
See, it's all about community, let's help ourselves
Cops brutalize us get dealt with shells
It's our turn, it's about time we win
Need somebody from the hood as my councilman."
Nas, "American Way," *Street's Disciple*, 2004

Attacks on rappers that supported the Hip Hop Summit Action Network continued. Evidence suggests that U.S. Intelligence used their "manufactured murderous rivalries" strategy to camouflage the continuation of their assault on rappers linked to activism. A U.S. congressional committee had previously documented the use of this strategy against the Black Panthers in the '60s, and other evidence supported its resumption between Tupac and Biggie in the 1990s (Ch.s 6, 21).[792]

The mainstream media's collaboration with U.S. Intelligence also continued in these operations (Ch.s 19-21, 28). After fostering the East/West rap feud between Tupac and Biggie, U.S. Intelligence and their media assets influenced the perception of near-fatal conflicts as a natural phenomenon in the rap community. The media failed to question police statements that the conflicts were due to these rap feuds, and failed to report evidence of police spy provocations, murders and attempted murders.

Police spokesmen and collaborative media had a harder time in trying to smear Jam Master Jay. He had successfully started his own JMJ music label under Def Jam, was known for writing positive lyrics, and he lived with his wife and two kids.[793] Nonetheless, *The New York Times* used a front-page article on Jam Master Jay's shooting to suggest in its headline that the murder may have stemmed from a "Music Industry Feud," and directly referred in the article to Tupac and Biggie. *The New York Times* also quoted a senior police official who made the dubious claim that the murder stemmed from someone trying "to get back at [Jam Master Jay's protégé] 50 Cent [because he] had a hit single that mocks gangsta rap."[794]

While a majority of the incidents that were labeled as part of the rap war took place in New York, police used the so-called rap war to explain mysterious attacks on rappers nationwide. In 2004, police claimed that murderous rap feuds took place in many areas, including the Midwest. For example they said that a rapper's murder in California stemmed from a rap war in Kansas City.[795]

At least one seemingly manufactured feud related to Russell Poole's lawsuit against the Los Angeles Police Department (Ch.21, 22, 27). Not long after filing the suit, Poole joined forces with Biggie Small's mother Voletta Wallace in her wrongful death lawsuit against the Los Angeles Police Department for her son's death. Two of Poole's and Wallace's top witnesses for their suits were Biggie's friends at the murder scene, Damien Butler and James "Lil' Caese" Lloyd.[796]

Five months after Poole filed his suit, Butler and Lloyd came under attack, and police claimed it was due to a rap feud. In February of 2001, two groups of entertainers met outside of New York's Hot 97 radio station in Greenwich Village to do radio interviews. One of the groups was connected to rapper Kimberly "Lil' Kim" Jones, while the other group was close with rapper Foxy Brown (Inga Marchand). Someone across the street from the radio station reportedly started firing a gun at both groups. Police said that nearly 30 bullets were fired from six guns. One woman was wounded. Damien Butler said he fired back when the bullets came at him, Lil' Cease Lloyd, Suif Jackson and Lil' Kim in front of the radio station.[797]

Two consecutive 2001 New York's *Daily News* cover story headlines read, "Rap Wars: Gunfire After Rap Party," and, "Foxy Vs. Lil' Kim: Shoot-out Blamed on Feud." The articles blamed the violence on a war between two of the most successful female rappers, Lil' Kim and Foxy Brown. Kevin Liles, HSAN Board co-chair, directed Russel Simmons's Def Jam record label that produced Brown, and HSAN co-director Sean Puffy Combs' Bad Boy Record Label produced Lil' Kim.

The Daily News made a typically prejudicial assertion in the subheading of the second article, suggesting that a critical remark could lead to a vengeful murder attempt. They said "a recorded slap" one rapper made at the other caused the shooting. The article later referred to the recorded "scorching criticism," but it only detailed the lyrics at the end of the article. In the last paragraphs, *The Daily News* quoted these rappers' lyrics as "you ain't a star and your record company know that," and "you still sound lame, and my name still reign."[798] According to *The Daily News*, the first of the violent rap feuds in the music industry started between Tupac and his Death Row label and Biggie on Combs' Bad Boy label (Note that music channels have done specials magnifying East/West rap feuds that they said came before Tupac and Biggie. Even if these were present, they weren't murderous).[799]

During the trial rising from the incident involving the female rappers, at least one witness description contradicted the notion that an intergroup rivalry started the shooting. The rap group Capone-N-Noreaga, the alleged "rival" group linked with Foxy Brown, had come to the radio station at the same time as Damien Butler, Lil' Caese, Lil' Kim, and several others. Capone-N-Noreaga manager James Cruz said he saw Butler pull a gun and shoot. But Cruz described Butler's behavior as defensive, saying he was firing back at gunshots from an unknown source. Cruz also reportedly described Butler as pulling "me around…to protect me, [as] he started firing back across the street."[800]

Biggie murder witnesses Lil' Caese got 5 years probation for the February 2001 shooting, and Butler awaited sentencing after pleading guilty to gun possession for the same February 2001 incident. Lil' Kim's security guard Suif Jackson received a 12-year sentence on similar charges. After the February 2001 shooting, police arrested Lil' Caese Lloyd for possession of marijuana. Then, in August of 2001, another armed assailant attacked Damien Butler and Lil' Caese without provocation, leading to a shootout. Butler was sentenced to 3 years in jail for "attempted criminal possession of a weapon," in that incident.[801]

Like Tupac Shakur receiving a heavy sentence for touching the butt of a woman with whom he had consensual sex, other activist-linked rappers faced heavy sentences for trivial charges. In March of '05, a court found Lil' Kim guilty of three counts of perjury (making false statements) regarding the '01 radio station shooting incident. The court acquitted her of obstruction of justice and other weightier charges. Lil' Kim, who got her start in a Bedford–Stuyvesant, Brooklyn group produced by Biggie Smalls, was a first time offender, but she received a sentence of one year in jail.[802] Trivial legal cases against Foxy Brown also continued and Hip-Hop Summit Action Network's Dr. Benjamin Muhammad (formerly Chavis) tried to support her through them. Brown also went to jail for a year, reportedly for two conflicts with manicurists that didn't result in even the slightest of injuries.[803]

Such seemingly manufactured conflicts and follow up attacks on rappers continued. For example, mainstream media appeared to try and manufacture a conflict between New York rapper Nas (Nasir Jones) and Jay-Z. But Nas had experienced a set-up before this against Tupac that Death Row empolyees likely helped manufacture.

Someone had first appeared to influence Tupac against Nas. Nas said that he heard Tupac had criticized him in the song "Against All Odds," on Tupac's final album released just after his death. An Outlawz rapper backed Nas' claim that he talked with Tupac at the '96 MTV Music Awards, and Interscope executive Jimmy Iovine planned for them to meet in Las Vegas on the weekend of Tupac's murder, to discuss ending any conflict between them. Nas has had a number of socially conscious recordings, starting with his 1994 CD, *Illmatic*. Nas has spoken at Hip-Hop Summit Action Network (HSAN) Conferences and won a HSAN Heroes award for his socially conscious single and video "I Can."[804]

Later, years after Tupac's death, Nas had come back from a long stint away fron the music world. Mainstream media took up the cause of manufacturing conflicts with Nas at that point. Magazines such as *XXL* discussed the alleged conflict between Nas and rapper Jay-Z in the first page of its lead article on the rapper. It also hyped a conflict between Nas and rappers such as Memphis Bleek. Nas denied any conflict with Jay-Z. He said that neither he nor Jay-Z talked about any conflict, and he went on the NYC radio station Hot 97 to tell the public that there was no conflict between them.[805]

Police also arrested Nas for assault in 2003. A stranger approached the rapper, who was seated at a table in a VIP lounge of a New York nightclub, accused the rapper of grabbing him, starting a fight. Undercover police in Miami also arrested Nas's wife, singer Kelis, for disorderly conduct and resisting arrest after she shouted at them. Attacks on Nas continued, particularly in England, where evidence suggests that British Intelligence targeted a number of rappers (See Snoop Dogg, Ch.29). In March of 2005, someone fired several shots from the crowd as Nas performed at a concert in London, though noone was injured. One journalist remarked that it was "amazing that someone was able to smuggle a gun into the venue, as there were over 100 security guards checking attendees at the door with hand-held metal detectors."[806]

The following year, two concert ushers were shot for inexplicable reasons at a London show of political rapper Kanye West.[807] (Some say the U.S. is conducting trial run tactics in Britain, home of a top global spy network.[808]) The media had also set up a rivalry between West and rapper 50 Cent, but the two dispelled any gravity to a feud by sharing a concert stage together arm-in-arm. West defied the rap norms by speaking out to try and stop homophobia in rap. West won several Grammy awards for his CD *Late Registration* that included some radical leftist lyrics. West further spoke out politically by going off script on a live Hurricane Katrina benefit show, saying, "George Bush does not care about black people." NBC deleted his remark when it aired on the West Coast.

Several parties further brought seemingly specious lawsuits against West, though none reached the levels of those filed against Tupac, or even P. Diddy. People did wonder about events in 2007. That fall, West's mother and close adviser, Donda West, a former chairwoman of the Chicago State University English Department, died after plastic surgery. The autopsy declared that the "cause of death is inconclusive." It remains uncertain if foul play was involved.[809]

Regarding the manufactured rap feuds, a number of reporters' statements exemplified how journalists walked a fine line in suggesting that verbal volleys naturally lead to shootings between rappers. In

2005, someone fired shots at rapper The Game, who had recently left fellow chart-topping rapper 50 Cent's group, G-Unit. While some rap activists derided 50 Cent at times, he had made a Tupac song for, and helped support, Afeni Shakur's *Tupac: Resurrection*. Respected Queens rap activist Jam Master Jay had also produced 50 Cent's CDs. One journalist pitted 50 Cent against many fellow rappers besides just Kanye West. This reporter used language that implied a literal war. He wrote that 50 Cent took "shots" at several other prominent rappers, even though he meant criticisms. A second journalist was also referring to criticisms when he said that these rappers have "ammo stocked up" against each other. Other articles had already suggested that criticisms of each other led to a feud between 50 Cent and The Game. The articles further said this feud was the reason for unknown gunmen firing at them.[810]

Hip Hop Summit Action Network (HSAN) members prevailed in ending this media-built up feud. HSAN's Russell Simmons and his rapper brother, Reverend Run, helped bring 50 Cent and The Game together to show the public that there wasn't any violent feud between them. They all held a press conference in which the two rappers put an end to any conflict and together donated $250,000 to the cash-strapped Boys Choir of Harlem. A month later, The Game and 50 Cent each gave $100,000 to Compton, California's public school district for arts programs.[811]

But with his huge success and his tour with Eminem, the attacks on 50 Cent increased. 50 Cent's 2005 CD stayed on top of the pop music sales charts for over a month. By April he announced his summer tour with his current producer, Eminem. By May of 2005, gunmen shot two young black men in 50 Cent's childhood neighborhood of Jamaica, Queens. The men were sitting in a car that was said to be one of a dozen registered to 50 Cent's production company. A third man in the car immediately drove the two wounded men to the hospital. Police reportedly had these men under surveillance and watched the shooting without intervening, attempting an arrest, pursuing the gunmen, or aiding the victims. The third man, Leroy Pressley, apparently obtained a bulletproof vest, guns and ammunition only *after* the shooting. Reports claimed Pressley was "trading fire" with another gunman, yet these reports are contradicted by the fact that Pressley was not immediately arrested and was not charged with discharging a gun. Police waited 90 minutes after the shooting before arresting him and charging him with two counts of weapons possession.[812]

35-Past/Present CIA/LAPD Links in RFK Assassination and Tupac's Murder

> About civil rights and poverty issues: "I think people should be angry enough to speak out…It's not enough to allow dissent. We must demand it." To a Peruvian audience: "Why don't you just go ahead and nationalize the damn oil company? It's your country? [Ignore Rockefeller's Standard Oil ownership] David Rockefeller isn't the government." About his increasingly leftist politics and pursuit of the presidency, he said: "There's a lot of CIA guns between me and the White House. I play Russian roullette every time I get up in the morning."
>
> Robert F. Kennedy quotes, from *The Assassinations*.

As detailed in earlier chapters, key people in Death Row Records, including police officers in the LAPD's Rampart Division, had links to the CIA (Ch.s 22-25, 27-8).[813] The Rampart Division's CRASH unit in particular—the unit of Death Row associate Ray Perez—worked with the FBI under CIA direction against politicized gangs after the LA riots (Ch.13, 14, 23, 25). Researchers also implicated the LAPD's Rampart Division in helping the CIA cover up the assassination of Robert F. Kennedy in 1968, just after his presidential primary victory speech in LA.

In an odd coincidence, while U.S. Intelligence and Rampart police appeared to plan Tupac's murder with Suge Knight, news coverage that summer of 1996 focused on the cover-up of evidence in RFK's assassination. It was then that photographer Scott Enyart finally received a trial for his lawsuit against the LAPD. Enyart had spent 28 years struggling to obtain the photographs he took of RFK's assassination. Enyart claimed that Rampart precinct cops confiscated his photographic film and then destroyed it. An *LA Times* columnist ridiculed the city's use of private lawyers to defend the LAPD in that trial when it had hundreds of lawyers on the District Attorney's staff. Did the city bypass its DA staff to prevent discovery of Intelligence operations during the '60s *and* the '90s?[814]

Rampart, one of 18 LAPD divisions, destroyed most of the evidence around the RFK assassination soon after it occurred. A number of researchers claim they did this under orders of the CIA team that orchestrated the assassination. These researchers said it was the most blatant CIA cover-up of the decade's four notorious assassinations: JFK, Malcolm X, MLK and RFK.[815]

Why was RFK targeted? The 1963 assassination of the first Irish Catholic president, John F. Kennedy, "radicalized" his brother, who had the chance to become the nation's first leftist President. After JFK's assassination, Robert F. Kennedy, the former U.S. Attorney

General, was elected as a U.S. Senator from New York in the mid '60s. During that time, RFK developed an anti-war stance, joined civil rights marches and in 1968 won the all-important California presidential primary. Martin Luther King's associate, William Pepper (Ch.3), also said that RFK made contact with King in March of 1968. He said Kennedy was asking MLK to join on his ticket as Vice-President if RFK won the Democratic presidential nomination.[816]

The Los Angeles Police Department investigative report on the RFK assassination stated that Sirhan Sirhan, alone, fired eight shots in the presidential hopeful's murder. A mass of evidence contradicts this notion. For example, Los Angeles coroner Thomas Noguchi administered the autopsy. Understanding the gravity of the case, he invited national expert coroners to oversee his work. Noguchi declared that all three of the bullets striking Kennedy entered from the rear, in a flight path from down to up and right to left. Powder burns around the entry wound indicated that the fatal bullet was fired from less than one inch from the head and no more than two to three inches behind the right ear. A picture on *Citizine* magazine's website showed Noguchi at a press conference shaping his hand into a gun within an inch of his head to show from where the assassin must have shot.[817] This further brought into question the eventual conviction of Sirhan Sirhan as the assassin since virtually all witness accounts placed Sirhan no closer than three feet in front of Kennedy.[818]

William Harper, a criminalist with 35 years' experience that included U.S. Intelligence work, was brought in to examine the evidence by Sirhan's defense attorneys. Harper testified in court and wrote a long affidavit supporting the coroner Noguchi and other witnesses' accounts that someone else fired a gun from behind RFK and within an inch of him. Harper also found that the bullets fired only matched a second gun, not Sirhan's gun, while two of the bullets he examined had markings on them indicating they weren't fired from the same gun.[819] LAPD radio logs, eyewitnesses and media groups further reported sightings of fleeing shooting suspects other than Sirhan Sirhan, who was held at the scene.[820]

One pair of notable researchers working on this case, William Turner and Jonn Christian, had strong journalistic credentials along with military and intelligence experience. Turner worked for 10 years as an FBI agent before writing for high-circulation magazines. He also published two books on the FBI. Christian had served as a naval airman and then worked as a broadcast newsman for ABC until 1966. They encouraged defense attorney Vince Bugliosi to aid them. Bugliosi had formerly gained international fame as LA's top prosecutor, partly for attaining a conviction of Charles Manson's murder ring, and for his best-selling book on the Manson case, *Helter Skelter*.[821] In connection with the RFK case, Bugliosi defended a radio station that was being sued for defamation due to its manager's claim that an associate of Sirhan's had a role in RFK's assassination.

While the radio station's 1975 civil trial had only limited success in publicly exposing the U.S. Intelligence machinations around RFK's assassination, Turner and Christian's post-trial book, *The Assassination of Robert F. Kennedy*, revealed much more. Their book published archival photos and affidavits that demonstrated CIA involvement in RFK's assassination as well as the involvement of the LAPD in at least the cover-up. The authors revealed that the bigoted, right-wing John Birch Society said that it had over 2,000 LA County law enforcement officers among its membership in the 1960s. The LAPD also admitted training and working with the CIA in the '60s, and Manuel Pena, the director of the LAPD group investigating RFK's assassination, was a long-time LAPD/CIA agent.[822]

Turner and Christian's well-documented evidence revealed many aspects of RFK's assassination that showed several people took part in the shooting. Turner and Christian cited the FBI summary report, much of which remained classified until 1976. This report cited interviews of seven witnesses who claimed that Sirhan had accomplices. Many of them said they saw the accomplices flee the murder scene.[823]

Oliver Stone's film *JFK* reported still-sealed records regarding the president's assassination. Many public appeals led Congress to declassify the vast records related to President Kennedy, and a researcher named James DiEugenio helped found *Probe* magazine, which his colleague Lisa Pease edited, to analyze the released documents. Pease wrote essays with copious citations on RFK's assassination that named even more witnesses who saw several suspects in RFK's murder. The records also indicated five other people were shot besides Kennedy, one of them twice. Three bullets went into Kennedy while a fourth went through his coat in an upward angle that caused a hole in the ceiling panel, totaling at least 10 likely bullets. The final LAPD investigation report said Sirhan's eight-bullet capacity gun was the only one fired.[824]

Pease also cited other physical evidence from the RFK file photos and the FBI's report on them. The photos showed two bullet holes in the wall and a third bullet that was removed from a doorframe. The FBI also ran strings through many ceiling panel bullet holes.[825] In agreement with Pease, Turner and Christian also presented a mass of physical evidence on other gunmen. They published photos of the strings showing the paths of the bullet holes. One showed Los Angeles coroner Thomas Noguchi measuring the distance between bullet holes in the wall and pointing to other bullet holes in the ceiling. Another photo shows Los Angeles police Sgt. Robert Rozzi and Sgt. Charles Wright pointing to the bullet holes. These extra found bullets brought the total bullets accounted for to at least 13. Officers Rozzi and Wright had inadvertently come over from the Wilshire Division, adjacent to the Rampart Division that was suspected of leading the cover-up.[826]

Aiding Turner and Christian, attorney Vince Bugliosi obtained sworn statements from Rozzi and Noguchi. Bugliosi further obtained an affidavit from investigating FBI agent William Bailey, who also saw the bullet holes. Bugliosi submitted them as exhibits at the radio station's civil trial connected to the RFK assassination.[827]

The most important witnesses who saw the real assassin include CBS News employee Donald Schulman. He was positioned at an angle behind RFK that enabled him to see Sirhan, as well as two other shooters. Schulman told radio reporter Jeff Brant that after Sirhan started firing, "a Caucasian gentleman [security guard] stepped out and fired three times; the security guard hit Kennedy all three times." His and similar statements were confirmed in a related 1975 court hearing. The guard standing in that position was Thane Eugene Cesar. Cesar admitted pulling a gun out but denied firing it. The LAPD didn't test his gun to see if it was fired. Cesar also said at first that he owned the same caliber gun that killed RFK (.22 caliber), but then said his statement wasn't true because he sold the gun before the assassination. However, the person he sold it to had asked Cesar to write him a receipt, which was dated a month after the assassination.[828]

Furthermore, a picture of Kennedy on the ground facing up after the shooting shows a clip-on tie next to his right hand. This tie was apparently pulled off Thane Cesar as he was the only guard shown in another post-shooting picture without one. Cesar also worked for billionaire Howard Hughes who had a hand in many joint CIA operations through his military contracts. Cesar had clearance to work on Hughes' CIA projects. Cesar's security firm, Ace Security, was started shortly before the assassination and was subsequently headed by DeWayne Wolfer, the LAPD criminalist who covered up coroner Noguchi's findings.[829]

Probe editor Lisa Pease interviewed a direct assistant of Howard Hughes, John Meier. Meier apparently didn't know of the RFK operation but he knew Cesar was associated with Robert Maheu, the CIA's liaison with the LAPD and Mafia. CIA documents released in June of 2007 detail how Maheu had formerly aided the CIA/Mafia assassination attempts of Cuban leader Fidel Castro. Curious about RFK's assassination, Meier approached one of his powerful contacts about it. Meier said that he repeatedly asked FBI Director, J. Edgar Hoover, about RFK's shooting and Maheu. Hoover told Meier, "Yes, we know this was a Maheu operation. People think I'm so powerful, but when it comes to the CIA, there's nothing I can do."[830]

In late 2006 a British Broadcast Corporation (BBC) televised news report presented several former CIA associates identifying three senior CIA operatives at the hotel where RFK was assassinated. The BBC said that these operatives had no jurisdiction inside the U.S. They were supposed to be in Vietnam at the time and at least one had told friends "I was in Dallas when we got the son of a bitch [JFK] and I was in Los Angeles when we got the little bastard [RFK]."[831] These wtinesses identified the CIA operatives through uncovered film and photgraphs of the incident. A Hollywood movie, *Bobby*, which came out in 2006, covered several hours in the lives of the five other people wounded by the large number of shots fired at RFk in the hotel.

The LAPD's Rampart Division initially headed the assassination investigation, and many said they covered it up. For example, two witnesses at the scene gave Rampart Police Sergeant Paul Sharaga a description of two accomplices of Sirhan who were fleeing the scene. Sharaga said he put out an All Points Bulletin (APB) on the accomplices, and his Rampart precinct started broadcasting it, when suddenly there was a 15-20 minute radio black-out. After the communications came back, Sharaga said his Rampart Detective Inspector ordered the APB ended.[832] Lisa Pease published actual Rampart radio logs in which an officer cited yet another report of a fleeing suspect, before a Rampart commander ordered officers to disregard reports on other suspects.[833]

Sgt. Sharaga also said the LAPD investigation team confiscated and disposed of his report on the event. The Rampart Division further took all the physical evidence from the assassination scene, such as the ceiling panels and doorjambs with reported bullet holes, and an order ensured that it was all destroyed within a year, despite an appeals case in process. Police also destroyed the scientific reports on the victims' bullets. Furthermore, bullet fragments and photos of RFK and other victims' bullets were sent to the Rampart Division where someone tampered with them.[834]

Finally, the Rampart Division confiscated the only known photographs of Robert F. Kennedy's assassination in 1968. These photos were never used as evidence at Sirhan's trial. In the summer of 1996, the LAPD reported that the photos were stolen out of a courier's car as they were being taken to photographer Scott Enyart's civil suit trial against the LAPD. Enyart won that case but never obtained his photographs. With LA using many privately contracted lawyers rather than it's own government lawyers for the case, the Rampart Division remained safe from scrutiny while other operations were underway against Tupac Shakur and activist-converted gangs.[835]

36-CIA/Nazi/Chile Condor & CIA/NYPD vs. Rappers, Activist Black & Latino Gangs

As detailed earlier, the CIA also collaborated with special units in New York City. Researchers cited memoirs of officers in the New York Police Department's Bureau of Special Services showing that they did CIA work, amongst other sources supporting this.[836] Another possible example of CIA collaboration with the NYPD started by the end of the '90s. News groups revealed that Republican Mayor Rudolph "Rudy" Giuliani began a hugely expensive NYPD program called "Operation Condor." In 2000, New York's murder rate, which had been decreasing (along with virtually all major cities nationwide), increased about 13%. This increase happened after Condor began, and it occurred just after Condor added $100 million to overtime undercover police work over the course of the year.[837]

In the '70s, the CIA had titled their murderous work with brutal Latin American dictators "Operation Condor." *The New York Times* revealed in one 2006 article that when "Salvador Allende, the first Socialist to govern Chile and also a physician, was elected in 1970, the United States conspired with the military to overthrow him. That resulted in the 1973 coup that brought Gen. Augusto Pinochet to power."[838] In another article, *The New York Times* partially revealed Operation Condor's history of political assassinations of Latin American leftists and even U.S. citizens working with them. *The Times* said that through Condor, Chilean dictator Augusto Pinochet dispatched "death squads to kill critics at home and overseas." Condor murder victims "included Latin American government officials ousted in United States-supported military coups, trade unionists, rights advocates and suspected socialists."

The Times further reported that these murders took place around the world as part of Operation Condor. Condor murders even included the car bombing of an American who was with a Chilean leftist in Washington, D.C. Also according to *The New York Times*, U.S. Intelligence aided these murders, using an American communications installation to share intelligence. The FBI helped Condor's efforts "by investigating South American leftists who were arrested, and in at least one case, tortured." [839]

The New York Times article quoted Professor J. Patrice McSherry, who published her own more extensive findings about Operation Condor. McSherry's Condor findings, based on CIA documents, concurred with University of Pennsylavania-Wharton Professor Edward Herman who wrote a related book. Both authors found that the CIA admitted paying Chile's Directorate of National Intelligence (DINA), Manuel Contreras, as well as American DINA assassin Michael Townley. Townley later admitted to committing several of his highly publicized murders.[840] In one book written with

Professor Noam Chomsky, Herman showed how the U.S. financed and trained right-wing military forces who led the 1973 coup against Chile's democratically elected leftist leader Salvador Allende.[841] Seven other Latin American countries soon joined in DINA's Condor operations, including Argentina, Uruguay, Bolivia, Paraguay, Brazil, Peru and Ecuador.[842]

Another aspect of the Chilean-based Condor involves the Nazi intelligence enclave found there, called Colonia Dignidad. In 2005, *The New York Times* reported that a post-Pinochet government had arrested and was investigating a World War II Nazi doctor, Paul Schäfer, who founded the enclave in 1961. The enclave had several hundred German residents, a close partnership with the Pinochet dictatorship, intelligence files on political dissidents, and an army's worth of military equipment. The U.S. Congress eventually had passed legislation cutting off aid to Pinochet but the Nazi enclave helped the dictator continue the murderous Condor operations.[843]

U.S. Intelligence's longtime collaborative work with Nazis exemplifies their murderously prejudiced perspective regarding ethnic groups. By 2006, Chile put Schäfer on trial for working with Pinochet's military and intelligence services to kidnap and torture leftists (Schäfer was also charged and convicted for sexually abusing 26 young boys).[844] The aforementioned CIA Operation Sunrise protected Nazis and sent many of them to work abroad. Sunrise extended to most of the eight Condor-linked countries (Ch.19). *The New York Times* article on Chile's Nazi enclave supports evidence that the Nazi enclave, with CIA aid, helped direct the death squad fascism in other Condor countries. Klaus Barbie's years in Bolivia exemplify this.[845]

Two thorough 1986 research articles detailed how CIA-paid Nazis helped establish oppression and drug trafficking in Latin America. Prof. Peter Dale Scott of the University of California at Berkeley cited a whistleblowing former chief prosecutor of the Justice Department's Nazi War Crimes Unit, John Loftus, who said that under Operation Sunrise, CIA director Allan Dulles helped smuggle some 5,000 Nazi Gestapo and SS agents to South America. Scott's sources backed Loftus' claim. Archival records cite how the [CIA precursor] OSS falsely claimed that Nazis such as Adolph Eichmann, Joseph Mengele, and Klaus Barbie had died in the 1940s. In fact, Eichmann was deported from Argetnina and went on trial in Israel in 1961. The Auschwitz "Angel of Death" Mengele was sent to do CIA work in Ecuador and Paraguay, and "Butcher of Lyon" Barbie went to Bolivia.[846]

Germany's *Stern* magazine published a multi-year investigation that involved a reporter spending a year in Bolivia. He used eyewitness sources to report Barbie's part in the aid given by the Nazi networks to anti-leftist coups in Chile, Argentina and Bolivia. Barbie planned and directed the military aspect of the Bolivian coup.

Many post-coup Bolivian pictures show Nazi flags. Together, these research findings, the report by *The New York Times*, and other sources show how the CIA and former Nazis covertly orchestrated the Latin American dictators' Condor death squad operation.[847] In the '90s, Justice Department prosecutor John Loftus, also a former Intelligence officer, published claims of an even earlier elite families/CIA leadership support of Nazis,[848] and others published similar or more far-reaching research (see notes).[849]

In 2006, *The New York Times* published Pinochet's former DINA intelligence chief's claims that the Chilean dictator and his son were also central to cocaine manufacturing and smuggling. This claim is backed by other researchers' extensive investigations. The Nazi networks in South American countries and elsewhere worked with these dictators which they helped install partly to aide the CIA drug trafficking detailed earlier (Ch.s 9, 10, 22).[850]

The same American officials involved in the Chilean Nazi-aided Condor work later advised Giuliani on New York's Operation Condor. CIA director Allan Dulles and fellow CIA associates, particularly Reagan/Bush's future CIA director, William Casey, worked on transporting the Nazis to Latin America with Sunrise and bringing many Nazis to the U.S. with other operations, such as Paperclip (Ch.19). Paperclip partly worked through a front group directed by Casey--The International Refugee Committee in New York.[851] *The New York Times* noted that William Casey later started the Manhattan Institute in 1978, which they cited as shaping George W. Bush's political views. *The Times* also said that the Manhattan Institute "has become the nation's most influential, though not best known—as befits a CIA operation—right wing think tank."(Also note, Bush's Vice-President Dick Cheney and Secretary of Defense Donald Rumsfeld worked in top national policy positions while Republicans presidents Nixon, Ford, Reagan and Bush, Sr. held office during Condor).[852]

Another *New York Times* article about the New York-based Manhattan Institute suggests that Mayor Giuliani's use of the name Operation Condor in 2000 was likely no coincidence. In the fall of 2002, *The Times* reported that the Manhattan Institute had regularly advised Mayor Giuliani's administration and was leaving to advise conservative opposition politicians in Latin America. The Institute had sponsored a conference in Latin America a decade before and counseled top Latin American conservatives, including presidents, former presidents, and opposition leaders in Honduras and Venezuela as well as Condor site Argentina and Condor's central base, Chile. The Manhattan Institute still advises NYC Mayor Bloomberg's Police Department.[853]

Other details on Chile's Condor support why New York's Condor would focus on rap stars. Professor Patrice McSherry reported that Chile's Condor had several phases. She quoted the FBI as saying that Phase III of Condor was aimed at "leaders especially feared for their potential to mobilize world opinion or organize broad opposition to the military states." McSherry noted that these influential targets of Condor forces included priests, nuns, students, teachers and politicians.[854] Chomsky and Herman said that Chile's most popular folk singer, Victor Jara, was an early torture and murder target.[855] Similarly, U.S. Intelligence likely viewed internationally popular radical rap stars, as well as activist-converted black and Latino gangs, as a threat.

The New York Police Department began their Operation Condor after they "reformed and decentralized" the Street Crime Unit, which had started in 1971, the year that the NYPD's Panther-targeting BOSS disbanded. As reported earlier, BOSS agents and leaders had also worked for both the FBI and the CIA (Chs.3, 4). CIA documents showed this work with local police Intelligence Divisions.[856]

Undercover Condor agents (dressed in street clothes) replaced the plainclothes Street Crime unit cops in 2000. Statistics on the NYPD's Condor suggest that one of its goals was harassment arrests. Since Condor's inception coincided with the forming of the Hip-Hop Summit Action Network, rappers appeared to be one of the activist-linked groups of color that it targeted. Operation Condor also coincided with the increased work of the NYPD's rap intelligence unit in 2000.[857] With their rap intelligence unit and its overlapping units, local and federal, the NYPD vastly increased the number of rappers they arrested from 2000 to 2003. The fact that judges dismissed many of these charges adds weight to the notion that the NYPD was pursuing a harassment arrest strategy. Charges not dismissed against less wealthy rappers and activist-converted gang members generally resulted in lengthy jail time. Wealthier rappers could afford lawyers who more often gained evidence to exonerate them.[858]

Outcry from New Yorkers and many police officers walking the streets ended New York's Condor in 2001. Nevertheless, newly elected Republicans had appeared to continue Giuliani's practices through other means.[859] Condor appeared to use the tactic of throwing a wide net over the city's people of color, and training its undercover cops to use particular brutal force. Condor's sweep contributed to 60,000 arrests in 9 months, with 40,000 for drug misdemeanors and 7,000 for violations, offenses "that do not rise to the level of a crime."[860] The more famous cases of brutality likely became so because they weren't political targets and the media allowed their coverage. Under Condor, the Street Crime Unit's brutality, such as the 41-bullet murder of unarmed Amadou Diallo in 1999, continued. For example, in 2000, police murdered Patrick Dorismond, reportedly after an undercover cop offered him drugs, beat him when he refused, and then allowed arriving cops to shoot him.[861]

The Manhattan Institute's Operation Condor-type policies appeared even more prevalent before it took on the official name. The Institute's focus on opposing Latino leftists continued inside the U.S. New York Mayor Giuliani Administration's police worked with federal agents to target the Latino activist-converted gang, the Latin Kings, in the mid-1990s. Called "the largest and most powerful street gang in New York," the 3,000-member Latin Kings changed its name to the Almighty Latin King and Queen Nation in 1994. Several media sources published articles on how The Young Lords, a former Latino activist group that modeled themselves after the Black Panthers, aided the Latin Kings' transformation into a leftist political group.[862]

A *Village Voice* article provided details that supported civil rights lawyer Ron Kuby's description of how the NYPD used what was likely a harassment arrest strategy on Latin Kings' leader Antonio "King Tone" Fernandez. Kuby said the NYPD's tactics included falsifying information and evidence to arrest King Tone a half dozen times without gaining a single conviction. Kuby also told the *Voice* that police targeted King Tone because *The New York Times* was giving him publicity for turning the group into "a progressive revolutionary force."[863] Former Young Lords member and Latin King advisor, Vincent "Panama" Alba, said that after the group's activist conversions, the NYPD further started arresting Latin Kings and Queens in larger numbers with street sweep-type roundups.[864]

Many other New York community activists said the NYPD and FBI teamed up to target King Tone and the Latin King and Queen Nation for murder because of their activist conversion. Another former Young Lord, Richie Perez, who moved on to chair the National Puerto Rican Resistance organization, said police targeted King Tone after he started settling conflicts peacefully. Father Luis Barrios, a priest and professor at John Jay College, said the government didn't mind when the Kings were killing each other. But, he said, once they turned to activism the FBI started a massive undercover surveillance of the group.[865]

King Tone claimed police first tried to kill him and then settled on keeping him in prison for many years, starting in the later '90s. King Tone said that *The New York Times* noted how strangers who shot at him were caught with a 9-mm handgun and a fully loaded machine gun but were released from jail with no charges. Yet cops searched Tone's car, arrested him because they found a bullet shell in his trunk, and put him on trial for possession of ammunition. On a different occasion they arrested Tone and 24 other Latin Kings. Despite not finding a beer, a joint or anything illegal, police charged them with disorderly conduct and unlawful assembly. Bail before their court dates was set at $15,000 for Tone and $500 for the others.[866]

In May 1998, the NYPD initiated their largest attack on King Tone and the Latin King and Queen Nation. At 5 a.m., in reportedly the largest coordinated New York City raid since the prohibition of alcohol in the 1920s, 1,000 U.S. Marshals spanned out across NYC and arrested Latin King and Queen leaders in what they called "Operation Crown." They found no drugs or guns on that raid, yet they arrested the 90 top male and female Kings and Queens for drug dealing and "criminal association." A judge set Tone's bail at $350,000. Community activists such as Father Douglas, Richie Perez, and Black Liberation leader-turned rap producer, Sonny Carson, put up their cars and payroll checks as collateral for Tone's bail.[867] Prosecutors used similar tactics against "King Tone" Fernandez as they used against Tupac, and Tone received a 10-15 year prison sentence.[868]

The U.S. Intelligence war on the Almighty Latin King and Queen Nation continued amidst the NYPD's Operation Condor in 2000, as did the targeting of the activist-converted United Blood Nation and rappers.[869] New York's *Daily News* noted that Latin King and Queen "elder spokesman" Hector Torres took part in a seminar at John Jay College of Criminal Justice in May of 2001, in which he warned of ways police try to turn people of color against each other. He also said police were waging a fake war on gangs to justify a war on youth of color. In that *Daily News* article Torres announced his nationwide travels to help gangs transform "into positive political voices for disenfranchised communities."[870]

When George W. Bush (Jr.) started his presidential term in January of 2001, and New York Mayor Mike Bloomberg took office the following year, Operation Condor practices continued through different means. Joint operations were conducted under these two Republicans, and this period was also notable because the closest associates of George H.W. Bush (Sr.) regained official power under his newly elected son. These associates included Iran-Contra-crack scandal cohorts John Poindexter, Elliot Abrams, Richard Armitage, Dick Cheney, Otto Reich, Colin Powell and John Negroponte.[871] The second Bush administration began to both expand and legitimize U.S. Intelligence's repressive operations.

Such work fell in line with the Bush family legacy. The first President Bush apparently had a longer CIA tenure than he has ever admitted. *The Nation* magazine had a lead article and picture of an FBI document identifying George Bush as part of the CIA in the '60s. In the document, FBI Director Hoover said an FBI agent briefed "Mr. George Bush of the Central Intelligence Agency," about President John Kennedy's assassination the day after it occurred in 1963. A *Nation* reporter wrote that an intelligence source who worked for the CIA in the '50s and '60s said George Bush was involved with the CIA. The source said "I know he was involved in the Caribbean... [and] the suppression of things after the Kennedy assassination," regarding Cuban groups.[872] President Ford then appointed George Bush as CIA Director in 1975.[873]

George H.W. Bush also led a number of particularly racist actions starting early in his political career. Bush won a Texas election to the U.S. House of Representatives in the late 1960s. Rep. Bush invited many speakers to address Congress on the issue of population control with a focus on non-white Americans.[874] He further organized the campaign to expel black Harlem Rep. Adam Clayton Powell from the U.S. Congress.[875] Many then credited Bush with leading the CIA operations that brought crack cocaine in record amounts, mostly in black and Latino neighborhoods while he oversaw the National Security Council as Vice-President in the '80s (Ch.10, 22).

While U.S. Intelligence began the targeting of Tupac Shakur under Republican President George H.W. Bush, some wouldn't believe it could continue under Democratic President Bill Clinton. While chances are that Democrat President Bill Clinton did know about it, previous events show that the top U.S. Intelligence faction could have waged their war on rappers and activists behind Clinton's back. Ex-CIA director George Bush, Sr. and the people who joined his son's administration, such as Dick Cheney, had formerly run such operations behind the back of Democrat, President Jimmy Carter. [876] Evidence supports that George Bush, Sr. helped many leftover CIA leaders from his administration hide their operations from Clinton. This evidence includes findings of Bush, Sr. talking to other world leaders on behalf of the FBI director without Clinton's knowledge.[877]

Iran-Contra Pulitzer Prize-winning writer Robert Parry detailed the activities of the Bush CIA clique. William Casey, later Reagan and Bush's CIA director, helped engineer the secret CIA office behind President Carter's back.[878] Parry detailed how Casey then created a clique of CIA officers that maintained over two decades of dominance, including Robert Gates, George Tenet, David Cohen and John McLaughlin, among others.[879]

Some believe that expanded New York Intelligence operations occurred only as a response to the World Trade Center 9/11 tragedy. More and more researchers believe Bush at least allowed, if not orchestrated, 9/11, due to his preplanned military intelligence goals locally to oppress poor Americans, and globally with the invasions of Afghanistan and Iraq. Some researchers also cite the occurrence of 9/11 on a Tuesday as a threat-timing type tactic since U.S. Intelligence helped orchestrate Pinochet's coup in Chile that launched Condor, on a Tuesday of that same date in 1973. While space precludes appropriate exploration of 9/11, the ever-growing list of people believing the Bush administration helped orchestrate 9/11 includes: over 50 professors and other university instructors, former CIA and Pentagon officials, top officials in Bush's administration, a long-time British Minister of the Environment, as well as a U.S. Congresswoman, a German Cabinet member, radio personalities and others (see notes). [880]

Whether its true or not that Bush officials orchestrated 9/11, Bush officials began running a vastly expanded police state apparatus. Bush family CIA loyalist David Cohen proceeded to run a global police operation out of New York after Republican Mayor Bloomberg appointed him to head New York's police intelligence.[881] From 1991 to 1995, Cohen had been the CIA's deputy director of the Directorate of Intelligence. He then headed their Directorate of Operations, overseeing the CIA's global network of offices and personnel until 1997. Cohen also said that for several years in the '90s he was the highest-ranking CIA agent working in New York City.[882]

One of Cohen's first actions in 2003 was to dismantle the New York "Handschu" restrictions on police intelligence that Barbara Handschu, lead lawyer for the group of activists that included Afeni Shakur, had fought for years to attain.[883] Also by 2003, New York upped the number of officers in the state's Joint Terrorist Task Force (JTTF) from 17 to 120, and the JTTF included officers from 35 other agencies. Cohen vastly expanded the NYPD intelligence division to global proportions, including 74 overseas offices.[884]

His office also targeted a throng of anti-Republican activists. Eighteen months after the Republican National Convention for the presidential election of 2004, *The New York Times* published an exposé that New York Police used undercover agents to infiltrate the 100,000+ marchers among the largest of the protests at the Republican convention. These undercover police agents started conflicts that police used as an excuse to conduct mass arrests at that event and other protest events.[885]

Further details of Cohen's expanded NYPD intelligence division show its global dimensions, as well as its focus on black and activist American neighborhoods. Cohen increased one intelligence unit from a handful of cops to 600 officers working from Brooklyn's "Park Slope to [the country of] Pakistan." [886] The largely white Park Slope Brooklyn activist neighborhood borders the Bedford-Stuyvesant area that spawned top rappers from Biggie Smalls to Jay-Z. As rap had become popular amongst most countries with large communities of people of color, the nationalized rap intelligence unit had potential for an international reach. NYPD detectives started working in the international police offices of Interpol from Tel Aviv to London, France and Canada.[887]

With the "Project Crown" Latin King and Queen arrests, the U.S. Intelligence war on activist-converted gangs appeared even larger and more overt than their war on rappers. This war on gangs grew in direct proportion to the increasing threat to the racist, conservative U.S. Intelligence interest of keeping the ethnic communities politically inert so they wouldn't erode wealthy white dominance of political power. As previously detailed, the Bloods and Crips gang peace truce and conversion to left-wing activism that started in 1992 spread eastward with the help of older activists.[888] Bloods and Crips leaders even talked to a socialist black group in England (Ch.14).[889]

The gang conversion movement spread to New York City. New York police joined the Los Angeles police in clamping down on these gangs only *after* they converted to activism. The clampdown applied particularly to gangs that had gained publicity for their activist transformation. This may be due in part to the fact that publicity increased the activist membership of these groups as it did with the Black Panthers in the '60s. *The New York Times* brought some publicity to an activist Bloods gang chapter. According to *The Times*, when top East Coast gang leader Omar "O.G. Mack" Portee founded the United Blood Nation, he pledged devotion to political and cultural solidarity with Latino activists, selling shirts with "Black and Latino Love" emblazoned on them. Portee said his education came from the LA peace truce and reading books about his heroes: Black Panthers Bobby Seale, Huey Newton, and George Jackson.[890]

While the NYPD was running Operaton Condor, police officials said Portee lied about his activist conversion, but *The Times* journalist appeared to support Portee's claims. A senior member of the NYPD's gang intelligence unit said skeptically that Omar Portee's conversion "isn't about reform, its about control" and enhancing drug sales. *The Times* said that the police kept Portee under close surveillance, and Portee claimed that they had his phone tapped. *The Times* further reported that because of this, one of Portee's relatives attempted to call a reporter from a pay phone and sugested that she was nearly shot while doing so. A half dozen other Bloods, their faces covered with bandannas, met with Portee and the *Times* reporter. They said that "The Bloods now model themselves after the Black Panthers and hope to 'help the community.'" [891]

Fifteen months after *The New York Times* printed their article on the United Blood Nation, police arrested many of them. They jailed Omar Portee and the female leaders of the United Blood Nation, along with 13 other male and female members. In a "gang sweep," a joint federal and local police force indicted them on anti-Mafia-type racketeering charges. The group wasn't charged with murder or attempted murder, but "conspiracy to commit murder, attempted murder, extortion, robbery and a string of other crimes."[892] The FBI had applied the charge of "conspiracy" to commit a crime, rather than its actual commission, to many activists, including Tupac's stepfather Mutulu Shakur. A federal court convicted Portee of racketeering and conspiracy to commit murder, leading to a 50-year prison sentence.[893]

37-Police & Federal Agents Target Black/Latino Police Groups, Activists & Leaders

Attacks on black and Latino groups of color that posed the threat of effective social activism continued, even against such groups within the New York Police Department. In 1997, officials from 100 Blacks in Law Enforcement Who Care and the Latino Officers Association, the two main police officer organizations representing black police officers and Latino officers, said that the NYPD was illegally spying on them. NYPD superiors denied the accusation. But the black and Latino police groups presented reporters' evidence that included a photo of a political gathering where undercover police officers were caught on film outside the Latino police group's location.[894]

NYPD Deputy Chief Raymond King, who headed the Internal Affairs Bureau (IAB), also contradicted the earlier NYPD denial of such spying. In court King stated, "Surveillances were conducted. Phone records were obtained," in two years of secret probes against 100 Blacks and its leader, Lieutenant Eric Adams. This included illegally obtaining their personal phone records from Verizon. An IAB member told Eric Adams that someone had planted a secret camera in his office and taped his private phone conversations. 100 Blacks in Law Enforcement filed a federal lawsuit against both New York City and Verizon. Furthermore, Yvette Walton, a member of both 100 Blacks and the Street Crime Unit, anonymously testified in 2000 for the family of Amadou Diallo after the Street Crime Unit fired 41 bullets at him. The police then fired her, but she filed and won a civil lawsuit against the NYPD.[895]

The NYPD targeting continued. In 2006, the 22-year NYPD veteran Adams, who had gained a promotion to Captain, faced departmental charges for criticizing the city on a television news program. Adams said that the NYPD delayed a terrorism alert for four days in order to distract the public from Mayor Bloomberg's failure to appear at a candidates debate in Harlem. Adams, scheduled to retire within a month of the department charges, risked losing his pension if the department charges resulted in a dismissal. A judge only found him guilty of one charge and docked him 15 days vacation.[896]

The NYPD continued its attacks on activist groups, such as the Black Panther and Black Liberation Movement-inspired Zulu Nation.[897] The *New York Times* reported on how the hip hop activist group Zulu Nation had chapters worldwide, including Germany, Switzerland and Japan, that extended to 10,000 members in 20 countries by the year 2000.[898] In 2002, despite having no evidence of any illegal activities, the New York Police Department declared that Zulu Nation was a gang. The NYPD kept Zulu Nation under surveillance and then arrested 34 of its members for tutoring students in a Staten Island park. Police declared it illegal for over 20 people to gather in a public park (either an uncertain or arcane political unlawful assembly charge).[899] More ominously, a gunman fatally shot a Hunter College sophomore who was volunteering at Pacifica's WBAI radio (a leftist radio station), just as he walked out of a Zulu Nation meeting.[900]

A mere sampling of other attacks on black leaders and activists further supports the continuation of U.S. Intelligence targeting. At the end of the '90s, powerful institutions in Atlanta attacked Ralph Abernathy, Jr., the son of Martin Luther King's closest associate in the civil rights movement. These forces helped get Abernathy out of his Atlanta leadership position in the Georgia State Senate after serving three terms. In 2000, a court convicted Abernathy of a "scheme in which he bilked the state out of $5,700 by filing false expense reports." For this he received four years in jail and six years probation (this appears as small change and a setup when, for example, Vice-President Cheney still has stock options in the company that couldn't account for over $1 billion of contract money he helped get them in Iraq).[901]

In 2002, conservative media attacked black leader Rev. Al Sharpton. HBO played a 1983 tape of an FBI agent posing as a drug trafficker promising to get kilos of coke for Sharpton. While the tape never showed Sharpton accepting the offer, *The New York Times* suggested that he had. Sharpton said that HBO aired the tape just as he was exploring a presidential run to dissuade him from running and voicing left-wing views in the televised presidential debates.[902]

In 2003, prosecutors in the Atlanta, Georgia area revisited a 30 year-old charge regarding the murder of a Georgia police officer that wasn't thought to have had enough merit in the '70s. They charged Kamau Sadiki (formerly Freddie Hilton) with the murder. Sadiki had worked with Tupac's aunt Assata Shakur in the New York Black Panthers. He also fathered a girl with Assata. Sadiki rejected government attempts to have him lure Assata back from her political exile status in Cuba.[903] Two years later, New Jersey offered a $1 million bounty for Assata Shakur's capture, after a court had convicted her there of shooting a police officer, despite strong evidence to the contrary (Ch.9).[904]

At the Atlanta trial, revisting the dropped charge against Kamau Sadiki, in the anti-Muslim climate of the post 9/11 World Trade Center attack, a judge sentenced Sadiki to life plus ten years. A writer for the daily *Atlanta Journal-Constitution* also insinuated that Sadiki killed police for no reason. The writer said that Sadiki "shot [the cop] at random" as he sat in his car at a gas station.[905]

A second example of a 2003 attack on a black leader took place in the City Council chambers of New York City Hall. Othniel Askew reportedly shot seven bullets into a black police officer-turned New York City Councilman, James Davis, in the City Hall chamber balcony. Prominent black activist Alton Maddox, unfairly discredited for the Tawana Brawley case (see endnote), claimed police intelligence assassinated Davis. He said their motive was to stop Davis' unifying liberal agenda in opposition to reactionary legislation by Republican Mayor Michael Bloomberg and the council speaker (Maddox didn't necessarily say they ordered it, only that Davis threatened the build-up of the huge New York spy operation).[906] This reactionary agenda likely included Intelligence Director David Cohen's spy operations (Ch.36). Geoffrey Davis also said, "The system killed my brother [but] we're going to keep fighting."[907]

Reports suggest that politicians, police and reporters attempted to cover up evidence that the murder of Councilman James Davis was an Intelligence operation (it was also the first-ever shooting in City Hall). The final widely-accepted report on the murder said that Othniel Askew, wearing a light-colored suit, shot Davis while with him in the chamber balcony, and that a white undercover cop, standing 45 feet away down on the chamber floor, fatally shot Askew four times, seconds later.[908]

This was contradicted by many initial reports. First, a newspaper article quoted the police commissioner as saying, "somebody in the balcony pulled a gun and shot two people." Another report cited a witness saying two people sat with Davis in the balcony, suggesting that the second person fired all the shots, killed Askew after he killed Davis, or at least was never asked what happened.[909] Mayor Bloomberg reportedly said the killer was still at large wearing a dark blue suit, and the city stopped all transit to shut down escape routes for the gunman, two hours later.[910]

Other factors also suggest U.S. Intelligence foul play. The FBI said Othniel Askew called them hours before the murder, claiming that James Davis threatened, coerced and bribed Askew not to run against him for office. Askew had moved to New York two years prior, had never run for any office and failed to get enough signatures to run in the recently held election. Thus, the FBI should have been able to know Askew had made a false claim by simply calling the Board of Elections or the Democratic Party office.[911]

Askew's alleged action of calling the FBI, his purported claim about Davis, and the FBI's reporting of it as a valid claim are all bizarre aspects of this incident that only a U.S. Intelligence-orchestrated media campaign could pass off unscrutinized (Ch.19). Nevertheless, police tried to bolster the FBI's claim and newspapers repeated it nationwide. Police said they found an unsigned, positive letter Davis wrote to Askew in his pocket that allegedly supported the FBI-stated Askew claims (The ultra-conservative *New York Post* stretched the allegation further to say it was a grant Askew got for Davis). Davis staffers said Davis didn't write the letter, and nothing else substantiated the alleged Askew claims.[912]

Several more odd aspects of this story further suggest U.S. Intelligence work. Othniel Askew had just finished a tour in the Air Force in the summer of 2001, and he had a previous arrest for a violent physical assault. [913] Also, the weapon that killed Davis was a Kahr MK40, invented in 1995 and approved for NYPD undercover work.[914]

Signs of U.S. Intelligence targeting incidents continued into 2004. During a mayoral election, the FBI placed listening devices in the office of black Philadelphia Mayor John F. Street, a Democrat. They also "bugged" the office of a Street supporter, top Philadelphia Muslim leader Shamsud-din Ali.[915] Mayor Street signed a bill that made Philadelphia one of the first cities in the United States to demand reparations from banks that had benefited from slavery. Revolutionary Action Movement (RAM) founder Muhammad Ahmad (Maxwell Stanford, Jr.) taught at Temple University and organized with the National Coalition of Blacks for Reparations (NCOBRA). NCOBRA led the cause that influenced Philadelphia's City Council Ordinance, which Street signed.[916]

Other targeting involved the presidential elections. NAACP leader Kweisi Mfume sat on the board of the Hip Hop Summit Action Network. His NAACP coleader, Julian Bond, criticized George Bush's policies and his refusal to meet with the group, the country's oldest black improvement organization. The IRS quickly launched an investigation into whether Bond's critique should exempt the NAACP from its non-profit status, which bars lobbying.[917] The IRS had previously acted on behalf of U.S. Intelligence during the Vietnam War when it conducted illegal searches on Huey Newton's home while focusing on the Black Panther Party, in addition to aiding U.S. Intelligence spying on other leftist groups similarly registered as legitimate political organizations.[918]

That same year, suspicious attacks on a different kind of black leadership came to light. *The Washington Post Magazine* covered various machinations used by the U.S. Department of Agriculture (USDA) to destroy thousands of black farmers' livelihoods. In the summer of 2004, the Environmental Working Group said the USDA spent $12 million on legal fees to thwart the transfer of $2 billion in settlement money awarded to thousands of black farmers in 1999 for USDA discrimination from 1981-1996.[919] The National Black Farmers Association leadership filed another suit in 2004, claiming that racist discrimination by the U.S.D.A. against black farmers continued.

The Black Farmers' leadership also experienced violent attacks. For example, the National Black Farmers' vice-president, Rick Haynie, experienced a long history of discrimination that included violent threats before the end of the '90s. He said that in 1981 he was suddenly refused loans after a white USDA supervisor took over the position of a black USDA supervisor working with Haynie who had approved them. Haynie had accumulated over 2,000 acres of farmland by that time. Soon after, Haynie found bullet holes in his farm equipment, and mysterious fires burned down thousands of dollars in livestock and equipment. Banks then charged Haynie exorbitant interest rates and delayed his commercial loans, decimating much of his holdings well into the '90s. Nothing changed until a USDA agent was suspended for threatening Haynie with a gun in '98.[920]

By 2005, conservative government officials again decided to retry old cases against Black Panthers. They formed a grand jury that ended up charging eight men for a 1971 killing of a San Francisco police officer, along with "conspiracy" charges that encompassed many other acts between 1968 and 1973. Similar charges had been thrown out in 1975 due to the fact that the evidence used to indict the men in 1971 had been extracted through torture. While the government had kept two of the men incarcerated as political prisoners for the past 30 years, the other six had lived regular lives, working and raising families. Seven of the men lived in several different states and one lived abroad in 2005. As of July 2007, all eight of the men, Herman Bell, Ray Boudreaux, Richard Brown, Henry Jones, Jalil Muntaqim (Anthony Bottom), Richard O'Neal, Harold Taylor, and Francisco Torres were in jail, each with a bail of $3 million.[921]

In 2005, the government also dealt another blow to gang peace truce leaders. California authorities had long-time death row inmate Stanley "Tookie" Williams executed. Williams had founded The Crips gang in the early '70s. Some historians claimed that the Crips started as revolutionary activists before getting involved in violence and murders. Nonetheless, Williams changed after his imprisonment in the early '80s. Williams had written several children's books that tried to teach peace and had helped organize the peace truces between the Bloods and the Crips. Williams was nominated for the Nobel Peace Prize. Celebrities such as Snoop Dogg, Bianca Jagger, Rev. Jesse Jackson, Judge Greg Mathis, Daz Dillinger and Jamie Foxx tried to gain a stay on his execution. Foxx had played the part of Williams in a television movie, "Redemption: The Stan Tookie Williams Story."[922] The government executed Williams by the end of 2005.

Also in 2005 and 2006, the FBI led a large attack on the Puerto Rican Independence movement. The movement's recent successes included a push for the U.S. Navy to stop testing bombs on the Puerto Rican island of Vieques. In more threat-timed targeting, the FBI led attacks on September 23, 2005, the anniversary of the day Puerto Rico declared its independence from Spain. Harvard-educated attorney and radio host, Juan-Manuel Garcia-Passalacqua, said that 200 agents surrounded the home of 72 year-old Puerto Rican independence activist Filiberto Ojeda Rios.

In 1983, the FBI had claimed Ojeda Rios was tied to a bank robbery. Garcia-Passalcqua said that Ojeda Rios was tried in a federal courtroom in Puerto Rico and unanimously absolved by a jury. Garcia-

Passalacqua further explained how bullet shell evidence from the 2005 attack showed that the FBI agents fired 100 shots into Ojeda Rios's home. Ojeda Rios fired 10 shots back. After he was badly wounded, the FBI wouldn't allow anyone in or out of the house for 12-15 hours as he bled to death.[923]

This brought an end to the longtime assault by the FBI on Rios, but they didn't end their attack on the movement. The FBI had previously pushed for "preventive detention" of Filberto Ojeda Rios and other political activists by denying them bail. Officials had jailed Ojeda Rios for six years before a jury aquitted him of FBI charges. Within months of Ojeda Rios's death, the FBI raided 5 independence organizers' homes, seized files, and arrested several organizers and their family members.[924]

38-Past Parallel: Jimi Hendrix's Panther Support, Spy Manager & FBI Targeting; Richard Wright

> "Get your Black Panthers...not to kill anybody, but to scare them. It's hard to say...I know it sounds like war, but that's what's gonna have to happen, it has to be a war if nobody is going to do it peacefully. Like quite naturally, you say, make love not war, and all these other things, but then you come back to reality and there are some evil folks around and they want you to be passive and weak and peaceful so that they can overtake you...you have to fight fire with fire."
>
> Jimi Hendrix, *Teenset*, 1969.

In light of the Vietnam War era U.S. Intelligence document discussing tactics for targeting political musicians (Ch.13), past cases of black political musicians' deaths deserve more scrutiny. Investigations reveal that U.S. Intelligence and its Cold War allies in British Intelligence used similar intelligence targeting tactics on Tupac Shakur as they had previously used on legendary guitarist Jimi Hendrix.

In the U.S, Hendrix received little fame in the mid-1960s while he toured with music legends such as Sam Cooke, but he did get an indirect message that doing things independently could get you in trouble. Cooke was famous for many hits such as "You Send Me," "Twistin the Night Away," and "Working on the Chain Gang." Purportedly, a desk clerk shot Cooke for attacking her in 1964. Some believe he was murdered due to CIA-linked Genovese Mafia resentment that he was the first black to produce his own records and that he would lead other black artists to do the same (see endnote).[925]

Jimi Hendrix then moved to England where he would first reach stardom. In England, a "former" spy named Mike Jeffery coerced his way into managing Hendrix. Jeffery had worked for MI6 (British CIA). Jeffery's continued partnerships with CIA-linked figures, his sudden huge wealth, and his skills at acquiring CIA-type tax havens in the Bahamas suggests he maintained MI6 work undercover.[926] As previously detailed, Frances Stonor Saunders, in *The Cultural Cold War,* described how the arts were a huge area of Intelligence undercover work from the '50s on. MI6 collaborated with the CIA's work in trying to control writing and music to counter any influences that went against the CIA's conservative hyper-capitalist agenda. The U.S. Government gave the CIA vast resources to oppose the Soviet and communist Eastern European influences.[927]

Black artists were a particular Intelligence focus because of left-wing radicalism amongst them. For example, the FBI and CIA closely monitored American black writer Richard Wright and French/Algerian black writer, Franz Fanon. Researchers highly suspected U.S. Intelligence actions in Wright's early death. In her book, *The Cultural Cold War*, British magazine editor Frances Stonor Saunders said that after Wright moved to Paris, the CIA and FBI monitored him closely until "he died in mysterious circumstances in 1960."[928]

Many close to Richard Wright, the first best-selling African-American novelist, believe he died young due to his radical leftist activism. In the 1930s, the House Un-American Activities Committee (HUAC) denounced Wright, before the FBI began their surveillance of him.[929] The State Department confiscated his passport soon after he published his classic novel, *Native Son,* in 1940.[930] By the mid- 1940s, the FBI put Wright on a Security Index of subversives to be rounded up in a national emergency.[931] After many appeals to the State Department, Wright finally regained his passport in 1946. Within the next two years, Wright moved his family to Paris, France to avoid the infamous McCarthey anti-Communist congressional hearings.[932]

In France, Wright wrote important books about black liberation, including *Black Power* and *White Man Listen!* Meanwhile, Time, Inc.'s magazines published smear articles on Richard Wright, calling him a "drunkard at 6,"[933] while also attributing a false quote to him years later.[934] U.S. Intelligence further surrounded Wright with spies in Paris, and they were highly suspected of writing the fake letters that came between him and other leftist activist leaders.[935] Wright also believed U.S. Intelligence aided the planting of several microphones he found hidden in his home.[936] The U.S. embassy again confiscated his passport in Paris, though Wright threatened to alert international press and gained it back.[937]

From Paris, Wright befriended British socialist George Padmore. Wright aided Padmore in mentoring future African Independence leaders. These included Ghanian leftist Kwame Nkrumah who helped lead The Gold Coast to gain its independence from England by 1957 (Wright detailed to friends why he believed British and U.S. Intelligence assassinated some of these potential leaders).[938] When Wright's wife and daughters moved to London, with the writer soon to follow his family, the British government refused to allow Wright residence.[939]

In 1960, Richard Wright elaborated on the tactics U.S. Intelligence used against him in the first of a broadcast series on French national television.[940] Wright's closest friend in Paris, acclaimed political cartoonist Ollie Harrington, and Wright's daughter, Julia, believe U.S. Intelligence helped orchestrate his death on the day of that broadcast, which black newspapers covered around America.[941] Richard Wright died in a small Paris hospital the night after he gained a clean bill of health at the age of 52.[942]

Similar to their targeting of Wright, U.S. and British Intelligence appeared to collaborate against Jimi Hendrix. By 1968, Hendrix became popular worldwide. The assassination of Martin Luther King that year led Hendrix to engage in more radical-left activism, such as supporting the Black Panthers. Hendrix promoted them in interviews, played benefits for Panther Bobby Seale and the Chicago Seven, and dedicated his last album to the Panthers.[943] Former Air Force Secretary Townsend Hoopes said one of the government's greatest fears was "the fateful merging of anti-war and racial dissension."[944] The universally admired Jimi Hendrix aided the bridge between these groups.

FBI and police targeting soon began against Hendrix in the U.S. and other countries aided their efforts when Hendrix went abroad. Such collaboration is common through the International police group "Interpol." Also, while British and U.S. Intelligence collaboration is well-known, at least one fomer MI6 agent said that the CIA actually looked to his agency for orders as the CIA was partly created by British Intelligence.[945] (The British Intelligence's 300+ year head start on the CIA offers some support to this claim). The FBI started a closely guarded file on Hendrix and placed him on a security list of subversives to be rounded up for detainment in case of a national emergency.[946] Police detectives began round the clock surveillance of Hendrix and his band.[947]

When Hendrix traveled north of the border, Canadian federal police arrested him at an airport, claiming that he transported drugs.[948] Hendrix biographers Harry Shapiro and Caesar Glebbeek cited Hendrix saying he'd never take such a risk and that his manager, Mike Jeffery, set up that airport arrest. The biographers described many ways Jeffery stole from Hendrix and tried to sabotage him. Also, regarding Hendrix and drug use, Shapiro and Glebbeek said that, contrary to popular belief, Hendrix produced his first classic album, *Are You Experienced?*, with virtually no drug use. Then, after using drugs recreationslly for awhile, Hendrix gave it all up except for social use of alcohol and weed.[949]

These Jimi Hendrix biographers and Hendrix fiancée Monica Danneman also claimed that manager Mike Jeffery consistently sabotaged the guitar legend's political activist work. She believed Jeffery dosed his drink before one political benefit show that caused Hendrix to end his set early.[950]

These authors also accused Jeffery of setting up a Mafia kidnapping of Hendrix in Manhattan in 1969. Jeffery's Mafia connections were extensive, and he apparently took part in this bizarre Mafia kidnapping of Hendrix. He did this in collaboration with a former [CIA supported] Haitian dictator's propagandist-turned band manager, Jerry Morrison.[951] Hendrix's bandmates described how Jeffery brought over a Mafia marksman to intimidate Hendrix regarding one business deal. In another incident, Mafia figures kidnapped Hendrix for several days in Manhattan in 1969. Jeffery and Morrison miraculously got Hendrix free, supposedly with "tougher" Mafia.[952] Researchers have previously noted Death Row Records links with Mafia to target Tupac, and CIA/Mafia links in the MLK and RFK assassination. In Hendrix's targeting, Intelligence agents appeared to use this Mafia kidnapping to intimidate Hendrix not to leave Jeffery.

Multiple reports cited how Mike Jeffery tried to undermine Jimi Hendrix's career while the media smeared Hendrix during his life and after his death. These incidents, like the intelligence connections of people who inserted themselves into their careers, are some of the many parallels in the targeting of Tupac Shakur and Jimi Hendrix. Both of these music icons also lost their lives when they officially signaled the end of their relationships with their business partners who were suspected intelligence agents. Tupac was murdered days after sending a letter firing Death Row co-owner Dave Kenner and Jimi Hendrix suffered a similar fate when he officially tried to separate himself from the former MI6 agent Jeffery.[953]

Rumors continue as to how Jimi Hendrix died. His live-in fiancée, Monica Danneman, appeared to give the most reliable account. Danneman reported that on September 17, 1971, the day after Hendrix finally fired Jeffery, she found her fiancée unconscious in their London apartment bed before noon. Hendrix had been at a party the night before and took sleeping pills to counter unusually bad insomnia he had that night. Danneman called an ambulance and Hendrix died either before arriving at the hospital or an hour after arriving, according to differing reports. While biographers Shapiro and Glebbeek had some discrepancies with Danneman's account of Hendrix's last 24 hours, most of their eyewitnesses' reports backed Danneman's general description.[954]

The coroner said that what Hendrix had in him shouldn't have killed him. The coroner found a non-fatal dose of sleeping tablets, a small amount of alcohol, a trace of the barbiturate Seconal, and 20 mg of amphetamine (speed). The coroner declared that Hendrix should have recovered from the pills, so the official cause of death was "inhalation of vomit due to Barbiturate intoxication."[955]

Reports claimed Hendrix had chronic insomnia problems and had ineffective results from the Vesperax sleeping pills he took that night. Danneman said Hendrix showed her a handful of pills people had given him at the party he attended the night before he died. He had then flushed them down the toilet in front of Danneman. This supports that someone likely spiked Hendrix's drink with the speed that was found in his system. He also likely tried to take more of the tablets to get to sleep.[956] While this may have supported a somewhat "accidental" overdose, more factors support that British authorities played a part in his murder.

Danneman's memoir and Shapiro and Glebbeek's biography described how government officials' foul play abounded thereafter. Danneman said that when police investigated her place they failed to take anything and warned her to not say anything about the death. Then, an official British inquest resulted in the London coroner and the inquest members declaring an open (inconclusive) verdict on Hendrix's death. The inquest had only called three witnesses to testify: Danneman, Hendrix's road manager and the coroner. They failed to have the ambulance workers, the people Hendrix saw at the party, or the hospital doctors testify.[957]

Police also presented false information on Hendrix, supporting erroneous media reports that Hendrix was suicidal. For example, police said that Hendrix left a message on his friend and former manager Chas Chandler's answering machine in which he said, "Help me, man," the night he died. Chandler said that he never owned an answering machine.[958]

But Danneman came upon the most disturbing evidence later. The coroner found an unidentifiable compound in Hendrix's body. Top doctors told Danneman that because the coroner waited several days to do Hendrix's autopsy, any poisons in his system may no longer have been in a detectable state.[959]

Groups reexamined Jimi Hendrix's death at least twice in later years. In 1975, the magazine *Crawdaddy* investigated and concluded that a death squad of undercover intelligence agents killed Hendrix.[960] While that magazine's sources are uncertain, in 1992, England's Attorney General ordered an inquiry, and Scotland Yard (British FBI) also re-examined the case. Danneman, Shapiro and Glebbeek easily contradicted Scotland Yard, exposing their cover-up. For example, Scotland Yard claimed to quote Hendrix's attending doctor, Dr. John Bannister, saying Hendrix was "dead on arrival... [dying] in the ambulance or at home."[961] The ambulance workers denied this.[962]

In addition, the hospital's official report had Hendrix's hospital arrival time as 11:45, and it said he was pronounced dead at 12:45.[963] If Hendrix was dead on arrival, what happened during that hour? Scotland Yard couldn't give Danneman an answer on that. When she asked what Dr. Bannister had to say about it, Scotland Yard told her he had been struck off England's official list of all doctors in the country, the medical register, without any further explanation.[964]

Several other similarities occurred after both Jimi Hendrix's and Tupac's deaths. Time Warner partly funded, highly promoted and had a controlling share of upstart Death Row Records. Death Row went against a judge's orders in never giving all of Tupac's 200-300 unreleased songs to Tupac's mother, Afeni Shakur. As previously detailed, Time Warner's political past included a Vice-President who also headed U.S. Intelligence's Psychological Warfare Division. Death Row and Time Warner kept the publishing rights to the songs, forcing

Afeni to split the tens of millions of dollars earned by the Tupac CDs she put out after his death (Ch.s 20, 22, 29).[965] Similarly, Mike Jeffery confiscated all of Hendrix's recordings and belongings in his New York studio (see similar New York incident with the late Peter Tosh, Ch.39). It took 25 years for Al Hendrix to gain the rights to his son's music from Warner Records. And then, on albums and memorabilia that made over $100 million in sales, he was only given $2 million.[966]

And finally, like associates of Tupac's, several close to Jimi Hendrix died in uncertain ways after him. Close friend Devon Wilson last saw Hendrix at the party the night before he died. Months later, she died of a reported overdose, but friends who saw the scene of her death said it looked like a violent murder.[967]

Several groups sued Hendrix's manager, Mike Jeffery, for money he owed them. A judge allowed Jeffery to travel for business during the trial, and he reportedly died in a plane crash in 1973. Because a witness only saw Jeffery's jewelry to identify him, some believe he escaped with the shell company fortunes he created (similar to the shell company Tupac's Death Row lawyer made). Jeffery created his tax haven shell with the same Bahamas institutions that worked later with George H.W. Bush's CIA in the BCCI/Iran-Contra scandal.[968]

Another Hendrix-linked death occurred much later. Monica Danneman said Jeffery threatened to kill her if she published her memoir about Hendrix that she wrote in 1971. She said she lost her book manuscript twice between 1971 and '73, first to a thief she believed Jeffery sent, and then to a Jeffery associate.[969] In 1995, she finally published a book about Hendrix's activist political plans, Jeffery's sabotage, and government cover-up. News reports said Danneman killed herself in '96. Her close friends believe she was murdered. They said Danneman had continued getting death threats over the years and had just finished a long interview for a film on Hendrix (of uncertain release).[970]

In 2009, new information came out which further supports how Mike Jeffery worked on behalf of British and U.S. Intelligence in their orchestration of Jimi Hendrix's murder. One of Jimi Hendrix's roadies, James "Tappy" Wright, published a memoir, *Rock Roadie*. Wright claimed in print that Mike Jeffery made a drunken confession in Wright's apartment one night in 1971. Wright said that Jeffery confessed to having Hendrix murdered.

James Wright quoted Mike Jeffery as saying, "I had to do it. You know damn well what I'm talking about." Jeffery reportedly said that he had taken out a life insurance police on Hendrix worth $2 million, with Jeffery as the beneficiary. Wright further quoted Jeffery as saying:

> "I was in London the night of Jimi's death and together with some of our old friends...we went round to Monika's hotel

> room, got a handful of pills and stuffed them into his mouth…then poured a few bottles of red wine deep into his windpipe. I had to do it. Jimi was worth much more to me dead than alive. That son of a bitch was going to leave me."[971]

The emergency room doctor who worked on Jimi Hendrix confirmed this account. After James Wright's book release in 2009, reporters interviewed the emergency room doctor, John Bannister. Bannister supported Wrights's claim, saying it was "plausible" that he was murdered. Bannister detailed that "The amount of wine that was over [Hendrix] was extraordinary. Not only was it saturated right through his hair and shirt, but his lungs and stomach were absolutely full of wine…He had really drowned in a massive amount of red wine."[972]

Bannister's description would seem to contradict a medical report that Hendrix had very little alcohol in his bloodstream at his time of death. [973] But the two reports do support business manager Mike Jeffery's satement of forcing the wine down his throat. This apparently killed Hendrix before his body could circulate the alcohol in his bloodstream.

Police investigating Hendrix's death failed to report Bannister's account. They also appeared to purposely overlook Mike Jeffery's motive for murdering Hendrix, despite Hendrix's lawyer, Henry Steingarten, and his fiancee, Monika Danneman, knowing that Hendrix had just fired his manager. While it's widely reported Jeffery "formerly" worked for MI6, a *London Times* reporter also wrote that Jeffery "flaunted his connections with organized crime and the FBI."[974]

39-CIA Links to Reggae Revolutionary Bob Marley and Peter Tosh's Early Deaths

"This morning I woke up in a curfew;
Oh god, I was a prisoner, too!
Could not recognize the faces standing over me;
They were all dressed in uniforms of brutality.
How many rivers do we have to cross.
Before we can talk to the boss?
All that we got, it seems we have lost;
we must have really paid the cost
(that's why we gonna be)
Burnin' and lootin' tonight."
Bob Marley, "Burnin' & Lootin'" *Burnin'*, 1973.

"So, my friend, I wish that you could see,
Like a bird in the tree, the prisoners must be free
Never make a politician grant you a favor;
They will always want to control you forever.
It takes a revolution to make a solution."
Bob Marley, "Revolution," *Natty Dread*, 1974.

Blacks around the world hailed reggae super star Bob Marley for his revolutionary lyrics. Having grown up poor in Jamaica and rising quickly to musical stardom, Marley never forgot his humble beginnings as he sang for people to "Get Up, Stand Up" for their rights against exploitation and government oppression. The CIA particularly worried about Marley helping a socialist prime minister win re-election against the candidate they backed. Evidence also supports that conservative government forces killed Marley's bandmate Peter Tosh for his leftist politics.

Bob Marley and Peter Tosh both grew up in squalid Jamaican homes. They met and formed a singing group called The Wailers in the mid-60s. By the mid-70s they broke into the American and British music world. Their 1974 *Burnin'* album was known for its Black Power songs such as "I Shot the Sheriff," "Burnin' and Lootin'," and the aforementioned "Get Up, Stand Up." His next album's "Revolution" was particularly incendiary in saying that there was no political change without revolutionary struggle.[975]

Bob Marley, Peter Tosh and their friends in the Rastafarian community preached that Jamaicans should resist American interventions. (They also, for better or worse, preached for the use of marijuana. While likely part of a rationalization of abusive use, some say it was to resist the use of heroin and coke that conservative political forces had contributed to becoming part of the country's trade).[976] Reports claimed that the CIA gained right-wing allies within a

Jamaican police department who attacked Tosh. While Tosh separated from the Wailers in about '75, he continued producing solo Reggae albums. Tosh had his door knocked in by conservative police figures twice in the '70s, and they dislocated several of his ribs in a beating.[977]

Democratic socialist leader Michael Manley had won the 1972 election as the Prime Minister of Jamaica with his People's National Party (PNP). Manley lived near Bob Marley and was friends with him, spending many nights at his house.[978] Despite U.S. government denials, researchers found covert interventions used against Manley's government that included arson, bombing and assassination. Manley's forces intercepted at least one shipment of 500 machine guns coming from a right-wing paramilitary faction with CIA roots and leaders convicted of drug trafficking. This right-wing group reportedly aided the trafficking of cocaine and heroin into Jamaica.[979]

Evidence supports that the CIA acted on increasing concerns about Bob Marley, who singled out the CIA with revulsion in political songs such as "Rat Race," where he sung, "Rasta don't work for no CIA!" In 1976, Prime Minister Michael Manley said the CIA-supported groups fueled unrest to influence the results of the upcoming elections. The Governor-General of Jamaica declared a state of emergency. The government police fought this unrest that Manley claimed was organized by CIA-backed opposition leader Edward Seaga and his Jamaica Labour Party (JLP).[980]

Close to the day of the 1976 election, Prime Minister Manley planned a free concert with Bob Marley sponsored by the Jamaican Ministry of Culture. A number of weeks before the concert, The Concrete Jungle, a paramilitary group that supported the Jamaica Labour Party, had held Marley at gunpoint and extorted regular payments from him. Manley's People's National Party (PNP) sent gunmen to guard Marley's home and ward off the extortionists. Days before the concert, Concrete Jungle gunmen broke into a neighbor's home where they shot Marley, his wife Rita, and his manager.[981]

Miraculously, they all survived after hospitalization. Police scared off the attackers before they could kill the Marleys. Prime Minister Manley had police, soldiers and Rastafarians escort the Marleys and Wailers band members to a secluded mountain encampment where they were guarded. Several days after his recovery, Marley appeared at the concert on stage with Manley. He and his PNP handily won the election.[982]

Those present at the encampment said an unarmed right-wing agent did get past the guards to attack Marley covertly. A group was making a documentary on Marley and the concert. Unknown to anyone on the film crew at the time, cameraman Carl Colby was the son of CIA director William Colby.[983]

Cinematographer Lee Lew-Lee, a former Black Panther of half-Asian descent, was part of the film crew. Lew-Lee, who later gained acclaim as cameraman for the Academy Award-winning documentary *The Panama Deception,* was close with members of the Wailers. Present when Carl Colby came into the encampment, Lew-Lee said that Colby brought a new pair of boots for Marley. The reggae star tried the boots on immediately—a reported customary gesture among Rastafarians. Sticking his foot in, the singer exclaimed "Ow" as something jabbed him. Marley pulled out a length of metal wire that was embedded in the boot.[984]

Lew-Lee said he thought nothing of the boot incident at the time but then became suspicious when Marley was playing soccer five months later and broke his toe on that same foot. When the bone wouldn't mend, doctors found it had cancer. The cancer quickly metastasized throughout Marley's body. Marley's manager Don Taylor also claimed in his memoirs that a "senior CIA agent" had been planted among the pre-election concert film crew as part of a plan to "assassinate" Marley. Many suggested that the wire in Colby's gift boots was either made out of a radioactive metal or contained a highly carcinogenic chemical element on its tip (*The New York Times* cited a recent use of carcinogens for asssassination regarding a former KGB spy who died within three weeks of the suspected poisoning).[985]

Several journalists, including Pulitzer Prize winner Gary Webb and Daurius Figueira, along with former CIA agent, Philip Agee, stated that the CIA opposed Jamaica's Democratic Socialist Prime Minister Michael Manley. Webb, Figueira and Agee said that the CIA used money, guns and cocaine to undermine Manley's administration. Webb detailed how Norman Descoteaux, the CIA station chief in Jamaica, began a program which included assassinations. That program worked with various opposition groups, including the Jamaican Labour Party and their supportive gangs, such as the Shower Posse (also called the Concrete Jungle). Shower Posse member Cecil Connor claimed he was trained by the CIA to fight political wars for the JLP. [986]

This supports the report of Bob Marley's manager, Don Taylor, who the Shower Posse shot in the same incident in which they shot Bob and Rita Marley. Taylor said that Rastafarians captured several of the gunmen who shot him and Marley before the Smile concert. The Rastafarians brought Taylor and Marley to the gunmen where the attackers confessed. Taylor described the situation:

> "Three young men were tied and bound in the gully when we arrived. One, a young man I knew only as Leggo Beast, told the ghetto court that four of them had been trained by the CIA and given guns and unlimited supplies of cocaine to do the assassination. Claiming that they had been caught up in a situation in which they had no control, the prisoners tried to explain their involvement while pleading with me and Bob for mercy. But ghetto justice had to prevail… The court, as constituted, listened to every plea and then passed sentence on

> the three accused, who confirmed that four men had been involved in the shooting....Two of the accused were hanged and one shot in the head sometime between 5 and 6p.m. on that Wednesday afternoon...Before shooting the last victim, the ghetto generals offered the gun to Bob, saying, 'Skip, yuh waan shoot the blood chaat here?' As I watched, Bob refused without emotion."[987]

Researchers claim that one of the gunman who shot Bob Marley was Lester Coke, also known as Jim Brown and likely the fourth man. Cecil Connor worked with Coke and ended up testifying against him. One writer claimed Coke was burned to death in jail, reportedly so as not reveal any more secrets about the CIA and JLP's criminal activities.[988] Don Taylor had a different report on the fourth man. He stated learning that the fourth man "went insane over the attempted assassination and died afterwards of a cocaine overdose."[989]

By 1980, despite dying of cancer, Bob Marley had become a hero for Africans. A New York radio network owner said in 1980 that in Europe and Africa, Marley was "bigger than Christ and Muhammad combined." Marley played concerts for leftist leaders such as Marxist Robert Mugabe in Zimbabwe. Marley also supported leftist struggles in Angola, Mozambique and South Africa. New York's Black Liberation Movement-aligned WLIB radio worked to get Marley's next album, *Uprising*, nationwide play on conservative-controlled black radio.[990]

The CIA and its collaborating forces, bent on defeating the democratic socialist People's National Party (PNP) in Jamaica in the 1980 elections, threatened Marley in his last days and democracy thereafter. Marley held shows despite his approaching death and CIA operatives' threats to not come back to Jamaica before the election. *The Daily Gleaner* helped the pro-Reagan Jamaica Labour Party (JLP) finally defeat Manley's socialist PNP election (The CIA reportedly worked inside the Inter-American Press Association to influence the right-wing transformation of the Jamaican newspaper, *The Daily Gleaner*). Bob Marley died in May of 1981, and 30,000 mourners attended his Jamaican wake.[991] The JLP-linked Concrete Jungle paramilitary group resumed perpetrating violence after the PNP regained leadership in 2000.[992]

Former Wailer Peter Tosh collaborated with Rolling Stone's lead singer Mick Jagger after Marley's 1981 death. Tosh continued his political "message music" until he was murdered with two friends by gunmen in 1987's JLP-led Jamaica. Tosh's producer, Wayne Johnson, cited an unnamed government official who told him that one of Tosh's murderers was a police officer. The government ended up only arresting and convicting one man, who reportedly wasn't carrying a gun. Similar to Jimi Hendrix's spy manager clearing out Hendrix's New York studio after his death and then claiming important song tapes had been stolen, Tosh's New York apartment was cleared out by "burglars." A New York public administrator then gained possession of Tosh's master tapes and hid them in a warehouse for years.[993]

40: Belafonte; Rep. McKinney & Tupac; Sports; Hampton's POCC; FBI Deputizes the Rich

> "I call President Bush a terrorist. I call those around him terrorists, as well: Condoleeza Rice, Rumsfeld, Gonzales in the Justice Department and certainly Cheney. ...It is tragic that the dubious way in which this president acquired power should have begun to unravel the Constitution and the peoples of this country. ...Yes, I say there are people in this country who live in terror. Poverty is terror. Having your Social Security...your livelihood as an elderly person slowly disappearing with no replenishment is terror. ...watching drugs permeate our communities and destroy our young, it's a life of terror. And men who sit in charge of that distribution mechanism, which can help the American people overcome these problems and refuse to do so, while giving the rich more money ...redirecting resources from those who are truly in need...going into the Middle East, bombing at will.... over 100,000 have already been killed... That is unacceptable."
>
> Harry Belafonte, *Democracy Now!* WBAI New York, 2006.

One of the earliest black entertainer activists, Harry Belafonte, outlived the above-mentioned three activist entertainers that followed him. Belafonte was born in Harlem in 1927 and spent five of his first 13 years in his mother's birthplace of Jamaica. After enlisting in the U.S. Navy during WWII, Belafonte came back to develop a career in acting. When he acted in a musical, it opened the door for a new singing career. Belafonte had award-winning success in both acting and music, selling millions of records.[994]

While Harry Belfonte said that his conscience led him into WWII, his mentor Paul Robeson may have further jumpstarted his sense of activism. The older, multi-talented, internationally reknowned Robeson was a college All-American football player, graduated from Columbia Law School, and won many awards for his music and acting. As an activist, Robeson fought for anti-lynching laws and many progressive causes, but was black-listed and had his passport revoked for defending communism.[995]

After regaining his passport in 1958, Robeson sung in concerts around the world in the next three years. In 1961, Robeson had planned a trip to Cuba, just after Fidel Castro and Che Guevera's revolution.[996] Paul Robeson, Jr. said that shortly before this trip, the CIA dosed his father's drink with LSD, or the more powerful hallucinogen BZ. When Robeson, Jr. went to check on his father, someone dosed Robeson, Jr's drink too.[997] These types of actions, well-documented as part of the CIA's Project MK-ULTRA, led Robeson, Sr. to feel suicidal.[998]

Robeson, Sr. experienced a flashback—the symptoms of tripping again—several months later. Doctors and associates talked Robeson's wife into having him go into a psychiatric hospital near London where they gave him fifty-four Electric Convulsive Treatments (ECT). Robeson, Jr. found that this, along with drug therapy used at the British hospital, matched the CIA's Project MK-ULTRA "mind depatterning" technique.[999] A leading study in 2007 showed that ECT, even in its more refined uses today, can cause "permanent amnesia and cognitive deficits."[1000] Paul Robeson, Sr kept a more isolated existence between his British hospital stay and his 1973 death.

Belafonte quickly followed in Robeson's footsteps by using his stardom to connect with the international community. He made links with African leaders early on, while also fighting to end segregation and gain equal access to voting for blacks in America. During one trip to Africa, the FBI visited Belafonte's home in the early '50s. The agents told Belafonte's wife and kids that they were investigating the entertainer for treason.

Belafonte persevered and regularly aided his friend Martin Luther King, Jr. Belafonte provided his New York home to King, bailed him out of jail, and funded the Freedom Summer student bus riders in the early '60s. U.S. Intelligence kept a regular wiretap on his and King's conversations.[1001]

At some point the CIA took the lead in these efforts. As stated earlier, they inserted Jay Richard Kennedy, cited as one of their top civil rights spies, into Belafonte's life as his manager. Jay Kennedy then mentored widely suspected Panther spy, Elaine Brown (Ch.s 4, 6, 10). As also previously noted, evidence supports that U.S. Intelligence had inserted agents into the lives of other black musicians, including Jimi Hendrix, Tupac and Wu Tang Clan (Ch.s 22-5, 31, 38). It's unknown how much Jay Kennedy may have sabotaged Belafonte's work before the entertainer fired him.[1002]

Belafonte continued to work on many other causes. He helped initiate the "We Are the World," project to raise millions of dollars for starving Africans. Belafonte also aided South African anti-apartheid leader Nelson Mandela, amongst other African leaders over many decades, and he worked against the U.S. embargo of Cuba. Belafonte started serving as UNICEF's Goodwill Ambassador in 1987 while remaining an outspoken critic of U.S. war policies and global oppression.

In 2006, Harry Belafonte led a black delegation that visited Hugo Chavez's Venezuela, where he denounced President Bush, later saying that all members of Bush's administration are terrorists. He cited them for killing over 100,000 Iraqis without just cause (later estimated as over 650,000 by Johns Hopkins School of Public Health, printed in Britain's top medical journal *Lancet* by 2006), as well as squandering billions while U.S. citizens were left to die in Hurrican Katrina and the poor in general are left without health care.[1003] Belafonte helped develop the community of conscience that shaped the politics of future black entertainers such as Jimi Hendrix, Tupac Shakur, and Bob Marley.

Of these entertainers, Tupac Shakur may have been the most prolific. Considering that Tupac died several months after his 25th birthday in June of 1996, his rate of creative output appears historically unmatched. Two of his five chart-topping CDs (which sold the most worldwide in a week) came out when he was alive.[1004] He produced five solo rap CDs (and his fourth recording was a double CD) and one group CD before he died. Death Row released the fifth CD just after his murder. Tupac had left hundreds of unreleased songs. Afeni Shakur then produced, or allowed production of, ten CDs of his unreleased recordings (four single CDs and three double CDs). Several of these posthumous CDs topped the pop music charts and most of them sold over a million copies.[1005]

Tupac also worked on a vast amount of other art in his short, Intelligence-beleaguered life. He produced dozens of music videos and acted in six films, five of them in lead roles. He further wrote a books-worth of poetry. His first manager, Leila Steinberg, produced Tupac's book of poetry, *The Rose That Grew From Concrete,* releasing it after his death (many celebrities read or interpreted these poems for 2 CD releases of the same name).[1006]

And finally, Tupac Shakur, Jimi Hendrix and Bob Marley were the youngest of the *Forbes* Magazine's "Richest Deceased Celebrity" top ten list. While Tupac ranked tenth in 2001, dying at age 25, Jimi Hendrix ranked ninth dying at age 27 and Bob Marley sold enough in 2001 for an eighth ranking, dying at age 35. All three were also the only black members of that celebrity list, which was topped by Elvis Presley. The $12 million Tupac's work generated in 2003 moved him up to number 8 on the *Forbes* list that year.

Albeit a morbid list, it shows how hard the three worked in their abbreviated lives. This gives a final support for U.S. Intelligence motives to murder them. As noted, U.S. Intelligence, in coordination with police intelligence of American allies, represents the very wealthiest sectors of society, helping them maintain their economically superior place at the expense of the poor. The *Forbes* wealthiest deceased celebrity list reveals people's devotion to the creative work of Tupac, Hendrix and Marley. In part, the three singers' work served as a vehicle for their attempt to better the world for the poor and less-empowered.

In November of 2005, U.S. Congresswoman Cynthia McKinney (D-Georgia) wrote legislation to obtain and analyze all government records on Tupac Shakur. She modeled her H.R. 4210—The Tupac Amaru Shakur Records Collections Act of 2005—after the John F. Kennedy legislation, H.R. 2554. The act would create a Tupac

Amaru Shakur Records Collection at the National Archives and Records Administration (NARA), and a copy at an archive approved by the Tupac Shakur Arts Center in Stone Mountain, Georgia. Afeni Shakur started the Center on behalf of her son and holds a performing arts camp there among other activities. (Note that McKinney also opposed the Iraq war and had further held a congressional hearing where she invited investigators who testified that the Bush administration orchestrated 9-11. More in Ch.36).[1007]

In April of 2006, Capitol Hill police and federal prosecutors led Rep. McKinney in front of a grand jury where prosecutors came close to charging her with assaulting a police officer who grabbed her in the Capitol Hill lobby. She wasn't arrested or charged with anything in the lobby and police reportedly apologized to McKinney in her office after the incident.[1008] Rep. McKinney held a press conference when reports arose that police would later charge her with assault. Entertainer activists Harry Belafonte and Danny Glover appeared there to support McKinney, as did visiting Atlanta supporters who held signs saying, "Is Cynthia a Target?" One of McKinney's attorneys suggested that top Republican lawmakers may have been behind the accusations and possible criminal charges. Involved in much previous targeting (Ch.31), the Fraternal Order of the Police (FOP) officially commended the Capitol Hill officer and condemned McKinney. A Dekalb county (Atlanta) police officer, the police division involved in targeting Tupac and H. Rap Brown, introduced this motion at the FOP national board meeting.[1009]

Police groups and prosecutors used the Capitol Hill incident to target Cynthia McKinney with opportune timing—just before the Georgia Republican Party waged a huge crossover vote campaign to unseat her in 2006. This ended a long conservative establishment targeting of Rep. McKinney which ranged from an earlier crossover vote that briefly unseated her in 2002, to a failure to investigate and protect her from a stalker for years. For months at a time McKinney had to live constantly in the dark with all of her shades down, due to a man that terrorized her and tried to break into her home.

In the 2006 election, Republican voters were recruited by a huge media campaign to vote for McKinney's Democratic opponent in the Congressional primary (her district is largely Democrat and Georgia is one of the only states that allows crossover voting). There were also unverified reports that voting machines (manufactured and programmed by Republican-owned companies) discarded votes for her en masse.[1010]

On the first of several final notes, other groups that U.S. Intelligence may have targeted deserve examination. Similar to the expedited drafting and jailing of anti-war Muslim boxing champ Muhammad Ali, U.S. Intelligence has appeared to target top black athletes with any activist links. Attacks, that include flimsy police charges, have come against the top athletes of various sports who are involved in activism or who have set up foundations for poor black communities.

One of many examples of charitable athletes includes basketball star Allen Iverson. Soon after he won the MVP award, police made domestic charges that were eventually dropped. Iverson said he was considering moving out of Philadelphia because police were targeting him. A white police officer backed Iverson's claim, telling reporters that a group of officers at a social gathering toasted their gaining an initial felony charge against Iverson. The white whistleblowing cop was physically assaulted by his superiors and kicked off the force within a year. A gunman then shot at Iverson. Later, the same woman who tried to censor Tupac attempted to get an Iverson rap CD banned.[1011]

Amongst other examples, authorities also appeared to target Hall of Fame football star Jim Brown. Brown organized many activist projects throughout his career but his last project, Amer-I-Can, likely contributed to police charges and a jail sentence in 2002. The judge sentenced Brown to six months in jail for misdemeanor vandalism of a car he bought for his wife. A jury acquitted him of making a "terrorist threat" against his wife during an argument in the same 1999 incident. Brown hired about 95% of the Amer-I-Can staff from at-risk youth who leave gangs or are ex-convicts. Along with Tupac and Mutulu Shakur, Brown aided the Los Angeles Bloods' and Crips' gang truce.[1012]

The CIA and FBI further targeted white leftist musicians, such as former Beatles singer/lyricist, John Lennon. Respectable researchers and family members of anti-war musician John Lennon, a one-time proclaimed socialist, support that the CIA orchestrated his murder. Police foul play and media cover-up also suggest more investigation is needed into any U.S. Intelligence aid in the documented police cover-up of Nirvana lead singer Kurt Cobain's death in 1993, due to his little-publicized radical leftist politics (space precludes further details here).[1013]

Some believe that the massive sweep of this targeting relates to recently increasing fascism against all Americans and the diminishing global energy resources that could drastically change the way we live (see footnote).[1014] Examples of governmental attacks on the communities mentioned above remain mere glimpses of their totality. Conservative forces have continued their onslaught against rappers, activists, entertainers and athletes. Meanwhile, the Bush Administration successfully pushed forward new intiatives such as the Military Commissions Act that shreds the Bill of Rights for all Americans, with U.S. Congress passing it. More specifically to Tupac's support network, a Mississippi judge suspended the law license of New Afrikan People's Organization chairman, Chokwe Lumumba, for a year around 2005. Lumumba, Tupac's national legal adviser, received this for a contempt of court charge. Lumumba had worked on the cases of Geronimo Pratt, Assata Shakur, and Mutulu Shakur.[1015]

As this book headed for its first perfect-bound printing in 2007, New York's Pacifica radio station, WBAI, reported that a group of police beat Tupac's New York trial lawyer Michael Tarif Warren (also Mutulu Shakur's lawyer) and his attorney wife Evelyn Warren. The two human rights lawyers came upon a group of police kicking a handcuffed young black man. The police then punched and brutalized the couple for asking about it, taking them into custody. New York Councilman Charles Barron (a fomer Black Panther) talked to the precinct commander as 100-200 supporters demonstrated outside the precinct chanting "Freedom Fighters," upon their release. Charges against Michael Tarif Warren for "obstructing governmental administration" and resisting arrest, if successful, could have jeopardized his law license. The state ended up dropping all charges.[1016]

Fred Hampton, Jr.'s Prisoners of Conscience Committee (POCC) remains continuously under attack by the legacy of the brutal Chicago political establishment that murdered Fred Hampton, Sr (Ch.s 5, 13). This establishment, blamed for ordering the brutal "police riot" at the 1968 Democratic National Convention, took orders from Mayor Richard Daley. Richard Daley, Jr. took over where his father left off. While State's Attorney, in charge of Illinois' prosecutors in the 1980s, Chicago police used former Vietnam War military police torturer Jon Burge to use (or supervise use of) torture interrogation tactics. These tactics included suffocation as well as the use of electric cattle prods on the ears and genitals of at least 108 black and Latino suspects. A groundswell of bad publicity eventually led Chicago police chiefs to suspend Burge for these actions by 1991.[1017]

POCC's Minister of Defense Aaron Patterson spent 17 years on death row after a confession gained through Burge-supervised suffocations and beatings. Illinois Governor George Ryan pardoned Patterson in January of 2003, at which time he jumped into his activist leadership position. By that year, Richard Daley Jr. had gained a longtime position as Chicago's mayor. Patterson regularly spoke at anti-war rallies and anti-police brutality forums, while organizing with POCC.[1018]

Within 20 months, Chicago police culminated an operation with Federal Alcohol and Tobacco and Firearms (ATF) agents against Patterson. POCC Chairman Fred Hampton Jr. said they labeled this Operation Revolving Door, and Joe Gorman Jr. headed it. Hampton also named the connections to his father's murder in this operaton. He said that Mayor Ricahrd Daley Sr. had personally hired Michael Cronin, who headed the gang narcotics unit, while Joe Gorman Sr. used a machine gun to help kill Panther Chairman Fred Hampton Sr and Mark Clark. The ATF, the same group involved in murderously targeting Tupac, Biggie, Wu Tang Clan, MOVE, Panther leader

Eldridge Cleaver and Ceasar Chavez, arrested Patterson wth Michael Cronin present. They had paid someone to offer Patterson guns and drugs for sale. Hours before they arrested Patterson, a federal judge had brought Lt. Jon Burge to Chicago from his retirement in Florida, reportedly to testify on a case.[1019]

Judge Rebecca Pallmeyer, who had presided over a trial that removed Gov. Ryan from office, sentenced Patterson to 30 years in jail. Prosecutors did not charge Patterson with selling drugs or guns, nor possession of drugs and guns, but merely "conspiracy" to do so. Prosecutors alleged Paterson intended to become involved in these activities.[1020]

In September of 2007, Fred Hampton Jr. said that he and his fellow POCC members heard that Chicago police shot two black youths. The POCC decided to conduct a people's investigation of it. They came upon the police and got out of their cars to observe what was happening. The police beat Hamtpon and other POCC members for reportedly "attempting to disrupt the police investigation of an aggravated battery." Hampton was acquitted in mid-October of 2007.[1021]

As of February 2008, the FBI and Homeland Security had over 23,000 representatives of private corporations working with them as part of a group called InfraGard. According to InfraGard's website, these members come from 350 of the nation's Fortune 500 companies. Director Robert Mueller told an InfraGard convention, whose members came from 86 chapters nationwide, that they were to alert the FBI of any "suspicious activity or an unusual event." In turn, Mueller said, "they could sic the FBI on 'disgruntled employees who will use knowledge gained on the job against their employers.'"[1022]

More importantly, an InfraGard member blew the whistle on a very ominous role spelled out for his group. This whistleblower told *The Progressive* magazine editor Matthew Rothschild that agents of the FBI and Homeland Security addressed his chapter recently. The whistleblower said the agents told his chapter that "when—not if—martial law is declared, it was our responsibility to protect our portion of the infrastructure, and if we had to use deadly force to protect it, we couldn't be prosecuted."

While the FBI and a national leader of InfraGard denied this claim, Rothschild interviewed another chapter member, Christine Moerke, who confirmed it. A third chapter member, a CEO of a Wisconsin business, wouldn't deny that the agents made these statements, but lauded the InfraGard's "public-private partnership." The American Civil Liberties Union (ACLU) claims that the FBI folded "22,000 corporate bigwigs…into its domestic surveillance machinery," and that they are beyond the reach of the Freedom of Information Act under the "trade secrets" exemption.[1023]

For the reasons mentioned above, virtually all media organizations have long maintained various degrees of censorship over many of these issues. Gaining justice and a final peace on these issues may take a variety of tactics for which some of the organizations described in this book may be consulted. Defying imperial forces' "divide and conquer" strategy and salvaging a humane way of life will require a concerted effort by all racial and ethnic groups to oppose malevolent multinational corporate forces and their mercenary government puppets rather than each other.

Endnotes

[1] The FBI refused to release 97% of their 4000+ page FBI file on Tupac Shakur. Told to this author with information on Freedom Of Information Act (FOIA) response, by Tawanda Monroe of the FBI headquarters on 5/10/2000. FOIA request on these documents released 99 pages, FBI letter to this author, May 18, 2000, Request no. 911992, Re: Shakur, Tupac.

[2] See, for example, Frances Fox Piven and Richard A. Cloward, *Why Americans Don't Vote* and *Poor People's Movements* (New York: Vintage, 1977) pp.99-100. For example, see police intelligence's brutal beatings of striking workers in, Philip Foner, T*he Autobiographies of the Haymarket Martyrs* (New York: Monad Press, 1977), pp. 1,2,10. Referenced in Huey Newton, W*ar Against the Panthers*, (New York: Harlem Press/Writers & Readers, 1996), pp.6-8, 15-16. Also see the origins of the Secret Service and the Bureau of Investigation (later FBI) for these purposes, detailed in U.S. Congress. Senate. Book II: Final Report of the Select Committee to Study Governmental Operations with Respect to Intelligence Activities, 94th Cong., 2nd sess. 1976, p.21, and Michael R. Belknap, "The Mechanics of Repression: J. Edgar Hoover, the Bureau of Investigation and the Radicals 1917-1925," *Crime and Social Justice* (Spring-Summer 1977), p.50. Both referenced in Newton, *Panthers*, pp.16,17,24. And finally, see Charle Lane, "Book Details U.S. Protection for Former Nazi Officials," *Washington Post*, 5/14/04, p. A2.
[22] Frances Stonor Saunders, *The Cultural Cold War: The CIA and the World of Arts and Letters* (New York: The New Press, 1999),
[3] Frances Stonor Saunders, *The Cultural Cold War: The CIA and the World of Arts and Letters* (New York: The New Press, 2000), pp.34-36, 41.
[4] See, for example, Michael Parenti, *Inventing Reality*, (New York: St. Martins Press, 1986), p. 233. Carl Bernstein, "The CIA and the Media," *Rolling Stone*, 10/20/77; Stuart Loory, "The CIAs Use of the Press: A Mighty Wurlitzer," *Columbia Journalism Review*, September/October, 1974, pp.9-18. Cited in Parenti, p232-3. Morton Mintz & Jerry Cohen, *Power Inc.* (New York: Bantam Books, 1976), p.364. *The New York Times*, December 25, 26, 27, 1977. Ralph McGehee, *Deadly Deceits: My 25 Years in the CIA* (New York: Sheridan Square Publications, 1983).
[5] Personal interview with Tupac Shakur's long-time family friend and business manager, Watani Tyehimba, 5/10/00. Tyehimba was a Black Panther in Los Angeles who was a founding Director of Security for the New Afrikan People's Organization. On gangs' leftist politicization that started mostly with the Bloods and Crips gangs peace truce, see Alexander Cockburn, "Beat the Devil," *The Nation*, June 1, 1992, pp.738-9. Mike Davis, "Who Killed LA? A Political Autopsy," *New Left Review*, 197, 1993, p.7. Mike Davis, "Who Killed LA? Part Two: The Verdict is Given," *New Left Review* 198, 1993, p.34. Connie Bruck, "The Takedown of Tupac," *The New Yorker*, 7/7/97, p.53. Mutulu Shakur reportedly started organizing the truce in the Lompoc Penitentiary. http://www.hitemup.com/tupac/family.html .
[6] On Penal Coercion, see "Biderman's Chart on Penal Coercion," *Amnesty International Report on Torture, 1983*. Reproduced and discussed in Ward Churchill and Jim Vander Wall, *The Cointelpro Papers: Documents from the FBI's Secret Wars Against Dissent in the United States* (Boston: South End Press, 1990) pp.321-323. On use of Death Row Records as police intelligence front to continue Penal Coercion tactics as well as orchestrate Tupac's murder upon his leaving the company, see FBI agent and police detective disclosures in Sundance Award-winning documentary filmmaker Nick Broomfield's documentary, *Biggie and Tupac* (2001), as well as their disclosures in Randall Sullivan, *LAbyrinth: A Detective Investigates the Murders of Tupac Shakur and Notorious B.I.G., the Implications of Death Row Records' Suge Knight and the Origins of the Los Angeles Police Scandal* (New York: Atlantic Monthly Press, 2002). On targeting

rappers, see New York's rap intelligence unit, Dasun Allah, "NYPD Admits to Rap Intelligence Unit," *The Village Voice*, 3/23/04.
[7] Bobby Seale, exceprt from speeches and *The Black Panther*, collected in ed. Philip Foner, *The Black Panthers Speak* (New York: Da Capo Press, 1970,95), p.161
[8] See, for example, Huey P. Newton, *War Against the Panthers: A Study of Repression* (New York/London: Writers and Readers Publishing,1981/96). Bobby Seale, *Seize the Time* (New York: Random House,1968,70), p.59.
[9] "Top black... 1900-1950." Top black intellectual and socialist, W.E.B. Du Bois, had started the longest-running black improvement organization, the NAACP, in 1910. The Federal Bureau of Investigation's predecessor, the Bureau of Investigation, quickly dubbed the NAACP's journal *Crisis* as inflammatory. Ed.s Mari Jo Buhle, Paul Buhle, and Dan Georgakas, *Encyclopedia of the American Left* (Chicago: University of Illinois Press, 1992), p.203. On 5,000 lynchings, Piven and Cloward, *Poor People's Movements*, p.186.
[10] For example, see Kenneth O'Reilly, *Racial Matters: The FBI's Secret Files on Black America, 1960-1972* (New York: The Free Press, 1989), pp.112, 217, cited in Ward Churchill and Jim Vander Wall, *The COINTELPRO Papers: Documents from the FBI's Secret Wars Against Dissent in the United States* (Boston: South End Press, 1991), p.170.
[11] Howard Zinn, "Student Nonviolent Coordinating Committee," in Eds. Mari Jo Buhle, Paul Buhle, and Dan Georgakas, *Encylcopledia of the American Left* (Chicago, IL: University of Illinois Press, 1992), pp.75-6.
[12] Ward Churchill and Jim Vander Wall, The COINTELPRO Papers: *Documents from the FBI's Secret Wars Against Dissent in the United States* (Boston: South End Press, 1990), p.105. These authors cite H. Rap Brown, Die Nigger Die! (NY:The Dial Press, 1969) as their key reference for this information.
[13] "SNCC...mid-1966." Muhammad Ahmad (Maxwell Stanford, Jr.*) We Will Return in th Whirlwhnd: Black Radical Organizations 1960-1975* (Chicago, IL: Charles H. Kerr Publishers, 2007), pp.120-124. Churchill and Vander Wall, Agents of Repression, pp.44-6. M. Newton, *Bitter Grain: Huey Newton and the Black Panther Party* (Los Angeles: Holloway House, 1980), p.15. On RAM and Williams, see Dan Geogakas, "Armed Struggle—1960s and 1970s," *Encylcopledia of the American Left*, p.57. Included in Georgakas' references is Robert Williams, *Negroes with Guns* (NY: Marzani & Munsell, 1962).
[14] "Later in... for Self Defense." See Michael Newton, *Bitter Grain: Huey Newton and the Black Panther Party*, pp.12-14 (no known relation to Huey Newton). Ward Churchill and Jim Vander Wall, *The COINTELPRO Papers: Documents from the FBI's Secret Wars Against Dissent in the United States* (Boston: South End Press, 1990), pp112, 123 and Churchill and Vander Wall, *Agents of Repression: The FBI's Secret War Against the Black Panther Party and the American Indian Movement* (Boston: South End Press, 1991), pp.45, 52, 63. More information comes from former Panther Lee Lew Lee's documentary *All Power to the People* (1996) and information from former Panthers such as George Edwards, personal interview, 8/10/00. Note that in writing the history while in prison, ex-Panther Sundiata Acoli said Herman Ferguson and Max *Stamford* started RAM. S. Acoli, "A Brief History of the New Afrikan People's Struggle," p.8 www.prisonactivist.org . Also see, Bobby Seale, *Seize the Time* (New York: Random House, 1970), p.34, and Afeni Shakur, "We Will Win," in ed. Phil Foner, *The Black Panthers Speak* (New York: Di Capo/Perseus, 1970), p.161.
[15] "They decided... membership." See, for example, Seale, *Seize the Time*, pp.28-9.
[16] "Huey Newton... group." Ex-Panther Lee Lew-Lee's *All Power to the People* (documentary, 1996). On politcal organization and philosophy, see Huey Newton, *War Against the Panthers: A Study of Repression* (New York/London: Writers and Readers Publishing,1981/96), pp.28-35. Also see, Seale, Seize the Time, p. 82 and Afeni Shakur, "We Will Will," in ed. Phil Foner, *The Black Panthers Speak* (New York: Di Capo/Perseus, 1970), p.161.
[17] "Seale and Newton... 1970." Huey Newton, *To Die for the People: Selected Writings and Speeches*, ed. Toni Morrison, (New York: Writers and Readers Publishers, 1972,

1999), pp.3-6. Also see Michael Newton, *Bitter Grain: Huey Newton and the Black Panther Party*. Churchill and Vander Wall, *Agents of Repression* and *The COINTELPRO Papers*. Also, Lumumba Shaakur et al. *Look for Me in the Whirlwind*.. On Panther newspaper circulation, see Seale, *Seize the Time*, p.179.
[18] "U.S. Intelligence… Cointelpro." Peter Zimroth, *Perversions of Justice*, pp.73-4. Churchill and Vander Wall, *Agents of Repression*, pp.39-40, and *The COINTELPRO Papers*, p.xi.
[19] "On the second… of Information." Cleaver's detailed description in Newton, *Bitter Grain*, p.24.
[20] "U.S. Intelligence…cities." Newton, *Bitter Grain*, p.38, 173. Churchill and Vander Wall, *The COINTELPRO Papers*, p.126. *Agents of Repression*, p.64, Newton, *Bitter Grain*, p.38
[21] "For…arrest." Seale, *Seize the Time*, pp.106-7.
[22] M. Newton, *Bitter Grain*, pp.31, 35-6.
[23] "On October…him" For details, see Michael Newton, *Bitter Grain: Huey Newton and the Black Panther Party*, pp.29-31, 42-65.. For lesser details, see Ward Churchill and Jim Vander Wall, *Agents of Repression* (Boston: South End Press, 1990) and their *The Cointelpro Papers.*
[24] "After over…attempt." On CIA file and 'hit list,' see "National Security, Civil Liberties and the Collection of Intelligence: A Report on the Huston Plan," reported in *U.S. Congress, Senate, Book III. Final Report of the Select Committee to Study Government Operations with Respect to Intelligence Activities*, 94th Cong. 2d sess., 1976, pp.936-960. Cited in Huey Newton, *War Against the Panthers* (New York: Harlem River Press/Writers and Readers, 1991), pp.43, 93n. On charges dismissed see, Newton, Bitter Grain, p.65.
[25] See Frances Fox Piven and Richard A. Cloward, *Why Americans Don't Vote*.
[26] "CIA…target." Clayborne Carson, David Gallen ed, *Malcolm X: The FBI File* (New York:Carroll and Graf, 1991), p. 17.
On effort to "destroy King," see memorandum in CIA file for Chief, Security Research Staff, from Allan Morse, one Jay R. Kennedy report. 6/9/65, p.7, in this writer's possession (Thanks to New Haven Black Panther founding member, George Edwards, for providing copies of these documents, originally obtained in a FOIA filing by filmmaker, Lee Lew-Lee. Also see, Wallace Turner, "FBI Taps Called Plan to Discredit Dr. King," *The New York Times*, Monday, May 21, 1973, p. A18. William Pepper, *Orders to Kill* (New York: Warner Books, 1998), p294-295.
[27] "Historians… 1964." Frances Fox Piven and Richard A. Cloward, *Poor People's Movements: Why they succeed, how they fail* (New York: Vintage, 1979) p.244-8.
[28] Lewis Killian, *The Impossible Revolution?* (New York: Random House, 1968), p. 601.
[29] "Blacks… Brown." William Pepper, *Orders To Kill: The Truth Behind the Murder of Martin Luther, Jr.* (New York: Warner Books,1998). p. 446.
[30] William Pepper, *Orders To Kill: The Truth Behind the Murder of Martin Luther, Jr.* (New York: Warner Books,1998). See Foreward by Dexter Scott King.
[31] "King had won…election." This poor people's march was called an "extremely explosive situation." Memorandum from Howard Osborn, Director of Security to Deputy Director of Support. 3/27/68, copy in this writer's possession. Also, the fact that MLK was assassinated on the exact day anniversary of his official anti-Vietnam War announcement attests to that stance as a major reason for his assassination. See more on this tactic below.
[32] "Pepper…balcony." See both, William Pepper, *Orders to Kill* (New York: Warner Books, 1998) and *An Act Of State: The Execution of Martin Luther King* (New York: Verso, 2003). Also see, Clayborne Carson, ed. by David Gallen, *Malcolm X: The FBI File* (New York: Carroll and Graf, 1991), p. 17. Pepper, *Orders to Kill*, p.82. Also see, DiEgenio and Pease, *The Assassinations*, "MLK" pp.432-529.
[33] In support…death." On McCollough as undercover Military Intelligence agent, see William F. Pepper, *Act of State: The Execution of Martin Luther King* (London/New York: Verso, 1993) p.74. On McCollough racing to MLK's body to check for life signs,

Pepper, *Act of State*, p.160. Also see James DiEugenio and Lisa Pease, *The Assassinations*, p.413. They refer to McCollough as a deep cover operative for the Memphis police, which he was while also working for military intelligence according to William Pepper, p.424 n.191. McCollugh even confirmed the picture of the first person kneeling over the shot MLK was him, a a Congressional report. Pepper, Act of State, p.12.

[34] "A former Naval...Pentagon." See photograph of these snipers' orders that day in photo no.33, Pepper, *Orders to Kill.*, with explanation at pp.424-5. MLK Papers director, Stanford professor Clayborne Carson read from the interview at the trial, Pepper, *Act of State*, pp.129, 283-91. On third SFG verifying first two, see, for example, William Pepper, *An Act Of State: The Execution of Martin Luther King*, pp.72-4, 129-31.

[35] Pepper, *An Act of State*, pp.66-7. Also see William Pepper, "An Act of State: The Execution of Martin Luther King: Talk given at Modern Times Bookstore, San Francisco, CA," 2//4/03 p.14. www.ratical.org/ratville/JFK/WFP020403.html

[36] See Pepper's *Act of State* book tour talk at Modern Times Bookstore on 2/4/03.

[37] "The BBC...it." Pepper helped validate Billet's story by presenting Billet a nameless photo line-up from which he identified various Mafia bosses at the scene Pepper, *Orders To Kill*, pp.145-7, 160, 174, 275. *Act of State*, p.118.

[38] "The BBC doumentary...claims." Pepper, *Orders To Kill*, pp.145-7, 160-2, 174.

[39] "As Pepper...responsibility." Pepper, Orders to Kill, p.539.

[40] "Pepper...*Show*." Pepper, *Orders To Kill*, pp.301, 304-305.

[41] "Out of...*Live*." Pepper, *Act of State*, pp.323-5. The *Prime Time Live* show was on 12/16/93.

[42] "Jowers gave...MLK." Pepper, *Act of State*, pp.73-4, 110-112, 137-9.

[43] Spates gave a deposition and signed an afidavit to this statement. Pepper, *Act of State*, p.138.

[44] "Glenda...assassination." Grabow had been injured in a car accident just prior to the trial an couldn't testify in person but her husband testified to the authenticity of her affidavits. Pepper, *Act of State*, pp.53-61, 122-3.

[45] "Witnesses...King." Pepper, *Act of State*, pp.73-4, 110-113.

[46] "Amongst much...in his office." Pepper, *Act of State*, pp.127-8.

[47] Pepper, *Orders to Kill*, p.431.

[48] "Furthermore, videotape...Ray.'" Pepper, *Act of State*, p.74, 142,. On Kyles as police intelligence informant, Pepper was told Kyles did that from '67-'68, *Orders to Kill*, 391-2.

[49] "Other testimony came... bathroom." Pepper, *Act of State*, pp.117-118.

[50] "Testimony continued... thereafter." Pepper, *Act of State*, pp.117-118.

[51] "Two...MLK." Pepper, *Act of State*, pp.30, 119-120.

[52] "And finally... hiding." Pepper, *Act of State*, pp.71-3, 129-30. Also see, Ei Eugenio and Pease, *Assassinations*, pp.502-3. Note that at p.71, Pepper tells how Terrell was used by ABC as a highly credible source and how Terrell believed Hill was murdered in what was described as a "professional killling." This caused the two snipers Pepper's investigative team interviewed, 'Warren' and 'Murphy,' to remain in Latin American exile (p.73).

[53] "Stanford...King." See interviews with those snipers read at the trial MLK's family held vs. government co-conspirator, Lloyd Jowers with Pepper representing them. William Pepper, *An Act Of State: The Execution of Martin Luther King*, pp.67-71,129, 283-91. Also see William Pepper, *Orders to Kill*, pp.418-29, 481. Further see, James DiEugnio and Lisa Pease, eds, *The Assassinations: Probe Magazine on JFK, MLK, RFK and Malcolm X* (Los Angeles: Feral House, 2003) pp.406-7, 502-3. On "friendlies not wearing ties...McCollugh only one close to MLK without tie, see Pepper, *Act of State*, p.286 and *Orders to Kill*, p.476 and photo #36. It further should be noted that a picture of witnesses at the scene appear to be pointing upward at the shooter as if the lethal shot may have come from another location. Some have suggested this came from a sniper on top of another higher building. Pepper shows evidence for several shooters aiming at

King so this scenario allows for a different shooter. Also see photo of Army orders photo no.33, Pepper, *Orders to Kill.*, with explanation at pp.424-5.
[54] "Stanford History…hotel." See, Pepper, *Act of State*, pp.129, 283-91. Also see Pepper, *Orders to Kill.*.
[55] "The jury…support." On the verdict, see the complete trial transcript at the King Family's The King Center website www.thekingcenter.org/new/trial/Volum14.html . On Pepper and media see Pepper's *Act of State* book tour talk at Modern Times Bookstore on 2/4/03. www.ratical.org/ratville/JFK/WFP020403.html On Ramsey Clark's view of the media, see his group the International Action Center www.iacenter.org
[56] "Coretta…importance." William Pepper, *An Act Of State: The Execution of Martin Luther King*. Kevin Sack and Emily Yellin, "Dr. King's Slaying Finally Draws a Jury Verdict, but to Little Effect," *New York Times*, 12/10/99, pp.A1, A26.
[57] See www.thekingcenter.org and click on "News and Information" and then click on "Trial Transcript."
[58] These and other Panther Quotes from Ed. Philip Foner, *The Black Panthers Speak* (New York: De Capo Press, 1995), pp.100, 146. Eldridge xcerpt from "The Black Man's Stake in Vietnam," *The Black Panther*, 3/23/69. Kathleen excerpted from "Liberation and Political Assassination," *The Black Panther*, 5/18/68.
[59] "After over…in '67." On CIA file and 'hit list,' see "National Security, Civil Liberties and the Collection of Intelligence: A Report on the Huston Plan," reported in *U.S. Congress, Senate, Book III. Final Report of the Select Committee to Study Government Operations with Respect to Intelligence Activities*, 94th Cong. 2d sess., 1976, pp.936-960. Cited in Huey Newton, *War Against the Panthers* (New York: Harlem River Press/Writers and Readers, 1991), pp.43, 93n. On charges dismissed see, Newton, Bitter Grain, p.65.
[60] "The documents…thereafter." See the text of a memorandum report on this strategy dated 8/30/67, Philadelphia FBI office Special Agent in Charge (SAC), to the FBI Director, Ward Churchill and Jim Vander Wall, *Agents of Repression* (Boston: South End Press,1990), pp.44-46. Also see a copy of an FBI document from 8/25/67, headed SAC Albany, Director, FBI on COUNTERINTELLIGENCE PROGRAM, BLACK NATIONALIST-HATE GROUPS, INTERNAL SECURITY. It was routed to over 20 listed city offices including Oakland area's San Francisco office and discussed strategies for "disrupting" and "neutralizing" black activist organization's activities. These "hate" organizations included Martin Luther King's Southern Christian Leadership Conference. In Churchill and Vander Wall, *The COINTELPRO Papers*, pp.92-3.
[61] "U.S. Intelligence…Hilliard." On Peace and Freedom Party, Churchill and Vander Wall, *The COINTELPRO Papers*, p.128. On raid of Cleaver's home and arresting 25 other Panthers, Newton, *Bitter Grain*, pp.68-9.
[62] "After Martin…their membership." On riots in over 100 cities, see *BBC News*, "On This Day: '1968: Martin Luther King Shot Dead.'"
http://news.bbc.co.uk/onthisday/hi/dates/stories/april/4/nesid_243000/2453987.stm . Panthers keeping Oakland blacks from rioting, see M. Newton, *Bitter Grain*, pp.71-2. Newton said the Panthers saw how 1967 riots in Detroit and Newark led to murderous police responses.
[63] "Police took matters…shot." Mostly from Newton, Bitter Grain, pp.74-78. Also see Robert Scheer, "Introduction," in *Eldridge Cleaver, Post-Prison Writings and Speeches* (New Yor: Rampart/Vintage boks, 1969), p.xix. Cited in Churchill and Vander Wall, *The COINTELPRO Papers*, p.128-9. Hutton's early membership appeared to increase his risk since police murderously targeted at least half of the original Panthers by the 90s. Bobby Seale in Lee Lew Lee's *All Power to the People* (documentary, 1996).
[64] "With Hutton's…1971." See Tackwood, *Glass House Tapes*, and note that Tackwood also passed a polygraph about his account, as cited in Churchill and Vander Wall, *Agents of Repression*, p.95 note 205. This source also cites former FBI agent M. Wesley Swearingen's deposition taken in Honolulu, Hawaii, October 1980, p.2 in his discussions with FBI undercover agent Darthard Perry, a.k.a. Othello.

[65] AIRTEL, dated 5/15/69, from Director, FBI to 27 SACs (names deleted; locations deleted other than Chicago, Albany, captioned BLACK PANTHER PARTY (BREAKFAST FOR CHILDREN PROGRAM), cited in Churchill and Vander Wall, *Agents of Repression*, pp.68, 399n.
[66] "The leadership…lines." Murray Kempton, *The Briar Patch: The People of the State of New York v. Lumumba Shakur et al.* (New York, Dell, 1973) p.57. This book was a National Book Award winner. Also see, M Newton, *Bitter Grain: Huey Newton and the Black Panther Party* (Los Angeles: Holloway House, 1991, p.176.
[67] "With membership… Wisdom')." On Panther New York estimates and courthouse beating, M. Newton, *Bitter Grain*, p.174, 176. Newton also described Brooklyn entrapment, but best source for that is Paul Chevigny, *Cops and Rebels: A Study in Provocation* (New York: Curtis/Pantheon, 1972). Tupac mentions McCreary as his "Uncle Thomas" along with Pratt and Odinga in "Words of Wisdom" on *2Pacalypse Now* (1991). He mentions "Huey" in "Changes" *2Pac: Greatest Hits* (1997). He also mentions Pratt and Odinga in "White Manz World" on *Ma.k.a.veli: Don Kiluminati, the 7 day theory* (1996). The Panther membership estimates are likely well below actual numbers as the New York Panthers reported gaining 800 new members in a single month. On New York as largest chapter, see Gene Marine, *The Black Panthers* (June, 1969), cited in Peter Zimroth, *Perversions of Justice: The Prosecution and Acquittal of the Panther 21* (New York: Viking, 1974), p.46
[68] "BOSS…activism." Zimroth, *Perversions of Justice*, pp.16, 48.
[69] "The Shakurs…chapter." On Abbah Shakur as well as the Shakurs and Odinga in the OAAU, see several sources. Personal interview with former Black Panther and Shakur family friend, Watani Tyehimba, 5/10/00. Also, Lumumba Shakur et al., *Look for Me In the Whirlwind: A Collective Autobiography of the New York 21* (New York: Vintage) pp.241-2, 264-5. On Abbah Shakur as a former Garvey follower, Jasmine Guy, *Afeni Shakur: Evolution of a Revolutionary* (New York: Atria, 2004), p.70. On Mutulu, Committee to End the Marion Lockdown, *Can't Jail the Spirit: Political Prisoners in the U.S.* (Chicago: CEML, 2002), pp.147-50.
[70] For example, Lumumba chose his first name in tribute to an important African leader whose rise and fall typified African history. Patrice Lumumba had won election to the presidency of the Congo and vowed to liberate it from Europe's Belgium. Belgium conquered the Congo with advanced weaponry developed during the European industrial revolution. While Belgium followed many European countries that invaded, colonized, and divided up virtually the whole of the African continent, Belgium's King Leopold's particular brand of brutality included chopping off the hands of any Africans caught stealing. Lumumba's independence from Western--European or American--control lead to his assassination, by former CIA agent accounts, through Western covert operations. John Stockwell, *In Search of Enemies* (New York: Norton, 1978), p.172. Cited in Noam Chomsky and Edward Herman, *The Washington Connection and Third World Fascim* (Boston: South End Press, 1979), p.50. Sekou Odinga came out and adopted his first name from the son of a poor farmer who became a labor movement activist and then the Marxist president of the African nation Guinea in 1958. Ed.s William Harris and Judith Levey, *The New Columbia Encyclopedia* (New York: Columbia University Press, 1975), p.2768. Sekou Odinga came out and adopted his first name from the son of a poor farmer who became a labor movement activist and then the Marxist president of the African nation Guinea in 1958.
[71] Peter Zimroth, *Perversions of Justice: The Prosecution and Acquittal of the Panther 21* (New York: Viking, 1974), p.46
[72] "By November…convictions." M. Newton, *Bitter Grain*, pp.180-1.
[73] "Tupac…charges." Lumumba Shakur, Afeni Shakur et al, *Look for Me in the Whirlwind: The Collective Autobiography of the New York 21* (New York: Vintage, 1971) p.292. Note that Lumumba Shakur and Sekou Odinga adopted their names from African nationalist leaders, Patrice Lumumba of the Congo, and Sekou Toure of Guinea. Frivolous arrest, see Newton, *Bitter Grain*, pp.180-1. Afeni's birth name was Alice Williams. On journalism award, see above and Peter Zimroth, *Perversions of Justice: The*

Prosecution and Acquittal of the Panther 21 (New York: Viking, 1974), p.12. Journalism award in Zimroth, p.13.

[74] "Meanwhile, three hours south... life plus 30 years." Marshall Edward Conway, *The Greatest Threat: The Black Panther Party and COINTELPRO.* (Baltimore, MD: iAMWE Publications, 2009), pp.55, 126-7,133, 135. For information from Baltimore Sun, Conway cited the book, *Black Radicalism and Political Repression in Baltimore*. Conway's *The Greatest Threat* was part of a masters thesis.

[75] Fred Hampton speech, originally printed in The Movement, January, 1970. Collected in ed. Philip Foner, *The Black Panthers Speak* (New York: Da Capo Press, 1970,95), pp.138-44.

[76] "The second... 1969." M. Wes Swearingen, *FBI Secrets: An Agent's Expose* (Boston: South End Press, 1995), pp.82-4.

[77] The irony of the United Slaves abbreviation as US is apparent. This work with Karenga came from undercover police Louis Tackwood & Citizens Research-Intelligence Committee, *The Glass House Tapes: The Story of an Agent Provocateur and the New Police-Intelligence Complex* (New York: Avon Books,1973). Cited in *Agents of Repression*, p63. The "drugs" provided by Tackwood was reported in M. Newton, *Bitter Grain*, p. 97.

[78] "Tackwood testified... assassination." M. Newton, *Bitter Grain*, p.95-97.

[79] Swearingen, *FBI Secrets*, pp.82-4.

[80] From two affidavits, one given to attorney Fred Hiestand and the other to Charles Garry, filed in *Black Panther Party v. Levi*, No. 76-2205 and interview with Fred Hiestand, 1/9/80. Also cited in information given to Ernest Volkman, Penthouse magazine, April, 1980. All cited in Huey P. Newton, *War Against the Panthers* (New York: Harlem River/Writers and Readers, 1996) pp.81,101n. FBI undercover agents George and Larry Stiner were tried and convicted of the murders. They did four years in prison before escaping and not being heard from again. Hubert was never apprehended. *War Against the Panthers*, p.81. And Swearingen, *FBI Secrets: An Agent's Expose*, p.84.

[81] Personal Interview with George Edwards, 7/24/07.

[82] Churchill and Vander Wall, *Agents of Repression*, p.79.

[83] "Years later... member." *Human Rights in the United States: The Unfinished Story, Current Political Prisoners—Victims of Cointelpro,* Issue Forum, U.S. Congressional Hearing, 9/14/00, 1:25 p.m. Rayburn House Office Building, Washington, D.C. Room 2000. http://www.ratical.org/co-globalize/CynthiaMcKinney/news/if000914HR.html Also, Personal interview, Michael Warren, attorney for Tupac Shakur and Mutulu Shakur in New York, 9/2/03.

[84] "Pratt gave a... chapters (Ch.s 6,10)." http://whosemedia.com/drums/2007/05/09/was-elaine-brown-an-agent/

[85] "All credible... informers'" M. Wesley Swearingen, *FBI Secrets: An Agent's Expose* (Boston, MA: South End Press,1995) pp.82-4.

[86] Perry's claim, Swearingen, *FBI Secrets*, p.83. George Edwards, personal interview, 6/12/07.

[87] See Malcolm X speech in American Experience: "Malcolm X: Make It Plain." PBS and The Autobiography of Malcolm X cited in Assassination, p.411. Also note that Swearingen testified on behalf of Pratt, Perry testified on behalf of other Panthers, and Tackwood made sweeping disclosures.

[88] Swearingen, *FBI Secrets*, pp.82-4.

[89] "A police... (Ch.s 22-5)." Randalll Sullivan, *LAbyrinth: A Detective Investigates the Murders of Tupac Shakur and Notorious B.I.G. the Implications of Death Row Records' Suge Knight and the Origins of the Los Angeles Police Scandal* (New York: Atlantic Monthly Press, 2002). Nick Broomfield, *Biggie and Tupac,* film documentary, 2002. Also see FBI agent whistleblower Kevin Hackie's statements in this book and film, as well as Gary Webb, *Dark Alliance* (New York: Seven Stories, 1998), on Death Row silent partner Michael Harris. All elaborated more on below.

[90] "Several... City." From two affidavits, one given to attorney Fred Hiestand and the other to Charles Garry, filed in *Black Panther Party v. Levi,* No. 76-2205 and interview

with Fred Hiestand, 1/9/80. Also cited in information given to Ernest Volkman, *Penthouse* magazine, April, 1980. All cited in Huey P. Newton, *War Against the Panthers* (New York: Harlem River/Writers and Readers, 1996) pp.81,101n. FBI undercover agents George and Larry Stiner were tried and convicted of the murders. They did four years in prison before escaping and not being heard from again. Hubert was never apprehended. *War Against the Panthers*, p.81.

[91] "Furthermore... precinct." Kempton, *Briar Patch*, p.77-8. Zimroth, *Perversions of Justice*, p.179-83. M. Newton, *Bitter Grain*, p.182.

[92] An attempt by the FBI to murder Lumumba that day is uncertain but possible. BOSS undercover agent Ralph White admitted shooting his gun *inside* the Harlem office with Lumumba there, though he said it was several days before the 17th. White said Lumumba warned him to never do that again, but White made the false claim Shakur said this due to his storing dynamite in the office Zimroth, *Perversions...*, p.187

[93] "These mid-January... visit." M. Newton, *Bitter Grain*, pp.181-5. Kempton, *The Briar Patch*, p.75-8. Zimroth, *Perversions of Justice*, pp.179-83. Note that police said they only accidentally came upon Odinga and the other Panthers who were there to shoot at a police precinct. Evidence suggests this was a complete fabrication. New York police officers Roland McKenzie and Louis Scorzello told of coming upon Sekou Odinga, Kuwasi Balagoon and Joan Bird while the three were involved in suspicious activity. McKenzie and Scorzello reported said they had a gun battle with Odinga and Balagoon. While reportedly six feet away from the officers, only McKenzie's summons pouch was allegedly hit by a Panther's bullet. Odinga and Balagoon escaped after the officers "immunized" their car with gunfire. After shooting up the car, the officers found 19 year-old Joan Bird huddled under the dashboard. When they took her to the nearest police precinct the admitting officer asked McKenzie, "Did you work her over?" in reference to her black eye and bruises. Kempton, *Briar Patch*, pp.75-78.

[94] "It appears... visit." M. Newton, *Bitter Grain*, pp.181-5. Kempton, *The Briar Patch*, p.75-8. Zimroth, *Perversions of Justice*, pp.179-83. Note that it's specifically Kempton, in his National Book Award-winning account, who said that the Panthers wanted to upstage Karenga, which he implied was the U.S. governement's claim, for why the Panthers set up bombings and shootings of police that day. Of course, a jury found that it was only U.S. Intelligence that set up bombings and shootings that day of Karenga's speech.

[95] Personal interview with George Edwards, 1/17/06.

[96] "The FBI... Huggins?" Zimroth, *Perversions of Justice: The Prosecution and Acquittal of the Panther 21*, pp.3-5., 17, 187-8, 193. Kempton, *The Briar Patch: The People of the State of New York v. Lumumba Shakur Et Al*, pp.2-12, 73, 199, and M. Newton, Bitter Grain, 185.

[97] "FBI agent... asylum." Odinga was said to jump 35 feet down to the ground to make his escape. Kempton, *The Briar Patch: The People of the State of New York v. Lumumba Shakur Et Al*, pp.2-12, and M. Newton, Bitter Grain, 185. Also see Zimroth, *Perversions of Justice: The Prosecution and Acquittal of the Panther 21*, pp.3-5. Lumumba Shakur, Afeni Shakur et al, *Look For Me In the Whirlwind: the Collective Autobiography of the New York 21.*

[98] "The FBI's... them." Senate Select Committee staff interview with Panther Deputy Minister of Defense Bobby Rush on 11/26/75; reported at p.198 of *The FBI's Covert Action to Destroy The Black Panther Party*. In U.S. Senate Select Committee to Study Governmental Operations, Final Report, Book III*: Supplementary Detailed Staff Reports on Intelligence Activities and the Rights of Americans*, Books, , 94th Congress, 2nd Session, (U.S. Government Printing Office, Washington DC., 1976}. Referenced in Churchill and Vander Wall, Agents of Repression, p.66, note 18. On promotion, see p.66 note 19: See documents and evidence in the case of *Iberia Hampton, et. al. Plaintiffs-Appellants v. Edward V. Hanrahan, et al., Defendants-Appellees*, Transcript at 21741-62 and 21807-18. (Later referred to as *Appeal* or *Transcript*). Appeal PL #306 showing that the pay increase was sought by [FBI Special Agent Roy] Mitchell, with [FBI supervisor Marlin]Johnson's endorsement, in late February, and approved by FBI headquarters on

March 11; Appeal, PL WON #3 shows the raise was to $450/month plus $125 monthly expenses.

[99] "Chicago's ... groups." Fred Hampton, "You Can Murder a Liberator, but You Can't Murder Liberation." In Philip Foner ed. *The Black Panthers Speak* (New York: Da Capo Press, 1970) , pp.146-50.

[100] See documents and evidence in the case of *Iberia Hampton, et. al. Plaintiffs-Appellants v. Edward V. Hanrahan, et al., Defendants-Appellees*, Transcript at 21741-62 and 21807-18. (Later referred to as *Appeal* or *Transcript*). Churchill and Vander Wall, *Agents of Repression*, pp.64-5, .notes 5, 8.

[101] Over 40 chapters estimate given by 'law enforcement experts' to Peter Zimroth in his *Perversions of Justice: The Prosecution and Acquittal of the Panther 21* (New York: Viking Press, 1974) p.39. That account reported 2,000 members by the end of '68 while historians and Panther sympathizers Ward Churchill and Jim Vander Wall reported 5,000 members in over a dozen cities that year. By most accounts, these numbers increased significantly up to 1970.

[102] FBI Memorandum, SAC Chicago to Directro, FBI, 12/20/68, COUNTERINTELLIGENCE PROGRAM, BLACK NATIONALST—HATE GROUPS, RACIAL INTELLIGENCE MATTER (BLACK PANTHER PARTY). In Churchill and Vander Wall, *Agents of Repression*, p.65 note11.

[103] "After... Maus." *Appeal*, PL #16-17 and *Transcript* at 4113-4. Churchill and Vander Wall, *Agents of Repression*, p.66, .notes 15,16.

[104] "O'Neal... 1969." Kirkpatrick Sale, *SDS* (New York: Vintage, 1973), p.664. Churchill and Vander Wall, *Agents of Repression*, p.66, note 21.

[105] *Appeal*, #26-30 and WON 5. Also see *Transcript* at 6579 and 8907. Churchill and Vander Wall, *Agents of Repression*, p.66, .notes 22-3..

[106] "The FBI had... Tupac." On Panthers, see, *Appeal*, PL WON #3 showed that FBI Chicago SAC Mitchell personally posted bond on one of O'Neal's charges and neither of his charges were prosecuted. On FBI collaboration with gang intelligence, see *Appeal*, PL #413 and *Transcript* at 26909. Churchill and Vander Wall, *Agents of Repression*, pp.64-6, .endnotes 5, 24. On Tupac, personal interview with his ex-Panther business manager, Watani Tyehimba, on gang radicalization plan. On Suge Knight let off charges and work with gang police unit against Tupac, see Randalll Sullivan, *LAbyrinth* (New York: Atlantic Monthly Press, 2002) and Nick Broomfield, *Biggie and Tupac* (BBC, 2002). Tupac info elaborated on later.

[107] Elaine Brown, *A Taste of Power: A Black Woman's Story* (New York: Anchor/Doubleday,1992), picture caption on p.216. While Brown's book is problematic in many ways, this fact doesn't appear politically motivated as her false accounts of Huey Newton do.

[108] "Heavy... teen." Lumumba Shakur et al., *Look for Me In the Whirlwind: A Collective Autobiography of the New York 21* (New York: Vintage) pp.139-40, 148-150. Lumumba Shakur said that his Brooklyn and Queens-based Chaplains gang, for example, had about 10,000 members and was as well armed as some countries.

[109] "It's... gangs." Kempton, *The Briar Patch*, p. 72.

[110] "By December... talks nationwide." *Transcript* at 28911-15, 29037-8 and 29183-4. *Agents of Repression*, page69 endnotes, 59, 60.

[111] Wes Swearingen, *FBI Secrets: An Agent's Expose*, pp.88-9.

[112] "Trial... Clark." Documents introduced as evidence in case of *Ibera Hampton, et al., Plaintiffs-Appellants v. Edward Hanrahan, et al., Defendants-Appellees* (Nos. 77-1968, 77-1210 and 77-1370) Transcript at 33716. In *Agents of Repression*, pp.73, 403n. On FBI falsely telling police that the Panthers killed a cop and O'Neal drugging his punch, see *Me and My Shadow: Investigation of the political left by the United States government*, Executive Producer Tarabu Betserai, Pacifica Radio Archives, track 4. Hampton's drugging also comes from Hampton's mother's testimony that Hampton was talking on the phone with her and fell asleep mid-sentence, and from an FBI agent's trial admission.

[113] "A future... million." Levin, S.K., "Black Panthers Get Bittersweet Revenge," *Colorado Daily*, November 10, 1982. Also see *Plaintiffs Motion for Sanctions Against*

Certain Defendants and Lawyers for Violations of the Rules, Abuse of Privilege, Bad Faith and Obstruction of Justice, Nos. 70-C-3026, 70-C-1384, Northern District of Illimois, United States District Court, 1982 (inclusive). Cited in *Agents of Repression*, p.77, endnote 128.

[114] "Richard... war." A Los Angeles FBI agent and a police intelligence agent both detailed aspects of these attacks on Pratt. Intelligence agent Louis Tackwood cites the attempted execution of Pratt and his unit's FBI supervision in Louis Tackwood & Citizens Research-Intelligence Committee, *The Glass House Tapes: The Story of an Agent Provocateur and the New Police-Intelligence Complex* (New York: Avon Books,1973) pp.104, 237-8. Cited in Churchill and Vander Wall, *Agents of Repression*, pp.79, 80-1,84, 213-4n.also see, Churchill and Vander Wall, *Cointelpro Papers*, p.225. For other attacks on Pratt, see M. Wesley Swearingen, *FBI Secrets: An Agent's Expose* (Boston: South End Press, 1995), pp.82-3. Swearingen worked in the LA FBI Cointelpro unit and said the FBI selected Pratt to be "neutralized," p.87.

[115] "In... this." M.Newton, *Bitter Grain*, p.164.

[116] "George Sams... shot." Edwards told this author this and the fact that he was in the 8th Air Force Strategic Air Command during the Cold War from 1955-1961, repairing bombing and navigation systems on B-4 bombers.Personal Interview, George Edwards, 7/8/00. Also see, M. Netwon, *Bitter Grain*, p.165. Raided other chapters after visits, Donald Freed, *Agony in New Haven: The Trial of Bobby Seale, Erika Huggins and the Black Panther Party* (New York: Simon and Schuster, 1973), p.25, cited in Churchill and Vander Wall, *The COINTELPRO Papers*, p.25.

[117] Huey Newton, *To Die for the People*, p.224.

[118] "Several aspects... up." See Donald Freed, *Agony in New Haven: The Trial of Bobby Seale, Erika Huggins and the Black Panther Party* (New York: Simon and Schuster, 1973), p.25, cited in Churchill and Vander Wall, *The COINTELPRO Papers*, p.25.

[119] "Several aspects... chapters." Donald Freed, *Agony in New Haven: The Trial of Bobby Seale, Erika Huggins and the Black Panther Party* (New York: Simon and Schuster, 1973), p.25, cited in Mumia Abu-Jamal, *We Want Freedom: A Life in the Black Panther Party* (Boston: South End Press, 2004), p.140. Sams traveling around country with seemingly limiteless money and settting up Panther chapters for raids is detailed in Churchill and Vander Wall, *The COINTELPRO Papers*, p.360, note114.

[120] "Also, when... Sams." Churchill and Vander Wall, *COINTELPRO Papers*, p.360, notes 113, 114.

[121] "The judge... him." Chucrhill and Vander Wall, *COINTELPRO Papers*, p.360 note 118.

[122] Mumia Abu-Jamal, *We Want Freedom* (Boston: South End Press,2004), p.151.

[123] "The FBI... sources." See, for example, published copies of FBI documents on this strategy against the Panthers and SNCC in Churchill and Vander Wall, *The COINTELPRO Papers*, pp.126-8, including FBI memorandums dated 10/10/68 and 7/1068. Also see FBI memorandums from SAC, Chicago to Director, 1/10/1969, 3/24/69, 4/8/69 in *Agents of Repression*, pp.43-4, 49, 66. And, 10/10/68 memorandum. *COINTELPRO Papers*, pp118-19,127.

[124] "But a... effort." See text of FBI COINTELPRO memorandum from G.C. Moore to W.C. Sullivan, dated 5/14/70, copied in Churchill and Vander Wall, *The Cointelpro Papers*, p149.

[125] "The FBI... figures." See copies of FBI memorandums dated 2/2/71 sent to about 30 offices that attempts to split Newton and Cleaver as well as an Airtel memo that attempts to split Newton and Afeni Shakur's New York Panther 21, Churchill and Vander Wall, *The COINTELPRO Papers*, pp.160-1. M. Newton told how this was turned into an East Vs. West Panther war, *Bitter Grain*, p.203. For FBI manipulation of the media in this regard, see copy of FBI memorandums dated 7/768 and 8/5/68 in which Albany, NY comments on Miami's success with a television station's Panther coverage that was sent to approximately 40 other cities' offices. Also see 10/10/68 memorandum. *COINTELPRO Papers*, pp118-19,127.

[126] "Murders of important Panthers…East/West war's murders." See *COINTELPRO Papers*, pp148-50, 362 notes 129-131. Kathleen Cleaver, Personal interview, 11/10/02.
[127] Pratt description which was delivered through an email of Kathleen Cleaver's. http://whosemedia.com/drums/2007/05/09/was-elaine-brown-an-agent/
[128] "Whiel Pratt…murders." See *COINTELPRO Papers*, pp148-50, 362 notes 129-131. On Kathleen Cleaver, Personal interview, 11/10/02.
[129] "Lumumba…underground." Assata Shakur, *Assata* (New York: Lawrence Hill, 1987), p.231.

[130] One of the last Oakland Panther National Chairs, David Hilliard, also went to trial in '71. Police charged David Hilliard with the attempted murder of officers as part of their allegation that he and fellow Panthers, Eldridge Cleaver and Bobby Hutton, had a "shootout" with them. As stated above, sources described it as a police onslaught without resistance. Nonetheless, Hilliard faced the prosecuting Assistant District Attorney (ADA) Frank Vukota in court three years later. Covering the trial, the *San Francisco Chronicle* said that Vukota introduced no evidence of Hilliard ever having a gun. They also commented on ADA Vukota consistently pointing his finger a number of times at Hilliard.

The Chronicle detailed one of several farcical moments in that trial when they reported particular interactions between ADA Vukota, David Hilliard and his defense attorney Vincent Hallihan. First, Hilliard had to sit through Hallihan describing him and his fellow Panthers as dim-witted when addressing the jury: "we have to think how these rather simple people felt at the time (of the shootout)." *The Chronicle* then said that when Hilliard was sitting on the witness stand, ADA Vukota "went over near Hilliard, and pointing his finger once again, said, 'he has hatreds.' Hilliard, cool and restrained during most of the trial, leaned forward and said to the prosecutor, 'you've got hatreds.'" While Vukota admitted that Hilliard may not have had a gun, Hilliard received a several year jail sentence as a result of that trial. Donovan Bess, "Case Goes to Jury: Hilliard Trial's Bitter End," *The San Francisco Chrnonicle,* 6/11/71, p.5. On sentence, see M. Newton, *Bitter Grain*, pp.78,210.
[131] Afeni Shakur, "We Will Win: A Letter from Prison," originally in *Rat,* January 7-20, 1970, collected in ed. Philip Foner, *The Black Panthers Speak* (New York: Da Capo Press, 1970,95), p.161
[132] "Indivduals from…groups." See Churchill and Vander Wall, *Agents of Repression: The FBI's Secret War Against the Black Panther Party and the American Indian Movement.* Also see their, *The COINTELPRO Papers: Documents from the FBI's Secret Wars Against Dissent in the United States.* American Indian Movement (AIM) representatives as well as Young Lords representatives had said they modeled some of their programs on the Panther survivial programs. Lee Lew Lee, *All Power to the People* (documentary film, 1996).
[133] "While space…inside (see notes)." Of the many brutal assaults on the American Indian Movement, the story of John Trudell, AIM's last national leader is particularly heart-wrenching. This FBI-targeted AIM leader had been warned in the late 70s that if he didn't stop his Indian rights work that his family would be killed. Trudell protested on the Washington DC Capitol steps and someone burned down his house within hours. His wife, Tina, his mother-in-law Leah Hicks-Manning, and his three young children were all killed in that incident. *Agents of Repression*, pp.362-3. When he finally got out of mourning, Trudell went on to become a musician. His albums include *Grafiti Man.* On other horrors in American indian history, see *Agents of Repression*, and for example, on thousands died in Trail of Tears see www.pbs.org/wghb/aia/part4/4h1567.html . For other info, see Howard Zinn, *A People's History of the United States.*
[134] Jon Lurie, "The Wiping of the Tears: 25 Years after the era of A.I.M. Militancy on Pine Ridge, " reprinted from *The Circle*, 8/1/00. www.geocities.com/crazyoglala/WipingTears_Lurie.html?200721
[135] "The fear…reasons)." The most comprehensive source for information on SDS is Kirkpratick Sale, *SDS* (New York: Vintage, 1974), p.664. On memebership numbers see p.664. Also see, former SDS president Todd *Gitlin's The Sixties: Years of Hope, Days of*

Rage (New York: Bantam, 1989). On see, for example, their *Prairie Fire: The Politics of Revolutionary Anti-Imperialism; Political Statement of the Weather Underground*, (Communications Co., 1974), published in hiding.

[136] "Other civil... supporters." While black radicals bore the brunt of FBI tactics, the FBI violence against White radicals, too. For example, an FBI-sponsored group, The Secret Army Organization, shooting up the house of a White radical, San Diego State economics professor Peter Bohmer The Secret Army Organization leader, FBI infiltrator Howard Godfrey, was in the car from where the shots were fired. A grand jury in Chicago found that the FBI and Army Intelligence had cooperated in funding and directing a right wing terrorist organization against left wing activists throughout that city. Zoccino, Nanda, "Ex-FBI Informer Describes Terrorist Role," *Los Angeles Times*, Janurary 26, 1976. Also see Parenti, Michael, *Democracy for the Few*, (New York: St. Martin's Press, 1980), p.24. Cited in Churchill and Vander Wall, *Agents of Repression*, p.203, 377

[137] Frances Fox Piven and Richard A. Cloward, *Poor People's Movements: Why They Succceed, How They Fail* (New York: Vintage, 1977).

[138] "At least... harm." Jane Alpert, *Growing Up Underground* (New York: Citadel, 1989).

[139] "The Weather Underground... time." On their list of bombings, see *Prairie Fire: The Politics of Revolutionary Anti-Imperialism*, (CommunicationsCo., 1974) p.16. This book was published by the Weather Underground leadership in hiding. These was part of an estimated 2,800 student-linked political bombing incidents in a 15 month period at this time to fight racism and stop the Vietnam War, according to Kirkpatrick Sale, *SDS* (New York: Vintage, 1974), p.632. Sale used figures drawn from an Alcohol, Tobacco and Firearms of the Dept. of Treasury survey to come up with these figures.

[140] "The Weather... bail." See for example, Hayden and Fonda in M. Wesley Swearingen, *FBI Secrets*; Chisolm and Bernstein, Zimroth, *Perversions of Justice*; Hendrix in "Jimi Hendrix, Black Power and Money," *Teenset*, January, 1969; and, Constantine, *Covert War Against Rock*, p.61. Douglas Pringle, *The Jimi Hendrix Companion* (New York: Simon & Schuster, MacMillan, 1996), p.63. Brando in Lee Lew-Lee, *All Power to the People* (documentary, 1995). Southerland, Robert Sam Anson, "To Die Like a Gangsta," *Vanity Fair*, March 1997. Lennon in Fenton Bresler, *Who Killed John Lennon?* (New York: St. Martins, 1989). Regarding Bernstein's support, its interesting to note that an FBI memorandum dated 5/21/70 was directed at Bernstein, who was Jewish, for his Panther support. It discussed manufacturing anti-Semitic literature that would be attributed to the Panthers and sent to Bernstein. Another FBI memo discussed success with this tactic in setting the Jewish Defense League against the Panthers. See *COINTELPRO Papers*, pp162-3.This was another strategy duplicated later against Tupac in the 90s.

[141] "The New York... each." Zimroth, *Perversions of Justice*, pp.9-12, 297-9. Jasmine Guy, *Afeni Shakur: Evolution of a Revolutionary*, pp.107-110. Kempton, *Briar Patch*, and Lumumba Shakur, Afeni Shakur et al: *Look for Me in the Whirlwind*..

[142] "After several... U.S." Note from publisher of autobio, *Look For Me In the Whirlwind*, p363. Also see Jasmyn Guy, *Afeni Shakur: Evolution of a Revolutionary* (New York: Atria, 2004), pp.110-11.

[143] "Afeni was up... movie.')." Zimroth, *Perversions of Justice: The Prosecution and Acquittal of the Panther 21*,, pp.160, 289-92.

[144] "But Afeni's legal... trial." Kempton, *The Briar Patch*, 246-8. This and jurors comments this remark, Peter Zimroth, *Perversions of Justice*, pp.288, 368, 376-7.

[145] Afeni said that she and the other Panthers were upset about Dharuba Moore and Cetewayo Tabor failing to help raise more bail for the others. The Panthers then worried that the two skipping bail for Algeria would hurt their case. Jasmine Guy, *Afeni Shakur: Evolution of a Revolutionary*, pp.107-110. But they weren't so upset that they couldn't get some entertainment from Tabor and Eldridge Cleaver during the trial. Just before closing his case, ADA Joseph Phillips brought up the issue of Dharuba Moore and Cetewayo Tabor in Algeria. ADA Phillips presented a taped phone call he had of Tabor. He introduced the tape stating, "He threatens to kill me. You know what he must have thought, 'To hell with the other defendants. I'm clear. I can say anything I want.' " With

his back to the defendants, Phillips played the tape, which began with, "Mr. Tabor, this is ADA Phillips in New York County, and we have a number of problems that you have created as a result of your leaving New York."

Tabor responded, "Hello, motherfucker, who is this?... *the* Phillips?" "Yes the Phillips, the one you refer to as 'pig Phillips.' " "Yes, pig Phillips, yeah. Right on." "How do you like Algiers, Mr. Tabor? [Pause ten seconds.] Mr. Tabor, hello, hello, Mr. Tabor." "Joe? Joe Blow." "Who is this?" asked Phillips. "This is Eldridge Cleaver, who is this?" "ADA Phillips... we have to advise him of his rights." "Are you recording this?" asked Cleaver. "Yes, I am," said Phillips. "So are we," said Cleaver, "and I want to inform you of the charges against you." Phillips laughed, "I don't want to be informed of any charges. I've got enough problems with my own case without getting any additional cases today, Mr. Cleaver." Cleaver continued, "You are wanted for crimes against the people." "Now wait a minute, I, uh, uh [laugh]. If you say so," Phillips responded. "We plan to see to it that you die for your crimes... Joe Blow," said Cleaver.

"May I speak with Mr. Moore?" asked Phillips. "Take that shit off your fucking calendar because we're through with your fuckin' courts. We're through with you from now on. It's war. Do you understand that?" Cleaver asked rhetorically. "Mr. Cleaver, do you believe a man of your, uh, of your purported intellect and writing ability has to degenerate to that type of argument or vilification?" "You're no good... death to all fascist pigs and that includes you," Cleaver concluded and passed the phone over to Ceteweyo [Tabor]. "What did you say, Joe?" "I thought you might be able to give us some assistance in finding Mr. Moore," said Phillips. "You know I wouldn't give you any assistance of any kind, Joe." "My opinion, Mr. Tabor, is that in talking to me and authorizing us to tell the court... you have rendered considerable assistance to us."

"I'll be seeing you soon, Joe, and, uh, what has to be done is just something that has been decreed by the masses of the people. You see, you know and I know that you are guilty... and give Murtagh my regards too... and tell him we'll get back; I'll be knocking at your door one night... 'Power to the People' and death to the fascist pig."

"Uh, Mr. Tabor, uh, I'm surprised that after all that we have gone through you can still utter threats to kill people. It's rather remarkable; you think you would have learned that, uh, killing people is not the solution to any problem. [Five second pause.] Are you still there, Mr. Tabor? [Seven second pause.] Hello. Hello."

Phillips concluded that this tape had proven his point and nailed the Panthers on trial. He expected shock and worry from the defendants he had his back to. But when he turned in triumph to look upon them, the thirteen Panthers were laughing.Kempton, *The Briar Patch*, pp.189-94.

[146] "Many revolutionary ... bomb." M. Newton, *Bitter Grain*, p.191. Also on Weather Underground bombing judge's home, see Zimroth, *Perversions of Justice*, p52. The Weather Underground's leadership didn't list this among their bombings cited in a later book, *Prairie Fire*, which they published in 1974.

[147] "In the end... crimes." On courtroom scene, jury time of deliberations, etc. see quoted trial transcript and spectator Zimroth in Zimroth, *Perversions of Justice*, pp.308-9. On jury and writer's opinion's crediting Afeni with winning case for Panthers, see Zimroth's interviews, pp.310 on, particularly pp.367-8, 377 and Connie Bruck "The Takedown of Tupac," *The New Yorker*, 7/7/97, p. 47. On Lumumba and others' stay in jail after verdict, Zimroth, *Perversions of Justice*, p.310.

[148] Zimroth, *Perversions of Justice*, pp.16, 48.

[149] "After... chair." Murray Kempton, *The Briar Patch: The People of the State of New York V. Lumumba Shakur Et Al.* (New York: Dell Publishing, 1973). p. 200. Also see Peter Zimroth, *Perversions of Justice: The Prosecution and Acquittal of the Panther 21.* (New York: The Viking Press, 1974), pp172-3.

[150] Clayborne Carson, ed. by David Gallen, Malcolm X: The FBI File (New York: Carroll and Graf, 1991), p. 17.

[151] "The murderous racism... blacks." On FBI document, FBI memorandum, March 4, 1968. In Clayborne Carson, *Malcolm X: The FBI File* (New York: Carroll and Graf, 1991), p. 17. On 5,000 lynchings, Piven and Cloward, Poor People's Movements, p.186.

On bombings, see Poor People's Movements, p. 243.Also see, Kenneth O'Reilly, Racial Matters: The FBI's Secret Files on Black America, 1960-1972 (New York: The Free Press, 1989), pp.112, 217, cited in Ward Churchill and Jim Vander Wall, *The COINTELPRO Papers: Documents from the FBI's Secret Wars Against Dissent in the United States* (Boston: South End Press, 1991), p.170.
[152] "Earl Little... suicide." Malcolm X, *The Autobiography of Malcolm X*, as told to Alex Haley (New York: Ballantine, 1964,'65,'99), pp.1-11. Afeni's accounts from North Carolina in the 50s, *Look for Me in the Whirlwind*, pp. 49-50. Also see other similar accounts of varying degrees of racism in that book form Boston to New York. Also see
[153] "Afeni... blacks." First sentenced explained later. Malcolm's birth and father, Malcolm X, *The Autobiography of Malcolm X*, as told to Alex Haley (New York: Ballantine, 1964,'65,'99), pp.1-9. On Afeni's father in law in Garvey's group, Jasimine Guy, *Afeni Shakur: Evolution of a Revolutionary* (New York: Atria, 2004), p.70. On James Coston's name and change, Lumumba Shakur, Afeni Shakur et al, *Look for Me in the Whirlwind: The Collective Autobiography of the New York 21* (New York: Vintage, 1971) pp.22-3. On million members in Garvey's UNIA, see Michael Lewis, "The Negro Protest in Urban America." In *Protest, Reform, and Revolt*, edited by Joseph Gusfield (New York: John Wiley and Sons, 1971), p.158. This source and fact is cited in Frances Fox Piven and Richard A. Cloward, *Poor People's Movement: Why They Succeed, How They Fail* (New York: Vintage, 1979), p.203.
[154] "Garvey... work." Ed.s Mari Jo Buhle, Paul Buhle, and Dan Georgakas, *Encyclopedia of the American Left* (Chicago, Illinois: University of Illinois Press, 1992). Also see his accomplishments listed on a Marcus Garvey commemorative poster, Harlem 1947, in Timothy White, *Catch a Fire: The Life of Bob Marley* (New York: Owl/Henry Holt,1996), p.104. On Garvey's reach to countries such as Belize, see Peter Eltringham, *The Rough Guide to Belize* (New York: Rough Guides, 2004), p.296.
[155] "Earl Little... suicide." Malcolm X, *The Autobiography of Malcolm X*, as told to Alex Haley (New York: Ballantine, 1964,'65,'99), pp.1-11. Afeni's accounts from North Carolina in the 50s, *Look for Me in the Whirlwind*, pp. 49-50. Also see other similar accounts of varying degrees of racism in that book form Boston to New York. Also see
[156] "By the... blacks." On FBI document, FBI memorandum, March 4, 1968. In Clayborne Carson, *Malcolm X: The FBI File* (New York: Carroll and Graf, 1991), p. 17. Also see, Kenneth O'Reilly, *Racial Matters: The FBI's Secret Files on Black America, 1960-1972* (New York: The Free Press, 1989), pp.112, 217, cited in Ward Churchill and Jim Vander Wall, *The COINTELPRO Papers: Documents from the FBI's Secret Wars Against Dissent in the United States* (Boston: South End Press, 1991), p.170.
[157] Clayborne Carson, *Malcolm X: The FBI File*, p.18.
[158] "The CIA grew... deals." On United Nations and CIA concern, see Douglas, *Assassinations*, pp.379-80. On European nations and Africa, see, for example, Ed.s William Harris and Judith Levey, *The Columbia Encyclopedia*, (New York: Columbia University Press, 1975), pp. 29-30. On threatening multinational corporations' deals with African leaders, see Malcolm X's speech titled by one editor, "I Don't Mean Bananas," in the Audubon Ballroom, 1964. *New Left Reader*, pp.208-222. Other bibliographical information on this previously copied source unavailable.
[159] "Malcolm... 1964." Malcolm X, as told to Alex Haley, *The Autobiography of Malcolm X* (New York: Ballantine, 1965), pp.316 & 322, for example.
[160] FBI Memo, 9/17/64, Carson, *The FBI Files*, pp.289, 299.
[161] Evanzz, *Judas*, pp.249-50. Cited in Douglas, *The Assassinations*, p.396.
[162] See, Corretta Scott King, *My Life with Martin Luther King, Jr*, revised edition (New York: Henry Holt, 1993), p.238. Cited in Douglas, *Assassinations*, p.403. Also see PBS's *American Experience*, "Malcolm X : Make It Plain," Archival footage of Malcolm pledging his group's support for Martin Luther King in an interview. Ossie Davis discussed Malcolm's day-long strategy meeting with other civil rights leaders. And in an interview Pacifica radio held with Mississippi-based Fannie Lou Hamer, she said Malcolm was her best friend and mentored her during her civil rights work.
[163] Muhammad Ahmad (Mazewell Stanford, Jr.), *We Will Return in th Whirlwind*, p.30.

[164] "The Shakurs…chapter." On Abbah Shakur as well as the Shakurs and Odinga in the OAAU, see several sources. Personal interview with former Black Panther and Shakur family friend, Watani Tyehimba, 5/10/00. Also, Lumumba Shakur et al., *Look for Me In the Whirlwind: A Collective Autobiography of the New York 21* (New York: Vintage) pp.241-2, 264-5. On Abbah Shakur as a former Garvey follower, Jasmine Guy, *Afeni Shakur: Evolution of a Revolutionary* (New York: Atria, 2004), p.70. On Mutulu, Committee to End the Marion Lockdown, *Can't Jail the Spirit: Political Prisoners in the U.S.* (Chicago: CEML, 2002), pp.147-50.
[165] "Information revealed …Panthers." See, for example, an NYPD BOSS undercover agent's memoir on his duel work with the FBI against Malcolm X, Tony Ulasewicz, with Stuart McKeever, the President's Pirvate Eye (Westport Connecticut: MACSAM Publishing), p.145, cited in James Douglas, "The Murder and Martyrdom of Malcolm X," James DiEugenio and Lisa Pease, eds, *The Assassinations: Probe Magazine on JFK, MLK, RFK and Malcolm X* (Los Angeles: Feral House, 2003) p.390-1. One historian said BOSS was known amongst Intelligence as "the little FBI and the little CIA." Frank Donner, Protectors of Privilege (Berkeley: University of California Press, 1990), p.155. B.O.S.S. Cointelpro-type tactics were described by a federal judge in *Handschu, et al vs. Special Services Division a/k/a Bureau of Special Services*, U.S. District Court, S.D.N.Y., 71 Civ. 2203 (CSH) Memorandum Opinion and Order, Mar. 7, 1985, p.26. Against the Panthers, B.O.S.S. agents worked closely with the FBI-paid Roland Hayes, a key to the frame-up of the Panther 21. In his book *The Briar Patch: The People v. Lumumba Shakur Et Al*, a National Book Award winner, Murray Kempton said that Roland Hayes provided the FBI with five reports a week, and BOSS accompanied the FBI on raids. *The Briar Patch*, p.73-4. Former assistant district attorney Peter Zimroth said that federal law-enforcement officials told him that Hayes was on the FBI payroll when he helped frame the Panther 21 by transporting dynamite to the Panther office, after which BOSS agents reported it. Zimroth, *Perversions of Justice*, p.193. For other reports on Roberts work for BOSS, see Peter Zimroth, *Perversions of Justice: The Prosecution and Acquittal of the Panther 21* (New York: Viking, 1974) p.48. Murray Kempton, *The Briar Patch: New York vs. Lumumba Shakur et al.*(New York: Delta, 1973) p.202.
[166] Karl Evanzz, *The Judas Factor: The Pot to Kill Malcolm X* (New York: Thunders Mouth, 1992) p.73 and Karl Evanzz, *The Messenger: The Rise and Fall of Elijah Muhammad* (New York: Pantheon, 1999) pp.187-8, 192. Also see, Louis Lomax, *To Kill a Black Man* (Los Angeles, Holloway House, 1987) p.103. All cited in Douglas, "The Murder and Martyrdom of Malcolm X," DiEugenio and Pease, eds, *The Assassinations* (Los Angeles: Feral House, 2003), pp.380-1.
[167] See Louis Lomax, *When the Word is Given* (New York: Signet Books, 1964), p.82 and the firestorm his claim created but was later confirmed by FBI documents cited in Evanzz, *The Messenger*, p.317. Cited in Douglas, "The Murder and Martyrdom of Malcolm X," DiEugenio and Pease, eds, *The Assassinations* (Los Angeles: Feral House, 2003), pp.378-79.
[168] See interview of Nation Of Islam Captain Joseph X in Spike Lee, *By Any Means Necessary: The Trials and Tribulations of the Making of Malcolm X* (New York: Halperion, 1992) p.63 and *On Brother Minister: The Assassination of Malcolm X*, a 1997 film directed by Jack Baxter and Jefri Aallmuhammed. Also see black Fire Marshall Victor Canty informing Malcolm X that fire department officials tried to frame him for that, in press statement, 2/18/65, "We Are Demanding an Investigation," *Malcolm X: The Last Speeches*, ed. by Bruce Perry (New York: Pathfinder, 1989) p.179. All cited in *Assassinations*, pp.381, 406. A PBS documentary on Malcolm X showed NOI Capt. Joseph X and Philbert X who also said John X Ali was the National Secretary of the NOI in the last years of Malcolm's life.
[169] "NOI leader Elijah…by FBI documents." Author James Douglas' interview with Wallace Muhammad, now W.D. Muhammad, 2/2/99 and Evanzz, Messenger p.317, both cited in Douglas, Assassinations, p.379. Wallace himself, accepted FBI money for information after fearing his half-siblings actions for Wallace aiding Malcolm X

[170] "Malcolm X believed... capacity." Jan Carew, *Ghosts in Our Blood* (Chicago: Lawrence Hill, 1994) p.39. Cited in *The Assassinations*, p.396.
[171] African diplomat's statement made to Eric Norden, "The Murder of Malcolm X," *The Realist*, 2/67, p.12. Cited in The Assassinations, p. 404
[172] FBI Director J. Edgar Hoover, February 4, 1965, memorandum. Besides the intelligence agencies mentioned, Hoover also sent this memo to the Attorney General and the Foreign Liaison Unit, Zak A. Condo, *Conspiracies: Unraveling the Assassination of Malcolm X* (Washington: Nubia Press, 1993) pp.271-2, endnote 491.
[173] August 11, 1964, CIA memorandum fro Deputy Director of Plans, titled "ACTIVITIES OF MALCOLM POSSIBLE INVOLVEMENT OF AFRICAN NATIONS IN U.S. CIVIL DISTRUBANCES," cited by Zach Kondo, *Conspiracies: Unravellling the Assassination of Mlacolm X* (Washington: Nubia Press, 1993) pp.49 and 242 endnote 280 and Evanzz, *The Judas Factor*, p.254. In *Assassinations*, p.398-9 endnote 118.
[174] Peter Goldman, *The Death And Life of Malcolm X* (Urbannam, Illinois: University of Illinois Press) 2nd ed.1979), pp.314. Also in the *New York Times*, 3/3/66, p.24. Cited in *Assassinations*, p.410-11.
[175] On police conspicuously absent from the scene, see eyewitness Patricia Russell's account she wrote for *The Baltimore Afro-American*, 2/27/65, in George Breitman, The Assassination of Malcolm X (New York: Pathfinder, 1991) pp.58-9. Then, police calmly filled the hall within 15 minutes, without drawing their guns. In Earl Grant, "The Last Days of Malcolm X," *Malcolm X: The Man and His Times*, ed. by John Henrik Clark (New York: McMillan, 1975), p.96 and Lee, *By Any Means Necessary: The Trials and Tribulations of the Making of Malcolm X*, p.42.
[176] Kempton, pp.200-201. "What appeared to be twenty minutes later," Roberts finished "police finally got there and took him over to the medical center." This disclosure contradicts police officer Henry's attempt to call backup officers and Police Inspector Taylor's claim of 20 police officers at the Ballroom.
[177] Malcolm X's daughter, Ilyasah Shabazz, in Corey Kilgannon, "Remembering Malcolm X In the Place Where He Fell," *The New York Times*, 2/21/05, p.B1.
[178] On Joan Roberts restraining Betty Shabazz and Shabazz throwing her into a wall, see Eugene Roberts interview in the 80s with Elaine Rivera, "Out of the Shadows: The Man Who Spied on Malcolm X," *Newsday*, 7/23/89, cited in James W. Douglass, "The Murder and Martyrdom of Malcolm X," in ed.s James DiEugenio and Lisa Pease, *Assassinations* (Los Angeles: Feral House, 2001) p.413. Roberts said he calmed Joan Roberts down and escorted her to a taxi after the incident, suggesting he was with her but didn't take the taxi home with her because he had more to do at the scene.
[179] On checking Malcolm X's pulse, see author Douglas' interview with Gene Roberts, 7/7/2000, in Douglas, *Assassinations*, p.413. On turning to Betty Shabazz and saying Malcolm's dead, Murray Kempton, *The Briar Patch: New York vs. Lumumba Shakur et al.* (New York: Delta, 1973) pp.200-203.
[180] Roberts admission... disengage." William Pepper, *Orders to Kill: The Truth Behind the Murder of Martin Luther King, Jr.* (New York: Time Warner, 1998), pp.128, 431, 481, 485.
[181] "A police... assassination." As quoted from the *Herald Tribune*, 2/23/65. Cited in Breitman, Porter & Smith, *The Assassination of Malcolm X*, p.54.
[182] "For example, New York's *Herald*... accounts." See copies of New York's daily *Herald Tribune*'s 2/22/65 front page early edition headline and description of two men being grabbed and beaten by the mob before police took custody of them. This was changed without explanation in the later edition. Also see *New York Times*, 2/22/65. All in George Breitman, Henry Porter and Baxter Smith, *The Assassination of Malcolm X* (New York: Pathfinder, 1976,'91), p.52-4. . As elaborated on below, U.S. Intelligence stated in their internal documents having that king of censorship control over media organizations. For one of many examples, see, Joseph Crewden, "Worldwide Propaganda Network Built by the CIA," *New York Times*, 12/26/77, p.1. Also, former 25 year CIA operative Ralph McGehee obtained documents from 1991 through the Freedom Of

Information Act (FOIA) in which the CIA's Public Affairs Office (PAO) said, "PAO now has relationships with reporters from every major wire service, newspaper, news weekly, and television network in the nation. This has helped turn some 'intelligence failure' stories into 'intelligence success' stories... In many instances, we have persuaded reporters to postpone, change, hold, or even scrap stories...." As referenced from Lisa Pease, "The Media and the Assassination," *The Assassinations* (Los Angeles, CA: Feral House, 2003), p.311.

[183] Breitman, Porter and Smith, *The Assassination of Malcolm X*, p.16.

[184] FBI teletype, 2/23/65, FBI Files, p. 368.

[185] "Interview from Lompoc Federal Prison with Tyehimba Jess of WHBK Radio in Chicago," www.mutulushakur.com/lompoc.html

[186] "Arguably... Cointelpro." On Media break-in, Churchill and Vander Wall, *The COINTELPRO Papers*, pp.xi, 332. See for, example, *The FBI's Covert Program to Destroy the Black Panther Party*, 94th Congress, 2nd Session, U.S. Government Printing Office, Washington, D.C., 1976. Seymour Hersh, "CIA Reportedly Recruited Blacks for Surveillance of Panther Party," *New York Times*, March 17, 1978, p. A1, A16. quoted in Huey P. Newton, *War Against the Panthers* (New York: Harlem River Press/Writers and Readers Publishing, 1996), p.90.

[187] Deposition of former FBI agent M. Wesley Swearingen, taken in October 1980, in Honolulu, Hawaii, p.2, in Churchill and Vander Wall, *Agents of Repression*, p.62

[188] *Handschu, et al vs. Special Services Division a/k/a Bureau of Special Services, U.S. District Court*, S.D.N.Y., 71 Civ. 2203 (CSH) Memorandum Opinion and Order, Mar. 7, 1985, p.26. Ibid, Memorandum Opinion and Order, May 24, 1979, p.3. Connie Bruck, "The Takedown of Tupac," *The New Yorker*, 7/7/97, p.54.

[189] "More and more... England." Citizens Research and Investigation Committee and Louis Tackwood, *The Glass House Tapes: The Story of an Agent Provocaeur and the New Police-Intelligence Complex* (New York: Avon Books, 1973). Phil Agee, *Inside the Company* (New York: Bantam, 1975). Victor Marchetti and John Marks, *The CIA and the Cult of Intelligence* (New York: Dell,1974).

[190] "Afeni... godmother)." Connie Bruck, "The Takedown of Tupac," *The New Yorker*, 7/7/97, p.47. On Assata Shakur, see editorial, "Thoughts and Notes on Tupac," *The Amsterdam News*, 12/17/94, p.24.

[191] Wes Swearingen, *FBI Secrets: An Agent's Expose* (Boston: South End Press, 1995), p.86.

[192] "An FBI-paid... years." Amnesty International, *Proposal for a commision of inquiry into the effect of domestic intelligence activieites on criminal trial in the United States of America* (Amnesty International: New York,1980), p.25. Cited in Churchill and Vander Wall, *Agents of Repression*, p.91.

[193] "Afeni regularly... U.S." On Pratt's legal settlement, Todd Purdum, "Ex Black Panther Wins Long Legal Battle," *The New York Times*, April 27,2000, p.A18. On CIA joining forces with FBI against Pratt, with CHAOS against Pratt, see Alex Constantine, *The Covert War Against Rock* (Venice, CA: Feral House, 2000), pp.15,18; and Angus McKenzie, *Secrets: The CIA's War at Home* (Berkeley: University of California Press, 1999), p.69. CIA spying on Americans, Seymour Hersh, "Huge C.I.A. Operation Reported in U.S. Against Antiwar Forces, Other Dissidents in Nixon Years," *New York Times*, 12/22/74, p.A1.

[194] "Afeni... activities." Speaking at colleges, Connie Bruck, *The New Yorker*, p.47. *Handschu, et al vs. Special Services Division a/k/a Bureau of Special Services*, U.S. District Court, S.D.N.Y., 71 Civ. 2203 (CSH) Memorandum Opinion and Order, December 16, 1981, p.6. Benjamin Weiser, "Threats and Responses: Law Enforcement" *New York Times*, 2/12/03, p.17. Also, Associated Press, "Judge Backs Expanded Police Surveillance," *New York Times*, 3/22/03, p.2.

[195] Personal interview, Watani Tyehimba, 5/10/00. Former Panther Teyhimba is a friend of Afeni's since that time. Also see, *Can't Jail the Spirit: Political Prisoner in the U.S.* (Chicago: Committee to End the Marion Lockdown, 2002), p.65.

---

[196] "The RNA...released." On RNA alignment with Panthers, see Huey Newton, "To the Republic of New Afrika: September 13, 1969," *To Die for the People* (New York: Writers and Readers Publishing, 1972,99), pp.96-101. On RNA founding, Chokwe Lumumba, "20th Anniversary Commemoration of the Historic New Bethel Incident," *By Any Means Necessary!* Vol.5, No.2, 1989, NAPO, Box 31762, Jackson, MS 39286, p.11. On New Bethel Attack, Dan Georga.k.a.s and Marvin Surkin, *Detroit: I Do Mind Dying* (New York: St. Martin's Press, 1975), pp.664-8. Both of these last two sources and their information was obtained in the essay "A Brief History of the New Afrikan Prison Struggle," by Sundiata Acoli, p.10-11. Acoli is an imprisoned former New York Panther 21 member who was attacked in a car with Zayd and Assata Shakur. This essay can be found at www.prisonactivist.or/pubs/brief-mst-naps.html. His bio and contact info can be found in *Can't Jail the Spirit: Political Prisoner in the U.S.* (Chicago: Committee to End the Marion Lockdown, 2002), p.65.

[197] On Zayd Shakur and Sekou Odinga as founding the BLA, see Churchill and Vander Wall, *The COINTEPRO Papers*, pp. 306-7. On snipers, Lee Lew Lee, *All Power to the People*.

[198] "Afeni and Zayd's...his aunt." Assata Shakur, *Assata*, pp.231-4. On Tupac's aunt Assata, Cathy Scott, *The Killing of Tupac Shakur* (Las Vegas: Huntington Press, 1997), p.65

[199] "Afeni would...Assata in 1972." *The COINTELPRO Papers*, p.308

[200] Lennox Hinds, on behalf of the National Conference of Black Lawyers, in a petition to the United Nations Commision on Human Rights. 12/11/78. "The Injustice of the Trial." In *Covert Action Quarterly*, #65, Fall 1998, p.43.

[201] "In May... thereafter." On torture, see Assata Shakur, *Assata* , pp.3-11, 82-3. On mass of evidence supporting her innocence, see Lennox Hinds, on behalf of the National Conference of Black Lawyers, in a petition to the United Nations Commision on Human Rights. 12/11/78. "The Injustice of the Trial," In *Covert Action Quarterly*, #65, Fall 1998, p.43. Also, *The COINTELPRO Papers*, p.308. Assata Shakur, *Assata*, pp.3,5, 9-10, 82-3.

[202] See chart of trial charges and outcomes in Assata Shakur, *Assata*, p.xiv.

[203] Assata Shakur, *Assata,* p.247.

[204] "At... stop." Lennox Hinds, "The Injustice of the Trial." *Covert Action Quarterly*, Fall 1998, #65, p.43.

[205] "Mutulu Shakur's... Chicago." Committee to End the Marion Lockdown, *Can't Jail the Spirit: Political Prisoners in the U.S.* (Chicago: CEML, 2002), pp.147-50.

[206] "Afeni was the first... settlement as it affects Black activists.'" Handschu, et al vs. Special Services Division a/k/a Bureau of Special Services, U.S. District Court, S.D.N.Y., 71 Civ. 2203 (CSH) Memorandum Opinion and Order, December 16, 1981, p.6.

[207] Ibid, Memorandum Opinion and Order, May 24, 1979, p.3. Also see, Handschu, et al vs. Special Services Division a/k/a Bureau of Special Services, U.S. District Court, S.D.N.Y., 71 Civ. 2203 (CSH) Memorandum Opinion and Order, Mar. 7, 1985, p.26. And on widest restrictions, *New York Sun*, 12/5/02, and Benjamin Weiser, "Threats and Responses: Law Enforcement" *New York Times*, 2/12/03, p.17. Also, Associated Press, "Judge Backs Expanded Police Surveillance," *New York Times*, 3/22/03, p.2.

[208] Barbara Handschu et al, plaintiffs, Rev. Calvin Butts, Sonny Carson, C. Vernon Mason, Michael Warren, Intervenors v. Special Services Division a/k/a Bureau of Special Services et al, Memorandum Opinion and Order, Kudge Charles Haight, U.S. District Court, Southern District of New York. 71 Civ.2203-CSH, p.34.

[209] See, *Can't Jail the Spirit: Political Prisoners in the U.S.* (Chicago: CEML, 2002), pp.147-50.

And, for example, Alfred McCoy, *The Politics of Heroin: CIA Complicity in the Global Drug Trade* (New York: Lawrence Hill, 1972,1991).

[210] On Lincoln Detox success, it was reportedly "recognized as the largest and most effective of its kind by the National Institute of Drug Abuse [NIDA], National Acupuncture Research Society, and the World Academic Society of Acupuncture." This and Zimbabwe travels, CMEL, *Can't Jail the Spirit*, pp.147-8. Mutulu Shakur noted that

SDS/Weather Underground leader Bernardine Dohrn's sister, Jennifer, worked with him at Lincold Detox. "Live from Lompoc Federal Prison with Tyehimba Jess of WHBK Radio in Chicago: On the History of the Use of Acupuncture by Revolutionary Health Workers to Treat Drug Addiction, and US Government Attacks Under the Cover of the Counterintelligence Program (COINTELPRO). www.mutulushakur.com/lompoc.html

[211] "Reports... activists." Churchill and Vander Wall, *The Cointelpro Papers*, pp.309, 410-11, note 24. *Agents of Repression*, p.364. Assata Shakur, "Assata Shakur: The life of a revolutionary," *Covert Action Quarterly* #65, Fall 1998, p36. Some reportedly linked to RATF and serving long political prisoner sentences include white Weather Underground radicals Kathy Boudin, Dave Gilbert, Sara Evans, Susan Rosenberg, Marilyn Buch and Judy Clark. A doctor who aided some of the wounded RATF members, Allan Berkman, MD, was jailed. This was the first time a doctor was jailed for such a charge since the doctor who aided John Wilkes Booth after he shot Abraham Lincoln. Italian activist Silvia Baraldini was arrested as linked to RATF, as was black activists (mostly former Panthers) Sekou Odinga, Chui Ferguson, Edward Joseph Anthony Laborde, Bilal Sunni-Ali, Iliana Robinson and Kuwasi Balagoon. The Puerto Rican independistas who formed the Movimiento de Liberacion National (MLN) were Ricardo Romero, Maria Cueto, Steven Guerra, Julio Rosado and Andres Rosado. All from *COINTELPRO Papers*, pp. 310-11, 322, 411-12. On Lincoln Detox success, it was reportedly "recognized as the largest and most effective of its kind by the National Institute of Drug Abuse [NIDA], National Acupuncture Research Society, and the World Academic Society of Acupuncture." In, CMEL, *Can't Jail the Spirit*, pp.147-8.

[212] "The FBI said... 'co-conspirator.'" Churchill and Vander Wall, *The COINTELPRO Papers*, p.309. On BLA Multinational Task Force, see Sundiata Acoli, "A Brief History of the New Afrikan Prison Struggle," 2/19/92. www.prisonactivist.org

[213] "It's likely...rights." On Street Crim Unit, see *New York Times*, 2/15/99, in Frank Morales, 'The Militarization of the Police," *Covert Action Quarterly*, Fall/Summer, 1999, p.46. On Joint Terrorist Task Force, Churchill and Vander Wall, *The COINTELPRO Papers*, pp. 309-11.

[214] "By 1981... better'" On Mutulu undergrund on FBI's Most Wanted list and FBI queries of Tupac, see Cathy Scott, *The Killing of Tupac Shakur*, p.65. On Tupac attending political meetings with Mutulu and experiencing the death of his parents' friends, see Mutulu Shaku's interview discussing Tupac's Post-traumatic Stress from that time, *Tupac: Resurrection* (DVD, Paramount, 2004). On Rev. Daughtry's quotes, see transcript of his 1996 memorial speech, Armond White, *Rebel for the Hell of It: The Life of Tupac Shakur* (Nw York: Thunder's Mouth Press, 1997), p.2.

[215] "The FBI... Pena." On FBI keeping Afeni unemployed, see Testimony of Tupac Shakur's attorney, Michael Warren, former Black Liberation Movement leader, New York vs. Tupac Shakur, sentencing hearing transcript, pp. 46-50. The use of this FBI tactic is backed by Michael Swearingen, *FBI Secrets: An agent's expose* (Boston, MA:South End Press,1995), p. 116. On Afeni moving dozens of times, see Scott, *The Killing of Tupac Shakur*, p.66. On Afeni writing chapter of book with Chomsky et al, see Marilyn Vogt, "Letter: Re: *Human Rights for Everybody*," New York Review of Books, Volume 24, Number 21 & 22, January 26, 1978. Other authors included poet Allan Ginsburg Latino activists Armando Gutierrez and Juan Jose Pena; as well as feminist activist Kate Millet .

[216] Cathy Scott, *The Killing of Tupac Shakur* (Las Vegas, NV: Huntington Press, 1997), p.66. On Legs Saunders, the major motion picture release, *Tupac: Resurrection* (Paramount/MTV Films, 2003).

[217] Ronin Ro, *Have Gun Will Travel: The Spectacular Rise and Violent Fall of Death Row Records* (New York: Doubleday, 1998), p.139.

[218] KSAN radio reporter Richard Boyle, on the CD, *Me and My Shadow: Investigation of the political left by the United States Government*, producers Tarabu Betserai and Adi Gevins from "The Pacifica Radio Archives." Track 3.

[219] Robert Sam Anson, "To Die Like A Gangsta," *Vanity Fair*, March 1997, p.248. Also, Cathy Scott, *The Killing of Tupac Shakur* (Las Vegas, Nevadea: Huntington Press, 1997), p.66.
[220] "Mutulu Shakur…'Mr. Untouchable.'" According to a 1976 "Top Secret" Justice Department report. Jefferson Morley, "The Kid Who Sold Crack to the President," *The City Paper*, 12/15/89, p.31. On Barnes acquittals and *New York Times* label, see Hank Messick, *Of Grass and Snow* (Englewood, CA: Prentice-Hall, 1979), p.148. Both cited in Clarence Lusane, *Pipe Dream Blues: Racism and the War on Drugs* (Boston, MA: South End Press, 1991), pp.41-42, notes 76 and 79. Mutulu Shakur also alluded to Nicky Barnes as a "rat," suggesting that he, too, thought Barnes worked for the government. See the momentary display of Mutulu's Thug Life Code in *Tupac:Ressurrection* DVD at the Mutulu Shakur interview.
[221] "Afeni…attack." Cathy Scott, *The Killing of Tupac Shakur*,.p.66
[222] "About…Ross." On CIA's California based trafficking, see Gary Webb, *Dark Alliance: The CIA, the Contras, and the Crack Cocaine Explosion* (New York: Seven Stories, 1998). The CIA's trafficking revealed by Webb was later disclosed in the CIA's Inspector General Report of 1998, cited in Dale Russakoff, "Shifting Within Party to Gain His Footing," *The Washington Post*, A1, A8, 7/26/04.
[223] "A…CDs." On Harris learning from Ross, see Gary Webb, *Dark Alliance*, p.148. Webb detailed the CIA cocaine trafficking network, and a CIA Inspector General backed his findings in 1998. On Inspector General's findings, see Dale Russakoff, "Shifting Within Party to Gain His Footing," *The Washington Post*, A1, A8, 7/26/04. On Harris providing Death Row seed money, see Ronin Ro, *Have Gun Will Travel* (New York: Doubleday, 1998), p.78. The courts later acknowledged this by ordering Suge Knight to pay Harris's wife, Lydia, $107 million in 2005 for her and her husband providing that seed money. Remmie Fresh, "Suge Ordered to Pay $107 Million," AllHipHop News, 3/30/05. www.allhiphop.com/hiphopnews/?ID=4247 .
[224] "*The New York Times*…treatment." Mike Wilson, "For Malcolm X's Grandson, a Clouded Path," *New York Times*, p. A1.
[225] "Of the many…Newton." Earl Anthony, *Spitting in the Wind: The true story behind he violent legacy of the Black Panther Party* (Malibu, CA: Roundtable, 1990), p122. Coming out in 1990, following Churchill and Vander Wall's extensively more revealing accounts, Anthony's book appears as part fact and part subterfuge. Among other undecover agents that got involved with the Oakland Black Panther office, LA Panther Melvin "Cotton" Smith eventually admitted he had been an undercover police intelligence agent. Smith travelled up to Oakland an worked in that Panther office before then traveling to the New York office where Assata Shakur he continually tried to get Panthers drinking liquor with him.See Churchill and Vander Wall, *Agents of Repression*, pp.86, 404n. #130, and 408n, #166. Also Assata Shakur, *Assata: An Autobiography*, pp.228-230.
[226] "Seale…drugs." Stated by Bobby Seale at the first Black Panther Film Festival, New York, 1999. On Newton's claims, for example, see "Teletype from FBI San Francisco to director, 2/16/74. FBU "Informative Notes," 2/16/74, prepared for "J.L.B." FBI Memorandum from Supervisor Gary L. Penrith to SAC San Francisco, 4/13/73. Newton noted here that these documents said he might be "shaking down" drug dealers to donate money rather than buying or selling drugs with them. Huey Newton, *War Against the Panthers* (New York: Harlem River/Readers and Writers, 1991), pp48-9.
[227] Newton quote from a description writen by Geronimo Pratt and sent by Kathleen Cleaver's email http://whosemedia.com/drums/2007/05/09/was-elaine-brown-an-agent/ Also see personal interview, Watani Tyehimba, 5/10/00. Tyehimba, a former LA RAM-based Black Panther who supported Pratt's defense, said he understood that Pratt helped Newton with withdrawal symptoms when they ended up in prison together. See more notes below on agents trying to get Newton using drugs.
[228] "Evidence supports…release." Personal interviews with Kathleen Cleaver, 10/5/02 and George Edwards, 8/20/00. Cleaver also made a strong implication of Brown's spy work when directly asked about it by an audience member at the 2nd Black Panther Film Festival. Churchill and Vander Wall also stated that "Elaine Brown, widely suspected among former

[Panther] party..." *COINTELPRO Papers*, p.153, 362 note 131. Note also the FBI memos on pp.151-2 that discuss the split in Panther factions that Brown was believed to have influenced between Newton's Oakland office versus the still united Cleaver faction in Algeria, Pratt in LA and the Shakur-led chapter in New York. This became known as the "East/West" split. These memos discussed trying to stop Kathleen Cleaver coming from Algeria to re-unify Huey Newton's national Oakland office with these other key chapters. "FBI Memo, 2/17/71, To: Director (100—448006) From: San Francisco (157-601) COINTELPRO—BLACK EXTREMISTS, RM.," *COINTELPRO Papers*, pp. 151-2. On Brown as Newton's one-time lover, she also apparently visited Newton in prison befort that, see Elaine Brown, *A Taste of Power* (New York: Doubleday, 1992), pp.242, 246, 258. Much thanks to Kathleen Cleaver for her information and support. On Brown's cocaine conviction, see Xeroxed clipping of a California news article from April 24, 1976, supplied by ex-Panther George Edwards.

[229] "Evidence...lessons." Xeroxed clipping of a California news article from April 24, 1976, supplied by ex-Panther George Edwards. Thanks to one of New Haven's former top Black Panthers, George Edwards, for his very compelling stack of evidence first compiled and reported in Lee Lew Lee's powerful Panther documentary *All Power to the People* (1995). Edwards then kindly donated his information, time, and insights to this author. Personal interview, George Edwards 8/22/00.

[230] On Pratt and his wife's expulsion and murder see, Churchill and Vander Wall, *Agents of Repression*, pp.87-8; *COINTELPRO Papers*, p. 153, 362 note 131. Researchers also claim that Brown heavily aided the FBI's manufacture of the East/West war. Former Panther National Communications Director Kathleen Cleaver further cited belief in Brown's possible connection to the murder of two LA Panther leaders and Black revolutionary George Jackson. Personal interviews with Kathleen Cleaver, 10/5/02 and George Edwards 8/22/00.

[231] "Geronimo reported...type.')" Newton quote from a description writen by Geronimo Pratt and sent by Kathleen Cleaver's email
http://whosemedia.com/drums/2007/05/09/was-elaine-brown-an-agent/

[232] "While Earl Anthony's...description." This writers's copies of CIA documents on Jay Kennedy, for example, were FOIA-obtained by ex-Panher turned filmmaker Lee Lew Lee and given to George Edwards and then this writer. See, for example, CIA internal memorandum in CIA file for Chief, Security Research Staff, from Allan Morse, one Jay R. Kennedy report. 6/9/65, p.7. On Jay Kennedy as Brown's ex-lovers, Elaine Brown, *A Taste of Power* (New York: Doubleday, 1992), pp.79-86. Earl Anthony, *Spitting in the Wind: The True Story Behind the Violent Legacy of the Black Panther Party* (Malibu, CA: Roundtable, 1990) pp.79, 151. Jay Kennedy as CIA's "Principal source," David Garrow, *Bearing the Cross: Martin Luther King, Jr. and the Southern Christian Leadership Conference* (NY: Quill, William Morrow, 1986), p285. William Pepper, *Orders to Kill: The Truth Behind the Murder of Martin Luther King, Jr.* (New York: Warner Books,1995) pp.82, 445.

[233] "The CIA...him" This writers's copies of CIA documents, for example, were FOIA-obtained by Lee Lew Lee and given to George Edwards and then this writer. See, for example, CIA internal memorandum in CIA file for Chief, Security Research Staff, from Allan Morse, one Jay R. Kennedy report. 6/9/65, p.7. Memorandum from Howard Osborn, Director of Security to Deputy Director of Support. 3/27/68. Also see Pepper finding that Jay Kennedy was the CIA's "Informant A"-- William Pepper, *Orders To Kill: The Truth Behind the Murder of Martin Luther King, Jr.* (NY:Warner Books, 1995), p.82.

[234] Rosemary Bray, "A Black Panther's Long Journey," *New York Times Magazine*, 1/31/93, p.68. J. R. Kennedy as "Principal source"-- David Garrow, *Bearing the Cross: Martin Luther King, Jr. and the Southern Christian Leadership Conference*, p.285. Brown's *Taste of Power* also mentions discussion with Jay Kennedy while she was a Panther, several times in the book, see, pp.175, 262.

[235] Ex-CIA agent John Stockwell in Lee Lew-Lee, *All Power to the People* (Documentary, 1996).
[236] "Earl Anthony…accounts." In *A Taste of Power*, Brown's 1992 published account, she said Newton physically abused her, which no other source collaborated as Newton having done to anyone. Newton wrote his doctoral thesis in 1980, based on his FBI and CIA file. His surviving wife published it in 1991 and one FBI document detailed the same kind of smear they would attempt on Newton as Brown carried out. In Brown's later memoir, she described Newton's early '70s, post-prison apartment as a "twenty-fifth-floor penthouse…[with] many balconies." An FBI document described how an FBI media collaborator Ed Montgomery helped the FBI smear Newton with a false report in a front page *San Francisco Chronicle* article as one of it's "counter-intelligence activities." The article characterized Newton's apartment as "luxurious," in contrast to "the ghetto-like BPP 'pads' and community centers." Other FBI memorandums detailed their intent to carry out this smear campaign. The FBI also created a fake letter from an anonymous Panther they sent from the Oakland Panther office to Panther offices nationwide complaining about Newton's alleged luxurious apartment. Elaine Brown, *A Taste of Power: A Black Woman's Story* (New York: Anchor/Doubleday, 1992), p.9. FBI memorandum from San Francisco to hqtrs., 11/24/70, and from SAC New Orleans to director, 12/11/71, in Newton, *War Against the Panthers*, p.61-2. Afeni Shakur in Jasmine Guy, *Afeni Shakur: Evolution of a Revolutionary* (New York: Atria, 2004), p.77, and Kathleen Cleaver, personal interview, 10/5/02. Many other books on the Panthers also contradict Brown's accounts.
[237] "Elaine Brown's later…question." This writer attended Brown's 2004 lecture in Washington D.C. Brown wrote and article and signed an advertisement on behalf of former honorary Black Panther, Imam Jamil Al-Amin (formerly H. Rap Brown, Elaine Brown, "Black Panther Party Long Victimized by Campaign of Lies," *Atlanta Journal-Constitution*, 3/25/00.
[238] "In the mid-80s…education." On Harlem acting, see Michael Eric Dyson, *Holler If You Hear Me: Searching for Tupac Shakur* (New York: Basic Civitas, 2001), p.33. 17 year-old Tupac Shakur in video, *Tupac Shakur, Thug Angel, Life of an Outlaw*, QD3 Entertainment, 2002.
[239] "While living…nationwide." Personal interview, Watani Tyehimba, 5/2/00. Personal interview with Chokwe Lumumba, 5/10/00. Teyhimba was a former Revolutionary Action Movement-based Los Angeles Black Panther who befriended Afeni Shakur working on Geronimo Pratt's case.
[240] Churchill and Vander Wall, *The COINTELPRO Papers*, pp.309-315.
[241] Personal Interview with Watani Tyehimba, 11/8/02.
[242] Churchill and Vander Wall, *The Cointelpro Papers*, pp.411-12. Footnote 29.
[243] "Three…hiding." http://www.hitemup.com/tupac/family.html
[244] Connie Bruck, "The Takedown of Tupac," *The New Yorker*, 7/7/97, p.54.
[245] "Still…undertaking." Churchill and Vander Wall, *The COINTELPRO Papers*, p.309. On BLA Multinational Task Force, see Sundiata Acoli, "A Brief History of the New Afrikan Prison Struggle," 2/19/92. www.prisonactivist.org
[246] Cathy Scott, *The Killing of Tupac Shakur* (Las Vegas, Nevada: Huntington Press, 1997)p.66.
[247] Michael Eric Dyson, *Holler If You Hear Me* (New York: Basic Civitas Books, 2001), pp.84.
[248] "Tupac…psychology." Michael Eric Dyson, *Holler If You Hear Me: Searching for Tupac Shakur* (New York: Basic Civitas, 2001). Dyson details the incredible library of books that Steinberg showed him as part of Tupac's mass of readings, pp.93-99. Also see some of Tupac's incredibly precocious and insightful political analyses in the pages before, pp.77-84.
[249] "Tupac further…insert." Personal interviews, W. Tyehimba, 5/10/00 and C. Lumumba, 5/5/00. On poetry see Tupac Shakur, *The Rose That Grew from Concrete* (New York: MTV Books, 1999), p.111. Tupac Shakur, *The Lost Tapes* (Herb N' Soul, 2001).

[250] "During... Morrison." Huey Newton, *To Die for the People* (New York: Random House/Writers and Readers, 1972/95) ed. by Toni Morrison. Huey Newton, *Revolutionary Suicide* (New York: Harcourt Brace/Writers and Readers, 1973/95). Erik Erickson and Huey Newton, *In Search of Common Ground* (New York: W. W. Norton & Co., 1973).
[251] "In prison... outside." *Last Man Standing*, new Pratt biography. Personal interviews with former Black Panthers Watani Tyehimba, and George Edwards. Torri Minton, "Huey Newton Gives In, Gets Out of Quentin," *San Francisco Chronicle*, August 27, 1988, A3. Torri Minton, "Prison Protest by Ex-Panther Newton," *San Francisco Chronicle*, August 24, 1988, B8. Paul Liberatore, "How Huey Newton Let a Panther Down," *San Francisco Chronicle*, September 16, 1988, p. A13. On the continued targeting of Newton with seeming frame-ups, see examples in M. Newton, *Bitter Grain*, pp.210-16. On doctorate, see his published doctoral thesis, War Against the Panthers, which gained him his doctorate at the University of California at Santa Cruz in the History of Conscience. On Panther school, Newton, *Bitter Grain*, p218..
[252] "Once out... generations." On black political prisoner starting to identify themselves as New Afrikans, see *Can't Jail the Spirit: Political Prisoners in the U.S.* a collection of biographies (Chicago: Committee to End the Marion Lockdown, 1st ed.1988, 5th ed.2002). Newton's work for Pratt, see Paul Liberatore, "How Huey Newton Let a Panther Down," *San Francisco Chronicle*, 9/16/88, p.A13. On Tupac's quote, see *Tupac Shakur, Thug Angel, Life of an Outlaw,* QD3 Entertainment, 2002. On Newton reuniting Panthers, personal interview, Billy X, *Black Panther* newspaper editor, 2nd International Black Panther Film Fest. Also, Newton attended African People's Socialist Party (a.k.a. Uhuru Movement) meetings. Personal interview of Watu of Afrikan People's Socialist Party, 10/28/03.
[253] "On August 22... execution." On shooting details, Lori Olszewski and Rick DelVecchio, "Huey Newton Shot Dead On West Oakland Street," *San Francisco Chronicle*, Wednesday August 23, 1989, pp. A1, A14. Clarence Johnson and Lori Olszewski, "Friends Say Huey Newton Had Financial Problems." *San Francisco Chronicle*, 8/24/89. On "known military-style... " A Special Forces Group military commander described how after dropping the assassination victim with the first shot, he then puts two bullets in their head. Stephen Kinzer, "Commandos Left a Calling Card: Their Absence," *New York Times*, 9/26/01, p. B6.
[254] "Then, the *San Francisco*... charged one." Churchill and Vander Wall, *the COINTELPRO Papers* pp.320, 417, 418.
[255] "He also was said to have... was found at the scene." Ward Churchill and Jim Vander Wall, The Cointelpro Papers (Boston, MA: South End Press, 1990), pp.320, 417, 418.
[256] "Also, witness... plans." "Witness Michelle... Newton." Michelle Johnson directly quoted in Clarence Johnson and Lori Olaszewski, "Friends Say Huey Newton Had Financial Problems," *San Francisco Chronicle*, 8/24/89, A1.
[257] Newton's bother, Melvin newton said this, as did Omali Yeshitela, a leader of the Uhuru House, a Black nationalist group in Oakland. Yeshitela dismissed the police version of Newton's murder as ludicrous. Omali believed that the government signed Newton's death certificate when they pressed the weapons charges, leaving him unarmed and defenseless. Both cited in Sharon McCormick, "Mourners Pay Respects to Huey Newton," *San Francisco Chronicle*, August 28, 1989, p. A3
[258] Newton's friend Pat Wright, in Clarence Johnson and Lori Olszewski, "Friends Say Huey Newton Had Financial Problems." *San Francisco Chronicle*, August 27, 1989. CIA agent John Stockwell in Lee Lew-Lee, *All Power to the People* (Documentary, 1996).
[259] William Pepper, *Orders to Kill*, p.5.
[260] Antoine Roger Lokongo, "Hands Off the Democratic Republic of Congo, Now!" *The Burning Spear*, October 2003, p.17. Also heard on Pacifica's WBAI radio in New York. On CIA assassinating Lumumba, see, for example, Ed.s James DiEugenio and Lisa Pease, *The Assassinations* (Los Angeles, CA: Feral House, 2002), pp.162-3. Also see, Alexander Cockburn and Jeffrey St. Clair, *White Out: The CIA, Drugs and the Press* (New York: Verso), excerpted in Dave Greaves, "The CIA, Drugs and Big Media" *Our*

Times Press, 9/98, p.8. On CIA attempting/aiding Patrice Lumumba assassination, see Mark Mazetti and Time Weiner, " Files on Illegal Spying Show CIA Skeletons from Cold War," *New York Times*, A1, 6/27/07.

[261] "Another key figure... activists." Ward Churchill and Jim Vander Wall, *Agents of Repression*, p.84, and *The COINTELPRO Papers*, pp.320, 417, 418. Swearingen, *FBI Secrets: An Agent's Expose*, p.87. Swearingen worked in Held's LA Cointelpro unit.

[262] "The FBI... '80s (Ch.8)." Ward Churchill and Jim Vander Wall, *Agents of Repression*, p.84. Swearingen, *FBI Secrets: An Agent's Expose*, p.87.

[263] Ward Churchill and Jim Vander Wall, *The COINTELPRO Papers*, pp.320, 417, 418.

[264] Ward Churchill and Jim Vander Wall, *The COINTELPRO Papers*, pp.320, 417, 418. Eyewitness Michelle Johnson directly quoted in Clarence Johnson and Lori Olaszewski, "Friends Say Huey Newton Had Financial Problems," *San Francisco Chronicle*, 8/24/89, A1.

[265] "A year later... him.'" On the Bari quote, this writer heard it on tape of her played on WBAI radio, NYC, 3/3/00. On other information, see Ward Churchill, "The FBI Targets Judi Bari" *Covert Action*, Winter 1993-94, Number 47. Robert J. Lopez, "Bomb victims jailed," *Oakland Tribune*, May 26, 1990; and Dean Congblay, "Police Say Car Bomb in the Back Seat: How Earth First! victims became suspects," *San Francisco Chronicle*, May 28, 1990. Sgt. Michael Sitterud, Oakland Police Follow-Up Investigation Report (1) RD No. 90-57171, May 2, 1990, pp.1, 3.

[266] "The government... tactic." n Churchill, *CovertAction*, p. 5. Darryl Cherney on "Better Living," with Gary Null, WPFK, Pacifica radio, 7/29/03. Bari vs. Sims, U.S. Court of Appeals for the Ninth Circuit, Case No. 97-17375, dated filed, 9/24/99, CV-91-01057-CW, Opinion of Judge Reinhardt, pp.5, 24. Circuit Judge Schroeder concurred, 12178. Bill Weinberg, "Victory in Judi Bari Case: FBI Agents & Oakland Police to Pay $4.4 million in California Terrorism Coverup," *The Shadow* #46, July-August 2002, p.11. Dennis Cunningham and Ben Rosenfeld, "Snatching Victory From the Jaws of Death," Covert Action Quarterly #75, Fall 2003. More information on the Judi Bari/Darryl Cherney case can be found at www.judibari.org.

[267] See her five-page printed speech, Judi Bari, "Community Under Seige," 5/8/91, in which she details Held's Cointelpro tactics against the Panthers, the American Indian Movement and then her Earth First! She listed and described a least 8 key tactics against her and her group. www.things.org/~jym/ef/community-under-siege.html

[268] "Judi Bari's... area." Held's former colleague M. Wesley Swearingen called the Bari bombing another example of the FBI's continued Cointelpro as "an effort by the FBI to neutralize Judy Bari." Swearingen, *FBI Secrets*, p.06. On Bari's lawsuit leading to Held's early retirement, see Swearingen quote in Ward Churchill, "The FBI Targets Judi Bari" *Covert Action*, Winter 1993-94, Number 47. On Richard Held later leading a top credit card company, see Covert Action Quarterly's founding co-publisher Louis Wolfe, *Human Rights in the United States: The Unfinished Story, Current Political Prisoners—Victims of Cointelpro*, Issue Forum, U.S. Congressional Hearing, 9/14/00, 1:25 p.m. Rayburn House Office Building, Washington, D.C. Room 2000. http://www.ratical.org/co-globalize/CynthiaMcKinney/news/if000914HR.html Wolfe said his investigation led him finding out that Held was CEO of a major credit card company in California. This underscores the revolving door between U.S. Intelligence and the wealthiest families in the United States, discussed in Ch.19.

[269] "Many aspects... Pratt." On FBI/Held's work against Pratt and his legal team in 1985, see *Pratt V. D.J. McCarthy, et al.*, NO. CR. 81-3407-PAR (K), United States District Court, Central District of California, 1985; Vol.3[A], pp.452-53. Cited in Chuchill and Vander Wall, *Agents of Repression*, p. 92 note 195. Also see Swearingen, *FBI Secrets*, p.167. On music benefits for Pratt, see Bruck, The Takedown of Tupac, *The New Yorker*, 7/7/97, p.49.

[270] "Tupac Shakur... leaders." Bruck, *The New Yorker*, 7/7/97, p50, 52.

[271] "As soon as... later." "Claim Against the city of Oakland, California, Claimaint: Tupac Shakur" by John Burris, Esq. Photocopied for Ed.s Jacob Hoye and Karolyn Ali, *Tupac: Resurrection* (New York: Atria Books, 2003), pp78-9. Danyel Smith "Introduction,"

Vibe editors, *Tupac Shakur* (New York: Crown Publishing, 1997), p.17. Personal interview, Watani Tyehimba, December 11, 2002. Robert McFadden, "At Two Rallies, Protesters Accuse Police in Killings," *New York Times*, 8/3/03, p.32. Several other deaths in police custody have occurred via choking.

[272] "The timing... hit." Drive-by shooting on limousine described by Tupac's friend, Troy, who was in imousince, on video *Thug Immortal* (Video, Xenon Entertainment, 1997).

[273] "Evidence and witnesses... shooting." Police cadet Darell Harts' supporters said police harassed Harts with many visits. The day police fatally shot him, two officers claimed they responded to a call about Harts shooting a neighbor's dog. A police spokesman said they exited their unmarked car wearing police uniforms and identified themselves as police after which Harts shot at them and they fired back. The *Los Angeles Times* reported that an eyewitness told a different story under anonymity for fear of police reprisal. This person said they didn't hear anyone yell "Halt" or "Police," they merely heard a barrage of shots all at once from a gray unmarked moving car. An autopsy found no drugs in Harts' system, no gunshot residue on his hands, and an Animal Regulation log said the neighbor's dog was "shot by LAPD." Months of candlelight vigils brought on an FBI investigation that failed to reach a conclusion of police fault in the case. Harts was to testify that a white police officer knocked the teeth out of black former LA Rams football player Austin Shanks after stopping him on a motorcycle with a white woman. Edward Boyer, Henry Weinstein, R. Serrano, "Questions Raised in L.A. Man's Death," *Los Angeles Times*, 5/4/93, A1,3. Richard Serrano, "Probe of Slaying by Officers Widened," *L.A. Times*, 5/5/03, B3. Nenry Wienstein, "Tests on Man Killed by Police Fuel Controversy," *LA Times*, 5/28/93, B1,8. Henry Weinstein, "FBI Launches Investigation of LAPD Shooting," *LA Times*, 9/11/93, B3.

[274] See youtube.com type in Fred Hampton, Jr. on Hip Hop.

[275] "Tupac Shakur gave... gatherings." Personal interview, Watani Tyehimba, 5/20/03 and also see added features of Sarah Lazin, *Tupac: Ressurrection* (MTV,2003)

[276] "While Tupac... cities." John Singleton and Veronica Chambers, *The Making of Poetic Justice* (New York: Delta, 1993). Alexander Cockburn, "Beat the Devil," *The Nation*, June 1, 1992, pp.738-9. On smaller riots in several other cities, see Pacifica Radio's *Democracy Now!* DemocracyNow.org "From COINTELPRO to the Shadow Government: As Fred Hampton, Jr. Is Released from 9 Years of Prison, a Look Back at the Assassination of Fred Hampton," 3/5/02.

[277] "Historically, U.S. Intelligence... him." Regarding 60s investigation on who influenced rioters, see William Pepper, *Order to Kill* (New York: Time Warner, 1998), p.446. On riots as one of the few disruptive mobilizations tactics that helped get national legislation passed for the poor, see Frances Fox Piven and Richard A. Cloward, *Poor Peoples' Movements* (New York: Vintage, 1979).

[278] "Mike Davis... Panthers." On attack of gang truce leaders see, for example, Gang truce leader Dewayne Holmes received a 7 year prison sentence for allegedly stealing $10 at a gang unity dance. Mike Davis, "Who Killed Los Angeles? Part Two: The verdict is given," *New Left Review* 199/1993, p.34-5. Operation Hammer work to break up legal gang peace summit meetings also discussed by LA activist on WBAI Radio, 4/15/02. FBI work with LAPD in Operation Hammer in Megan Garvery & Rich Winton, "City Declares War on Gangs," *Los Angeles Times*, 12/4/02. Kody Scott (a.k.a. Sanyika Shakur), Monster: The Autobiography of an L.A. Gang Member (New York: Penguin, 1994), pp.vii-viii, 347-9. Tupac planned activist projects with Scott, Vibe ed.s, *Tupac*, '97, p.51. Mitchell Landsberg & John Mutchell, "In Gang's Territory, a Weary Hope," The Los Angeles Times, 12/5/02, p.A.1. "Rival Gangs Extend Reach to Small Cities," Houston Chronicle, 9/20/94, p.20. Reuters New Service, "Gangs Found in Military, Magazine Says," *St. Louis Post –Dispatch*, 7/17/95, p4A. Mike Davis, "Who Killed LA? A Political Autopsy," *New Left Review*, 197, 1993, p.7.

[279] "After the... father." Personal interview, Fred Hampton, Jr. at Third Black Panther Film Festival, New York, 8/1/03. Also written about in "Framed! For Defending the Rights of the Black Community," www.inpdumchicago.com/framed.html . Fred Hampton Jr, as told to Heru, "Assassination Attempt on Fred Hampton,. Jr." 10/2/02,

Davey D's Hip-Hop Corner: the New Source for the Hip-Hop Generation, http://www.daveyd.com/FullArticles/articleN1274.asp On walking with daughter, Heru, "Fred Hampton, Jr. Interview," AWOL Magazine 2002.
[280] "Police accused... activist)." Personal interview, Fred Hampton, Jr. 8/1/03. Also written about in "Framed! For Defending the Rights of the Black Community," www.inpdumchicago.com/framed.html . Fred Hampton Jr, as told to Heru, "Assassination Attempt on Fred Hampton,. Jr." 10/2/02, Davey D's Hip-Hop Corner: the New Source for the Hip-Hop Generation, http://www.daveyd.com/FullArticles/articleN1274.asp On pictures of assassination attempts, J.R. "Young Chairman Fred Hampton Jr. Pictorial," *San Francisco Bay*, www.sfbayview.com/022603/manyhaveforgotten022603.shtml On Hampton citing Tupac's importance, see reprint of 12/3/04 *Vibe Online* Exclusive: Interview with Chairman Fred Hampton, Jr."
[281] "U.S. Intelligence also... death.'" As noted above, one intelligence document a Senate committee found included strategies for use against political musicians such as "Intelligence Activities and Rights of Americans," Book II, April 26, 1976, *Senate Committee with Respect to Intelligence Report*. Excerpted in Alex Constantine, *The Covert War Against Rock* (Los Angeles: Feral House, 2001), p.9. U.S. Senate Select Committee to Study Government Operations, *The FBI's Covert Program to Destroy the Black Panther Party*, U.S. Government Printing Office, Washington. D.C. 1976.
[282] "Buchanan Call For Winning Back 'Soul of America'" *Los Angeles Times*, 5/28/92, p.A5.
[283] Tupac Shakur, "Souljah's Revenge," *2Pacalypse Now* (Interscope, 1991).
[284] "*Rolling Stone*... cake.'" Allan Light, "L.A. Rappers Speak Out," *Rolling Stone*, June 25, 1992, p.15.
[285] "In the... government.'" *Thug Immortal* (Documentary, Xenon Entertainment, 1997). Also see lyrics for "Panther Power" Tupac Shakur, *The Lost Tapes,* (HerbNSoul, 1989/2000). This footage also seen in Laura Lazin and Karolyn Ali, *Tupac: Resurrection* (MTV, 2003).
[286] "Marku Reymolds... Tupac's hands." Mostly Marku Reynolds in video, *Thug Immortal,*
[287] Veronica Chambers, "Ain't Nothing Changed but the Weather," *Premiere*, August, 1993, p.84.
[288] "The assailants then... gun." Marku Reynolds in video, *Thug Immortal,* Don't Back Down Productions, 1997. Also, Robert Sam Anson, "To Die Like A Gangsta," Vanity Fair, March 1997, p.248.Connie Bruck, "The Takedown of Tupac," *The New Yorker*, July 7, 1997, p.47.
[289] "Reynolds saw... charge." Marku Reynolds in video, *Thug Immortal,* Don't Back Down Productions, 1997. Also, Robert Sam Anson, "To Die Like A Gangsta," *Vanity Fair*, March 1997, p.248.Connie Bruck, "The Takedown of Tupac," *The New Yorker*, July 7, 1997, p.47.
[290] Veronica Chambers, "Ain't Nothing Changed but the Weather," *Premiere*, August, 1993, p.84. On Harding living in Marin, Attorney Michael Warren, personal interview, 4/10/00.
[291] See also, Robert Sam Anson, "To Die Like A Gangsta," *Vanity Fair*, March 1997, p.248.Connie Bruck, "The Takedown of Tupac," *The New Yorker*, July 7, 1997, p.47.
[292] Reprinted from a Booneville, CA speech, Judi Bari, "Community Under Siege," 5/8/91. www.things.org/~jym/ef/community-under-siege.html
[293] M. Newton, *Bitter Grain: Huey Newton and the Black Panther Party*, p.224
[294] See copied FBI memorandum of Held's in his LA FBI Cointelpro team member, M. Wesley Swearingen's memoir, *FBI Secrets: An Agent's Expose*, pp.118-127. Also see Churchill and Vander Wall, *Agents of Repression*, p.80. Sophisticated media work against LA Panther supporters, see FBI memorandum, "To: Director, FBI (100-448006), From: SAC, Los Angeles (157-4054) Date 4/27/70," against Jane Fonda and more damaging Held work against Jean Seberg, FBI memorandum dated 4/27/70 (Ch.5). Memorandum copies published in Ward Churchill and Jim Vander Wall, The

COINTELPRO Papers (Boston: South End Press, 1990). pp.212-216. "Specialized," p.214.
[295] "Reynolds and at least…Marin Fest." Mostly Marku Reynolds in video, *Thug Immortal,* (Xenon/Don't Back Down Productions, 1997). Also, the interwiew quote from Robert Sam Anson, "To Die Like A Gangsta," Vanity Fair, March 1997, p.248.The "I hated myself…" from Connie Bruck, "The Takedown of Tupac," *The New Yorker*, July 7, 1997, p.47.*Thug Immortal*, video also showed quotes of the spin on the interview in the local paper. More came from "Yo! MTV Raps Top Ten" from MTV preview of *Tupac: Resurrection* 11/13/03.
[296] "Reynolds saw… charge." Marku Reynolds in video, *Thug Immortal,* Don't Back Down Productions, 1997. Also, Robert Sam Anson, "To Die Like A Gangsta," *Vanity Fair*, March 1997, p.248.Connie Bruck, "The Takedown of Tupac," *The New Yorker*, July 7, 1997, p.47.
[297] Veronica Chambers, "Ain't Nothing Changed but the Weather," *Premiere*, August, 1993, p.84. Also, Bill Hewitt, "Rapper sheet: hip-hop hitmaker Tupac Shakur is busted for sexual assault." *People Weekly*, 12/6/93, p.89 (2).
[298] Chris Morris, "Quayle's 2Pac/Interscope Attack Puts New Heat On Time Warner," *Billboard*, October 3, 1992, pp.5, 86.
[299] Micheal Eric Dyson, *Holler If You Hear Me*, pp.80-82.
[300] "A little-known… each other." Mike Davis, "In L.A., Burning All Illusions," *The Nation*, 6/1/92, p.745. Mike Davis, "Who Killed LA? A Political Autopsy" *New Left Review*, 197/1993, p.7. Personal interview, Watani Tyehimba, 10/17/02. Jesse Katz, "Man Freed in Death of Gang Leader Courts: Rodney Compton is to get one year probation in the slaying of Tony Bogard, who helped reach a truce between the Crips and Bloods," *The Los Angeles Times*, 6/1/94, p.3. His cousin, Dewayne Holmes, worked with ex-Black Panther Michael Zinzun and local Shiite Muslim leader Mujahdid Abdul-Karim to rally Bloods and Crips factions against the LAPD instead of each other. Jesse Jackson and others helped the gangs increase the factions engaging in the peace truce and working against racist police attacks on their community. Mike Davis, "Who Killed LA: Part Two: the Verdict is Given," *New Left Review* 198, pp.34-5.
[300] Sullivan, LAbyrinth, p.34 and photo.
[300] Sulivan, LAbyrinth, p.152.
[300] Randalll Sullivan, *LAbrynth*, pp.205-207, 225.
[300] OJJDP Summary, August 2000—Youth Gang Programs and Strategies, "Suppression Programs" www.ncjrs.org/html/ojjdp/summary_2000_8/suppression.html
[301] On Jackson, see Mike Davis, "Who Killed LA: Part Two: the Verdict is Given," *New Left Review* 198, pp.34-5. On Belafonte and other black activists see, Joe Garofoli, "Singer Belafonte feels the beat of antiwar sentiment/ Keynote speaker at Oakland rally hears international criticism," *San Francisco Chronicle*, 4/5/03, pA.15.
[302] Mutulu reportedly started organizing the truce in the Lompoc Penitentiary. http://www.hitemup.com/tupac/family.html . He was considered highly revered in the prison system as a political activist. Connie Bruck, "The Takedown of Tupac," *The New Yorker*, 7/7/97, p.53.
[303] "Then, he… class." Personal interviews with Tupac's business manager, ex-Black Panther and NAPO security director, Watani Tyehimba, 5/10/00. And, Chokwe Lumumba, national chair of NAPO, 5/5/00. On other Thug Life goals, also see Bruck, *New Yorker*, p. 50 and Tupac Jacob Hoye and Karolyn Ali, eds, Afeni Shakur, concept, *Tupac: Resurrection* (New York: Atria, 2003), pp.116-17. A final note on the name came from an interview Mutulu Shakur gave to *AllHipHop.com*. He said that Tupac called himself a "thug." Tupac had said he did that because that's what all the adults called him and his friends. Mutulu said that the British called the young citizens of India, whom the British colonized, "thuggies." These Thuggies ended up accepting this name and organizing as a major factor that fought for India's independence from Britain. Sone excerpt "masses… " from Tupac Shakur, "Wordz of Wisdom," *2Pacalyspe Now*, 1991.
[304] "Tupac's later increased… anti-abuse.' " Vibe eds., *Tupac Shakur*, pp.17, 43. bell hooks prefers to spell her name in lower case letters but an editor overruled this writer.

---

[305] "One defense…support." Connie Bruck, "The Takedown of Tupac," *The New Yorker*, 7/7/97, p.56.
[306] "Tupac and Mutulu…LIFE." From literature, "Code of THUG LIFE" by Tupac Shakur and Mutulu Shakur. Provided to this author by former New Haven Black Panther George Edwards.
[307] "Writers…socialism." Kody Scott (a.k.a. Sanyika Shakur), *Monster: The Autobiography of an L.A. Gang Member* (New York: Penguin, 1994), pp.vii-viii, 347-9. Tupac planned activist projects with Scott, Vibe ed.s, *Tupac*, '97, p.51. Mutulu "revered," Bruck, *New Yorker*, p.53.
[308] "After the…leaders." Alexander Cockburn, "Beat the Devil," *The Nation*, June 1, 1992, pp.738-9.
[309] "Government…publication." See transcript of Sanyika Shakur's speech videotaped and presented at a 1995 forum he was to speak at after his 1994 publication, when his parole was revoked and he was imprisoned again. http://www-unix.oit.umass.edu/~kastor/fallprogram/fall-shakur.html
[310] "Gang peace…Latinos (Ch.36)." On Atlanta, personal interview with eyewitness Tony Parker, 7/7/03. On Latin Kings, see Jennifer Gonnerman, "Throne Behind Bars: The Latin King Leader on Love, Law Enforcement, and Landing Back in Jail," *Village Voice*, 4/7/98, p.61. Also, see video, *Black and Gold*, Big Noise Films, 1999. On New York Bloods, Chris Hedges, "Old Colors, New Battle Cry: Gang's Founder Calls for Focus on Community, Not Crimes," New York Times, 1/31/00, pp.B1, B6.
[311] Tim King, "US street gang leaders to address London rally," *The Guardian*, 10/28/94.
[312] Mitchell Landsberg & John Mutchell, "In Gang's Territory, a Weary Hope," *The Los Angeles Times*, 12/5/02, p.A.1.
[313] "Rival Gangs Extend Reach to Small Cities," *Houston Chronicle*, 9/20/94, p.20.
[314] Reuters New Service, "Gangs Found in Military, Magazine Says," *St. Louis Post – Dispatch*, 7/17/95, p4A.
[315] "U.S. Intelligence…Weed and Seed." Alexander Cockburn, "Beat the Devil," *The Nation*, June 1, 1992, pp.738-9. For example, Gang truce leader Dewayne Holmes received a 7 year prison sentence for allegedly stealing $10 at a gang unity dance. Mike Davis, "Who Killed Los Angeles? Part Two: The verdict is given," *New Left Review* 199/1993, p.34-5. WBAI Radio, 4/15/02. FBI work with LAPD in Operation Hammer in Megan Garvery & Rich Winton, "City Declares War on Gangs," *Los Angeles Times*, 12/4/02. Mitchell Landsberg & John Mutchell, "In Gang's Territory, a Weary Hope," *The Los Angeles Times*, 12/5/02, p.A.1. On Bush's Weed and Seed, see Mike Davis, "Who Killed LA? A Political Autopsy," *New Left Review*, 197, 1993, p.7. Also, Watani Tyehimba said that a lecturing LA black activist said it was commonly believed that Weed and Seed stood for weeding undercover agents into the gangs to seed conflict and end the truce. Personal interview, 11/02/03.
[316] "Also, by a Presidential…control.'" see Colonel William W. Mendel, US Army (retired), book review of *Fires and Furies*, by James D. Delk, *US Army Foreign Military Studies Office* (FMSO), Fort Leavenworth, Kansas, 1996. See also by Mednel, Combat in Cities: The LA Riot and Operation Rio," *FMSO*, July 1996. Major Christopher m Schaubelt, "Lessons in command and Control, from the Los Angeles Riots," *Parameters Magazine*, Summer 1997. William V. Wenger and Frederick W. Young, "The Los Angeles Riots and Tactical Intelligence," *Military Intelligence*, Oct-Dec. 1992. *The Federation of American Scientists Military Analysis Network*, "Garden Plot," November 1998. All cited in Frank Morales, "U.S. Has Been Preparing to Turn America into a Military Dictatorship," *What Really Happened*, www.whatreallyhappened.com/suppression.html Similar Morales article appeared in print, such as Frank Morales, "The Militarization of the Police," *CovertAction Quarterly*, Spring–Summer 1999, #67, pp.45-50.
[317] "Prison…Colorado." A warden's memo said that Mutulu's transfer to the nation's most maximum-security prison was due to his influence over young Blacks through his "outside contacts." Bruck, *The New Yorker*, p.54.

---

[318] Personal interview with Tawanda Monroe of the Department of Justice, Federal Bureau of Investigation, May 9, 2000. Letter from Department of Justice acknowledged this communication and this author's willingness to pay for the copying fee of $405 (see Monroe). Ms. Monroe also disclosed that they charged 10 cents per page, copying 10 and copied 10 at a time, fitting her "over 4,000 page disclosure. Ms. Moroe originally said "I'm not allowed to tell you how many pages are in that file," but then stated the number a few minutes later. The Los Angeles FBI File Number for the Tupac Shakur file is 266A-LA-201807.
[319] "Reagan…operatioins." Michale Montalvo, "Prisoner of the Drug War: An Inside Report from a former Inside Player," *Prevailing Winds* #8, 2000, pp.76-82.
[320] On September…earlier." Chris Morris, "Quayles' 2Pac/Interscope Attack Puts New Heat On Time Warner," *Billboard*, October 3, 1992, pp.5, 86.
[321] "Ice-T had… Killer'" Allan Light, "L.A. Rappers Speak Out," *Rolling Stone*, June 25, 1992, p.15. Ice-T, "Cop Killer," on Body Count, *Body Count* (Self-titled debut on Sire/Warner, 1992).
[322] "The case of… months." All from Barry Shank, "Fears of the White Unconcious: Music, Race, and Identification in the Censorship of 'Cop Killer.'" *Radical History Review* #66, Fall 1996. http://chnm.gmu.edu/rhr/article1.htm . This article cites several articles regarding police groups' and Republicans' protest. These include Bruce brown, "Quayle Boosts 'Cop Killer' Boycott Campaign," *Washington Post*, 6/20/92, ppB1,5; Avis Thomas-Lester & Marylou Tousignant, "Reaction to Ice-T Song Heats Up: 60 Congressmen Join Complaint," *Washington Post*, 6/25/92, pp.C1,3. On Time Warner dropping Ice-T, Irv Lichtman, "The Billboard Bulletin: Sire/Warner Drops Ice-T," *Billboard*, 2/6/93, p.82.
[323] "Tupac was also… 50%." Robert Sam Anson, "To Die Like a Gangsta," *Vanity Fair*, March 1997, p.251. Connie Bruck, "The Takedown of Tupac," *The New Yorker*, 7/7/97, p.57. Tupac lyric from "Keep Ya Head Up, "*Strictly 4 My N.I.G.G.A.Z* (Interscope, 1993).
[324] "Tupac likely… election." Tupac Shakur, *2Pacalypse Now* (Interscope, 1992). *Strictly 4 My N.I.G.G.A.Z* (Interscope, 1993). This CD was ready for release but held up for a year by Time Warner. Personal interview, Watani Tyehimba, 5/5/00.
[325] Other Republican… Tupac." Nick Broomfield, *Biggie and Tupac*, documentary film, 2002. Cathy Scott, "The Death of Tupac Shakur One Year Later," *Las Vegas Sun*, September 6, 1997. Meanwhile, the William Bennett, "United States' pre-eminent moral crusader," who wrote *The Book of Virtues*, reportedly lost $8 million at casinos over the Nineties, "Bennett Acknowledges Gambling Large Sums, But Says He is Quitting," The Sun, 5/6/03, p.2A.
[326] "Politicians… year." Nick Broomfield, *Biggie and Tupac* (documentary, 2002). Broomfield had previously won a best documentary award at the Sundance Film Festival.
[327] "The U.S.… into rivalries' (Ch.12)." "Intelligence Activities and Rights of Americans," Book II, April 26, 1976, *Senate Committee with Respect to Intelligence Report*. Excerpted in Alex Constantine, The Covert War Against Rock (Los Angeles: Feral House, 2001), p.9.
[328] "It eventually… below)." Dasun Allah & Joshua Fahiym Ratcliffe, "Law and Disorder," *The Source*, June 2004, p.44. Nicole White and Evelyn McDonnell, "Police Secretly Watching Hip-Hop Artists," *Miami Herald*, 3/9/04, p.1A.
[329] See August 30, 1967 FBI Memorandum from Philadelphia's Special Agent in Charge to the FBI Director, reprinted in Churchill and Vander Wall, *Agents of Repression*, pp.44-7.
[330] "In line… dismissed." Associated Press, "Rapper Shakur Hit with a Gun Arrest Encore," *The Daily News*, May 1, 1994. Personal interview with Ken Ellis, Esq. 5/20/00. Karen Zekan, "4 Sought in Shakur Shooting," *Las Vegas Sun*, September 9, 1996 from www.lasvegassun.com/sunbin/stories/text/1996/sep/09/505068709.html . On celebrities and guns, see, for example, "Names and Faces: Pistol Packing Big Shots," compiled by Chris Richards, *Washington Post*, 8/5/03, p.C3. While it names many celebrities among the 3,600 New Yorkers with liceneses to carry a loaded weapon, its interesting that Steven Seagal was denied a permit renewal after his films exposed much U.S.

Intelligence drug trafficking. The Mafia also tried to extort Seagal around 2000. On Tupac's many arrests for mostly minor charges in areas particularly focusing on Tupac and other rap starts, see "Rapper's Rap Sheet: 10 Arrests," *The New York Post*, 12/22/93 and Associated Press, "Rapper Shakur Hit with a Gun Arrest Encore," *The Daily News*, May 1, 1994.

[331] "These harassment... gun." Deborah Russell, "Rapper 2Pac Faces Assault Charge in LA," *Billboard*, v105 March 27, 1993, p.94. Also see *New York Post*, and Vibe Editors, *Tupac Shakur*, pp.29, 138.

[332] "Similar circumstances... charges." Personal interview with Tupac's Atlanta trial lawyer, Ken Ellis, Esq. 5/20/00.

[333] "The FBI apparently... occuring." Tupac said shows cancelled in Vibe eds *Tupac Shakur* (New York: Crown, 1997) p.46. Rage Against the Machine lead singer Zach De La Rocha detailed how police used this tactic against his group when they went on tour with rap group Wu Tang Clan, personal interview, 5/5/99. On the FBI's fax campaign to get police canceling NWA shows, see Bruce C. Brown, "Quayle Boosts 'Cop Killer' Campaign," *Washington Post*, 6/20/92, pp.B1,5. Cited in Barry Shank, "Fears of the White Unconcious: Music, Race, and Identification in the Censorship of 'Cop Killer.'" *Radical History Review* #66, Fall 1996.

[334] *Me and My Shadow: Investigation of the political left by the United States Government*, producers Tarabu Betserai and Adi Gevins from "The Pacifica Radio Archives." Track 5.

[335] "Over a dozen... life." On "frivolous" lawsuit, personal interview with attorney Dan 5/9/05.C. Dolores Tucker, who formed an anti-rap campaign with President Bush's Drug Czar, William Bennett, filed a lawsuit claiming that "her sex life with her husband was adversely affected because of some of Shakur's lyrics." Cathy Scott, "The Death of Tupac Shakur One Year Later," *Las Vegas Sun*, 9/6/97. Randalll Sullivan, *LAbyrinth* (New York: Atlantic Monthly Press, 2002), p.87-88.
Also see, Johnnie Roberts, "Grabbing at a Dead Star," *Newsweek*, September 15, 1997, p.56. "C. Delores tucker Files $10 Million Lawsuit Against Tupac Shakur's Estate," *Jet*, September 1, 1997, p.62. On over a dozen lawsuits, see "Another in a long line... nothing about the lawsuit." Associated Press, "$16.6 M of Shakur Estate Sued," *Las Vegas Sun*, November 20, 1996.
http://www.lasvegassun.com/sunbin/... nov/20/112100529.html?Tupac+Shakur

[336] "Most of these... trooper.'" Veronica Chambers, "Ain't Nothing Changed but the Weather," *Premiere*, i1 v6 August, 1993, p.84-88. Also on Quayle-backed lawsuit claiming lyrics caused teen to kill cop, see Chuck Phillips, "2Pac's Gospel Truth," *Rolling Stone*, 10/28/93, p. 22. Chris Morris, "Quayles' 2Pac/Interscope Attack Puts New Heat On Time Warner," *Billboard*, 10/3/92, pp.5, 86. Barbara Ross, "Cops Widow Sez It's Time to Dump Star," *The Daily News*, 11/24/93.

[337] "The Atlana... case." On Atlanta suit, see Personal interview with Ken Ellis, Esq. 5/15/00, and Karen Zekan, "4 Sought in Shakur Shooting," *Las Vegas Sun*, 9/9/96 from http://www.lasveagasu\sun.com/sunbin/stories/text/1996/sep/09/505068709.html

[338] Ibid, Scott, *Las Vegas Sun*, September 6, 1997.

[339] Michael Eric Dyson, *Hollar If You Hear Me* (New York: Basic Civitas Books, 2001), p.170.

[340] "Tupac said... in jail." Dream Hampton, "Hellraiser," *Source*, September 1994, pp. 82, 84, 88.

[341] "Tupac had... there." Affidavit by Tupac Shakur, p.1, *New York vs. Tupac Shakur, Supreme Court of State of New York*, Appelate Devision, First Department, Indict. No. 11578/93. Sonia Murray, "Rapper's Career Taking Off in Film, Recording Industries," *The Atlanta Journal/the Atlanta Constitution,* November 2, 1993, p.C5.

[342] "Tupac's car... him." Personal interview with Tupac's Atlanta trial lawyer, Ken Ellis, Esq, 5/12/00. Ellis reported that his investigator luckily got a hold of the black motorist and interviewed him.

[343] "White and black... at him." Partly from eyewitness Watani Tyehimba, parked next to black motorist first focused on by the plainclothes cops. Personal interview, 11/5/03.

Also from witness interviews--personal interview, Ken Ellis, 5/12/00. Long after the trial's end, Ellis told this writer about his interviews with the prosecutors' top witness, Edward Fields, who was also cited in Danzy Senna, "Violence is Golden," *Spin Magazine*, April, 1994, p43-47. Ellis further told this writer about the white couple wintesses he interviewed that he never needed to call to trial as the case never went far enough in court. This writer conducted a personal interview with Tupac's other lawyer, Chokwe Lumumba, 5/5/00. Lumumba's reported interview quotes of the white couple's account were also reported in Danzy Senna, "Violence is Golden," *Spin Magazine*, April, 1994, p46. The daily *Atlanta Journal Constitution* gave exact quotes of the police report in which Edward Fields is quoted as saying that "one of the White males... pull out and point a black handgun... started yelling 'Get Down! Get Down! And then fired one shot towards the Mercedes." Kathy Scruggs and Scott Marshall, "Witness says off-duty cops fired first shot: Claims rapper's return fire caused brothers' wounds." *Atlanta Journal Constitution*, 11/03/93, p. D12. Ellis said that the prosecutor spent a long cross-examination to get Fields to say that the officer's shots could have been warning shot and the newspaper then reported it that way.

[344] "Tupac's reaction... homicide." Personal interview, Billy Lesane, April, 10,1999. Also reported by Edward Fields in describing person looking like Tupac shooting back. Scruggs and Marshall, "Witness says off-duty cops fired first shot," *Atlanta Journal Constitution*, 11/03/93, p. D12.

[345] "The white officers... at them." On "Niggers came by and..." Ronin Ro, *Have Gun Will Travel* (New York: Doubleday, 1998), p.146. On white officers' account, see their lawyer in "Witness says off-duty cops fired first shot." *Atlanta Journal Constitution*, 11/03/93, p. D12.

[346] Personal interviews with, Ken Ellis, Esq. 5/20/00 and Chokwe Lumumba, 5/5/00. On not announcing, "police," common knowledge that killing a cop can bring a death penalty and cops would say "Police" in order to help protect themselves. Ellis supported that Atlanta cops would normally say "police," off duty or not, and Chokwe Lumumba supported this notion that the cops would have protected thmselves this way unless they wanted to hide the fact. Personal interview with Chokwe Lumumba, 5/5/00. Also, eyewitness accounts of Tupac's biological cousin, Billy Lesane, personal interview, 4/10/99, and Watani Tyehimba, 5/10/00.

[347] "The oficers... surveillance." Caught lying, saying no guns on them, Scruggs & Marshall, "Witness says off-duty cops fired first shot." *Atlanta Journal Constitution*, 11/03/93, p. D12. On going right to hotel room despite aliases, personal interview with, Ken Ellis, Esq. 5/20/00. Personal interview with Chokwe Lumumba, 5/5/00.

[348] "Most importantly, locker." Cathy Scott, *The Killing of Tupac Shakur* (Las Vegas, Nevada: Huntington Press, 1998), p.77. Ken Ellis, Esq. Tupac's Atlanta trial lawyer, and *Spin*, p.46.

[349] New York City Police Officer Craig McKernan, *People of the state of New York vs. Charles Fuller and Tupac Shakur,* Indictment no. 11578-93, Trial Excerpt of People's Witness—P.O. McKernan cross-examination, pp.8-9. Cross-examination by Michael Warren, Esqu.

[350] Personal interviews with, Ken Ellis, Esq. 5/20/00 and Chokwe Lumumba, 5/5/00. On not announcing, "police," common knowledge that killing a cop can bring a death penalty and cops would say "Police" in order to help protect themselves. Ellis supported that Atlanta cops would normally say "police," off duty or not, and Chokwe Lumumba supported this notion that the cops would have protected thmselves this way unless they wanted to hide the fact. Personal interview with Chokwe Lumumba, 5/5/00. Also, eyewitness accounts of Tupac's biological cousin, Billy Lesane, personal interview, 4/10/99, and Watani Tyehimba, 5/10/00.

[351] On Oakland National office shooting, see Churchill and Vander Wall, *Agents of Repression*, p.78. On mid-town New York Panther chapter assault, M. Newton, *Bitter Grain*, p.176.

[352] "The FBI... leader." On Brown as 60s Cointelpro target, see FBI memorandum from SAC Albany to Director, FBI, August 25, 1967, "COUNTERINTELLIGENCE

PROGRAM, BLACK NATIONALIST-HATE GROUPS," Copied in Chuchill and Vander Wall, *The COINTELPRO Papers*, pp.92-3d. Also see important FBI document of concern that SNCC'sCharmichael or Brown, SCLC's MLK, RAM's Max Sanford, or NOI's Elijah Muhammad could become the new black "messiah." See "AIRTEL, To: SAC Albany, From: Director, FBI (100-448006), COUNTERINTELLIGENCE PROGRAM, BLACK NATIONALIST HATE GROUPS, RACIAL INTELLIGENCE, 3/4/68. Copied in Churchill and Vander Wall, *The COINTELPRO Papers*, pp.108-111, particularly Brown et. al. at p.111. On Brown's honorary East Coast pantehr status, see Churchill and Vander Wall, *The COINTELPRO Papers*, p.126. The writer of this FBI War on Tupac book also saw Seale say this in a documentary. Newton's printed speeches officially declared SNCC's Charmicheal an honorary field marshall, in Huey Newton, *To Die for the People*, pp.7-9. The "Nonviolent" in the SNCC title was changed to "National" around 1966.

[353] "In 1967… riot." On black officers shooting Brown, see eyewitness Gloria Richardson, interviewed by Gil Noble on ABC television's *Like It Is*, March 17, 2002. This, Rap Brown's quoted response, and Rap Brown Amendment discussed in Carl Schoettler, "A Whole New Rap," *The Baltimore Sun* , 8/19/95, p.1D.

[354] "When prosecutors… 1990 (Ch.12)." Manning Marable, *Race, Reform and Rebellion: The Second Reconstruction in Black America, 1945-1982* (Jackson, Mississippi: Univ. of Mississippi Press, 1984), p.125. Cited in Ward Churchill, "The FBI Targets Judi Bari," *CovertAction Quarterly*, Winter 1993-94, p.55.

[355] Carl Schoettler, "A Whole New Rap," *The Baltimore Sun*, 8/19/95, p.1D. Also see Peter Slevin, "Police Seek Ex-Millitant in Slaying," *The Washington Post*, 3/18/00, p.A1, 12.

[356] Imam Jamil… mosques." Fareed H. Numan, a Washington research analyst who has consulted for the American Muslim Council, in Schoettler, *The Baltimore Sun*, August 19, 1995. Also, see David Firestone, "For Former Radical, Old Battleground Became a Refuge," *The New York Times*, March 22, 2000, p. A21.

[357] Joshua B. Good and Richard Whitt, "Eye on Al-Amin: FBI, Police Tracked Militant, Inner Circle in '90s Homicides," *The Atlanta Journal-Constitution*, April 1, 2000. From http://www.accessatlanta.com/partners/ajc/newsatlanta/alamin/0402.htm.

[358] "Imam Al-Amin 'has been… Al-Amin with these crimes." Joshua B. Good and Richard Whitt, "Eye on Al-Amin: FBI, Police Tracked Militant, Inner Circle in '90s Homicides," *The Atlanta Journal-Constitution*, April 1, 2000. From http://www.accessatlanta.com/partners/ajc/newsatlanta/alamin/0402.htm.

[359] "In 1995… him." Carl Schoettler, *The Baltimore Sun*, 8/19/95.

[360] An analysis of a many media accounts support how evidence contradicted police claims. For example, see Peter Slevin, "Police Seek Ex-Militant In Slaying," *The Washington Post*, March 18,2000, p.A12. Gloria Richardson on *Like It Is*, March 17, 2002. Fareed H. Numan, a Washington research analyst who has consulted for the American Muslim Council, in Schoettler, *The Baltimore Sun*, August 19, 1995. Also, see David Firestone, "For Former Radical, Old Battleground Became a Refuge," *The New York Times*, March 22, 2000, p. A21. Joshua B. Good and Richard Whitt, "Eye on Al-Amin: FBI, Police Tracked Militant, Inner Circle in '90s Homicides," *The Atlanta Journal-Constitution*, April 1, 2000. From http://www.accessatlanta.com/partners/ajc/newsatlanta/alamin/0402.htm. *The Revolutionary Worker*, April 9, 2000, p.7. Associated Press, "Former Black Panther May have Fled Georgia," *The New York Times*, March 20, 2000, A10. Peter Slevin, "Police Seek Ex-Militant in Slaying," *The Washington Post*, March 18, 2000, A1. Jack Warner, "Note Had Warning on Al-Amin," *The Atlanta Journal-Constitution*, 4/1/2000. David Firestone, "For Former Radical, Old Battleground Became Refuge," *The New York Times*, March 22, 2000, p.A21. Kevin Sack, "A Legacy of Achievement and Also of Investigation," *New York Times*, January, 15, 2001, p.A10. Personal interview, Watani Tyehimba, 10/15/02. Ernie Suggs, "Trial of Al-Amin May Test Community," *The Atlanta Journal-Constitution*, September 9, 2001. http://lw3.hotmail.msn.com/cgi-

bin/getmsg?curmbox=F000000001&a=a65da032e64'. Alvin Benn, "Former Black Panther Arraigned," *Montgomery Advertiser*, October 2, 2002. http://lw3fd.hotmail.msn.com/cgi-b... SG1034043255.239&start=1554351&len=9272.

361 "Jamil... a cop." Honorary officer, see *The Revolutionary Worker*, April 9, 2000, p.7. Theft and impersonation charge, Associated Press, "Former Black Panther May have Fled Georgia," *The New York Times*, March 20, 2000, A10.

362 "Police then said... officer." Peter Slevin, "Police Seek Ex-Militant in Slaying," *The Washington Post*, March 18, 2000, A1. Jack Warner, "Note Had Warning on Al-Amin," *The Atlanta Journal-Constitution*, 4/1/2000.

363 "But much... appeals." David Firestone, "For Former Radical, Old Battleground Became Refuge," *The New York Times*, March 22, 2000, p.A21. Also, Personal interview with Watani Tyehimba, 11/2/02.

364 "For example... King, Jr." Kevin Sack, "A Legacy of Achievement and Also of Investigation," *New York Times*, January, 15, 2001, p.A10

365 James Dao, "With Heady Days in the Past, Ex-Atlanta Mayor Faces Trial," *New York Times*, 1/23/06.

366 Brenda Goodman, "Ex-Atlanta Mayor Given 30-Month Term and Financial Penalty in Tax Case, " *The New York Times*, 6/14/06, p.A16.

367 "Also, at least one racist... group." Robert Keating, "Atlanta, Who Murdered Your Children," *SPIN*, 1986. Robert Keating and Barry Michael Cooper, "A Question of Justice," *SPIN*, 1986.

368 The FBI and Atlanta... Williams." Chet Dellinger wrote a book called *The List*, which detailed the continuation of murders of Atlanta's black children, even while local black deejay Wayne Williams was incarcerated and on trial for killing several black adults. Williams was only implicated with specious evidence for killing children, but never tried for it. An FBI agent said that the evidence on Williams killing the adults was also actually falsified. Furthermore, two other Atlanta child murder investigators, Dekalb County Sheriff Sidney Dorsey and Fulton County Police Chief Louis Graham, both Atlanta homicide investigators at the time of the murders, said on "Dateline NBC" June 2, 1998, that they believe Wayne Williams is innocent. On the GBI and KKK drug dealing and arms dealing collaboration for which no arrests were ever made, as well as the other information, see Robert Keating, "Atlanta, Who Murdered Your Children," *SPIN*, 1986. Robert Keating and Barry Michael Cooper, "A Question of Justice," *SPIN*, 1986. Bob Guiccione, Jr. "Atlanta: Still A Question of Justice," *SPIN*, p.20, 1986. Alicia Banks, "Atlanta Child Killings Revisited," News Service, pp.1, 3. http://www/mumia.org/wwwboard/messages/914.html.

369 "Cold-case Squad to Probe Decades-ld Atlanta Murders: Police chief still things Wayne Williams is innocent," CNN.com, 5/7/05. www.cnn.com/2005/LAW/05/07/wayne.williams . On Graham being part of original police task force, Ernie Suggs and Mae Gentry, "Some Cases form Atlanta Child Murders" to be Reopned," *San Diego Union-Tribune*, 5/12/05.

370 Recorded by Prison Radio (www.prisonradio.org); Noelle Hanrahan, 1995.

371 "Regarding... shooting." Personal interview, Chokwe Lumumba, 5/10/00.

372 Ex-CIA agent John Stockwell, in Lee Lew Lee's *All Power to the People* documentary film, 1996. Lee previously worked as the cinematographer for the Academy Award winning documentary *The Panama Deception*.

373 "One strong... apartment." *Oakland Tribune*, 2/22/73, p.1.FBI occupancy seen in memorandum from J.G. Deegan to W. R. Wannall, 8/26/74, saying "there has been no indication that the BPP was aware of our occupancy of the apartment next door to Newton's." Stinette reportedly fired two shots through door after police knocked but didn't hit cops before rifle jammed, according to FBI memorandum from Special Agent Wilbert J. Weiskrich to SAC San Francisco, 2/28/73. In Huey Newton, *War Against the Panthers* (New York: Harlem River Press/Writers and Readers, 1991) pp.64, 98n. Also see, Interview of attorney Charles Garry reviewing FBI file made available in Delligner v. Mitchell, Civ. Action No.1768-69, Fed. Dist. Ct. (D,C.1969). *Oakland Tribune*, 2/22/73, p.1.

[374] "Evidence also…The Move." Mumia Abu-Jamal's journalism accomplishments included becoming chairman of the Pensylvania Black Journalists Association and published articles in prestigious journals such as the *Yale Law Review*. On FBI labeling him a top threat in 1973 and Rizzo threat, see C. Clark Kissinger, "Why Mumia Abu-Jamal Deserves a New Trial" a compilation of articles that originally appeared as a series in the *Revolutionary Worker*, January-April, 2000. On FBI picture with dead written on back, personal interview with Mumia's European spokesperson, Michael Warren (Tupac's lawyer), 2/5/96.
[375] "Virtually everyone…Faulkner." For some examples, see Jill Smolowe "Mumia on Their Mind," *Time*, 8/7/95, p.33. Peter Noel and Danielle Douglas, "The Fleeing Man," *The Village Voice*, 11/30/99, Vol.44, #47, pp.61-65. Don Terry, "Key Witness Alters her Testimony in Death Row Case," *New York Times*, 10/2/96.
[376] "Mumia Abu-Jamal's trial…chambers." On Judge Sabo barring Mumia's self-representation and removal from court, see "Executive Summary," of the trial by C. Clark Kissinger, Septermber, 2001. On $800 provided to public defender for Mumia defense and Judge Sabo giving most death sentences in nation, Jill Smolowe "Mumia on Their Mind," *Time*, August 7, 1995, p. 33.
[377] Affidavit of Terri Maurer-Carter, August 21, 2001, Philadelphia, PA. This and the other affidavits quoted can be found at www.refuseandresist.org/mumia/idx.php
[378] "After years…expert." On Mumia's hand not tested for nitrate from fired gun, see Texas Criminalist and Crime Laboratory Director, Ronald Singer, —"Affidavit of Ronald Singer," U.S. District Coutt. Murmia Abut-Jamal, Case No.99 Civ 5089 (Yohn), Petitioner vs. Martin Horn, Commissioner of the Pennsylvania Dept. of Corrections. On not testing Mumia's gun, see "Executive Summary," C. Clark Kissinger, April 1999, revised Sept. 2001.
[379] On Mumia's .38 caliber gun and a .44 fatal bullet, see Jill Smolowe "Mumia on Their Mind," *Time*, August 7, 1995, p. 33. On not testing Mumia's gun or hiding the results, see "Petition for Post-Conviction Relief" Court of Common Peas of Philadephia v. Mumia Anu-Jamal. Criminal Devision Nos 1357-1358 (january Sessions, 1982), pts 37-9.
[380] "Executive Summary," C. Clark Kissinger, 9/01.
[381] Helen Halyard, "*Live from Death Row*: Political prisoner Mumia Abu-Jamal speaks from prison," 4/21/99 World Socialist Website. Mumia's lawyers obtained his 800 page FBI file through a FOIA request. www.wsws.org/articles/1999/apr1999/mumi-a21.shtml
[382] "In the following…pressure." Ibid, Common Pleas court Petition, Pennsylvania v. Mumia Abu-Jamal, Petition for Post Conviction Relief. Also see longtime legal writer and investigator Michael "Affidavit of George Michael Newman," Court of Common Pleas, Commonwealth, Case No. 8201-1357-59 vs. Mumia Abu-Jamal. Newman conducted a telephone interview of key prosecution witness, cabdriver Robert Chobert, who recanted his testimony of seeing Mumia shoot Faulkner. Newman said he was prepared to testify on this reanting but Attorney Weinglass, to fellow attorney Rachel Wokenstein's dismay, didn't call Newman to testify. Mumia subsequently fired Weinglass for this and other reasons. Newman said Weinglass had said he'd been threatened by Ken Freeman's relatives and wasn't willing to take more of a risk in pursuing Freeman as the murderer.
[383] "Another…cases." Noel and Douglas, *The Village Voice*, 11/30/99, pp.61-65. Police had pressured prostitutes to falsely testify against both Newton and Mumia at trials and appeared to use psychological profiling to lure them both into gunfire. On Newton see M.Newton (no relation), *Bitter Grain*, pp.213-14, and Huey Newton, *War Against the Panthers* (New York: Harlem River Press/Writers and Readers, 1991. On Mumia, see Don Terry, "Key Witness Alters her Testimony in Death Row Case," *New York Times*, October 2, 1996.
[384] "Also, regarding police…confession." Ibid, Common Pleas court Petition, *Pennsylvania v. Mumia Abu-Jamal*, Petition for Post Conviction Relief. The doctors who testified to no statement made by the barely conscious Mumia were Dregina Cudemo MD and Anthony Colletta MD. Also see, Appeals hearing transcript from August 1, 1995, p.38, cited in Mumia trial "Executive Summary," C. Clark Kissinger, 9/01. On Bell and

Durham alleging to hear Mumia confess, see "Why Mumia Abu-Jamal Deserves a New Trial: An Analysis of Jamal's Petition for a Federal Writ of Habeus Corpus" *Revolutionary Worker*, January-April, 2000, reprint at p.9. C Clark Kissinger was a former National Secretary of the largest student anti-war organization in the country, the Students for a Democratic Society (SDS).

[385] "A startling... getaway." Affidavit by Arnold R. Beverly on the Events of December 9, 1981. U.S. District Court, Eastern District of Pennsylvania, *Mumia Abu-Jamal, Case N. 99 Civ 5089 (Yohn) vs. Marin Horn, Commissioner, Pennsylvania Department of Corrections*, 6/8/99.

[386] Personal Interview, Pam Africa, 1/4/08.

[387] "An affidavit of Mumia's brother... army." Billy Cook in "Affidavit by William Cook on the Events of December 9, 1981." U.S. District Court, Eastern District of Pennsylvania, *Mumia Abu-Jamal, Case No. 99 Civ 5089 (YOHN) Petitioner, vs. Martin Horn, Commissioner, Pennsylvania Department of Corrections, and Connor Blaine, Superintendent of the State Correctional Institution at Greene, Defendants* (hereafter, "U.S, District Court, Abu-Jamal vs. Horn & Blaine").

[388] "In his own affidavit, Mumia... knees." , "Affidavit by Mumia Abu-Jamal on the Events of December 9, 1981," *Mumia Abu Jamal vs. Martin Horn, Comissioner, Pennsylvania Dept. of Correstions,* U.S. District Court, Eastern District of Pennsylvania. Posted, 5/5/01.

[389] "Billy Cook said that... army." Billy Cook in "Affidavit by William Cook on the Events of December 9, 1981." U.S. District Court, Eastern District of Pennsylvania, *Mumia Abu-Jamal, Case No. 99 Civ 5089 (YOHN) Petitioner, vs. Martin Horn, Commissioner, Pennsylvania Department of Corrections, and Connor Blaine, Superintendent of the State Correctional Institution at Greene, Defendants* (hereafter, "U.S, District Court, Abu-Jamal vs. Horn & Blaine").

[390] "Other witnesses and... Freeman." Peter Noel and Danielle Douglas, "The Fleeing Man," *The Village Voice*, 11/30/99, Vol.44, #47, pp.61-65.

[391] "Further cover-up... jailed." See "Technology Transfer From Defense: Concealed Weapons Detection," *National Institute of Justice Journal*, Issue #229, Aug. 1995, pp.42-43. Frank Donner, *Protectors of Privilege: Red Squads and Police Repression in Urban America* (Berkeley, California: University of California Press, 1990), pp.242-43. "25 Years on the Move," published by MOVE, P.O. Box 19709, Philadelphia, PA 19143, p.49. Richard Poe, "Preemptive Strike: A New Kind of Policing, " *East Village Eye*, June 1986, p.12.

[392] "Further... circumstances.'" Peter Noel and Danielle Douglas, "The Fleeing Man," *The Village Voice*, 11/30/99, Vol.44, #47, pp.61-65.

[393] "Witnesses added... scene." C. Clark Kissinger, "Why Mumia Abu-Jamal Deserves a New Trial: An Analysis of Jamal's Petition for a Federal Writ of Haeas Corpus," *Revolutionary Worker*, January-April, 2000. Kissinger cited testimony from prosecution witnesses Mark Scanlon about the beating and the police officers who said Cook had fresh blood running down his face. Also see Mumia attorney Leonard Weinglass make this same report in excerpts of his book *Live From Death Row. People* magazine called this beating only a "scuffle" between Faulkner and Cook. Marjorie Rosen and Anne Longley, "Fight to the Finish," *People*, 8/14/95, pp.49-50.

[394] "Credible witness William... scene." Noel and Douglas, *The Village Voice*, 11/30/99, pp.61-65.

[395] Some of these people and groups calling for justice for Mumia include: the African National Congress, Amnesty International, the European Parliament, the International Parliament of Writers, the National Lawyers Guild, the National Black Police Association, U.S. Congressional Representatives John Conyers, Charles Rangel, Ron Dellums and Ckaka Fatah. Writers Maya Angelou, Barbara Kingsolver, E.L. Doctorow, Alice Walker, Elie Wiesel, Howard Zinn and Salman Rushdie, along with actors and activists.

[396] "By the end... 70s." See, for example, "Affidavit by Mumia Abu-Jamal on the Events of December 9, 1981," *Mumia Abu Jamal vs. Martin Horn, Comissioner, Pennsylvania*

Dept. of Correstions, U.S. District Court, Eastern District of Pennsylvania. Posted, 5/5/01. Mumia's new legal team obtained many of the above affidavits from the confessed shooter, Arnold Beverly, as well as Mumia's brother, Billy Cook, and Mike Newman. Newman said that Mumia's lead lawyer, Leonard Weinglass, lied to him about getting retracted testimony from a key witness and that Weinglass told him he wouldn't pursue Ken Freeman's role in the murder of Officer Faulkner because of threats by Freeman's relatives. Affidavit of George Michael Newman, 10/16/01, in the Court of Common Pleas for the Commonwealth of Pennsylvania first Judicial District. Billy Cook said that another Mumia lawyer, Rachel Wolkenstein, tried to have Cook testify but Weinglass didn't allow it. Affidavit by William Cook on the Events of December 9, 1981. 4/29/01 in Philadelphia.

[397] "Two weeks…hotel." See Ayanna Jackson in New York v. Charles Fuller and Tupac Shakur, Indictment No. 11578-93. Also Det. Slimak, People's Witness, p.352. New York v. Tupac Shakur, Notice of Motion Pursuant to CPL 530.45 Ind. No. 11578/93 by Michael Warren, p.8, cites trial testimony at 33-38, 40, Jackson's confirming consensual oral and vaginal sex at hotel room. On Jackson's date at club, see New York vs. Tupac Shakur, Sentencing hearing, p.36.

[398] "In the several…arrest." Ayanna Jackson in New York v. Charles Fuller and Tupac Shakur, Indictment No. 11578-93. See Jackson's admission in Fuller's defense attorney cross examination of Jackson at p.232. Also Det. Slimak, People's Witness, p.352. New York v. Tupac Shakur, Notice of Motion Pursuant to CPL 530.45 Ind. No. 11578/93 by Michael Warren, p.8, cites trial testimony at 33-38, 40, Jackson's confirming consensual oral and vaginal sex at hotel room and then leaving telephone message "I like the way you fuck."

[399] Dr. M. Diana of St. Lukes Roosevelt Hospital, cited as testifying in *New York v. Tupac Shakur*, Notice of Motion., p.9.

[400] "Tupac had become…Guilty.'" Tupac Shakur "Changes," *MTV*, video, 1999.

[401] Barbara Handschu et al, plaintiffs, Rev. Calvin Butts, Sonny Carson, C. Vernon Mason, Michael Warren, Intervenors v. Special Services Division a/k/a Bureau of Special Services et al, Memorandum Opinion and Order, Kudge Charles Haight, U.S. District Court, Southern District of New York. 71 Civ.2203-CSH, p.34.

[402] Karen Freifeld, "Judge dumps convictions in New York jogger case," *The Baltimore Sun*, 12/20/02, p.3A.

[403] "Michael Warren…Agnant." Personal interviews, Michael Warren, 12/25/94, 10/15/96, 11/8/98.

[404] Connie Bruck, "The Takedown of Tupac," *The New Yorker*, 7/7/97, p.55.

[405] Personal interviews, Michael Warren, 12/25/94, 10/15/96, 11/8/98.

[406] As noted above, one intelligence document a Senate committee found included strategies for use against political musicians such as "Intelligence Activities and Rights of Americans," Book II, April 26, 1976, *Senate Committee with Respect to Intelligence Report.* Excerpted in Alex Constantine, *The Covert War Against Rock* (Los Angeles: Feral House, 2001), p.9. U.S. Senate Select Committee to Study Government Operations, *The FBI's Covert Program to Destroy the Black Panther Party*, U.S. Government Printing Office, Washington. D.C. 1976.

[407] "Another sign…semen." Jackson Trial Testimony p. 239, Detective Slimak's Cross-examination by M. Warren , p.344, *New York vs. Tupac Shakur*, Indictment No. 11578-93, p.10.

[408] Al Guart, "Tupac-tape Tamper Alleged," *New York Post*, November 24, 1993. Salvatore Arena, "Sex Tapes Erased, Says Shakur Lawyer," *Daily News*, November 24, 1993. Cross-examination of Ayanna Jackson, by Ken Ellis, Esq. *New York vs. Charles Fuller and Tupac Shakur*, Indictment no. 11578-93, Nov. 14, 1994, p.232.

[409] Rob Speyer, "Rapper, Minor Had Sex in Video: Cops," *Daily News*, November 26, 1993. Al Guart, "Shakur's Lawyer Raps Cops," *New York Post*, November 30, 1993, p. 15.

[410] Al Guart, "Tupac Terrorist Twist," *New York Post*, December 17, 1993, p.3.

[411] "Among many... destroyed." Judge J. Dunn's disenting remarks, *In Re: Pratt, 112 Cal. Ap.3d. 795;--Cal. Rptr.—(Crim. Np. 37534. Second Dist., Div. One. 3 December 1980).* In Ward Churchill and Jim Vander Wall, *Agents of Repression* (Boston: South End Press, 1989), p. 90.
[412] "At Tupac's trial... in." See *New York v. Tupac Shakur and Charles Fuller*, Cross examination of Det. Cragi McKernan, p.23-5. On Det. Slimak, see Cross-ezamination (Warren), p.331-2, 345 and Redirect/Recross, p.356.
[413] But the state's... sperm." See for example, Jackson contradicting many former statements regarding time of arrival and gold jewelry left at the scene and who called her to come there, despite many pretrial meetings with ADA Mourges where details are usually reviewed. New York vs. Tupac Shakur and Charles Fuller, Cross-examination of Jackson by Robert Ellis , pp.215, 230, 240-41, 254 compared to Recross of Det. Slimak by Micheal Warren at p. 359.. On evidence examined for semen and found negative, despite Jackson's claim of spitting semen on it, see Cross-examination of Jackson/Ellis, p.239, and Warren's Cross-eamination of Det. Slimak pp.342-6, and (Trial Testimony at 239) cited in New York vs. Tupac Shakur Moton of Motion Pursuant to CPL 530.45 for Bail Pending Sentence, p.10, pt.26. On Mourges saying different underwear checked, see same—p.10, pt.26. On guns, see same at p.8, pt.22 (citing Affidavit Testimony p.14 at lines 18-23 and Trial Testimony at p.226).
[414] "ADA... claim." On Mourges saying different underwear checked, see *New York vs. Tupac Shakur* Moton of Motion Pursuant to CPL 530.45 for Bail Pending Sentence, p.10, pt.26. Stockings, p.23 pt.50 A iv. On judicial bias, see same, p.21 , pt.50 A I (Trial Testimony 60-8 and indictment counts Exhibit C).
[415] "While the jury... suit." Richard Perez-Pena, "Wounded Rapper Gets Mixed Verdict In Sex-Abuse Case," *New York Times*, 12/2/94, pp. A1, B4. Also, Personal interview, Michael Warren,4/7/99.
[416] "The jury found... will." *New York v. Tupac Shakur, Ricardo Brown (a.k.a. Jacques Agnant) & Charles Fuller*, Exhibit A. 2. PL 130.65 Sexual Abuse 1st Degree "forcing contact between the... buttocks of informant and the hands of defendant Shakur, Brown." Also, Richard Perez-Pena, "Wounded Rapper Gets Mixed Verdict in Sex Abuse Case," *New York Times*, 12/2/94, p.B4.
[417] "Michael Warren... time." On District Attorney's large, successful effort to keep Tupac from gaining bail, see Letter to Judge Ernst Rosenberger, from ADA Francine James, 2/3/95. And, for example, Robert Morgenthau, District Attorney, Petitioner, for a Judgement of Prohibition Pursuant to Article 78 of the Civil Practice Law and Rules, against Honorable Ernst Rosenberger, Justice of Supreme Court, Appellate Division, First Department, and Tupac Shakur, Respondents, New York, 5/9/95. On judicial bias, see New York vs. Tupac Shakur Moton of Motion Pursuant to CPL 530.45 for Bail Pending Sentence, same, p.21 , pt.50 A I (Trial Testimony 60-8 and indictment counts Exhibit C).
[418] "First, Warren... easy." On everything regarding ADA Mourges, see Connie Bruck, "The Takedown of Tupac," *The New Yorker*, 7/7/97, p.54-5. On Warren's comment, personal interview, 11/8/98.
[419] See, for example, one study found that "Nearly one-fifth of women (18 percent) reported experiencing a completed or attempted rape at some time in their lives." National Institute of Justice and Centers for Disease Control and Prevention, *Prevalence, Incidence, and Consequences of Violence Against Women: Findings from the National Violence Against Women Survey*, November 1998. Another study found that 48% of those 12 and over experiencing rape or sexual assault reported it to the police. While that study said assaults by strangers are reported 18% more than adults by intimates or relatives, this doesn't account for the high percentage of these case that may be children. Bureau of Justice Statistics Speacial Report, Reporting Crime to the Police, 1992-2000, March 2003. All found at http://endabuse.org/programs .
[420] "First, by her own admission... will." On not leaving scene when could, see *New York vs. Tupac Shakur*, Notice of Motion Pursuant to CPL 530.45 for Bail Pending Sentence #27 p.11. On high profile lawyer speaking for her immediately, Tom Raftery, Sal Arena

and Miguel Garcilazo, "Rapper Nabbed in Sexual Assault," *Daily News*, November 20, 1993. This backs Warren's closing statement citing Jackson's testimony in New York vs. Tupac Shakur Ind. No. 11578/93, p.44. On Jackson seeing Tupac's movie later see, New York V. Tupac Shakur and Charles Fuller, Cross examination of Ayanna Jackson by Attorney Ken Ellis, pp.222-3.
[421] Also... wealth." On only filing a civil suit against Tupac, Bruck, *New Yorker*, p.55. "Free sex to entrap," in "Intelligence Activities and Rights of Americans," Book II, April 26, 1976, *Senate Committee with Respect to Intelligence Report*. Excerpted in Alex Constantine, *The Covert War Against Rock*, p.9. U.S. Senate Select Committee to Study Government Operations, *The FBI's Covert Program to Destroy the Black Panther Party*, U.S. Government Printing Office, Washington. D.C. 1976.
[422] "Then, in 1995... sodomy." Vibe ed.s *Tupac Shakur*, p.54. A further interesting note about Jackson was her employment at the Brooklyn Naval Yard. While the Navy Yard was sold to New York state by the federal government by 1970, it would seem that similar functions would be maintained. Trial Testimony 24-33, cited in *New York v. Tupac Shakur, Notice of Motion Pursuant to CPL 530.45 for Bail Pending Sentence, Indictment No. 11578/93*, p.7. Jackson said she had sex with Tupac until 5 a.m. before going back to Brooklyn because she had to work at 9 a.m. at the Brooklyn Naval Yard that day. Naval Intelligence collaboration with FBI efforts is well documented against Malcolm X and MLK. And, Panther leader Lumumba Shakur had said that when he was a gang leader, the Brooklyn Naval Yard appeared to purposely let gangs pilfer all the guns they wanted for years, with which to kill each otherKempton, *The Briar Patch*, p. 72.
[423] Tupac's biological cousin, Billy Lesane, said that his sister told him she saw Agnant following her and Tupac after Tupac stopped hanging with Agnant, just before the Times Square shooting. Personal interview, Billy Lesane, 4/10/99
[424] "Several... rapper." Tupac interview with Kevin Powell in Vibe eds. *Tupac Shakur*, p.46.
[425] "Upon... floor." On bullets through head while on ground, see Deposition of Barbara Justice, MD, New York v. Tupac Shakur, December 21, 1994. On military execution, see Stephen Kinzer, "Commandos Left a Calling Card: Their Absence," *New York Times*, 9/26/01, p. B6.
[426] "Many... lobby." On, police statement, Gladwell, *The Washington Post*, 12/2/94, p. F2. On Quad's hit records, Cathy Scott, *The Murder of Biggie Smalls* (New York: St. Martin's Press, 2000), p.65.
[427] On, police statement, Gladwell, *The Washington Post*, 12/2/94, p. F2.
[428] "These... them." On police outside lobby doors Warren said cops present when they looked out glass doors, personal interview, Michael Warren, 12/25/94. Also in *Vibe*, eyewitness Randy "Stretch" Walker said cops were slowly rolling up just after gunmen fled, Vibe editors, *Tupac Shakur* (New York: Crown,1996), p.61. Police presence is backed by news accounts of police having Tupac under surveillance at that time. In, "Thoughts and Notes on Tupac," *Amsterdam News*, 12/17/94, p. 24. On Rolex watch left, see Vibe eds. *Tupac Shakur*, p.41
[429] Malcolm Gladwell, "Shakur Guilty of Sex Abuse," *The Washington Post*, 12/2/94, p. F1, F2.
[430] Officer Heinz, Midtown North precinct, personal interview, May 4, 1999. This writer told Officer Heinz he was writing a piece on an incident where the Street Crime Unit wasn't involved in a violent offense and so he'd like to talk to Officer Joseph Kelly about such an incident he was involved, in December of '94. She said, "Let me get this straight. You want to talk to a member of the Street Crime Unit about an incident where they *didn't* end up involved in any violence?" "Yes." "Well, Joe Kelly works until midnight tonight so you can try calling back at 11pm." Several writers have stated the belief that Street Crime Unit took over for the NYPD's Cointelpro BOSS unit in starting the year Cointelpro and BOSS 'officially' end. For one, see Frank Morales, "The Militarization of the Police," *CovertAction Quarterly*, no. 67, Spring/Summer, 1999,p. 48.
[431] Cathy Scott, *The Murder of Biggie Smalls* (New York: St. Martin's Press, 2000), p.65.

[432] Charisse Jones, "For a Rapper, Life and Art Converge in Violence," *New York Times*, 12/1/94, pp. A1, B3. Personal interview, Michael Warren, 12/20/01.
[433] "They moved... survived." See Deposition of Barbara Justice, MD, New York v. Tupac Shakur, December 21, 1994, Vibe ed.s *Tupac Shakur*, p.48, and Scott, *The Murder of Biggie Smalls*, p.66.
[434] "Tupac first... up."" Tupac first rejecting the notion, personal interview with Michael Warren, 2/4/00. Song quote from "Against All Odds" on Tupac Shakur (a.k.a. Ma.k.a.velli), *Don Killuminati: The Seven Day Theory*, 1996.
[435] "Intelligence Activities and Rights of Americans," Book II, April 26, 1976, *Senate Committee with Respect to Intelligence Report.* Excerpted in Alex Constantine, *The Covert War Against Rock* (Los Angeles: Feral House, 2001), p.9.
[436] "For example... assailants." On New Afrikan Panthers, Armond White mentioned it but either he, or an editor, failed to explain that its significance as the young adult section of the New Afrikan People's Organization, Armond White, *Rebel For the Hell of It* (New York: Thunders Mouth Press), p.38. A *Vibe* magazine article after Tupac's death mentioned it as a kids' art organization. On lobby's security videotape, Cathy Scott, *The Murder of Biggie Smalls* (New York: St. Martin's Press, 2000), p.65.
[437] "Michael Warren... incident."" On Warren's claim, personal interview, Michael Warren, 12/15/94. On Toure' quote, Toure, "The Professional: Tupac Shakur gives the performance of his life," *The Village Voice*, 12/13/94,pp75,85.
[438] In a personal interview with Toure, 12/27/94, several weeks after Tupac's shooting, Toure said he wasn't covering Tupac's shooting so he didn't know many details of it. Five-to-ten minutes later he said that if the gunmen were trying to kill Tupac, they would have used higher caliber bullets, a detail unfound in the press for several more weeks.
[439] Kevin Powell interview, reprinted in Vibe editors, *Tupac Shakur*, p.46. Also, personal interview with Warren, 11/2/98.
[440] Personal interview with Michael Warren, 4/4/2000.
[441] "While some information... conservatives." Daniel Akst, "No Alternative," *Wall Street Journal*, 1/10/03. For example, the *Village Voice* is owned by one of two major chains which is partly owned by Goldman Sachs, one of the largest Wall Street Investment firms. Another key owner is the anti-abortion rights multi-millionaire owner of Hartz pet supplies. On Voice editors replaced, see Kate Brlingham and Maura Keanny, "Muffled Voice: Village Voice Cashes in on Hip," *Modern Times* 10/5/95, p.1.
[442] Ben Bagdikian, *The Media Monopoly*, 4th Ed. (Boston: Beacon Press, 1992), p.25. Bagdikian won a Pulitzer Prize and was dean of the University of California-Berkeley School of Journalism.
[443] "Investigative... it." Personal interview, Michael Warren, 1/4/95.
[444] "The history... 2000)." Victor Marchetti and John D. Marks, *The CIA and the Cult of Intelligence* (New York: Dell, 1974), p.96. On changes after 2000, see Michael Ruppert, *Crossing the Rubicon: The Decline of the American Empire at the End of the Age of Oil* (Gabriola Island, BC Canada: New Society Publishers, 2004), pp.427-36.
[445] "The highest ranking... claim." Victor Marchetti and John D. Marks, *The CIA and the Cult of Intelligence*, pp.44-46, 266-9. And, British magazne editor Frances Saunders, also backs this claim. Frances Stonor Saunders, *The Cultural Cold War: The CIA and the World of Arts and Letters* (New York: The New Press, 2000), p.34-6.
[446] "The CIA was... agents" Book *U.S. Intelligence and the Nazis*, written on by, Thom J. Rose, "Files Show Nazi Criminals' U.S. Intel Role," *United Press International*, 5/13/04. Tim Reid, "Files Show CIA Gave Jos to Nazi Criminals," *The Times* (London), 5/14/04, Overseas News p.20. Elizabeth Olson, "Documents Show U.S. Relationship with Nazis During Cold War," *The New York Times*, 5/13/04, p.5. Sarah Helm, "MI6 Protected Nazi Who Killed 100 British Agents," *The Times* (London) 5/14/05, www.timesonline.co.uk
[447] "Researchers had... genocide." Christopher Simpson, *Blowback:The First Full Account of America's Recruitment of Nazis, and Its Disastrous Effect on Our Domestic and Foreign Policy* (New York: Weidenfeld and Nicolson,1988). Simpson was also a visiting scholar at the Institute for Policy Studies and research director for famed French film director Marcel Ophuls' film on Nazi Klaus Barbie. On Paperclip and similar coded

operations, see pp.35,36, 38-9, 73. On prologue summary, p.xv. On Lovett and Dulles, pp.4, 8, 92-3, 100, 104. On U.S., Europe, Latin American and Middle East, see, for example, Italy in pp.88-94; Egypt/Middle East, 244, 248, 260; Latin America, 179-80, 186, 189, 194. On Brunner, also see as an example of Simpson's vast research and careful endnotes, pp.248-9, endnote 7. Citations in that endnote include "Eichmann quote, see Simon Wiesenthal Center, Membership Report, Summer 1985. On Brunner's wartime career, see Berlin Document Center dossier on Alois Brunner, NSDAP no. 510,064; SS no. 342 767. See also Alois Brunner, U.S. Army INSCOM dossier no. XE064584 17B025." On Lovett and Dulles as lawyers for several Bush, Harriman and Rockefeller family concerns, see Webster G. Tarpley and Anton Chaitkin, *George Bush: The Unauthorized Biography* (Washington, D.C.: The Executive Intelligence Review, 1992), pp.31,55, 66-8.

[448] Shaila Dewan, "Widow Recalls Ghosts of '64 At Rights Trial," *The New York Times*, 6/17/05, p.A1.

[449] "*The Baltimore Sun*... crimes." Michael Ollove, "The FBI's Mole in Klan was Horrifyingly Brutal as the Rest," *The Baltimore Sun*, 6/5/05.

[450] "Truman started... annually." Frances Stonor Saunders, *The Cultural Cold War: The CIA and the World of Arts and Letters* (New York: The New Press, 2000), p.40-1, 129. Also see Marchetti, *The CIA and the Cult of Intelligence*, pp.45-6.

[451] "In *The New York*... media." Joseph Crewden, "Worldwide Propaganda Network Built by the CIA," *New York Times*, 12/26/77, p.1, cited in Pease, *Assassinations*, p.300.

[452] See Dennis Mazzocco, *Networks of Power* (Boston: South End Press, 1994).

[453] National Security Council Directive, 10 July 1950, quoted in *Final Report of the Select Committee to Study Governmental Operations with Respect to Intelligence Activities* (Washington: United States Government Printing Office, 1976). Cited in Stonor Saunders, *The Cultural Cold War*, p.4 notes 5,6.

[454] "The CIA, OPC... CIA." Stonor Saunders, *The Cultural Cold War*, pp.34-36, 371, 427. Saunders is a documentary film producer and arts editor for *The New Statesman* in London. For other sources on its continuation, see Noam Chomsky and Edward Herman, *Manufacturing Consent: The Political Economy of the Mass Media* (New York: Pantheon, 1988), p.20, for example.

[455] Saunders, *The Cultural Cold War*, p.241.

[456] "The MCEA... students." On personal interview with Toure, see endnote 162 above. On recruitment and co-optation of minority youth, see Miles Seligman and Cymbre Simpson, "Behind Right-Wing Campus Newspapers," *EXTRA!*, September/October, 1991, p.9. This EXTRA! Article noted that by 1991, corporate funders such as Mobil Oil, Dow Chemical and Chase Manhattan Bank. Conservative foundation support comes from Olin, Scaife, Coors, and Smith Richardsonmaintained MCEA's huge treasure chest. Also see, Carol Innerst, "Collegiate Network of Campus Newspapers Gets New Home," *The Washington Times*, 12/3/95, pA6. Ron Chepesiuk, "Alternative Voices: Liberal and conservative newspapers are emerging anew on college campuses; includes excerpts from commentaries on multiculuralism; Special report Campus Redux," *The Quill*, Vol. 80, No. 3, April 1992. Thanks to Steve Rendall of FAIR (Fairness and Accuracy In Reporting, which publishes *Extra!*) for providing these articles.

[457] On 5% journalists of color, Kevin Kelley, "In Black and White—But Mostly White," *Guardian*, December 12, 1984. Referenced in Alex Parenti, *Inventing Reality* (St. Martin's Press, 1986), p.11. On MCEA's Student Forum, Seligman and Simpson, *Extra!*, p.9.

[458] Carol Innerset, "Collegiate Network of Campus Newspapers Gets New Home," *The Washington Times*, December 3, 1995, p.A6.

[459] "In a... sake." Personal interview with Toure, 12/27/94. Toure, "The Professional: Tupac Shakur gives the performance of his life," *The Village Voice*, 12/13/94, pp75,85.

[460] On CIA spy work on Americans locally, see Seymour Hersh, "Huge C.I.A. Operation Reported in U.S. Against Antiwar Forces, Other Dissidents in Nixon Years," *New York Times*, 12/22/74, p.A1. On blacks, Seymour Hersh, "CIA Reportedly Recruited Blacks for Surveillance of Panther Party," *New York Times*, March 17, 1978, p. A1, A16, quoted

in Huey P. Newton, *War Against the Panthers* (New York: Harlem River Press/Writers and Readers Publishing, 1996), p.90.

[461] "Suspected U.S.... Jackson." Natasha Stovall, "Death Row" *Village Voice*, September 24, 1996, p. 29. On *People*'s statement, Calvin Baker, Karen Brailsford, Tom Cunneff, and Brooke Stachyra, "Living Dangerously," *People*, 9/23/96, p.75. This writer believes Toure influenced Stovall because of this writer's past acquaintances with Stovall, Stovall's past commitment to activist politics, and few other such indiscretions in Stovall's writing. It's also interesting to note the possible use of "astroturf" media work. This term applies to the known use of fake grassroots marketing by corporations. *The Village Voice* and other media used a mural in New York's East Village to back up their claims that the word on the street was that Tupac got himself killed because of his murderous lifestyle. The mural had Tupac and said 'Live by the Gun Die by the Gun." Police spokemen and Newspaper headlines repeated similar such phrased regarding Tupac. On Astroturf marketing, see John Stauber and Sheldon Rampton, *Toxic Sludge is Good For You! Lies, Damn Lies and the Public Relations Industry* (Monroe, ME: Common Courage Press, 1995), pp. 95,

[462] "It bears... there." *The People of the State of New York vs. Tupac Shakur, Ricardo Brown, Charles Fuller, Defendants*. Robert Morganthau, District Attorney. Exhibit C.

[463] "U.S. Intelligence... news." On Wisner's "Wurlitzer," Joseph Crewden, "Worldwide Propaganda Network Built by the CIA," *New York Times*, 12/26/77, p.1. On McGehee, a former 25 year CIA operative, he obtained documents from 1991 through the Freedom Of Information Act (FOIA) in which the CIA's Public Affairs Office (PAO) said, "PAO now has relationships with reporters from every major wire service, newspaper, news weekly, and television network in the nation. This has helped turn some 'intelligence failure' stories into 'intelligence success' stories... In many instances, we have persuaded reporters to postpone, change, hold, or even scrap stories...." As referenced from Lisa Pease, "The Media and the Assassination," *The Assassinations* (Los Angeles, CA: Feral House, 2003), p.311.

[464] "Also, Watergate... mandate." Carl Bernstein, "The CIA & the Media" *Rolling Stone*, 10/20/77. On more than 400, see p.55; on virtually all leading media companies, p.56; on Senate Intelligence Committee forcing the dislcosure, p.65; on "far" more than 400 see CIA "officials most knowledgable about the subject say that figure of 400 American journalists in on the low side," p.66 On "living double lives," see one-time CIA Deputy Director William Bader and other saying "reporters had been involved in almost every concievable operation," p.66. On reprinting CIA-writen story under their name, see example of Cy Sulzberger, p.59. On some first worked for media, some CIA, p.63. On work as "covert operations" vs. "foreign intelligence," p.66. On CIA spy work on Americans locally, see Seymour Hersh, "Huge C.I.A. Operation Reported in U.S. Against Antiwar Forces, Other Dissidents in Nixon Years," *New York Times*, 12/22/74, p.A1. On blacks, Seymour Hersh, "CIA Reportedly Recruited Blacks for Surveillance of Panther Party," *New York Times*, March 17, 1978, p. A1, A16, quoted in Huey P. Newton, *War Against the Panthers* (New York: Harlem River Press/Writers and Readers Publishing, 1996), p.90.

[465] "Ben Bagdikian... company.'" Ben Bagdikian, *The Media Monopoly* (Boston: Beacon Press, 1992) pp.ix, 24-5. Other researchers have elaborated on how the top corporations control the general political state of the nation, partly through their dominance in the National Association of Manufacturers. For example, see an essay by Alex Carey, "Managing Public Opinion: The Corporate Offensive," (University of New South Wales1986, mimeographed), pp. 1-2. This essay had also been referenced in Noam Chomsky and Edward Herman, *Manufacturing Consent: The Political Economy of the Mass Media* (New York: Pantheon Books, 1988), p.342 n. *The Media Monopoly* cited a 1979 study by Peter Dreier and Steven Weinberg that listed the New York Times interlocked Board of Directors as including Merck, Morgan Guaranty Trust, Bristol Meyers, Charter Oil, Johns Manville, American Express, Bethlehem Steel, IBM, Scott Paper, Sun Oil, and First Boston Corporation. Time, Inc. (before becoming Time Warner) "had so many interlocks it almost represented a Plenary Board of directors of American

business and finance, including Mobil Oil, AT&T, American Express, Firestone Tire and Rubber Company, Mellon National Corporation, Atlantic Richfield, Xerox, General Dynamics, and most of the major international banks.

[466] "Money for war…" from "Keep Ya Head Up," Strictly for My N.I.G.G.A.Z (Interscop, 1993). This CD and his first, 2Pacalypse Now, had lyrics advocating for groups helping the poor and preaching for armed self defense, in his parents' Black Panther vein.

[467] Michael Parenti, *Inventing Reality: The Politics of the Mass Media* (New York: St. Martin's, 1986), p.xi.

[468] Bagdikian, The Media Monopoly, pp.210-11.

[469] Albert Einstein, "Why Socialism," Monthly Review, 1949, www.monthlyreview.org/598einst.htm

[470] "For example…by 1982." "DOD Kills 205 Periodicals; Still Publishes 1,203 Others," *Armed Forces Journal International* (August 1982), p.16. in Noam Chomsky, *Manufacturing Consent: The Political Economy of the Mass Media* (New York: Pantheon, 1988), p.20

[471] "In the mid-70s…*Times*.'" On first Senate intelligence report quote, Michael Parenti, *Inventing Reality: The Politics of the Mass Media*, (New York: St. Martins Press, 1986), p.233. This information is also referenced in Morton Mintz & Jerry Cohen, *Power Inc.* (New York: Bantam Books, 1976), p.364. On *The Times* expose, Joseph Crewden, "Worldwide Propaganda Network Built by the CIA," *The New York Times*, December 25, 26, 27, 1977. On CIA agents in *New York Times* reviewing CIA books, see Senate Select Committee on Intelligence Activities, *Final Report*, April 1976, cited in Mintz and Cohen, *Power, Inc.*, p. 364. Also see *Columbia Journalism Review*, July/August 1976, pp.36-7 and David Wise & Thomas Ross, *The Invisible Government* (New York: Bantam, 1965), pp.134-5, 267, both cited in Parenti, *Inventing Reality*, p.233 note 28.

[472] "Disclosures from…the advertisers." Norman Bauman, "Newspapers: More or Less Put Together by the Advertisers?" unpublished monograph, 1977, p.24. Referenced in Parenti, *Inventing Reality*, p.48.

[473] Interview with CBS veteran, Herman Keld, Todd Gitlin, "When the Right Talks, TV Listens," *Nation*, October 15, 1983, p.335. Referenced in Parenti, *Inventing Reality*, p.49.

[474] A clip of rather saying this was included in the film *Why We Fight* (2005) Sony, dir. Eugene Jarecki. This film won the Grand Jury Prize for documentary at the Sundance Film Festival. Rather's quote was reprinted on www.mediaresearch.org/cyberalerts/2002/cyb20020517_extra.asp

[475] "Various writers…war.'" See, for example, Alex Constantine, *The Covert War Against Rock*, p.12 on U.S. Intelligence focus on music. On rap, see Nick Broomfield stating that a congressional committee convened to discuss rap's subversive element in '93 and how the FBI began spying on rappers at least that early, *Biggie and Tupac* (Documentary, 2002). Constantine also stated that samples of FBI files on Elvis, Jimi Hendrix and Jim Morrison can be found in their reading room. Also see, Fenton Bressler, *Who Killed John Lennon* (New York: St. Marks, 1989), p.9. Quote by Reed in James Ridgeway, "The End of the Road?Convention '96," *The Village Voice*, August 20, 1996, p.25.

[476] "In the early '50s…suit." Frederic Dannen, *Hit Men* (New York: Vintage Books, 1991), pp.42-3, 46. On Freed widely credited with coining the term rock and roll from the black community's slang for sex, see "Allan Freed" at www.history-of-rock.com/freed.htm . It cites The Dominoes "Sixty Minute Man," for the slang. This source also told of small stations imitating Freed, and actually used the words "eventually forcing large stations to follow suit."

[477] On 25,000 people showing up, http://groups.msn.com/Teddyboyrock/biographyofallanfreed.msnw . This source cites a book on Freed by John A. Jackson, *Big Beat Heat: Allan Freed and the Early Years of Rock and Roll.* Jackson has written many books on music and this book was made into an NBC movie.

---

478 "Some researchers... stations." Alex Constantine, *Covert War Against Rock* (Los Angeles, Feral House, 2000) pp.19-22.
479 "Events... history." Constantine, *Covert War Against Rock*, pp.19-22. On Mafia, particularly Genovese, and U.S. Intelligence collaboration in WWII and then drug trafficking, see Alfred McCoy, *The Politics of Heroin: CIA Complicity in the Global Drug Trade* (New York: Lawrence Hill Books, 1991), pp.30, 35-7, 73-4. Also see, Clarence Lusane, *Pipe Dream Blues: Racism and the War on Drugs* (Boston: South End Press, 1991), pp.38-42. McCoy is a professor of Southeast Asian History at University of Wisconsin-Madison and Lusane is a professor at University of the District of Columbia.
480 "Fredric Dannen's... Records)." On Levy and Freed, see, Fredric Dannen, *Hit Men* (New York: Vintage Books, 1991), pp.37-8, 42-6. see, for example, Dannen, pp.164n, 272-99. On charge of Roulette for heroin traficking, p.53. On McCaw, Constantine, *Covert War Against Rock*, pp.19-22.
481 "After Freed... menus." Rick Sklar, *How the All-Hit Radio Stations Took Over* (New York: St. Martin's Press, 1994), pp.11, 17 19.Cited in Constantine, *Covert War Against Rock*, pp.19-22.
482 http://groups.msn.com/Teddyboyrock/biographyofallanfreed.msnw, from John A. Jackson, *Big Beat Heat.*
483 "in 1958... lives)." Jackson, *Big Beat Heat*, cited above.
484 "While charges... day." On Boston inciting riot charge, "Allan Freed" at www.history-of-rock.com/freed.htm , also in http://groups.msn.com/Teddyboyrock/biographyofallanfreed.msnw . John A. Jackson, *Big Beat Heat.* On gunman looking to kill Freed in the music studio, Rick Sklar, *Rocking America: How All Hit Radio Stations Took Over* (New York: St. Martin's, 1984), p.46, cited in *Covert War Against Rock*, pp.19-22. Rick Sklar's wife was at the scene when a gunman came to the station looking for Freed that day. McCaw firing Freed for unknow reasons, Constantine and Dannen, *Hit Men*, p.
485 "Freed... career." Constantine, *Covert War Against Rock*, pp.19-22. Fredric Dannen, *Hit Men*, pp.37-8, 42-6. and on. Payola wasn't illegal at that time, Congress only made it a misdemeanor thereafter, and noone else besides Freed was penalized.
486 "McCaw's... each." Constantine, *The Covert War Against Rock*, pp.22-3, cites *Forbes* magazine regarding the McCaw sons and also cites the McCaw family's billion dollar investment in Nextel Communication and along with the McCaw's merge with AT&T.
487 For example, Miles Copeland was a founding member of the CIA. His son, Miles Jr., organized concerts starting in the 1960s, and started a record label that represented musicians such as Tina Turner and hundreds of others. He also produced dozens of movies. His brother, Ian Copeland, started Frontier Booking International (F.B.I.), representing hundreds of successful bands. Stewart Copeland started the band, The Police, as their drummer and songwriter. He co-founded a film company with his brothers. http://en.wikipedia.org Also see, "New Wave music impressario Ian Copeland dead at 57," 5/24/06, http://news.yahoo.com There are two other aspects of this family which this writer read but can't find the citation on. Most importantly, Fenton Bresler, a British barrister (lawyer) and crime reporter for London's *Daily Mail* published, *Who Killed John Lennon?*—a seven-year investigation of his findings that the CIA orchestrated John Lenneon's murder. Stewart Copeland wrote a newspaper review panning the book. Of minor importance, Police singer Sting reportedly broke the group up due to Copeland wanting to continue as exclusive songwriter.
488 "The Mafia continued... Union." On label ownership and promotion, see Dannen, *Hit Men*, pp.34, 59, 164n, 272-99. On Mafia control of Teamsters, Harry Shapiro and Caesar Glebbeek, *Jimi Hendrix: Electric Gypsy* (New York: St.Martin's Griffin, 1990), p.295.
489 Personal interview with Louis Wolfe, 5/10/04. Wolfe has copublished Covert Action Quarterly for over 20 years. This leftist political magazine was co-founded by Phil Agee, a longtime CIA employee who published a memoir tell-all about the CIA, *Inside the Company: CIA Diary* (New York: Bantam, 1975).
Covert Action has won numerous annual Project Censored awards and published this writer's Tupac article.

[490] Besides music and magazines, Time Warner further had vast holdings in dozens of Cable TV stations, book publishing, video production, Warner Brothers motion pictures, Warner Brothers (WB) Television, and a half dozen book publishers. Time Warner's merge with Turner Broadcasting around this time brought them another half dozen film production companies, a dozen cable networks such as CNN, and many other entertainment holdings. They had the most media holdings of the four companies that dominated what *The Nation* magazine called, "The National Entertainment State." Mark Crispin Miller, pullout "The National Entertainment State," *The Nation.* 1996.
[491] "Bothe Time and Warner... policies." Ben Bagdikian, *The Media Monopoly,* 4th edition, pp.31-33.
[492] "Of the 17... services.'" Carl Bernstein, "The CIA and the Media," *Rolling Stone*, p.63.
[493] "British editor Frances..arts." Frances Stonor Saunders, The Cultural Cold War: The CIA and the World of Arts and Letters (New York:The New Press, 1999), pp.116-17, 146-9, 152-3. See citations that include, C.D. Jackson, 'Notes of meeting,' 3/28/52 (CDJ/DDE) and Dwight D. Eisenhower, quoted in Blanche Wiesen Cook, *The Declassified Eisenhower: A Divided Legacy of Peace and Political Warfare (New York: Doubleday,1981).* C.D. Jackson to Henry Luce, 3/28/58 (CDJ/DDE), C.D. Jackson to Abbott Washburn, 2/2/53 (CDJ/DDE) and Lawrence de Neufville, telephone interview, Genevea, March 1997. Note that CDJ/DDE stands for C.D. Jackson Papers and Records, Dwight D. Eisenhower Library, Abilene, Kansas.
[494] See, for example, Victor Navasky, *Naming Names* (NY:River Run Press,1991). On blacklisted musicians such as Pete Seeger, see www.writing.upenn.edu/~alfilreis/50s/seeger-bio-2.html
[495] Raobert D'Attilio, "Sacco-Vanzetti Case," in ed.s Mari Jo Buhle, Paul Buhle, and dan Georgakas, *Encyclopedia of the American Left* (Chicago, Ill: Universtiy of Illinois Pres,1992), pp.667-70.
[496] "C.D. Jackson... Rosenbergs." Stonor Saunders, The Cultural Cold War, pp.180-183, 291. Saunders' citations on Rosenbergs include Douglas Dillon to State Department, 5/15/53, (CJD/DDE). Charles Taquey to C.E. Johnson, Psychological Strategy Board, 3/29/53 (CJD/DDE), and C.D. Jackson to Herbert Brownell, 2/23/53 (CJD/DDE). On blacks and the arts, see C.D. Jackson to Nelson Rockefeller, 4/14/55 (CDJ/DDE). The Rosenberg children's adopted father, Abel Meeropol, a folk musician, had written Billie Holiday's classic song, "Strange Fruit," about rampant lynchings from trees in the South. http://www.law.umkc.edu/faulty/projects/ftrials/rosenb/ROS_BMER.HTM
[497] "C.D. Jackson... artists." Stonor Saunders, The Cultural Cold War, pp.180-183, 291. Saunders' citations on Rosenbergs include Douglas Dillon to State Department, 5/15/53, (CJD/DDE). Charles Taquey to C.E. Johnson, Psychological Strategy Board, 3/29/53 (CJD/DDE), and C.D. Jackson to Herbert Brownell, 2/23/53 (CJD/DDE). On blacks and the arts, see C.D. Jackson to Nelson Rockefeller, 4/14/55 (CDJ/DDE). In this letter Jackson warned his CIA colleagues not to get the 'smarty pants' idea of using these artist as intelligence sources—'I don't think that these people are emotionally capable of playing a double role'—but he did agree that 'After they return they can of course be skillfully debriefed.'
[498] Robert Sam Anson, "To Die Like a Gangsta," *Vanity Fair*, March 1997, p.251. Connie Bruck, "The Takedown of Tupac," *The New Yorker*, 7/7/97, p.57.
[499] One of the songs they censored was "Holler If Ya Hear Me," *Strictly 4 My N.I.G.G.A.Z*, Interscope Records, 1993. Tyehimba stated that Time Warner/Interscope heavily censored the lyrics to this single along with its accompanying video. The CD *Strictly...* was not allowed to be released for more than a year after it was finished. Personal interview, Watani Tyehimba, May 20, 2000. Tupac's public relations assistant said that his third release, the group project he titled, Thug Life, was also held up for a year. Barbara Ross, "Cops Widow Sez It's Time to Dump Star," *Daily News*, November, 24, 1993, p.27. New Yorker editor Connie Bruck also reported on Interscope/Time Warner forcing songs off that CD, Bruck, "The Takedown of Tupac," *The New Yorker*, 7/7/97, p.52

[500] Associated Press, "Hip-Hop Magazines Taking Off," Sunday, July 5, 1998. http://search.newschoice.com/AngTr_storydisplay.asp?story=d:\inetpub\wwwroot\newsarchives\angrtr\bus\19980705\98-07-05_a5ds405.txt

[501] "Jones said… issue." Quincy Jones, "Vibrant Thing: A Letter from Qunicy Jones," *Vibe*, December, 1998, p.38. Jones' letter addresses the partnership, without this writer's opinion stated here.

[502] Among previously cited personal interviews with Tyehimba and Warren.

[503] Ted Demme, the nephew of noted film producer Jonathan Demme, influenced MTV to let him start a rap show in 1988, which he titled, *Yo! MTV Raps*. That same year, NWA's *Straight Outta Compton* sold 2 million copies and Public Enemy was becoming one of the top rap bands among both Whites and Blacks. Filmmaker Spike Lee featured Public Enemy's radical political songs including, "Fight the Power," in his late Eighties movie, *Do the Right Thing*. One of the first rappers, Grandmaster Flash, started things off in the late Seventies, while Run DMC was the biggest rap group in the mid-Eighties. Russell Simmons, a borther of one of the Run DMC trio, produced their group and distributed Public Enemy on the Def Jam label he co-owned.

[504] In the nineties, Time Warner would expand its music holdings even more. Warner Music merged with EMI music, combining over six well known music labels—Warner Brother Records, Elektra Entertainment Group, Atlantic Group, Capitol, Virgin, and Priority, which they aggregately called WEA. These companies each owned a multitude of independent labels, including rap labels, No Limit, Rap A Lot, Qwest, Rawkus, Hoo Bangin', etc. They made up a quarter of the total music sales with three other companies controlling the other part of 84% of all music sales.

Warner EMI became the top music company dominating the market with three other companies—Universal Music, BMG entertainment, and Sony Music. *The Source* magazine noted that these four became an oligopoly—a handful of companies with considerable control over an entire industry. Such oligopolies could act like a cartel and unanimously decide to do anything they wanted in the industry.

Time Warner further had vast holdings in dozens of Cable TV stations, book publishing, video production, Warner Brothers motion pictures, Warner Brothers (WB) Television, and a half dozen book publishers. Time Warner's merge with Turner Broadcasting around this time brought them another half dozen film production companies, a dozen cable networks such as CNN, and many other entertainment holdings. They had the most media holdings of the four companies that dominated what *The Nation* magazine called, "The National Entertainment State." Mark Crispin Miller, pullout "The National Entertainment State," *The Nation*. 1996.

[505] Chuck Phillips, "Putting the Cuffs on 'Gangsta' Rap Songs," *Los Angeles Times*, 12/10/92, p. F1.

[506] Tuma Musango, "And Then There Were Four: The Fight For Independents," *The Source*, April 2000, p.50.

[507] "Time Warner bought… labels." In the nineties, Time Warner would expand its music holdings even more. Warner Music merged with EMI music, combining over six well known music labels—Warner Brother Records, Elektra Entertainment Group, Atlantic Group, Capitol, Virgin, and Priority, which they aggregately called WEA. These companies each owned a multitude of independent labels, including rap labels, No Limit, Rap A Lot, Qwest, Rawkus, Hoo Bangin', etc. They comprise a quarter of all music sales with three other companies controlling the other part of 84% of all music sales.

Warner EMI became the top music company dominating the market with three other companies—Universal Music, BMG entertainment, and Sony Music. *The Source* magazine noted that these four became an oligopoly—a handful of companies with considerable control over an entire industry. Such oligopolies could act like a cartel and unanimously decide to do anything they wanted in the industry. As shown above, Time Warner had many other entertainment holdings. They had the most media holdings of the four companies that dominated what *The Nation* magazine called, "The National Entertainment State." Mark Crispin Miller, pullout "The National Entertainment State," *The Nation*. 1996. On Time Warner's rap censorship, see Chuck Phillips, "Putting the

Cuffs on 'Gangsta' Rap Songs," *Los Angeles Times*, 12/10/92, p. F1. On music consolidation, also see Tuma Musango, "And Then There Were Four: The Fight For Independents," *The Source*, April 2000, p.50. On *Vibe* and other rap magazines rise, see Associated Press, "Hip-Hop Magazines Taking Off," Sunday, July 5, 1998. http://search.newschoice.com/AngTr_storydisplay.asp?story=d:\inetpub\wwwroot\newsarchives\angrtr\bus\19980705\98-07-05_a5ds405.txt

[508] One source reported that Time Warner's initial funding of Death Row Records was $10 million. Robert Sam Anson, "To Die Like a Gangsta," *Vanity Fair*, March 1997, p.252. A later book by Ronin Ro reported a lesser, but still substantial, $1.5 million initial financing. Ro, *Have Gun Will Travel*, p.315. Time Warner said it sold all links to Death Row in late '95 but it still keeps publishing rights, Sullivan, *LAbyrinth*, p.173.

[509] "Tupac Shakur's severe... sheet." Tupac's criminal record of two misdemeanors were for weapons possession and simple assault when someone came on his stage in Lansing, Michigan and tried to take the microphone away from him. Notice of Motion or Bail Pending Sentence New York v. tupac Shakur, Indictment no. 11578/93, Michael Warren, Attny for Depfendant-Petitioner Tupac Shakur. p.19 point 48.

[510] See Peter Zimroth, *Perversions of Justice: The Prosecution and Acquittal of the Panther 21*, p.289-292. Zimroth worked for the Justice Department before teaching at New York University Law School while watching the Panther 21 trial and interviewing all involved in the case.

[511] "Tupac's judge... this." Several Affidavits regarding bail money raised include those noted from court documents New York v. Tupac Shakur New York County Indict. No. 11578/93 in Supreme Court of N.Y. Appellate Div. 1st Dept. Tupac Shakur told of $350,000 put up by his actress friend Jasmine Guy and by Bert Padell. Watani Tyehimba told of $850,000 put up by Time Warner, which Asst. District Attny Francine begrudgingly acknowledged in a letter to the judge, 2/3/95, and Ahadi Tyhimba told of $36,000 Tupac gave her as a down payment for Tupac's sister Sekyiwa's $115,000 house for which Ahadi had to purchase because of Sekiywa's insufficient work record. The house was Tupac's and put up as part of bail package. On other information, also see Bruck, *The New Yorker*, 7/7/97.

[512] "Also, 45 days... off." On sales, see Vibe *Tupac*, p.140. On quote, see Michael Eric Dyson, *Holler If You Hear Me: Searching for Tupac Shakur* (New York: Basic Civitas Books, 2001), p.125.

[513] Eugene Robinson, "Exiles," *The Washington Post Magazine*, 7/18/04, pp.23-4, 33-7.

[514] "The increase... visits." On Clinton, see Jacob Hoye and Karolyn Ali, ed.s *Tupac: Resurrection* (New York: Atria, 2003), p.153. Cathy Scott, *The Killing of Tupac Shakur* (Las Vegas: Huntington Press, 1997), p.83. Tupac's prison card, *Tupac: Resurrection*, p.152. Album release date, Vibe eds, *Tupac Shakur*, p.140.

[515] Reporter Mark Schwartz, covering prison legislative reform, CD, *Me and My Shadow: Investigation of the political left by the United States Government*, producers Tarabu Betserai and Adi Gevins from "The Pacifica Radio Archives." Track 5.

[516] "U.S. Intelligence and prison... penal coercion.'" On guards, Tupac told of the better treatment he received from the black female guards at Rikers Prison in New York City, Vibe eds. *Tupac Shakur*, pp.50-1. U.S. Intelligence influence on judges and prison situations, see Mike Ryan, "The Stammheim Model: Judicial Counterinsurgency," *New Studies on the Left*, Vol. XIV, Nos. 1-2, Spring-Summer 1989, pp.45-69. On political prisoners, see treatment of Weather Underground activists linked to Mutulu, Black Liberation activists and Plowshares activists. On "torture" See *Amnesty International Report on Torture, 1983*. Also see, Thomas Benjamin and Kenneth Lux, "Soliltary Confinement as Psychological Torture," California Western Law Review, 13(265), 1978, pp.295-6. And, on "brainwashing," see Dr. Edgar Schein discussing methodology with federal maximum-security prison wardens in 1962, quoted in National Committee to Support the Marion Brothers, *Breaking Men's Minds,* Chicago, 1987. see Churchill and Vander Wall, *The COINTELPRO Papers*, pp.321-4.

[517] "In a…Biderman." Alfred McCoy, *A Question of Torture:CIA Interrogration, from the Cold War to the War on Terror* (New York: Metropolitan Books, 2006), pp.31-33, 40-43,50-52.
[518] See, "Biderman's Chart on Penal Coercion," *Amnesty International Report on Torture, 1983.* Reproduced and discussed in Ward Churchill and Jim Vander Wall, *The Cointelpro Papers: Documents from the FBI's Secret Wars Against Dissent in the United States* (Boston: South End Press, 1990) pp.321-323. Also see tactics used on Tupac's mother, Joan Bird, Afeni Shakur, Lumumba Shakur et. al., *Look for Me In the Whirlwind: The Collective Autobiography of the New York 21* (New York: Vintage Books, 1971), pp. 319-325.
[519] Bruck, *The New Yorker*, p.56.
[520] "Biderman's Chart on Penal Coercion," Churchill and Vander Wall, *The COINTELPRO Papers*, p.323.
[521] "Prof. McCoy…pain.'" McCoy, *A Question of Torture*, p.52.
[522] Affidavit of Barbara J. Justice, M.D. , *New York v. Tupac Shakur, Indictment No. 11578/93*, pp.2-4.
[523] Robert Sam Anson, "To Die Like a Gangsta," *Vanity Fair*, March 1997, p.280.
[524] Bruck, *The New Yorker*, p.56.
[525] "Tu Klux Klan," *Melody Maker*, November 11, 1995, p.4. Ronin Ro, *Have Gun Will Travel* (New York: Doubleday, 1998), pp.246-247.
[526] Anson, *Vanity Fair*, p.280. Tupac's sister, Sekiyawa Shakur also said his Panther uncle looked out for him in prison.
[527] "Of the other…Caryn James, "The Things That People Say," *New York Times*, December 15, 1995, pp. C15, C19. On length of time, see *Tupac: Resurrection*, p.162. Shower for Madonna visit, p.173.
[528] Several close to Tupac before and after prison attest to this. Actress Jada Pinket Smith, his best friend from high school, said "he went to jail and turned into a totally different person…part of Pac just died right there." Tupac's first manager and continued friend, Leila Steinberg, said Tupac had a brutalizing prison experience and his shining light and wit happy persona "was completely changed, dimmed." Michael Eric Dyson, *Holler If You Hear Me: Searching for Tupac Shakur* (New York: Basic Civitas, 2001) pp.215-16. Political prisoner George Edwards noted psychological damage in what he sensed was put in his prison food. He said that prison officials appeared to take the Penal Coercion to new levels with Huey Newton at one particular prison that caused a noticeable change in the Panther cofounder. Personal Interview, 8/10/00.
[529] Personal interviews with Tupac business manager Watani Tyehimba, 5/10/00, national lawyer Chokwe Lumumba, 5/5/00 and New York lawyer, Michael Warren, 11/8/00. Nick Broomfield also said this after discussions with Tyehimba, noted in his credits, Nick Broomfield, *Biggie and Tupac* (BBC funded documentary, 2002).
[530] Of the many examples cited of FBI's use of fake letters and undercover agents to set up East vs. West Panther war between Afeni Shakur's New York Panthers and Huey Newton's West Coast Panthers, see New York Black Panther Assata Shakur, Assata: An Autobiography (Chicago: Lawrence Hill Books, 1987), pp.230-232. Also see, copies of FBI correspondence obtained through the Freedom Of Information Act (FOIA) or confiscated in an FBI office raid by activists in 1971. Some of these were reprinted in Ward Churchill and Jim Vander Wall, The COINTELPRO Papers, pp.160-61. Such as, "From: Director, FBI (100-448006) COINTELPRO – BLACK PANTHER PARTY (BPP) – DISSENSION RACE MATTERS 2/10/71," and "Airtel to Albany et al Re: COINTELPRO – Black Panther Party (BPP) – Disssension 100-448006 Newton's …(deletions)…New York 21…San Francisco and New York are already involved in counterintelligence operations…creating dissension between local branch and/or its leaders and BPP national headquarters." Also see FBI undercover agent Louis Tackwood's admissions, Louis Tackwood, Churchill and Vander Wall, *Agents of Repression*, p.80. Tackwood, Lewis E., "My Assignment was to Kill George Jackson," *Black Panther*, April 21, 1980.

[531] See former FBI Cointelpro agent M. Wesley Swearingen, FBI Secrets: An Agent's Expose (Boston: South End, 1995, pp.82-3.
[532] "But Congress... into rivalries.'" "Intelligence Activities and Rights of Americans," Book II, April 26, 1976, *Senate Committee with Respect to Intelligence Report.* Excerpted in Alex Constantine, The Covert War Against Rock (Los Angeles: Feral House, 2001), p.9.
[533] "The FBI remains... shot." Cathy Scott, *The Killing of Tupac Shakur* (Las Vegas, NV: Huntington Press, 1997, p.153. On anonymous letters, see Tupac's road manager, Charles "Man-Man" Fuller in Connie Bruck, "The Takedown of Tupac," *The New Yorker*, p.58. In personal interviews with Tupac business manager Watani Tyehimba, 5/10/00, national lawyer Chokwe Lumumba, 5/5/00 and New York lawyer, Michael Warren, 11/8/00 the writer of this FBI War on Tupac book proposed these theories to these close associates of Tupac's and they wholeheartedly agreed. Nick Broomfield also said this after discussions with Tyehimba, noted in his credits, Nick Broomfield, *Biggie and Tupac* (BBC funded documentary, 2002).
[534] Reporter Mark Schwartz, covering Special Investigative Committee of California Legislature reviewing U.S. Intelligence tactics in prisons, *Me and My Shadow: Investigation of the political left by the United States Government*, Tarabu Betserai and Adi Gevins from "The Pacifica Radio Archives." Track 5.
[535] Personal interview, Billy Lesane, 3/26/99. Billy Lesane is Tupac's biological cousin.
[536] "But this... war." On media role, see, for example, Cheo Hodari Coker, "How the West was Won," *Vibe*, Vibe eds, *Tupac Shakur*, p.39, also see suspected intelligence agent Booker. Jacques Agnant's associate who called Tupac to Times Square shooting scene and then "spun" Tupac's first interview to help make it much more contentious and accusatory to aid the rap war's start, in Vibe eds, *Tupac Shakur*, p. 59. Adario Strange, "Death Wish," *The Source*, March 1996, pp.87-88. *Source* in Ro, *Have Gun Will Travel*, p.163.
[537] "One of Penal... as '93." Penal Coercion goal, *Amnesty International Report on Torture, 1983* in Churchill and Vander Wall, The COINTELPRO Papers, p.323. $200,000 for one song, Ro, *Have Gun Will Travel*, p.146. Time Warner push for Tupac on Death Row, Connie Bruck, "The Takedown of Tupac," *The New Yorker*, 7/7/97, p.57.
[538] After over... 1995." On 90% of Tupac's bail already raised, see Tupac's aunt, Jean Cox, and mother, Afeni, put up personal bonds. His actress friend, Jasmine Guy put up $350,000 with a man named Bert Padell. Tyehimba got Atlantic Records to agree that if Tupac promised $850,000 from his next CD, they'd put that much into the bail package to bring it to $1.2 million. See, New York v. Tupac Shakur, Sentencing hearing transcript, p.70 and Affidavits from Tupac Shakur, 2/2/95, Watani Tyehimband Ahadi Tyehimba. Atlantic is a Time Warner subsidiary.On, Tupac's release just after signing to Death Row, see, eds. Jacob Hoye and Karolyn Ali, *Tupac: Resurrection* (New York: Atria, 2003) pp.193-4, and Bruck, *New Yorker*, p.58 for some of many citings.
[539] Ronin Ro said Knight actually only provided $250,000 of the bail money with Interscope and Time Warner providing the rest. Ro, *Have Gun Will Travel*, p.250. also see Bruck, *New Yorker*, p.58.
[540] Gary Webb, *Dark Alliance: The CIA, the Contras, an the Crack Cocaine Explosion* (New York: Seven Stories, 1998), p.148. On Harris as silent partner, Ronin Ro, *Have Gun Will Travel: The Spectacular Rise and Violent Fall of Death Row Records* (New York:Doubleday, 1998) pp.76-80. Bruck, *New Yorker*, p.58.
[541] Murray Waas and Craig Unger, "In the Loop," *New Yorker*, 11/2/92, p.64ff. Referenced in Craig Unger, House of Bush, House of Saud (New York: Scribner, 2004), pp.74. One writer, Michael Montalvo, described Bush's role and how the Reagan/Bush administration could set a new standard for cover-up of their cocaine trafficking. Montalvo said that Marine Lt. Col. Olver North's own diary entries disclosed much of his role in supervising the transportation of "over 500 tons of cocaine... to the poor masses of the inner cities and across the USA," purportedly only for saving Central America and the U.S. from Communism. Montalvo said that former CIA Director George Bush, the Vice-President at the time, was heading the National Security Council (NSC) for the

White House, with North as a National Security Advisor. They were able to keep documentation of these operations under wraps through President Reagan's Executive Order 123333. The order "'privatized' NSC intelligence operations and permitted agencies other that the CIA to carry out 'special operations' without reporting its activities... [allowing] any private enterprise the NSC set up, to carry out covert operations." Michale Montalvo, "Prisoner of the Drug War: An Inside Report from a former Inside Player," *Prevailing Winds* #8, 2000, pp.76-82.
[542] Dale Russakoff, "Shifting Within Party to Gain His Footing," *The Washington Post,* A1, A8, 7/26/04.
[543] Webb, *Dark Alliance*, p.558.
[544] "Ricky... Bush." Nelson's background came from the Department of State's Biographical Register, 1973, and from CIA-BASE, a computer database operated by former CIA officer Ralph McGehee, in Garry Webb, *Dark Alliance*, pp.196-7, 513n.
[545] On National Security Council overseeing U.S. Intelligence, see Victor Marchetti and John D. Marks, *The CIA and the Cult of Intelligence* (New York: Dell, 1974), p.117. The authors are CIA and Intelligence veterans, respectively. On Bush directing the National Security Council, see Michale Montalvo, "Prisoner of the Drug War: An Inside Report from a former Inside Player," *Prevailing Winds* #8, 2000, pp.76
[546] "This became... others." On U.S-backed brutal dictator, Webb, *Dark Alliance*, pp.22-3, 46-7. On officials and CIA-linked assoaciates indicted, conivted and pardoned, Webb, pp.553-561. On Bush directing Iran-Contra and the drug trafficking operations, as well as Bill Gates part, see, Al Martin, *The Conspirators: Secrets of an Iran-Contra Insider* (Pray, Montana: National Liberty Press, 2002).
[547] "The real... control." Ronin Ro, *Have Gun Will Travel*: *The Spectacular Rise and Violent Fall of Death Row Records* (New York:Doubleday, 1998) pp.76-80.
[548] "Mutulu Shakur... 'Mr. Untouchable.'" According to a 1976 "Top Secret" Justice Department report. Jefferson Morley, "The Kid Who Sold Crack to the President," *The City Paper*, 12/15/89, p.31. On Barnes acquittals and *New York Times* label, see Hank Messick, *Of Grass and Snow* (Englewood, CA: Prentice-Hall, 1979), p.148. Both cited in Clarence Lusane, *Pipe Dream Blues: Racism and the War on Drugs* (Boston, MA: South End Press, 1991), pp.41-42, notes 76 and 79. Mutulu Shakur also alluded to Nicky Barnes as a "rat," suggesting that he, too, thought Barnes worked for the government. See the momentary display of Mutulu's Thug Life Code in *Tupac:Ressurrection* DVD at the Mutulu Shakur interview.
[549] Elaine Brown, *Taste of Power*, p.86. William Pepper, *Orders to Kill*, p.82.
[550] Police Detective Russell Poole said this on film in Nick Broomfield, Biggie and Tupac (documentary, 2002), as well as Randalll Sullivan, *LAbyrinth: A Detective Investigates the Murders of Tupac Shakur and Notorious B.I.G., the Implications of Death Row Records' Suge Knight and the Origins fo the Los Angeles Police Scandal* (New York: Atlantic Monthly, 2002). Poole lists many of the cops' names working in Death Row throughout this book.
[551] Randalll Sullivan, *LAbrynth*, p.166.
[552] Ro, *Have Gun Will Travel*, pp.36-7. Sullivan, *LAbyrinth*, "Timeline," p.301
[553] "For example, after... his own record label." Ro, *Have Gun Will Travel*, p.118, 130-1, 154.
[554] "Later trial... infiltrator work." See, *Appeal*, PL WON #3 showed that FBI Chicago SAC Mitchell personally posted bond on one of O'Neal's charges and neither of his charges were prosecuted. On FBI collaboration with gang intelligence, see *Appeal*, PL #413 and *Transcript* at 26909. Churchill and Vander Wall, *Agents of Repression*, pp.64-6, .endnotes 5, 24.
[555] Some writers... case)." Sullivan, *LAbrynth*, p.107. Ro, *Have Gun Will Travel*, p.197. And secondly, lawyers working on the case said Longo had nothing to do with the settlement because he was "the low man on the totem pole" in that case. Ro, *Have Gun Will Travel*, p.197. Furthermore, Death Row hadn't signed a contract with Longo's daughter Gina, until January of '96, while Knight's continued arrests, convictions, and jail-free suspended sentences included several as early as 1990. Gina Longo's brother

reportedly first met with David Kenner in June of 1995 to talk about an Eazy-E film project, when he first mentioned his sister. In 1996, Kenner also rented a home from Longo, before Kenner had Knight stay there. Longo had only submitted plans for the home to be built in December of 1994. Ro, pp. 300-303. It's also interesting how Knight received a glowing probation report despite having nine separate charges with many convictions by that time of '95, particularly compared to a probation report supervisors changed from positive to negative in Tupac's sexual assault case.
[556] "Tupac's signing ... lawyer." Personal interview, Tyehimba, 5/10/00. Bruck, *New Yorker*, p.58.
[557] See, "Biderman's Chart on Penal Coercion," *Amnesty International Report on Torture, 1983.* Reproduced and discussed in Ward Churchill and Jim Vander Wall, *The Cointelpro Papers: Documents from the FBI's Secret Wars Against Dissent in the United States*, pp.321-323.
[558] Ro, *Have Gun Will Travel*, p.271-272, 319-20. Randalll Sullivan, *LAbrynth*, pp.35-38.
[559] Bruck, *The New Yorker*.
[560] "As previously... Belafonte." Elaine Brown, *Taste of Power* (New York: Doubledaay, 1992), p.86. Pepper, *Orders to Kill*, p.82.
[561] See, for example, Bruck, New Yorker, p.58. Robert Sam Anson, "To Die Like a Gangsta," Vanity Fair, March 1997, p.280. Alcohol and weed at Death Row, also see Ro, *Have Gun Will Travel*, pp.104, 110. 116.
[562] This writer has close over ten years experience as an addictions counselor and has taken several certification classes on the subject.
[563] Kevin Powell interview with Tupac, Vibe editors, *Tupac Shakur*, p.45-6. On Tupac as well-read and always teaching her, see Dyson, p.71. Pinkett Smith described him as brilliant and incredible, crying about his death on an interview for the promo outtakes of *Tupac: Resurrection*, DVD (MTV, 2003).
[564] "Others also... all the time.'" This writer bases this assessment on his own work for over 10 years in the field of addiction. On Tupac as well-read and always teaching Pinkett Smith, see Michael Eric Dyson, *Holler If You Hear Me* (New York: Basic Civitas, 2001), p.71. Pinkett Smith described him as brilliant and incredible, crying about his death on an interview for the promo outtakes of *Tupac: Resurrection*, DVD (MTV, 2003). Second part from Dyson, *Holler If You Hear Me*, p.240.
[565] Rob Marriott, "Ready To Die," *Vibe*, November 1996, p. T3.
[566] "Suge Knight... *Chronic*." With his former rap group, NWA, Dre rapped against marijuana use on his 1988 NWA song "Express Yourself." Death Row influenced Dre to devote a whole CD to marijuana, which he titled with its slang for potent weed, *The Chronic*. Ro, *Have Gun Will Travel*, pp.97, 109. On FBI letter to, and attempt to cancel concerts of, NWA, see On the FBI's fax campaign to get police canceling NWA shows, see Bruce C. Brown, "Quayle Boosts 'Cop Killer' Campaign," *Washington Post*, 6/20/92, pp.B1,5. Cited in Barry Shank, "Fears of the White Unconcious: Music, Race, and Identification in the Censorship of 'Cop Killer.'" *Radical History Review* #66, Fall 1996.
[567] Ronin Ro, *Have Gun Will Travel*, pp.83-4.
[568] "Death Row next set....advances." Ro, *Have Gun Will Travel*, pp.122-3, 158, 174-6. On Death Row and Wu Tang, also see Sullivan, *LAbyrinth*, p.85. Zulu Nation Afrika Bambata said his Zulu hip hop activist organization partly modeled itself after the Panthers, Black Panther Film Fest III, CUNY, NYC, 2002. Zulu Nation founder Afrika Bambatta reported first organizing the group around principles of the Black Panthers, Third Black Panther Film Festival, CUNY, 2003. The Black Liberation Movement leader was Sonny Carson, who had a recording studio. He worked with Tupac's New York lawyer Michael Warren in the 80s when New York police illegally targeted them with their Black Desk unit.
[569] "Death Row next set....Miami." Ro, *Have Gun Will Travel*, pp.122-3, 158, 174-6. On Death Row and Wu Tang, also see Sullivan, *LAbyrinth*, p.85.
[570] "Similarly, Death... behavior." Ro, *Have Gun Will Travel*, pp.156-157, 226-227, 232, 258. And, Cathy Scott, *The Murder of Biggie Smalls* (New York: St. Martin's, 2000) pp.54-5.

[571] "Knight and his…answer." Knight and his Death Row employees had been charged with many violent crimes for which much evidence existed but they were rarely charged with them. Also many witnesses said Death Row employees beat a Crip gang member to death unprovoked. Sullivan *LAbyrinth*, pp.37-9, 190-1.
[572] "Knight and…records." On Tupac's change from promoting unity amongst rapper to divisiveness, see, for example, the first CD *2Pacalypse Now*'s naming of activist rappers on "America's Nightmare," and then "Representin' '93" on his second CD, *Strictly for My N.I.G.G.A.Z.* Despite the divisive sounding CD title, Tupac promotes White and Hispanic rap groups House of Pain and Cypress Hill along with Black rappers in this song. On his Death Row CDs, especially over half the tracks he produced within days of leaving prison, he has attacks on his former friend and top rapper, Biggie Smalls (Notorious BIG). His next CD then included attacks on many other New York rappers. Also see for example, Tupac's quotes of Knight's advising him to beat down Biggie and Puffy if they don't respect him. Vibe eds. *Tupac*, p.102.
[573] Ro, *Have Gun Will Travel*, p.267-268.
[574] "Furthermore…laundering money." Randalll Sullivan, *LAbrynth* , pp.40, 124, 192, 197.
[575] "Furthermore, highly…acted on." Sullivan, *LAbyrinth*, pp.40, 124, 169-70, 191.
[576] Mike Davis, "Who Killed Los Angeles? Part 2," *New Left Review*, #199, 1993, p.35. Davis authored the *New York Times* best-selling book, City of Quartz, on the history of Los Angeles.
[577] Jesse Katz, "Man Freed in Death of Gang Leader Courts: Rodney Compton is to get one year probation in the slaying of Tony Bogard, who helped reach a truce between the Crips and Bloods," *The Los Angeles Times*, 6/1/94, p.3.
[578] "The LA…riots." Mike Davis, "In L.A., Burning All Illusions," *The Nation*, 6/1/92, p.745. For example, Gang truce leader Dewayne Holmes received a 7 year prison sentence for allegedly stealing $10 at a gang unity dance. Mike Davis, "Who Killed Los Angeles? Part Two: The verdict is given," *New Left Review* 199/1993, p.34-5. WBAI Radio, 4/15/02. FBI work with LAPD in Operation Hammer in Megan Garvery & Rich Winton, "City Declares War on Gangs," *Los Angeles Times*, 12/4/02. One activist was taped speaking to a large assembly and broadcast on the Pacifica Radio Network. He told how the LAPD's Operation Hammer—an "anti-gang operation" disrupted the gang peace summit meetings. He said that while he was helping run the peace summit meetings, it was only then that this operation had their police officers break up the meeting with a charge of "unlawful assembly. Heard by this writer on 99.1, WBAI radio station in New York City, April 29, 2001.
[579] Sullivan, *LAbyrinth*, pp.197, 201-7.
[580] OJJDP Summary, August 2000—Youth Gang Programs and Strategies, "Suppression Programs" www.ncjrs.org/html/ojjdp/summary_2000_8/suppression.html
[581] On Wright, Sr. as Gang chief, see Nick Broomfield, *Biggie and Tupac*. On Wright, Jr. working with his father on Compton police force, Sullivan, *LAbyrinth*, p.191.
[582] Churchill and Vander Wall, *Agents of Repression*, p.465 n.86
[583] Ro, *Have Gun Will Travel*, pp.88, 102, 105, 111, 114-115,
[584] Mike Davis, "Who Killed Los Angeles? Part Two: The Verdict is Given," *New Left Review* 198/1993, p.35.
[585] Ro, *Have Gun Will Travel*, pp. 68, 92, 104-5, 120, 193-4.
[586] "At least one…reports." Sullivan, *LAbyrinth*, pp.37-39. Also see, Ro, *Have Gun Will Travel*, pp.208-11.
[587] Ro, *Have Gun Will Travel*, p.166.
[588] "U.S. Intelligence…Quincy Jones." Robert Sam Anson, *Vanity Fair*, p.281. Scott, *The Killing of Tupac Shakur*, p.81.
[589] Frank Alexander with Heidi Siegmund Cuda, *Got Your Back: Protecting Tupac in the world of gangsta rap* (New York: St. Martin's Griffin, 1998, 2000) p.144.
[590] "In Tupac Shakur's…nation.'" Tupac under pseudonym, Ma.k.a.veli, *don kiluminati: the 7 day theory* (Death Row, 1996).

[591] Robert Sam Anson, "To Die Like a Gangsta," Vanity Fair, March 1997, p.280. On organizing around independent electoral politics, see Vibe eds. *Tupac Shakur*, p.280.
[592] Rob Marriott, "Last Testament," Vibe Editors, *Tupac Shakur*, pp.125-126.
[593] Vibe Editors, "Inside the Mind of Tupac Shakur," *Tupac Shakur* (New York: Crown Publishing, 1996), p.97. Armond White, *Rebel for the Hell of It* (New York: Thunder's Mouth Press, 1997), p.168. "Bits and Pieces," The Source, October 1996, p.6. Rob Marriott, "Last Testament," Vibe Editors, *Tupac Shakur*, pp.125-126.
[594] Ro, Have Gun Will Travel, p.281.
[595] Fula ran Tupac's record company, Euphenasia, Bruck, *New Yorker*, p.61. Molly Monjauze, Tupac's 4 hour personal assistant, also helped run this company. On Odinga's fathering Yafeu Fula with Yaasmyn, see a letter by Mutulu Shakur in Alex Constantine, *The Covert War Against Rock* (Los Angeles: Feral House, 2001), p.159. Yaasmyn Fula had also done jail time in connection to Mutulu Shakur's indictment in the 80s. See Kuwasi Balagoon, *A Soldier's Story: Writings by a Revolutionary New Afrikan Anarchist* (Montreal: Solidarity, 2001), p.34.
[596] Both of Tupac's personal bodyguards, Fran Alexander and Kevin Hackie, reportedly said this in Det. Russell Poole's interviews. In Sullivan, *LAbyrinth*, pp.188, 192.
[597] "Tupac had immediate exit…Death Row co-chair Dave Kenner." Connie Bruck, "The Takedown of Tupac," The New Yorker, 7/7/97, pp.61-63. Also see a copy of Tupac's handwritten contract signed in jail, ed.s Jacob Hoye and Karolyn Ali, *Tupac: Resurrection 1971-1996*, pp.192-93.
[598] See both Yaasmyn Fula in Bruck, *New Yorker*, p.62 and Kidada Jones in Anson, *Vanity Fair*, p.281.
[599] On Kenner's East Coast Mafia ties, Sullivan, LAbyrinth, p.192. Las Vegas gambling had a notorious Mafia history. Organized crime figures made Las Vegas their "Mafia money machine." Cathy Scott, *The Murder of Biggie Smalls* (New York: St. Martin's Press, 2000), p.130.
[600] See the booklet of documents created by Michael Rupert on Albert Carone, with assistance from Carone's daughters. Michael Ruppert, *Albert V. Carone: The Missing Link Between CIA and the Mob* (Los Angeles, CA, From the Wilderness Publications, 1998). www.fromthewilderness.com .
[601] William Pepper, *Orders to Kill: The Truth Behind the Murder of Martin Luther King* (New York: Warner, 1998), p.146-7, 485. Also note that despite Warner Books' republishing of Pepper's book originally published by Carrol and Graf, this author needed to order the book from Warner's warehouse and Warner generally appeared to buy the rights to it in order to keep it hidden. Other Mafia overlap with the FBI in Boston and the NYPD have also received wide press.See for example, CBS News/Associated Press, "Ex-FBI Agent Charged in Mob Hit," www.cbsnews.com/stories/2003/11/21/national /main584890.shtml. FBI documents also cited their attemtps to provoke a Mafia hit on Panther-supporting comedian, Dick Gregory. See FBI letter From: SAC, Chicago, To: FBI Director,(100-4480006). 4/15/68. Copied in Churchill and Vander Wall, *The COINTELPRO Papers*, p.104.
[602] Randalll Sullivan, *LAbrynth* (New York: Atlantic Monthly Press, 2002), p.99. And, Ronin Ro, Have Gun Will Travel, book flap. An associate of Ro's told this author that much information was censored out of the American reprinting of his book originally published in Britain. Anson also mentioned this connection, Anson, *Vanity Fair*, p.281. *New Yorker* editor Connie Bruck also mentions Death Row's connections to New York organized crime families, Bruck, *The New Yorker*, p.64.
[603] For Genovese Mafia family and U.S. Intelligence work, see Lucky Luciano and his Lieutenant, Vito Genovese. They led the New York's five largest Mafia families that controlled heroin traffic in the Fifties while helping oppose Communists/Socialists. *Newsday* Editors, *The Heroin Trail* (New York: Signet, 1973), p.199, cited in Clarence Lusane, *Pipe Dream Blues: Racism and the War on Drugs* (Boston, South End Press, 1991), p.39, 117-18. When Luciano, Genovese and Meyer Lansky exited due to death and old age, the next leading member of their network, Santo Trafficante, furthered business with CIA and U.S. military supported drug trafficking Vietnamese generals.

Alfred McCoy, *The Politics of Heroin: CIA Complicty in the Global Drug Trade* (New York: Lawrence Hill Books, 1991), pp.32-9, 43-4, 73-7, 255-6.
[604] "Death Row… attorney." Scott, *The Murder of Biggie Smalls*, p.81, 130. Scott told how Goodman and Chesnoff worked as Death Row's lawyers. Sullivan also told how Goodman billed himself as the "mouthpiece for the Mob." *LAbyrinth*, p.99. Cathy Scott was a veteran police reporter for *the Las Vegas Sun* who has written for the New York Times and written for or appeared on a dozen other newspapers and television news programs. She has also won a dozen journalism awards. Randalll Sullivan has written articles for *Rolling Stone* and *Esquire*. On Chesnoff, see Sullivan, *LAbyrinth*, p.99
[605] Released CIA documents on contracting Roselli orchestrate assassination of Castro can be found at www.gwu.edu/~nsarchiv/NSAEBB/NSAEBB222/index.htm or google it at george washington university CIA family jewels. See CIA document—MEMORANDUM FOR: Executive Director—Comptroller, SUBJECT: Roselli, John, 15 FEB 1972. Howard J. Osborn, Director of Security. Also see Jack Anderson, "Castro Stalker Worked for the CIA," *Washington Post*, 2/23/71, p.B11.
[606] "Tupac finally… revoked." Dyson, *Holler If You Hear Me*, pp.247-8.
[607] "The biggest… setup." Sullivan, LAbyrinth, pp.192-3.
[608] "That weekend… battery." Sullivan, *LAbyrinth*, pp.188, 192-3. In official notes taken by Los Angeles Detectives Russell Poole and Frank Miller, cited within. See, LAPD notes of interview of Frank Alexander, written by Det. Russell Poole, dated 4/28/98 7 pages. Most comments of Alexander's come from this source, except where otherwise noted. Alexander was also an auxillary police officer in Los Angeles. Also see, Scott, *Tupac*, p.5. Anson, *Vanity Fair*, p.282.
[609] On alcohol and weed at party, Anson, *Vanity Fair*, p.282. On the Vegas moonlighting cops joining the LA moonlighting cops that night, Scott, *The Killing of Tupac Shakur*, p.6.
[610] "After watching a … scene." Eyewitness Frank Alexander in Sullivan, *LAbyrinth*, p.188. Tupac was likely more easily influence to get involved in this scuffle partly because of his likely post-party intoxicated state and partly because he had previously been punched by some Crip gang members for no reason. Cited in Dream Hampton, "Hellraiser," *The Source*, September 1994, p.85.
[611] "Many disclosures… Tupac." Bruck, *New Yorker*, p.63.
[612] Stated in Broomfield, *Biggie and Tupac*. Hackie's "informant," meaning paid, work for the FBI also came out in many new sources when they reported on rapper Biggie Small's family wrongful death trial. See, for example, Charlie Amter, "B.I.G. Revelations in Biggie Trial," *Yahoo! News*, 7/24/05.
[613] Cathy Scott, *The Murder of Biggie Smalls* (New York: St. Martins, 2000), p.94.
[614] Sullivan, *LAbyrinth*, pp.157, 159, 162-5. "security detail," p.165.
[615] "Knight and Tupac… apprehended." This scene has been described in many ways by many sources. Cathy Scott did excellent work, particularly in uncovering many police irregularities regarding this scene. The only weak point in her depiction came in regards to Suge Knight. Scott claimed Knight was hit by a bullet "fragment," implying a ricocheting fragment,Scott, *The Killing of Tupac,* Shakur, p.7. Scott later changed the wording to Knight being "hit by a bullet," in Scott, *The Murder of Biggie Smalls*, p.72. This small difference is important in people's attempt to defend Knight. Investigating Police whistleblower, Det. Russell Poole, documentary filmmaker Nick Broomfield, and *LAbyrinth* author Randalll Sullivan, all believe that Knight was only injured as described in this writer's paragraph, by flying debris. Sullivan, LAbyrinth, p.144. *New Yorker* editor Connie Bruck did an extensive article saying "Knight's forehead was grazed," without saying by what. Connie Bruck, "The Takedown of Tupac," *The New Yorker*, 7/7/97, p.63. Vibe's Rob Marriot said "bullet fragments" grazed Knight, Vibe ed.s, *Tupac Shakur*, p.120. On Travon Lane's car also blocking Tupac in, *documentary Tupac Assassination* (2007) dir. Ricahrd Bond, co-produced with Frank Alexander
[616] Knight argued that he got a bullet lodged in his head that required an overnight hospital stay, though most researchers say he was merely grazed by ricocheting glass or shrapnel. Of the many researchers' insistence of Knight's not getting directly hit by a

bullet, see Sullivan, *LAbyrinth*, Broomfield *Biggie and Tupac*. Scott, *The Killing of Tupac Shakur*, p.8. Knight's walking around fine a day or two later attests to to no direct shots hitting him. For their approximate weights, see his prison identity card in Tupac: Ressurection 1971-1996, p.152, where it also lists him as 5'11". For Knight, he's listed as 6'4" and 330 lbs. Scott, *The Murder of Biggie Smalls* (New York: St. Martin's, 2000) p.52.

[617] "Tupac reportedly... label." Bruck, *New Yorker*, p. 63.

[618] "Knight then raced... dashboard." Scott, *The Killing of Tupac Shakur*, pp.9, 41, 95.

[619] "Knight drove... hospital." Scott, *The Killing of Tupac Shakur*, pp.7-10.

[620] Scott, *The Killing of Tupac Shakur,* p.59.

[621] "First... calls." Scott, *The Killing of Tupac Shakur*, pp.8-9, 39, 42-43.

[622] "Then, police lost... photos." Scott, *The Killing of Tupac Shakur*, pp.9, 40, 43. Also see, "Investigative Reports: Interview with Cathy Scott," *XXL Magazine,* October, 2000, p.131.

[623] Scott, *The Killing of Tupac Shakur*, p. 40.

[624] Scott, *The Killing of Tupac Shakur*, pp.18-19, 35-39, 112. Scott, *The Murder of Biggie Smalls* (New York: St. Martin's Press, 2000), p.89.

[625] "Tupac's backup... assertions." Chuck Phillips, "2 Say They Saw Attackers of Slain Rapper; Members of Tupac Shakur's entourage say they haven't been asked to view photos of suspects." *The Los Angeles Times*, 2/28/97, A3.

[626] "Police then failed... line." Scott, *The Killing of Tupac...*, pp.47-8, 59.

[627] "Furthermore... there." Sullivan, *LAbyrinth*, pp.157, 159, 162-5. "security detail," p.165.

[628] See official police documents that confirm witness statements about McCauley's promotion just after Tupac's murder, as well as his work permit revocation before the murder. For example, LAPD "Intradepartmental Correspondence" from Commander Keith D. Bushey of Human Resources Bureau, Personnel Group, "Subject: Work Permit Revocatin, Police Officer III Ricahrd McCauley," dated 1/8/95 2 pages. And, LAPD "Supplemental Investigation to Personnel Complaint Investigation IA No 96-1408," resulting in "one additional allegation of midsconduct against Sergeant I Richard McCauley," dated 6/25/97 5 pages. p.157, 163, 316-17. Police superiors only punished McCauley after other police joined Knox and Poole in complaints about McCauley.

[629] Sullivan, *LAbyrinth*, pp.161-2. Like the FBI's Richard Helds father and son team, such father and son teams appeared to be used by U.S. Intelligence in many cases, possibly for the father to help provide his son direction and ensure his loyalty loyalty. The LAPD only finally suspended McCauley when another police detective, Lt. Alba, followed up on Knox and Poole's findings and pushed the issue.

[630] "Las Vegas... murder." Sullivan, *LAbyrinth*, p.143.

[631] "U.S. Intelligence... influence." Robert Sam Anson, *Vanity Fair*, p.281. Scott, *The Killing of Tupac Shakur*, p.81.

[632] "Tupac's expanding... rapper." See fashion modeling picture and film list, Vibe ed.s Tupac Shakur, pp.114, 141. Also see, picture of Tupac with Donatella Versace in Frank Alexdander, *Got Your Back.* On judge, see Dyson, *Holler If You Hear Me*, p.248. Tupac's last film include *Gridlock'd* with actor Tim Roth, and, ironically, *Gang Related*, with Jim Belushi. The latter movie used the same theme most media used to cover up corrupt police murders of blacks, in saying it was "gang-related."

[633] "Tupac promised... alarms." On community centers after each CD, military philosophy and Monster Kody, Vibe ed.s, *Tupac*, '97, p.51, 97-8. LA community center was for "at-risk youth," Robert Sam Anson, "To Die Like a Gangsta," *Vanity Fair*, March 1997, p.280.

[634] Sullivan, *LAbyrinth*, pp.188-189.

[635] Nick Broomfield, *Biggie and Tupac*, 2002. Sullivan, *LAbyrinth*, p.189.

[636] Jullianne Shepherd, "Death Row Bodyguard=Undercover FBI Agent," Vibe.com http://www.vibe.com/news_headlines/2007/10/death_row_undercover/

[637] "Kevin Hackie's... jail." Hackie appeared to originally be a cog in the FBI operation against Tupac. Expert researchers have said agents in such positions are usually given

only partial knowledge of the entire operation. See former Panther attorney, Paul Chevigny, Cops and Rebels: A Study of Provocation (New York: Curtis/Pantheon Books, 1972), p.113, Called "One of the year's best books," by the *N.Y.Times* Book Review. On Afeni's description of Tupac's business relationship with Knight, as well as Fula and Jones about Atlanta, see Bruck, *The New Yorker*, pp.61, 63. Hackie said authorities set him up for that arrest in Broomfield, *Biggie and Tupac*.

[638] Jullianne Shepherd, "Death Row Bodyguard=Undercover FBI Agent," Vibe.com http://www.vibe.com/news_headlines/2007/10/death_row_undercover/

[639] Richard Bond, dir. *Tupac Assassination* (2007), Bond-Age Films/Ste N' UP Enterprises, produced with Frank Alexander.

[640] "Within several... often traveled there." Scott, *The Killing of Tupac*, p.105. Knight's Vegas lawyer, David Chesnoff, claimed Knight went to police headquarters a second time to register as an ex-convict. Chesnoff said the FBI "reminded" Knight of this because of a Nevada law saying you had 72 hours to do so. This reason for the FBI talking to Knight seems dubious. Knight had driven the 300 miles from LA to his Las Vegas mansion many weekends. Since Knight had a home in Las Vegas and spent much time there, why wouldn't they have asked him to register in the past? This makes the reported "registration as an ex-con" reason for Knight's contacts with the FBI and police sound like a cover story for a debriefing and consultation on how to handle the murder aftermath. Scott, *The Killing of Tupac*, p.104.

[641] "But most curious... shootiing." Sullivan, *LAbyrinth*, pp.141-143.

[642] "In LA... Tupac." Sullivan, *LAbyrinth*, pp.141-143. On Travon Lane reporting Anderson and Crips killing Tupac, *Tupac Assassination* (2007) documentary, Rich Bond and Frank Alexander producers.

[643] "Police said... Bloods." Sullivan, *LAbyrinth*, p.145.

[644] Davis, "Who Killed Los Angeles? Part Two: The Verdict is Given," *New Left Review* 199/1993, p.35.

[645] Mike Davis, "Who Killed Los Angeles? Part Two: The Verdict is Given," *New Left Review* 199/1993.

[646] "In Las Vegas... 1996" Anson, *Vanity Fair*, p.282. Some of the people that came to Tupac's bedside included These included Jesse Jackson, Al Sharpton, Jasmine Guy, Diana Ross, MC Hammer and Mike Tyson. Tyson left his post-boxing match press conference without talking to reporters so that he could rush to the hospital and come to Tupac's bedside. On Afeni deciding to not revive him, Scott, *Biggie*, p.102.

[647] "Twenty... shootings." Sullivan, *LAbyrinth*, pp.141-143. Crips Darnell Brims was shot three times on 9/9/96. A Blood working for Death Row's Wrightway security was shot several times by a Crip. 30 yr-old Bobby Finch was fatally shot on Compton's Southside. Police found arms and ammunition inside the homes of Jerry Bonds and Orlando Anderson. On many in mourning, the movie *Tupac: Resurrection* showed people mourning worldwide. In the U.S., Princeton Professor Cornel West said his son attended a Tupac memorial of hundreds at Howard University that had people crying. West also asked for a moment of silence for Tupac on the anniversary of his death, at the start of West's keynote address at the AFL-CIO Labor Conference at Columbia University this writer attended. Personal interview, 9/13/97. Many white activists appeared not to understand why West cared.

[648] "The cover-up of... months." On police ignoring Fula, Scott, *The Killing of Tupac Shakur*, pp.18-19, 35-37, 112-113. On police saying murder drug-related..., Scott, *The Murder of Biggie Smalls*, p.88. Media repeated this lie. *Time Magazine*, "The Year in Review," 12/30/96, p.130. This police/media concoction is a worse case cover-up than that around Newton's death.

[649] On details of killing, Scott, *The Killing of Tupac Shakur*, p.112.

[650] "In November of... record.." On police saying murder drug-related, Scott, *The Murder of Biggie Smalls*, p.88. Media repeated this lie. *Time Magazine*, "The Year in Review," 12/30/96, p.130. This police/media concoction is a worse case cover-up than that around Newton's death.

[651] "There are several... company." Scott, *The Killing of Tupac Shakur*, pp.11-115, *The Murder of Biggie Smalls*, pp. 70-1, 89.
[652] "There are several... Odinga." Walker was killed by three gunmen after a high speed car chase in Queens. Scott, *The Murder of Biggie Smalls*, pp. 70-1, 89.
[653] LAPD notes of interview of Frank Alexander, written by Det. Russell Poole, dated 4/28/98, 7 pages. LAPD notes of interview of Frank Alexander, written by Det. III Fred Miller, dated 4/28/98, 2 pages. Referenced in Randalll Sullivan, *LAbyrinth* (New York: Atlantic Monthly Press, 2002), pp.188-189.
[654] "For one... cool.'" On ticket purchase day of match and saying he got free MGM room as a big gambler without a known source of income, see Scott, *Murder of Biggie*, p.81. On Orlando's actions and quote after scuffle, see Sullivan *LAbyrinth*, p.147.
[655] "Reports on... shooting." Scott, *Murder of Biggie*, pp.80-83, 157-158.
[656] "Also, within... fled." Sullivan, *LAbyrinth*, pp.142-147.
[657] "Det. Russell Poole... Crips." Sullivan, *LAbyrinth*, pp.147,189,193.
[658] "Filmmaker... murder." Darrin Keene, "Nick Broomfield Blows the Lid Off of Biggie and Tupac," *ChartAttack.com*, October 15, 2002.
wysiwyg://25/http://chartatack.com/damn/2002/10/1502.cfm
[659] Cathy Scott, *The Murder of Biggie Smalls* (New York: St. Martin's Press, 2000), pp.80, 157.
[660] "Further investigation... financing." Scott, *Murder of Biggie*, p.158. Sullivan, *LAbyrinth*, p.146.
[661] Scott, *Murder of Biggie*, pp.155-157.
[662] "Russell Poole... shooting." Sullivan, *LAbyrinth*, p.193.
[663] "While investigating... Smalls." Nick Broomfield, *Biggie and Tupac* (2002, documentary film) and Sullivan, *LAbyrinth*.
[664] "LAPD... investigation." Sullivan, *LAbyrinth*, pp.6, 44,116, 200, 248, 322-4. Broomfield, Biggie and Tupac. On Stallone's project, Joseph Patel, "Actor Will Play LAPD Detective Russell Poole in 'Rampart Scandal.' MTV.com 6/6/03. Conservative forces apparently stopped that project.
[665] "Poole's investigation... investigation." Sullivan, *LAbyrinth*, pp.208-209. Broomfield, *Biggie and Tupac*.
[666] "Biggie's murder... car." Cathy Scott, *The Murder of Biggie Smalls*, pp.1-5, 8, 14-15. Sullivan, *LAbyrinth*, p.120, 136.
[667] "Biggie's friends... leaked." Scott, *Murder of Biggie Smalls*, pp.9-10, 120-1.
[668] Scott, *Murder of Biggie Smalls*, p.120.
[669] "Another witness... murderer." Broomfield, *Biggie and Tupac*. Sullivan, *LAbyrinth*, pp.180-4, 282-3.
[670] "Furthermore, Damien... home." Sullivan, *LAbyrinth*, pp.180-4.
[671] "Furthermore, Damien... home." Sullivan, *LAbyrinth*, pp.180-4.
[672] Scott, *Murder of Biggie Smalls*, p.120 and Sullivan, *LAbyrinth*, p.184.
[673] Broomfield, *Biggie and Tupac*. Sullivan, *LAbyrinth*, pp.282-3. Also see Cathy Scott, *The Murder of Biggie Smalls*, pp.5-6. On Davis, see Sullivan, *LAbyrinth*, p.126.Also, "Investigative Reports: Interview with Cathy Scott," *XXL Magazine*, October, 2000, p.131.
[674] "Other... LA." Nick Broomfield, *Biggie and Tupac*. Also, Sullivan, *LAbyrinth*, pp.279-80.
[675] Chuck Phillips, "Officers May Have Seen rap Killing; Crime: Off-duty Inglewood police member was behind vehicle when rap star Notorious B.I.G. was slain and undercover New York agents were trailing the singe that night, sources say." *The Los Angeles Times*, 4/23/97, B,1:2.
[676] Nick Broomfield, *Biggie and Tupac*
[677] Scott, *The Murder of Biggie Smalls*, pp.94, 128-9. "Investigative Reports: Interview with Cathy Scott," *XXL Magazine*, October, 2000, p.131.
[678] "Evidence placed... scene." See Sullivan, *LAbyrinth*, p.136, and "LAPD photocopies of business cards of Det. Oldham, New York Police Department, and Timothy Reilly, Special Agent, U.S. Department of Treasury, Criminal Investigation Division, with

handwritten notes, dated 3/9/97 1 page." This was under section, "Documents: Biggie Smalls Murder," *LAbyrinth*, pp.313-4. ATF as Division of the Treasury Department, Christopher Lee, "ATF Eyes Bargaining Exemptions," *Washington Post*, 6/24/03, p.A19. Also, Nick Broomfield, *Biggie and Tupac.*

[679] "That the FBI... murdered." Nick Broomfield, *Biggie and Tupac*

[680] "A former Bureau... time." ATF agent Larry Shears in court, on Channel 23, Los Angeles, CA, news broadcast, 12/17/71. Drew McKillips, "Amazing Story by Hell's Angels Chief," *San Francisco Chronicle*, 12/12/72, p.1. "ATF Agent Says He Was Part of Coast Plot to Kill Cesar Chavez," *New York Times*, 1/ 2/72, p.31. All referenced in Alex Constantine, *The Covert War Against Rock* (Los Angeles, CA: Feral House, 2001), pp.55-59. George Bush Sr, oversaw U.S. intelligence when the Hells Angels twice attempted to kill the Rolling Stones and Barger got paroled early due to a Republican senator.Karen Brandel, "Angles in Arizona," *Tuscon Weekly*, 8/15/96, p.1. A.E. Hotchner, *Blown Away: A No-Holds-Barred Portrait of the Rolling Stones and the Sixites Told by the Voices of the Generation* (New York: Fireside, 1990), p.320.
On Newton see, Edward J. Epstein, *Agency of Fear: Opiates and Political Power in America* (New York: G.P. Putnam's Sons, 1977), pp201-201, 207, 213-215. Cited in Huey Newton, *War Against The Panthers* (New York: Harlem River/ Readers and Writers, 1991), pp50-52.

[681] See, for example, *The Federation of American Scientists Military Analysis Network*, "Garden Plot," November 1998. Cited in Frank Morales, "U.S. Has Been Preparing to Turn America into a Military Dictatorship," *What Really Happened*, www.whatreallyhappened.com/suppression.html .

[682] "Police incidentally... story." Sullivan, *LAbyrinth*, p.136.

[683] "But Lil' Cease also said... said he couldn't remember." Nick Broomfield, Biggie and Tupac, 2002. Nick Broomfield interviewed Biggie's friend and rap partner, Lil' Cease, who was present at the murder. Broomfield said that "these are FBI photos," putting them on the film screen. Broomfield then said that, "I called the FBI agent who took the photos. Broomfield addressed him "Hello is that Detective...," blanking out the name with a car horn. But the "FBI agent" responded affirmatively to his title and name, saying "That would be, yes." I was wondering if I could talk to you, because I understand that you were following Biggie Smalls and Puffy Combs at the time of Biggie's... " "Who are you?" My Name's Nick Broomfield and I saw some photographs that I believe you might have taken. What do you do for a living. I'm a documentary filmmaker. Okay. . Let me call you back, I'm in court now." I discovered he was attending Puffy's trial for the night club shooting. I was just wondering what it was that you were investigating at the time?" "Right. Well, I wouldn't discuss it with you." Oh, you wouldn't discuss it, even though it was some time ago. Well it hasn't finished yet." It hasn't finished?"

[684] "Both Hackie and... killed." Sulivan, *LAbyrinth*, pp.192-4. Broomfield, *Biggie and Tupac* (2002). On Alexander's book and film, Frank Alexander with Heidi Siegmund Cuda, *Got Your Back: Protecting Tupac in the world of gangsta rap*. The book appears to be mostly to cover up the damage done by his initial disclosures. But it is interesting that Alexander said and MGM security guard stood next to Orlando Anderson when Tupac and the Death Row entourage attacked him, yet no one was stopped by the police. *Got Your Back,* p.155.

[685] "Thes acounts... Records." Sullivan, *LAbyrinth*, pp.166-7, 284-5.

[686] "The largest apparent... Smalls." Chuck Philips, "Who Killed Tupac Shakur; How a fight between rival Compton gangs turns into a plot of retaliation and murder," *The Los Angeles Times*, September 6, 2002, p.A1. On Phlip's vow to vindicate Knight, Sullivan, *LAbyrinth*, p. 285.

[687] "*Vibe* further... mentioned it." Sam Anson, "Reasonable Doubt," *Vibe*, December, 2002, p.148-156. On Biggie's mom, Voletta Wallace, Salim Muwakkil, "The Sad Saga of Biggie and Tupac," *Chicago Tribune*, 9/16/02, p.1.15.

[688] "*Vanity Fair*... mentioned it." On Biggie's mom see, Salim Muwakkil, "The Sad Saga of Biggie and Tupac; the latest rap on two unsolved murder mysteries fingers a gang element and corrupt cops," *Chicago Tribune*, September 16, 2002, p.1.15. Sam Anson,

"Reasonable Doubt," *Vibe*, December, 2002, p.148-156. Anson has written articles on Tupac Shakur for *Vanity Fair* and *Esquire* magazines. Quotes, *Rolling Stone* and *Vanity Fair* writer Randalll Sullivan. On timeline that contradicts Phillips' account, Geoffrey Gray, "Time Bomb," *Vibe*, December 2002, pp.152-156. The many reprints include: Michele Orecklin, "Who Killed Tupac," *Time* magazine, 9/16/02, p.91. Chuck Philips, "The Rap on B.I.G.: Rival reportedly paid $1M and supplied gun to kill Tupac Shakur," *Newsday*, p.A3.

[689] *Davey D's Hip Hop Corner*, FNV Newsletter, "Former Vibe Writer Kevin Powell Speaks Out…" www.daveyd.com/fnvsept62002.html

[690] Chuck Philips, "An attack on Tupac Shakur launched a hip-hop war," *Los Angeles Times*, 3/17/08. James Rainey, "For the Record: The Times apologizes over article on rapper," *Los Angeles Times* 3/27/08. "For the Record: Times retracts Shakur story, " *Los Angeles Times*, 4/7/08.

[691] "Meanwhile, it seems…him." David Walker and Zach Dundas, "Living and Dying in L.A: Interview with Randalll Sullivan." www.mumblage.com/story.php?id=27

[692] "Furthermore, Death Row's…Division." Sullivan, *LAbyrinth*, pp.180-184, 279-80.

[693] "When Det. Russell…precinct." Sullivan, *LAbyrinth*, pp.205-8. On Rampart Scandal in mainstream news, see Don Terry, "Rackets Law Can Be Used Against Police in Los Angeles," *The New York Times*, August 30, 2000, p.A14. Scott Glover and Matt Lait, "30 L.A. Officers Called to Testify Before Grand Jury," *Los Angeles Times*, 4/14/2000.

[694] "Poole said the…cops did." Sullivan, *LAbyrinth*, pp.201-212, 228. Also see PBS's *Frontline* report crediting Poole and his investigation opening the lid on the Rampart Scandal and how Frontline also suggested that the Rampart Task Force diverted the focus of the corruption away from what Poole originally found. PBS, *Frontline*, "LAPD Blues, Interviews: Detective Russell Poole."
www.pbs.org/wgbh/pages/frontline/shows/lapd/interviews/poole.html .

[695] "The LAPD…still awaits trial." Sullivan, *LAbyrinth*, p.292. While the *LAbyrinth* ends with Poole saying the FBI told him they're investigating Suge Knight in his part in setting up the murder of Tupac and Biggie in 2001, nothing has come of it as of February 2005 as Voletta Wallace's lawsuit against the LAPD awaits trial in April 2005.

[696] "Wallace's…trigger." Nolan Strong, "Victory for B.I.G., Family Closes in on Rogue Cop Theory," 7/8/05, www.allhiphop.com .

[697] "Biggie's family…detective." Associated Press, "Judge Orders LA to pay 1.1M to family of Notorious B.I.G." *Boston Herald.com*, 1/21/06.
http://news.bostonherald.com/national/view.bg?articleid=122328

[698] "A month…off." Randall Sullivan, "The Notorious B.I.G.: The Murder and Cover-up," *Rolling Stone*, 12/15/05, pp.142-4.

[699] "A month…2006." Sullivan, "The Notorious B.I.G.: The Murder and Cover-up," *Rolling Stone*, 12/15/05, pp.138,140,147.

[700] "Filmmaker…murder." Darrin Keene, "Nick Broomfield Blows the Lid Off of Biggie and Tupac," *ChartAttack.com*, October 15, 2002.
wysiwyg://25/http://chartatack.com/damn/2002/10/1502.cfm

[701] "Judges had…murder." Sullivan, *LAbyrinth*, Timeline, pp.301-9. Cathy Scott, *The Murder of Biggie Smalls*, pp.82-4, 97. *Ro, Have Gun Will Travel*, pp.323-4. Broomfield, *Biggie and Tupac*.

[702] Former FBI agent, LA cop, and Tupac's whistleblowing bodyguard Kevin Hackie told Poole that no matter what else he heard, Reggie Wright ran Death Row while Knight was in jail. Sullivan, *LAbyrinth*, p.193.

[703] "Det. Russell…member." Sullivan, *LAbyrinth*, pp.278-9. PBS *Frontline*, "LAPD Blues:The Rampart Scandal Timeline,"
www.pbs.org/wgb/pages/frontline/shows/lapd/scandal/cron.html . Also see, John S. Gordon, U.S. Attorney, Central Distict California press release, "Former LAPD Oficer Raphael Perez Sentenced to Two Years fro Federal Civil Rights Violations," 5/6/02. Matt Lait and Scott Glover, "Secret LAPD Testimony Implicated Nine Officers," *Los Angeles Times*, 2/26/03.

---

[704] Knight gained…jail." Associated Press, "Rap Mogul Out of Jail," 8/7/01. *CBS News.com*. Reuters, "'Suge' Knight Arrested After Police Find Marijuana in Truck," *HighTimes.com*.
[705] "Death Row actions…activism." Veronica Lodge, "Jackin' beats," *Rap Pages*, September 1998, pp.65-71. Also, Cathy Scott, *Biggie*, p.106. Ben Charney, "Family of Tupac Sues Rapper's Bootleg Recordings," December 2, 1999. http://search.newschoice.com/AngTr_storydisplay.asp?story=d:\inetpub\wwwroot\newsarchives\angtr\fpg\19991202\52686_t2as202.txt. Personal interview, Watani Tyehimba, 5/10/00.
[706] Michael Datcher, "The Good Die Young: Snapshotz from the Outlawz Photo Album," *The Source*, October 2000, p.195.
[707] See picture of Snoop with Tupac at rally in ed.s J Hoye and K. Ali, *Tupac: Resurrection*, p.232.
[708] Cathy Scott, *The Murder of Biggie* Smalls (New York: St. Martin's, 2000), p.56.
[709] Ro, *Have Gun Will Travel*, p.119-20. Sullivan, *LAbyrinth*, p.194.
[710] Randalll Sullivan, *LAbyrinth* (New York: Atlantic Monthly Press, 2002), p.194.
[711] "Then Suge…2003." Suge Knight and Death Row website, Nick Broomfield, *Biggie and Tupac*, 2002. Police unarming Snoop's guards, Rodd, McLeod, "Above the Law," July, 2000, *XXL Magazine*, p.86. Gunmen shooting at Snoop's car. Wire Reports, "Snoop Dogg in Convoy of Cars Shot at in LA," *The Baltimore Sun*, April 12, 2003, p.2D.
[712] On Snoop's ban, Roman Wolfe, "Snoop Dogg Permanently Banned From UK," 5/16/06, www.allhiphop.com/hiphopnews On MIA's denied entry, Bhavna Malkani, "British Rapper MIA Denied Entry Into U.S.," 5/26/06, www.allhiphop.com/hiphopnews
[713] "In 2005…2003." Lawrence Van Gelder, "Arts, Briefly: Accuser Drops Rape Case Against Snoop Dogg," *The New York Times*, 8/12/05, p. E5.
[714] "With virtually…Coast." On Kurupt history, see Dan Deluca, "Taking his Rap from Death Row to Phila.\Former Dogg Pound Member Kurupt Has Big Plans: His Own Label, a Double CD, and Forthcoming Collaborations," *The Philadelphia Inquirer*, 10/7/98, p.E1. On real name as Ricardo Brown, *Jr.*see Sullivan, *LAbyrinth*, p. 291. On Jacques Agnant as Ricardo Brown, Sr., see New York vs. 1. Tupac Shakur (M 22) 2. Ricardo Brown (M 30) 3. Charles Fuller (M 23), Defendants, Deposition of Police Officer Craig McKernan by ADA Mourges, 11/19/93. Kurupt was raised by his mother in Philadelphia. While the elder Brown listed his age as 30 in 1993, Warren suggested he was older, believing Tupac first saw Agnant as a substitute father figure. Tupac had a hard time initially accepting that Agnant was likely an agent until after his trial started a year after the sex assault charge.Kurupt was 20 at that time of 1993. Michael Warren's investigations found out Brown, Sr.'s real name of Agnant, as well as his dismissed charges up and down the East Coast.
[715] "Kurupt had moved…time." Deluca, "Taking his Rap from Death Row to Phila…" *Philadelphia Inquirer*, 10/7/98, p.E1. Elon Johnson, "Kurupt is 'Calling Out' DMX," *MTV.com*, 10/8/99. Shaheem Reid, "Kurupt Hits Big Screen, Talks Lisa Lopes Album, Tha Row: Rapper puts music aside for roles on big screen and as senior VP of Tha Row," *MTV.com*, 11/11/02.
[716] "In 2005, police…Afeni Shakur." On Dre, Ronin Ro, *Have Gun Will Travel*, pp269-279. On Eminem and 50 Cent, see Tupac's posthumous CDs, *Tupac: Ressurrection* and Tupac following CD, *Loyal to the Game*.
[717] "The Vibe…threats" Nolan Strong, "Man Who Assaulted Dr. Dre Claims Suge Knight Paid for Punch," 1/16/05 www.AllHipHopNews.com . Johnson's brother also reportedly owed Knight money.
[718] As noted above, one intelligence document a Senate committee found included strategies for use against political musicians, "Intelligence Activities and Rights of Americans," Book II, April 26, 1976, *Senate Committee with Respect to Intelligence Report*. Excerpted in Alex Constantine, *The Covert War Against Rock* (Los Angeles: Feral House, 2001), p.9. U.S. Senate Select Committee to Study Government Operations, *The FBI's Covert Program to Destroy the Black Panther Party*, U.S. Government Printing Office, Washington. D.C. 1976.

[719] "Starting in the... behavior.' " Andrew Lee and Carl Swanson, "NYPD Raps," *New York*, 4/30/01, p.13.
[720] Nicole White and Evelyn McDonnell, "Police Secretly Watching Hip-Hop Artists," *The Miami Herald*, 3/9/04, p.1A. Nicole White and Evelyn McDonnell, "Monitoring of Rap Stars Disputed," *Miami Herald*, 3/17/04, p1B.
[721] Evelyn McDonnell and Nicole White, "Arresting Data in Rap Binder," *Miami Herald*, 5/14/04, p.1B.
[722] "Rock and Rap Confidential... are allowed to perform." Dave Marsh, "And the Beat(ing) Goes On... Counterpunch, 11/9/2002, http://www.counterpunch.org/marsh1109.html Also, www.daveyd.com
[723] Dasun Allah, "NYPD Admits to Rap Intelligence Unit," *The Village Voice*, 3/23/04.
[724] Dasun Allah & Joshua Fahiym Ratcliffe, "Law and Disorder," *The Source*, June 2004, p.44.
[725] Houston Williams, "Former Editor-In-Chief of the The Source Jailed," 5/25/06 www.allhiphop.com/hiphopnews
[726] "Dasun Allah, who... on the rappers.'" Dasun Allah, "The Hiphop Cop," *The Village Voice*, 4/6/04
[727] "The Street Crime... studio." As mentioned in a previous note, this writer had a personal interview with an Officer Heinz of Midtown North precinct, 5/4/99, who inadvertently implicated one of several cops who came to Tupac's Times Square shooting and his sexual assault charge hotel scene. See endnote 231. Also see report of three cops at that scene all at hotel scene, Vibe ed.s Tupac Shakur, p.41. Salvatore Arena, "Sex Tapes Erased, Says Shakur Lawyer," *Daily News*, November 24, 1993. On refusing surveillance videotape, Cathy Scott, *The Murder of Biggie Smalls* (New York: St. Martin's Press, 2000), p.65.
[728] Dasun Allah, "The Hiphop Cop," *The Village Voice*, 4/6/04
[729] "Events support... owner." Nicole White and Evelyn McDonnell, "Police Secretly Watching Hip-Hop Artists," *Miami Herald*, 3/9/04, p.1A.
[730] Nicole White and Evelyn McDonnell, "Police Secretly Watching Hip-Hop Artists," *Miami Herald*, 3/9/04, p.1A.
[731] Broomfield, *Biggie and Tupac*, and Sullivan, LAbyrinth, pp. 136, 314.
[732] "But Congress... into rivalries.'" As noted above, one intelligence document a Senate committee found included strategies for use against political musicians such as "Intelligence Activities and Rights of Americans," Book II, April 26, 1976, *Senate Committee with Respect to Intelligence Report.* Excerpted in Alex Constantine, The Covert War Against Rock (Los Angeles: Feral House, 2001), p.9. U.S. Senate Select Committee to Study Government Operations, *The FBI's Covert Program to Destroy the Black Panther Party*, U.S. Government Printing Office, Washington. D.C. 1976.
[733] "A radical... videos." Michael Franti with Amy Goodman, Democracy Now, broadcast on FISTV, Comcast Cable Ch.5, Baltimore, MD, 5/16/03, 7:30 p.m. On friend of Tupac's, Franti told this writer in discussion as he stopped in New York on activist tour funded by Zach De La Rocha in 2000.
[734] "While U.S. Intelligence... Killa.'" On the FBI's fax campaign to get police canceling NWA shows, see Bruce C. Brown, "Quayle Boosts 'Cop Killer' Campaign," *Washington Post*, 6/20/92, pp.B1,5. Cited in Barry Shank, "Fears of the White Unconcious: Music, Race, and Identification in the Censorship of 'Cop Killer.'" *Radical History Review* #66, Fall 1996. On Tupac, see Vibe eds *Tupac Shakur* (New York: Crown, 1997) p.46. On Paris, see "Sonic Jihad release from Paris," http://polsong.gcal.ac.uk/news_archive.html . Also see attempted use against Jimi Hendrix, Harry Shapiro and Caesar Glebbeek, *Jimi Hendrix: Electric Gyspy* (New York: St. Martin's Griffin, 1995) pp.190, 426.
[735] Personal interview with Rage Against the machine lead singer, Zach De La Rocha, May 5, 1999.
[736] This writer attended that Rage Against the Machine benefit concert, just outside New York City in New Jersey. Radio stations such as KROK discussed police attempts to cancel the show in 2000.

---

[737] "U.S. Intelligence...Nation." On Carson as founding member of Republic of New Afrika, see Dasun Allah, "Sonny Carson Dies: Legendary Black Nationalist Figure in Bedford-Stuyvesant," *Village Voice*, 1/1-1/7/03. www.villagevoice.com On, Zulu Nation, personal interview, this author heard Zulu nation founder Afrika Bambata say this at the Third Black Panther Film Festival at CUNY in New York City, 2002, then talked briefly with him afterwards. On Zulu's worldwide status see, Shaila Dewan, "At a Live Homage, Hip-Hop Is King but 'Rapping" is Taboo," New York Times, November 13, 2000, p.B3. Also see articles on Zulu Nation at www.daveyd.com which said the Zulu Nation had 10,000 members.

[738] "U.S. Intelligence had many... break up." Andy Soages, "Hip Hop Fridays: Vibes of the Pro Black: A Conversation of Brother J. of X-Clan Part 1 (May 27-30), 2005. www.blackelectorate.com

[739] Personal interviews with June of Shaka Shakur's Maroon Records and "Panther Cub" Orlando Green, who also organizes the Hip Hop Convention www.hiphopconvention.org 3/4/06. In an interview with Davey D, Porfessor Griff also claimed that Public Enemy's former Def Jam label claimed that the group owed them $2 million. He further said that the industry changed the laws making sampling of other's music require royalty payments and that this went into effect retroactively. http://odeo.com/audio483066/view

[740] "In 1999, events... survived." Peter Noel, "A Bullet for Big Baby Jesus," *Village Voice*, 2/2/99, pp.45-6.

[741] "Possibly using... fled." Most details of this event described in Noel, *Village Voice*, 2/2/99, pp.45-6. On cops shooting at ODB in Street Crime Unit, see *Vibe*, May 1999. Noel, *Village Voice*, cited a Criminal Court complaint saying that these cops were part of the Street Crime Unit.

[742] "Other cops... vest." Patrice O'Shaughnessy, "Rapper Vows Suit, Sez Cops Did Him Dirty in Shooting," New York's *Daily News*, February 5, 1999, p.4. *Vibe*, May 1999. Noel, *Village Voice*, 2/2/99, pp.45-6. On arrest for vest, Associated Press, "Rapper's in the Clink," New York *Daily News*, 3/11/99, p.3.

[743] "Also, in 2000... a crime." Frank Owen, "The Rap Group and the Rat; Gunrunning, the Feds, and the Wu-Tang Clan," *The Village Voice*, May 30, 2000, pp.43-48. Caruso disclosed being personal manager for two Wu Tang rappers. "Music Matters; Family Ties," *The Source*, October 2000, p.56

[744] "Music Matters; Family Ties," *The Source*, October 2000, p.56. Frank Owens, "Letters: Response," The *Village Voice*, June 13, 2000, p.6.

[745] Nolan Strong, "Ol' Dirty Bastard Dead," 11/12/04. Roman Wolfe, "Ol' Dirty Died From Cocaine and Prescription Painkillers," 12/15/04. Both from *AllHipHop.com*: News. The listed painkiller was Tramidol.

[746] Odd names do run in the family but his appears to have a positive purpose. Remmie Fresh, "Family, Friends, Say Goodbye to Ol' Dirty Bastard," *AllHipHop.com: News* 11/19/04.

[747]"Police groups... blacks." Chisun Lee, "Taking the Rap; City Clubs Ban Hip Hop Radicals," *The Village Voice*, 9/12/00, pp.47-8. pp.47-8. See quote on FOP and PBA by Police lieutenant Eric Adams, president of 100 Blacks in Law Enforcement Who Care.

[748] "The PBA... Committee." On PBA hounding Dead Prez, Chisun Lee, "Taking the Rap; City Clubs Ban Hip Hop Radicals," *The Village Voice*, 9/12/00, pp.47-8. On Dead Prez supporting Uhuru Movement, this writer saw him speak of his support at the 3rd Black Panther Film Fest, NYC, 2003.

[749] "Other rap... him." On Riley's activism, see www.speakoutnow.org/People/BootsRiley.html On Jackson and his murder, see Houston Williams, "Paris Not Dead, Memer of The Coup Killed," 11/17/05 www.allhiphop.com/hiphopnews

[750] "By 2001,... neighborhoods." Hip-Hop Summit Action Network, www.hsan.org/Content/main.aspx?pageid=27

[751] Kristin Jones, "Rocking the Hip-Hop Vote," *The Nation*, 12/1/03, p.7-8.

[752] Lola Ogunnaike, "Soldier of Fortune," *Vibe*, December, 2002, p.101

[753] Felicia Lee, Hip Hop is Enlisted in Social Causes," *New York Times*, p.B9.

[754] For one of many examples, Baltimore news channels covered his speech against Bush's Patriot Act and interviewed him on 4/17/03.
[755] Scott, Murer of Biggie Smalls, p.192. Katherine Finkelstein, "Hip Hop Star Cleared of Charges in Shooting at Manhattan Club," The New York Times, March 17, 2001, p. A1, B2. Peter Noel, "The 'Bad Boy' Curse," *Village Voice*, April 3, 2001, p.45
[756] He donated much money, giving $500,000 to the largely Black college he attended, Howard University, $50,000 to the 100 Black Men think tank, as well as $125,000 for his after-school and summer programs out of the Harlem YMCA. He further donated a100 computers in Harlem and fed 30,000 as part of an Atlanta project started by civil rights leaders. Scott, Murder of Biggie, pp.166. Peter Noel, "Guns, Bribes, and Benjamins," *Village Voice*, December 12, 2000, p.53. Karen Hunter, "Wrist Slapped Puffy a Magnet for Tribulation," *Daily news*, 1/15/01, p.8. The 10 Black Men think tank rejected Puffy's donation to avoid bad publicity since a member of the think tank, attorney Johnnie Cochran, represented Puffy.
[757] Cathy Scott, The Murder of Biggie Smalls, pp.94, 129. *Rock and Rap Confidential* Dave Marsh reported that New York cops put rappers under surveillance and quoted hip-hop journalist, Davey D, about national rap surveillance and banning of rap shows. On FBI arrest, see Randalll Sullivan, *LAbyrinth* (New York: Atlantic Monthly Press, 2002), p.289. Cathy Scott reported the criminal mischief conviction as '96, Cathy Scott, *The Murder of Biggie Smalls* (New York: St. Martin's, 2000), pp.188-9.
[758] See "Puffy's Studio Hit by Street Shooting," MTV.Com news, cited in Tina Johnson, "Kurupt's Security Guard Killed, Two Other Injured in Studio Shooting," www.mtv.com/news/articles/1431071/19991018.story.jhtml .
[759] "Combs ahd helped... bystanders." Dan Barry and Juan Forero, "Between High Life and Street Life," The New York Times, December 29, 1999, p.B1.
[760] "Prosecution ended... robbing Combs." Katherine Finkelstein, "Judge in Combs Case Permits Statement by Missing Witness," *New York Times*, 3/6/01, B2.
[761] "The DA... Cochran." Peter Noel, "Daddy Under the Gun," *Village Voice*, January 9, 2001, p.21.
[762] Nick Broomfield, *Biggie and Tupac,* 2002.
[763] Heard by this writer on WB11 News at 11p.m., 3/14/01.
[764] "A veteran... time." Noel "Daddy Under the Gun," *Village Voice,* p.21
[765] "Furthermore, police... innocence." Barbara Ross and Leo Standora, "Puffy Linked to Gunshot," *Daily News*, January 10, 2001, p.7.
[766] "On March... sentence." Katherine Finkelstein, "Hip Hop Star Cleared of Charges in Shooting at Manhattan Club," *The New York Times*, March 17, 2001, p. A1, B2.
[767] "Shooting victim... time." Katherine Finkelstein and Dexter Filkins, "Combs Trial Jurors Consider Gun Case Against Rap Star," *New York Times*, 3/15/01, p.B3.
[768] Jody Miller and Ellen Golden, "Record Breaking Houston Hip-Hop Summit Registers & Encourages Over 20,000 Youth to Vote," 2/3/04. Also see, Jody Miller and Ellen Golden, "St. Louis Hip-Hop Summit Announces 114,000 New Voter Registrations in Missouri," 2/23/04. www.hsan.org
[769] "That year... home" Nolan Strong, "Kimora Lee Simmons Arrested," 7/28/04, *All HipHop.com*: News.
[770] Clover Hope and Clarence Burke Jr. "AHH Stray News: Kimora Pleads Guilty," 8/10/05 www.allhiphop.com/hiphopnews
[771] "New York Targeting... under surveillance." Professor Griff, *Analytixz: 20 years of conversations and enterviews with Public Enemy's Minister of Information* (Atlanta, GA: Rathsi/Heirz to the Shah, 2009). Regarding: Surveillance of Public Enemy p.79; Toure email ending career of Public Enemy, p.110, gas causing explosion (note that Griff's studio was in his house and all his belongings were sadly lost)pp.197-8, poisoning of Griff p.33, shooting at Griff's office p.123 comments against Jews p.63, Creating Bridging the Gap between Blacks and Jews p.106, Aiding Free Mumia movment, It's stated in book along with a Mumia essay. This writer of FBI War on Tupac has also talked several times with the head of the Free Mumia movement, Pam Africa, about this.

[772] Personal interview with attorney, Murray Richman. Articles covering videotape supporting Jay-Z include kris ex, "Jay Z: The Trial and Tribulations of S. Carter," *Vibe*, February 2000, p.136. The record producer was Lance "Un" Rivera.
[773] "Jay-Z is hardly... acquitted." Kim Odorio, "Police is Watching," *The Source*, July 2001, p.49. Regarding other mentioned rappers in this paragraph, the writer of this Tupac essay has found what appear to be frivolous arrests of many of them but a lack of space and time precludes more research on them.
[774] DMX may have shown his political leanings in collaborating with top radical activist band Rage Against the Machine. Shaheem Reid, "DMX Teams Up With Rage Against the Machine," MTV News: Headlines, 8/5/02,
http://www.mtc.com/nes/articles/1456432/20020802/dmx.jhtml?headlines=true
[775] Shaheem Reid, "DMX Teams Up With Rage Against the Machine," MTV News: Headlines, 8/5/02,
http://www.mtc.com/nes/articles/1456432/20020802/dmx.jhtml?headlines=true
[776] "Evidence also supports... charges." Jacob Ogles, "Hard Knock News: Where's DMX's Dogs At," Vibe, October, 1999, p.73.
[777] "The following year... it wasn't DMX's." Rodd McLeod, "Above the Law," XXL Magazine, July 2000, p.86. Also, personal interview with Murray Richman, 7/12/2000.
[778] Shaheem Reid, with Larua Lazin, "Eminem: Reconstructing Tupac," mtv.com. www.mtv.com/bands/t/tupac/news_feature_102703/ . On Tupac film in top 10, Nielson, New York Times movies.nytimes.com/pages/movies/boxofffice/weekend_us/index.html .
[779] "Names and Faces," *The Washington Post*, 12/6/03, p.C3.
[780] Shaheem Reid, with Larua Lazin, "Eminem: Reconstructing Tupac," mtv.com. www.mtv.com/bands/t/tupac/news_feature_102703/
[781] Michael Kane, "Hip-Hop and the 911 Truth Movement," Guerilla News Network, 12/22/04. This article discusses many rappers who blamed the Bush administration for 9/11 in their raps, including Jadakiss, Paris, Immortal Technique, Mos Def, etc. Immortal Technique did a particularly eloquent job in his rap with samples of Mos Def, Eminem, Jadakiss, etc, titled "Bin Laden."
http://www.gnn.tv/print/1016/Hip_Hop_and_the_9_11_Truth_Movement
[782] *The Source*, February 2004. CEO of The Source is Dave Mays and the next highest position as Editor in Chief is Ray "Benzino" Scott. An editor quit in 2005, due to the heavihandedness of Mays and Scott, Aqua Boogie, "The Source's Editor-In-Chief Resigns," 8/16/05, www.allhiphop.com/hiphopnews
[783] The writer of this book took a University of Pennsylvania Masters of Social Work class titled American Racism and Social Welfare with Prof. Rufus Sylvest Lynch, PhD, who presented this idea with much supportive evidence.
[784] While all of America has varying degrees of racism, Eminem attended all Black schools along with having virtually all-Black friends and music collaborators throughout his life.
[785] "Starting at... death (Ch.40)." On Obie Trice, Associated Press, "Emimen's friend killed in nightclub shooting on Eight Mile Rd," *Star Tribune*, 4/11/06. www.StartTribune.com . On Proof, see EM News, "Proof Shot to Death Outside Detroit Club," 4/11/06. www.allabouteninem.com/news.html . On 4 million in sales, AP, "Rapper killed in nightclub shooting," *CNN.com* 4/11/06.
[786] "Details... Tupac (Ch.s11,18)." On former U.S. Army, Nolan Strong, "Man Suspecte of Fatally Shooting Rapper Proof Surrenders, Pool Game May Have Sparked Fight," 4/12/06, www.allhiphop.com/hiphopnews On three shots fired in chest and head, Lawrence Van Gelder, "Arts, Briefly: Rapper Who Was Killed Fired First Shot, Police Say," *New York Times*, 4/14/06, p.E5.
[787] On MTV's Video Music Awards incident, yotube.com carried a video of the incident seen by this author. Also see Minister of Information JR, "Mos Def goes to court for POCC MOD Aaron Patterson," 8/1/07. http:blog.myspace.com/P.O.C.C. On work with Hip-Hop Summit Action Network see, for example, "Global Hip Hop Summit and Jam Session 2006," http://commitments.clinton.org/projects.htm?mode+view&rid=42905

---

[788] "Also, women...*Malcolm X*." A former model accused Hip Hop Summit Action Network board chair, Damon Dash, of rape, saying it occurred a year earlier. "Dash of Controversy," *The Source*, March 2004, p.42. A Temple University employee accused Bill Cosby of groping her a year earlier Glenn Collins, "Cosby to Be Questioned," *New York Times*. And a makeup artist filed a $25 million lawsuit accusing Snoop Dogg of raping her two years after the alleged incident occurred Nolan Strong, "Makeup Artist Files a $25 million Rape Lawsuit Against Snoop," 2/1/05, www.AllHipHopNews.com . On Cosby, Democratic Socialist Princeton University Professor Cornel West said Bill Cosby has been a friend of the peoples' struggle for years. Joseph Phillips, " The Cosby Firestorm Just Won't Die," Drumbeats Magazine 6/3/04 www.dvercity.com/drumbeats_entertainment.html

[789] From Wire Reports, "Run-DMC D.J. Killed in Shooting at Studio," The Sun, October 31, 2002, p.3A.

[790] "Witnesses said... shooting." On JMJ, Andy Newman and Al Baker, "Was It a Bad Business Deal Or a Music Industry Fued?" *New York Times*, p.B4. On Tupac's watch, Vibe ed.s *Tupac Shakur*, p.41. A Special Forces Group military commander described how after dropping the assassination victim with the first shot, he then puts two bullets in their head. Stephen Kinzer, "Commandos Left a Calling Card: Their Absence," *New York Times*, 9/26/01, p. B6.

[791] Shaheem Reid and Jim Fraenkel, with Rahman Dukes and Tim Kash, "Who Shot Jam Master Jay? Were Killers Caught on Video?" MTV News, 12/13/07. www.mtv.com/news/articles/1576390/20071213l/jam_master_jay.jhtml

[792] "Manufactured murderous rivalries... 60s." U.S. Senate Select Committee to Study Government Operations, *The FBI's Covert Program to Destroy the Black Panther Party*, U.S. Government Printing Office, Washington. D.C. 1976. Also see copies of FBI memorandums dated 2/2/71 sent to about 30 offices that attempts to split Newton and Cleaver as well as an Airtel memo that attempts to split Newton and Afeni Shakur's New York Panther 21, Churchill and Vander Wall, *The COINTELPRO Papers*, pp.160-1. M. Newton told how this was turned into an East Vs. West Panther war, *Bitter Grain*, p.203.

[793] From Wire Reports, "Run-DMC D.J. Killed in Shooting at Studio," The Sun, October 31, 2002, p.3A.

[794] A. Newman & A. Baker, "Was It a Bad Business Deal Or... Feud?" *New York Times*, p.B4.

[795] Nolan Strong, "Police Say Rap War Could Be Brewing in the Mid West," 11/10/04 www.AllHipHopNews.com .

[796] "This was the... LAPD." Sullivan, *LAbyrinth*, p.262. Broomfield, Biggie and Tupac. On Wallace's wrongful death suit, see Launch News Nework, "The Notorious B.I.G. Estate Cleared to Move Forward with LAPD Lawsuit," http://music.yahoo.com/read/news/12062379 .

[797] "Five months... station." Julia Preston, "Prosecutor Says Lil' Kim Lied to Protect 2 of Her Associates," *New York Times*, 3/2/05, p.B6. Clove Hope and Nolan Strong, "Lil' Kim Found Guilty," *AllHipHop.com.*

[798] "Several articles provide... still reign.'" Alice McQuillan, "Rap Wars: Gunfire After Rap Party," *Daily News*, pp.1, 3. Alice McQillan, Ralph Ortega & Corky Siemaszako, "Foxy Vs. Lil' Kim: Shootout is Blamed on Feud," *Daily News*, 2/26/01, pp. 1,2 & 3.

[799] Alice McQuillan, Rap Wars: Gunfire After Rap Party," *Daily News*, pp.1, 3. Alice McQillan, Ralph Ortega & Corky Siemaszako, "Foxy Vs. Lil' Kim: Shootout is Blamed on Feud," *Daily News*, pp. 1,2 & 3. Also see the way the District Attorney used the above shooting incident against Lil' Kim or years. The DA tried to charge her with perjury and obstruction of justice as of 2005. Julia Preston, "Security Tape Shows Lil' Kim Next to Manager Before Shooting," *The New York Times*, 3/3/05, p..B8.

[800] "When the... street.'" Cruz, "Lil' Kim's Trial Proceeds... Testify," http://www..i.kimstyle.com/main.html .

[801] "Lil'... incident." Yves Salomon, "Lil' Cease Arrested and Questioned About Shootout," http://music .yahoo.com/read/news/12032051 . Yves Erwin Salomon, "Lil' Kim's Former Manager Headed to Jail," http://music.yahoo.com/read/news/12053708 .

[802] "Like Tupac Shakur's…press)." Julia Preston, "Lil' Kim Guilty of Telling Lies About Gunfight: Jury Acquits Rapper of Obstruction Charge," *New York Times*, 3/18/05, pp.B1, 6. Lola Ogunnaike, "Prospect of Jail May Enhance a Rap Resume," *New York Times*, 3/18/05, p. B6.
[803] Meanwhile, more legal cases came upon Foxy Brown. Nail salon workers charged Brown with misdemeanor assault, claiming she struck them with a cell phone in a dispute over payment for a manicure in August of 2004. Hip-Hop Summit Action Network's Dr. Benjamin Muhammad (formerly Chavis) watched in support of Brown in court as a judge ordered her handcuffed to a court bench. As of January 2006, Brown still faced sentencing, with sources saying she could receive up to a year in jail. Brown also strangely lost her hearing for many months around that time. On hearing loss and Chavis in court with Brown, see Houston Williams, "Foxy Brown Nearly Totally Deaf," 12/6/05 and Eben Gregory and Nolan Strong, "HSAN's Min. Ben Offers Eyewitness Account of Foxy Brown Incident, Chastises Judge," 12/24/05 www.allhiphop.com/hiphopnews . On Brown facing one year sentence, "Foxy Brown Turns Down Second Plea Deal for Salon Assault," 8/7/05, www.ballerstatus.net . "Arts, Briefly: Can You Hear Me Now?" *The New York Times,* p.A18, 1/19/08.
[804] "Eminem, Nas Speak Out at Hip-Hop Summit in Detroit," LAUNCH Radio Network, 4/28/03, http://music.yahoo.com/read/news/12030387 Young Noble, from Tupac's backup group The Outlawz, said this in "2Pac: straight spittin'" *XXL Magazine* October 2003, pp.121.
[805] "Such seemingly… them." Bonsu Thompson, *XXL* magazine, April 2001, pp.91-103.
[806] On arrests, Andrew Dansby, "Nas Arrested for Assault: Rapper accused of throwing bottle in club," 12/18/03 www.rollingstone.com Shaheem Reid, "Nas Shrugs Off Kelis Arrest, Gets His 'Greedy On' With Tour, New Album," www.mtv.com 3/12/07. On gunshots from crowd despite 100 security guards with metal detectors, Stephany Jourdrey, "Shots Fired During Nas Concert in London," 3/22/05, Chartattack.com She cited *NME.com*, the website of one of the top British music magazine's, *New Music Express*. One report wrote about a man shooting from the stage and rumor of Nas somehow behind it was worded as "Nas was heard boasting that he had made everyone look, which he apparently believed would make the audience 'slaves' to the pages in his rhyme book." Posted by jsmooth995 3/21/05, www.hiphopmusic.com/archives/000905.html
[807] On Kanye West, see Reuters, "Two shot at Kanye West concert," CNN.com 3/1/06. Also see, CBC Arts, "Ushers shot at Kanye West concert in U.K." 5/1/06, Canadian Broadcasting Corporation www.cbc.ca
[808] See, for example, Steve Jones, "GCHQ—Government Communications Headquarters: Europes most powerful intelligence gathering agency." 10/6/05. http://globalresearch.ca GCHQ is Europe's version of America's National Security Agency (NSA). One former MI6 agent (British CIA), James Casbolt, said that MI6 actually oversees the CIA and other Intelligence agencies. This would make sense in terms of British's centuries-longer Intelligence history, though it would mean that the U.S. corporate dominance has no allegiance to its own country. James Casbolt, "MI6 Are the Lords of the Global Drug Trade," 5/20/06, available on a number of websites, such as http://z13.invisionfree.com/THE_UNHIVED_MIND
[809] Lisa de Moraes, "Kanye West's Torrent of Criticism, Live on NBC," www.washingtonpost.com 9/3/05. "Star says rap is 'too homophobic,' " *BBC News*, 8/19/05. Alicia Chang, Associated Press, "Records: Doctor arrested for DUIs, targeted by malpractice suits," *North County Times,* 11/14/07. "West Autopsy: 'Cause of Death is Inconclusive," San Francisco Gate, www.sfgate.com 11/14/07. "50 Cent Reignites West Feud," Rapweekly.com 8/31/07. Shaheem Reid, "Jay-Z, Kanye West, 50 Cent, Diddy, TI, Ciara, Swizz Beatz Make Hip-Hop History at NYC Show," www.mtv.com 8/23/07. It's interesting to note that the article by Chang said that the plastic surgeon doing the procedure, Jan Adams, MD, had two DUIs and was thus would have been more susceptible to influence by the police. This doctor had also been the subject of two malpractice suits. But no other support has been found to suggest that Adams was

directly involved in any foul play. Another doctor did say that she refused West for plastic surgery unless West had a physician clear her since she had a heart condition that could cause a heart attack during surgery. On lawsuits against West, Associated Press, "Kanye West Sued by Chicago Deejay," www.foxnews.com 11/10/05. Associated Press, "Evil Knievel Sues Kanye West over video," www.msnbc.com 12/12/06. Associated Press, "Evel Knievel, Kanye West Settle Lawsuit," abcnews.go.com. Associated Press, "Kanye West Sued Over Car Lease Deal," www.washingtonpsot.com 5/10/06.

[810] "Another example showed... them." On media instigation, see Nolan Strong, "Jadakiss Responds to 50 Cent," AllHipHop.Com, 3/10/2003. William Rashbaum, "Police Heighten Scrutiny of Rap Performers," *New York Times*, 3/3/05, p.B6. Also see the way the District Attorney used the above shooting incident against Lil' Kim. On quick end to 50 Cent and The Game's feud, see Lola Ogunnaike, "Feuding Rappers Make Peace, and Donations, " *New York Times*, 3/10/05, p.B1.

[811] "Hip Hop... Harlem." William Rashbaum, "Police Heighten Scrutiny of Rap Performers," *New York Times*, 3/3/05, p.B6. Also see the way the District Attorney used the above shooting incident against Lil' Kim. On quick end to 50 Cent and The Game's feud, see Lola Ogunnaike, "Feuding Rappers Make Peace, and Donations, " *New York Times*, 3/10/05, p.B1.

[812] "By May of 2005, gunmen... possession." On police having the men under surveillance and waiting 90 minutes after the shooting to make the arrest, Warren Woodberry, Jr. and Jonathan Lemire, "50 Cent Pals get popped," New York Daily News, 5/20/05. On Pressley "trading fire" Nolan Strong, "Alleged Members of G-Unit Wounded in Shootout In Queens," 5/23/05, *ALLHIPHOP.com*. Strong said that Pressley traded fire "despite the presence of police." While these articles revealed important details, neither of these articles stated the exact charges. *The New York Post*, on the other hand, left out details except that it gave the exact charges of weapons possession. Muray Weiss, Michael White and Phillip Messing, "Rap War Bust," *New York Post online edition.*. "Vioence Erupts Outside of Two NY Clubs," *Eurweb.com* said the arresting officers were members of the NYPD Gang Unit.

[813] William Webster, *The City in Crisis: A Report by the Special Advisor tot eh Board of Police Commissioners on the Civil Disorder in Los Angeles*, Los Angeles, 10/21/92, two volumes. Cited in Mike Davis, "Who Killed Los Angeles? Part 2," *New Left Review*, 198, '93, p.32. Also, *Los Angeles Times*, 3/17/93, cited in Davis, "Who Killed Los Angeles?" *New Left Review*, p.32

[814] "Rampart police also... division." Regarding Scott Enyart, pp.619-621, Bill Boyarsky, *Los Angeles Times*, 7/9/96in James DiEugenio, "The Curious Case of Dan Moldea," ed.s James DiEugenio and Lisa Pease, *The Assassinations*, (Los Angels, Feral House, 2003) pp.619-21. Also see, Pease, "The RFK Plot Part I" *The Assassinations*, pp.544,546, 548, 553, 554. On CIA operation vs. RFK, see *The Assassinations*, pp. 530-633. Los Angeles Times columnist z Bill Boyarsky ridiculed the city's use of private lawyers in that suit. Could they have been worried that a DA representative hunting around the Rampart Division might have stumbled upon Death Row cop's illicit activities?

[815] "Rampart, one... RFK." Rampart as one of 18 LAPD divisions, see Sullivan, *LAbyrinth*, pp.29. On most blatant CIA cover-up, see Ed.s James DiEugenio and Lisa Pease, *The Assassinations*, (Los Angels, Feral House, 2003), p.530.

[816] William Pepper, "An Act of State: The Execution of Martin Luther King: Talk given at Modern Times Bookstore, San Francisco, CA," 2//4/03 p.5 www.ratical.org/ratville/JFK/WFP020403.html

[817] "Other experts involved... shot." Los Angeles *Herald-Examiner*, 5/13/74, cited in Turner and Christian, *Kennedy*, p.162.

[818] See, for example, sworn statement to Vince Bugliosi by eyewitness, Martin Patruski, 12/12/75, and Turner and Christian, Kennedy, pp.350-1. Also,

[819] "The Los Angeles... court." On official LAPD investigative report, see copy of it in William Turner and Jonn Christian, *The Assassination of Robert F. Kennedy: The Conspiracy and Coverup* (New York: Thunders Mouth Press, 1993), Appendix, pp.376-7. On Harper's affidavit, see copy of it in Turner an Christian, pp.378-9. On Harper's

U.S. Intelligence work, he was in the CIA precursor, OSS, Pease, "RFK Plot Part I," *Assassinations*, p.565. Pease cited researchers' findings of different types of bullets used at the scene, pp.556-562. For example, see witness Martin Patrusky's signed statement in Turner and Christian, *The Assassination of Robert f. Kennedy*, p.350; cited in Pease, "RFK Plot Part I," *Assassinations*, p.550. William Harpsaid the bullets he examined weren't fired from the same gun." Pease, "RFK Plot Part I," *Assassinations*, p.555-7, 560-1.

[820] Reports first cited at least two shooting suspects as well as several people shot. Turner and Christian, pp.167-8, sourcing a KFWB transcript, & Paul Hope, "Senator Felled in Los Angeles; 5 Others Shot," *The Evening Star*, 6/5/68. Both cited in Pease, "The RFK Plot Part II," *Assassinations*, pp.534, 602-3. These reports were quoted from LAPD files, radio broadcasts and even Intelligence Division log entries, with witness names and dates provided. Pease, "RFK Plot Part I," *Assassinations*, pp.544-5.

[821] "One pair of notable...*Helter Skelter*." William Turner, The Assassination of Robert F. Kennedy: The Conspiracy and Coverup (New York:Thunder's Mouth Press,1978,93). See about the authors. On Bugliosi, see pp.10, 243-4.

[822] "While that...assassination." Turner and Christian, *The Assassination of Robert F. Kennedy*, pp.60, 64-66 (*Kennedy*, herein). On John Birch report they cite the group's national public relations director, John Rousselot. On LAPD admissions to CIA work, the cite LAPD Detectives Chief Hugh McDonald's consistent talk about his CIA work in Hugh McDonald, *Appointment in Dallas* (New York: Hugh C. McDonald Publishing, 1975). On other CIA training of local police, Morton Kondracke, *The Chicago Sun-Times*, 2/8/73, both in *Kennedy*, pp.64-6. On LAPD's RFK investigation members, Lt. Manuel Pena and Sgt. Enrique "Hank" Hernandez, see Robert Houghton, the LAPD Detectives Chief who replaced McDonald and headed the RFK investigation team called *Special Unit Senator*. Robert Houghton, *Special Unit Senator* (New York: Random House, 1970), pp.95-6. Turner and Christian's final and best source Manuel Pena who truly controlled the LAPD's RFK team was an old Turner colleague who headed the FBI investigation on the RFK event, Roger LaJeunesse. He said the LAPD excluded his group and revealed Pena as CIA. *Kennedy*, pp.62-5.

[823] Turner and Christian's...scene." Lonny Worthey, interview 6/7/68, unpaginated in FBI Summary Report by Special Agent Amedee Richards, Jr., 8/1/69. Susanne Locke interviewed 6/7/68, pp.405-5, FBI Summary report. Cathy Sue Fulmer, interview 6/8/68, unpaginated section of Summary Report. Sandra Serrano, interview 6/8/68, in Summary Report pp.464-7. Darmell Johnson, 6/7/68, pp.406-9. Thomas Dipierro, interviewed 6/8/68, pp.432-34. George Green, interviewed 6/7/68, unpaginated section of Report. All in Turner and Christian, *Kennedy*, pp.68-73.

[824] "Oliver Stone... fired." On *Probe*, DiEugenio and Pease, Preface, *Assassinations*, pp.xii-xiii.. On bullets and victims, Pease, "The RFK:Plot Part 1: The Grand Illusion," *Assassinations*, pp.540-43. On other witnesses seeing more suspects, see, for example, LAPD interview of Roy Mills, 8/9/68. Joe Klein, interviewed by LAPD, 7/3/68. Pease, *Assassinatioins*, p.545.

[825] "Pease...holes." On *Probe*, DiEugenio and Pease, Preface, *Assassinations*, pp.xii-xiii.. On bullets and victims, Pease, "The RFK:Plot Part 1: The Grand Illusion," *Assassinations*, pp.540-43. On other witnesses seeing more suspects, see, for example, LAPD interview of Roy Mills, 8/9/68. Joe Klein, interviewed by LAPD, 7/3/68. Pease, *Assassinatioins*, p.545.

[826] "In agreement... cover-up." See photos on inserted photo pages:10,11,12. Credits for these photos were 6/5/68, Official LAPD photo, AP Wirephoto, Los Angeles County Coroner's Office, and Official FBI Photos taken under supervision of Special Agent Al Grenier and verified by Special Agent William Bailey. Turner and Christian, *The Assassination of Robert F. Kennedy*. Also see pp.180-81, 316-17.

[827] "Aiding... assassination." See photos on inserted photo pages:10,11,12. Credits for these photos were 6/5/68, Official LAPD photo, AP Wirephoto, Los Angeles County Coroner's Office, and Official FBI Photos taken under supervision of Special Agent Al

Grenier and verified by Special Agent William Bailey. On sworn statements to Vince Bugliosi, see pp.180-81, 316-17, 345-47. Copies of statements in appendix.
[828] "This security… times.'" Turner and Christian, *Kennedy*, pp.161, 165-6. Schulman's testimony and statements, along with similar witness statements, were introduced at official hearings in Los Angeles Superior Court in late 1975. Pease citd Schulman first making part of this statement in a radio interview on 6/5/68 and then repeating it in the District Attorney's office in 1971. Pease, *Assassinations*, p.545. Cesar first said he had told a police sergeant about his .22 gun when he was interviewed after the assassination, but then he said he must have been mistaken as he had already sold it. His revised statements was cited by Turner/Christian from a reporter's transcript, Room 113, Bureau of Investigation, DA's Office, 524 North Spring St., Los Angeles, 7/14/71, pp.47-8. In *Kennedy*, p.165. Also see dogged investigato, Ted Charach, who produced the documentary, *The Second Gun*.
[829] "Another of many… Wolfer." Lisa Pease, "The RFK Plot Part 1: The Grand Illusion," pp.544-5, and "RFK Plot Part II: Rubik's Cube," pp.602-6. In DiEugenio and Pease ed.s *The Assassinations*. The above book cites Noguchi detailing this for his book *Coroner*. On Cesar's security clearance to work at CIA site, see interview with fellow employee and engineer, Jim Yoder, who sold Cesar a gun,Turner and Christian, *Kennedy*, p.Ted Charach, who produced the Golden Globe nominated documentary claiming Thane Cesar killed Kennedy, showed a picture of Noguchi at a press conference reenacting how the gun killing Kennedy was practically touchin his ear from behind his head. Charach also offered videotape copies of eyewitness Don Shulman telling a KNXT newsman (now KCBS)that he saw the security guard, Cesar, shoot Kennedy. Charach offered it to any media groups, though most ignored Charach's press conference. David Manning, "Ted Charach's Press Conference: Thane Eugene Cesar's Gun Found," Probe V2 n.3. www.webcom.com/ctka/pr795-2gun.html
[830] "A direct assistant… can do." Pease, "RFK Plot Part II," *Assassinations*, pp.607-8. Also, Maheu hiring Mafia boss Johnny Roselli to direct Castro assassination attempt, Brad Ayers, *The War That Never Was* (Indianapolis: Bobs-Merrill, 1976) and private correspondence, in Pease, *Assassinations*, p.575. Released CIA documents on Maheu as CIA/Mafia liaison to attempt assassination of Castro can be found at www.gwu.edu/~nsarchiv/NSAEBB/NSAEBB222/index.htm or google it at george washington university CIA family jewels. See CIA document—MEMORANDUM FOR: Executive Director—Comptroller, SUBJECT: Roselli, John, 15 FEB 1972. Howard J. Osborn, Director of Security. Also see Jack Anderson, "Castro Stalker Worked for the CIA," Washington Post, 2/23/71, p.B11.
[831] "CIA Role Claim in Kennedy Killing: New video and photographic evidence that puts three senior CIA operatives at the scene of Robert Kennedy's assassination has been brought to light," *BBC News*, 11/20/06. http://news.bbc.co.uk/1/hi/programmes/newsnight/6169006.stm
[832] "The LAPD's Rampart Division… ended." On Sgt. Sharaga, Art Kevin's taped interview with Sharaga, KMPC radio, Los Angeles, 12/20/74. In Turner and Christian, *Kennedy*, pp.67, 73-77.
[833] Telephone and Radio Transmissions Log (H-XIII), Radio transmission, reel 6 from the Californial State Archives SUS Files Microfilm Collection. Cited in Lisa Pease, "The FK Plot Part 1: The Grand Illusion," *Assassinations*, pp.347-8.
[834] "The LAPD's Rampart Division… bullets." On Sgt. Sharaga, Art Kevin's taped interview with Sharaga, KMPC radio, L.A., 12/20/74. In Turner and Christian, Kennedy, pp.76-77. On destroyed evidence, see Deputy Chief Daryl Gates' interview on NBC network, 8/22/75, *Kennedy*, pp.178-9. On bullet photos and bullet fragments sent to Rampart, Pease, Assassinations, p.554.
[835] "And finally, the… gangs." On Rampart and Enyart photos, Lisa Pease, *Assassinations*, pp.619-21. Pease cites Bill Klaber and Phil Melanson, *Shadow Play: The Murder of Robert F. Kennedy, the Trial of Sirhan Sirhan, and the Failure of American Justice* (New York: St. Martin's Press, 1997), pp.301-310.

---

[836] See, for example, an NYPD BOSS undercover agent's memoir on his duel work with the FBI against Malcolm X, Tony Ulasewicz, with Stuart McKeever, the President's Pirvate Eye (Westport Connecticut: MACSAM Publishing), p.145, cited in James Douglas, "The Murder and Martyrdom of Malcolm X," James DiEugenio and Lisa Pease, eds, *The Assassinations: Probe Magazine on JFK, MLK, RFK and Malcolm X* (Los Angeles: Feral House, 2003) p.390-1. One historian said BOSS was known amongst Intelligence as "the little FBI and the little CIA." Frank Donner, Protectors of Privilege (Berkeley: University of California Press, 1990), p.155.

[837] "Another possible…year." William K. Rashbaum, "Rising Murder Rate Defies Latest Push Against Crime," *The New York Times*, April 5, 2000, p.B3. On the decreasing murder rates in "New York and other cities nationwide," see Yale Law School Professor John Donnohue, Letter to the Editor: "Rudolph Giuliani, Nobel Nominee," *New York Times*, 6/6/05. He and MIT Professor Steve Levitt published this research that showed other reasons for the crime drop nationwide in their best-selling book, *Freakanomics*. On Condor adding $100 million to overtime undercover… Kevin Flynn, "Feeling Scorn on the Beat and Pressure From Above," *The New York Times* on the web, December 26, 2000, posted on http://www.nycpba.org/press-nyt/00/nyt-001226-morale.html

[838] Larry Rohter, "Visit to U.S. Isn't a First for Chile's First Female President," *The New York Times*, 6/8/06, p.A3.

[839] "*The New York Times*… tortured." Diana Jean Schemo, "New Files Tie U.S. to Deaths of Latin Leftists in 1970's," *The New York Times*, 3/6/01, p.A7. Orlando Letelier, the former Chilean foreign minister, and Ronni Mofit, an American colleague were killed in 1976.

[840] "McSherry's Condor… murders" Patrice McSherry, "Operation Condor: Deciphering the U.S. Role," *Crimes of War*, July 6, 2001, pp. 1-6, http://www.crimesofwar.org/special/condor.html McSherry is an Associate Professor of Political Science at Long Island University and author of Incomplete Transition: Military Power and Democracy in Argentina (new York: St. Martin's Press, 1997). She's written numerous articles on Condor and the Latin American military, conducting her research in Chile, Paraguay, Argentina and the U.S.

[841] The U.S. provided Chile with $216 million in military aid from 1946-1975 and trained 6,328 military personnel from 1950-1975 and Chile used that training for torture on an administrative basis. On military aid, see the Agency for International Development (AID), *U.S. Overseas Loans and Grants and Assistance from International Organizations*, 1976 ed. Number of client military trained in the U.S., see "The Pentagon's Proteges, U.S. Training Programs For Foreign Military Personnel," *NACLA's Latin America and Empire Report*, January 1976, p.28. Police aid or training to clients, see Michael T. Klare, Supplyng Repression, Field Foundation, December 1977, pp.20-21. All cited in Noam Chomsky and Edward Herman, *The Washington Connection and Third World Fascism* (Boston: South End Press, 1979), p.44.

[842] Patrice McSherry, "Operation Condor: Deciphering the U.S. Role," *Crimes of War*, July 6, 2001, pp. 1-6, http://www.crimesofwar.org/special/condor.html

[843] "Another interesting aspect… out." Larry Rohter, "At Cult's Enclave in Chile, Guns and Intelligence Files," *New York Times*, 6/17/05, p.A9.

[844] Larry Rohter, "World Briefing; Chile: Cult Leader Gets 20 Years," *New York Times*, 5/25/06, p.A14. On sexually abusing young boys, see Becky Branford, "Secrets of ex-Nazi's Chilean Feifdom," BBC News, 3/11/05. Also, "New Charges for Cult Leader," BBCNews, 3/22/05, and final sentencing on 5/24/06 for sexaully abusing 25 children, attaining 20 years in jail and paying the equivalent of $1.5 million, en.wikipedia.org, Paul Schaefer.

[845] See, for example, U.S. government's Nazi hunter Allan Ryan's 600 page report, *Klaus Barbie and the United States Government* (Washington, D.C.: Government Printing Office, 1983), p.212. And, Allan Ryan, *Quiet Neighbors* (New York: Harcourt Brace Jovanovich, 1984), pp.280-4. Also, correspondence obtained via Freedom Of Information Act (FOIA) for documentary background: Representative Peter Rodino to comptroller general, 2/17/83; Allan Ryan to Joseph Moore (FBI), 2/18/83; and GAO Director

William Anderson to FBI Director William Webster, 3/2/83. A sanitized version of Barbie's FBI file available via FOIA inclues similar internal DOJ correspondence on this investigation; see FBI File No. 105-221892 on Klaus Barbie. All cited in Christopher Simpson, *Blowback: The First Full Account of America's Recruitment of Nazis, and its Disastrous Effect on Our Domestic and Foregin Policy* (New York: Weidenfeld and Nicholson, 1988), pp.192-3, notes 33,34.

[846] Peter Dale Scott, "How Allen Dulles and the SS Preserved Each Other," *Covert Action Information Bulletin* No.25, Winter 1986, pp.4-14. Scott, a former Canadian diplomat with a Ph.D in political science, was a Professor of English at the University of California at Berkeley who has published numerous books. The 90 citations he used in this article include the following reference sources from around the world: U.S. National Archives, *The Washington Post, Le Mond Diplomatique, Der Spiegel,* and whistleblowing books by Justice Department insiders such as John Loftus, *The Belarus Secret* (New York:Knopf, 1982). On Loftus statement of "Dulles aided the smuggling of some 5000 Nazis" Jerry Meldon, The Jewish Advocate, 9/20/84, citing John Loftus, Boston Globe, 5/28/84. On O.S.S. false claims, U.S. National Archives, Record Group 165, 250.401. Sect. XIX; letter of 19 Jamuary 1948 from Brig. Gen. Telford Tayloer, OCCWC, OMGUS. And U.S. National Archives, Record Group 319, CIC File No. V-2399, XE 012547 D20D216; *Washington Post,* 3/15/85, p.A10. The Simon Wiesenthal Center in Los Angeles released documents from the U.S. Army under the Freedom of Information Act saying Mengele "may have ben arrested by U.S. authorities in Austria in 1947 and released," *The Nation,* 3/2/85, p.231. Former WWII intelligence agent William Stevenson wrote about Mengele accumulating huge assets after gaining Parguayan citizenship in 1957, Stevenson, *The Bormann Brotherhood* (New York: Harcourt, Brace, Jovanovich, 1973), p.228. In Scott, p.7. On Barbie and other Nazis drug and arms trafficking, see, for example, "Barbie's reported dealings with August Joseph Ricord of Parraguay whose 'Corsican' drug ring was 'linked to networks of former Nazis in Europe and Latin America." Alain Jaubert, *Dossier D... comme drouge* (Paris: Alain Moreau, 1973), p.296. In Scott, "How Allen Dulles..." *Covert Action Information Bulletin,* p.9 note 33.

[847] "Germany's... flags." Kai Herman, "Klaus Barbie: A Killer's Career," *Stern,* May and June, 1984. Herman allowed the reprinting of this article in *Covert Action Information Bulletin,* No.25, Winter 1986, pp.15-20. For some of Herman's sources, see interview with Argentinian intelligence agent, Alfredo Mingolla, pictures of Barbie in Bolivia, iincluding his fake name on his intelligence ID, Klaus Altmann Hansen. On post-coup Nazi flags in Bolivia, see pp.3,17.

[848] Note that one of Loftus's books making some of these claims, *The Belarus Connection,* was nominated for a Pulitzer Prize. Also, Publishers Weekly noted that Loftus and co-author Mark Aarons interviewed some 500 former intelligence officers of various nationalities for their book, *The Secret War Against the Jews: How Western Espionage Betrayed the Jewish People* (NY: St. Martin's Griffin, 1997). The authors included 115 pages of references for this book and, as of seven years after its printing, reportedly noone brought a libel or defamation suit against the authors, www.amazon.com/Secret-War-Against-Jews-Espionage/ and www.amazon.com/Unholy-Trinity-Vatican-Nazis-Swiss/ . During his investigations of the end of WWII Justice Department, John Loftus also found that a circle of elite families, mostly in the U.S. but also in England, actually bankrolled the Nazis from their inception. In his book, *The Secret War Against the Jews,* Loftus detailed that these elite families included the Rockefellers, Harrimans, and Bushes and they worked with the German industrialist Fritz Thyssen (his memoir *I Paid Hitler*). Loftus said they took advantage of the fact that WWI impoversished Germany, which allowed them to pay for vast propaganda and a mercenary army of brownshirts for Hitler. John Loftus and Mark Aarons, *The Secret War Against the Jews* (New York: St. Martin's Press, 1994). And, Fritz Thyssen, *I Paid Hitler,* 1941, reprinted in (Port Washington, NY: Kennikat Press, 1972), p.133. Thyssen said that his contributions began with 100,000 marks given in October 1923 for Hitler's attempted "putsch" against the constitutional government. Also see www.john-loftus.com With Loftus's compliments of George W. Bush and mainstream acceptance, on that

website, he may have been "compromised." This term applies to whistleblowers who have to compromise what they say they believe, usually out of U.S. Intelligence orchestrated blackmail. Loftus also may have just been threatened, or its remotely possible he actually likes George W. Bush.
849 In *George Bush: The Unauthorized Biography*, researchers Tarpley and Chaitkin published a copy of the 1942 government document ordering the government seizing of the Union Banking Corp., an American bank jointly owned by the above named families, for funding the Nazis. Under the U.S. *Trading With the Enemies Act,* the Justice Department further seized these families' German shipping and steel companies. London's *Guardian* also published this information. Ben Ari and Duncan Campbell, *The Guardian*, 9/25/04. Document citations found in Tarpley and Chaitkin, *George Bush*, pp.26-44, include "Office of Alien Property Custodian, Vesting Order No. 248. The order was signed by Leo T. Crowley, Alien Propert Custodian, executed 10/10/42; F.R. Doc. 42-11568; Filed 11/6/42; 7 Fed. Reg. 9097 (11/7/42). Fritz Thyssen, *I Paid Hitler*, 1941, reprinted in (Port Washington, NY: Kennikat Press, 1972), p.133. Thyssen said that his contributions began with 100,000 marks given in October 1923 for Hitler's attempted "putsch" against the constitutional government.

George H.W. Bush's father, Prescott Bush, played a key role in managing a joint elite British-American banking venture, Brown Brothers Harriman (BBH). The group worked behind the back of the British government on behalf of the government's opponents—British royalty. Former Brown Brothers' partner Montagu Norman, a Bank of England Governor, was reportedly a Hitler supporter. BBH also worked behind the back of President Franklin D. Roosevelt's administratioin. BBH and several Bush-Harriman steel and shipping companies kept up joint ventures with German steel mogul, Fritz Thyssen. In his autobiography, *I Paid Hitler*, Thyssen boasted of financing Hitler's rise to power with a several-hundred-thousand-strong private army. On Brown Brothers Harriman and Montagu Norman see, Andrew Boyle, *Montagu Norman* (London: Cassell, 1967). Sir Henry Clay, *Lord Norman* (London, McMillan & Co., 1957), pp.18, 57, 70-71. John A. Kouwenhouven, *Partners in Banking... Brown Brothers Harriman* (Garden City: Doubleday & Co., 1969

Among other Nazi supporters, Chase Bank (later J.P. Morgan Chase) helped the Nazis exchange their money stolen from Jewish bank accounts, IBM helped track Jews, noted Jew-hater Henry Ford kept business ties with Hitler, and the Rockefeller's Remington Arms worked with Germany's I.G. Farben on war materialsMost of this material is in both Ari and Campbell, *The Guardian*, 9/25/04 and Tarpley and Chaitkin, *George Bush*, pp.26-44. On Morgan Chase Bank aid of Nazis, see Tim Reid, "Files Show CIA Gave Jobs to Nazi Criminals," *The Times* (of London), 5/14/04 reprinted at http://blog.zmag.org/rocinante/archives/000392.html . Note on Henry Ford from James Pool and Suzanne Pool, *Who Financed Hitler?* (New York: The Dial Press, 1978), Ch.3, as cited in Jonathan Vankin, *Conspiracies, Cover-ups and Crimes* (New York: Dell,1992), p.292. Tarpely and Chaitkin include a picture of the Library of Congress/Law Department's copy of the U.S. government WWII "vesting order" #248 seizing the Union Banking Corporation as a front for Fritz Thyssen and his Nazi Steel Trust, see pictures between pp.114-5. The information on IBM has been widely printed in *The Washington Post* and other dailies. John D. Rockefeller, historically America's wealthiest man when adjusted for inflation, owned Standard Oil (which spawned Exxon) and his brother, William, owned National City Bank (later Citibank).
On Rockefeller as richest man, William Grimes, "Heartless Robber Baron or Visionary Financier," *New York Times*, 7/22/05, p.E11.

Tarpley and Chaitkin present evidence that this elite circle of families funded the Nazis rise due to their similar racist beliefs, reflected in their Eugenics movement. William helped E.H. Harriman buy Union Pacific Railroad in 1898. Part of the reason these company owners had an easy time dealing with the Nazis is that they shared the same violently racist philosophy--eugenics. The Rockefellers funded eugenics leaders through the 1920s and '30s. They became the top Nazi ideologues. The Harrimans organized the Third International Congress on Eugenics in 1932 and the Bush family was close with various eugenics proponents and practictioners. Text from the Eugenics Congress discussed the importance of "racial purity" and dealing with the "dangers" to the "better" ethnic groups by sterilizing or "cutting off the bad stock" and elimination of the "unfit" by means including violence. Tarpley and Chaitkin, *George Bush,* pp.14, 45-62.

Some of the citations in th 3rd Int. Eugenics book include, A Decade of Progress in Eugenics: Scientific Papers of the Third International Congress of Eugenics held at American Museum of Natural History New York, Aug. 21-23, 1932. (Baltimore: William and Wilkins Company, Sept. 1934). Paraphrased ideas from this book include "the stubborn persistence of African-Americans and other allegedly 'inferior' and 'socially inadequate' groups in reproducing... It was reccommended that these 'dangers' to the 'better' ethnic groups and to the 'well-born,' could be dealt with by sterilization or 'cutting off the bad stock' of the 'unfit.'

Tarpley/Chaitkin also cite the Rockefeller Institute's Alexis Carrel, Man the Unknown (New York: Halcyon House with Harper & Brothers, 1935), pp.318-19. Carrel said "unfit" included those "who have... misled the public." Also see summaries of letters from George Herbert Walker, 39 Broadway, NY to W.A. Harriman, London, 2/21/25, in WAH Papers. They discussed "'breeding thoroughbreds' among horses and humans." And see Averell Harriman to Dr. Charles Davenport, President, The International Congress of Eugenics, Cold Spring Harbor, L.I., NY 1/21/32, on bringing German colleagues to the eugenics and genetics conference. The congressional hearings in 1934 established that Hamburg-Amerika Line of the Bush-Harriman company gave free passage to those carrying out Nazi propaganda chores. See Investigation of Nazi Propanda Activities and Investigation of Certain Othe Propaganda Activities: Public Hearings before a Subcommittee of the Special Committee on Un-American Activities, U.S. House of Representatives, 73rd Congress, New York City, July 9-12, 1934—Hearings No. 73-NY—7 (Washington: U.S. Govt. Printing Office, 1934). See testimonies of Capt. Frederick C. Mensing, John Schroeder, Paul von Lillienfied-Toal, and summaries by Committee members. Tarpley and Chaitkin, *Bush,* pp.61 notes, 9-11 and p.44 note 32.

Loftus claimed their motives were merely for profit. Others have claimed the had political economic reasons in opposition to Soviet Communism, though Loftus also backs his claims of the money motive by saying some of these families also funded the Russian Bolsheviks. While this claim appearrs more bizarre, it might be explained by a particularly weak Russian Czar, a predicted revolution, and the Bolsheviks being the most favorable of the various factions vying for post-revolutionary leadership.

[850] Larry Rohter, "Former Aide says Pinochet and a Son Dealt in Drugs," *New York Times*, 7/11/06, p.A3. Also see Peter Dale Scott, "How Allen Dulles and the SS Preserved Each Other," *Covert Action Information Bulletin* No.25, Winter 1986, pp.8, 14. Scott, a former Canadian diplomat, has a Ph.D. in political schience and was a Professor of English at University of California at Berkeley.

[851] Thierry Meyssan, "The Center for Security Policcy: Washington's Manipulators," *Voltaire*, 11/13/02 www.voltairenet.org/article30118.html Meyssan citation for this appeared to be "Group Goes from Exile to Influence," *The New York Times*, 11/23/81.

[852] "Bush Culls Campaign Theme From Conservative Thinkers," *The New York Times*, 6/12/00. On Cheney and Rumsfeld, "Donald Rumsfeld, Former Secretary of Defense, www.defenselink.mil and www.whitehouse.gove/vicepresident/ . Cheney worked within Nixon's White house from 1969 on, was named Ford's Chief of Staff in 1975, and was Chairman of the Republican Policy Committee from 1981-1987. Rumsfeld also was Bush, Sr.'s Secretary of Defense. Rumsfeld joined Nixon's cabinet in 1969, was Ford's Chief of Staff in 1974-1975, and was the youngest-ever Secretary of Defense from 1975-1977. Between the Reagan and Bush years of 1982 and 1992, Rumsfeld served on more than a half dozen presidential advisory committees and international policy commissions while heading international pharmaceutical and technology companies. Also see years of Condor and Italian judge attempt to extradite top Republican Henry Kissinger, Bill Van

Auken, "Italian judge seeks trial of 140 over Operation Condor repression," www.wsws.org 1/15/08.

[853] "Another...Department." Anthony DePalma, "The Americas Court a Group that Changed New York," *The New York Times*, 11/11/02. On Manhattan Institute advising Bloomberg's police, Nicholas Confessore, "Giuliani Guide is Bloomberg Gladfly," *New York Times*, 10/25/05.

[854] "What Prof. McSherry reported...politicians." J. Patrice McSherry, "Operation Condor: Deciphering the U.S. Role" from her website, Crimes of War.

[855] See, Amnesty International, *Report on Torture* (U.S. Edition, Farrar, Straus and Giroux, 1975), pp.206-7, cited in Chomsky and Herman, *The Washington Connection and Third World Fascism*, p.9.

[856] See p.27 of CIA documents known as "Family Jewels at www.gwu.edu/~nsarchiv/NSAEBB/NSAEBB222/index.htm

[857] "Statistics on Condor...crime." "NYC Police Suspend Extra Patrols for 10 Days," American Civil Liberties Union News, Source reportedly *The New York Times*, October 12, 2000, http://archive.aclu.org/news/2000/w101200z.html

[858] "The NYPD...them." See, for example, "Operation Lockdown," *The Source*, March 2004.pp.107- 127. That article cites many of the notable rap arrests in a timeline and short essays from 1986 to 2003. Adding them up, significantly more arrests occurred in the four years between 2000-03 then occurred in the 14 years from '86-'99. Also see, "Actual Facts," *XXL* magazine, July 2000, p.35. Of the many other examples besides Tupac, Biggie and ODB targeted in California, "Oakland hometown favorite, Seagram Miller, a.k.a. Seagram, age 26 was shot in the head...[after] illustrating the dangers of the violent and criminal lifestyle he'd denounced." "Bits and Pieces," *The Source*, October 1996, p.6. And Oakland graffiti artist and rap collaborator Mike "Dream" Francisco, who had organized the first-ever Bay Area gallery installment—a response to the Rodney King verdict called "No Justice No Peace," was fatally shot. Leah Rose, "360: Street Dream" *XXL* magazine, p.36.

[859] "The NYPD...them." See, for example, "Operation Lockdown," *The Source*, March 2004.pp.107- 127. That article cites many of the notable rap arrests in a timeline and short essays from 1986 to 2003. Adding them up, significantly more arrests occurred in the four years between 2000-03 then occurred in the 14 years from '86-'99. Also see, "Actual Facts," *XXL* magazine, July 2000, p.35. Of the many other examples besides Tupac, Biggie and ODB targeted in California, "Oakland hometown favorite, Seagram Miller, a.k.a. Seagram, age 26 was shot in the head...[after] illustrating the dangers of the violent and criminal lifestyle he'd denounced." "Bits and Pieces," *The Source*, October 1996, p.6. And Oakland graffiti artist and rap collaborator Mike "Dream" Francisco, who had organized the first-ever Bay Area gallery installment—a response to the Rodney King verdict called "No Justice No Peace," was fatally shot. Leah Rose, "360: Street Dream" *XXL* magazine, p.36.

[860] "Statistics on Condor...crime." "NYC Police Suspend Extra Patrols for 10 Days," American Civil Liberties Union News, Source reportedly *The New York Times*, October 12, 2000, http://archive.aclu.org/news/2000/w101200z.html

[861] "Under Condor...Dorismond." Bill Vann, "The Killing of Patrick Dorismond: New York police violence escalates in wake of Diallo verdict," March 22, 2000, http://www.wsws.org/articles/2000/mar2000/nyc-m22.shtml For deaths in police custody, see case of teenager Anthony Baez's chokehold death after his football hit a police car, as one of hundreds of examples.

[862] "Called the largest...group." For example, see Jennifer Gonnerman, "Throne Behind Bars; The Latin King leader on love, law enforcement, and landing back in jail," *Village Voice*, 4/7/98, p.61. and, see, Big Noise Films, *Black and Gold: The Latin King and Queen Nation*, AK Press Catalog, 2003, p.155.

[863] "Civil rights...force.'" Gonnerman, *Village Voice*, 4/7/98, p.61.

[864] Personal interview, Vincent Panama Alba, 10/15/96 and 5/15/98. Arrest of King Tone and 23 other Latin Kings was also reported in Jennifer Gonnerman, "Thrown Behind Bars," *The Village Voice*, 4/7/98, p.61.

[865] "Many other... group." *Black & Gold: The Latin King and Queen Nation,* a documentary, Big Noise Films, 1999.
[866] "King Tone... court dates." *Black & Gold: The Latin King and Queen Nation,* a documentary, Big Noise Films, 1999. Arrest of King Tone and 23 other Latin Kings was also reported in Jennifer Gonnerman, "Thrown Behind Bars," *The Village Voice*, 4/7/98, p.61.
[867] "In May... bail." *Black & Gold: The Latin King and Queen Nation,* Big Noise Films, 1999.
[868] Personal interview with Hector Torres, 9/12/98. Hector Torres, called the "elder spokesman" for the Latin Kings and Queens, also worked for New York activist, Reverend Al Sharpton. In describing how King Tone's probation officer didn't believe Tone's probation should be violated, Torres described a similar situation as had happened to Tupac before his sentencing hearing. Torres said that the probation officer's high level superiors came in and took the case from her, rewrote her report to the judge and recommended that Tone be violated and imprisoned. For Tupac's case, see Sentencing hearing transcript—New York vs. Tupac Shakur and Charles Fuller, defendants, February 14, 1995, pp. 8-9. A Daily News article referring to Torres as the Latin King and Queen elder spokesman also said Torres headlined a seminar at John Jay College of Criminal Justice. Torres said police use intimidation and false information to turn gang members against each other in Torres said he would travel nationwide to transform gangs "into positive political voices for disenfranchised communities." Maki Becker, "Latin King vows to aid gang kids," *Daily News*, 7/9/01.
[869] Robert Gearty and Bill Hutchinson, "Sweeping Up Street Gang," Daily News, May 9, 2001, p.7.
[870] "New York's *Daily*... color." Maki Becker, "Latin King vows to aid gang kids," *Daily News*, 7/9/01.
[871] "George Bush, Sr.'s... Negroponte." Michael Ruppert, *Crossing the Rubicon: The Decline of the American Empire at the End of the Age of Oil* (Gabriola Island, BC Canada: New Society, 2004), p.453.
[872] "*The Nation* magazine... 1975." Joseph McBride, *The Nation*, July 16, 1988, pp.37, 41-2. In that article, a CIA spokesman "wouldn't confirm or deny" the information. A Bush spokesman first said Bush responded without a full denial, before the spokesmen later gave a denial for him. In.the next issue of *The Nation*, 7/30/88, p.80, the editors said a C.I.A. representative claimed the George Bush was another George William Bush, but refused to provide documents proving that. "'63 Bush CIA Link Reported," *The New York Times,* 7/11/88; "'63 Memo Seen as Case of Mistaken Identity," New York Times, 7/21/88; articles cited in Vanken, Conspiracies, Cover-ups and Crimes, pp.235, 349n. On letter from other Bush, Tarpley and Chaitkin, *Bush*, photo captiion between pp.238-9. Also cited by Wayne Madsen, "Another Insult from Bush and the Pentagon Neo-cons," *From the Wilderness,* 11/22/2004. Bureau of Intelligence memo's subject "Assassination of President John F. Kennedy, November 22, 1963," dated, November 29, 1963. Madsen also said that for the Bay of Pigs the CIA use Zapata ex-Navy landing craft, named Barbara J. and Houston, for Bush's wife and city. www.fromthewilderness.com . *The New York Times* also published an article about this document but ten days later they cited a CIA source saying said this was a different George Bush. Researchers said this other Bush was a lowly technical assistant who wrote a letter claiming no meetings with the FBI in '63.
[873] Joseph McBride, *The Nation*, July 16, 1988, pp.37, 41-2.
[874] Webster Tarpley and Anton Chaitkin, *George Bush: The Unauthorized Biography* (Washington, D.C.: Executive Intelligence Review, 1992), pp. 193-205.
[875] *White House Chronicle,* WHUT TV, Ch19, 9/12/04. Remembrances of Rep. Adam Clayton Powell.
[876] Craig Unger, *House of Bush, House of Saud* (New York: Scribner, 2004), pp.41, 50-1, 309-310n. Unger noted how Carter's CIA Deputy Director set up a separate Arlington complex to run these operations. Other key figures in these operations included Reagan/Bush's future CIA director, William Casey, Republican congressman Dick

Cheyney, Zbigniew Brzezinski, and James Baker. Unger's footnoted sources include Gary Sick, *October Surprise*, p.24; "Unauthorized Transfers," Committee on the Post Office and Civil Service, pt. 1, pp.36, 39, 55, 100, 102,124, 1086, 1105; United Press International, July 24, 1983; Laurence I. Barrett, Gambling with History, p.383; and former congressman Donald Albosta, telephone interview.

[877] "Evidence supports that... without Clinton's knowledge." On Bush's leftover CIA leaders, see Pulitzer Prize-winning reporter, Robert Parry, "The CIA's DI Disgrace," 7/13/04, www.consortiumnews.com. This article was adapted from Parry's upcoming book, *Secrets and Privilege: The Rise of the Bush Dynasty.* On, Bush, Sr. working behind Clinton's back, see FBI director Freeh's "well-known" antipathy to Clinton, in Benjamin and Simon, The *Age of Sacred Terror*, p.301. 'Bush as a secret emissary,' for some reason on behalf of Freeh in discussions with an arab leader, Robert Siegel interview with Elsa Walsh, *All Things Considered*, National Public Radio, 5/7/01. Cited in Unger, *House of Bush House of Saud*, pp.176-7. Jane Perlez, "Bush Senior, on His Son's Behalf, Reassures Saudi Leader," *New York Times*, 7/15/01, pp.1, 6. Also, Michael Ruppert, *Crossing the Rubicon: The Decline of the American Empire at the End of the Age of Oil* (Gabriola Island, BC Canada: New Society, 2004), p.453.

[878] "Iran-Contra Pulitzer... back." Unger, *House of Bush...*, pp.41, 50-1, 309-310n. Unger noted how Carter's CIA Deputy Director set up a separate Arlington complex to run these operations. Other key figures in these operations included Reagan/Bush's future CIA director, William Casey, Republican congressman Dick Cheyney, Zbigniew Brzezinski, and James Baker. Unger's footnoted sources include Gary Sick, *October Surprise*, p.24; "Unauthorized Transfers," Committee on the Post Office and Civil Service, pt. 1, pp.36, 39, 55, 100, 102,124, 1086, 1105; United Press International, July 24, 1983; Laurence I. Barrett, Gambling with History, p.383; and former congressman Donald Albosta, telephone interview.

[879] "Robert Parry detailed how Casey... his second presidential term." Robert Parry, "The CIA's DI Disgrace," 7/13/04, www.consortiumnews.com. This article was adapted from Parry's upcoming book, *Secrets and Privilege: The Rise of the Bush Dynasty.* Parry said that before George Bush left the presidency in '92, he appointed Robert Gates as CIA director and David Cohen as deputy director of the Directorate of Intelligence. Many CIA administrators petitioned President Bill Clinton for a housecleaning of all the Bush/Reagan leftover intelligence leaders. While Clinton let go of Gates, he left Cohen and others in their powerful positions. He also appointed a neo-conservative democrat who was close to Bush, James Woolsey, as CIA director. Clinton then appointed another Gates ally, George Tenet, as CIA director in his second presidential term.

[880]"While space... others(see notes)." In 2004, one of the top pollsters, Zogby International, found that 41% of New York State residents and 49% of New York City residents believed Bush at least had foreknowledge of the 9/11 attack and could have stopped it.[880] While space precludes further exploration, by 2006, researchers presented much evidence that the Bush administration actually orchestrated 9/11. See, for example, Michael Meacher, "This War on Terrorism is Bogus: The 911 attacks gave the US and ideal pretext to use force to secure its global domination," *The Guardian*, 9/6/03. Meacher was Britain's Minister of the Environment from 1997-2003. www.guardian.co.uk Congresswoman Cynthia McKinley got voted back to Congress 2004 after accumulating 911 commission reports supported some of her assertions.

Some of the most convincing documentaries on the Bush administration orchestrating 911 can be found at http://911revisited.infad.net/video.html And "Loose Change (2nd edition)" www.loosechange911.com/ Further see www.911proof.com/ On radio personalities, actress turned Air America radio host, Janine Garofalo announced that she finally felt she saw enough proof to publicly say the Bush administration orchestrated 911, Reportedly said on 2/23/06, at 739 amEST, radio channel 167, Air America Radio, The Majority Report, "911 was an inside job! I have come to this conclusion about that. I think all Air America phone-in caller should open by saying, '911 was an inside job. We can all agree on that.' Then get on with their specific uestion

or comment... accept the truth about 91 as the gospel... to inspirre research."
www.total411.info/2006/02/garofolo-911-was-inside-job.html

Professors and others formed groups such as Scholars for 911 Truth. For example, recently retired Religion professor, David Ray Griffin's two books and talk on the subject that was nationally televised on C-Span in the spring of 2005. On their website, 911 Scholars, that include physics and engineering professors, state "books and articles by members and other associates have established that the World Trade Center was almost certainly brought down by controlled demolitions and that... the government not only permitted 9/11 to occur but may even have orchestrated these events to facilitate its political agenda. www.scholarsfor911ruth.org

While numerous books and films have come out on this subject, one that goes much further with this idea is Michael Ruppert's *Crossing the Rubicon: The Decline of the American Empire at the End of the Age of Oil* (Gabriola Island, BC Canada: New Society, 2004). It uses meticulously documented research from many, including professors, journalists and former politicians, to argue that the Bush administration orchestrated the 9/11 attacks in order to create a police state. Ruppert convincingly argues that pending oil shortages brought on the urgency for such dire action, but that the narco-traffickers in higher office had a history of such covert operations, or plans for such. He includes declassified government documents for a similar plan, Operation Northwoods, detailing attacks on U.S. cities as an excuse to invade Cuba. Ruppert's web magazine gives more information on these issues. www.fromthewilderness.com

Note that some websites esposing 911 have also, purposely or not, bought into the "divide and conquer" strategy ranging from exagerated critiques of each others projects or outright prejudice regarding certain minority groups. From the Wilderness, to which this author subscribes, has been a front runner in bringing the 911 Truth issue to light, especially regarding Peak Oil, but it also has appeared to be a bit regrettably too farreaching in its critiques of others' projects, as well as less radical media sources such as Pacifica's Democracy Now. Whatreallyhappened.com offers both excellent and timely information, while also regretably offering broad-sweeping Holocaust denial information that contradicts their denials of anti-Jewish prejudice. Atheists of Jewish ancestry, such as this author, have enough evidence of lost family in the Holocaust to understand its validity. Granted, communist, gypsy and gay Holocaust victims have not gotten enough attention, though Jews were among two of these groups. Centuries of anti-Jewish media have attempted to scapegoat Jews, as documented in the movie *The Protocols of Zion*, about the anti-Jewish book, *The Protocols of the Elders of Zion.* While Israel's Mossad, amongst other country's intelligence units, certainly helped U.S. Intelligence at times, What Really Happened claims Israel is taking over America. Israel has less than 1% the population of the U.S. and Jews in America are about 2-3% of the population.

[881] "Bush family... intelligence." "A Spymaster Joins the NYPD," *The New York Times*, 1/23/01, p.B3.

[882] "He spent... City." David Cohen, "The Cohen Declaration: Facing 'Heightened and Unjustifiable Risk'" *The New York Sun*, 12/5/02. A few years after leaving his '97 CIA position, Cohen appeared to continue his CIA work in the private sector. During that time, Cohen worked for the American International Group (AIG). AIG, officially a global financial group, employed Medellin drug cartel co-founder Carlos Lehder's wife. Researchers found AIG tied to covert operations since "World War II and conclusively linked to the heroin trade," with the world's largest fleet of airliners and cargo planes. See, "Mayor Michael R. Bloomberge and Police Commissioner Raymond W. Kelly Announce Appointment of David Cohen in Newly-Created Post of Deputy Commissioner of Intelligence," PR-020-02, www.nyc.gov. "(AID) aglobal financial... Lehder's wife," see Michael Ruppert, Crossing the Rubicon, p.57, Ruppert said he had lunch with Lehder's wife near the office. "AIG tied to covert... to the heroin trade," see "Hostages, Part II—A.I.G., *From The Wilderness*, Vol. IV, no. 5, August 14, 2001. "Largest flee of airliners..." Ibid; see also AIG Financial Report, www.aigcorporate.com/corpsite/about/content/realfinancial.htm.

[883] Cohen's declaration, New York Sun, 12/5/02. "Red Squad" and "restrictions modified and eased," Benjamin Weiser, "Threats and Responses: Law Enforcement" *New York Times*, 2/12/03, p.17. Also, Associated Press, "Judge Backs Expanded Police Surveillance," *New York Times*, 3/22/03, p.2.
[884] "By 2003…Pakistan.'" Brad Hamilton, " 'Blue Spies' for City: Kelly's Anti-Terrorism Cops Go Global for Higher Intelligence," *New York Post*, 6/29/03, News, p.3. On FBI overseas offices, see Raymond Bonner, "World Briefings: Australia: FBI Opens Office," *The New York Times*, 11/9/06, p.A22.
[885] Jim Dwyer, "New York Police Covertly Join In at Protest Rallies," *The New York Times*, 12/22/05, pp.A1, B10.
[886] "By 2003…Pakistan.'" Brad Hamilton, " 'Blue Spies' for City: Kelly's Anti-Terrorism Cops Go Global for Higher Intelligence," *New York Post*, 6/29/03, News, p.3
[887] "The largely white…Canada." Brad Hamilton, " 'Blue Spies' for City: Kelly's Anti-Terrorism Cops Go Global for Higher Intelligence," *New York Post*, 6/29/03, News, p.3
[888] "The Bloods…nationwide." Many Black activists would be credited with bringing the truce about, including singer/actor Harry Belafonte who worked hard on behalf of Martin Luther King fifteen years earlier. Joe Garofoli, "Singer Belafonte feels the beat of antiwar sentiment/ Keynote speaker at Oakland rally hears international criticism," San Francisco Chronicle, 4/5/03, pA.15.
[889] Tim King, "US street gang leaders to address London rally," The Guardian, 10/28/94.
[890] "The gang… Jackson." Chris Hedges, "Old Colors, New Battle Cry; Gang's Founder Calls for Focus on Community, Not Crimes," *The New York Times*, January 31, 2000, pp.B1, B6.
[891] "While police… community.'" Chris Hedges, "Old Colors, New Battle Cry; Gang's Founder Calls for Focus on Community, Not Crimes," *The New York Times*, January 31, 2000, pp.B1, B6.
[892] "Fifteen months…crimes.'"Robert Gearty and Bill Hutchinson, "Sweeping Up Street Gang," *New York Daily News*, 5/9/01, p.7.
[893] Laura Mansnerus, "Gang Crackdown in New Jersey Leads to More Than 60 Arrests," *New York Times*, 7/26/06, p.B6
[894] "In 1997, officials…location.' " Melissa Grace, "Black, Latino Cops Demand Spying Probe," New York *Daily News*, 7/31/00, p.13.
[895] "NYPD Deputy… the NYPD. " Ginger Adams Otis, "Spying Behind the Shield," *Village Voice*, January 1, 2002, p.23. At the trial, King said he used an "administrative subpoena" to get Adams' personal phone records. Presiding Judge Alvin Hellerstein asked King, "What is an administrative subpoena?"
[896] "In 2006… dismissal." Andrew Jacobs, "Captain Critical of City May Face Dismissal," *New York Times*, 2/20/06, p.B3.
[897] Zulus' Panther inspiration heard by this author when Afrika Bambatta said this at the third Black Panther Film Festival in New York and he confirmed it in later discussion with this author. See Black Liberation Movement leader Sonny Carson's mentoring From Zulu Nation's website and articles on Zulu Nation at www.daveyd.com
[898] Shaila Dewan, "At a Live Homage, Hip-Hop Is King but 'Rapping" is Taboo," *New York Times*, 9/13/00, p.B3. See articles on Zulu Nation at www.daveyd.com . Also see articles on Zulu Nation at www.daveyd.com
[899] "Also by 2002, the New… charge)." Dave Marsh, "And the Beat(ing) Goes On…And That's the Way It Is," Counterpunch, 11/9/2002, http://www.counterpunch.org/marsh1109.html For NYPD surveillance and calling the group a gang, also see Fahiym Ratcliff, "Can't Stop, Won't Stop" *The Source*, November 2003, p.39.
[900] Tina Kelley, "Hunter College Sophomore Dies After Being Shot on a Street Corner in Harlem," *New York Times*, 9/26/03, p.B3.
[901] "Former Georgia senator released from prison early." *Jet*, 11/10/2003. While this book was going to press, this writer could also only find a conservative opinion on this matter, presented by Michael King, "Setting the Struggle Back," New Visions Commentary: The National Leadership of Conservative African-Americans, October, 1999.

[902] In 2002, HBO...debates." Marc Santoro, "Sharpton Says F.B.I. Tape Distorts Truth," *New York Times,* 7/24/03, p.B6.
[903] "In 2003, prosecutors...Cuba." Safiya Bukhari, "Kamau Sadiki (formerly known as Fred Hilton)," www.itsabouttimebpp.com/Political_Prisoners/Kamau_Sadiki.html .
[904] Houston Williams, "U.S. Government Declares $1 Million Bounty for Assata Shakur, Tupac's Godmother," *AllHipHop News,* 5/2/05. www.allhiphop.com . This well-written article seems to only run afoul in that it claims Assata was Tupac's godmother, and Mutulu his godfather. Mutulu was Tupac's stepfather and Assata was seen as his aunt.
[905] "At the Atlanta...impulses." Beth Warren, "Ex-BLA Member Gets Life Plus 10 Years for Killing a Cop," *Atlanta Journal-Constitution,* 11/12/03. From www.inforshop.org/inews .
[906] "A second example...speaker." On Askew leaving Air Force in North Carolina in the summer of 2001, Michael Daly, "Rev. Moon Son Made Gun," *New York Daily News,* 7/27/03, p.7. On prominent black activist put Davis's assassination on par with MLK's, Alton Maddox, Jr. "Something Smells in Councilman Davis' Assassination," *Amsterdam News,* 7/31/03, p.12. . It should be noted that Alton Maddox and Al Sharpton were heavily punished for defending a 15 year-old girl, Tawana Brawley, who said a group of white men raped her over several days. The District Attorney's office and mainstream media apparently got the jury, as well as much of the country including this writer, to believe the girl's claim was a hoax. The state disbarred Maddox and heavily fined both he and Sharpton when one of the accused men filed a defamation lawsuit. An alternative view of the whole case was barely mentioned elsewhere besides grafiti in Spike Lee's film, *Do The Right Thing.* On a wall in that movie it said, "Tawana told the truth." In August of 1998, a small Brooklyn newspaper, *Our Time Press,* published a long piece laying out why Tawana likely did tell the truth. It interviewed Graham B. Weatherspoon, a retired 20-year veteran of the New York Police Department, 10 years as a detective. He said he sat through the whole trial and stated the evidence provided in court. Tawana Brawley was an honor student, a cheerleader, and sang in the church choir. He said the paramedics found Tawana Brawley in a clinical state of shock, almost dead, in a trash bag. They verified the "Nigger" and "KKK" written on her back and torso, along with shit packed in her hair. There do drugs in her system that could have caused the shock. One of the men accused was the son of the top cop in the state of New York. When a police detective interviewed her, she gave ten pages worth of description about how she was raped by 5-6 men, at least one of them being a white police officer. A police woman in court said she gave no substantiative answers with which to follow up on. The examining doctor said she had blood pooling near her pevic bone and wrote down sexual assault. A postal worker described one man, Hary Christ, in a group of four cruising in a police car near the area who ended up dead within several days. Brawley identified him as one of the assailants when she saw his photo in the paper. Another of the accused, Steve Pagones, said he was Harry Christ the night before he died, as did another of the accused, Scott Patterson. Pagones said he was friends with Christ, but also admitted Christ had recently pulled a gun on him. Pagones provided a handwritten shopping mall sales receipt for where he was the day Brawley was found. The police said they found a suicide note that lacked Christ's fingerprints and really read as a letter to his girlfriend. No other evidence said suicide, but evidence did point to his murder out of fear he'd tell about the assault on Brawley, because someone may have identified him as a perpetrator. For more details, contact *Our Times Press,* Brooklyn, NY editors@ourtimepress.com (718)599-6828.
[907] Anthony Harwood, "Assassinated; Rival Shoots Anti-gun Politician 12 times at City Council Meeting," *The Daily Mirror* (London) 7/24/03, p.27.
[908] Also on cop shooting Askew from chamber floor moments after he shot Davis, see NY Post reporting team, Larry Celona et al. "Deranged Rival Blows Away Pol—Cop in City Chamber Takes Down Killer with 4 Shots," *New York Post,* 7/24/03, p.2. Also see, Josh Getlin, "The Nation: New York Honors a Fallen Public Servant," *Los Angeles Times* 7/29/03, p.A8.

[909] Witness Arielle Altman in Michael Cooper, "Councilman is Fatally Shot in City Hall," *The New York Times*, 7/24/03, p.A1.
[910] "and a media report... later." Alton Maddox, *Amsterdam News*, 7/31/03. Report on Bloomberg shutting down city to stop gunman from getting away is supported by reports by others, such as *The New York Times* saying "officials initially believed that a gunman was still loose," and that Bloomberg ordered the Brooklyn and Manhattan Bridges to be closed, streets barricaded, and subways to bypass City Hall. Cooper, "Councilman is Fatally Shot in City Hall," *New York Times*, 7/24/03. The *New York Daily News* also reported this, though both sources downgraded the amount of time after the shooting that this was done.
[911] "Other factors... office." "Deranged Rival Blows Away Pol—Cop in City Council Chamber Takes Down Killer with 4 Shots," *New York Post*, 7//24/03. On FBI claims of Askew calling them and police claim of supportive Davis letter in Askew's pocket, a Davis spokesman said it sounded like a letter Askew had sent to Davis and Davis never wrote or signed anything like it. Detailed in Dianne Cardwell and Kevin Flynn, "Volunteer Accused of Making Threat to Councilman," *The New York Times*, 7/26/03, p. B1.
[912] "Askew had... election." "Deranged Rival Blows Away Pol—Cop in City Council Chamber Takes Down Killer with 4 Shots," *New York Post*, 7//24/03. On FBI claims of Askew calling them and police claim of supportive Davis letter in Askew's pocket, a Davis spokesman said it sounded like a letter Askew had sent to Davis and Davis never wrote or signed anything like it. Detailed in Dianne Cardwell and Kevin Flynn, "Volunteer Accused of Making Threat to Councilman," *The New York Times*, 7/26/03, p. B1.
[913] "A second example... speaker." On Askew leaving Air Force in North Carolina in the summer of 2001, Michael Daly, "Rev. Moon Son Made Gun," *New York Daily News*, 7/27/03, p.7. On prominent black activist put Davis's assassination on par with MLK's, Alton Maddox, Jr. "Something Smells in Councilman Davis' Assassination," *Amsterdam News*, 7/31/03, p.12.
[914] "Several more... work." The Bureau of Alcohol, Tobacco and Firearms was quoted about the gun in two articles. On gun firing Davis' fatal shots NYPD undercover weapon, see Michael Daly, *New York Daily News*, 7/27/03, p.7. This and other articles also discuss Askew's violent criminal history and Askew leaving the Air Force in 2001.
[915] "In Philadelphia, the... Shamsud-din Ali." David B. Caruso, "Philadelphia Mayor Seeks Explanation of FBI Bugs," *Washington Post*, 10/10/03, p.A15. Bugging Ali's phone, From News Services, "News In Brief: Philadelphia," *Washington Post*, 8/27/04.
[916] "Mayor Street... signed." Muhammad Ahmad, *We Will Return in the Whirlwind: Black Radical Organizations, 1960-1975* (Chicago, IL: Charles H. Kerr Publishing, 2007), pp.299-302.
[917] "Other targeting... lobbying." On Kweisi Mfume, see www.hsan.org. On IRS targeting NAACP and other groups, see Stephanie Strom, "Nonprofit Groups Question Motive for Federal Actions," *The New York Times*, 3/21/05, p.A10.
[918] Memoradum from IRS Assistant Commissioner D.W. Bacon to chief counsel and other officers, re "Activist Organizations Committee," 7/18/69. Memoradum for file by D.O. Virdin, IRS, re "Activist Organizations Committee," 7/24/69, p.1. In H. Newton, *War Against the Panthers* (New York: Harlem River Press/ Writers and Readers Publishers, 1996), pp.86-7.
[919] "For one, *The Washington*... 1981-1996." Wil Haygood, "The Promised Land," *The Washington Post Magazine*, 10/3/04, p.14.
[920] "National Black Farmers... 1998." Haygood, *Washington Post Magazine*, 10/3/04, pp.24-30.
[921] By 2005, conservative... Torres." Ron Jacobs, "Free the San Francisco 8: Former Black Panthers in Prison Need Your Support," *Znet*, 7/30/07, www.zmag.org Committee for the Defense of Human Rights, www.freethesf8.org
[922] "In 2005... Story.'" Eben Gregory, "Crips Founder/Children's Author to Be Executed," 10/26/05 and Nolan Strong and Eben Gregory "Gov. Schwarzenegger

Refuses Clemency, Tookie Executed," 12/12/05 www.allhiphop.com/hiphopnews HBO showed a film on the Crips, *Bastards of the Party*, dir. By Cle Shaheed Sloan, (2006) that said they started as revolutionaries, which might also be documented in Mike Davis, *City of Quartz*.

[923] "Also in 2005 and 2006... bled to death." Amy Goodman interview of Juan-Manuel Garcia-Passalacqua, "FBI Assassinates Puerto Rican Nationalist Leader Filiberto Ojeda Rios," Democracy Now! 9/26/05. Amy Goodman and Juan Gonzalez interview Jorge Farinacci and Juan-Manuel Garcia-Passalacqua, "FBI Killing of Puerto Rican Independence Leader Filiberto Ojeda Rios Sparks Outouring of Anti-US Sentiment," Democracy Now! 9/26/05. www.democracynow.org

[924] Francesca Manning, "FBI raids homes of Puerto Rican pro-independence organizers," The Dominion, 3/1/06. http://dominionpaper.ca/international_news/2006/03/01/fbi_raids_.html

[925] "Legendary guitartist... same." On Hendrix, see Harry Shapiro and Caesar Glebbeek, Jimi Hendrix: Electric Gyspy (New York: St. Martin's Press, 1995), pp.70-1, 106-110. On Cooke, Pra.k.a.sh Gandhi, "Sam Cooke," *AMI Specials: Rock Secrets and Scandals*, March 14, 2000, p.30. Frederic Dannen, *Hit Men* (New York: Vintage, 1991), p.34. Sam Cooke's popular songs included "You Send Me," "Chain Gang" and "Twistin' the Night Away." A hotel desk clerk claimed Cooke attacked her so she shot him, while others believe the Mafia murdered Cooke for being the first black musician to take music ownership from Mafia hands and police failed to investigate. On government-linked Mafia, see details on Genovese frontman Mo Levy's huge Black recording industry control in Fredric Dannen, Hit Men (New York, Vintage, 1990). On Genovese Mafia family's CIA links, see for example, Vito Genovese as lieutenant for Charles "Lucky" Luciano, who worked with U.S. Naval Intelligence and then the CIA, in Alfred Mcoy, *The Politics of Heroin: CIA Complicity in the Global Drug Trade* (New York: Lawrence Hill, 1991) pp.36, 38, 43, and Clarence Lusane, *Pipe Dream Blues* (Boston: South End,1991), p.117.

[926] On Jeffery's British MI6 work, possible continued MI6 work, and his later associates with likely CIA background, Shapiro and Glebbeek, *Electric Gypsy*, pp.120-121, 280, 480-5. Alex Constantine, *The Covert War Against Rock* (Los Angeles, CA: Feral House, 2001), p.63-4. Mike Jeffery's college study following his intelligence work was focused on learning more languages than the Russian he learned as an official agent. His other major, sociology, focused on the psychology of the masses. Such study would attract both left-wing radicals and high-level intelligence operatives. Also, Besides managing The Animals and The Jimi Hendrix Experience, Jeffery inserted himself into managing several other bands. They all reported Jeffery's negative manipulations and control over their careers. Mike Jeffery then developed Carribean tax havens with banks that did U.S. Intelligence work. He created similar shell companies as Death Row Records owner Dave Kenner. On such Carribean bank work as CIA and Pentagon-type work through BCCI as part of the Iran Contra scandal, see "Banks and Nacotics Money Flow in South Florida," US Senate Banking Committee report, 96th Congress, June 5-6, 1980, p.201. Jonathon Kwitney, *The Crimes of Patriots: A True Tale of Dope, Dirty Money, and the CIA* (New York: Touchstone, 1987), p.153. Both cited in Constantine, Covert War on Rock, p.64. On Jeffery associate Jerrry Morrison likely being CIA, he had done five years of public relations work for Haiti's Pentagon-backed brutal dictator, "Papa Doc" Duvalier. See Shapiro and Glebbeek, *Electric Gypsy*, pp.279-280. *The New Columbia Encylcopedia* described Duvalier as army-backed and in office through a "sham election," after which he declared himself "president for life." It further said he led a "reign of terror... summarily executed his political opponents" and had his son succeed him in 1971. Ed.s William Harris and Judy Levey, *The New Columbia Encylcopedia,*(New York and London, Columbia University Press, 1975) p.815. For Pentagon backing see, Noam Chomsky and Edward Herman, *The Washington Connection and Third World Fascism* (Boston, South End Press, 1979) inside chart "The Sun and Its Planets: Countries Using Torture on an Administrative Basis in the 1970s, With Their Parent-Client Affiliations." Sites U.S. military training 567 Haitian military

personnel from 1950-1975. U.S. also gave $4,200,000 in military aid. Source: *Amnesty International Report on Torture* (U.S. edition, Farrar, Straus and Giroux, 1975), as backed by other extensive evidence and numbers tortured over 500. Amount of military aid obtained from Agency for International Development (A.I.D.), *U.S. Overseas Loans and Grants and Assistance from International Organizations*, 1976, ed. Number of client military trained in the United States, 1950-1975, from "The Pentagon's Protoges, U.S. Training Programs For Foreign Military Personnel," *NACLA's Latin America & Empire Report*, January 1976, p.28, and police aid or training from to clients from Michael T. Klare, *Supplying Repression*, Field Foundation, December 1977, pp.20-21.

[927] Frances Stonor Saunders, *The Cultural Cold War: The CIA and the World of Arts and Letters* (New York:The New Press, 1999), pp.68-69, 167, 174, 376.

[928] "Black artists... death." Saunders, *Cultural Cold War*, pp. 68-69.

[929] Richard Wright, A Father's Law (New York: Harper Perrenial, 2008), Biographical Timeline, p.11-12. Also see, Addison Gayle, *Richard Wright: Ordeal of a Native Son* (Garden City, NY: Anchor Press/Doubleday, 1980)),p.125,132. Also see FBI Files, document, 100-157464-1, 12/9/42.

[930] FBI Files, April 4, 1958, p.6 From Washington Field Office, WFO, 100-15433, Office of Origin, New York. Also see Gayle, p.128.

[931] FBI Memorandum, SAC New York, Director , FBI Richard N. Wright Security Matter-C September 8, 1946. 100-157464.

[932] Gayle, 194-5.

[933] FBI documents. Copy of picture with Life magazine photography credit. Article/picture undated.

[934] Gayle, p.295, Fabre, p.509.

[935] Addison Gayle, *Richard Wright: Ordeal of a Native Son* (New York: Anchor Press/Doubleday, 1980) p.295. Michael Fabre, *The Unfinished Quest of Richard Wright* (Chicago, IL: University of Illinois Press, 1993), p.509. Father's Law timeline, p.16

[936] Dir. Madison Davis Lacy, *Richard Wright-Black Boy*. Co-producers include: Mississippi Educational Television, the Independent Television Service, Madison Davis Lacy and the British Broadcasting Corporation (BBC), 1994. It first aired on PBS in 1995.

[937] Gayle, p247.

[938] Harrington, p.8, p.24

[939] Richard Wright, *Haiku: This Other World* (NY: Arcade Publishing, 1998), pp.viii, ix, (Introduction by Julia Wright). Fabre, *Wright: Unfinished Quest*, pp.493-4.

[940] Harrington, pp.15-16.

[941] Gayle, p.273. Fabre, pp.516-19.

[942] Dir. Madison Davis Lacy, *Richard Wright-Black Boy*. Co-producers include: Mississippi Educational Television, the Independent Television Service, Madison Davis Lacy and the British Broadcasting Corporation (BBC), 1994. It first aired on PBS in 1995. Also, Harrington, p.25. Personal Interview, Julia Wright, 6/20/08.

[943] "But it took... Panthers." in Monica Danneman, *The Inner World of Jimi Hendrix* (New York: St.Martin's Press,1995) pp.40,116. Shapiro and Glebbek, *Electric Gypsy*, pp.271-2. On interviews supporting the Black Panthers and political benefit for Bobby Seale and the Chicago 7, see "Jimi Hendrix, Black Power and Money," *Teenset*, January, 1969; and, Constantine, *Covert War Against Rock*, p.61. Danneman also quoted from part of this interview, though she cited Jacob Atlas, *Circus*, March 1969, in Monica Danneman, *The Inner World of Jimi Hendrix*, p.123. It could have been a press conference quoted by both magazines. On Hendrix dedicating his last album to the Panthers, see Douglas Pringle, *The Jimi Hendrix Companion* (New York: Simon & Schuster, MacMillan, 1996), p.63.

[944] Todd Gitlin, *The Whole World is Watching* (Berkeley: University of California Press, 1980) p.55, cited in Martin Lee and Bruce Shlain, *Acid Dreams: The Complete Social History of the CIA, LSD, the Sixties and Beyond* (New York: Grove Press, 1985), p.210.

---

[945] James Casbolt, "MI6 Are the Lords of the Drug Trade." Copyright James Casbolt, 2006. Note that Casbolt's father Peter was also an MI6 agent. This article has been reprinted on a dozen or more websites. One is http://icssa.org dated May 22, 2006. After this article, an article purportedly by Casbolt has been printed on extraterestials or UFOs. This appears to be a fake article by Intelligence to discredit Casbolt.
[946] "The FBI started... emergency." Santa Barbara University campus newspaper filed a FOIA request and obtained this information in 1979, Constantine, *Covert War Against Rock*, p.61. FBI surveillance of Hendrix also noted by Fairness and Accuracy In Reporting (FAIR) cofounder Martin Lee & Bruce Shlain, *Acid Dreams* (New York: Grove, 1985), p.226.
[947] Danneman, p.78; Shapiro and Glebbeek, p.360.
[948] Shapiro and Glebbeek, pp.359-361. Danneman, pp.48, 76-78.
[949] "Hendrix biographers... weed." Shapiro & Glebeek, p.335, 361. Danneman, p.49. Danneman claimed, and this was backed by Shaprio and Glebbeek, that Hendrix's first album, Are You Experienced, considered a masterpiece by most, was done six months before Hendrix ever used LSD. Purple Haze, for example, was the name of diffused light in a Hopi Indian folklore book. A batch of LSD out of San Francisco then took on that nickname. Shapiro and Glebbeek, p.148
[950] On Jeffery sabotaging Hendrix's political benefits, see Shapiro and Glebbeek, pp.190, 426. Dsneman, p.48.
[950] "Jimi Hendrix's lawyer, Steve... Weiss represented Hendrix." Shapiro and Glebbeek, pp.294-296, Constantine, Covert War on Rock, p.62.
[950] "Hendrix percussionist Juma Sultan... played the Salvation club." Shapiro and Glebbeek, p.395.
[950] "Danneman, Shapiro and Glebbeek's... Mafioso and freed Hendrix." Shapiro and Glebbek, pp.393-396.
[951] Shapiro and Glebbeek, p.280.
[952] "Hendrix's bandmates... 'tougher' Mafia." On Jeffery's association with Mafia and intimidation of Hendrix with Mafia, see Shapiro and Glebbeek, pp.294-296, Constantine, *Covert War Against Rock*, p.62. Also see Mafia intimidation account of Hendrix percussionist Juma Sultan in Shapiro and Glebbeek, p.395. On Mafia kidnapping and Jeffery/Morrison part in freeing Hendrix, see Shapiro and Glebbek, pp.393-396.
[953] "Multiple reports... death." On Hendrix, see Danneman, *The Inner World of Jimi Hendrix*, pp.165-167. Hendrix firing Jeffery also in Shapiro and Glebbeek, *Electric Gypsy*, pp.461-2. On Tupac, see Connie Bruck, "The Takedown of Tupac," *The New Yorker*, 7/2/97, p.63.
[954] "His live-in fiancee... description." Danneman, pp.165-167. Shapiro and Glebbeek, pp.461-7, 473.
[955] "The coroner said... intoxication.'" Danneman, pp.167-170, 175-178.
[956] "Reports claimed Hendrix... did." Constantine, *Covert War Against Rock*, p.67.
[957] "Danneman's memoir... testify." Danneman, pp.175-178. Shapiro and Glebbeek, pp.463-467, 473.
[958] "Police presented false... answer-phone." Danneman, pp.176-177; Shapiro and Glebbeek, pp.468-472.
[959] "Secondly, Danneman... state." Danneman, *Jimi Hendrix*, p.178.
[960] John Swenson, "The Last Days of Jimi Hendrix," *Crawdaddy*, January, 1975, p.45, cited in Constantine, *The Covert War Against Rock*, p.72.
[961] "While that magazine ... home.'" Danneman, *Jimi Hendrix*, pp.188-9.
[962] "The ambulance men ... dead.'" Danneman, *Jimi Hendrix*, Shapiro and Glebbeek, *Electric Gypsy*, p.475, and Constantine, *The Covert War Against Rock*, pp.65-66.
[963] Danneman, p.188-9. Shapiro and Glebbeek, pp.466-7.
[964] "If Hendrix was... register." Danneman, p.188.
[965] "For one, Time... death." On Death Row and Time Warner maintaining publishing rights over many of Tupac's 300 unreleased songs, see Veronica Lodge, "Jackin' beats," *Rap Pages*, September 1998, pp.65-71. Also, Cathy Scott, *Biggie*, p.106. On tens of millions of dollars made on Tupac's songs, see Ed. Betsy Schiffman, "Earnings from the

Crypt: Top Earning Dead Celebrities," Forbes Magazine, 2002. http://www.2paclegacy.com – 2PAC in top 10 for earnings. On Time Warner keeping publishing rights to Death Row material, see Ro, *Have Gun Will Travel*, pp217-219. Also, Betsy Streisand, Thom Geier, "Time Warner Moves to Unload its Stake in Interscope Records," *U.S. News and World Report*, 8/21/95, p.48.

[966] "Similarly, Mike Jeffery confiscated…$2 million." Shapiro and Glebbeek, pp.473, 477-491, particularly 490.

[967] "And finally,…like a violent murder." Shapiro and Glebbeek, pp.473, 477-491. Wilson's death, also Danneman, p. 185. Also see, Chuck Phillips, "Father Gets Hendrix Song, Image Rights," *Los Angeles Times* (home ed)7/26/95, p.1, cited in Constantine, *Covert War Against Rock*, p. 73.

[968] "Several groups sued…BCCI/Iran-Contra Scandal." On lawsuit trial and death, Shapiro and Glebbeek, pp.479. On Bahama shell company, see Constantine, John Swenson, "The Last Days of Jimi Hendrix," Crawdaddy, Jamuary, 1975, p.488. Also "Banks and Narcotics Money Flow in South Florida," US Senate Banking Committee Report, 96th Congress, June5-6, 1980, p.201, and Jonathon Kwitney, The Crimes of Patriots: A True Tale of Dope, Dirty Money, and the CIA (New York: Touchstone, 1987), p.153, all cited in Constantine, The Cover War Against Rock, 63-4. And, Shapiro and Glebbeek, pp.484-8.Wilson's death, also Danneman, p. 185. Also see, Chuck Phillips, "Father Gets Hendrix Song, Image Rights," *Los Angeles Times* (home edition), July 26, 1995, p.1, cited in Constantine, Cover War Against Rock, p. 73.

[969] "Hendrix fiancee…associate." Danneman, *The Inner World of Jimi Hendrix*, pp.184-5.

[970] "In 1995…release)." *Eastern Daily Press*, April 6, 1996, cited in Constantine, p.66,71.

[971] "In 2009, new information…for the JLP." James "Tappy" Wright and Ron Weinberg, Rock Roadie: Backstage Confidentia with Hendrix, Elvis, The Animals, Tina Turner and an All-Star Cast (New York: Thomas Dunne Book/St. Martin's Press, 2010) pp.231-2. James Tapper, "Jimmy Hendrix was murdered by his manager, claims roadie." 3/31/09 http://www.dailymail.co.uk/news/article-1189805/Hendrix-murdered-

[972] Aislinn Simpson, "Jimi Hendrix murder theory 'plausible' says ER doctor." 7/2/09 http://www.telegraph.co.uk/news/newstopics/celebritynews/5869491/J

[973] James Tapper, "Jimmy Hendrix was murdered by his manager, claims roadie." 3/31/09 http://www.dailymail.co.uk/news/article-1189805/Hendrix-murdered-

[974] Dominic Wells, "Was Jimi Hendrix Murdered?" *The London Times*, 7/4/09

[975] Blacks around the…struggle." On growing up poor, Timothy White, *Catch a Fire: The Life of Bob Marley* (New York: Henry Holt, 1996), pp.49-55. On his *Burnin'* album's songs, 260-1, 268. On CIA and conservative government forces, election and Tosh, see pp.264-5, 304, 317-18, 364-5. Also see Alex Constantine, *The Covert War Against Rock* (Los Angeles: Feral House, 2001), p.134-6, 144.

[976] White, *Catch A Fire*, p.307 and Clarence Lusane, *Pipe Dream Blues: Racism and the War on Drugs* (Boston, MA: South End Press, 1991) pp.112-3.

[977] "Bob Marley, Peter Tosh…beating." White, *Catch a Fire*, pp.268

[978] White, *Catch a Fire*, pp.264-5.

[979] "Despite U.S. government…into Jamaica." Ellen Ray and Bill Schaap, "Massive Destabilization in Jamaica," *Covert Action Information Bulletin*, no. 10, August-September 1980, pp.13, 16. William Blum, *The CIA: A Forgotten History* (London: Zed Books, 1986), p.301. Jerry Meldon, "The CIA's Dope-Smuggling 'Freedom Fighters,' Veterans of the CIA's Drug Wars, Profile: Luis Posada Carriles," *High Times*, December 18, 1998. All three cited in Constantine, *Covert War…*, pp.137-8.

[980] "Evidence supports that…no CIA!" White, *Catch a Fire*, pp285, 304.

[981] "Coming up to the…manager." White, Catch a Fire, p.318

[982] "Police and Rastafarians…election." White, *Catch a Fire*, pp.288-293.

[983] "But those present…William Colby." White, *Catch a Fire*, p.291.

[984] "Cinematographer Lee Lew-Lee…boot." Alex Constantine, *The Covert War Against Rock* (Los Angeles: Feral House, 2001), pp.135-6.

---

[985] "Lee Lew–Lee said he...poisoning)." Constantine, *The Covert War Against Rock*, p.136. On ex-KGB spy poisoning, see Alan Cowell, "Planes tested for radioactivity in link to death of the former Russian spy," *The New York Times*, 11/29/06.
[986] "Several journalists...Concrete Jungle)." Casey Gane-McCalla, "How the CIA Created the Jamaican Shower Posse," News One, 6/3/10.
http://www.antifascistencyclopedia.com/allposts/how-the-cia-created-the
[987] Don Taylor, **Marley and Me**: *The Real Bob Marley Story, Told by his Manager* (Fort Lee, NJ: Barricade Books, 1995), pp.168-9.
[988] Casey Gane-McCalla, "How the CIA Created the Jamaican Shower Posse," News One, 6/3/10. http://www.antifascistencyclopedia.com/allposts/how-the-cia-created-the
[989]

[990] "By 1980, despite dying...black radio." On ''bigger than Christ" quote, support for Mugabe in Zimbabwe, and WLIB radio support, see White, Catch A Fire, pp. 1-3, 304. On support of lefist struggles in Angola, Mozambique and South Africa, see Marley's song "War," in Constantine, *The Covert...*, p.135.
[991] "By 1980, Bob...wake." White, *Catch A Fire*, pp. 304, 317-18. In his bibliography, White cites Fred Landis, "The CIA and The Media: IAPA and the Jamaican *Daily Gleaner*." *Covert Action Information Bulletin* no. 7 (December 1979-January 1980), and "CIA Media Operations in Chile, Jamaica and Nicaragua." *Cover Action Information Bulletin*, no.16 (December 1981).
[992] David Gonsalez, "Violence Subsides in Jamaica, but Wounds Still Fester," *New York Times*, 7/11/01. This article also claims JLP leader Seaga as a victim of PNP police death threats, though in the context of JLP-linked murders of Marley, Tosh and others, the PNP reaction might be better understood.
[993] "Former Wailer Peter Tosh... years." Eric Williams, "Who Kiled Peter Tosh?" *High Times*, no.221, January 1994, p.18, for warehoused tapes. This and other facts cited in Constantine, p.144. On Hendrix's tapes stolen from N.Y. apartment, see Shapiro and Glebbeek, *Jimi Hendrix: Electric Gypsy*, p.477.
[994] "One of...records." "Harry Belafonte Biography on Yahoo! Music," Jason Ankeny http://launch.yahoo.com/ar-262982-bio—Harry-Belafonte
[995] "Biography: Paul Robeson," by Rob Nagel.
http://homepage.sunrise.ch/hompage/comtex/rob3.htm
[996] Personal Interview, Julia Wright, 6/18/08, Paris. Julia Wright met with Paul Robeson, Jr. as he was being interviewed on a radio program in Philadelphia. She read the transcript from that recorded talk at the Richard Wright Centennial Celebration in Paris. Also see Paul Robeson, Jr., "The Paul Robeson Files," *The Nation*, 12/20/99.
www.frankolsonproject.org/Articles/Robeson,%20Nation.html
[997] See Personal Interview, Julia Wright, 6/18/08, Paris. Julia Wright met with Paul Robeson, Jr. as he was being interviewed on a radio program in Philadelphia. She read the transcript from that recorded talk at the Richard Wright Centennial Celebration in Paris. Also see Paul Robeson, Jr., "The Paul Robeson Files," *The Nation*, 12/20/99.
[998] Martin Lee and Bruce Shlain, Acid Dreams: The Complete Social History of LSD—The CIA, the Sixties, and Beyond (New York: Grove Weidenfeld, 1985)pp. 35, 44-5, 52-3, CIA document from June 9, 1954, *Project MK-ULTRA, The CIA's Program of Research in Behavior Modification*, Joint Hearing before the Select Committee on Intelligence and the Subcommittee on Health and Scientific Research of the Committee on Human Resources, United States Senate, August 3, 1977.
[999] Martin Lee and Bruce Shlain, Acid Dreams: The Complete Social History of LSD—The CIA, the Sixties, and Beyond (New York: Grove Weidenfeld, 1985 Also see, www.frankolsonproject.org/Articles/Robeson,%20Nation.html
[1000] PRNewswire-USNewswire, "Electroconvulsie Therapy Causes Pernmanent Amnesia and Cognitive Deficits, Prominent Researcher Admits," *Forbes*, 12/21/06.
http:www.ect.org/electroconvulsive-therapy-causes=permanent-amnesia-and-cognitive-defeicits/

[1001] "Belafonte quickly…King's conversations." 1/30/06, "Harry Belafonte on Bush, Iraq, Hurricane Katrina and Having his Conversations with Martin Luther King Wiretapped by the FBI," www.democracynow.org
[1002] "The CIA…him" This writers's copies of CIA documents, for example, were FOIA-obtained by Lee Lew Lee and given to George Edwards and then this writer. See, for example, CIA internal memorandum in CIA file for Chief, Security Research Staff, from Allan Morse, one Jay R. Kennedy report. 6/9/65, p.7. Memorandum from Howard Osborn, Director of Security to Deputy Director of Support. 3/27/68. Also see Pepper finding that Jay Kennedy was the CIA's "Informant A"-- William Pepper, *Orders To Kill: The Truth Behind the Murder of Martin Luther King, Jr.* (NY:Warner Books, 1995), p.82. On J.R. Kennedy as Belfonte's manager, besides the many internet sources, see Elaine Brown, *A Taste of Power: A Black Woman's Story* (New York: Anchor Books, 1992), p.86.

[1003] 1/30/06, "Harry Belafonte on Bush, Iraq, Hurrican Katrina and Having his Conversations with Martin Luther King Wiretapped by the FBI," www.democracynow.org Other information from this section came from Belfonte's words at the National Black Summit Tavis Smiley organized in Houston in 2006.
[1004] "Considering that Tupac…when he was alive." On over 30 million copies sold, see John Jurgenson, Hartford Currant, "New CD extends Tupac's lucrative post-death career," The Mercury News, 12/18/04, www.MercuryNews.com . On third no.1 CD since death, see Ben Sisario, "Tupac Is Back, Again," *New York Times*, 12/23/04, p.B2. Also see "Tupac has a platinum 2003" which says two of his CDs, *Better Dayz* and *Resurrection* both went platinum. www.rapnewsdiret.com
[1005] Afeni Shakur kept them listed mostly under his industry spelling, 2Pac. She named her production company after Tupac's middle name, Amaru. These were, in chronological order, 2Pac, *R U Still Down? [rmember me]* (Interscope, double CD, 1997) ; 2Pac and Outlawz, *Still I Rise* (Interscope, 1999); Tupac Shakur, *The Lost Tapes* (Herb N'Soul: 2000); 2Pac, *Until The End of Time* (Amaru Entertainment, double CD, 2001); 2Pac, *Better Dayz* (Amaru Entertainment, doble CD, 2002); *Tupac: Resurrection* (Amaru Entertainment, 2003); 2Pac, Loyal to the Game (Interscope, 2004). Tupac's finished CDs while he was alive include his solo CDs: 1991's *2Pacalypse Now* (Interscope), 1993's *Strictly 4 My N.I.G.G.A.Z*, 1995's *Me Against the World* (Interscope), February of 1996 release *All Eyez On Me* (Death Row) and November of 1996 release under the pseudonym Ma.k.a.veli, *The Don Kiluminati: the 7 Day Theory* (Death Row). Tupac Shakur, The *Rose that Grew from Concrete* (New York: MTV/Pocket Books,1999). CD, Tupac Shakur, *The Rose that Grew from Concrete* (Amaru/Interscope, 2000).
[1006] Tupac Shakur, The *Rose that Grew from Concrete* (New York: MTV/Pocket Books,1999). CD, Tupac Shakur, *The Rose that Grew from Concrete* (Amaru/Interscope, 2000). Films include: *Juice, Poetic Justice, Above the Rim, Bullet, Gridlock'd, and Gang-Related.*
[1007] "In November…activities." On Rep. McKinney's Tupac Act, www.house.gov/apps/list/press/ga04_mckinney/PrsRlsTupacBill.html McKinney's congressional hearing on 9-11 was covered on CSPAN television in late 2005.
[1008] Deirdre Walsh and Terry Frieden, "Sources: McKinney case heading to grand juey," CNN, 4/5/06, CNN.com.
[1009] "Rep. McKinney…meeting." Bob Kemper, "McKinney accuses Capitol Hill cop of racism," *The Atlanta Journal-Constitution*, 4/1/06. www.ajc.com
[1010] On crossover vote campaign and McKinney being terrorized at her home, see *American Blackout* (2006) Guerilla News Production, dir. Ian Inaba. On voting machine issues, see 8/8/06 reports, www.cynthiaforcongress.com/news Also of interest, someone nominated Elaine Brown to run for U.S. president on the Green Party Ticket. When many brought up that Congresswoamn McKinney accused Brown of possibly being a spy, Brown attacked McKinney for using Cointelpro tactics. Brown also attacked Kathleen Cleaver and Geronimo ji Jaga (Pratt) of still having hatred over Panther divide. Cleaver and Prattt distributed an email as to why they believed Brown was a government spy. http://whosemedia.com/drums/2007/05/09/was-elaine-brown-an-agent/ In 2007,

Geronimo ji Jaga said that highly suspected spy Elaine Brown also attacked the "Fighter for True Justice Cynthia McKinney," regarding the Green Party presidential nomination.
[1011] "On the first...cases." On police whistleblower about police toasting their gaining a felony charge on Iverson, see Brian Hickey, "Did Bucceroni Blow It?" *Philadelphia Weekly*, 2/5/03. On shooting at Iverson, from wire reports, "NBA notes," 76ers. *The Baltimore Sun*, 5/14/03, p. 3D. On same person attempting to ban Iverson's CD as Tupac's, see C.Dolores Tucker heading the group in Staff at Associated Press, "Protesters Ask Radio Stations to Nix Iverson," 10/10/00. www.gfn.com/archives/story.phtml On Iverson's activism, see examples cited in Steve Argerie, "Iverson Charity Attracts Celebrities to Prince George's Stadium," *The Washington Post*, July, 2003. Date missing because article torn out of paper. The book covering Ali and other sports cases is *What's My Name Fool: Sports and Resistance*, by David Zirin, published by Haymarket Press.
[1012] "Amongst...truce." Associated Press, "Hall of Famer Brown surrenders for jail sentence," 3/13/02. Demetria Ricahrdson, "Amer-I-Can Justice," www.blackathlete.net/Football/040502.shtml 2006. Also see, for example, the case of Jamal Lewis who, after breaking the single game rushing record and nearly the season rushing record, was indicted on a charge from five years previous. Lewis set up the foundation to help poor communities in Baltimore. A judge said that "The government basically had only one witness [who was]... quite impeachable." She was a paid "informant with a criminal record...a string of aliases and fictitious birthdates and had been convicted of forgery, posed as a drug dealer and secretly recorded conversations with Lewis and a codefendant." Chief U.S. District Judge Orinda Evans said "the prospects were 'very high' that prosecutors would have been unable to convince a jury to convict Lewis." Jeff Barker, "Judge in Lewis case passes mild sentence: She doubts that a trial would end in conviction," *The Baltimore Sun*, 1/27/05. The book covering Ali and other sports cases is *What's My Name Fool: Sports and Resistance*, published by Haymarket Press.
[1013] "Other communities...here)." Regarding various black athletes, some that reached the top of their sport also had community helping foundations and fundraisers before their legal problems. Analyzing the above mentioned Intelligence memo of tactics used on musicians and the evidence around their cases shows the possible use of those tactics against certain black athletes. For more on U.S. Intelligence's targeting of Lennon and possible orchestration of his death, see Fenton Bressler, *Who Killed John Lennon* (New York: St. Martin, 1989). Bressler worked as both a lawyer and a writer for London's *Daily Mail* and *Sunday Express*. Also see Alex Constantine, *The Covert War Against Rock* (Los Angeles: Feral House, 2001) pp.117-130. Another source for the FBI's huge John Lennon file is Jon Wiener, *Come Together: John Lennon in His Time*. On dcoumented police cover-up in Kurt Cobain's death, see FOIA-obtained police papers compiled and discussed by mainstream news journalists Max Wallace and Ian Halperin, *Love and Death* (New York: Atria Books, 2004). Also see their first book on Cobain's alleged suicide, *Who Killed Kurt Cobain: The Mysterious Death of an Icon* (New York: Birch Lane/Carol Publishing, 1998). This latter book was an international bestseller. Wallace wrote several other books, had a documentary nominated for a Gemini Award (Canadian Emmy), was a guest columnist for the *New York Times* and contributed to the BBC. Halperin won a *Rolling Stone* magazine Investigative Journalism award with Wallace and wrote a bestseller on James Taylor, is a correspondent for Court TV and has contributed to *60 Minutes 2*.
[1014] A final factor worth mentioning as a possible motive for the heightened U.S. Intelligence targeting over the past decade involves the increasing number of researchers and politicians' statements on diminishing global energy resources. U.S. Congressional representatives, best-selling authors, scientists and top energy investors have publicly detailed their belief that oil depletion and other diminished energy resources will change the way we live and eat. They say that the amount of oil we can obtain has peaked and now diminishes while the demand steadily increases. They explain that oil not only fuels our cars but also, as the main ingredient in fertilizer, helps to grow our food, and goes into themaking of all our plastic products.

Some of these researchers detail how increased U.S. Intelligence fears about the diminishing energy resources predicament have increased the targeting of opposition at home and abroad. As agents of the top, conservative multinational corporations, Intelligence has led undercover operations against U.S. citizens and any international figures that show an indication of opposing U.S. nuclear and military dominance See Kenneth S. Defferyes, Professor Emeritus, Princeton University, Op-Ed, "What Happens Once the Oil Runs Out," New York Times, 3/25/05. Also see, Congressman Roscoe Bartlett's presentation to the U.S. House of Representatives in mid-March of 2005, cited in House congressional notes on online publications reprinted with source links at www.fromthewilderness.com . For one of the top sources on oil and energy depletion as a current, primary reason for increased U.S. Intelligence militance at home and abroad, see Michael Ruppert, *Crossing the Rubicon: The Decline of the American Empire at the End of the Age of Oil* (Gabriola Island, BC Canada: New Society Publishers, 2004). And see his website magazine, www.fromthewilderness.com that lists many other reputable sources for this information. Reuters, "Oil Surges $2 on 'Super-Spike' Prediction," *ABC News*, 3/31/05. www.ABCNews.com. Super-spike prediction of oil at least doubling its price per barrel made by the top trader in energy derivatives, Goldman Sachs bank. Further see Canadian professor Michael Chossudovsky's website, www.globalresearch.ca

[1015] "Examples of governmental ... all examples)." Nolan Strong, "Top Secret Documents Reveal Rappers Jay –Z, Diddy, others Monitored Before 2004 RNC, *All Hip HopNews*, 5/17/2007. www.allhiphop.com/hiphopnews/ "Immortal Technique's run in with the DEA" 9/30/*04 Hip Hop NewsDX.com*, "Mos Def Arrested after freestyling against Bush," www.youtube.com Julie Bosman (AP) "Metro Briefiing, White Plains: Warrants Issued for Rapper," *The New York Times*, 4/12/07. Claude Mills, "Who Tried to Kill Capleton?" *Xtra News*, Kingston, Jamaica, cover story, pp2-3, Arpil 4-10, 2007. Associated Press, Sports Briefing, Football: Bengals Coach Apologizes," *New York Times*, p.D6, 5/25/07. On Chokwe Lumumba see info.frontlinedefensders.org/news/1770

[1016] WBAI News evening of 6/22/07. Also, "Civil Rights Lawyer, Wife Claim Police Brutality, New York 1010 WINS www.1010wins.com 6/22/07. Furhter, http://nyprotest.flactivist.org. On "200" supporters number, see Mary Alice Miller, "Activist and Attorney Michael Tarif Warren and Wife Evelyn Arrested and Punched by Police," www.ourtimespress.com Note that police have also charged Evelyn Warren with resisting arrest. The trial date is March 3, 2008. www.justiceforwarrens.org

[1017] Sasha Abramsky, "Trial by Torture," *Mother Jones Online*, 3/3/00. http://www.truthinjustice.org/chicops.htm On the number "108 black and Latino," see Caryl Sortwell, "Aaron Patterson Targeted in Police and Fed Frame-up," Oct-Nov 2004 http://www.fightbacknews.org/2004/04/aaronpatterson.htm

[1018] John Conroy, "Aaron Paterson," *The Chicago Reader*, 12/3/99. www.ccadp.org/aaronpaterson-reader.htm Caryl Sortwell, "Aaron Patterson Targeted in Police and Fed Frame-up." *Fightback News*, Oct-Nov 2004.

[1019] Caryl Sortwell, "Aaron Patterson Targeted in Police and Fed Frame-up." *Fightback News*, Oct-Nov 2004. Minister of Information JR, " POCC Min. of Defense Aaron Patterson Sentencing Hearing Update: The Saga Continues in the Legal Lynching of Aaron Patterson; and Interview wit' Chairman Fed Hampton Jr. 8/31/07.

[1020] John Conroy, "Aaron Paterson," *The Chicago Reader*, 12/3/99. www.ccadp.org/aaronpaterson-reader.htm Caryl Sortwell, "Aaron Patterson Targeted in Police and Fed Frame-up." *Fightback News*, Oct-Nov 2004. Minister of Information JR, " POCC Min. of Defense Aaron Patterson Sentencing Hearing Update: The Saga Continues in the Legal Lynching of Aaron Patterson; and Interview wit' Chairman Fed Hampton Jr. 8/31/07.

[1021] Peronal Interview of Fred Hampton, Jr, 10/10/07 and myspace.com/ChairmanFredpart_2

[1022] Matthew Rothschild, "The FBI Deputizes Business," *The Progressive*, March 2008.

[1023] Rothschild, The Progressive.March 2008. www.progressive.org/mag_rothschild0308

Afterword

By **Fred Hampton, Jr.**

JUS' CURIOUS !?

How many more times are we to be buried before our time?
Framed up and chained up and placed behind enemy lines.
How many more Stokeleys to be snatched, Malcolms to be murdered, and Khallids to be killed?
How many more martyrs to go unremembered? And how many more monuments won't be built?
How many more Mumias, H. Raps, Sundiatas, & Peltiers?
How many more political prisoners? How many more fuckin' years?
How many more frame ups on Fred? And Merle Africas coming up dead?
How many more revolutionaries in the cemeteries? How many more blood stained beds?
How many more February 21's, August 7's, & December 4's?
How many more fallen comrades? How many more of us gotta go!?
How long before the Cinque' Magees, & Angola 3's are to be finally unleashed?
How many more Geronimos, COINTELPROS, & Shaka Sankofas to be dragged & body bagged on death row?
How many more set ups and wet ups, & FBI files?
How many more Assata Shakurs to be forced into exile?
How many more Mafundi Lakes must be taken away?
before you finally wise up & say enough is enough!
We've taken more than we can stand, and in all actuality,
that's been entirely too much. . .
How many more Khalfuni Khalduns to be beat by prison goons?
And bad negroes named Goode will you let drop bombs on MOVE?
By the way, should the Minnesota 8 simply sit back and wait,
for you to muster up the courage to say that they've
been framed by the state?
When will you demand the release of Jose' Louis, Ralph Lee,
and the rest of those who've been framed by the police?
How many more Sekous, Mutulus, & Ojure Nurus?
Lucasvilles, & Statevilles, & Attica 32's.
How much injustice can you stomach? How much more can you take?
How many more Bashir Hameeds, N.Y. 3's, Robert Hayes, & Eddie Conways?

How many more Azola Angolas & Sister Ramonas?
will you sit back and let be attacked for fighting while Black?
How many more Hugo Pinnels to be beat down in jail?
How many more resistors will you relinquish?
How many more Herman Bells?
How many more Maroon Shoats & Move 9's will you allow to be confined?
How many more FALN's, Death Row 10's?
And how long will justice be denied?

FREE 'EM ALL!

Chairman Fred Hampton Jr.,
Prisoners **O**f **C**onscience **C**ommittee,
P.O. Box 368255, Chicago, IL 60636.
myspace.com/P.O.C.C.
myspace.com/ChairmanFredpart_2

About the Authors

Author: John Potash did his undergraduate work at Swarthmore College where he was an Academic All-American. With a decade of activism behind him, he earned a masters in social work at Columbia University in 1998 where he concentrated in community organizing. He was founding publisher/editor of *Social Justice Action Quarterly*—a national social work school newspaper that lasted four years and won four honors in the Campus Alternative Journalism Awards. He also received a certification in acupuncture drug treatment at Mutulu Shakur's former clinic, Lincoln Detox, in the Bronx. While mostly working as an addictions counselor, he has published articles (*Z, Covert Action, Baltimore Chronicle*), poems and short stories. He is currently working on a political novel with some research that overlaps this book.

Foreword Author: Pam Africa Minister of Confrontation for the MOVE Organization, founded by JOHN AFRICA of whom she is a disciple. She is also the Co-Coordinator of the International Concerned Family and Friends of Mumia Abu-Jamal, spearheading the international movement to gain the release of Mumia, an innocent man, and a political prisoner who has been on death row since 1981. MOVE's founder JOHN AFRICA coordinated her work on his group and on behalf of Mumia. Pam also hosted a 13-week TV program in Philadelphia presenting Mumia's struggle on death row. She has further been featured on national television and radio programs, such as Pacifica Radio's *Democracy Now!*

Foreword Contributor: Mumia Abu-Jamal (pictured on cover and discussed in Chapter 17) was a founding Minister of Information for the Philadelphia Black Panther Party. He then worked as a radio journalist for National Public Radio, winning the Peabody Award for outstanding journalism. He further published articles in prestigious media such as the Yale Law Journal, consistently covering leftist activist issues. The FBI started a file on him at 14, of which he later obtained over 800 pages. After the Philadelphia Association of Black Journalists elected Mumia their chair, he was shot in 1981. Mumia has written several essays a week which have been recorded and broadcasted on radio stations around the country by prisonradio.org. He has also written several books, including *Death Blossoms* and *We Want Freedom.* He has since become a political prisoner cause celebré, with supporters that include a vast range of politicians and celebrities, including South African president Nelson Mandela, French president Francois Mitterand, actors Ed Asner, Danny Glover, and writers such as E.L. Doctorow, Barbara Kingsolver, Maya Angelou, Elie Wiesel and Salman Rushdie. Rage Against the Machine titled their song by his often heard label, "Voice of the Voiceless."

Afterword Author: Fred Hampton, Jr. (pictured on cover and discussed in Chapter 13) is the son of Fred Hampton, Sr., the famed Illinois Black Panther Party leader who was next in line to be on the Central Committee and as a national Panther spokesman. When Chicago Police killed Hampton in 1969, his wife Deborah Johnson was pregnant with Hampton, Jr. In 1990, Hampton became the president of the International People's Democratic Uhuru Movement. After an apparent frame-up in 1992 for "attempted" arson, a judge sentenced Hampton to eighteen years in prison. He was paroled in 2001 and is currently chairman of the Prisoners of Conscience Committee (POCC). Hampton speaks on behalf of activist causes worldwide. He has been featured on such shows as Pacifica radio's *Democracy Now!* and the documentary *Dave Chappelle's Block Party.*

Cover Photo credits in alphabetical order: Abu-Jamal, Mumia: Nolen Edmonston, courtesy of MOVE, *Covert Action Quarterly*, Spring-Summer 1999. Belafonte, Harry: William Morris Agency, all rights reserved, website, www.wma.com/harry_belafonte/imgs . Brown, H. Rap (Imam Jamil Al-Amin): Western States Black Research Center, in *Bitter Grain: Huey Newton and the Black Panther Party* (LA: Holloway House:1991). Carter, Alprentice "Bunchy:" *The Black Panther* newspaper, in Ward Chuchill and Jim Vander Wall, *Agents of Repression: The FBI's Secret War Against the Black Panther Party and the American Indian Movement* (Boston, MA: South End Press,1990), Cleaver, Eldridge: *U.S. New and World Report*, 1968, Churchill and Vander Wall, *Agents of Repression*, p.41. Cleaver, Kathleen: Ramparts, *Agents of Repression*, p.89. Combs, Sean "P-Diddy," Walter Weissmann/Globe Photos, 1995, Armond White, *Rebel for the Hell of It* (NY: Thunders Mouth Press, 1997) p.142. Hampton, Fred: Oct. 1969, *Agents of Repression*, p.64. Hampton, Fred, Jr.: Uhuru Movement Minister of Information, J.R. at fire@sfbayview.com from his article at *San Francisco Bay View*, 2/26/02. Hendrix, Jimi: Monika Dannemann, his fiancee, the afternoon before his death, 1970. Monika. Dannemann, *The Inner World of Jimi Hendrix* (NY:St. Martin's Griffin, 1995)p.163. Huggins, Jon: *The Black Panther, Agents of Repression*, p.78Ji Jaja, Geronimo (Pratt): *The Los Angeles Times*, in *Agents of Repression*, p.93. King, Martin Luther: Ben Fernandez, 1967, MLK is talking to author William Pepper in full photo #2, in William Pepper, *Orders to Kill: The Truth Behind the Murder of Martin Luther King, Jr.*(NY: Warner Books, 1998). Mizell, "Jam Master Jay" Jayson: Laura Levine, *New York Times*, 11/1/02, B4. Marley, Bob: Chuck Krall, 1972, In Timothy White, *Catch a Fire: the Life and Times of Bob Marley* (NY: Henry Holt, 1996)p.174. Newton, Huey: Roy Williams, early 1980s, *Oakland Tribune*, in Michael Newton, *Bitter Grain: Huey Newton and the Black Panther Party* (LA: Holloway House:1991)p.218. Odinga, Sekou: *Can't Jail the Spirit: Political Prisoners in the U.S.*(Chicago, IL: Committee to End the Marion Lockdown, 2002)p.142. Seale, Bobby: Ron Reisterer, *Oakland Tribune*, in *Bitter Grain*, p.32. Shakur, Afeni: Globe Photos, Inc. in *Tupac: Resurrection*, ed.s Jacob Hoye and Karolyn Ali(NY: Atria Books, 2003)p.4. Shakur, Assata (Joanne Chasimard): Zed Books, 1st publ. Cover of Assata Shakur, *Assata: An Autobiography* (Chicago: Lawrence Hill Books, 1987). Shakur, Mutulu: Rebel for the Hell of It, p.16. Shakur, Sanyika (Monster Kody Scott): Howard Rosenberg, cover photo of Sanyika Shakur, *Monster: The Autobiography of an LA Gang Member* (NY: Grove Press,1993). Shakur, Tupac: (full photo has him shaking hands with Chuck D of Public Enemy) Al Pereira/Michael Ochs Archives, *Rebel for the Hell of It*, p.190. Smalls, Biggie (Christopher Wallace): Walter Weissmann/Globe Photos, 1995, Armond White, *Rebel for the Hell of It, p.142.* Malcolm X: Oliver F. Atkins, courtesty of the Atkins Collection, George Mason University Libraries, posted at *We Shall Overcome—Malcom X Housesite.*

Other added photos—Ojeda Rios, Filiberto: Claridad, published with article by Miguel Guzman, "Comments on DOJ Report Regarding Ojeda Killing," *NY Latino Journal*, 8/12/06. Bari, Judi: placed on Judi Bari's door. Called a "standard FBI counterintelligence intimidation technique. Printed in Ward Churchill, "The FBI Targets Judi Bari: A Case Study in Domestic Counterinsurgency," *Covert Action Quarterly*, #47 Winter 1993-4, p.4. Kennedy, Robert F.: From William Turner and Jonn Christian, *The Assassination of Robert F. Kennedy* (New York: Thunders Mouth Press, 1993).

Shakur, Lumumba, AP/Wide World Photos, from Vibe eds. *Tupac Shakur* (NY: Crown) 1996, p.24. Toure, Kwame (Stokely Carmichael) photo from the internet.

Photos Credits on pages inside book, where not stated—1, 5:Vibe eds., *Tupac Shakur* (NY: Crown Publishers,1997). 1-Karla Radford, 5-AP/Wide World Photos. 2, 3 & 6: Armond White, *Rebel for the Hell of It* (NY: Thunders Mouth Press,1997). 2-Gary Miller and Globe Photos, 3-Reuters/Corbis-Bettmann. Photo 4 is from *Covert Action Quarterly (CAQ)* Spring/Summer 1999. 7- AP/Wide World, Elaine Brown, *A Taste of Power* (NY: Anchor/Doubleday, 1992). 8-Eddie Crespo, CAQ, Winter 1993-4. 9-William Pepper, *Orders to Kill* (NY: Warner Books, 1998). 10-Monika Dannemann, *The Inner World of Jimi Hendrix* (NY: St. Martin's, 1995).

Photos and documents on following pages come mostly from this author's files. But, the first document, Tupac's Euphanasia page, is from Jamal Joseph, Tupac Shakur: Legacy (NY:Atria, 2006). The CIA and the Media is from *Rolling Stone Magazine*, 10/20/77. RFK-related pictures and copied documents are from William Turner and Jonn Christian, *The Assassination of Robert F. Kennedy: The Conspiracy and Coverup* (Thunder's Mouth Press,1978,93). Thanks to George Edwards who copied the CIA documents which he attained after cinematographer/director Lee Lew-Lee (*All Power to the People,*documentary, 1996) attained them through a FOIA filing to get more substantiation for Edwards's researched claims.